The Hebrew Falcon

The Hebrew Falcon

Adya Horon and the Birth of the Canaanite Idea

ROMAN VATER

SUNY
PRESS

Published by State University of New York Press, Albany

Printed in the United States of America

For information, contact State University of New York Press, Albany, NY
www.sunypress.edu

Library of Congress Cataloging-in-Publication Data

Name: Vater, Roman, author.
Title: The Hebrew falcon : Adya Horon and the birth of the Canaanite idea / Roman Vater.
Description: Albany : State University of New York Press, [2024] | Includes bibliographical references and index.
Identifiers: LCCN 2023039402 | ISBN 9781438497662 (hardcover : alk. paper) | ISBN 9781438497679 (ebook) | ISBN 9781438497655 (pbk. : alk. paper)
Subjects: LCSH: Horon, A. G. (Adolph Gourevitch) | Zionism. | Canaanites (Movement) | Jews—Israel—Identity. | National characteristics, Israeli. | Israel—Biography.
Classification: LCC DS149 .V367 2024 | DDC 320.54095694—dc23/eng/20231201
LC record available at https://lccn.loc.gov/2023039402

10 9 8 7 6 5 4 3 2 1

Contents

Acknowledgments		vii
Note on Transliteration and Terminology		ix
Introduction		1
Chapter 1	Adya Horon's Life	19
Chapter 2	From Nation to Denomination: Adya Horon's Historiography	69
Chapter 3	From Denomination to Nation: Adya Horon's Politics	117
Chapter 4	The Hebrew Foundational Myth in a Comparative Perspective	161
Conclusion	What Counts as a Failure?	207
Appendix A		227
Appendix B		239
Appendix C		247
Appendix D		259

Acknowledgments

This book is the result of more than a decade of research spanning four countries and three universities. During these years I have accrued debts of gratitude to numerous sympathetic onlookers who generously extended a helping hand and words of advice, which I now take the opportunity to discharge.

At the University of Manchester's School of Arts, Languages, and Cultures I am grateful to Rachel Corbishley, Julie Fiwka, and Amanda Mathews, as well as to Moshe Behar and John Healey (under whose diligent supervision this research took on its initial shape as a doctoral dissertation), Jean-Marc Dreyfus, Stuart Jones, Daniel Langton, and Alex Samely, whose casual remark at the early stages of research set this work on the right path. At the Oxford Centre for Hebrew and Jewish Studies and the School of Interdisciplinary Area Studies, I thank Sue Forteath, Stephen Minay, Emma Darwall Smith, and Martine Smith-Huvers, and then Martin Goodman, Adriana X. Jacobs, David Rechter, and above all Derek Penslar, who remains a steady source of unwavering support. At the Faculty of Asian and Middle Eastern Studies at Cambridge, where this book was finalized, I thank Nadya Mullen and Susie Nightingale, and then Assef Ashraf, Amira Bennison, Khaled Fahmy, Geoffrey Khan, Andrew Marsham, Charis Olszok, Yaron Peleg, Michael Rand (of blessed memory), and Hans van de Ven. At St. Edmund's College and Woolf Institute, my thank you goes to Angela Coltman, and then to Catherine Arnold, Matthew Bullock, Judith Bunbury, Ed Kessler, Jonathan Mar, Philip McCosker, and Miriam Wagner. In Hughes Hall, I am grateful to Laurie Bristow, Becky Lawrence, Tori McKee, Alison J. Nicholson, Carole Sargent, and Nidhi Singal. Other Cambridge friends include Stanley Bill, Sabine F. Cadeau, Hank Gonzalez, and Moritz Mihatsch.

For their moral and practical support over the years, I thank Menna Abukhadra, Ilan Zvi Baron, Johannes Becke, Peter Bergamin, Emma and Eyal Clyne, Magdalen Connolly, Yael Dekel, Arie Dubnov, Sami Everett, Shai Feraro, Nathalie Frydman, Sara Yael Hirschhorn, Eran Kaplan, Nathaniel Miller, Marton Ribary, Avi Shilon, Colin Shindler, Dan Tamir, Yair Wallach, Ewa Węgrzyn, Elian Weizman, Casper Wits, and Jerzy Zdanowski.

I have benefitted from the Israeli and Middle Eastern Studies PhD studentship and maintenance grant during my postgraduate years in Manchester, from the Israel Institute postdoctoral fellowship in Oxford, and from the Leverhulme Trust & Isaac Newton Fund Early Career Fellowship in Cambridge. I am deeply grateful to all for providing a firm material basis and financial resources to conduct this research. I am also deeply indebted to the dedicated staff at the various archives I frequented in Israel, the United States, and the United Kingdom, including the Jabotinsky Institute Archive, the Ben-Gurion Archives, the Leopold Muller Memorial Library in Oxford, the Genazim Institute of the Hebrew Writers Association, the Houghton Library at Harvard University, the Central Zionist Archives, the National Library of Israel, and the Yad Vashem Archives in Jerusalem.

The book achieved its final shape thanks to the dedicated proofreading of Susan Kennedy and Camille Hale, and the advice and guidance of the anonymous reviewers and Michael Rinella and Diane Ganeles at the State University of New York Press.

Last, I wish to express my deepest gratitude to relatives, acquaintances, and affiliates of my protagonist, who selflessly dedicated their time and personal resources to help me in my queries: Henriette Asséo, Yigal Bin-Nun, Christine Blumberg, Uzzi Ornan (of blessed memory), Ami Shinar, and Esra Sohar (of blessed memory). Above all, I thank from the bottom of my heart the daughter of Adya Horon, Margalit Shinar, and her husband, David Woo. Without Margalit's trust, welcome, readiness to share her father's archive and her personal recollections with me, as well as her valuable critical comments on the final draft of this book, this research would not have happened in the first place. She knows how much I owe her.

None of the aforementioned carry any responsibility for any omission or error of fact or interpretation in this book.

Note on Transliteration and Terminology

The main protagonist of this book was born Adolphe Gourevitch, adopting the name Adya Gur in 1959. Throughout his life, he used numerous pseudonyms, including A. G. Horon, Adya G. Horon, Adolphe G. Horon, Adiag, AGH, Alraïd, and so on. For the sake of clarity and consistency, he will be referred throughout this book as Horon or Adya Horon, his best-known nom-de-plume. On the same grounds, Uriel Shelah (born Uriel Heilperin, also used the form Halperin) is referred to by his poetic pseudonym, which he also used in his political writings, Yonatan Ratosh. The movement both created (and Ratosh led) will be referred to interchangeably as the Young Hebrews, their original self-designation, and the "Canaanites." The latter is in quotation marks throughout to signify its initially pejorative meaning and to differentiate them from the historical Canaanites.

The book follows the Library of Congress standard for transliteration from Hebrew, wherever practically possible; the *International Journal of Middle East Studies* standard for transliteration from Arabic; and simplified phonetic transliteration from Russian. Exceptions are made for names and terms with established forms in English, such as Adya Horon, Yonatan Ratosh, Uzzi Ornan, Zeev Jabotinsky, Esra Sohar, Boas Evron, Hillel Kook, Baruch Kurzweil, Haskalah, and so on, unless they are transliterated directly from Hebrew sources in endnotes and bibliography—apart from non-Hebrew surnames (e.g., Jabotinsky).

Any translations from original languages (Russian, French, Hebrew), unless stated otherwise, are my own. Likewise, in direct citations, unless stated otherwise, all emphases are original.

Introduction

Revisiting "Canaanism"

This book is a critical examination of a person and an ideology. The person is Adolphe Gourevitch (1907–1972), who mostly wrote under the nom-de-plume Adya Gur Horon (and variations thereof), and the ideology is the strand of mid-twentieth century anti-Zionist Hebrew nationalism popularly known as "Canaanism." Given the original pejorative meaning of this label afforded it by its Zionist opponents, it may more accurately be called the Young Hebrews' ideology, a name that preserves the self-designation of the political-artistic movement that propagated an indigenous national Hebrew identity in Mandatory Palestine, and then Israel, from the early 1940s until the late 1970s. Gourevitch-Horon, whose writings influenced a limited but powerful circle of intellectuals and activists united by their critical attitude to the brand of Zionism espoused by the leadership of the Yishuv and, subsequently, of Israel, formulated the intellectual basis of the Young Hebrews' dogma but left the task of leading the movement to others—most notably the political activist Uriel Shelaḥ, better known as the poet Yonatan Ratosh. The initiation and evolution of the personal and intellectual connection between Horon and Ratosh, the author of a number of poetical classics in modern Hebrew literature as well as of several iconoclastic political treatises, is one of the topics explored in some detail in this book.

I have chosen to focus on Adya Horon's life and works because the circumstances of his biography and his thought offer themselves to a study of the relationship between an intellectual placed in a position to articulate a worldview and the social processes which, in their turn, this worldview reacts to and participates in shaping.[1] Thus, an individual's intellectual output, which in the course of events becomes largely forgotten, when rediscovered provides fresh insights into the ideology it helped to form, and consequently opens new perspectives on an entire mass of issues connected to the dynamics and dialectics of an intellectual debate unfolding within the tumultuous framework of nation formation and state-building. The geographical-historical setting in which this dynamic played itself out in the present case is twentieth-century Palestine/Israel, the history of which is overwhelmingly filtered through the binary perception of a protracted conflict between the Arab Palestinian and the Jewish-Zionist national movements.

My primary aim in this book is to reincorporate Horon's historiographical output into the "Canaanite" ideology's intellectual history. This will then permit me to conduct a deep comparative review of "Canaanism's" and Zionism's nationalist language and values, demonstrating that the former is a fully fledged ideological-political alternative to Zionism, which dissents from it on basic elements of nationalist discourse. The journey I take in analyzing the challenge the Young Hebrews posed to the hegemonic ideology of the Yishuv and Israel leads me ultimately to provide a reassessment of the nature of Zionism and the sociopolitical structures it erected. This I do by addressing the differences in the discursive strategies of "indigenization" between competing Hebrew and Jewish nationalisms in light of scholarly insights from the discipline of postcolonial studies regarding the attempt to construct a "New Jew" in Israel. I ask myself in which ways the vision of the past articulated by Horon determined the differences between the Zionist figure of a "New Jew" and the "Canaanite" figure of the "New Hebrew." And while my research is historical in nature, located as it is in the disciplinary "catchment area" of intellectual history, the lessons I personally draw from this voyage and that are briefly presented at the closing pages of this book pertain above all to the current condition of Israel and its perspectives into the twenty-first century as an entity that shares both definitive settler-colonial and some postcolonial traits.

One of the aims of this book's concluding chapters is to demonstrate that Israel's paradoxical condition as a state whose *raison d'état* mixes structural characteristics of settler colonialism with postcolonial political culture can be efficiently illuminated by the juxtaposition of the "Canaanite" and the Zionist positions on state- and nation-building, which were inspired by their targeted reading of historical evidence drawn from biblical antiquity. Given that it was Horon who made this reading for the Young Hebrews, his pivotal role in crafting the ideology is thus re-established. My rereading of the "Canaanite" idea is therefore made through the lens of Horon's specific input into it, unless stated otherwise—in which case I will clarify the differences in the interpretation of Hebrew history and "Canaanite" politics between Horon and his fellow Young Hebrews.

Unlike traditional Judaism, non-Zionist forms of Jewish nationalism (such as Bundism and territorialism), or assimilationism, "Canaanism" was not yet another Jewish rival to Zionism that declared itself relevant to Jewry at large.[2] The challenge posed to Zionism by the Young Hebrews was of an *indigenous* kind: Adya Horon and other "Canaanites" acted in the name of a putative Hebrew-speaking non-Jewish national community native to Palestine that demanded that Zionism withdraw from the land considered the target area for Hebrew self-determination. This would supposedly enable the Hebrew nation to break free from all premodern regressive inhibitions and Jewish particularistic residues—religious, confessional, tribal, and so on—that Zionism had allegedly preserved under the rhetorical cloak of modernizing nationalism. Placing itself on a crash course with what the Young Hebrews took to be rational, secular, and above all republican principles of modern nationhood, Zionism's "unresolved" nature over what Jewish identity meant in modernity,[3] invited, as it were, a "Canaanite"-type refutation of Jewishness as a defining characteristic of the state and its nation. Directing their critical gaze on what they saw as the greatest vulnerability at the core of the Zionist state- and nation-building project—its ultimate anti-modernism—"the Canaanites represented an existential threat to the ontological security of Jewish identity in its Zionist form."[4]

By adopting the principles and language of nationalism, the Young Hebrews attacked Zionism on its own terms, thereby eroding the latter's claim to be the sole agent of nationalism in Mandatory Palestine and after 1948 the single custodian of Israel's national sovereignty. They professed a typical modernist view that the most advanced and suitable social arrangement for the twentieth century was national sovereignty in a secular state, hailed as the guiding principle of universal modernity.[5] What the Young Hebrews perceived in Zionism or, what is equally important, Pan-Arabism was an inclination to the contrary. In brief, "Canaanism" was a rightist form of *Israeli nationalist anti-Zionism,* which introduced a third national factor between Jews and Palestinians with a moral claim to determine the nature of the sovereignty of Palestine and the *raison d'état* of Israel.

To make this claim intellectually compelling and politically valid, "Canaanism" formulated and operated a fascinating historiosophical conceptual grid, exemplifying the need of a modern political ideology for a myth of origins that would legitimize its contemporary practical pursuits and expose what it considered the ideological and practical bankruptcy of Zionism and Pan-Arabism. My research therefore constitutes an examination of the practical and moral function of a vision of the past in a future-oriented political program; in other words, this book is an essay in nationalism studies focusing on a segment in the intellectual history of the modern Middle East.

The primary tenets of the "Canaanite" ideology were formulated by Adya Horon and Yonatan Ratosh in the late 1930s in Paris, in a direct reaction to the national dynamics of the Hebrew Yishuv in Palestine under the British Mandate. The ideology took on organized shape in 1939 when Ratosh established the Committee for the Consolidation of the Hebrew Youth on his return to Tel Aviv. During the Second World War, the committee issued a number of statements of principle, among them "Epistle to the Hebrew Youth," "Opening Discourse," and "Letter to the Fighters for the Freedom of Israel" (directed at the LEHI underground), which were distributed clandestinely. During the 1948 war for Israel's independence, the Young Hebrews founded the political and literary journal *Alef*. Edited initially by Ratosh, and later by his disciple Aharon Amir, a poet, writer, and prolific translator, in 1951 it attempted unsuccessfully to enter the Israeli political scene by establishing the "Center for the Hebrew Youth." After *Alef* had ceased publication in 1953, the Young Hebrews largely acted individually. Their only common endeavor afterwards was the reissue of *Alef* in 1967–1972, when it became an exclusively political review, without the participation of Aharon Amir, with whom Ratosh had a falling-out.

Back in 1950, Ratosh's youngest brother Uzzi Ornan (a prominent Hebrew linguist by profession) cofounded the League against Religious Coercion to protest the tightening symbiosis of religion and state in Israel. However, its narrow and "reformist" focus failed to win it support from other Young Hebrews. Between 1958 and 1976 (and again from 2002 to 2008), Aharon Amir edited the literary-philosophical review *Ḳeshet*, which, by diluting sharp-edged "Canaanism" into a vague but pluralist "Mediterranean" orientation, became in time one of Israel's leading literary platforms. In the mid-1960s, Amir affiliated *Ḳeshet* with a discussion club named Club for Hebrew Thought, which accommodated both "Canaanites" and non-"Canaanites" and rivaled Ratosh's more "orthodox" "Club for Hebrew Guidance." The final publication under the "Canaanite" logo of a stylized ancient Hebrew grapheme Aleph appeared in 1976 in the form of a thick anthology of "Canaanite" writings primarily from the revived *Alef* and other newspapers. When Ratosh died five years later, he was recognized as a contemporary classic of Hebrew poetry, though his political thinking was held in decidedly lower esteem.[6]

Two impulses gave rise to the Young Hebrews' ideology in the late 1930s. One was the emergence and dissemination of the sentiment of an autochthonous and distinctive identity within the Yishuv in Palestine, which increasingly came to be placed within the discursive practices of nationalism, thus buttressing the proposal that the label "Hebrew" attached to it was in fact a national signifier separate and distinct from "Jewish." This in turn triggered reflections concerning the nature of identity and history related to the ongoing social transformation of the Hebrew-speaking society in Mandatory Palestine,[7] undertaken, at first separately and then in tandem, by the historian and philologist Adya Horon and the poet and publicist Yonatan Ratosh. Both men resided then in Paris and initially belonged to the Revisionist rightist wing of Zionism. Hence, their thinking was nourished by post-1789 European liberalism that hinged personal and collective liberty and prosperity on national sovereignty.

Examining the historical development of ancient Hebrew culture and Judaism and the prevailing political conditions in the Middle East and Palestine, Horon and Ratosh concluded that the Zionist idea in both its socialist and Revisionist iterations was inadequate to meet the cultural and political realities of the day. Starting with a political critique of Zionism, the two eventually ceased to identify with the ideology by coming to reject the intellectual foundations of Jewish nationalism. This struck at Zionism's very core, since a sine qua non of ideological adherence to Zionism is the acceptation of the national character of the Jews, notwithstanding their deterritorialization and ethnoreligious bonds.

The "Canaanite" movement that Horon and Ratosh went on to establish reformulated the difference between a Hebrew and a Jew as the difference between membership in a modern nation and membership in a premodern ethnoreligious community, respectively. They considered these two forms of social organization to be mutually exclusive and identified in the Zionist idea of ethnic communalism a denial of the liberal norms of what constitutes a nation. The Young Hebrews' concept of ethnogenesis (nation formation) was premised on the conflation between people, territory, language, and consciousness,[8] as opposed to Zionism's fusion of religion and biology as nation-shaping criteria. Since Jews the world over did not share the four traits listed above, Zionism's claim to speak in the name of a nation was deemed a priori fraudulent, as was Pan-Arabism's claim to speak in the name of a fictitious "Arab nation," whose only common trait was the literary Arabic language. A Jewish "false consciousness" derived from, and inspired by, a Diaspora denominational socioeconomic lifestyle served in the sovereign state of Israel, in the Young Hebrews' eyes, to blur the differences between a nation and a community, between participatory citizenship and patronage, and between geographically delimited nationality and a nonterritorial ethnoreligious identity.

The methodological starting point for this book is that since the Young Hebrews self-identified as nationalists, they ought to be analyzed as such. It is but intellectually honest to base the analysis of any phenomenon upon the terms it sets for itself, checking its claims against the relevant theoretical frame of reference and remaining wary of methodological frameworks that contradict (either implicitly or explicitly) the phenomenon's declared essentials. At the same time, these essentials should not be taken at face value to the detriment of a sound critical judgment.

And so, is the "Canaanite" idea a case of genuine nationalism? I accept that it is, not simply because the Young Hebrews claimed that it was, but because their ideology and activity fit the generic framework outlined by the academic literature on nationalism.[9] They possessed a robust and intricate nationalist doctrine, which they prioritized above their artistic and literary activity (despite being better known for the latter). The image and purpose of the Hebrew nation articulated by them contradicted Jewish and Pan-Arabist nationalist imagery and teleology. "Canaanite" writings repeatedly emphasized the urgency of defeating Zionism and Pan-Arabism if the Hebrews were to become sovereign. Never constituting a mass movement, "Canaanism" functioned largely as a circle of radical intellectuals and artists who came to occupy, sometimes posthumously, a prominent place in Israeli culture, and whose ideology was seen as an inspiration by a wider circle of supporters and as a menace by the mainstream Israeli intelligentsia and political establishment. Last, the Young Hebrews possessed a detailed political plan for the future, a searching sociopolitical and cultural analysis of the present, and a highly developed vision of the past, both recent and ancient.

The observation that "Canaanism" was a genuine national ideology carries a number of theoretical and methodological implications. First, it questions the teleological thrust of Zionism by which Jewish historical experience ineluctably leads to a Jewish political sovereignty. In consequence, the only available option to Israelis for political and cultural self-expression is in a "Jewish state," which means that an Israeli identity, insofar as such exists, is interpreted as just a modern variation of the historical premodern Jewish identity. Careful attention to the guiding principles of the critique of Zionism enunciated by the Young Hebrews leads me to an attempt to adopt a "neutral" position with respect to Zionist and "Canaanite" teleologies, as both are ideologically contingent. This book therefore rests on the premise that the "Canaanite" observation that a Hebrew national identity was in existence in the late years of the British Mandate in Palestine is essentially correct, but that this does not automatically validate any other proposals put forward by the Young Hebrews regarding the "contents" of the Hebrew identity or the paths that should determine its relationship to Jews and Arabs. This entails, of course, the problematization not only of Zionist teleology, which can no longer be taken for granted, but also of "Canaanite" teleology, which has its own innate biases and weaknesses that are explored in further detail in the conclusion.

Second, as indicated above, in order to properly assess the real meaning and significance of the "Canaanite" nationalist challenge to Zionism and Pan-Arabism, a shift in focus away from the towering figure of the Young Hebrews movement, its founder, leader, and most articulate public speaker and advocate, Yonatan Ratosh, to that of Adya Horon is in order. Horon, who was born in Kiev in 1907 as Adolphe Gourevitch and died in Tel Aviv in 1972 as Adya Gur, was neither a man of letters nor an artist: he thus stands out among the "Canaanites" as the only non-"bohemian" within the group that created and gave the movement its direction. Horon was a scholar of the ancient Middle East by education and training, and his participation in the deciphering of the Canaanite literary epics of Ugarit early in his career had a formative impact on his conceptualization of the long-term cultural-historical processes in the ancient Levant. He was, in addition, a versatile writer who moved between several genres: academic scholarship, popular scholarly essays, and political journalism, sometimes blurring the borders between them. Starting with a series of articles in the early 1930s published in the Russian-language Zionist Revisionist press—a seemingly innocuous excursion into ancient Hebrew history that, read with hindsight, can now be identified as the first exposure of a historiographical approach shortly afterwards to become "Canaanite"—and ending with his posthumous publications, Horon's entire adult life was dedicated to the construction of a narrative that would refute the Jewish-Zionist vision of history and offer a positive alternative to what he considered Zionism's suicidal course. His subversive secular reading of the Bible and other works of ancient Eastern Mediterranean literature, which absorbed many insights of biblical criticism and *Wissenschaft des Judenthums*, ran counter to the most essential premises of both Jewish and Zionist historiographies. It thus formed the basis for the "Canaanite" vision of the ancient Hebrew past, creating, in the words of Yael Zerubavel, an alternative "master commemorative narrative," which is "a broader view of history, a basic 'story line' that is culturally constructed and provides the group members with a general notion of their shared past." By "focus[ing] on the group's distinct social identity and highlight[ing] its historical development . . . ," Zerubavel explains, "[the master narrative] contributes to the formation of the nation, portraying it as a unified group moving through history."[10] In this way, national narratives provide a sense of long-term continuity and purpose that help allay contemporary social, cultural, or political anxieties.[11] They also determine what Ana María Alonso calls "national chronologies," which "establish both a historical right to a specific territory and a territorial right to a particular history."[12]

By producing a foundational myth for anti-Zionist Hebrew nationalism, Horon became, to use a Gramscian metaphor, "Canaanism's" organic intellectual. This book therefore asserts that due to his formative intellectual contribution to the "Canaanite" movement (as opposed to his practical participation, which was quite limited), Horon ought to be recognized as its central figure; otherwise the exact nature of the differences between "Canaanism," Zionism, and Pan-Arabism will remain beyond grasp. It is this book's contention that if one chooses to concentrate on the heated political disputes between the Young Hebrews and Zionists at the expense of Horon's discussions of ancient Hebrew history, difficult as they are to the layperson—thereby ignoring the political conclusions that arise from them—the only plausible but deficient conclusion would be that the Young Hebrews did nothing but develop the secularist and anti-Diaspora tenets of Zionism to their logical extreme.

This study asserts that the fundamental difference between Zionism, Pan-Arabism, and "Canaanism" lies in the *basically divergent commemorative narratives of the past* promulgated by the three ideologies, a divergence that transitions into political disagreements regarding the present and the future. To rephrase it in a formulaic form: if a disagreement obtains with respect to a society's past, a similar disagreement will most probably obtain with respect to that society's present and the future. Certainly, such core disagreements do not nullify per se any overlaps that may exist between the different ideologies vying for dominance in the same temporal or geographical space. Rather, these overlaps, however crucial they may be, must not obfuscate the fact that the intellectual roots of the contending ideologies are essentially distinct. In the present context, the clear intellectual, political, and even personal affinities between "Canaanites" and Zionists this book recognizes must not mislead to the conclusion that the ideologies they subscribed to sprang from the same source and thus constituted two variations of the same basic principle. On the contrary, the core principles underpinning Zionism, Pan-Arabism, and "Canaanism" are different because their respective approaches to the usefulness of history in modern politics are incompatible.

Given Horon's repeated admissions that the purpose of his studies of ancient Hebrew history was to advance the Hebrew national cause,[13] we need to briefly consider to what degree they can be considered academically legitimate. The question whether the scholarly findings of an anti-Zionist nationalist public intellectual can be judged on their own merits has indeed been raised more than once: expert commentators on "Canaanism" like Ron Kuzar[14] and Yehoshu'a Porat[15] argued that, ultimately, the historiography underpinning the Young Hebrews' ideology was solidly based. Some Israeli scholars of antiquity, like Ḥaim Rabin[16] and Iśrael Ef'al,[17] also agreed that Horon's scholarship was sound in its own right, though Ef'al warned against drawing "too far-reaching political conclusions" from ancient history. The archaeologist Ḥanan Eshel asserted in the preface to Horon's most comprehensive posthumous publication that discoveries made since his death had positively verified Horon's findings.[18]

Horon himself obviously never doubted his professional integrity as a historian, but what is crucial for our purposes is the societal function of the Hebrew commemorative narrative rather than its level of conformity with standard scholarly methods. To follow Asher Kaufman's directive, "[t]he main thrust here is to analyze how a community imagined itself and not whether this imagining was historically conceivable."[19] It is therefore not my intent to pass any judgment on the scholarly soundness of Horon's findings in the field of ancient Hebrew history. Not only do I lack the professional competence to do so, but also the establishment of his studies' "truth value" is beside my point of examining his oeuvre's function as the Hebrew national foundational myth.

With all the problematic attendant on entanglements of positionality and knowledge that tap into a much broader debate about the relations between knowledge, power, and sociopolitical standpoint,[20] most relevant debates conclude that sociopolitical biases driven by the researchers' biographical context do not of themselves nullify any merits their academic work might possess, and sometimes even enhance it.[21] Students of nationalism agree that foundational myth is effective as a motivator for collective action only insofar as it is perceived and acted upon as genuine representation of bygone reality. "Identity," writes Walker Connor, "does not draw its sustenance from facts but from perceptions; not from chronological/factual history but from sentient/felt history,"[22] hence "from an anthropological perspective, *myths that are believed become social facts.*"[23] The myth of the Hebrew "golden age" developed by Horon pursues a number of objectives meant to answer contemporary rather than historical questions: uncovering the nation's "spirit," "essence," and corresponding "destiny" (to use a mix of Hegelian and Herderian terms, both of whom played a very significant role in the formation of modern nationalism[24]); formulating the language by which the national idea would be elaborated, represented, and reproduced; mobilizing the people to the national idea; and reinforcing the national intellectuals' authority in society.[25] The golden age, which, as observed by John Coakley, if dated at all, is located in a very distant past (in Horon's case, in the prebiblical period), consists of three basic components, not all of which have equal weight in every national commemorative narrative: political and/or military greatness; cultural or social greatness; literary greatness, evidenced by the rediscovery (or, sometimes, fabrication) of ancient epics.[26] Mary Matossian comments that a golden age does not always entail an imperial potency and grandeur; it can also be imagined as a "pristine" agrarian past when the nation's immaculate essence was supposedly expressed to its fullest.[27] Nonetheless, in all variations, foundational myths of a golden age "provide a people that may be suffering from socio-economic and cultural deprivation with a self-validating image of former greatness . . . [and] imply a political project for the future."[28] As synthesized by Kaori O'Connor, these myths "reaffirm cultural values and assumptions, consolidate identity, create community, mobilize sentiments, validate social exclusions and inclusions and endorse a society's self-image—all with reference to a past which is presented as historic, but which is invariably largely or wholly mythic."[29]

Foundational myths are divided into two broad types that share basic structural characteristics such as an origin in a particular time and place, a lost golden age, and a teleology of its recreation. The first type stipulates an organic connection between the members of the nation and their presumed ancestors who lived during the golden age; this is therefore a myth of descent and the acquisition of certain collective faculties and desires through a blood link. The second type emphasizes a spiritual connection between the "ancestors" and the "heirs," drawing inspiration from past examples with no ascertainable biological connections between the "fathers" and their "sons." Anthony Smith[30] calls the first type *biological* and the second type *ideological*, paralleling Steven Knapp's dichotomy of myths of *continuity* as opposed to myths of *analogy*,[31] and John Coakley's myths of *biological descent* versus myths of *cultural affinity*.[32] It will be argued in this book that the Zionist myth of origins corresponds to the biological type, whereas the "Canaanite" myth of origins bears the characteristics of the ideological type. How these differences expressed themselves in the two ideologies' actual political platforms will be exposed below.

The central points of disparity between "Canaanism" and Zionism, understanding of which ensures a methodologically sound analysis of the Young Hebrews' ideology, can be summed up thus. First, the two ideologies' *visions of the past* were fundamentally irreconcilable, and so, in consequence, were their standpoints regarding Israel's present and future. Second, there was an essential disagreement regarding the *exact identity* of the nation to which the two ideologies directed their appeal: as this book will show, the Hebrew nation of the "Canaanites" only partly overlapped with the Jewish nation of the Zionists. Third, and perhaps most important, the ideologies' respective *concepts of a national identity and nation formation* were deeply incompatible: the "Canaanite" concept of national identity was civic and territorialist, whereas the Zionist concept of national identity remains ethnoreligious and primordialist. The true proportions of these differences cannot be appreciated unless Horon's historiography is re-appraised as the key element that made the Young Hebrews' ideology *nationalistically* anti-Zionist.

The "Canaanites" in a Zionist Mirror

Although the Young Hebrews stated their principles and objectives quite openly and repeatedly, many researchers remain perplexed by the question of what exactly the "Canaanite" ideology was. The cause of the glaring discrepancy between "Canaanism's" avowed goals and principles, and its image in the scholarly literature, seems to me the lingering (and, as will be shown immediately, highly detrimental) influence of the Israeli literary critic Baruch Kurzweil's interpretation of Hebrew nationalism. Kurzweil engaged for the first time with "Canaanism" (the idea rather than the movement per se) in 1947,[33] but it was his seminal essay on the Young Hebrews, first published in 1952, that set the tone of the debate for many years.[34]

Kurzweil, who had both traditional Jewish upbringing and modern academic education, placed "Canaanism" within the larger framework of a process that Jewish thought and letters had been undergoing since the age of the Haskalah (eighteenth to nineteenth centuries) and that resulted in the emergence of what he called "the antivocational" current in Jewish letters. This current expressed, according to Kurzweil, the rejection of Judaism's innate spiritual vocation by secularized Jewish intelligentsia, which had struggled to adapt to modern values ever since premodern values and religious outlook had ceased supplying it with existential certainty. Kurzweil's approach to Jewish history was highly pessimistic: while acknowledging that Enlightenment, nationalism, secularization, and Zionism were historically inevitable (and possibly even desirable), he regarded them as highly injurious to traditional Jewish culture, which could not survive the onslaught of modernity. The place Judaism occupied in the Jewish spiritual world was usurped, Kurzweil writes, by the *Wissenschaft des Judenthums*, which heralded a scholastic-secular approach to issues that had previously functioned within, and were inseparable from, the sacral-moral sphere. For Kurzweil, the "scientificization" of Judaism meant that its spiritual heritage was now being studied in the same manner as an anatomist dissects a cadaver, except that the anatomist does not pretend to resurrect the corpse, while the "science" of Judaism spuriously ascribed to itself the role of a direct and legitimate continuator of Jewish heritage. Kurzweil, who regarded biblical philology and Jewish studies as bogus substitutes for traditional Jewish values and fiercely opposed their claim to take over from Judaism, concluded that Jewish culture was seized by a suicide urge. In a way, he considered Zionism, one of the outcomes of traditional Judaism's collapse, a tormented attempt to simultaneously *destroy* Judaism and to *preserve* it in a transformed shape. "If one plays the game of secular nationalism, one must not be affrighted by its consequences," he noted melancholically.[35]

The Young Hebrews' ideology was for Kurzweil but a radical expression of the Haskalah antivocational tendency; thus, only historical ignorance precluded the "Canaanites" from realizing that they were mere epigones of Jewish Enlightenment. "The 'Young Hebrews,' " Kurzweil claimed, "in their attempt to establish a 'Hebrew Ideology,' are involved, to a degree they hardly suspect, in a complex of phenomena characteristic of Jewish thought in modern times; . . . from an ideological viewpoint, the 'Canaanites' constitute an Israeli variation of a well known Jewish *Galuth* phenomenon."[36] He derived their outspoken secularism from the Nietzschean concept of a "nation's spirit," whereby every nation possesses a collective desire to survive expressed in a unique cultural or social structure of values, norms, and behaviors. Jewish secularists simply regarded traditional Judaism as a premodern manifestation of their "nation's spirit." However, with the advent of modernity, this tool could be replaced by a new one—a secular ideology of national revival that would treat Judaism as "a supporting cloaking device for the real reason."[37] Kurzweil devoted a series of essays to the refutation of this idea, pointing to the Zionist thinker Aḥad-Ha'am as the main exponent of the concept that Jewish religion was secondary to the Jewish organic "survival drive"; in a dialectical feat he managed to link "Canaanite" anti-Zionism with the ideas of the founder of spiritual Zionism. Thus, in Kurzweil's reasoning, the Young Hebrews were Jewish culture's unacknowledged executioners in the name of an ideology wearing a nativist robe, though inspired by the Haskalah, that is, by purely Jewish Diaspora values. Their success and advance correlated to Jewish culture's agony; Kurzweil, by assuming Cassandra's role and blowing "Canaanism" out of all proportions, believed that the Young Hebrews charted the direction to which the entire Israeli secular culture was heading unless a meaningful dialogue with Jewish heritage is initiated within the framework of Jewish sovereignty.

The main fault in Kurzweil's otherwise penetrating analysis is, however, easily perceivable—namely, that Kurzweil contrasted Haskalah-age Jewish intellectuals, for whom secularized Jewish identity was only one option among several pathways offered by Jewish modernity and who were educated enough to make their choice, to the Young Hebrews, who never had to face such a dilemma. He admitted that the ascending generation of young Hebrew writers in Israel was born into a reality devoid of sanctity and never needed to tackle the preceding generations' existential impasse. In fact, they were quite ignorant of it; a secular-territorial identity was a natural and secure frame of identification for them: "The present generation . . . is far removed both by education and experience from that full-bodied Jewish life . . . Products of an environment, radically different in both a positive and negative sense, the 'Young Hebrews' transform the theoretical negation of *Galuth* Judaism into living reality."[38]

This means that the antivocational current in contemporary Hebrew letters was no longer a matter of intellectual exercise, but an expression of received reality. In effect, Kurzweil admitted that the post-Jewish identity, whose evolvement he so intensely deplored, was nonetheless authentic, its authenticity, moreover, pinned upon a fundamental ignorance of the Jewish tradition. An "aggressive confrontation with Jewish tradition," observes Yaacov Yadgar concerning the Zionist rejection of Jewish Diaspora heritage, "manifests a certain type of conversation with tradition, which is based on a familiarity with it."[39] This, however, was not the case with native Hebrew youth, who were brought up in a sentiment of disdain toward the Diaspora without any profound awareness of its spiritual life and legacy.[40] The endgame is a glaring internal inconsistency, since a confident and natural native Hebrew identity, which it indeed was by Kurzweil's own admission, cannot express at the same time a tormented Diaspora identity of an enlightened Jew struggling to release themself from their "vocation": the two are simply not one.

This major interpretative failure seems to have occured when Kurzweil substituted his own interpretation for understanding, that is, committed a "category error," which happens when "[people] place their own interpretative constructions upon other people's experiences and [. . .] confuse the two."[41] Kurzweil, who had personally experienced the full tragedy of the Jewish fate under the Nazi occupation of

Czechoslovakia (he fled in time to survive) and was consequently, in the words of Aharon Amir, "tormented by the decline of some Jewish historical existence,"[42] was simply not able to fathom how Hebrew people of letters could preoccupy themselves with something other than the question of the survival of the Jewish spiritual legacy and values—a question he made the centerpiece of his own intellectual pursuits.

A possible source, or inspiration, for this category error (aside from Kurzweil's personal grief over the hypothetical obliteration of Jewish heritage by modernity) is the philosophy of history developed by the prominent Jewish-Zionist thinker Gerschom Scholem. It was Scholem who coined the antinomic phrase "the violation of the Torah is its fulfilment" to describe the pseudomessianic drive of seventeenth-century Sabbateanism, inherited first by eighteenth-century Hasidism and then by late nineteenth-century Zionism, as a justification of their annulment of certain Jewish legal principles and regulations seen as Judaism's "outer shell" obscuring its innate essence these movements were supposedly reaching to.[43] It appears that Kurzweil's observation that "Canaanism" constitutes the extreme form of Haskalah-driven Jewish secular nationalism rises from a similar logic, as if "the violation of Zionism" (discarding the ideology's "Jewish" shell) was its "true fulfilment" (reaching the "Hebrew" essence). The unfortunate upshot is that the more insistent the "violators" are on their non-Jewishness, the more "Jewish" eo ipso they are—regardless of their own declared principles. Such logic is inherently foreign to the Young Hebrews, and it is ironic that Kurzweil, who attacked Gerschom Scholem especially savagely for his complicity as a senior Jewish scholar in burying the living Jewish heritage,[44] resorted to Scholem's line of reasoning when dealing with the "Canaanites."[45]

The most faithful exponent of Kurzweil's paradigm is Yaacov Shavit, who describes the ideology of Hebrew nationalism as "a heresy [vis-à-vis Zionism] and fantasy."[46] It is limited in his eyes to an intellectual game played by two Jewish right-wing intellectuals, Adya Horon and Yonatan Ratosh, in late 1930s' France, when fascination with ancient history allegedly implied fascistic sympathies. Shavit concentrates on the intellectual-theoretical aspect of the "Canaanite" idea and is certainly correct in observing that a historical vision of the past as a cultural text prefigures the emergence of a political vision for the present and the future.[47] At the same time Shavit dismisses Horon's historiography as "false" and "speculative," and the entire

"Canaanite" *vision de monde* as a priori artificial and imitative of Jewish secular discourse,[48] without applying equally strict critique to Zionist historiography, which developed, according to Shavit's own method, from the same source: modern historiographical interpretation of Jewish antiquity.[49]

James Diamond's *Homeland or Holy Land?* is premised on the perceptive observation that "Canaanism" was above all "a political and social ideology" rather than "a literary-cultural phenomenon."[50] Yet since Diamond's study of the Young Hebrews grew directly from his earlier work on Baruch Kurzweil,[51] he follows the latter's erroneous dictum that "Canaanite" historiography was "a quasi-historical view based on the absolutization of the present"[52] and suggests that "Canaanite" politics need to be considered separately from the "window-dressing" of historiography.[53] Kurzweil's paradigm is strongly present in Diamond's book, which opens with a discussion of Zionism's most acute dilemma—whether it was a continuation of historical Judaism or a revolt against it[54]—implying that the emergence of the Young Hebrews' ideology was just another attempt at resolving this dialectic. At a certain place, Diamond makes the Kurzweilian argument that "Ratosh bears more than a superficial resemblance to Berditchevsky and perhaps even to Ahad Ha'am,"[55] and elsewhere, he locates him at the end-point of an intellectual-biographical chain stretching all the way back to Spinoza. The two figures, Diamond opines, open and close "a clear and respectable line of Jewish nonbelievers, who thought themselves out of the Jewish religion,"[56] a judgment that implicitly evokes the words of the Babylonian Talmud: "Even though Israel [in this case—Ratosh] hath sinned, they are still called Israel."

Two fundamental factors are arguably answerable for the lasting influence of Kurzweil's Judeo-centric analysis of "Canaanism." First, by engaging above all with the ideology's aesthetic and literary aspects, Kurzweil was able to frame it as mostly a cultural phenomenon, avoiding tackling its politics in earnest. It is safe to say that beyond Diamond and Shavit the vast majority of scholarship devoted to the Young Hebrews concerns itself with the literary qualities of the poetry and prose of Yonatan Ratosh, Aharon Amir, Benyamin Tammuz, and 'Amos Ḳenan (or with tracing the connections between their literature and politics)[57], notwithstanding Ratosh's own declaration that he considered poetry writing merely a "hobby" that stood in the shadow of his political activism.[58] Second, as just pointed out, Kurzweil's paradox-play, encapsulated in his formula of "a literature that furiously negates what it seeks to renew in another form,"[59] legitimized the thesis that those pretending to be Hebrews were actually Jews, whether they liked it or not. Its eager acceptance by many commentators on "Canaanism"[60] manifests, in my opinion, a suppressed anxiety that a thorough engagement with the Young Hebrews' politics would inexorably bring to the surface painful questions regarding Israeli identity, its relationship with the Jewish Diaspora, and consequently the teleological justification of Zionism.

In this way the privileging of literary analysis in the study of "Canaanism" makes it a convenient measure for the deep and sometimes unconscious entrenchment of Zionism's principles in the Israeli scholarly community. These principles can be summarized as follows: a) Jewish identity is inviolable and inherited throughout the ages, which means that b) national identity is (at least for Jews) a matter of fate rather than of choice. Since most Young Hebrews were born to Jewish parents in the Diaspora and professed Zionism in their youth, it was inconceivable that they could no longer identify as Jews, ergo "Hebrew nation" was just a fabrication—while "Jewish nation," by implication, was somehow not. This way, any discussion of the burning issues of Israeli sociopolitical agenda takes the national character of the Jews for granted.[61] This book, contrariwise, refuses to entertain the proposal that any one of these identities is less "authentic" than the other, or a derivative thereof, since the central point to be made here, without venturing any advocacy on behalf of the "Canaanites," is that the Hebrew national identity is neither more nor less "constructed," "fabricated," or "imaginary" than the Jewish or the Arab national identity.

With this in mind, this book hopes to take the first step in an intellectually captivating voyage to uncover the intellectual sources of Israeli indigenous opposition to Zionism by meticulously tracing the transitions in Horon's historical and political thinking and how those were incorporated into the Hebrew national ideology. Chapter 1 is wholly devoted to Horon's biography, which took him from prerevolutionary Ukraine to Italy, France, the United States, and finally to Israel. This chapter highlights not only his lifetime achievement as the ideologue of "Canaanism" but also Horon's other endeavors, such as his quest to establish a Hebrew maritime force in the 1930s, his impact on Jewish anti-Nazi resistance in France and on the emergence of post-Zionist thinking during the 1940s, and his attempts to forge a "minorities union" across the Middle East to resist what in his eyes was a Pan-Arabist onslaught during the 1950s and 1960s.

The following two chapters contain an extensive discussion of Horon's own oeuvre. The analysis of his historical studies in chapter 2 precedes the examination of his political outlook in chapter 3, so as to identify the parallels between Horon's historiography and his political opinions, even when no such connection is made explicit by him. Chapter 4 makes a number of comparative inquiries, discussing at length the similarities and dissimilarities between "Canaanism," reconceptualized as nationalism in light of Horon's contribution to its theoretical structure, and Zionism; between "Canaanism" and post-Zionism, both the 1940s and the 1990s varieties; finally, between "Canaanism" and other national-territorial ideologies in the twentieth-century Middle East, mainly "Pharaonism" in Egypt and "Phoenicianism" in Lebanon, in order to locate Horon's thought in a wider regional perspective. The conclusion attempts to assess the reasons for "Canaanism's" ultimate failure to secure a mass following in Israel. It argues that Horon's deterministic approach and the Young Hebrews' lack of sensitivity to the intricacies of the emergent Hebrew-Israeli identity were accountable for the growing discrepancy between their worldview and the values of the national society they preached to. Finally, the appendices let Horon speak in his own voice by reproducing a number of original documents from the various stages of his life that are especially representative of his evolving yet at the same time remarkably stable outlook.

Chapter 1

Adya Horon's Life

Europe (1907–1940)

In the early 1960s, while preparing a biography of his father, Eri Jabotinsky requested a number of acquaintances to record in writing their personal and political connections with the founder of Revisionist Zionism. One of the accounts Jabotinsky received came from Adya Horon and, while it indeed concentrates mostly on his relationship with Jabotinsky the elder and the movement he founded, it offers at the same time indispensable information and insights into the early life of the writer himself, providing a comprehensive portrait of a "Canaanite" as a young man.[1] This was probably the most detailed (if not sole) attempt at autobiography undertaken by Horon, and for this reason, this chapter will rely quite heavily upon it. At the same time, it will endeavor, wherever possible, to complement the information provided by Horon with data from other sources, such as archival materials, memoirs, scholarly studies, and information personally supplied to the author by relatives of the chapter's protagonists.

Adolphe Gourevitch was born in 1907 on an estate near Kiev, son of Arie Noah (Leon or Lev in European tongues) Gourevitch. Born around 1865, Gourevitch the elder came of age during a stage in Russian Jewish history marked by two parallel developments: the economic decline of the East European Jewish town, the *shtetl*, that set in around mid-nineteenth century following the crushing of the Polish national rebellions of 1831 and 1863, as well as Russia's defeat in the 1853–1856 Crimean War[2] and the concomitant adoption by the Russian government of a "selective integration" policy directed at economically "valuable" Jews.[3] Benefitting from the temporary abolition of Russian state credit institutions after the Crimea disaster and from the centralization of the taxation system, by the 1880s a class of well-to-do Jewish merchants, private credit lenders and tax farmers on behalf of the government on the western outskirts of the Russian Empire rose to considerable fortunes. Winning a number of privileges not normally accorded to Pale of Settlement Jews, including the right to reside in large cities outside the Pale, they lobbied on behalf of their coreligionists remaining in the *shtetls*. Adopting the Russian language and culture, "[t]hey pondered their birthplace through the privileged lens of an acculturated individual who spoke the language of the state, dressed in European clothes, and no longer had use for kosher food, Talmudic debates, or the pious way of life."[4]

Thanks to an 1859 law that permitted Jewish first-guild merchants to reside and buy land in the Pale's major cities and in the interior of the Russian Empire (where limits on Jewish presence were otherwise strictly enforced),[5] Leon Gourevitch came to own extensive lands near Brest-Litovsk in the Grodno Governorate of the Russian Empire, on the Polish borderlands. Being practical minded, at times he attempted to curb his youngest son's intellectual pursuits. In contrast, Horon's mother, Rachel Gourevitch, who came from Odessa (a fact that provides a sentimental-personal background for Horon's early attachment to Odessa native Jabotinsky), was well-educated and, alone in her family, professed Zionist views. When Adolphe was seven, she hired him a personal teacher of Hebrew, whose only achievement, according to his own words, was to fill him with disgust for the Bible and for the traditional Jews who lived in the eight villages dispersed throughout the lands belonging to the Gourevitch family. They were poor, pious, and spoke Yiddish; the Gourevitches were wealthy, Russophone, nonobservant, and urban. A widespread mixture of an inferiority complex accompanied (and occasionally exacerbated) by a sense of cultural superiority toward traditional Jewry[6] led many Russophone secularized Jews to embrace Zionism as a Jewishly meaningful compensation for their loss of roots. Class background, in this case, had a major role in determining the political and identity choices made by Horon later in his life.[7]

On the last day of 1914, Horon's mother died of pleurisy, and his education was taken over by a Prussian governess, to whom Horon owed his knowledge of German. Following his wife's death, Leon Gourevitch decided to liquidate his businesses in Russia and take his family to Europe. A wartime stay in Switzerland was followed by Prussia and Italy. In 1924 Horon graduated from a gymnasium in Turin, where he learned classical Greek and Latin "and hardly anything else." Following graduation, the family relocated to Paris, where they remained until the Second World War. Leon Gourevitch died in New York in 1957 in the tenth decade of his life, two years after losing his second wife.[8]

The sociocultural setting of interwar Paris in which the Gourevitch family found itself was aptly described in a post-WWII obituary of Michael Berchin, an émigré Russian Jewish journalist who, like Horon, associated himself with Jabotinsky: "In [the 1930s] the Russian emigrant community consisted of two main elements: 1) the Russian royalists and 2) the liberals whose philosophy was libertarian and hence opponents of Bolshevist totalitarianism . . . Around this latter group concentrated also the Jewish intelligentsia. And it is strange to what degree this Jewish group made its impact upon the intellectual life of the Russian community in France."[9]

The latter group functioned in an ambiguous reality, between the Russian "White" emigration, whose blossoming cultural and social life they animated despite the presence of strong anti-Semitic sentiments among the Russians who had escaped the Bolshevik Revolution,[10] and the Zionist (or other Jewish political) activity, whose affairs were to a large extent conducted in Russian as well. The pioneering ethos of Labor Zionism failed to attract well-to-do (or formerly well-to-do) bourgeois Russian Jews, taken aback by its presumed resemblance to Bolshevik social engineering. Many of them considered Jabotinsky one of their own: a Russophone Jewish intellectual who had masterfully expressed the tragic identity dilemma of assimilated Russian Jewry on the eve of the Revolution in his novel *The Five*. The activist Russian Jewish youth, however, was largely drawn to the values enunciated in Jabotinsky's other novel, *Samson*, set in a semipagan biblical Palestine, which offered a comforting vision of physical and mental agility and power nurtured by natural connection to the land. Horon confesses in his account to being attracted to "Samsonism," which, according to his contemporary belief, expressed itself in the Betar Revisionist youth movement and in the ETZEL underground in Palestine. Moreover, he believed that Jabotinsky's true values were those encapsulated in *Samson*, while the entire Revisionist rhetoric, with its toned-down diplomatic jargon, was reserved for external consumption on the world political stage—by Jews and non-Jews alike.[11]

Two formative events that took place in 1921 rekindled Horon's interest in his origins. The first was a Scout meeting in France, when Horon (still living in Italy) was informed by a fellow "White" Russian Scout that, as a lowly Jew, he had no country to call a home and no nation to call his own. The second happened on the seventh anniversary of his mother's death, on December 31, 1921. On that day, the family story goes, Horon heard his mother's voice calling him in Hebrew in words from the Book of Genesis: "Get thee out of thy country and from thy kindred and from thy father's house unto a Land that I will show thee."[12]

Stories of Paulinian revelations setting men on an unexpected path that becomes their life mission have a venerable lineage; in Horon's case, this was as mystical as he ever got, remaining thoroughly rational and irreligious in his thought and writings. The event nonetheless did continue to inform his broad relation to the universe: his daughter attests that as a scholar, Horon was deeply aware of the inherent limitations of science and empirical enquiry and possessed "a sense of the sacred" or of awe toward the vastness of the natural world.[13] Horon's romantic side was expressed, above all, in veneration of Occidental canonical poets and poetry (the Bible, Pushkin, Dante, etc.) and, to a large degree, determined his attitude to Yonatan Ratosh, whose poetic genius he put above any personal differences.

It is worth considering that a similar mystical experience is evoked in the mytho-biography of Eliezer Ben-Yehuda, the person identified in popular memory with the revivification of spoken Hebrew.[14] Ben-Yehuda reveals in his autobiography that one midnight in 1877 "all of a sudden as if lightning flashed before my eyes, and my thought flew . . . to the Fords of Jordan in the Land of Israel, and I heard a strange internal voice calling unto me: The revival of Israel and its tongue in the land of our forefathers!."[15] The parallels are manifest, not only with regards to the content, but also to the story's function as a personal foundational myth. Both Horon and Ben-Yehuda became as a result engaged in the business of Hebrew national revival, against the grain of their respective societies.

An event such as this—authentic or not, this is immaterial—is useful in articulating one's position vis-à-vis the world, as Horon's next steps demonstrate. He was impelled to study his roots seriously (for which purpose he prevailed upon his father to bring him a Hebrew grammar book from a business trip to Paris),[16] and within a brief span of time he arrived at the conclusion that the ancient Hebrews were in antiquity a major civilization-driving force. Their historical glory, he came to believe, can and ought to be renewed. At this point, Horon makes a very significant remark in his record (which may be a post-factum rationalization): his search for Hebrew grandeur was an end in itself, and he did not pursue it in order to answer any Herzlian "Jewish question."

Another conclusion that Horon reached early on was that any political action must be grounded in a sound ideology, that "every event and step must be measured against [the idea]."[17] By his own admission, tactical thinking was alien to him; he was a person of "all or nothing," "now or never." This principle trumped for him any occasional political allegiances; moreover, it trumped his allegiance to Zionism itself. As Horon recalled in the mid-1940s,

> I began my life . . . by devoting myself completely to political and cultural activities in the service of the Hebrew ideal, of the yet indistinct Hebrew movement, and I joined, as a naïve youth, one of the Zionist parties, the most militant of course. I, also, under the stress of events which already seemed urgent, began with the very end, with the action. After five years of relentless action . . . I came to realize more and more that Zionism lacked completely any adequate ideology, that it had no principles, especially no historical foundations whatsoever. Therefore I devoted myself to the discovery of the necessary principles, to the study of our past, and became more and more a student of history. I did not retire from the fight. I felt that somebody had to do a job, a hard job, without which the fight itself would be hopeless. I felt that Zionism, as it was, must fail. Not just that it *may* fail, —but that it *must*. At least from the only point of view I was interested in, from the point of view of the *Hebrew* national revival.[18]

The "militant" movement mentioned by Horon was the Jabotinskian youth organization Betar, whose French branch he cofounded in 1928.[19] Given Horon's social milieu in Paris, this step was, perhaps, scarcely avoidable. Most of his friends and acquaintances were, like him, Russian-speaking secular Jews who hailed chiefly from Ukraine (in his account for Eri Jabotinsky, Horon commented on surrounding himself with Ukrainian Jewish friends: "I never lost touch with the clannish feeling, despite all my up-to-date theories") and who felt attracted to the national-secular ethos embodied by Jabotinsky. Two of them particularly stand out in Horon's biography: Boris Souvarine and Victor Mirkine. The former is quite a large name: a prominent communist activist and thinker whose growing doubts about the Soviet Union led to him being expelled from the French Communist Party in 1924 on accusation of "Trotskyism," and who later pioneered the analytical field that came to be known in the West as Sovietology.[20] Mirkine, however, is a more obscure figure: his biography can be partially reconstructed from handwritten notes scribbled on the margins of publications Horon contributed to in the early 1930s, references in Eri Jabotinsky's biography of his father, a 1951 memorial publication of Betar France, a number of contemporary press articles, and French online sources on military history. Mirkine was born in 1909 in Ekaterinoslav to a Jewish family that relocated to France following the 1917 Revolution. He held a degree in law from the Sorbonne and also studied at the French military academy of St. Cyr. On his Zionist side, Mirkine was in the 1930s a director in the Palestine Jewish Colonization Association, a member of the Maccabi sports club in Paris, and head of the sports section of Betar. Demobilized after France's capitulation in July 1940, he volunteered for the Free French and embarked upon a military career replete with battlefield achievements before being killed in November 1944 in a battle at Grosmagny in northeastern France.[21] A square facing the Caesarea train station in Israel now carries his name.

The importance of Mirkine to Horon's biography is twofold. It was he who introduced Horon to his close friend Eri Jabotinsky, through whom Horon became acquainted with his father, Zeev Jabotinsky. Mirkine also organized a group of Jewish students in Paris in the late 1920s to form a self-defense association against anti-Semitic attacks, to the creation of which Horon provided an intellectual backing. Out of this association grew the founding nucleus of Betar France, initiated in 1928 following a guest lecture by the head of Betar Palestine, Menachem Arber.[22] Among the first recruits to the new branch were Eri Jabotinsky's maternal cousin Serge Halperin, Halperin's stepsister Ada Steinberg, who later married Horon, and her friend Natalia Poliakova. His involvement in Betar France prevented Horon's planned departure to Palestine: faced with his son's determination to study Hebrew philology at the Sorbonne, Leon Gourevitch had obtained a Palestinian certificate for him, to put him out of what he considered folly's way. The certificate was never used since Horon first fell ill with scarlet fever and, upon recovery, was drawn into politics by Mirkine.[23] In the event, Horon did not settle in Israel until 1959.

With Mirkine at the helm of Betar France and Horon as the branch's informal chief ideologue, the organization pursued a "Samsonian" ideal of a "strong Jew" capable of active self-defense, both physically and intellectually. To this end, it established in early 1930 a self-defense school to provide training in military skills and martial arts to interested members. Victor Mirkine was tasked with heading the sports section and teaching jiu-jitsu, while Horon became the principal. The school apparently opened without obtaining prior approval from the world leadership of Betar (*Shilṭon Betar*) and its financial arm, the Tel Ḥai Fund. It took Zeev Jabotinsky's personal intervention to compel the Fund to support the school without insisting on oversight of its activities. A somewhat angry exchange of letters from February to May 1930 between Horon, the Tel Ḥai Fund management in London, Eri Jabotinsky, Zeev Jabotinsky, and the senior Revisionist official Meir Grossman attests to a measure of misunderstanding on the issue between Betar France and the Tel Ḥai Fund (there was possibly some greater disagreement between Betar France and the London offices of the Revisionist movement, of which the self-defense school was only one instance).[24]

The self-defense school was ultimately a footnote in the history of Betar France; in the present context, however, it is important for having launched a relationship that would prove crucial for Horon's future intellectual development. Listed among the students of the school is one U. Halperin, none other than the future founder and leader of the "Canaanite" movement, Yonatan Ratosh, whose true name was Uriel Halperin (later changed to Shelaḥ). Living in Paris for study purposes in 1929–1930, Ratosh became involved in the local Revisionist scene.[25] Both Porat and Aharon Amir suggest he was introduced to the local Betar activists, including Horon, by another Paris-based Palestinian Revisionist, Haim Abravaya, who subsequently became a prominent translator of French literature into Hebrew.[26] The contact established between Horon and Ratosh through the self-defense school was initially quite ephemeral; although the two exchanged some letters during the 1930s, Horon was not always capable of remembering the correct form of Ratosh's official surname.[27]

The next step initiated by Horon was the foundation in early 1931 of the youth movement named "Rodêgal" (a French variation on the Hebrew phrase Rodê Gal—"Lords of the Waves"). This movement, in which Eri Jabotinsky, Serge Halperin, and Zeev Malinov (the future chief mechanic of the Israeli naval company ZIM) were also involved, elevated the idea of "Samsonian" Jewish self-defense to a new level by marrying practical principles to a historical-ideological platform, which would become a benchmark of every endeavor Horon involved himself in for the rest of his life. The guiding idea behind this movement for "Jewish sea imperialism," as Zeev Jabotinsky himself put it,[28] is that by nurturing seafaring and aviation skills, the Jewish past of valiant naval exploration would be reconciled with the Jewish future, permitting the Jews to practice their right for self-determination that they had won in the Great War. Horon calculated that 25 percent of the contemporary Jewish population (amounting to around 4.2 million people in the early 1930s) lived in close proximity to major bodies of water, such as seas, rivers, or lakes, yet only 0.05 percent derived their income from water. This, Horon concluded, was an anomaly typical of the Diasporic condition, which stood in glaring contrast to Jewish antiquity, when Jewish seafarers were "lords of the waves" in the Mediterranean and beyond and founded colonies and trading stations on its shores. A claim to the restoration of this glory would therefore be a crucial step toward the redemption of Jews from their current oppression.[29] As Horon promised in a letter to Eri Jabotinsky, "the first thing we will build in the land [of Israel]—a seven meter long ship with two masts."[30] He also planned to write a booklet on aviation, for which he solicited Eri Jabotinsky's help in collecting relevant visual and written material in Palestine.[31] Horon, finally, was the author of Rodêgal's anthem.[32]

The movement's activities fused direct action with ideological preaching, a mode of political work favored by Horon. Between December 1930 and March 1931 Rodêgal produced three issues of the journal *Le Cran—Revue Juive d'Action et de Jeunesse* (*A Jewish Review of Action and Youth*[33]), in which texts on technical nautical matters mixed with ideological-historical articles. Each issue contained a section devoted to Rodêgal, detailing its ongoing activities and the principles driving them, and the first two issues also had a section on the Maccabi sports club. Other articles included discussions of the merits of jiu-jitsu (written by Mirkine, the jiu-jitsu instructor of Maccabi) and other sport disciplines, analyses of the contemporary political situation from what might be termed an extremist Revisionist perspective, book reviews, articles on history, and some attempts at literary prose. Horon wrote a large part of the content for all issues, sometimes under his own name, sometimes under pseudonyms (such as "Pelony," which means "Anonymous" in Hebrew, or "Leo Horwitz," probably a play on his father's name), and sometimes without signing them at all.[34]

Rodêgal organized public lectures and balls in Paris,[35] provided courses in swimming, nautical craft, aviation, and the Hebrew language, and even established a branch in Tunisia, where Betar enjoyed particularly strong following.[36] In 1932 it took part in organizing the worldwide Betar sports competition in southern France, which, if we are to believe Eri Jabotinsky, was meant as a rehearsal for a future rebellion against British rule in Palestine. On this occasion, Jabotinsky made an attempt to fly a glider, and Horon coined a Hebrew neologism for it, coming up with "daon." This word ultimately entered living Hebrew and displaced the term "maglosh" used by the non-Revisionist aviation clubs in Palestine.[37]

Rodêgal was defunct by 1932, but in the same year, Horon, Eri Jabotinsky, Abravaya, Malinov and a few others established The Hebrew Order ("Hagedor Ha'ivri," as Horon called it[38]). This organization, which apparently lasted an even shorter time than Rodêgal, was all ideology and no practice. It advocated the occupation of Palestine from the east and south by Betari youth trained in sports and martial and nautical arts, for which purpose Jewish settlements were to be established as beachheads on the Tiran Islands in the Red Sea and on the shores of Arabia. Preliminary geographic studies were initiated but abandoned quite quickly, and the daring plan (code-named "Te'uzza," a neologism by Horon for "courage" and therefore also a translation of "le cran") came to a halt.[39]

Nonetheless, this episode had some long-lasting effects. First, materials produced by Rodêgal—such as *Le Cran* or the *Manuel Nautique Élémentaire* (*Elementary Naval Manual*) authored by Horon and Malinov—were put to use by the Betar naval school founded in 1934 in the Italian harbor of Civitavecchia (where an Italian naval school had been operating since 1923) under the command of Yirmiyahu Halpern.[40] Second, Horon, as the head of Rodêgal, was invited by Zeev Jabotinsky to compose a series of articles in the Russian-language Revisionist newspaper *Rassviet* (*The Dawn*) laying out the historical conception of Hebrew antiquity that underpinned the movement's activity ("notwithstanding the 'elders' opposition," Horon notes in his record). These articles, most of which appeared under the headline *On History*, are examined in the next chapter, as they constitute the first appearance in print of a historicopolitical viewpoint that, by the end of the decade, had developed into the "Canaanite" ideology. To understand this ideology properly, it is important to point to its beginnings in a popular-scholarly exposition of a new approach to ancient Hebrew history published in the Russian Zionist press of 1930s' France.[41] Some of the tropes developed in *On History* can be identified in the historical articles that appeared on the pages of *Le Cran* (such as the Canaanites being kin to the ancient Hebrews and Judaism being a late phenomenon), and Horon continued to publish historical essays in the same spirit in Betari outlets in France during the 1930s.[42]

Yehoshu'a Porat suggests that the Betar leadership was suspicious of Rodêgal because of its refusal to merge with Betar and the concomitant potential for rivalry;[43] more suspicious than the head of Betar himself, in fact. At the Betar world convention in Danzig in April 1931, Zeev Jabotinsky proposed to reciprocate Rodêgal's greetings with a similar gesture since this movement "collected interesting statistical information on the Jewish people and its relation to the sea," whereas its activity in the field of naval sports might have constituted an example to emulate for Betar. However, Arie Disenchik from the Betar high command objected to this, pointing that Rodêgal was staffed by ex-Betar members. The dispute was handed over to a commission, resulting in a watered-down resolution by the Betar congress to officially acknowledge Rodêgal's greetings and to look into possible ways of cooperating with it.[44] The Civitavecchia school, it should be added, came into being partly to offset the advantage Rodêgal had over Betar in military sea training.

In spite of the above, Jabotinsky's interest in what Rodêgal represented, both in ideological and practical terms, never waned. This is confirmed by a number of letters he sent to people associated with the Revisionist movement in the 1930s, after Rodêgal had ceased to exist, which demonstrated his hope that a Rodêgal-like movement and spirit could be recreated within Betar.[45]

The Rodêgal episode is helpful in shedding light on the full extent of relations between Horon and Jabotinsky. As mentioned above, Horon had been a close companion of Eri Jabotinsky since the late 1920s and thus a frequent guest at his father's house. In 1935, he became a member of Jabotinsky's extended family by marrying Ada Steinberg.[46] "Since [my father] took interest in the moods of the young," testifies Eri Jabotinsky, "he conversed with this young fellow [Horon] as well."[47] Jabotinsky soon realized that Horon was "the most knowledgeable among his disciples and assistants, as well as the most far-sighted."[48] When Horon's historical articles were published in *Rassviet*, Jabotinsky felt compelled to react to them personally in print, which in itself is an indication of the weight he accorded to Horon's thinking at this early stage.

His take on Horon's output is contained in two articles, "The Mythology of Canaan" and "Israel and Carthage."[49] The former is a friendly satire poking fun at Horon's fascination with ancient paganism that leads him to fabricate a Hebrew equivalent of the Olympian pantheon, while the latter is a serious review of Horon's ideas. Although generally sympathetic in tone, Jabotinsky is reluctant to embrace Horon's historiography in its entirety, cautioning in the latter article that "the young scholar's scientific opinions [might be] largely influenced by his political views or his practical-national tendencies."

The intellectual differences between Horon and Jabotinsky were not limited back then to ancient history; in the record he wrote for Eri Jabotinsky, Horon states that in 1931 Rodêgal submitted an invasion plan of Palestine to Jabotinsky. This was turned down as unrealistic, as were Horon's explanations that no Arab resistance would be forthcoming since there were no authentic Arabs in the vicinity. Jabotinsky's fixation on language-based national identity, Horon writes in the record, made him quite an "Arab nationalist" (a grievous sin in Horon's eyes, as will be explained in chapter 3), leading him to reject this element of Horon's argumentation. Indeed, in everything relating to "direct action" in Palestine, Horon was significantly more radical than Jabotinsky.

All this meant that personal relations between the two could occasionally become strained, and it was only Jabotinsky's appreciation of Horon's intellect that prevented a full break for a time. Eri Jabotinsky admits that Horon was the only one among the Revisionist youth from whom his father could tolerate a constant and devastating critique, certainly not couched in diplomatic niceties.[50] He also considers perfectly plausible that Jabotinsky the elder came under the influence of some of Horon's ideas (as for himself, he leaves no doubt regarding his intellectual indebtedness to Horon; yet we will observe below that this influence was most pronounced in areas where Eri Jabotinsky diverged from his father).[51] Horon, for his part, wrote in his record that his attachment to Jabotinsky was based not on the latter's political role, but on his position as a Leader. This should be understood as a hint that Horon distinguished between Jabotinsky the person and the thinker (toward whom he maintained a reverential attitude throughout his life)[52] and Jabotinsky the politician, with whom he was eventually in strong disagreement. For several years, Horon entertained the hope that the "real" Jabotinsky was that of *Samson*, while to the outside world he displayed a moderate face; the ultimate disappointment, one guesses, was bitter. Nonetheless, Horon writes that Jabotinsky's death in 1940 was one of three personal disasters he experienced.[53]

The relations between the two reached their tipping point in September 1935, at the founding congress in Vienna of the New Zionist Organization (NZO) established and led by Jabotinsky after the Revisionist Party's withdrawal from the Labor-led World Zionist Organization (WZO). Moved by the pro-Revisionist stance of the chief rabbi of Palestine and the theoretician of religious Zionism Abraham Kook on the Arlozorov murder affair, Jabotinsky proposed at the congress an alliance with the religious-Zionist Mizraḥi party. To achieve this, he was ready to introduce into the NZO statute a paragraph on making "the sacred values of the Torah ruling in the national life" of the future Jewish state. The considerations behind such a move were primarily tactical; Jabotinsky made no secret of his belief that in a few generations, religion would become extinct, while as long as it existed, even secularists like himself could benefit from the "moral pathos" of Jewish religion and heritage without subscribing to its clerical features or legislation.[54]

Nevertheless, this proposal caused an uproar among a select number of committed anti-clericals attending the congress, who defied their leader openly. Horon argued from the pulpit that an alliance with the religious amounted to a backward step in relation to the rules of historical development, due to the regressive and anti-national character of organized religion. Acknowledging Judaism's role as the keeper of the Jewish "national flame," Horon denied at the same time that he adhered to a religion that had now become a hindrance to the Jewish national reawakening. He concluded his speech with a rhetorical bombshell, which, according to some eyewitnesses, "caused panic"[55] in the audience: "I am not a Jew from Yavneh, but a Hebrew from Samaria!."[56] Eleven delegates eventually voted against the alliance with the religious party, and it was under their pressure that the stated aim of the New Zionist Organization charter was reformulated to "to root in the sacred values of the Torah in national life" instead of "ruling."

Eri Jabotinsky perceptively remarks in his memoirs that Horon spoke not as an "old-fashioned" atheist (which he never was) but as a historiosopher. His objection to an alliance with the religious was grounded in considerations deeper than plain secularism: one might discern here an *ideological* attack on Zionism. What Horon perceived at the Vienna congress was a cardinal divergence between his concept of Jewish national revival, which inescapably entailed the destruction of traditional Judaism and the Diaspora way of life, and that of Zeev Jabotinsky, who was unwilling to go that far.

The latter, notably, saw that as much. Horon recalls with admiration Jabotinsky's gallant attitude since he personally sat next to him and tried to persuade him to withdraw his objection, citing the tactical considerations mentioned above. When Horon refused, Jabotinsky bade him farewell with the words "Go on *your own way*, as your conscience dictates, though you shall always have my esteem" (emphasis added). In a letter to his son, Jabotinsky stated that to his taste Horon's declaration that there was no connection whatsoever between Judaism and the ancient Hebrew-speaking Canaanites came "from a wholly different opera" (as compared to the speaker before Horon, who grounded his objection in an atheistic outlook).[57]

From this point on, relations between Horon and Jabotinsky moved on to a different plane. Horon ceased being a disciple of Jabotinsky or his formal subordinate in the structures of the Revisionist movement: "Gourevitch was no longer in the eyes of my father the talented friend of his young son, but simply an interesting and valuable thinker."[58] The two continued to meet and exchange letters until Jabotinsky's departure to the United States in early 1940.[59] It is worth recalling as well the one issue on which an agreement between Jabotinsky and Horon survived the latter's resignation from the Zionist movement—the advocacy of a shift from the Hebrew alphabet to a new one derived from the Latin. A large part of the correspondence presently mentioned was written in Hebrew while using an intricate version of the Latin alphabet, probably devised by Jabotinsky himself.[60]

In personal terms, the rift with Jabotinsky was disastrous for Horon: "He was literally thrown onto the street."[61] Previously a high-ranking functionary of the Revisionist movement and a key figure in Betar France, he had also served part-time as a private secretary to Jabotinsky, as a secretary of the Tel Ḥai Fund (with which he had previously quarreled over the self-defense school) established to buttress the Revisionist activities financially and break the Jewish National Fund's monopoly over the flow of resources within Zionism[62] and finally, as a technical secretary to the Betar leadership, in which role he was expected to disseminate his ideas regarding Jewish national renaissance via conquest of the sea. Outside the party, he worked briefly as a reporter for the newspapers *Paris-Midi* and *Paris-Soir* (arranged by Jabotinsky), attempted to become an arts dealer, and provided occasional language lessons and translations. When he was left to fend for himself, he found a job monitoring foreign radio broadcasts for the French Ministry of Posts and Telegraph. This post, he mentioned in a letter to Eri Jabotinsky, was an evening and night job, which left him plenty of time during the day to pursue his scholarly interests.[63]

What accounts for this radical shift in Horon's worldview, which he brought to the fore on the occasion of the Vienna congress and in defense of which he was willing to jeopardize his position in the Revisionist movement? To quote once again Eri Jabotinsky, who knew Horon like none other, he "was already then contemptuous of Zionism, and wished for something else instead: Zionism was [for Horon] an androgynous entity that attempted against all reason to forge in the name of a religious tradition something, which, if successful, must . . . deliver a mortal blow to this tradition and to the very existence of Judaism."[64] And what pushed him to such conclusion? Horon answers this himself, in his 1945 speech to the Hebrew Committee of National Liberation, cited above: "I came to realize . . . that Zionism lacked completely any adequate ideology, that it had no principles, especially no historical foundations whatsoever."[65]

Zionism's historical legitimization was revealed to Horon as bankrupt, and he sought an alternative legitimizing apparatus, drawn from Hebrew history but unblemished by Jewish Diaspora communal-religious values and worldview. This he found in the prebiblical past, which he investigated during his academic studies. The picture of Hebrew antiquity that he ultimately reconstructed (and that is explored in detail in the next chapter) fused a critical evaluation of biblical literature inspired by the *Wissenschaft des Judenthums* and biblical philological-historical query developed in German universities, with what David Ohana[66] defines as "promethean Nietzscheism," that is, the idea that a rediscovery of an ancient myth and its contemporary actualisation will result in the shaping of a new Jewish personality—a "New Jew," or, to revert to Jabotinskian vocabulary, a "Samsonian" Jew.

Operating a number of key conceptual terms, such as "nation," "denomination," "language," and "territory," this picture of the past presupposed a huge qualitative difference between the ancient Hebrews and contemporary Jews and held rabbinic Judaism, Diaspora's ultimate product, in contempt; it viewed the ancient Hebrews as creators of a far-flung civilization that dominated the Mediterranean from its eastern shores; it highlighted what the "Sons of Israel" and their Canaanite and Phoenician neighbors had in common; finally, it challenged Ernest Renan's proposal that all Semitic peoples originated in the Arabian Peninsula and were thus, one way or another, "Arab." Most crucially, it replaced what it saw as Zionism's parochialist-clerical definition of the "in-group" with a territorial-linguistic common denominator, one that is inherently more inclusive through its deliberate blindness to ethnic or racial origins.[67]

In 1929, Horon entered the Sorbonne as an undergraduate student of Semitic philology and literature, followed by courses in comparative history of religions, sociology, and mathematics at the École Pratique des Hautes Études. In 1937 he obtained his baccalaureate (Licence des Lettres) and started working on his doctoral dissertation, which he planned to complete by 1942 before moving to Palestine. In parallel, he devised publication plans, which included a scholarly article and a short book.[68] It was during his studies that Horon discovered his calling: having studied under the French luminaries of biblical criticism and Oriental sciences, Victor Bérard, Adolphe Lods, and Charles Virolleaud, he gradually internalized their approach to the history of the ancient Levant, which questioned the established truths of the Hebrew Scripture. Virolleaud, on whose seminars at the École Pratique Horon sat, was the recently retired head of the antiquities department in the French mandate of Syria. In this capacity he oversaw the initial explorations at Ra's ash-Shamra, the site of the ancient Canaanite city of Ugarit in northwestern Syria today, where cuneiform prebiblical Canaanite texts were discovered in 1929. He engaged Horon, who had a thorough preparation in Hebrew philology, to help him in deciphering them. This job was both unpaid and uncredited, since Horon as a stateless person was formally prevented from taking up paid employment at a higher education institution in France. Nonetheless, the experience of an intimate contact with ancient Canaanite literature suggested to him the historical legitimization tool that Zionism purportedly lacked. A friend from among the Revisionists, Benno Lubotzky (later known as Binyamin Eliav), recollected Horon's excitement at the discovery of an ancient cultural universe so closely affined to biblical Hebrew history and heritage yet free of any Judaic elements:

> I recall this youngster . . . strolling with me for many nights in the streets of Paris in order to relate this great discovery

> of the Semitic "Hebrew" pantheon found in Ugarit and to point out that herein lay the expansion of our historical consciousness; and to explain to me that it was the Phoenicians and their colonies from which the Jewish Diaspora later arose . . . Our historical consciousness [he believed] must from now on base itself on the Ugarit mythology, literature, and characters—no less than on the Bible and the Jewish history.[69]

When Eliav shared this recollection in the late 1960s, he had already come full circle in his own intellectual development: from a Revisionist in the 1920s–1930s ("totally submissive to Jabotinsky," in the words of Horon in his record) he drifted toward MAPAI, to finally become a fully pronounced "dove" in the wake of the 1967 war.[70] Perhaps this is why he never mentions Horon by name in his testimony and treats the entire "Canaanite" ideology extremely derogatively. Things, however, were not so at an earlier stage: while still a Revisionist Eliav actually came under a strong influence of "Canaanism"[71] (in that case, his subsequent ardent rejection of it may have a psychological background). What is certain is that he was completely fascinated by the *On History* series of articles in *Rassviet*, which summarized Horon's current academic knowledge. Eliav proposed to expand it into a four-volume book intended for distribution among the branches of Betar in order to educate its members in a "national" fashion.[72] If such an idea was indeed approved, or even merely entertained, by the Betar leadership, then its readiness to endorse a historiography that had the potential to overthrow the Zionist one speaks volumes about the movement's cultural and political orientation at that time.

Eliav was among the members of the Revisionist movement with whom Horon maintained contact after his own withdrawal from it.[73] Another high-standing Revisionist he met in Paris in order to preach his ideals was Avraham Tehomi, who between 1931 and 1937 headed the Hagana B split militia in the Yishuv, from which the ETZEL Revisionist underground subsequently developed. These conversations led nowhere; Eri Jabotinsky accuses Tehomi of duplicity owing to his tendency to agree with any interlocutor regardless of the content of the exchange.[74]

The most significant contact with an affiliate of the Revisionist movement that Horon cultivated after 1935 was with Uriel Halperin, the poet Yonatan Ratosh. We saw above that their acquaintance dated to the Betar self-defense school run by Horon and Mirkine in Paris in 1930 and persisted intermittently throughout the following decade. When Ratosh returned to Paris in 1938 to continue his education, he was a disillusioned Palestinian Revisionist, whose activist agenda, he felt, was time and again torpedoed by the movement's leaders, who had no intellectual or emotional understanding of the political, social, or cultural realities in the Yishuv, and in Palestine more generally. Neither did they share in his (and other radical Revisionists') conviction that Great Britain was a colonial overlord rather than an ally, and his attempts to persuade them otherwise fell on deaf ears. His objective in coming to France was to expand his knowledge on the ancient history of the Hebrews and the Middle East,[75] which suggests that he too, like Horon, felt the inadequacy of legitimizing a revolutionary break in Jewish life by reliance on Jewish tradition. He renewed his contacts with Horon, which in a very short time developed into close intellectual rapport (without always amounting to personal friendship). In an interview given shortly before his death, Ratosh recalled his impressions of Horon and reflected on what drew them together:

> We were more or less of the same age, but entirely different people, different in temperament, different in character, our backgrounds were entirely different as were our personal spheres of interest and points of view. He was, philosophically speaking, an idealist, while I was probably a materialist, he drew his vision from history, whereas at the sources of my worldview lay the geopolitics. He was essentially a scholar, I a writer. What brought us together was our common interest in the issues pertaining to the Land [of the Hebrews].[76]

The experience of conversing and working with Horon in 1938–1939, when he was introduced to Horon's vision of Hebrew history, was such a critical turning point in Ratosh's own intellectual and political upbringing that he did not hesitate to describe it many years later as a "liberating shock." The fusion of Horon's geopolitical doctrine based on rigorous historical research (Ratosh called it "articulate") with Ratosh's disdain for Britain and Zionism, along with his highly developed sentiment of nativeness to Palestine, resulted in the creation of an ideology that retained Zionism's nationalist component but redefined its addressee. Eri Jabotinsky testifies: "Adya must be acknowledged as the real founder and author of the ideology known as 'Canaanism.' I think that the 'Canaanite' movement was created when Adya met in Paris Uriel Heilperin, otherwise Uriel Shelaḥ, otherwise Yonatan Ratosh."[77]

What each of them particularly contributed to the final shape of the ideological edifice is now impossible to discern; after several decades of common toil, "it is difficult to say where the one's ideas end and the other's ideas begin."[78] Both Jabotinsky[79] and Porat[80] claim that before their decisive meeting Horon and Ratosh had already been expressing ideas that are usually considered the other's contribution to "Canaanism." Most sources agree that it was Horon who educated Ratosh on the "Jewish question" in light of his version of Hebrew history, whereas Ratosh instructed him on the "Arab question," persuading Horon that what was known as the Arab nation was neither Arab nor a nation (see chapter 3 for a full exposition of this theme).[81]

This intellectual link does not stop here; through Ratosh Horon came to know Avraham Stern, then a senior member of ETZEL. Porat reports a tripartite meeting that took place in Paris in 1939 between Horon, Ratosh, and Stern, at which Horon insisted on the formulation of a detailed plan for the shape of the future Hebrew state.[82] In the summer of 1940, Stern broke away from ETZEL to form an independent militia under the name "The ETZEL in Israel," which after its reconstitution in 1943 renamed itself Fighters for the Freedom of Israel (LEHI in Hebrew acronym).[83] Quite a few of Horon's and Ratosh's ideas (before the latter's conversion to "Canaanism") made their way into the LEHI's ideology, and Ratosh throughout his life took credit for "sowing the seed of the LEHI."[84] At the same time, many elements of Stern's ideology remained antithetical to atheistic "Canaanism"—first and foremost, his deep reverence for Jewish religious heritage and his messianic leanings[85]—and therefore the dialectical relationship between "Canaanism" and the LEHI, which itself underwent a series of profound ideological metamorphoses over its eight-year history that quickly made Stern's initial outlook obsolete, makes for a fascinating enquiry.[86] Eri Jabotinsky is certainly justified in suggesting that "it is worth looking one day into the Gourevitch-Shelaḥ-Yair [Stern] chain of connections and influences."[87]

In parallel with his meetings and conversations with Ratosh, in the summer of 1938, Horon occupied himself with setting up yet another discussion club on history and geopolitics, which adopted the name "La Renaissance Hébraïque" (The Hebrew Renaissance).

Unconnected to the Revisionist movement, this club acted under the auspices of the Association Amicale des Israélites Saloniciens (AAIS), the society of the Jews of Salonica in Paris, one of whose pillars was Yehouda (Leon) Jossua, a wealthy businessman who turned to supporting Horon financially. Jossua had an amateur interest in Hebrew history and linguistics and took a lively part in the activities of La Renaissance Hébraïque. At Jossua's invitation, Horon delivered a series of twenty lectures to the AAIS on the history, ethnography, and mythology of the Hebrews, which were afterwards published under the title *Canaan et les Hébreaux* (*Canaan and the Hebrews*),[88] followed in March 1939 by four lectures on geopolitics, subsequently published as *Perspectives du Mouvement National Hébreu* (*Perspectives of the Hebrew National Movement*).

Other participants in La Renaissance Hébraïque included George Blumberg, who lectured to the AAIS on the "Jewish question and the Hebrew renaissance," Leon (Lico) Ghedalia, and—apparently discreetly—Boris Souvarine. Concerning the latter, Horon writes in his record that he introduced him to Jabotinsky in 1938, resulting in Souvarine's "conversion" to the idea of a Hebrew national revival, as his life-long interest (with a "Canaanite" slant) in all matters related to Israel and the Middle East testifies. "It is curious to state," Horon adds, "that the 'conversion' to Hebraism (though not Zionism) of this former general secretary of the Leninist Third International is my work." Another participant was Yonatan Ratosh, who delivered ten lectures for the AAIS on the "Hebrew problem in the Near East."[89] Yehoshu'a Porat identifies the latter's broader input in the anti-Arabist and anti-British statements of La Renaissance Hébraïque,[90] as these topics were almost entirely absent from Horon's earlier writings and utterances.[91] Horon asserts in his own record that the intellectual sophistication of La Renaissance Hébraïque was in part due to these newly introduced elements.

Members of La Renaissance Hébraïque adopted semihumorous pseudonyms drawn from Hebrew or proximate languages to cultivate the spirit of a romantic coterie of dreamers fascinated by the picturesque Mediterranean antiquity, whose political relevance to the present day they attempted to articulate. Thus, George Blumberg became "Belial" or "Ben de Ben Ben"; Leon Ghedalia, "Humbaba"; Leon Jossua, "Gilgamesh";[92] finally, Gourevitch's life-long nom-de-plume "Horon" also probably originated in this milieu. His daughter suggests that it might have been coined by Eri Jabotinsky, "who had a hell of a sense of humor and an aptitude for punning."[93] Jabotinsky saw in the physical features of his friend a resemblance to a falcon and appropriated for him the name of the Egyptian falcon-god Horus (originally a totem of the pharaohs), which appears in several Hebrew Canaanite ethnonyms and toponyms (like Bet-Ḥoron), as well as in the name of the Canaanite vengeance deity.[94] As for the name "Adya," much later adopted as his official name, it derived from a Russian diminutive of his given name Adolphe (*Adia*), which he had come to dislike with the rise of Hitler, and forfeited gladly.[95]

In June 1939, members of La Renaissance Hébraïque published in Paris a first issue of *Shem: Revue d'Action Hébraïque* (*Shem: A Hebrew Action Review*). George Blumberg was listed as the editor since he was among the few in the group who was born in France (to Jewish Romanian parents) and therefore held French citizenship. *Shem* is the first known occasion of the use of the "Horon" pseudonym: the issue features an article signed by "Ammi-Horon," alongside an article signed by A. Gour. Horon's best-known quote from this journal is that "the event of the birth of a new nation should not be hidden behind a Jewish veil, as part of an attempt to convince the whole world that finally something Jewish was happening in Palestine at a time when . . . something Hebrew was occurring in Canaan,"[96] words that, as Horon explained in his record for Eri Jabotinsky, were uttered in the context of the breaking by ETZEL of the *havlaga* ("restraint") policy adopted by the official Zionist bodies in face of the Palestinian Arab Revolt of 1936–1939[97]—a "Samsonite" step in his view. George Blumberg also contributed two articles to this issue, one under his own name, the other under the pseudonym G. Belial.

This issue of *Shem* was designed as the platform for the ideology of a Hebrew national resurgence as envisioned by Horon after his break with Zionism and to develop further the ideas first hatched in Rodêgal. However, while Rodêgal, with all its ideological idiosyncrasy, still spoke of a Jewish national revival, *Shem* replaced it with a "Hebrew" revival, assuming that the concomitant destruction of the Jewish way of life and identity, and the subsequent reterritorialization of the Jews, necessitated a new national terminology. The "Hebrews" of *Shem* are therefore still not the Hebrews of the "Canaanite" brand that rejected any meaningful connection between them and the Jews. Porat[98] argues quite compellingly that the radical critique of Zionism in the pages of *Shem* conformed to the principles of Maximalist Revisionism as developed in the early 1930s by Aba Aḥimeir and his associates and did not therefore constitute a complete withdrawal from the ideological fold. It is for this reason that Horon wrote in his record for Eri Jabotinsky that La Renaissance Hébraïque was not a prototype of the Young Hebrews, but "something else—for better and worse."

These ideas were elaborated in an article written by George Blumberg using the alias of "Belial." Published as a separate brochure,[99] it can be considered the ideological manifesto of La Renaissance Hébraïque and therefore representative of the worldview espoused by its members. Sensing the darkening atmosphere of late 1930s Europe, Blumberg pictures a very gloomy prospect for the Jewish Diaspora. He assumes that the Jews will not survive as a group unless they take immediate and decisive steps, in defiance of both the Gentile world and unwilling Jews, to territorialize themselves in Palestine. This entails the complete overhaul of the components of Jewish identity, since the failure of assimilation demonstrates that Jews cannot choose a nation to join at their will. Rather, in order to become a nation again, as dictated by their historical fate and the fact of descent from ancient Hebrews, they must seek inspiration in the Hebrew national myth made available by recent archaeological discoveries. Recovering a Hebrew national identity, Blumberg asserts, is identical to the recovery of humanity by Jews, and that means that "Jews must cease being Jews, they must become human again, they must become a nation again, they cannot become but a single nation, the Hebrew nation."

The raison d'être of the Hebrew renaissance is, therefore, not to create an asylum for persecuted migrants, model farms, or a spiritual center for world Jewry. Its essential purpose is to transform landless Jews (*peuple sans terre*) into a Hebrew nation and Palestine (*terre sans peuple*) into a sovereign Hebrew state by the expulsion of the British Mandatory power.[100] There is no point in framing this struggle in terms of a "Jewish cause," Blumberg adds, since it will not arouse any sympathy from the outside world; neither is there any point in waging a war against anti-Semitism. The anti-Semites, he contends, assault Jewish interests, which are not similar to the interests of the Hebrew renaissance, since the latter has nothing in common with the chimeras of the so-called "Jewish vocation." The anti-Semites are obviously not interested in the Jews becoming a nation and therefore are less dangerous to the Hebrew cause than the British, who are busy fomenting the "Pan-Arabist mirage" in the Middle East. This article, then, written as it was on the eve of the Second World War, displays a severe underappreciation of the particular brand of Jew-hatred espoused by Hitlerism.

And so, while Blumberg, much like Horon in 1935, is adamant that the Jews' historical role and duty is to willingly sign the death warrant for Diaspora Jewish legacy and tradition, he clearly considers the Jews the direct descendants of the ancient Hebrews, whose only way of escaping the Jewish fate of perennial persecution is to become again "Phoenicians." At the core of his discussion is still the "Jewish problem," though he argues that Judaism, being responsible for the fact that there are still Jews, but no Hebrews yet (apart from Palestine), must cease to exist in its present form. Notably, Blumberg considers Zionism a highly flawed form of the Hebrew renaissance and treats it in his article only in passing, as if it were next to irrelevant to his postulates.

Such attitude was radical enough to deter some potential supporters who grasped well in advance the implications of these ideas. Uri Avnery quotes in his memoirs the Maximalist Revisionist Wolfgang von Weisl, who explained his withdrawal from La Renaissance Hébraïque in the following way: "At first I had thought they wanted to fool the Arabs, so I supported them, but then I realized that they wanted to fool the Jews!"[101] As for Avnery himself, his encounter with La Renaissance Hébraïque was the first step in a long voyage beyond the limits of Zionism, which ended up in his formulating an ideology that merged radical-left anti-Zionism with a staunch nationalist outlook. From October 1941 through March 1942, he published a number of articles on historical topics inspired by the first issue of *Shem* in the Revisionist journal *Haḥevra*, the last of which he signed with his adopted Hebrew name instead of his given name, Josef Ostermann.[102] The articles, by his own later admission, were "full of superlatives" in relation to *Shem*, and their Nietzschean spirit demonstrated how quickly Avnery internalized Horon's attitude to both ancient Hebrew history and contemporary Zionism. However, the personal relationship between Avnery and Ratosh, whom he soon met, quickly turned sour, as the ideological differences between the two became more and more pronounced. Avnery was never a "Canaanite" in the proper sense; yet he remained throughout his long life a strong supporter of the idea of the separateness of Hebrew Israelis from Jews around the world. The political conclusions he drew from this foundation ultimately went in a direction opposite to that of Horon and Ratosh, especially as he regarded Pan-Arabism a potential ally rather than an enemy.[103]

Belial's article was found on the desk of Avraham Stern on February 12, 1942, the day he was killed by the British police in Tel

Aviv,[104] which gives some indication of the direction Stern's thoughts were heading in the last months of his life. Alongside this article lay two Polish booklets published in Romania in 1940 describing the Polish army's retreat in face of the Wehrmacht in September 1939. Their author was Jerzy Łużyc, a pseudonym for one of the greatest Polish nonfiction writers of the twentieth century, Melchior Wańkowicz.[105] The fact that Stern obtained and took interest in such material points to possible connections between the Hebrew underground and the Polish exiled administration and military, some of whose units were deployed in Palestine. These contacts, such as they were, were based upon the prewar cooperation between ETZEL and the Polish government, and their continuation in wartime Palestine is undoubtedly a topic worthy of further scholarly attention.[106] After all, their best-known result was the appointment of Menachem Begin to the leadership of ETZEL after his release from the Polish army in exile in 1943.

A final matter to ponder is the location of La Renaissance Hébraïque and *Shem* on the left-right perimeter against the backdrop of the looming global clash between Nazism and the forces opposing it. Observers, both hostile, like Shavit,[107] Porat,[108] and Eliav,[109] and sympathetic overall, like Avnery,[110] tend to censure Horon for his supposed right-wing extremism, in which they identify the influence of the prewar French and Italian fascist right. Eliav goes as far as to accuse Horon of authoring "memoranda expressing sympathy toward the Axis states,"[111] by which he probably means Horon's 1939 opinion, given in *Perspectives du Mouvement National Hébreu*, that the Hebrew movement must be ready to strike a deal even with the Satan, let alone with Hitler, "who is not the Satan" (sic!).[112] Porat additionally contends that the subtitle of *Shem—Revue d'Action Hébraïque*—was borrowed from the *Revue d'Action Française* of Charles Maurras, the ultra-Catholic monarchist and anti-Semite, and suggests that Horon's loathing of de Gaulle as a British stooge (later on exacerbated by the French withdrawal from Algeria in 1962) by way of negation implies an acceptance of Pétainism and the Vichy regime as legitimate manifestations of French patriotism.[113]

It remains beyond any reasonable doubt that the late-1930s European zeitgeist speaks quite loudly from the pages of *Shem*.[114] But is the fact that Horon and his associates wilfully used the rhetoric and symbolism of the prewar Far Right (and took lightly the true nature of Nazism, as many others, including Zeev Jabotinsky, did) sufficient to identify speech with ideology? It seems to me that these accusations against La Renaissance Hébraïque are made with the benefit of hindsight that attributes guilt by association. Numerous political bodies in France that sprang up all over the country following the February 1934 political crisis profusely employed the designation *action*, including strongly left-wing anti-fascist committees. Treating *Shem*'s "fascist" vocabulary and spirit entirely literally leaves no room for possible nuance or irony (assuming that such might have been present), all the more so since as early as in 1933 George Blumberg copublished a harshly critical analysis of Nazism, diagnosing it as a "rebellion against reason."[115] Furthermore, when a newspaper article about Horon repeated Porat's allegation concerning his presumed attitude to de Gaulle and Vichy France,[116] his daughter angrily refuted it, insisting on his liberal-democratic credentials.[117]

The fate of the members of La Renaissance Hébraïque after the outbreak of the Second World War and the fall of France varied. Yonatan Ratosh returned to Palestine in September 1939, and Boris Souvarine fled to the United States. Meanwhile Horon (although not a French citizen) and George Blumberg were called up into the army. Horon entered the engineering corps, yet shortly afterwards he was suspected of being a "Soviet spy" (probably due to his proficiency in Russian, which his interrogators somehow linked to the operations of the NKVD on French soil in the late 1930s). This led to him being court-martialed and nearly sentenced to execution, from which he was saved by the intervention of his wife. Upon release, Horon was dispatched to an officers' training camp in Versailles, but he saw no combat action due to France's swift capitulation, as predicted by Blumberg. He then evacuated his family to Nice in the "Free Zone," whence he attempted to reach Palestine illegally with the help of Ratosh, but he failed to raise the necessary funds. On Souvarine's intercession, he managed to obtain American visas for his family from the Emergency Rescue Committee, a body established under the auspices of Eleanor Roosevelt with the purpose of saving Europe's intellectuals and artists from the Nazis.[118]

Jossua and Blumberg took refuge in Marseilles, where in late 1941 they set out to produce *Shem* clandestinely under assumed names, as part of their involvement in the French Jewish resistance. New authors who had also found shelter in southern France appeared on its pages, including Jossua's nephew by marriage Edmond Asséo, André and Jacqueline Amar, prominent members of the "Organisation Juive de Combat" ("Jewish Resistance Organization"), and Frédéric Max, the future diplomat and pioneer of the Roma Genocide studies. Leon Jossua took over the editorial tasks until his arrest by the Gestapo in March 1943 in Marseilles, whereupon he was taken to Drancy detention camp and murdered in Auschwitz in June 1943 at the age of forty-five.[119] The rest were tipped off in time and remained in hiding, restarting *Shem* in January 1944.

Wartime *Shem*, which merits separate research and is treated only cursorily here, manifested both continuity and change with regard to its prewar "legal" predecessor. The issues now came out irregularly and were reproduced by typewriter on poor-quality paper (procured by Jossua on the black market) without any professional typographic design. They were still mostly devoted to questions of Hebrew renaissance, now tinged with the disaster of the ongoing Holocaust. Each issue, of about one hundred copies each, was distributed mostly among other resistance groups. The subtitle of the journal was changed after its third issue in October 1942 to *Revue du Mouvement National Hébreu* (*Hebrew National Movement Review*), as a defiant statement of the will to struggle and to mock Vichy's "Révolution Nationale."[120]

The journal was discontinued after its twelfth issue in July 1945. George Blumberg, who became a military correspondent, settled in Palestine in February 1946.[121] He returned to France in December that same year entirely disillusioned with the Yishuv, which he described with disgust as "crabs in a bucket." He subsequently worked in commerce and as a translator and editor and became involved in local politics before his death in 1987. Leon Ghedalia, an antiquarian, died shortly afterwards, while Edmond Asséo, a physician, lived until 1999. The archives of La Renaissance Hébraïque, hidden after Leon Jossua's arrest and subsequently forgotten, were rediscovered in 1963, when the Israeli embassy in Paris was informed of their existence. The article that reported the discovery[122] was full of errors, such as confusing Horon with Blumberg, that were only partially corrected by a subsequent intervention from Israel's former ambassador to Belgium, Joseph Ariel.[123] The documents were then transferred to Yad Ṿashem, where they remain to this day.[124] However, as detected by Yehoshu'a Porat,[125] the Yad Ṿashem depository actually contains the archives of two separate groups: La Renaissance Hébraïque and the unconnected "Massada" group from the French concentration camp in Compiègne, led by the lawyer and right-wing Palestinian Zionist Yitzhak Kadmi-Cohen, whose final fate was similar to Jossua's (it remains unclear how the two became mixed).[126] "Massada," unlike the anti-Pétainist La Renaissance Hébraïque, advocated a form of

Hebrew renaissance with the presumed support of the Vichy regime. This difference in political disposition actually harked back to 1931, when the second issue of *Le Cran* published a negative review of Kadmi-Cohen's book, presciently titled *L'État d'Israël*, due to what it considered its binationalist leanings in the spirit of Brit Shalom.[127]

America with an Israeli Intermezzo (1940–1959)

In late 1940 or early 1941 the Gourevitch family settled in New York.[128] Their impression of 1940s' America was decidedly negative: what they encountered was small-mindedness and widespread xenophobia toward Jewish refugees from Europe. Horon was not drafted into the US Army following its entry into the Second World War, officially for medical reasons, though he suspected that this rejection was actually motivated by a scathing critique of the French military, and of de Gaulle in particular, in a memoir he wrote shortly after arrival (the US military officials supposedly could not swallow an eyewitness account of an allied army that still used bridge-building manuals from the Napoleonic era). In the academic sphere, the dominance of the American biblical archaeologist William Foxwell Albright, who allegedly detested Horon's *maître* Virolleaud, may have prevented him from obtaining a secure scholarly position.[129] Between 1944 and 1946, Horon worked as a lecturer in Semitic linguistics and ancient history at the expatriate French higher education institution, the École Libre des Hautes Études, housed in the premises of the New School for Social Research in New York, and gave counsel to Souvarine on biblical history for an annotated Bible the latter was tasked with preparing. Around 1947, Horon was appointed head of the Semitic languages department of the United Nations translation service,[130] remaining there until his move to Israel two years later. Additional funds came from public lectures and translation assignments and were sometimes provided by friends.[131]

Horon's employability was further undercut by a nervous breakdown he suffered after learning the full extent of the Holocaust, in which members of his extended family and friends perished. Among the latter was Leon Jossua, with whom Horon had continued to correspond for as long as the United States maintained diplomatic relations with Vichy France. Horon's letters to Jossua and Blumberg, uncovered among La Renaissance Hébraïque documents in 1963, attest to the mood on both sides of the Atlantic early in the war. Horon writes about his dissatisfaction with life in America and shares his income worries, exacerbated in his opinion by the American intellectual class's reverential attitude to all things Jewish and biblical, leaving the historical vision worked out by La Renaissance Hébraïque crying for audience. Horon therefore encourages the friends remaining behind in France to persevere in their struggle for their historical-political vision and promises on his own part to contribute writings, and even to compose a full utopian book that will do for the Hebrew renaissance what Herzl's *Altneuland* did for Zionism. He celebrates the news that traces of a Phoenician colony were identified in Brazil in June 1940, meaning that it was actually the Hebrews who "discovered" the American continent (given that Horon never took the issue further, we may assume that the "discovery" was soon disproved).[132] He sums up his reflections on the condition of the Hebrew idea and its bearers in La Renaissance Hébraïque by confessing that "the more I think about the meaning of events, the more I see at their center a small group that is a seed of the future."[133]

Horon's intellectual imprint during the 1940s was left most strongly upon the ETZEL delegation to the United States, dispatched there early in the war under the leadership of Hillel Kook, the most senior ETZEL member outside Palestine, who assumed the political pseudonym "Peter Bergson." Members of the "Bergson group" included old friends and acquaintances of Horon, such as Eri Jabotinsky and Yirmiyahu Halpern, as well as seasoned members of the Revisionist movement, such as Shmuel Merlin and Arieh Ben-Eliezer. During the war and in its immediate aftermath, the group established a number of advocacy lobbies that superseded each other, changing titles, aims, and sometimes strategies—among them The Committee for an Army of Stateless and Palestinian Jews, The Free Palestine Committee, The Emergency Committee to Save the Jewish People of Europe, and The Hebrew Committee of National Liberation, its last and longest incarnation (1944–1948).

The ETZEL delegation has earned some measure of notoriety in Zionist historiography due to its loud and at times deliberately provocative public relations tactics, particularly during the Holocaust, on behalf of European Jews and in the service of the Hebrew national idea. In Kook's interpretation, however, the Hebrew idea quite quickly drifted away not only from "mainstream" political Zionism but also from Revisionism. The reasons for this mostly have to do with the clash between democratic-civic nationhood as embodied by the American body politic (at least in theory) and the ethnonationalist principles brought from the Yishuv and Europe by the ETZEL delegation, which it could not repudiate without turning its back on Zionism itself. This transition is quite extensively analyzed in the available historical literature, which sometimes gives due credit to Horon for initiating it (or at least playing a central part in its triggering); nonetheless, the precise nature of Horon's impact and its results have eluded most scholars.[134]

What I wish to argue here is that the adoption of a liberal-civic form of nationalism by the Hebrew Committee of National Liberation was terminologically channeled into the distinction between "Hebrews" and "Jews" as articulated by Horon. This distinction became a practical discursive tool both among the members of the Committee and in conveying to the American public the associated rejection of what they perceived as the ethnonationalist illiberal founding principles of Zionism. By extension, this meant as well the abandonment of the objective of a "Jewish national sovereignty" that would jeopardize the Jews' position throughout the Western world and the advancement of full enfranchisement and emancipation—assimilation, effectively—as the best sought-after solution for those Diaspora Jews who were for reasons of their own uninterested in Hebrew national revival.

One of the results of this development was a complete breakdown of trust between the "Bergson group" and its mother organization, the Palestinian ETZEL. After 1948, this lack of mutual confidence expressed itself in the tension between the Ḥerut party leadership and those members of the Hebrew Committee who became Israeli parliamentarians, and which ended in the latter's purge from the party by Menachem Begin in 1950–1951.[135]

Horon was never an official member of the Hebrew Committee, though he did take part in some of its activities, contributed to its publications,[136] delivered a number of talks to its members[137] and received occasional remuneration for them.[138] In his lectures, Horon laid out both his views on current affairs and his historical opinions on Hebrew antiquity that legitimized his wartime politics. Here we encounter for the first time Horon's mature historiography that includes all the essential elements not only of the "Canaanite" ideology, but also that of the Hebrew Committee, and that he continued to develop for the remainder of his life. In one of these talks Horon concisely explained the nature of his connection to the Hebrew Committee and his "behind-the-scenes" role:

> I must say a word about my own position regarding this Committee. It is rather peculiar. I am not a member of it, yet I am not a real outsider either. Some of the most active men in this movement I have known for years, some of them I may call my friends and comrades-in-arms. Yet I had no part whatsoever in the creation of the Committee, and no influence on the shaping of its policies, for which I cannot feel responsible. And yet I feel very much responsible for the very name of this Committee, for the name of Hebrew, and *for the ideology which should be connected with such a name.*[139]

The contents of this ideology were elaborated in greatest detail by Eri Jabotinsky in a series of articles entitled "Jews and Hebrews," which he published between October 1947 and February 1948 in the Hebrew Committee's mouthpiece, *The Answer*.[140] These articles combine discussions of Hebrew history with the resultant political conclusions pertaining to the present day and are replete with profuse quotations from Horon's talks before the Committee and credit him with providing the historical background. Jabotinsky's objective is to expose the intellectual inconsistency and political decay of the Zionist movement (within which he also includes Revisionism) and to assert that the Hebrew/Jew dichotomy propagated by the committee is the authentic incarnation of the principles of the theoreticians of Zionism, Herzl and his own father, Zeev Jabotinsky. By stating that "the term Hebrew used by us is but a new and more definite name for an old concept," Jabotinsky actually makes his friend a canonical exegete of classical Zionism: "Horon's ideas were not immediately accepted. When he first outlined his theory in 'Shem' it aroused a storm in the Jewish intellectual circles in Paris. The war interrupted their further propagation and it was only in 1943, that they were taken up again by the Free Palestine Committee, which has been working in America since 1940 under Mr. Peter Bergson."

The crux of the distinction, in brief, between "Hebrews" and "Jews" as adopted by the Hebrew Committee is that the former denotes a territorial-linguistic nation, whereas the latter refers to a worldwide denomination, whose members belong to the different nations wherein they dwell. But—and this is the key theoretical innovation, albeit with a questionable empirical basis—in ruined Europe, Jews could no longer claim to belong to the nations that in the vast majority had turned against them. They are therefore classified as "Hebrews in exile," since the Hebrew Yishuv is by default the only national body to which they can and wish to claim allegiance. Therefore, the committee drew an ontological equivocation between a "Hebrew located today in Tel Aviv and a Hebrew found today in Bergen-Belsen,"[141] except that the former has brought their national identity into full realization, whereas the latter strives to do so but is prevented by adverse forces, mainly Great Britain, which blocks access to Palestine by refugees from postwar Europe:

> The Hebrews comprise today:
>
> 1. The Hebrew settlers already rooted in the Hebrew land, forming there the nucleus of a reviving nation.
> 2. Those who want to join the Hebrew nation through an act of free choice and will.
> 3. Those who are in need of a Hebrew Republic, and who must join the Hebrew nation as their only means of physical and spiritual salvation. This category includes mainly the hundreds of thousands, indeed the millions of oppressed or uprooted Jews and so-called "Non-Aryans," for whom there is no more room in the world outside the Hebrew nation—since nationhood is the law of the modern world. For every man and woman in this category the liberation of the Hebrew land and the creation of a Hebrew Republic is a question of life and death.
>
> The difference between the three categories, however, is purely academic. Whether forced by circumstance or impelled by conviction, or simply because they are Hebrews by birth, the Hebrews share a common interest which makes them a tangible political body.[142]

The Hebrew republic envisaged by the Hebrew Committee would emulate, in the formation of its body politic, the structural and principled solutions implemented by the United States of America. It would not therefore be an exclusionary Judenstaat, but would form a unitarian national society made up of the Hebrew Yishuv, the exiled Hebrews to be "repatriated" from Europe, and the native Arab Palestinians (whom the Hebrew Committee did not regard as possessing any national characteristics of their own): "The Hebrew movement strives neither for a 'Jewish Palestine' nor for a 'Moslem Palestine.' It strives to build *one* nation, *to create one single Republic*—the Hebrew Republic. This Republic will accept all those individuals who want to be part of it, and will grant a status of complete civil equality to every group, religious or other, that would prefer to retain its moral, social, cultural autonomy."[143]

The deviation from Zionism's principles and goals is evident. However, the Hebrew Committee's ideology is also removed from the "ideal type" of "Canaanism" developed at the same time in Palestine by Ratosh, who indeed attacked the committee very harshly for what he perceived as its midway stance toward Zionism.[144] This is due to three key precepts: a) the Hebrew Committee considered the Jews the direct descendants of ancient Hebrews, which explains the ease with which it reclassified Jewish refugees from the Holocaust as "exiled Hebrews"; b) it considered Zionism a legitimate and necessary historical stage in Hebrew modern history that had come to a natural end and wished to thrive on its achievements; c) the geographical scope of its vision was limited only to Palestine on both banks of the Jordan (as such, it agitated vehemently against granting independence to Transjordan in 1946). Furthermore, despite the impression one might gain from Eri Jabotinsky's reference to *Shem*, the Hebrew Committee was not a direct continuation of La Renaissance Hébraïque, which functioned in radically different historical circumstances and tackled a set of entirely different problems. Unlike *Shem*, the Hebrew Committee did not frame its Hebrew national vision in terms of solution to a "Jewish problem" conceptualized in national terms since any such problem, according to Kook and his associates, was immanently not a national one. An a priori assumption made by the committee was that Jews either unable or unwilling to follow the path of complete emancipation and assimilation in a liberal-democratic society automatically became Hebrews, whose national salvation lay in the establishment of a US-type secular egalitarian Hebrew republic in Palestine. In addition, the example of the United States as a national society consolidated around a common future rather than a local history that is foreign to most of its population made up of immigrants and their descendants was very different from the example of France, whose body politic derives its historical legitimization from common historical territorial-linguistic bonds. These two distinct sources of inspiration for Hebrew Israeli territorial nationalism make for some fascinating dialectics that become very pronounced in "Canaanite" writings.

The name chosen by Hillel Kook for the ideology promulgated by the Hebrew Committee, surprising as it may sound from today's perspective, was "Post-Zionism." He first used the term, in a meaning hardly different from the one in vogue today, on December 10, 1947, when the *New York Herald Tribune* published a short letter in which Kook explained the committee's stance on the Palestinian question following the United Nations' decision on the partition of Palestine, and outlined its ideas regarding the future shape and "human boundaries" of the imminent state.[145] This letter was followed by a number of polemical utterances, in which the committee and its spokespeople reaffirmed their self-designation as post-Zionists and offered more detailed elaborations on what this entailed for the Zionist movement and the future political arrangements in Palestine.[146] In brief, the committee called for the full disestablishment of all Zionist bodies and organizations now that their declared objective had been achieved and for an egalitarian secular Hebrew state that would both solve the problem of postwar Jewish displaced persons ("exiled Hebrews") and embody the political rights of the indigenous people of Palestine, Hebrews and Arabs alike.

Chapter 4 offers a deeper investigation of the 1940s' post-Zionism, its intellectual bonds to the "Canaanite" idea, and the significance of the fact that post-Zionism originated on the borderline between "Canaanism" and radical Revisionism, rather than in the liberal Left, for which it is so often mistaken today.[147] In the present biographical context, it is sufficient to note that by the time Kook declared himself post-Zionist, he had had a falling-out with Horon, resulting in a life-long mutual enmity. "They were at daggers drawn since then," says Horon's daughter,[148] who recalls that her father accused Kook of embezzling some funds collected by the Hebrew Committee. He also had a low opinion of him as an intellectual[149] and later condemned his apparent "reconversion" to "some form of Zionism" as a result of the anti-Semitic campaign waged in the USSR in Stalin's final years.[150] By the late 1940s, Horon's name had disappeared completely from the publications of the Hebrew Committee; instead, between October 1947 and March 1949, he placed a series of historical-political commentaries (under the name "Adiag") in *La Riposte*, the French-language counterpart of *The Answer*, which was edited in Paris by the veteran French Revisionist Albert Stara.[151]

Eri Jabotinsky suggests that Horon played a crucial role in expanding the Hebrew Committee's activities to Europe on the eve of Israel's independence thanks to his prewar contacts in France, and indeed there is a documentary evidence of Horon's presence in France during Israel's war of independence, when he was most probably involved in the dispatch of the ill-fated munitions ship Altalena to Israel in June 1948.[152] The bloody Altalena affair resulted in Kook being arrested and held without trial for several weeks by the Ben-Gurion administration. Perhaps even more interesting, while in France, Horon submitted to the European representation of ETZEL a brief historical-political essay, in which he argued that the ongoing Hebrew liberation war was just the first step in the liberation of the entire Land of the Hebrews despite the Zionist leadership's active attempts to curb this liberating thrust.[153] It very possible that this document reflects an attempt by the Hebrew Committee to influence the ETZEL into accepting a form of national non-Zionist Hebrew ideology and snatch battlefield initiative by announcing wide-ranging and long-term strategic goals of regional anticolonial liberation that would be incompatible with Israel's limited raison d'état as set out by Ben-Gurion. In such speculative scenario the ETZEL, guided by a broad historical vision of the ancient Hebrews' cultural greatness and spatial outreach, would become a truly oppositional armed militia that would defeat not only the Arab armies but also the Zionist establishment tainted with seclusionary "Jewish" historical consciousness that coveted the Land of Israel in separation from Canaan and the entire Land of the Hebrews. Begin's order "not to shoot" and let Altalena burn certainly quashed any such hopes.

The establishment of Israel marks the next major turn in Horon's life. Against Ada Gour's best advice, he quit his job at the United Nations and moved with his entire family to the new state. He arrived in mid-May 1949, with ambitious dreams to found a truly "Hebrew" university that would disseminate historical knowledge based on Horon's understanding thereof, but also with more realistic plans to establish a translation bureau and to work on his historical researches. In his suitcase lay the typescript of a recently completed book on Hebrew history, "Le Monde des Hébreux," which he intended to translate into Hebrew with the help of Yonatan Ratosh.[154]

Upon arrival, however, Horon found himself in constrained circumstances. The country was poor, with few job offerings for a person coming from an educational and political background like his own. Not only was Horon a former Revisionist, but he also was a stranger to the Ḥerut party establishment in Israel, which was in conflict with former members of the "Bergson group," who were still calling from the tribune of the Knesset and in party forums for the complete secularization of the state guaranteed by a constitution. Nor was he able to forge any productive political or personal relationship with Ratosh and other "Canaanites," whose experiences and opinions were very different from his own. In the event, Horon had to make do with odd translation jobs, while revising on behalf of Ṿa'ad Halashon (the Language Committee, a precursor to the Academy of the Hebrew Language) Zeev Jabotinsky's Hebrew study manual *Taryag Millim* (*613 Words*) for its second publication.[155]

Eri Jabotinsky assisted Horon in assuming the editorial supervision of the prehistory section in the *Encyclopaedia Hebraica*, for which he wrote several entries on prehistoric topics[156]: the closest that Horon's view of history has ever got into mainstream Israeli scholarship (in a private letter he expressed his surprise at "how the editorial board swallowed this and all of Horon's previous articles"[157]). However, he quickly ran into conflict with the editorial board of the *Encyclopaedia*, especially with the strictly observant Yeshayahu Leibowitz, whom Horon faulted with imposing a "rabbinic" spirit on the *Encyclopaedia*, and had no kind words to spare for the other editor-in-chief, Ben-Zion Netanyahu, as well.

Finding that resources for his work on the *Encyclopaedia* were lacking in Israel but abundant in the United States, and having fallen ill with rheumatic fever in early 1950, Horon resolved with a heavy heart to return to New York in April 1950, less than a year after his arrival.[158] If "[his] stay in Israel was a disaster," says his daughter, then abandoning the state "was one of the lowest points of [his] life: a kind of admission of defeat."[159] In a letter sent from New York in October 1950 to friends remaining in Israel, Horon compared his short stay to a Dantean descent into Hell and recalled George Blumberg's failure to accommodate to the Yishuv a few years earlier. He detailed the reasons that had pushed him back to America, both material and political. Having invested a significant amount of money in the move, he was unable to obtain a steady employment befitting his qualifications; living in the Judean Hills, close to the tension of the Jordanian border, and with their heavy climate, he felt he was putting his family in peril[160]; last, he found the social structure of Israel repugnant, describing it as a kind of feudal socialism, "a magnificent marriage of 'managerial socialism' with a High Middle Ages theocracy." Horon's low spirits are evident in this letter, which concludes with a description of his struggle to find a job back in New York and with the plea "Answer me. I am very lonely."[161] In his reply, Eri Jabotinsky invited Horon to cooperate on a project of a constitution for Israel, which he was advocating as a member of the Israeli parliament[162]; Horon however was not too excited about the offer given Jabotinsky's close personal contacts with former members of the Hebrew Committee and the fact that he did not resign his Knesset chair.[163]

Eventually, Horon returned to translation to make a living ("I am translating an average of 100 pages of psychoanalytical nonsense from German into English, as a substantial part of my livelihood," he complained to Eri Jabotinsky in October 1955[164]) and also became for a while a licensed agent of the New York Life Insurance Company.[165] In 1951 Horon managed through the intercession of the New York–based Egyptian naturalist and poet Ahmad Zaki abu Shady and art historian Meyer Schapiro to obtain a part-time lecturing position (albeit "unstable" and "rogue," in the words of his daughter[166]) in the Asia Institute founded by the prominent Persianist Arthur Upham Pope in New York, which offered evening courses in Oriental subjects.[167] The courses Horon delivered included Canaan in World History, Early Africa in Relation to Asia and Europe, Hebrew: Classical and Modern, The Hamito-Semitic Languages, and Israel and Lebanon Today.

Shortly, however, his relations with the Asia Institute ran aground. In late 1952 Horon organized two public meetings that he intended to devote to the explanation and analysis of the perils of Pan-Arabism (and, tapping into contemporary American anxieties, its possible or alleged links to communism), with the support of the French delegation to the UN and some Zionist bodies. For the second meeting the institute insisted for the sake of balance on inviting some pro-Arab speakers and the entire event, according to a French-language report compiled probably by Horon himself, transpired in a very tense atmosphere, with the anti-Arab speakers discriminated against by the unnamed moderator. This persuaded Horon that the Asia Institute became yet another Arab agency in the United States, and he severed his contacts with it. Instead, together with friends he bonded with through these events (such as the Moroccan advisor to the French delegation to the UN Muhammad Temsamani, who spoke at the first event, or the American-Zionist scholar Joel Carmichael), he started to look for avenues to continue their anti-Arabist activity independently of the Asia Institute. A draft proposal preserved in Horon's archive floats the idea of an American-based information and publication bureau that would work closely with like-minded public figures in Lebanon, France, and Israel, as well as with Lebanese expatriates in the United States.[168]

At the same time, now that Horon and Ratosh were physically out of each other's way, the two rediscovered their ability to work fruitfully together. Horon advised the Young Hebrews from America on geopolitical matters and since late 1950 had contributed original articles and translations to the "Canaanite" journal *Alef*. He also advocated *Alef*'s principles in public meetings in the United States and offered practical help in procuring print paper for *Alef* in America in order to circumvent the paper limits imposed by the Israeli government. In return, *Alef* undertook to publicize and disseminate in Israel the American publications Horon was involved in, while Horon would disseminate the output of the "Center for the Hebrew Youth."[169] In 1952, Ratosh's middle brother, Gamliel Heilperin (who adopted the pen-name "Svi Rin"), joined Horon in the United States, but the two failed to cooperate due to differences in political disposition and personal temper.[170] Rin, nonetheless, relied on Horon as well as on his brother in his own postgraduate studies of Hebrew antiquity.[171]

Quite soon, Horon grew distant from Ratosh as well. Though still appreciating him as a great mind and a friend who "should not be forgotten,"[172] he became impatient with his doctrinarian radicalism and lack of flexibility that was undermining their common objective. In his letters to the Young Hebrews in Israel, Horon warned against adopting a decolonial "Third-Worldist" position in the platform of the "Center for the Hebrew Youth," which he saw as a potentially procommunist "Oriental nationalism" that was drawing the unwelcome attention of Israeli censorship and intelligence. Moreover, while Horon was willing to accept mass Jewish immigration to Israel, or to tactically compromise on the ideal of separation of religion and state, Ratosh would not, thus earning from Horon the epithet of a "communist atheis[t]." In Horon's view, the most absurd aspect of Ratosh's behavior was that principles Ratosh had learned from him in Paris and toward which Horon himself maintained a degree of reflexive distance, Ratosh treated as sacrosanct. In a characteristic comment that Ratosh would have certainly found extremely offensive, Horon described his friend's ideological rigidity as actually very "Jewish." He saw the Young Hebrews consolidated around Ratosh as a closed group resembling the Baptists, busying itself with grand designs for the future and therefore not bothered with mundane tactics and day-to-day struggles and the accompanying political costs.[173] Unbeknownst to Horon, the same derisive label of "Jewishness" was attached to him in private by Aharon Amir, who took him in 1949 for a brainy Diaspora Jew who used the Hebrew idea to accommodate himself in Israel.[174]

For all these reasons, Horon preferred to focus on practical and intellectual cooperation with the "Kedem Club," established in the mid-1950s in Haifa by Eri Jabotinsky and the architect Shmuel Rosoff. In terms of political outlook this club largely continued the ideas of the Hebrew Committee of National Liberation through its declared post-Zionism, married to an idea popular among certain circles of the Israeli Right (and occasionally floated by David Ben-Gurion as well) of an anti-Arab "minorities union" in the Middle East. This idea, which probably originated in French colonial attitudes in the Middle East and North Africa,[175] challenged the supposedly British-inspired Pan-Arabist framing of the region by highlighting its ethnoreligious diversity as a core principle of policy making and state design. This mode of thinking portrayed the non-Sunni and non-Arab Middle Eastern societies as the descendants of the pre-Islamic autochthonous populations and therefore the addressees of a national revival project, whose claim to historical authenticity and hence to greater political and cultural rights would effectively contest the Arab Muslim cultural and political domination. The Kedem Club believed such a contestation could only be successful if the pivot of these minorities' consolidation were to be Israel. Israel in turn would need to shake off its Jewish-Zionist residues to lead the regional liberation struggle against Pan-Arabism as a Hebrew state, and therefore a genuinely organic part of the Eastern Mediterranean rather than a Diaspora outpost with an army and a fleet.[176]

The American organization that reflected these principles most closely and consequently served as the Kedem Club's opposite number in the United States was the "Levant Club." This club was established in the early 1950s by Lebanese Maronite expatriates in America, with branches in New York and Detroit, homes to significant Lebanese Christian communities. In truth, the Levant Club was hardly anything beyond a front organization for the Lebanese Phalange (Katā'ib) party, and the ideology it espoused was Lebanese "Phoenician" nationalism, which stipulated that the nation of Lebanon was not essentially Arab but hailed from the autochthonous Canaanite Phoenician populations of Mount Lebanon and its environs. It is therefore unsurprising that many Christian Lebanese nationalists admired Zionism and Israel (albeit not unreservedly) for its belligerent attitude toward all forms of Arab nationalism, and the history of practical, political, and intellectual cooperation between the Yishuv and Israel on the one hand and Christian Lebanese nationalist figures and movements on the other stretches from the beginnings of Zionism to at least the 1982 Lebanese War.[177]

It is not known when Horon had "discovered" Lebanese "Phoenician" nationalism, though its adherents were certainly present in Paris in the 1930s,[178] where he might have come to know them. The United States being neutral ground, the Levant Club was an instance of a post-1948 collaboration between "Phoenicianist" Lebanese and pro-Israeli (which is not the same as "pro-Zionist") Jews in America; American Betar apparently played some practical role in setting up the club. In one of his letters, Horon specified that among the members of the club's organizing committee, apart from himself, was a religious Jew, a straightforward Zionist, a Betar member, and a follower of MAPAI, the Israeli ruling party at that time.[179] Their common goal was to foster a Lebanese-Israeli strategic alliance that would do away with sectarian-denominational politics in both countries (though in the Lebanese case this actually meant the entrenchment of the domination of the Maronites over other ethnoreligious communities[180]). It would take Lebanon out of the Arab League and battle Pan-Arabism, which, in their interpretation, was fanning the anti-French struggle in Algeria, and would firmly ally Israel and Lebanon with the "Western world" in global geostrategic dynamics. The club's activity concentrated on producing political pamphlets, memoranda, statements, and periodicals, the first of them being *The Levant: Behind the Arab Curtain* in 1952 (in which both Horon and Eri Jabotinsky, then on a visit to the United States, had a part). These were distributed among policy and opinion makers in Lebanon, Israel (with the help of *Alef*, as mentioned above), France, the United States, and some Arab countries. The club also founded newspapers (or purchased existing ones) that circulated among the Lebanese diaspora in the United States, including the *Lebanese Gazette*, *Lisan al-'Adl*, and *aṣ-Ṣabāḥ*. To these newspapers, Horon, under various pseudonyms, was a constant contributor—the only known instance of the "Canaanite" ideology being laid out in print in the Arabic language.[181]

Horon's pen was dedicated at this time above all to combatting the Pan-Arabist ideology and, in addition to the Levant Club publications, he contributed a number of articles to various forums without paying particular attention to their ideological profile: the urgency was clearly too great.[182] He also corresponded with the American publisher F. Praeger regarding a projected book on the Middle East and North Africa, "The Hebrew Land by the Euphrates,"[183] as well as with the right-wing French publisher Roland Laudenbach concerning the potential updating and printing of his mid-1940s study, "Le Panarabisme."[184] Finally, Horon regularly contributed to the political periodicals *Est & Ouest* and *Le Contrat Social*, edited by Boris Souvarine, largely in the same vein.[185]

The Levant Club generated some curiosity in Zionist circles in America and in Ḥerut circles in Israel (as well as a probably passing interest in the government and intelligence services, who noted its cooperation with the Kedem Club[186]). Joseph Schechtman, a high-ranking Revisionist functionary in the United States, with whom Horon later cooperated on the production of Jabotinsky's biography,[187] was particularly interested, though Horon framed his interest as "spying" on them on behalf of the Zionist establishment. The party newspaper *Ḥerut* also devoted some attention to the club.[188] The most intriguing of the club's documents are the minutes of a discussion between its leadership (with Horon present) and the Israeli military attaché in the United States and Canada from 1954 through 1957 Katriel Śalmon (identified in the document only as Colonel Katriel S.), that took place on December 15, 1954.[189] The discussion concerned means of cooperation between Israel and Lebanon, and one learns from it that the Levant Club was planning to raise funds in America for the paramilitary training of members of the Katā'ib.[190] The first Lebanese civil war (1958) was just a few years away.[191]

The extensive correspondence between Horon and Eri Jabotinsky, especially from 1954 through 1956 (two samples of which are reproduced in the appendices), throws light not only on the evolving relations between the Levant Club in the United States and the Kedem Club in Israel, but also on the internal life of the two associations and the variances of opinion that gradually started to overshadow their common objectives. In time, the two clubs started to drift apart, largely due to local specifics in their respective areas of activity that were insufficiently clear to the other side. Horon criticized Eri Jabotinsky for his parochial, inward-looking tendencies, his apparent inaction, and his exaggerated emphasis on the issue of Palestinian refugees, which, he felt, was playing into the hands of left-wing critics of Israel abroad. On his own side, he implied a feeling of intellectual solitude among the Zionists and the Maronite nationalists in the leadership of the Levant

Club. Concerning the latter, he admitted that their nationalism and pro-Israeli inclinations were basically "Zionist" in tone and content, and that they could not accord any meaning or significance to what for "Canaanism" was the cornerstone—the ontological distinction between Hebrew and Jew. Horon also conceded that, Christianity being one of its fundamental building blocks, Maronite nationalism was quite clerical in character. For this reason, he found it necessary to downplay his own strong support for the principle of separation of religion and state and chastized the Young Hebrews for pressing the issue so strongly that they repelled potential partners.[192] Whether, and to what extent, Horon was aware of the actual effects of Maronite religious particularism on their national ideology, and the degree of their incompatibility with his own "Canaanite" outlook, remains an open question.

Despite these disappointments, the Levant Club provided Horon and his associates with numerous paths of contact with prominent public figures in the United States, Israel, Lebanon, Morocco (which until 1957 remained a French protectorate), and France, with the hope of rallying them behind the club's cause of achieving a "non-Arab" solution for the problems of the Middle East. Some of these contacts extended quite high: in his letters Horon mentions connections, or attempts to initiate ones via mutual acquaintances, with Menachem Begin, the Maronite bishop of Tyre (through Eri Jabotinsky), the French ambassador to the UN, and the aforementioned member of the Moroccan delegation to the UN Muhammad Temsamani. The latter, described by Horon as supporter of "Canaanism" and Maronite "Phoenicianism" and opponent of the "Anglo-Arabs" (as demonstrated by his speech in the event Horon organized in the Asia Institute in 1952, where he lambasted the Moroccan nationalist Istiqlal party as "irresponsible trouble-makers"[193]), suggested that Horon should make a political visit to northern Africa. Horon even attempted to approach the Moroccan sultan himself through the Jewish Moroccan engineer Idriss Belghi, in whose hands he deposited a report on Pan-Arab activity in the United States intended for the sultan.[194]

Thanks to the good services of Boris Souvarine, who undertook to distribute Horon's 1945 study of Pan-Arabism, "Le Panarabisme" (originally commissioned by the French government[195]) among French policy makers and public intellectuals, as well as building upon pre-existing contacts from the 1930s, Horon developed a particularly thick web of connections with members of the French political class, especially those involved in the struggle for l'Algerie Française. These included the French secretary of state for war, Jacques Chevallier, who was also for a time the mayor of Algiers; the vice-president of the French Union (the French equivalent of the British Commonwealth), Marie-Hélène Lefaucheux; Louis Gros, a senator representing French Morocco in the French National Assembly[196]; Camille Aymard, editor of the Casablanca journal *Paris: Organe de la Présence Française en Afrique du Nord*[197]; General Augustin Guillaume, French resident-general in Morocco[198]; and Jacques Soustelle, governor-general of Algeria in 1955–1956.[199]

The full-hearted engagement on behalf of the French in the Algerian conflict, which Horon interpreted as a clash between Soviet-backed Pan-Arabism and his own vision of liberal nationhood embodied by the French Republic, consumed a large part of his life during the 1950s. It is probably close to impossible to collect and enumerate all the pieces Horon published under different pseudonyms in defense of the French cause in Algeria; on that subject, Uri Avnery testifies to his shock at seeing a pied noir mouthpiece filled with contributions by Horon lying on Jacques Soustelle's desk.[200] Horon even participated in establishing an American weekly devoted to this single issue, called *Middle East & West*, apparently financed by the French consulate in New York.[201] The periodical, however, did not last long: with the downfall of the Fourth French Republic and the return to power of Horon's old nemesis Charles de Gaulle (in what Horon euphemistically described as "not . . . arbitrary circumstances, but unfortunately . . . more profound and unhappy ones"[202]), its sources of revenue dried up. Horon decided to use the funds that remained after the journal's closure to implement his dream of returning to Israel, where, he hoped, public atmosphere would be more conducive to this type of anti-Arabist activity. In early 1959, Horon followed his wife and daughters to Israel.[203]

Israel (1959–1972)

Horon arrived in Israel with dreams of taking up a chair in history at the University of Haifa,[204] yet—just as they had two decades earlier in the United States—his unorthodox views on history and politics obstructed his academic advance. Horon discovered that the Israeli intellectual class felt no differently from their American counterparts with regard to biblical history and its political meanings; in private, he referred to them as "idiots with a diploma" ("ḥamorim meduplamim," literally, "diplomaed asses") who lacked the moral courage to state out loud what clearly emerged from the historical evidence.[205] In the end, Horon returned to translating as his chief occupation for the remainder of his life in Israel (including, at one point, translations of radio broadcasts in Swahili[206]): in a letter written shortly before his own death in 1969, Eri Jabotinsky mentions his "friend Gour, a shy historian who is making his living by translations."[207]

In the early 1960s, Horon was one of the founders of the Israel Program for Scientific Translations, which later grew into the Keter Publishing House. Its purpose was to provide employment for the influx of highly qualified immigrants from Eastern Europe by commissioning translations of scientific works, mostly from Russian into English, for Western universities, think tanks, and, possibly, intelligence services. Horon was initially put in charge of the program's geology and geography department, but after suffering a debilitating stroke in 1961 that confined him to his home in Ramat Aviv, he relinquished all managerial duties and concentrated solely on translation. The best-known book he produced in this capacity was the English translation of a Soviet history of ancient Arabia,[208] which was quite coolly received by the Western academic community.[209] Other books translated or edited by Horon during his final years in Israel (or earlier) included Carlo Levi, *Fear of Freedom*, and Gilbert and Colette Charles-Picard, *Daily Life in Carthage*.[210] Some additional tasks that Horon undertook as a translator were, one might assume, less to his taste on account of their pro-Zionist bent, such as rendering entries from English into Russian for *The Shorter Encyclopaedia Judaica*, which started to appear in 1976, four years after Horon's death.[211]

Another source of income, as well as avenue for dissemination of his views, were public lectures. During the 1960s and early 1970s Horon delivered a considerable number of talks on Hebrew history and Israeli and Middle Eastern geopolitics to university and high school students, soldiers, nurses, members of the Jabotinsky Order, urban clubs, *'olim* societies (including North African Francophone immigrants and newcomers from the USSR), and, at least once, members of Betar France. Before 1962, most of the talks concentrated on the "Algerian question" and the necessity of defeating the Front de Libération Nationale (FLN). When put paid to this, Horon's talks turned to more general topics, united by the common theme of the imperative for internal reform in Israel to put it on liberal-democratic tracks as a Hebrew nation-state and the fulcrum of a regional alliance against Pan-Arabism. One such talk was given at an ideological seminar of the Greater Israel Movement in Jerusalem in December 1971, despite the movement's overtly religious and Zionist nature. Some talks were booked by official Israeli or Zionist bodies, such as the Ministry of Education or the Jewish Agency.[212]

Apart from these occasional invitations, Horon had ample opportunity to preach his ideas within discussion clubs organized by members or sympathizers of the Young Hebrews, with the explicit purpose of producing intellectual and political ferment in Israel by injecting their ideology into the state's public life. Three of them deserve particular attention: Club 59, Club for Hebrew Thought, and Club for Hebrew Guidance. The last two were established as rival organizations by Aharon Amir and Yonatan Ratosh respectively, and Horon's participation in both illustrates the twilight dynamics of the "Canaanite" movement.

The first, Club 59, is arguably the most mysterious initiative Horon involved himself in. As far as I know, it has left no traces in any official archival repository in Israel, and all that is known about it (and presented below) is drawn from materials preserved in Horon's personal archive. Club 59, so called after the year of its establishment, was probably the first organization Horon joined or cofounded on his return to Israel (the latter is more probable given that his archive contains drafts of its statutes and some other core documents, partly handwritten). At the same time, although it adopted Horon's historiography as its legitimizing apparatus and guide toward its objectives, Club 59 was not a "Canaanite" body. The tension between "Canaanite" and Zionist tendencies and values is evident in the documentary record, which contains criticism of "Canaanites" made by Horon himself, while criticism of Zionism remains more veiled. Its overall leaning is more post-Zionist, in the spirit of the Hebrew Committee of National Liberation and the Kedem Club, than anti-Zionist, as can be gauged from the questions from the audience that Horon scribbled down during the talks he gave to the club. Though no document in Horon's archive identifies its founders and members, it can be surmised that the club was made up of sympathizers of Ḥerut, disgruntled with what they might have considered Begin's betrayal of Jabotinsky's secularist-liberal legacy. This tendency comes across quite clearly in the club's founding documents, which I cite below *in extenso* due to their public unavailability (notably, most of them are in English). The club's declaration of aims, for instance, is phrased in the following way:

> The Club wishes to discuss the problems faced by the State of Israel in the light of a single task: the completeness of the homeland. [This] means both liberation of historical territories and demarcating strategic boundaries, and the accomplishment of the entire process of the Hebrew renaissance: a full return of the people, the consolidation of the people in the spirit of the renewed Hebrew culture and the joint participation of <u>all</u> the inhabitants of the homeland in the construction of the renewed Hebrew nation.

In December 1959, club members accepted the following charter:

> . . . 4. THE AIMS OF THE CLUB:
>
> a. To strengthen, deepen and broaden the Hebrew national outlook and movement in Israel, among its Jewish as well as non-Jewish population;
>
> b. To seek understanding, friendship and support for this movement abroad, both in the East and the West—especially in the Mediterranean world and quite particularly within Israel's own neighbourhood, i.e., in the Levant area;
>
> c. To help raise the cultural standards of human relations, while resisting all forms of bigotry, chauvinism or discrimination inimical to such standards;
>
> d. To further the development of an intellectual, social and political elite capable of providing guidance and leadership for the stated ends;
>
> [. . .]
>
> 5. THE PRINCIPLES
>
> a. We believe that nationhood is the basic form of collective existence in the modern world; that national life must enhance, not destroy the freedom and dignity of individual groups or persons; and that a nation, with

its component sections and individuals, should use the State as an instrument of harmony and fulfilment, not become enslaved to the State as to a master.

b. We also believe that the modern nation is a complex being, both spiritual and material, defined by a territorial framework and a cultural personality; and furthermore, that it is an open society, able to acquire, like any living thing, new cells, new elements from the outside world, and therefore not restricted to an exclusive, racially or religiously limited membership.

c. Man, we believe, does not live by bread alone; likewise, a nation has not only "needs" and "interests," but also ideals and a mission—in respect to itself and in relation to the universe. It follows that the several nations, far from being condemned to permanent mutual hostility, may cooperate on certain levels and even form supranational, regional associations.

d. On the other hand, and by the same token, none of the totalitarian ideologies, old or new, seems to us compatible with the existence of nations or the survival of free individuals. For us, as free men and members of the Hebrew nation, both Communism and Panarabism are, at present, the arch-enemies.

e. As applied to the case of Israel, the above principles can be expressed axiomatically as follows:

    i. The State of Israel is the first imperfect expression of the Hebrew national rebirth;

    ii. Israel must develop as a national Hebrew state, perforce multi-racial and multi-denominational, and not as a glorified Jewish ghetto;[213]

    iii. The mission of Israel is twofold: —to guide as many as possible among the dispersed Jewish people toward the normalcy of national Hebrew existence, —and to free from oppression as much as possible of the Levant (wherein lies the historic Hebrew territory);

    iv. The appeal of Israel must therefore be directed not only to its own citizens, and not only to the Jews;

> but also to the oppressed "minorities" in the Levant and to all those forces in the world, particularly the Mediterranean world, which are threatened by Panarabism, or by Communism, or both.
>
> Such are our vital ideals, and such also our material interests; any *Realpolitik* without corresponding "idealism" (or vice-versa) would be utterly unrealistic, and immoral.[214]

Since there is no further documentary evidence available at the moment relating to the activity of Club 59, we can assume that it fell dormant quite quickly without leaving any noticeable impact on Israeli public life. Subsequently, in the mid-1960s, Horon was drawn in by Aharon Amir to participate in his Club for Hebrew Thought, which, although established by a "Canaanite," accommodated a wide array of opinions, much wider than Ratosh, for example, would ever have endured. Among the participants in the club's discussions were public figures, parliamentarians, academics, and high-ranking military officials such as Nissim Rejwan, Rustam Bastūni, Yehoshu'a Palmon, Shim'on Shamir, or Ḥaim Beer, all of whom used the forum to voice their own ideas pertaining to Israel's raison d'être. These discussions were gathered under the title *Tsvat Rishona* (*First Pincer*), coedited in 1966 by Horon with Rejwan, Amir, and Esra Sohar.[215]

Amir also encouraged Horon to commit himself systematically to writing up his newest historical researches, which resulted in *A World in a Hebrew Outlook* series of articles that appeared in 1965–1966 in the literary review *Ḳeshet* published and edited by Amir. Those articles were supposed to become the core of a fifty-thousand-word book on Hebrew politics and history (*Ḳedem Ṿa'erev* being one of the proposed titles) of nine to twelve chapters that would summarize and bring up to date Horon's historical findings and political insights. The book, which was supposed to be submitted around 1969 to the "Canaanite"-friendly publisher Hadar, failed to ultimately materialize in full form.[216] Only five articles were eventually published in *Ḳeshet*, and many years later Amir confessed his frustration with Horon, who notoriously failed to meet deadlines due to his perfectionism. Ratosh, who had been in a protracted conflict with Amir since the early 1950s (and which was only partially healed in the early 1980s), reacted very negatively to the series, due to the ideological reservations he harbored toward Horon's methodology[217] and also on the grounds that Amir, as editor, refused to publish his comments on Horon's work, reluctant to expose any rifts in the minuscule "Canaanite" camp.[218]

After the 1967 war, Amir transformed his Club for Hebrew Thought into an Action Staff for the Retention of Territories (occupied by Israel), which briefly attempted to join forces with the Zionist Greater Israel Movement that appeared slightly later.[219] By that time, however, Horon had disengaged himself from Amir's enterprises. Dissatisfied with his propensity to "smooth things over" and to compromise on principal issues, Horon soon realized that in the long run it would be more fruitful to cooperate with Ratosh, who would not contemplate any collaboration with Amir. As Horon's daughter put it, her father admitted that "when push came to shove, Ratosh was a great intellect, and Amir a mediocre one."[220] Horon contributed to the "Canaanite" periodical *Alef*, which was restarted in 1967 without Amir—his last article there was dated May 1972—and delivered lectures on history and politics to Ratosh's Club for Hebrew Guidance, the final given only two months before his death. "Adya always came in carefully dressed, full of enthusiasm, a pile of books in his hands to illustrate his words with pictures from these books, a box of oddly-colored pencils, and various maps," recalled Ratosh's wife of these meetings.[221] These were reproduced posthumously (though not wholly faithfully, owing to Ratosh's editorial interventions) in the "Canaanite" anthology *From Victory to Defeat* in 1976.

All this points to mounting equilibrium in the relations between Horon and Ratosh. During his last years Horon finally gained recognition within the "Canaanite" circle and the wider public as being equal to Ratosh in the formation of its ideology. In a number of interviews, Ratosh acknowledged Horon's role in his own intellectual formation and drew on Horon in his study of ancient Hebrew history, published in 1971. In addition, Ratosh acquiesced in Horon's insistence that the movement's designation be changed from the "Young Hebrews" to "Canaanites" (similarly advocated by Svi Rin in the United States[222]) and asked him to review and comment on the draft of his booklet *1967—And What Afterwards?*,[223] incorporating most of his comments and insights into the final version (including the dropping of a reference to the victorious Israeli generals as the counterparts of Charles de Gaulle).[224] Horon reciprocated by submitting his talks to the Club for Hebrew Guidance for Ratosh's advance approval[225] and by accepting some of Ratosh's features of "Canaanism," which he had previously qualified as irresponsible radicalism (such as the inherent contradiction between Jewish and Hebrew identity), though on other key elements—such as the place of Carthage in Hebrew history—they remained at odds. Their personal contact, now growing closer, was as stormy as ever, tarnished by Ratosh's heavy drinking and both men's difficult characters. Margalit Shinar recalls scenes at home, where meetings between the two often took place: "[Horon] would walk about the house shouting that [Ratosh] was impossible, a devil . . . I heard my father repeat again and again: 'This man is draining me. He picks my brains, he picks my brains, but I let him: he is a genius who turns the pickings into extraordinary poetry.' "[226]

Around the same time, Horon took part in an attempt to resuscitate the "Canaanite" movement as an active political group under the title "Bene Kna'an" ("Sons of Canaan"). To support this initiative Horon published in 1970 the booklet *Erets-Haḳedem*, intended as a short and accessible review of his main ideas in historiography and politics. This booklet, written at the suggestion of Esra Sohar, who also provided the introduction, was to be Horon's final major publication. It was enthusiastically greeted by pro-"Canaanite" reviewers and disseminated among potential sympathizers by the younger "Canaanite" generation belonging to the "Nimrod" youth movement.[227] Plans to publish it in foreign languages did not materialize.[228]

In parallel, Horon was invited by Eri Jabotinsky to partake in the establishment of a research and advocacy institute on Middle Eastern affairs, to be modeled on Hillel Kook's American Institute for Mediterranean Affairs (Kook committed himself to providing the funds). On that occasion Jabotinsky revisited some political disagreements he had with Horon,[229] yet Horon remained reluctant to join as long as Hillel Kook was involved, describing himself in a letter to Jabotinsky as "totally sold to the Canaanites."[230] He also pressed Ratosh into avoiding direct contact with Kook despite the latter's willingness to give financial support to the Young Hebrews' activities.[231] Eventually, the entire project ground to a halt with Jabotinsky's death in July 1969.

Perhaps the most "Canaanite" statement-by-action made by Horon in Israel is revealed in a postscript to a letter he sent to Eri Jabotinsky in December 1964. He mentions there that six months earlier he had taken Israeli citizenship and officially changed his name to 'Adya Gour.[232] With Horon living in Israel since 1959, this means that he became an Israeli citizen through naturalization rather than through the Law of Return. He was the only one in the family to do so: Margalit Shinar clarifies that she, her sister, and her mother all became Israeli citizens immediately on arrival. The reasons for her father's initial refusal of Israeli citizenship may have been entirely prosaic, possibly to do with formalities related to his American citizenship or matters of taxation.[233] Yet given his explicit and very strongly worded denunciation of the Law of Return (see chapter 3), it is entirely plausible that one of his motives for opting for naturalization was his unwillingness to benefit from legislation modeled on the Nazi Nuremberg laws.[234]

When Horon died on September 19, 1972, the Young Hebrews paid him a tribute in a memorial announcement in *Haarets* (29.9.1972) and, apart from including some of his writings in *From Victory to Defeat*, dedicated the entire anthology to his memory,[235] though initial plans included a full memorial issue of *Alef*.[236] Horon was interred in accordance with his wishes in the old cemetery of the northern Israeli settlement of Rosh Pina, which permitted secular burials. "In his funeral and burial he managed to beat the Jewish establishment," writes Joanna Ratosh in her obituary, "winning the right to be brought to rest like a human being, like a free Hebrew in his country, without the Ḥevra Ḳadisha functionaries managing his funeral . . . (albeit here as well his victory was incomplete, since officially this was still a Jewish funeral, with a rabbi present for a few minutes, but given the circumstances this was the lesser evil)."[237] The funeral was attended by Hillel Kook, Menachem Begin, Natan Yalin-Mor of the LEHI,[238] and, in the language of a brief newspaper note, "writers, poets, officers and youngsters."[239]

"The place where Adya was buried is located high on the mountain, and it is symbolic that it is not fenced in from any direction, but is ascended by numerous steps with tombs here and there, and the whole place looks more like a grove than a cemetery."[240] His tombstone, which carries the image of the falcon of Horus and the inscription "He who uncovered the history of the Land of the Hebrews and foresaw the Kedem Union and the *Pax Hebraica*," was designed by his son-in-law 'Ami Shinar (then still known as Śenir), who also undertook to collect, edit, and publish Horon's writings.[241] Twenty-three years later, Ada Gour was laid to rest in the same place. *Ḳedem Ṿa'erev*, which saw light in 2000, is dedicated to her memory.

Chapter 2

From Nation to Denomination

Adya Horon's Historiography

Who Possesses a "National Outlook"? The Nation in History

In the opening paragraphs of the first article in the *On History* series, written at the very outset of his activity as a public intellectual in the early 1930s, Horon established that a "nation does not exist outside its history."[1] The entire series of articles, which introduced the reader to ancient Hebrew history in the light of the most recent discoveries in biblical archaeology and philology, was premised on strictly historicist foundations: that in order to collectively shape the future, the past must first be discovered and understood. Over the years, Horon repeatedly made his historicist leanings clear.[2] Yehoshu'a Porat, who regarded Horon's early historiography as essentially Zionist, albeit differently distributing certain accents, concluded that Horon initially viewed national identity as being shaped by long-term developments over time rather than by geographic-territorial location.[3]

However, right from inception, Horon's concept of ethnogenesis (nation formation) was more complex. While, indeed, assuming that a nation *was* shaped by history, in the same breath he referred to "Aztec history" as the only authentic history possible in contemporary Mexico. Thus, he made it clear that national history meant local-territorial history.[4] The same was applicable to the Hebrews: in April 1931 Horon wrote that "what is characteristic of our tribe: its language and psychological make-up, was shaped *exclusively* on the soil of a common homeland, between the Euphrates and the Nile, between the Mediterranean Sea and the Great Desert. And only after the common tongue and common psychical make-up had emerged, may we speak of a 'Hebrew nation.' "[5]

We can infer from the above that Horon's early model of ethnogenesis was in fact a mixture of historicism and environmentalism. Porat, however, is correct in observing that eventually the latter came to dominate Horon's thought, though only gradually: in a large typewritten draft of a never-published book, "Le Monde des Hébreux," dated to 1949, the discussion of the Hebrews' geophysical surroundings is preceded by a discussion of the Hebrews' language, culture, and faith, with both given roughly equal space.[6] In order to realize how this development came about, we must first place Horon's ideas regarding nation formation in a wider theoretical framework, looking in particular at the question of pre-modern nationhood.

The formation of national identities is extensively explored in a huge body of literature, of which only a nonrepresentative sample was used for the present study.[7] Conceptualizing its subject matter evokes some congruent dichotomies. Yasir Suleiman refers to the *cultural* and the *political* concepts of national identity, drawing an implicit parallel between them and the *objective* versus *subjective* definitions of a nation, respectively.[8] A nation defined *culturally*, Suleiman writes, draws on ostensibly *objectively* measured elements that constitute its purported essence over time and space. The best-known set of elements is proposed by Anthony Smith—common territory, historical heritage, culture, legal and economic systems—yet variations abound. A cultural nation is in most cases believed to be preceded by a premodern ethnic community (an *ethnie*, a group of presumed or real common ancestry and a specific cultural identity). The distinction between a nation and an *ethnie* is central for Anthony Smith's ethnosymbolic approach: "An *ethnie* [is] a named human population with myths of common ancestry, shared historical memories and one or more common elements of culture, including an association with a homeland, and some degree of solidarity."[9] An *ethnie* "graduates" to a nation, according to Smith, when it produces a mass standardized culture and legal and economic frameworks, normally embodied in a sovereign state.[10] Therefore, even to such a strong believer in the premodern origins of nations as Smith, nationhood, unlike ethnicity, is an essentially modern phenomenon.

Conversely, for the *political* nation defined *subjectively*, the nebulous border between nation and *ethnie* is of lesser significance. What matters is the common *will to be* a nation, regardless of empirical grounding and putative premodern sources; the nation, claim the adherents of this concept, argues itself into existence. As expressed by Craig Calhoun, "Nationhood . . . cannot be defined objectively, prior to political processes, on either cultural or social structural grounds. This is so, crucially, because nations are in part made by nationalism. They exist only when their members understand themselves through the discursive framework of national identity, and they are commonly forged in the struggle carried out by some members of the nation-in-the-making to get others to recognize its genuine nation-ness."[11] The political nation is described as forming voluntarily by a chosen identification with a group, which manufactures its own traditions and rituals, though mindful on occasion of their dubious historical basis (as the title *The Invention of Tradition* by Hobsbawm and Ranger[12] suggests). In such a framework, intellectuals who articulate the principles of nationalism—in our case, Adya Horon—come to play a key role.

Disagreements notwithstanding, both supporters of the "cultural/objective" and the "political/subjective" nation largely concur that national identity in the modern sense cannot be identified prior to the early nineteenth century, when the Industrial Revolution, the French Revolution, and the liberation wars in the American continent popularized the idea of a conscious, active, and solidary citizenry. Even the latest intervention in the debate by Azar Gat,[13] who robustly attempts to tip the balance in favor of the "cultural/objective" concept, ultimately concedes that a modern nation is precisely just that. The resulting agreement is that national identity, however "new" or "invented," did not emerge ex nihilo, but utilized pre-existing cultural elements, some of them quite authentically ancient.[14] Suleiman borrows from George Schöpflin the notion of "resonance," implying a dialogue between modernity and premodernity, whose purpose is to place national identity upon authentic foundations: "Imagination, invention and mythologizing work only to the extent that they can successfully exploit authentic . . . aspects of the culture of those for whom a particular national identity is being constructed."[15] Ultimately, the "cultural/objective" and the "political/subjective" conceptions of nationhood are now accepted not as dichotomous poles but as the endpoints of a continuum. Therefore, in debating Horon's attitude to nation formation, this book will juxtapose the "cultural/objective" nation to "political/subjective" nation only insofar as its protagonist made this juxtaposition the operational lever of his political argument.

It is this juxtaposition's *discursive* character that is methodologically utilized here, not as a faithful depiction of reality.

Can it justifiably be argued that Horon's synthesis of historicism and environmentalism constituted usage of the "resonance" method? Horon's statement that "the nation is a wholly modern form of political organization; but the principle upon which it is based, —the homeland and a people sharing a consciousness of a common destiny, —is as old as the world"[16] suggests a positive answer. Horon employs three different terms in his discussion of Hebrew ethnogenesis that we must follow him in distinguishing: *'am*, which in Hebrew means "people," and *umma* and *leom*, which are both habitually translated as "nation." Horon writes that all three initially denoted blood ties and are therefore partially congruent; the difference between them stems from the various kinship levels reflected in each term and in their sources. *'Am* is explained as denoting above all a patrilineal extended family of cousins linked through their fathers (hence the Arabic word for paternal uncle, *'āmm*).[17] In ancient Hebrew the word was rich in meanings and nuances and could signify a group of clans forming a political-national identity, noblemen related by a cult or mythical origin to a certain deity, and, finally, a military formation such as infantry.[18] Conversely, *umma* (which, Horon indicates, shares its root with the Hebrew word *emm* and the Arabic word *umm*—"mother"[19]) denotes a matrilineal society, and is therefore more ancient. Finally, Horon interprets *leom* to mean a group of people tied by allegiance to an eponymous ancestor who usually bequeathed his name or some feature to his reputed descendants.[20] He emphasizes that *leom*'s ancestors might be mythical, originating in prehistorical animal totems that later transmuted into anthropomorphic gods, and lists some of the most significant totems in ancient Hebrew mythology that survived into Judaism as figures in the biblical narrative. Thus, Rachel is a sheep; Judah is a lion; Dan is both lion and snake; Naḥor (Abraham's grandfather) is a dolphin, the marine symbolism indicating North African rather than Mesopotamian origins, and so on. Numerous important totems of the Hebrews, Horon says, derive from the cattle family: Jacob is an aurochs; the golden calf is a relic of an ancient animalistic cult; the chief deity of the Canaanite pantheon, El, is also known as Shor-El, the Bull-God, worshipped throughout Western Asia (whereas Northern Africa worshipped the Sheep-God, reflecting differing agricultural conditions giving rise to differing myths of origin); finally, cattle symbolism abounds in Canaanite sacral art.[21]

Mindful of the contemporary connotations of the word *leom* (which in Hebrew routinely denotes a modern nation), Horon proposes to use the word *umma* when speaking of a premodern group united by common characteristics that can be perceived as nation forming: "We are in doubt," he writes, "whether it is possible to find a common term . . . for what . . . is nowadays referred to as a *leom*. When dealing with a distant past it is perhaps better to indicate the difference by using a less modern term, such as *umma* (. . . here meaning . . . a wide 'ethnic' unit)."[22]

Similar terminological ambiguity characterizes Horon's earliest attempt to address the question of Hebrew ethnogenesis in the *On History* series. Written in Russian, it employs terms that open up a particular field of references and connotations in the language of origin, not easily transferred into either Hebrew or English. For example, the word *narod*, which Horon uses very liberally, is normally translated as "people" (*'am* is the Hebrew equivalent in Horon's later vocabulary) but may less often denote a modern nationhood. Other terms we encounter in *On History* in the context of ancient Hebrews are *narodnost'* ("nationality," "peoplehood," or something like "volkisch essence") and *natziya* ("nation"), which in Russian cannot be partitioned into modern *leom* and the supposedly premodern *umma*.[23] The Latin loanword *natziya* in Russian has the precise meaning of "modern nation"; therefore, had the *On History* articles been written in Hebrew, the only correct equivalent would have been *leom*, a term that Horon took care not to apply to the ancient Hebrews in the 1960s and 1970s.[24]

References to what makes a nation are interspersed in Horon's writings,[25] but the only document that stands alone as a discussion of the essence of a national identity is a handwritten affidavit Horon composed for friends in the early 1960s and never intended for publication.[26] In it he says:

> A "Nation" [*leom*], in living Hebrew, is the modern equivalent of the Latin term *natio* . . . defined back in the age of the Franco-American Revolution . . . Unlike other names for social groups, such as folk, tribe, caste, race, etc., "nation" refers to a particular connection between the humans and their land . . . It denotes both the mental and the factual connection that obtains between a sovereign population and the boundaries of its sovereignty. This means that "nation" relates the entire human settlement, or at least its decisive

> part (*natio politico*), to an inhabited land, a particular geographical territory where its cultural and material values were and are created. This way, "nation" gives expression to the human contents of the geographical term "land."

At the same time, Horon concedes that a nation does not remain locked into its domain: mass migrations within and without are frequent, ethnicities mix, and foreign influences are imported to be creatively adapted by indigenous populations. "We cannot establish universally," he admits, "an indisputable relation between a historical nation [*umma*] and the geographical space wherein it exists . . . There are even nations for whom geography constituted a step-mother, who nevertheless rose to independence despite the lack of natural borders."[27]

It seems rather clear that Horon accepted as possible the existence of a national, or at least ethnic, identity in antiquity. We must not, however, simply assume that he took the presence of an ancient Hebrew nation for granted: quite early in his career, Horon became aware of the impossibility of ruling out any differences between the ancient and modern nation, as evidenced by his declaration in *On History* that "the [notion of a] sentiment of the Hebrew unity . . . should not be treated in too modern a way."[28] In the early 1930s, Horon traced the emergence of a Hebrew "national consciousness" to an ages-long process of consolidation that the Hebrew-speaking tribes underwent in Canaan. Likewise, in his 1960s writings, Horon insists, "This awareness of everything's dependence upon everything [meaning forces of nature intertwined with historical processes, which is the cornerstone of a national feeling] . . . was no less typical of the ancient peoples' sensation of the world."[29] His midcareer proposal for an overall definition of a nation is a community sharing language, civilization (here probably a substitute for "culture"), and aspirations on a native territory,[30] thus not merely ". . . an arbitrary item, dependent on such or such will."[31]

Horon's primordialist definition of a nation highlights the continuity between *umma* and *leom*. Constituting a nation means for Horon the acceptance and realization of certain values—irrespective of time and place. Therefore, what distinguishes the modern *leom* from the premodern *umma* is merely a higher form of political organization—which is exactly the distinction that Anthony Smith draws between a nation and an *ethnie*. A casual remark by Horon hints in fact at such a distinction: "All the 'forefathers' are apparently 'national' [*leumiim*] in the ancient sense—name-givers ('eponyms') to peoples [*'ammim*] and places."[32] That is, an ancient nation coalesces around a myth of familial origin, but it is also similar to a modern nation through the attachment to its ancestral territory.[33]

To conclude, to Horon's mind, it is not enough to believe in a mythical ancestor, or to simply dwell in a country. The ancestral myth and the group's relation to its native environment must form a *conscious synthesis* in order for this group to become a *leom/umma*.[34] Let us examine more closely the nature of this synthesis.

Yasir Suleiman recalls "the role of the physical environment in shaping the character of a people . . . Broadly speaking, the environment delivers this function through the boundaries it provides between regions, the climatic conditions which obtain in each region, the kind of soil each region has, and, finally, its topography. This view is generally dubbed 'environmental determinism' in the literature."[35] Environmental determinism holds that particular geophysical units, delimited by natural boundaries (such as seas, mountain ridges, rivers, or deserts), have the power to influence social identity in a way that brings about the development of a sentiment of belonging both to the inhabited land and to the people sharing it. A collective separated from other collectives by geography would coalesce over time to finally emerge as a national group expressing a unique form of attachment to its land through culture mediated via a unique linguistic medium.

With the adoption of environmental determinism, Horon's concept of ethnogenesis did away with racial and biological theories of nation formation. An authentic national consciousness is conditioned by a full and natural congruence between the history of a land and the history of the nation occupying it, which renders the issue of genetic bonds between ancients and moderns (whether or not such exist) redundant.[36] By making the Hegelian allusion that a "nation is not a casual populace and surely not a biological 'race' . . . [but] . . . constitutes the action of the spirit in nature, a historical-geographical phenomenon,"[37] Horon abandons radical primordialist nationalism. Hence, any idea of "genetic preservation" is a fable: "race" anyway is a vague concept that denotes biological traits common to human groups, which change not only genetically but also under environmental influence,[38] whereas "racial purity" is impossible in any country not bereft of culture and history.[39]

Other elements are at play in shaping a national identity: "We should denote—especially in modern reality—among the factors mediating between a land and its inhabitants . . . the political framework (a social-territorial regime) and the national tongue (as a national tool of expression and custodian of historical memories)." Yet "[t]heir importance notwithstanding, neither of these characteristics carries the determining weight in its own right, that is, outside the territorial identity . . . Elements of language or statehood are acceptable insofar as they are secondary."[40]

Thereby Horon dissents from numerous ideologues and theoreticians of nationalism who have observed the intimate link between a nation and its language.[41] Acknowledging the importance of language in shaping a national culture, he argues that a nation cannot simply be correlated with its speech, stating that "language by itself is not a national identity card."[42] Most nations are more than monolingual; the choice of language can be dictated by convenience, and not every language spoken by a nation is indeed its *national* tongue (like English for the Irish, or, closer to home, Arabic for the Egyptians). There are nations for whom more than one language is their own (the Swiss, for example), or nations that share to different degrees their language with other nations (like Anglophone, Hispanophone, or Francophone societies). Finally, some culture-shaping languages perform roles that are demonstratively nonnational (such as Latin for Christianity or literary Arabic for Islam).[43]

To awaken national consciousness an element of spirit must be present; or, in Horon's poetic words, "nature shall prepare for us a place on Earth—this is Land; but only human history will turn it into a 'homeland.'"[44] A group unified by identification with its land will develop unique forms of conceptualizing its location, which will give rise to cultural expressions of both belonging and exclusion. The nation articulates a collective conception of its physical world; that is, a particular weltanschauung or a "comprehensive, sunny conception of the Universe,"[45] which Horon terms "national outlook" (*hashkafa leumit*), takes root.[46] A national outlook is expressed by Horon in the following terms:

> A nation in its homeland exists only . . . in reciprocal relationship, as well as in a relation to the wide world. For the "Land" consists not only of its soil, its mountains, valleys, rivers, but also of the skies above or the sea and its routes . . . The land's location under the sun, its situation relative to seaways, the relation of the land-dwellers

> to these natural conditions, the world's influence on the land's population, and the population's influence on the world from within—all these belong to the manifold unity called *leom* (or *umma*) . . . We can add to the definition of "nation and homeland" as a wholeness other participants in this great natural unity: the nature's forces . . . the sun's rays and the showers, the waters of the sea and ground, the processes of universal history.[47]

Horon's definition of a national weltanschauung makes it both anthropocentric and geocentric. It is founded upon a vital and harmonious relationship between the one and the whole: between the single human being and the collective, between the collective and the land, between the land and the universe, in an ever-expanding circle of cultural references.

But why call this outlook "national"? It was suggested above that environmental determinism admits no distinction between modernity and premodernity since societies are influenced by their geophysical environment irrespective of historical age. Therefore, *any* group related culturally to its space is, in Horon's method, potentially a nation and hence is suited to no other outlook. In Horon's words: "The existing world does not present itself to people (or societies) from a vacuum . . . but from particular vantage points upon earth. Therefore, only national outlook constitutes a *true factual* theory."[48] A national outlook emerges out of the native soil and shapes a concept of the universe on material grounds—the only grounds known empirically to humans, especially ancients, who viewed their world with their feet firmly set on their land. The centrality of the material aspect for the ancient national outlook stems from the physical impossibility of beholding the earth from above, unlike modern cosmography, whose observing eye, Horon writes, "floats out there in the outer space, accompanying the Lord of Creation, or like a satellite camera."[49] Correspondingly, national outlook is a unity of time and space viewed from *within*, a unity encapsulated in the Hebrew word for "Universe," *'Olam*.[50]

The Hebrew national outlook was remarkable because of the ancient Hebrews' location at the center of the antique universe[51] and the early development of culture in their homeland. The Hebrews, Horon says, observed their country facing the rising sun with their backs to the Mediterranean Sea. In their perspective, east was to the front, west was to the rear, north was to the left, and south was to the right. Front/East was identified with higher geomorphological forms, therefore Hebrew *hara*—"to the mountain"—also meant "eastwards," while *yama*—"to the sea"—also meant "westwards."[52] The Hebrew name for Yemen (Teyman), Horon continues, comes from the root *ymn*, which indicates both "south" and "right," as well as "seashore," given its common etymology with the word *yam*, "sea."[53] Another indication of "seashore," this time designating the Atlantic West, is the Berber word *ataram*, which in Hebrew survives in the word for "south," *darom*.[54] Thus, when the Bible says "left to Damascus" it means "north to Damascus," and "in front of Egypt" is actually "east to Egypt."[55]

Other contemporary cultures had different dispositions: the Egyptians looked southwards to the sources of the Nile (therefore for them west was to the right and east was to the left), while the Sumerians and Babylonians looked northwards. Horon suggests that the origin of these differing orientations might have been the initial direction of the respective cultures' spread: the Hebrews spread eastwards, the Egyptians southwards, and the Mesopotamian civilizations northwards.[56] It is the latter's orientation derived from Chaldean astronomy that modern culture eventually adopted, identifying north quite arbitrarily with the topmost direction.

The Hebrew national outlook gave rise to plethora of cultural expressions. One of them is the division between the "red" and the "white" domains. The "Red" (*Adom*, from the root *'dm*, whose derivatives denote also "land" and "human being") stretched, according to Horon, from North Africa to Canaan, while the "White" (*Lavan*, from the root *lvn*, which also denotes "moon") began in the snowy mountain tops of *Lebanon* and continued northwards.[57] Watching the sun circling the area to their right and moving from the front to the back, the Hebrews identified the south as the sun's dwelling, naming it "the Land of Ḥam" (hence the Hebrew *ḥama*, "sun"[58]). To the north/left (in the "white" domain) was the "Land of Japheth," behind whose mountain-peaks the sun "hid" at night. In between lay the land of the "sons of Shem," which, despite its intermediary position, was closer to the Ḥamitic geo-astronomic circle, due to its location in the sun area.

Over the years Horon kept returning to the etymologies of the "three sons of Noah," which, as he asserted, when interpreted incorrectly, caused serious confusion in historical knowledge and consequently distorted moral and political worldviews. In true fact, Horon contends, the three names designate mythological godlike ancestors, who bequeathed them to ethnolinguistic groups that articulated their identification with those ancestors in cultural and cultic forms. The names' function was therefore both linguistic and ethnohistorical. Focusing particularly on the name "Shem" and its derivative "Bene Shem" ("sons of Shem," otherwise Semites), Horon translated the latter as "those who carry names," and therefore stand above the commoners. Having a name to cherish meant that the society identifying itself as Semitic was, as Horon puts it, "a society of patricians, of noblemen. The very legend of their origins, the very name they gave to their mythical ancestor—Shem, the very title which belongs to them, —Bene Shem, from which derives the modern word 'Semites,' means, in plain Hebrew, 'the Noblemen,' —men having a noble name and caring for it."[59]

Thus, the Hebrews from their earliest days considered themselves aristocrats in the ancient sense of the word—ennobled by a mythical-symbolic forefather, who many centuries later was incorporated into the legend of Noah and the deluge—and their clans were not just ethnic or familial units, but associations of noblemen, which later gained military significance.[60] The Hebrews are therefore the true original Semites, whereas neighboring populations (including the Arabic-speaking Bedouins) are "Semites" only insofar as they internalized certain characteristics of the Hebrews upon the latter's migration to the Arabian Peninsula. Ultimately "Semites" came to denote people speaking languages identified as Semitic—that is, Hebrew and its closest relatives—irrespective of their ancestry. Contemporary ethnolinguistics, which classifies as Semites peoples only because they speak languages related to Hebrew, though they had never identified themselves as such, are guilty in Horon's opinion of conflating linguistic identity with "race" and thereby lending scholarly legitimacy to various racial theories (including the most perfidious of all, anti-Semitism).[61]

Another cultural expression of the Hebrew national outlook is termed by Horon "admiration toponyms," meaning nouns that, without the definite article, signify general geographical terms, but with the definite article are reserved for particular locations that underpin the national outlook. These were common among the ancient Hebrews: for example, "the Land" or "the Country" meant the Land of the Hebrews; "the Sea" was the Mediterranean Sea; "the River" was the Euphrates, and so on. Such linguistic forms highlighted the geocentricity immanent in the national outlook, facilitating cognitive unity between the general and the singular, between the whole and the one.[62]

Developing a national outlook is contingent upon obtaining appropriate epistemological tools to analyze properly the relationship between the nation and its land. Although Horon did not produce a stand-alone methodological treatise on historiography, he extensively deliberated the question how to write history to facilitate nation-building in several works. Horon's approach to the issue was not entirely consistent: he acknowledged on the one hand that "[s]cience must be for its own sake," since a "'[s]cience that serves the nation' is an extremely dangerous phenomenon,"[63] and cautioned as early as in *On History* that popular memory creates legends, not history.[64] On the other hand, he was adamant that historical science must support the formation of a national outlook and contribute to the solution of contemporary questions of politics, economy, society, and so on. Moreover, national history is anything but parochial since it actually means a *universal* historical vision from a *particular* national vantage point that provides a correlation between the researcher's analytical methods and their own view of the world and the nation. A genuinely global or universal history *must* be anchored in a particular vantage point; otherwise there would be no truth or value to it. Hebrew history, for instance, is not a history *of* the Hebrews, but History as such, *viewed* by Hebrews.[65] Such attitude to the past positions one's own group as a living and active agent of history and therefore master of its own fate. This entails

> viewing the past, present and future of your nation, or even the world to which you and your nation belongs, from the very inside, from the very center of events, from the vantage point of your own consciousness. You grasp and judge and feel and believe in a way which differs entirely from the "objective" or "scientific" method, from the method of analyzing strange bodies, looked upon as dead bodies . . . [A] history of [this] type . . . alone can provide the mainspring of consciousness to a living nation. [66]

The series of articles Horon published in *Ḳeshet* from 1965 through 1966 becomes a blueprint for an authentic Hebrew national historiography, as its general title suggests ("A world in a *Hebrew outlook*"). Hebrew antiquity is not merely an age to be studied; it is *the* Hebrew golden age, which, as Horon makes amply clear, should inspire political action here and now: "The Hebrew nation will not develop adequately without self-consciousness, that is, without recognizing its own self and might. This is why we must base ourselves . . . on national historical-geographical background and scholarship . . . We should concentrate on antiquity—not merely because it is longest, but . . . [because it] accords with our particular points of view. For we are like a man rising from slumber . . ."[67]

To the nationally conscious and nationally informed "intrinsic" historiography, Horon juxtaposes the "extrinsic" view of history, which, to his pronounced chagrin, characterizes most, if not all, works on the history of the Hebrews, especially those by Jewish historians. A Jewish historian, Horon qualifies, need not be explicitly hostile to Hebrew pagan antiquity; it is enough to profess Jewish values and outlook to distort the picture of ancient Hebrew nation making. For such a historian, "the Hebrews will be a dead people, the Hebrew language, —a dead language, and the name of the Hebrews, —a dead name, meaningless in the present and unfit for any use. Or, if you want, fit for any and every use, —as a pompous synonym to the prosaic name of Jews."[68]

The main moral and methodological failing in an "extrinsic" history of the Hebrews is that its subservience to the grand idea of a historical "Progress" voids proper historical awareness. Works in this vein are not interested in the nation for its own sake, Horon avers, but instrumentalize it for such twentieth-century "prejudices" or abstract ideals as liberalism, nationalism, Marxism, or fascism. The Hebrews and their history are effectively treated in much the same way as Judaism was treated by *Wissenschaft des Judenthums* in Baruch Kurzweil's perspective: as a cadaver that cannot inspire any significant moral choices of contemporary pertinence.

This theme appears quite early in Horon's thought, since the *On History* series begins with a criticism of the available historical literature produced chiefly by Jewish historians enthralled by macro-historical paradigms.[69] It portrays Jews (which Horon did not then differentiate from Hebrews the way he did later) "either as god-seekers, or revolutionaries, or salesmen, truth-seekers, peaceful sheep, agents of cosmopolitism," and so forth. In effect, "there are plenty of books on our history[;] . . . however . . . they all lack the sense I am looking for, they lack *history*."[70] The situation remained equally woeful when Horon moved his attention from Jews to Hebrews: "[T]here are thousands and thousands of [books on the ancient Hebrews]," he stated in the mid-1940s, "but not a single one was written by an author who was, or tried to be, a Hebrew."[71]

A Hebrew historiography marred by Jewish historical consciousness (which in modernity, Horon remarks, tends to imitate Christian historical consciousness) will be focused on the role of Hebrew antiquity as a precursor to Judaism. It will therefore play down the intrinsic value or importance of Hebrew pagan heritage, treating it instead as an obscure introduction or background to the truly "momentous" historical chapter of Judaism as the world's first monotheistic creed. "Imagine, for the sake of comparison," Horon tells his readers, "a history of Ireland, where all the ancient and glorious past of the Celts is summarized in a hundred pages, while the following nine hundred are devoted to the occupation and colonization of Ireland by the English."[72]

A historiography that is unable to appreciate Hebrew history in its true proportions inevitably makes a caricature out of it. Guided by the "Messianic principle" (which is answerable for the Jews' infamous passivity in the Diaspora), Jewish historiography regards Judaism as a religion specific to Judea and its followers a "race" of the descendants of the exiles therefrom. Such a perspective, Horon asserts, cannot satisfactorily explain the factual history of Judaism, its dissemination in the Canaanite and Mediterranean geo-cultural spheres, the conversion of both Semitic and non-Semitic populations to it, and the various Judaic proselytizing movements around the world, from Yemen to Khazaria. It cannot explain how Judaism managed to preserve the Canaanite language and traditions ("a Hebrew consciousness") that enabled the Hebrew renaissance in the twentieth century. Similarly, Christian historiography of the Hebrews treats their antiquity as an introductory stage to Christianity and its *historia sacra*, with King David, to take an example, being reduced to no more than a precursor of Jesus. "This being so," Horon concludes, "what can we expect from our Jewish historians? They are describing what they perceive in the midst of the night. But it is the daylight we want, the broad daylight of the pre-Jewish, of the Hebrew past, —in order to see ahead, and prepare for the dawn to come."[73] Therefore, from a Hebrew national perspective, King David will be a Caesar, while Solomon will be an Augustus.

Horon thoroughly details the shortcomings he identifies in "extrinsic" Western scholarship of Hebrew and Middle Eastern history, both Jewish and non-Jewish. The problem starts at the basic level of interpreting the Bible: for Jews, Horon argues, this is a collection of various writings with different degrees of sanctity, while Christian historiography treats it homogeneously. Neither, however, sees it as a genuine source of knowledge about ancient paganism. Nonnational Western scholarship applies to the African Semitic world its own criteria of development, progress, and modernity, which it contrasts to equally Western conceptions of "Middle Ages." The Hebrew world and its broader environs emerge deformed from this treatment. Some of the widespread mistaken conceptions (originating with Ernest Renan) include an essentialised picture of "Semitic race," "pan-Babylonism," "a romanticism which uses the Bible to identify the 'eternal unchanging East,'" and the idea that the Hebrew people and language originated in the Arabian Peninsula.

Hebrew history is not analyzed in an authentically synthetic way that would place the Hebrews integrally in what Horon terms both the "Euroafrican space" and the "Semito-African world." Instead, different members of this geo-historical community are all examined separately: Hebrews are reduced to being the Jews' "racial" ancestors; ancient Bedouins are portrayed as the oldest of Semitic peoples; Islam is perceived as an exclusively Arab religion; the Eastern churches are largely ignored, and so are the deep-seated connections between the Hebrews, Europe, and Northern Africa;[74] the Hebrews as daring sea-roaming explorers are either forgotten or suppressed by malicious design.

To make matters worse, these historiographical and philosophical falsehoods pervade Israeli cultural and political discourse. Traditional Jewish historiography, which is busy cataloguing the miseries that befell the Jews during their alleged two-millennium dispersal, underpins the Israeli scholarly curriculum, alongside biblical romanticism and European scholarly paradigms drawn from Oriental archaeology and biblical criticism. With regard to the Hebrew land and identity, none of them promulgates a view from within and are thus either irrelevant to the Hebrew national outlook or overtly hostile to it.[75]

In spite of all these deficiencies, Horon never denied his own indebtedness to Western scholarship, in particular to biblical criticism and archaeology (as the bibliography to *Ḳedem Ṿa'erev* demonstrably shows). On a number of occasions, he even stressed the valuable contribution of Protestant-inspired critical study of the Bible to the demythologizing of the biblical text.[76] Indeed, given the profusion of Western academic sources in Horon's works, we cannot assume that he is free from their paradigmatic influence. Horon's style of historical writing largely corresponds to what Hayden White calls the "Organicist" form of historical explanation, whose teleological leanings make it characteristic of the national school of European historiography, and that of Leopold von Ranke in particular.[77] Then, the distinction between the earlier pagan Israelites and the later monotheistic Jews is a fundamental tenet of biblical criticism and also undergirds the thought of both Friedrich Nietzsche[78] and Oswald Spengler,[79] with whom Horon was undoubtedly familiar. Next, there are a number of easily observable parallels between some of Horon's principles and the ideas advanced by Gottfried Herder. Although they disagreed on the role of language in nation formation (Herder believed it to be of primary importance, Horon, as we have seen, relegated it to the background), some of their assumptions remain strikingly similar. Although a cleric, Herder treated the Bible as a collection of folklore rather than a revealed truth, an idea that became the starting impulse for biblical criticism. He was also fascinated by ancient German paganism, deploring Christianity's effect upon the German national "essence," quite similar to Horon's dislike of monotheism and Judaism in particular.[80] Some of Herder's ideas lie at the root of environmental determinism, such as his contention that the more a nation is secluded geographically, the stronger is the impact of geophysical conditions upon its identity.[81] Finally, Horon's antiracism brings to mind Herder's denial of superiority and inferiority among races and nations (also reflected in Horon's assertion that languages cannot be inherently "backward" or "advanced").[82] The unacknowledged influence of one of the fathers of modern nationalism is thus highly visible in the output of the father of "Canaanite" Hebrew nationalism.

Last, Horon's thinking on both ancient Hebrew and Arab history, as well as on nation formation, seems to engage in a tacit dialogue with the legacy of Ernest Renan. With Horon adopting a variation of the "cultural/objective" definition of the nation through national outlook, it is unsurprising that his explicit references to Renan, the main theoretician of the nation as a voluntary association of individuals, are meagre and utterly negative.[83] However, there appears to be a deeper influence here that contributed to Horon's understanding of how nations are formed and why neither Jews nor Arabs qualify as such. Renan's prejudiced attitude to Muslims was a matter of notoriety back in Horon's time, as was his conviction that ancient Hebrews were Hebrew-speaking Bedouins. These ideas Horon rejected due to their incompatibility with historical knowledge, but their moral thrust, which situated "tribal" Jews and Arabs as inferior to the "civic" nations of Europe (and France in particular), has to large extent shaped the "anti-Jewish" and Arabophobic tendencies of radical rightist Zionism, which Horon carried over into "Canaanism."[84] More importantly, while it was above all the territorial environmental determinism that eliminated racialist thinking from Horon's notion of nation formation almost entirely, the Renanist conception of the territorial rather than the exclusively ethnic nation participating in a "daily plebiscite" strongly echoes in the "Canaanite" critique of the nondemocratic and illiberal characteristics of Israel, to which Horon contributed his own share, as the next chapter will demonstrate.

Kedem: The Land in History

Horon's statement that "a nation is equivalent to its land"[85] is indicative of the centrality of geography to his thinking. His treatment of the notions of Land and Homeland, and especially of the Hebrews' national territory, is articulated in a way that makes the Land an active autonomous agent of history, whose significance is equal to that of the Nation; so much so that, as Horon's colleague and disciple Esra Sohar points out, he was actually more a historian of a Land than of a Nation.[86]

The geo-historical area at the heart of Horon's enquiry is named the "Land of Kedem" (Erets Haḳedem), a name that intertwines three meanings, each indicating a separate set of values vested symbolically in the land. The Hebrew word *ḳedem* denotes "east": in the context of Horon's analysis, it refers to the land participating in the Land-Sea continuum in the eastern Mediterranean basin. Second, *ḳedem* means "front," "fore." Our discussion of national outlook renders this meaning easily understandable: the Hebrews stood facing the Land with their backs to the Sea and looking forward. Third, *ḳedem* is also "antiquity." This meaning invokes the historical uniqueness of the Land and its culture, legitimizing the modern quest for it as a suitable golden age. Last, *ḳedem* also connotates the Hebrew word for "progress," *ḳidma*. In sum, three cognitive domains are encoded in this short word: the *geographical*, the *cosmological*, and the *temporal*.[87]

Equally important is the fact that the Hebrew toponym Ḳedem expresses a *national* view from *within*. Other names used for the area, such as "Orient" or Ash-Shām, denote for Horon "East" or "North" respectively, and thus reflect foreign (British or Arab) outlooks and conceptual systems.[88] Curiously, in the early 1950s, Horon at least once professed dissatisfaction with the term "Land of Kedem," calling it in a private letter a "bad notion, fictional, unscholarly and erroneous,"[89] a sentiment that to my knowledge is not repeated elsewhere in his writings. The "Land of Kedem" is actually a typical Horon term when writing in Hebrew, while Ratosh's favorite was the "Land of Euphrates." In his non-Hebrew writings, Horon opted for somewhat less nuanced names, such as "the Levant," meaning "the country of Sunrise."[90] The Land, he wrote, "may be defined as the Euphrates country, because of the great river which crosses its entire hinterland. Or, by combining its two main features, one may call it the *Levant and Euphrates* region . . . ; [moreover, the Land], as a geographic and ethnic name, could be rendered in English as *Hebrewland*."[91]

Horon begins his historical narrative with the Land's formation, approximately twenty million years ago, when the African continent, to the northeastern tip of which the future Land of Kedem was attached, started to merge with Euro-Asia.[92] This process shaped the Land as a pass between the three continents of Africa, Asia, and Europe, lying precisely in the midst of the "Old World" (meaning the "world" as imagined in antiquity: without the American continent and surrounded by the Ocean): "Our Land is the in-between land of the Old World, on the crossroads of Asia, Africa, and Europe, at the juncture of the routes of the Nile and Mesopotamia, the Red and the Mediterranean Seas, up to the external Ocean. Such localization determines future fate: it is a Land of multitude of influences, absorbing elements from without and exporting elements from within, in recurrent cultural waves, in various epochs."[93] Horon informs his reader that "our natural zone, 'the Land,' meaning the land of the Hebrews, is *not* the state of Israel, nor is it the Land of Israel [*Erets Iśrael*], but an extensive geographical unit."[94] This pronouncement contrasts Hebrew national geography with its Zionist equivalent, revealing the implicit political character of the demarcation of the Land of Kedem. Horon defines the Land as "a geographical division stretching between sea and desert, from the boundaries of Egypt to the river Euphrates—in accordance with the extensive, *ancient Hebrew outlook*. By this we mean a *natural* unit, divided today between *so-called* 'Israel,' 'Jordan,' 'Syria,' 'Lebanon,' etc.—and encompassing them all."[95] Being "both sea-and-desert," the geomorphological elements of the Land of Kedem configure a unique territory with naturally defined, though ultimately vague, boundaries (more like marches than precise borderlines). Its natural make-up is as follows:

> Our Land is located at the crossroads of the two major lines: the sea-and-desert space and the Rift. These lines'

> conjunction determines the Land's shape as a geomorphologic unit; furthermore, it is the source of its visible internal division into five parts. They stretch northwards and southwards in parallel and lie adjacent to each other from west to east; a) the sea-shores (lower in "southern" Canaan, higher beginning with the Carmel peak); b) the "Mountain," that is, the mountains of the western part . . . ; c) the Rift . . . ; d) the mountainous plateaus in the eastern part . . . ; e) the eastern desert . . . over most of the "Land of Kedem"; and "the great river Euphrates" [which] flows near its north-eastern edge.[96]

The Land of Kedem is not "neutral" with respect to its location: Horon states that culturally and mentally, it is closer to the Mediterranean basin than to the eastern desert. The Land and the Sea are described as naturally extending one another: "Our area of belonging . . . is not particularly 'Semitic' . . . but wider and richer, more to the west and north, African and Mediterranean in essence."[97] The Land is therefore an integral and pivotal part of what Horon terms the "Euroafrican space," although the climatic catastrophe that hit the northern African continent between 8000 and 3000 BCE, turning it into a desert, spared the Land.[98]

The Land stretches over eight hundred thousand square kilometers and was inhabited in Horon's time by approximately 15 million people ("an average country," Horon concedes, "yet large enough by European standards"[99]). He devotes particular attention to Canaan, which encompasses the seashore, the Rift, and the mountain ridge on the edges of the desert and is the Land's most watered area. Horon mentions that the toponym probably denoted initially the area where yearly precipitation was above five hundred millimeters (that is, from Gaza northwards[100]). Though constituting only 10 percent of the whole Land of Kedem, Canaan remains its pivotal part due to its proximity to the sea and its centrality to the national outlook since it is from its shores that the ancient Hebrews beheld the Land of Kedem: "[T]he geographic feeling of the Hebrew-speaking peoples [*'ammim*] . . . is based upon the western positions within their world"[101]; "Canaan, or Phoenicia . . . is almost synonymous with 'The Hebrew Land' and designates the essential western half of it."[102] Canaan also functions as a miniature version of the entire Land of Kedem: the former is centered on the Jordan River, in the same way as the latter is centered on the Euphrates. The Jordan, Horon adds, has not two but *three* banks: the western (the contemporary West Bank and Israel), the eastern (modern-day Kingdom of Jordan), and the northern (the sources of the Jordan River in Lebanon and Syria). All three constitute *one* geopolitical unit—a statement whose political implications are not difficult to discern.[103]

Certain Hebrew synonyms for the "Land of Kedem" that we encounter in Horon's writings, such as "Riverland" ('Ever-hanahar) or "the Land of 'Ever" (Erets-'Ever), are equally politically weighty. Erets-'Ever is actually a tautology; as explained by Horon, the Hebrew word 'Ever denotes "Land": "This is a noun signifying a space along a natural line, such as sea or river, on both its banks as well . . . *'Ever* might refer to an extensive territory . . . or to a particular territory that is being traversed."[104] In Horon's lexicon, 'Ever is chiefly a topographical notion, and he suggests that initially it denoted only the hills of Canaan, expanding later to cover the whole Land of Kedem. Smaller 'Evers exist within the greater Land of 'Ever, such as "Riverland" East and "Riverland" West (the territories on each side of the Euphrates), the "'Ever of Jordan" (Canaan), the "'Ever of the Sea" (the Mediterranean), and so on.

The most significant aspect of this onomastic decision is the linguistic kinship Horon identifies between 'Ever and "Hebrews," both derived from the same root (*'vr*). Thus, Hebrews ('Ivrim) are "inhabitants of 'Ever," that is, "people of the Country," otherwise "those who stay." Stated simply, the word "Hebrews" denotes an *indigenous, autochthonous* population characterized by three symbolic designations: *Adam*, representing soil (*adama*); Shem, representing status; and 'Ever, representing country. The Hebrews are therefore Sons of the Land, red-blooded, noble people of their own country. The term, Horon writes, acquired its meaning probably in the late third millennium BCE, which makes it one of the world's earliest ethnonyms.[105]

This element of Horon's geo-historiography utterly negates the received biblical image of the Hebrews as wanderers. Hebrew tales of passage (such as the migration of the household of Abraham from Mesopotamia to Canaan, or the Exodus from Egypt) are all myths; and although they reflect a certain historical reality, Horon says, the biblical narratives in the form they came down to us cannot be treated as trustworthy sources.[106] The fundamental fact of Hebrew history is that "the Hebrew nation formed in its *own* land, whose backbone is Canaan; yet this is a complex and mixed nation by the very nature of its consolidation; it possesses local elements, and the rest came from all directions."[107] The soil remains the basic element of Hebrew ethnogenesis: though the proto-Hebrews maintained cultural and economic ties with other areas of western Asia and northern Africa, and migrated to and fro, Horon insists that the assimilatory power of the Land of Kedem was potent enough to supersede foreign cultural influences, however strong.

Horon's geo-historical narrative starts at the Upper Pleistocene (45,000–40,000 BCE), when the Carmel Neanderthals introduced into the Land the first elements of what later became culture: speech, worship, and burial rituals (which subsequently transmuted into the cult of the dead and the "forefathers"). Truly indigenous culture began evolving in the Land only during the Upper and Middle Holocene (between 10,000 and 3000 BCE), with the appearance of grain agriculture (earlier than in any other part of the world, Horon claims), the domestication of bovines, and the emergence of pottery, seafaring, and the first cities. By the third millennium BCE the Semito-Hamitic family of languages, comprising Libyan, ancient Egyptian, early Hebrew/Canaanite, and Akkadian, came into being (Cushitic and Hausa African languages were more distantly related). This stage signifies the shift from *pre-history* to *history*: with a written culture in place, historical research into Hebrew antiquity is no longer exclusively dependent on voiceless geological and archaeological findings. A Hebrew Canaanite world formed around the Eastern Mediterranean and Northern Africa five to six thousand years ago, shaping this space culturally, linguistically, socially, and politically. It became firmly established at the outset of the Bronze Age, in parallel to the rise of Egypt and Sumer.[108] Earlier than anywhere else, History begins its course in the Land of Kedem, Horon asserts: "[H]uman 'civilization' starts in our part of the world."[109]

Hebrew National History

Having introduced and scrutinized Horon's theoretical framework, we can now move on to his actual historiographical discourse, which grounds the Young Hebrews' political ideology in a uniquely elaborate vision of the past. The following review makes no claim of doing full justice to Horon's rich excursion into ancient Hebrew history, nor does it pass judgment on the scholarly validity of his findings. My aim is above all to throw light on the main ideological positions and statements that are interspersed throughout his writings, whether explicitly or, more often so, implicitly. While the present section will chiefly focus on Horon's later and more developed works (1960s–1970s), collected posthumously as *Ḳedem Ṿa'erev*, I shall also trace the transformations in Horon's historical opinions by starting my treatment with the 1930s *On History* series and the writings that came in its wake. Other works will be referenced more occasionally, insofar as they contribute new insights to the main body of Horon's mature output.

Horon admitted more than once that his purpose was to facilitate Hebrew national consolidation by undoing the existing historiography of the Jews.[110] This was equally true in the early 1930s, when he set out to share some of his initial insights into Hebrew history with the Russophone Zionist Jews who constituted the main readership of *Rassviet*. Though following the conventions of popular journalism, *On History* is nevertheless a very intricate and nuanced work, which puts forward some bold proposals on how pre-Exile Hebrew and Jewish history ought to be viewed in light of the Jewish national renaissance of the twentieth century. Its tone is quite "Zionist," both in its approach to ancient history and to its contemporary political implications, insofar as it lacks the strong anti-Judaic bent characteristic of Horon's later works and is therefore not yet a sustained attack on the entire body of Jewish-Zionist historiography.

Viewed comparatively, *On History* contains several elements and tropes that challenge contemporary historiographical knowledge and that can be identified in a more developed form in Horon's later writings, alongside a number of tropes that subsequently vanished from his version of the Hebrew past as his historical knowledge developed along with his growing distance from Zionism. Although *On History* already conspicuously differentiates an ethnonym—"Hebrews"—from a political term—"Israel,"[111] its most important Zionist residue is its author's contention that his narrative of ancient Hebrew history (which Horon closes at the collision between the Jews and Rome around the turn of the first millennium), framed in largely geographical terms, is *contemporary Jews' national history*. Given that *On History* is missing the analytical notion of "national outlook," it comes as no surprise that Horon considers Jews ("us") the direct descendants and historical heirs of the ancient Hebrews.[112] In fact, not only does Horon not make any qualitative distinction between Diaspora Jews and the Yishuv, he does not mention the latter even once.

Other features that later became central to Horon's historiography but are not yet visible in *On History* include the broad delimitation of the Land of Kedem and the Land's prehistory and its geomorphological composition; instead, Horon concentrates on Canaan, which he defines quite vaguely as lying "between the Red Sea and Euphrates," or "between the Euphrates and the Nile, between the Mediterranean Sea and the Great Desert,"[113] and begins his narrative in the thirteenth to twelfth centuries BCE, associated with the Exodus and early Judges period. Among the crucial features of *On History* later dropped as either incompatible with Horon's updated historical knowledge or as "too Zionist" (or both) is his acceptance of the historical veracity of parts of the biblical story, such as the Exodus from Egypt (which Horon considers a mythologized reflection of a long-term internal consolidation by the Hebrews, yet a fact nonetheless[114]) or the reference to Abraham ("semi-sedentary chieftain"[115]), Moses, and Jacob as historical figures. The conflict between Jews and Romans, which is portrayed as a centuries-long clash of two world civilizations taking place "from Libya's sands in the west to Iran's ridges in the east" rather than as a suppression of a provincial mutiny, is the central event in the history of the Western World,[116] and one of its unexpected products is Christianity, which broke with Judaism only after the crushing of Bar Kochba's rebellion in 135 CE.[117] Finally, and possibly most peculiarly, Horon regards the tension between Hebrew imperialism during the age of David and Solomon and the parochialist tendencies expressed by some prophets as the prototype of the tension between the universal and the particular in Jewish history, up to and including Zionism.[118]

In parallel Horon published a historical essay in an internal Betar periodical in France.[119] There is nothing outstandingly remarkable in this short piece, which is basically a condensed retelling of the *On History* cycle, with its "Zionist" elements intact. Yet only two years later, in 1934, Horon published in the same journal an updated sketch of his historical findings, which contains an outline of his newer approach to ancient Hebrew history.[120] Although he retained his *Rassviet* pseudonym Alraïd, his decision to continue his exploration of ancient Hebrew history in French rather than in Russian is a portent of things to come. Though not yet appearing in this particular piece, the differentiation between "Hebrew" and "Jew" that was soon to become central to Horon's worldview could not be as effectively expressed in Russian as it could in French (or English and Hebrew for that matter).[121] This essay, on the one hand, maintains certain elements of established Jewish historiography (such as the unification of the Hebrew tribes by the tribe of Judah, which created the Hebrew monotheistic faith), yet on the other hand asserts that new archaeological discoveries made in

Ugarit necessitate a revision of the historical picture of ancient Canaan. It introduces in a very rudimentary form both the "national outlook" and the "Land of Kedem" concepts, by stating that Palestine is only a small part of the Hebrew land. We can therefore conclude that the decisive shift in Horon's historical views took place between 1932 and 1934, when he studied the Ugarit epics under Charles Virolleaud. In 1935, he abandoned the Zionist movement.

Another crucial element of Horon's worldview, that of the Hebrews' cultural and historical connection to the sea as explorers and conquerors, appeared in print as early as 1931, in the Rodêgal journal *Le Cran*.[122] An article signed by S. G. (most probably Serge Halperin, a nephew of Jabotinsky, step-brother of Horon's future wife, Ada Steinberg, and a member of Rodêgal, who used the French-style transliteration "Galperine") lays out in a detailed form the idea that the ancient Hebrews were a seafaring nation and so should be their descendants and historical heirs, the Jews, if Zionism is to achieve any success. The author notes the centrality of the Mediterranean to ancient Hebrew history, allegedly evidenced by the Bible, and introduces several motifs that we encounter in Horon's later writings. Among them are the Sea (an "admiration toponym") as the true "home" of the Hebrews, who gave it such names as "Sea of the Dawning Sun," "Last Sea," or "Great Sea," and the bipolar ancient political order, with Jerusalem as the capital of the Hebrew eastern Mediterranean and Carthage as the capital of the Hebrew western Mediterranean. At the same time, the article is explicit that the Jewish Diasporic condition is above all a result of the Jews' detachment from the Sea and that Zionism's success is conditioned upon the reestablishment of this connection, most importantly for the Sephardic and North African Jews who still abide by its shores. The author concludes that the chances of this happening increased with the shift in the United States' immigration policy in 1924, which limited the inflow of migrants from Eastern and Southern Europe to North America.[123]

The underlying historiographical motif of Horon's mature works, around which his entire enquiry revolves and which demonstrates most clearly his disagreement with the Jewish commemorative narrative, is contained in the following quotes: "The [ancient] Hebrew society was not born of the 'slaves' which 'we were in Egypt,' but from a long chain of free generations in the Land of Kedem . . .[124] This is important to us, —this knowledge that we started in life as a strong and free people, conscious of the greatness and the beauty of the world, master of its own world, second to none of its neighbors."[125] These statements deeply contradict Jewish historiography, whose basis in the biblical picture of the "Sons of Israel" as slaves and wanderers nourishes a myth of a persecuted people that is elevated to the position of "chosen" by a demiurge that presents itself as omnipresent but actually behaves like a local deity. To such historiographical paradigm the idea of potent Hebrews living their own independent polytheistic life was, of course, anathema. Horon explained that "[t]he Bible's late editors were disinterested in this period of glory [lived] by the Hebrew 'pagans' in their Land and universe; its memory could only hamper the secluding Judaism."[126] Therefore, "they succeeded in depriving Canaan of its Semitic parentage—for reasons which have little in common with ethnography, but everything to do with theology."[127] The tactic of the Jewish compilers of the Bible, who could not simply disregard the all too obvious Hebrew paganism, was to besmirch it. The result is that most of what we know about Hebrew spiritual life before Judaism reaches us in the distorted shape of Jewish polemics, which castigated the Hebrews for deviating from a moral-religious framework quite unknown to them:

> Much stress is laid in the Bible on the paganism of the Ancient Hebrews. Again and again, the Jewish editors and authors reproach their forerunners with this sin, and hardly anybody is spared. Even the greatest Kings, such as Solomon, are said to have sinned incessantly against the later conceptions of Judaism. Sometimes, it is true, the Jewish censorship has attempted to go the other way round, in imagining a few virtuous heroes, in the dim past, and in putting in their heart, quite anachronistically, the fire of the yet unborn Jewish faith . . . Nevertheless, the pagan past of the Hebrews was a fact too obvious to be denied. On the whole, it was not denied, but represented as a sin.[128]

"In brief," Horon concludes, "the Bible is a Hebrew work . . . which underwent a Jewish censorship."[129]

Horon's treatment of the Bible as an investigable historical source is premised on secular-rationalist foundations, which see it first as a human-made collection of various large or small books, fragments, quotes and pieces of texts of every imaginable genre: regnal chronicles, official documents, memoirs, speeches, historical romances, legendary stories, novels and literary essays, geographical aide memoires, hagiographies, magical formulas, metaphysical treatises, legal texts, ritual codes, poetry, epopeias, mythological, religious, and national anthems, erotic poetry, fables and popular proverbs, philosophical dialogues, scholarly commentaries, polemical proclamations, editorial remarks and interventions, and so on, that mostly bespeak of a Canaanite Hebrew pagan world and culture.[130] Therefore, ancient Hebrew tales, even if corrupted beyond repair by the Jewish editors of the biblical source material, *do contain some tangible historical truth*, and by removing the layers of later legendary-ideological accretions on ancient Hebrew folklore Horon believes himself to be able to reveal the reality behind the earliest myths: "In order to reach the source of the ancient myth we must dig up the layers of additions, adornments, and commentaries, amassed during the ages . . . ; we must concentrate on [the 'remains' which preceded Judaism] if we want to uncover some reality under the strata of mythology."[131]

In tracing the sources of the sociocultural reality encoded in Hebrew beliefs, symbols, and archetypes, Horon utilizes his knowledge of the history, archaeology, and, above all, linguistics of the ancient Near East. Competent in Libyan/Berber, old Egyptian, ancient Hebrew, and other Eastern Semitic languages and acquainted throughout with the Ugaritic epic literature, Horon produces an etymological-historical analysis of the onomastics of the Land of Kedem, connecting the emergence and migration of symbols, mythical motifs, and names to prehistorical or historical events, which he then places in a wide geo-cultural context.

Krinka Vidaković Petrov observes that oral folk traditions tend to develop in time into sophisticated literary forms; that is, an initially chaotic legendary material undergoes standardization to emerge as written epopees.[132] In his study, Horon attempts to trace the process backwards, identifying the oral sources of the written culture canonized in the Ugarit epics and the Bible. His enquiry consists of two central elements: deciphering the ancient Hebrew myths and cultural codes on the one hand, and proposing on the basis of his findings an alternative historical narrative for the rise and development of the ancient Hebrew culture and nation on the other. This narrative is organized into general repetitive cycles of rise and fall, or into cyclical transmutations of a "golden age" into an "age of demise" and then again into an "age of renaissance," quite in accordance with the three-tiered nationalist system of historical periodization, which seeks a "golden age" in the past to inspire a speculative "golden future" on the ruins of the oppressive "present."[133]

To repeat, the key idea in Horon's historiography is the Hebrews' indigenousness to the Land of Kedem. Three native elements are involved in making the Hebrew *umma*, in descending order: territory, language, and religious tradition. Canaan is the core of the Hebrew domain, which upon first sight conforms to traditional Jewish historiography; yet by insisting on complete synonymy between the linguistic terms "Hebrew" and "Western Semitic," Horon pictures the Hebrew culture as more far-flung than is normally accepted by Jewish historians: "Western-Semitic is nothing but Hebrew . . . ; the whole [Western Semitic linguistic] family spread only on the western territories of the Land of Kedem, with its eastern frontier reaching the Euphrates mid-stream . . . ; [the Western Semitic group] is nothing but the Hebrew tongue in its ancient form: the Canaan language and related dialects[134]; Canaanite, Phoenician and Hebrew are equivalent terms designating a single language."[135] Horon also notes that the linguistic label "Semito-Hamitic" (to which the Western-Semitic group of languages belongs) is a misnomer since it suggests the existence of two different branches within a single family of languages. This false division originated with the fifth-century BCE scribes of Judaism, who were the first to introduce the separation between "Semitic" (monotheistic) Sons of Israel and "Hamitic" pagan Canaanites. Actually, he states, no more substantial differences exist between "Hamitic" and "Semitic" languages than between languages within these two "branches."[136]

While Riverland West was entirely Hebrew, Eastern Semitic languages, related to Hebrew more distantly, were spoken in Riverland East. Here Horon describes the Hebrews as primarily a linguistic community, which allows him to attack another aspect of Jewish historiography that limited the Hebrews to the "twelve tribes" of Jacob's progeny. The clans that formed the Israelite tribal union, Horon states, were kin to other Hebrew-speaking pagans, who shared with them land and culture: "The Hebrew nation [*umma*] included not only the Sons of Israel but all the "Sons of 'Ever," dwellers of the Land of Kedem who spoke Western-Semitic dialects similar to the tongue of Canaan . . . ; the Amalekite, the Midianite, the Ishmaelite, etc., are all sons of 'Ever . . . the sons of Canaan were Hebrews for all intents and purposes."[137]

Back in the early 1930s Horon claimed that various group titles one encounters with reference to the inhabitants of Canaan (like the "seven Canaanite nations") did not denote ethnic identity, but a political entity or a social class.[138] This way he undid another idea underpinning Jewish historiography: that the terms "Hebrews," "Jews," and "Israelites" were synonymous. Horon regards this as a terminological abuse, since he strictly distinguishes between "Hebrews" as an ethnonym, "Canaan" as a toponym, and "Israelites" as a political term that signified complex and above all fluid tribal coalition. As for "Jews," this was an anachronistic phrase, wholly irrelevant to early biblical times. The word "Jews," meaning "followers of Judaism," is entirely absent from ancient Hebrew writings or the Bible. Instead, Horon says, we have "Judeans" (*Bene Yehuda*), noblemen belonging to a Hebrew pagan tribe under the house of David.[139]

Although the Land of Kedem experienced invasions and migrations, Horon asserts that the incoming elements did not supplant or destroy the existing ones, but joined them to enrich the local ethnocultural tapestry. Of particular significance were several long-term migratory waves from North Africa that were assimilated into the Hebrew ethnocultural space, but also brought with them their own lingering influences, such as African totems or the taboo on pig meat. In parallel, the Hebrews migrated from Canaan northward to Asia Minor and farther; the Arameans, for example, bequeathed their ethnonym to the land that became Armenia.[140] Ethnocultural continuity was never broken in the Land: unity of territory, language, and faith prevailed on the stage of the ancient Hebrew drama over its *longue durée*.

Insisting that any sacral content springs from a material source, Horon argues that the Hebrew totems and deities (as well as the place-names honouring them, dispersed throughout the Land of Kedem) originally represented astronomic-geographic elements and retained an onomastic connection with them having morphed into cult entities detached from their natural origins. The ancient Hebrews, he says, perceived their cosmic order as pervaded by various dichotomies of both geographical and religious significance, such as east/west, sun/moon, land/sky, sea/land, day/night, morning/evening, "red"/"white," bull/sheep, dog/falcon, and so on. Every Canaanite god was associated with some of these dualist sets, by name, location, or activity.[141] For instance, Baal was the god of the sky-waters and was therefore identified with "high" geographical elements: sky, clouds, mountains, and so on, while his "low" counterpart was the sea-abyss monster Leviathan.[142] A "red/white" duality, which we have already encountered, appears in the myth of Jacob, who marries into the family of Laban ("white"), while his brother Esau becomes the "red" Edomites' progenitor.[143] A "sun/moon" duality persists until today in the toponyms Bet-Shemesh (literally "House of the Sun") and Bet-Yeraḥ or Jericho, both derived from the root signifying "Moon."[144] However, the most intriguing (and politically significant) etymological observation by Horon is that the theophoric place-and-tribe-name "Judea" (*Yehuda*) honors the Canaanite Baal, otherwise known as *HDD*.[145] In the ancients' time concept, these dualities represented recurrent seasonal changes; therefore, Horon concludes, the Canaanite sacral calendar reflected the local agricultural cycle.[146]

Some prehistorical or early historical cataclysms found their way into the Bible, becoming formative experiences for the ancient Semites. These, however, mostly appear in a distorted form or are misattributed geographically. For example, the tale of "the plagues of Egypt" is a reminiscence of the ecological, and in consequence social, catastrophe that befell Egypt in the closing centuries of the third millennium BCE; the deluge myth is an echo of a dim memory of local floods that were caused by the glacial recession at the end of the last ice age (the Land of Kedem remained untouched by those floods, Horon remarks, so the myth has foreign origins); finally, the tale of Sodom and Gomorrah destroyed by fire and earthquake is an import from the central Mediterranean, where volcanoes were active, and therefore such events could take place. The positioning of those two legendary cities in the Dead Sea vicinity stems from a linguistic error since tribe and place names derived from the root *'mr/ghmr* (whence the name of Gomorrah originates) were present in the territory of today's Tunisia. This territory also abounded with salty lakes, hence the conflation with the Dead Sea.[147]

These cataclysms triggered huge waves of migration from North Africa to the Land of Kedem, the last among them occurring, by Horon's calculations, in the second half of the third millennium BCE. All of them imported memories of disaster dressed in a legendary garb, which were incorporated into the local Canaanite (not only Israelite) mythology in the form of the stories of Adam's children, the travels of Cain and Noah, the "Exodus from Egypt" tale, and so on.[148] Thus, some of the Hebrews' totemic forefathers, like Abraham or Moses, are the result of the fusion of North African and Hebrew mythical motifs. Following Peter Burke, who traces how collective memory transforms historical or semihistorical figures into mythical archetypes,[149] we can suggest that Horon follows the same process not with persons but with protohistorical events. To sum up in Horon's own words: "All those tales . . . testify to a movement of Libyan 'sea-peoples' through Egypt to Canaan . . . stressing the connection between this movement and a natural disaster . . . along the Mediterranean coast."[150]

Horon dates the entry of the Land of Kedem into history roughly to 2500 BCE, when written sources appear in the Land, although primeval state-like entities can be identified even earlier. Shinar (a synonym for Riverland East) witnessed the emergence of the royal Semitic city-states of Mari and Kish, followed by the non-Semitic Sumer, to be finally conquered between 2300 and 2200 BCE by Akkad, which became the first Semitic Mesopotamian superpower both politically and culturally. Simultaneously, weakened by internal instability and internecine warfare in the late third millennium BCE, Egypt faced ravaging bands of Canaanites (a memory of which was preserved in the recurrent biblical theme of "descent" to Egypt by the forefathers and their progeny's "ascent" back to Canaan). In about 2000 BCE, Egypt finally managed to fortify its border against the Hebrew intruders, and in consequence, the Hebrews directed their attention eastwards.[151] In the twentieth to nineteenth centuries BCE Hebrew-speaking Canaanite tribes known as *Amurru* or *Mar-tu* (the Amorites) began penetrating Riverland East in consecutive waves of migration and conquest. Those tribes founded upon the ruins of Akkad the first kingdom of Babylon, whose sociocultural build-up was more Western Semitic than Mesopotamian.[152] Hebrew Canaanite culture was brought to the eastern part of the Land of Kedem, enabling livelier and easier communication between Riverlands East and West and enhancing their unity.[153]

The early second millennium BCE opened an age of deep reform and reconstitution in the social, cultural, and political spheres. After several centuries of chaos, the Land of Kedem entered a period that Horon describes as an age of prosperity: commerce, crafts, and metallurgy flourished, making travel simpler and, in consequence, cultural exchange became swifter and more lasting. During this first Hebrew "golden age," cohesive centralizing processes were set in motion in the Land of Kedem.[154] The decentralized tribal system was little by little replaced with protofeudalism: fortified cities were led by chieftains and princes who, thanks to the introduction of a hereditary kingship over a wider realm, wielded their power more effectively than the tribal chiefs who preceded them (this period is mentioned in the Bible as the "age of the Elders," which, Horon argues, was much longer than one can infer from the biblical text, "bowdlerized" by Jewish editors).

Especially important is Horon's observation that in these new conditions a protopolitical identity began to form among the city dwellers. It was expressed more vividly along the Canaanite coastline, which enabled a sociocultural differentiation between the coast and the hinterland, whose inhabitants maintained stronger attachment to their tribal system. The Hebrews' social structure became more complex, facilitating the emergence of a single cultural-religious identity despite their political disunity, a situation resembling that of ancient Greece where political disunity existed alongside ethnocultural unity.[155] The Canaanite tribes and classes came together around a vitalistic agricultural cult of a legendary eponymous ancestor (usually an animalistic totem) that augmented their sense of territorial belonging.

This development resulted in the reshaping of the tribal coalition, a key social tool in which both the ethnocultural unity and the political diversity of the Land were reflected. Egalitarian and loose coalitions were replaced by hierarchical and centralized alliances of Hebrew tribes. Tribal unions and confederations abounded in the Land of Kedem, sharing similar language and mythological beliefs and thereby facilitating the emergence of early Canaanite high culture. In approximately 1750 BCE the first phonetic alphabet was developed in the Canaanite city of Byblos (modern-day Jubayl in Lebanon). Thence it gradually spread all over the "Old World," giving rise to such alphabets as the Aramaic, the Libyan, the Greek, the Etruscan, the Latin, and the Iberian. The first known works of Hebrew Canaanite literature date to the same period.[156]

Biblical literature is described by Horon as a continuation of earlier Canaanite literary legacy, meaning that it did not represent an independent tradition[157]; hence the importance of the Canaanite epos for Horon's study, which, though discovered in the thirteenth-century BCE ruins of Ugarit and written in a North Syrian dialect of Hebrew, is of a more southern and earlier origin. Since it predated the Bible, the Canaanite literary tradition was supposedly not tainted by monotheistic biases and is therefore a more reliable source, especially for philological comparative analysis that is the kernel of Horon's method.[158]

The increase in the Hebrews' might tempted the Canaanite chieftains to invade Egypt once again around 1730 BCE. The new rulers became known in Egyptian as ḤḲ'U ḤS'T, which is interpreted by

Horon as a corruption of the ancient Hebrew phrase "lawgivers of a hilly and forested country" (a coded description of Canaan).[159] This, in turn, was corrupted by the Greeks to Hyksos, who ruled Egypt for two centuries. The Hyksos were expelled in the mid-sixteenth century BCE by the Pharaohs of the Eighteenth Dynasty, who chased the Hebrew invaders back to Canaan, laid siege to their cities, and eventually subjugated Canaan for the next few hundred years. This leads Horon to conclude that in the second half of the second millennium BCE, Egypt and Canaan constituted a single polity (as much as the term is applicable to ancient history), a development resulting in a significant expansion of the Hebrew cultural space at the cost of the Hebrews' independence. This fact was edited out of the Bible since it undermined the eschatological value of the myth of Exodus and release from "Egyptian bondage."[160]

At the same time, a process of an even greater import took place. Faithful to the principle of the Hebrew-Mediterranean cultural bond, Horon pictures the Hebrews as mighty seafarers, whose most important naval base was Tyre. The Hebrews embarked on their sea voyages in the twentieth to nineteenth centuries BCE, gradually disseminating their culture all over the Mediterranean, reaching as far as the Apennine and the Iberian Peninsulas, and perhaps even beyond. One of the foci of the spread of Hebrew culture was the Aegean archipelago, where the Hebrews became known as Phoenicians ("red people" in Greek[161]). Horon is adamant that the Greek (that is, foreign) designation "Phoenicians" was meaningless to the designated themselves, since no major ethnic or linguistic differences existed between them and other Hebrews. Therefore, "[t]here are no Phoenicians—only seagoing Hebrews: there is no Phoenician language, it is just good plain Hebrew, with, of course, some dialectal shades."[162] "Phoenician," Horon repeats in an afterword to Jabotinsky's Hebrew study manual, "is merely one of several Hebrew dialects."[163]

In order to validate the Canaanite/Hebrew/Phoenician Greek connection, Horon performs a backward analysis of Greek mythology, similar to his deconstruction of the Hebrew myths. This analysis is performed with a pronounced ideological accent, since Horon accuses contemporary Greek studies of exaggerated philhellenism, which pictures the ancient Greek culture as contained in itself (and—in effect—of "phoenicophobia," implied to be similar to the Jewish Bible editors' abhorrence of anything "pagan"). Such an attitude, Horon believes, reflects anti-Semitic prejudices that accounted it impossible for Hebrew speakers to have played any role in the shaping of the supposed cradle of Western civilization, though he duly warns against the opposite extreme as well.[164] His own position is that "[t]he modern notion of a classical Antiquity as purely Greco-Roman or Indo-European needs to be revised" to include the various branches of Hebrews,[165] given that Greek mythology testifies to a reality in which Hebrew and Greek commercial and cultural contacts were quite extensive.

Horon provides plenty of supporting evidence for this thesis: common totemic or linguistic sources for deities (like the bull cult[166] or the etymological siblings Adonis/Adonay[167]); a common linguistic heritage (the Cretan Linear A script possibly being Hebrew in origin); and migrating toponyms and ethnonyms (Horon points to the etymological kinship between the Hebrew Yaṿan ["Greece"] and Greek Ionia,[168] the Hebrew "sons of Dan" and the Greek Danaans,[169] the legendary Canaanite king Caret as the eponym for Crete,[170] and so on.). Horon dates the beginning of the Hebrew colonization of the Greek archipelago roughly to the Hyksos invasion of Egypt, that is, to the eighteenth century BCE. The Hyksos' demise two centuries later sent waves of Hebrew-speaking refugees all around the Aegean Sea and even to mainland Greece; and it is this migration that left the deepest mark upon Greek culture, Horon claims, rejecting the possibility of Greek borrowing from Canaanite culture as the result of the Greeks' own voyages to the Levant.[171]

The most intriguing aspect of Horon's analysis of Greco-Hebrew contacts is the cosmic symbolism he reconstructs from Greek Hebrew-inspired myths. Analysing the tale of Cadmus and Europa, he identifies these two names as personifications of a typically Canaanite duality of east/west, borrowed from the Hebrew Ḳedem ("east") and its opposite 'Erev ("west"/"evening"). Thus, "the myth of Cadmos [*sic*] and Europa [is a myth] of an Eastern brother seeking a sister who is the very embodiment of the West";[172] its Canaanite counterpart is the myth of Shaḥar and Shalem, the morning and the evening star respectively.[173] Implied here is the Hebrew etymology of *both* "Europe" and "Maghreb," two adjacent areas lying to the west of the Land of Kedem. In this way, Horon argues, modern toponymy and cartography preserve the ancient Canaanite cosmic-mythical dichotomy of east and west, sunrise and sunset.[174] Other traces of Hebrew toponymy beyond the Land of Kedem that survived the ages include Ibiza (originally I-bośem, "Perfume Island"), Iberia and Eire (whose origins Horon traces to 'Ever, though he also acknowledges possible

Berber influence), Cadiz and Agadir (both derived from the Hebrew Gader, "Fence"), and Haifa ("harbor"), which appears in a number of variations as Hebrew Carthaginian colonies in northern Africa.[175]

The centuries after the Hyksos' downfall (approximately 1500–1200 BCE) are another "era of darkness" in Hebrew history, a "Middle Ages" period that followed the "golden age" of the twentieth to sixteenth centuries BCE. The Land of Kedem was divided between two powerful foreign peoples: Egyptians from the south and Indo-Europeans (mainly Hittites) from the north. Whereas outside the Land the Indo-European ethnocultural element survived in the long term (hence the huge Iranian and Kurdish populations in western Asia), within the Land the Indo-Europeans were affected by environmental determinism, and, being anyway less numerous, ultimately assimilated into the Hebrew population.[176] In 1200 BCE, an extremely destructive invasion of another Indo-European people, the Philistines, laid the cities of Canaan waste but also weakened the Hittites and Egypt.

Horon determines that this experience of foreign occupation lay at the roots of the Hebrew *ummic* identity, which had been formed by the end of the second millennium BCE. The transformation from a tribal to a city-state structure, initiated a few centuries earlier, bore fruit in the Hebrew monarchy of Saul, who was capable of uniting and leading the emerging nation in a liberation struggle against the foreign powers. Thus, Horon emphasizes, a *state ideology* appeared for the first time in Canaan, whose unifying symbol became YHWH, the divine patron of the royal house. Social stratification among the Hebrews became more pronounced, with the elites comprising the old tribal family heads, the new city lords, and the monarchical nomenclature.[177] Early in his career, Horon gave weight to this period of Hebrew history, claiming that the foreign occupation taught the Hebrews the art of political organization and stimulated their national consciousness: "[I]n its Israelite form the Hebrew people becomes a nation [*natziya*]."[178]

It is important to mark here two contentions that stand out on account of their explicit anti-Jewish/Zionist bent. One, that the Israelite tribal confederation, which formed in about 1250 BCE, was merely the latest and best-known iteration of the Hebrew tribal leagues; therefore, its emergence was not the *beginning* of a new historical stage characterized by a Jehowist statehood and religion but the *pinnacle* of a millennium-long sociocultural development deeply immersed in paganism. The existence of the Israelite coalition, described by Horon as "a political and cultic federation of Hebrew clans,"[179] and the ensuing statehood was "an important episode in Hebrew history, but only an episode."[180] Two, that the Israelite confederation, though united by the YHWH cult, was far from being "Jewish" in any way. YHWH, Horon clarifies, was back then no more than a regionally identified member of the Canaanite pantheon, son of the supreme god El and sibling to Asher.[181] Contemporary political structure, based on notions that reflected a magical conception of the world, fused the management of a city-state with a territorial pagan cult, with no separate terms for either religion or state.[182] Though the prophets spoke in the name of YHWH, their teachings did not resemble any monotheism, and the political formation "Israel," whose human limits were quite fluid and included at some point the Amorites rather than the legendary "twelve tribes," retains a Canaanite theophoric component. "Iśrael," Horon explains, is actually a corruption of Asher-El, and therefore the Jewish etymology of "Israel" as an alternative name for the patriarch Jacob, himself a legendary totemic forefather, is anachronistic.[183] The Israelite confederation embodied in Horon's eyes a vitalistic pagan culture, exuding "a giant vital power, a desire for expansion in almost all spheres of human activity, an extreme individualism."[184]

This period of the eleventh to tenth centuries BCE, which we might term the second Hebrew "golden age," is associated above all with the names of kings David and Solomon. Under David's leadership (Horon suggests that Daẏid is a title meaning "warlord," rather than a proper name[185]) the Israelite confederation rose to the status of a regional superpower. David's son and heir, Solomon (whose name Horon traces to the root *shlm,* which suggests a "peaceful" inclination; both names are thus more archetypical than strictly historical), preferred diplomacy and commerce over military politics. He extended the regional system of tribal alliances through intermarriage, sent his ships all over the Mediterranean and beyond, and established further Hebrew coastal colonies and outposts, so that Hebrew power reached both the Atlantic and the Indian oceans.[186] The Hebrews, who now possessed a highly advanced political structure, became the predominant cultural element in the Mediterranean.

The prolonged Hebrew *umma* building resulted in the emergence of one of the mightiest civilizations of antiquity, which occupied a chronological and geographical middle ground between Egypt and Sumer on the one hand, and classical Greece on the other, and matching Greece in philosophy, Egypt in arts, and Assyria in military power.[187] Describing this stage of Hebrew history at the outset of his career, Horon did not attempt to moderate his enthusiasm: "The rule of the first Davidides spread over one of antiquity's greatest empires; it was probably the first colonial empire ever upon Earth . . . It was a logical conclusion . . . of Hebrew evolution . . . Two millennia had to pass before the Arab expansion and the great American discoveries overseas provided us with a spectacle of an enterprise whose verve matched Canaan's expansion."[188]

The post-Solomonic age marked yet another period of decline, when the Israelites split into two rival kingdoms and the Hebrew city-states witnessed internecine warfare and palace revolts that drove more refugees from Canaan to its Mediterranean colonies. One of the colonies, "the New City" (*ḳrḥdsht*), established on the northern coast of Africa, was destined to play a major role in the later stages of Hebrew history. Known by its Greek corruption of Carthage, it was founded in the ninth century BCE by Tyrean exiles. A dual political balance gradually formed in the Mediterranean basin, with the eastern focus of power centered on Jerusalem and Samaria (capitals of the kingdoms of Judea and Israel, respectively) and the western organizing itself around Carthage.

Carthage's allegiance to Tyre was quickly reduced to nominal, turning it to a major Hebrew cultural and political stronghold, mightier than Rome or Alexandria. Allied with the Etruscans, Carthage radiated throughout the western Mediterranean and beyond. Horon mentions that traces of Carthaginian Hebrew influence can be identified as far away as Senegal, Niger, and Cameroon in sub-Saharan Africa on the one hand, and the British Isles on the other, but was especially pronounced in the Maghreb and the Iberian Peninsula, where in time a Carthaginian colony, "the new New City" (*ḳrḥdsht ḥdsht*), grew into the city of Cartagena.

Carthage's downfall in the Third Punic War did not signify the extinguishment of Hebrew presence in the area since a Hebrew Canaanite linguistic culture survived in North Africa till the coming of Islam, and even left a trace in Rome with the Severan dynasty. At some point there was even a linguistic resurgence of Hebrew, which Horon believes was comparable to the twentieth-century phenomenon.

After a period of relative stabilization and prosperity under kings Omri and Jehoash, Canaan irretrievably lost its geopolitical pre-eminence to newer and stronger formations, like Assyria, in parallel with a spiritual transformation in the Land of Kedem. Sensing the Hebrews' exhaustion from maintaining the vast empire and their discontent with the imperialist ideology promulgated by the ruling houses, the YHWH prophets channeled this sentiment into pacifist agitation, abandoning the image of YHWH as Adonay Tsva'ot, "Lord of Hosts," and turning what had previously been Jehowist state-ideology into a subversive rallying cry. Though Isaiah reverted to supporting the royal policy, the road was thrown open to the crystallization of a wholly new form of YHWH cult, the effects of which would be lethal for Hebrew national identity.[189]

In 740 BCE, Assyria launched a military expedition against Canaan, reducing the Hebrew kingdoms into vassal states. In 722 BCE, the occupier deposed the last king of Israel and exiled the elites of Samaria (and *not* the whole ten tribes, as recorded in the Jewish tradition; those, according to Horon, remained in place and continued to profess their pagan cults). The last remnant of Hebrew independence was destroyed in 586 BCE, when the kingdom of Babylon conquered Jerusalem; in consequence, former Hebrew colonies in the Eastern Mediterranean began to Hellenize. The sacking of Tyre by Alexander of Macedon less than three centuries later put an end to the Hebrew naval dominance of the eastern Mediterranean and in the long haul enabled the creation of a Judaic Second Temple state. Thus ended the period of Hebrew glory in the Land of Kedem, and the balance was finally tipped in favor of Carthage, which emerged as the sole remaining champion of Hebrew culture and might, with the focus of world history gradually shifting to Greece and Rome. When Rome embarked on its conquest of the Mediterranean, it faced two different Hebrew powers of differing strength and national vigor, a struggle that defined Roman history until approximately 150 CE.[190]

One of Horon's most strongly held convictions was the immediate relevance of Carthage to Hebrew history. In his eyes, modern Hebrew was actually closer to the language of Carthage than to the ancient dialect of Judea, and therefore "if there is anything written in Phoenician in Tunis this is still our heritage, at least linguistically, *or perhaps even otherwise*."[191] This aspect of Horon's historical narrative demonstrates his greater intellectual flexibility over that of his Israel-based "Canaanite" colleagues. In a personal letter, Horon vented his frustration with their excessive concentration on a narrowly delimited "homeland," whereby anything that happened outside the Land of Kedem was foreign by definition. This, he felt, was an absurd doctrinarism that resembled the Jewish obsession with the "legacy of forefathers" and made the Young Hebrews self-professed parochialists potentially verging on the anti-Semitic: "A narrowly 19th-century French conception of purely territorial nationhood (which Shelaḥ had learned in Paris, and partly from me—though I use it *cum grano salis*, and he doesn't) led to the Aharon Amir type of exaggeration: (Hannibal *not* part of the Hebrew stream, because it is out of 'our' territory, as if people were merely plants; and had no feet to travel with.)."[192] On his part, Aharon Amir identified in Horon's views on history a decisive influence of the French ideological principle of "France d'outremère," which he regarded as "nationalism of the water" rather than the supposedly genuine "Canaanite" "nationalism of the soil."[193] After Horon's death, Ratosh used the opportunity to expunge most of the references to Carthage and post-Hebrew history in Horon's posthumous publication in *Minitsaḥon Lemapolet*.[194]

The Arrival of Judaism

Tracing the evolution of YHWH cult from pagan-territorial to monotheistic-universal, Horon ties it to the transformation of the Hebrew Levi tribe into a class of priests. His claim is that the mythical Levitic historiography, though Hebrew-pagan in origin, was absorbed into the nascent monotheistic Judaism as its core paradigm, subsuming the surviving Hebrew commemorative narratives. Of the latter, only traces are preserved in the Bible, but a connection between the two traditions persists on a deeper level, since Judaism incorporated the characteristics of Canaanite deities either into YHWH attributes or into its demonology and angelology.[195]

The dominant motif of Levitic historiography is the Exodus from Egypt, a tale known in Canaan long before Judaism but deformed in the Bible into a legend of wonders. Scrutiny of the surviving pre-Jewish elements in the Exodus tale and etymological analysis help Horon to establish the Levites' origin. The "sons of Levi" arrived in the Land of Kedem during the latest phase of migration from North Africa (circa 2500–2200 BCE) as a strong and warlike tribe. The name "Levi" (from the root *lvy*) points to the tribe's eponymous sacral totem: the sea-monster Leviathan, probably a huge lizard-like dragon.[196] The same root also discloses the Levites' native domain: the territory stretching between Egypt and the Maghreb along the Mediterranean coast, otherwise Libya. Horon explains that the literal meaning of the root *lvy/lby*, common to both Hebrew and Libyan/Berber, is "water."[197] Hence, water motifs occupy a central place in Levitic mythology, to name Moses's deeds alone: saved from water in infancy, commands the Red Sea, produces water by hitting a rock, and so on. "It is no wonder," Horon comments, "that in biblical myths Moses and Aharon the Levites wielded power over water from the rock, the Red Sea, and all that dwells in the Great River: for they are descended from the monster ruling over waters of sea and abyss."[198]

The figure of Moses is central to the Levites owing to his position as their legendary forefather. Horon emphasizes that the heavy Jewish reworking of the biblical Mosaic legends makes it close to impossible to distinguish between mythical additions and authentic historical traces. What is certain, nonetheless, is that the name "Moses" belongs *etymologically* to northern Canaan, where an Ugaritic tale tells how Baal impregnated a cow by Lake Hula, who gave birth to a magical calf called Mush. This tale, Horon adds, is another instance of cosmic dichotomies remade by the Canaanites into mythological tropes: the linguistic roots used in this tale (*mvsh* versus *ḥvl*) denote the contrast between evening/west and morning/east respectively.[199] *Narratively* though, Moses comes from North Africa: the Levitic-Libyan tale of his deeds reuses some Egyptian folk plots, while its place of action leaves no doubt as to its origins. Horon concludes that at a certain point, when the Levites took root in the Land of Kedem, there occurred a fusion of these traditions, or rather a fusion of an African narrative with Canaanite onomastics.

Horon argues that the Levites were initially an ordinary tribe that settled all over the Land and adopted the Canaanite agricultural cults without joining the Israelite tribal confederation. Subsequent political upheavals deprived the Levites of most of their territorial possessions, which resulted in a growing attachment to the tale of their ancestors' travels through the desert, now infused with Canaanite sacral motifs. Little by little, the Levites became professional sorcerers and experts in witchcraft, mutating from a tribe to a caste. The event that sealed their fate was another invasion from North Africa, this time by the tribe of Ephraim, led by the legendary Joshua, son of Nun. Horon is emphatic that the Levitic and Ephraimic migrations to the Land of Kedem were separate and unrelated developments, despite the biblical argument to the contrary. Ephraim's putative African origin is proven etymologically: the Berber word "Afri," Horon explains, denotes "cave-dwellers," hence "Africa" in Latin and "Efraim" in

Hebrew.[200] Joshua, like Moses, is for Horon a non-historical figure, whose accomplishments put him somewhere between a mighty sorcerer and a warrior-angel.[201] The Ephraimides brought from Libya the cult of the Sinai-god (which originates in the Maghreb and not in the misidentified peninsula adjacent to Egypt) that in Canaan was absorbed into the cult of YHWH.[202]

When the Israelites adopted YHWH as the patron of their confederation and kingdom, the Levites became identified with its cult and began rising in prominence as a hereditary professional priestly class. Later on, when YHWH became the unifying symbol of the masses discontented with Davidic imperial politics, the prophets associated with the Levites became their tribunes, thwarting subsequent attempts to restore the empire. The road was open, Horon concludes, to impose Levitic historiography upon the Hebrews.

This process reached its finale after the destruction of the Hebrew statehood, when yesterday's lords of the Mediterranean yearned for a cohesive symbol to uphold their broken spirits.[203] At this stage, it was not yet the monotheistic religion encountered by the Romans several centuries afterwards, but a new form of Hebrew solidarity and a new stage in the development of the Hebrew *ummic* spirit, which expressed "[f]eelings of despair, and hope, and self-criticism, and the will not to surrender, but to struggle for a new and better Hebrew world."[204] It is within this setting that the Deuteronomic reform was undertaken by the Judean king Josiah starting from 620 BCE, which made YHWH a strong unifying symbol in face of the Assyrian peril.[205]

Only in the sixth century BCE did the Levitic paradigm finally mutate into Judaism. This happened when the Persian King Cyrus subdued Babylon in 538 BCE and emerged as the ruler of a vast empire. Its enormous territorial expanse, which encompassed numerous lands and peoples, each with their own pantheon, induced Cyrus and his successors to seek a source of legitimacy other than functioning as the supreme king-priest of the local deity. To solve the problem of authority, the Persian Empire resorted to a previously unknown model of social relations: it replaced regional and tribal alliance-making under particular deities with religious freedom conditioned upon political loyalty. The Persian kings particularly encouraged beliefs that sought "universal" abstract truths and were uninterested in pagan territorial theology and its intimate connection with tribal politics. In effect, the mental connection between the land and the deities identified with it, which lay at the base of national outlook, was undermined. "A political world, founded upon allegiance to the material homeland, became cosmopolitan, yearning for a 'celestial Jerusalem.' "[206]

Persia in Horon's portrayal appears as a precarious multireligious, multicultural, and multiethnic empire, facilitating the emergence of a communal-denominational outlook and the transformation of territorial *ummas* into congregations whose legally codified faith could be practised universally. Horon characterizes the new zeitgeist thus: "The Kingdom of Persia signifies the shift from territorial-ethnic societies to a wholly different organization, one that is religious-confessional, where not the geographical location and the roots in the land constitute the decisive elements, but the ideology, the heavenly-ordained discipline of the spirit."[207] New universal faiths and philosophical systems sprang up all over the ancient world, supplanting "outdated" magical-natural cults and preaching worship of abstract omnipresent entities: Buddhism, Zarathustrianism, Pythagoreanism, Aristotelianism, Platonism, and so on. The Persian Empire became the first non*ummic* polity in the ancient world, "a prototype for all that followed, up to the Ottoman Empire."[208]

These conditions enabled the conversion of YHWH cult, now detached from its Canaanite ground, into a monotheistic religion, with its own "holy scripture" and cosmic outlook. Horon emphasizes that Judaism and its community of believers (the first Jews) arose *not* in Canaan but in Babylonia, translating the Jerusalem elites' shock of exile into a messianic dream of return. However, only a limited number made their way back to Canaan once King Cyrus made the return possible, establishing in the environs of Jerusalem an enclosed community of nonidolatrous YHWH worshippers ("a tiny Church-state"[209]), hostile to the local pagan population, with whom only a few decades beforehand they had shared culture, language, and faith.

Canaan was thus transformed from a real homeland for the Hebrews into a "holy land" for the Jews, constituting mainly a spiritual point of reference (also for those who actually returned, whose center of political attachment and loyalty remained the Persian court). The Persian Empire also replaced Jerusalem as the metropolitan hub for the Hebrew colonies in the Mediterranean, turning Hebrew ports in the Eastern Mediterranean into vassal entities that could be used in case of war with Greece. Under the guidance of Ezra the Scribe, old Hebrew folktales pervaded by Levitic mythology were canonized as the Bible after a heavy editing had adjusted the legendary material to the new and anachronistic dogma of YHWH as the only supreme demiurge.[210]

The numerous monotheistic glosses and interpolations within the biblical text disclose this interference, though many polytheistic traces remain, mainly, according to Horon, due to the Jewish editors' linguistic ignorance (such as the "covenant of the pieces" [Genesis 15], which is concluded between Abraham and *both* YHWH and Asher).[211] Other editorial interventions by Jewish writers resulted in the fabrication of genealogical links between totemic "forefathers" and later historical persons or groups, such as the identification of Moses and Aharon as Levites, who in this way also became "related" to Abraham and the house of David; the "incorporation" of the twelve mythical tribes into the Israelite tribal confederation and tracing their pedigree back to the "house of Jacob"; the composition almost from scratch of the Torah and Joshua books, which, Horon observes, radically differ in style, language, and content from the much earlier Book of Judges; and, perhaps most importantly, the reworking of the Exodus myth (for which no evidence exists in historical, literary, and archaeological sources) to suit the needs of a monotheistic community returning to Canaan under Persian patronage and with Persian blessing. In Horon's uncompromising words: "The mythology of the 'Exodus from Egypt' is not simply a re-rendering of semi-totemic myths from the distant past. This is a very particular 'reconstruction,' made to disseminate a message; an ideological tale."[212] The Exodus fable became in Judaism an ideal type for later events: "The Bible is full of schematic and some of the events narrated in it are presented as re-enactments of earlier ones," as noted by Burke.[213] Thus reconstructed, a historical analogy was drawn by the Jewish editors between the Exodus and the return from Babylon, suppressing the Hebrew commemorative narrative in favor of the emerging Jewish historiography.[214] The new Jewish mythology not only disowned its Canaanite heritage; based on nonnational assumptions, it also professed an outward hostility to the Hebrews' pagan past. And this hostility was easily transferred to the contemporary heirs of Canaanite polytheism, such as the Samaritans.

Horon decries the disintegration of the *umma* and its replacement by a confessional community typical "of a tired world, of declining societies, of a Dark Age."[215] In this way, he dissents from received historiographical opinion that the transition from polytheism to monotheism amounted to a progressive development. Echoing Herderian sentiments, he muses melancholically on "how wrong are those who assume that the new religions and philosophical currents, which have prevailed amongst us since Ezra and among the Greeks since Plato, are more 'enlightened' than the ancients' beliefs."[216] The truth is quite the opposite, he asserts. Judaism could only emerge in a monarchy organized into a complex hierarchical structure of classes, castes, and religious communities ("churches"), discriminated and played off against each other by the ruling house, the Persian Empire being the prototype. In conditions such as these, the first Jewish communities could not but adopt a zealous and xenophobic outlook, exemplified in the activity of Ezra and his successor Nehemia. In the following generations, Jewish xenophobia was augmented by the Pharisee sect, the progenitors of Diaspora Rabbinic Judaism. Horon describes the Pharisees as thriving exclusively under foreign patronage, following the Persian model, and opposing the mixture of spiritual and profane authorities.

At the same time, Horon cannot disregard the speedy and massive spread of Judaism all over the Old World (especially in the Mediterranean basin) relatively shortly after the religion's emergence. Since the number of Jews around the Mediterranean in the first century CE was anywhere between 6 and 8 million, making them almost 10 percent of the population of the Roman Empire and therefore 7–8 percent of the population of the entire ancient world from India to the Atlantic,[217] they could not obviously all descend from the supposed "exiles" from Canaan. Horon attributes the growth of the Jews into one of the largest demographical, economic, and political powers in antiquity to the replacement of Persian religious tolerance with an assimilationist approach promulgated by the Hellenic successors of Alexander of Macedon. Ptolemaic Egypt, which became a propaganda center for Greek language and culture, attracted Jews who preached the YHWH monotheistic cult. Either way, the true homeland of Judaism—whether in its xenophobic or missionary form—was not Canaan, but Persia and Egypt. And this is Horon's key point: Judaism from its very inception was a religion shaped by, and accommodated to, physical and spiritual distance from Canaan (or from any land, for that matter). A universal cosmopolitan outlook such as the Jewish one is focused on transcendent causes, while upon earth it becomes ossified in a myriad of ceremonial rules and legal principles, as Halakhic Judaism demonstrates so expressly.

To redress somewhat this gloomy picture, Horon asserts that the flame of Hebrew nationhood was not extinguished in the Land of

Kedem straightaway. The Jews, he says, were initially a tiny minority among pagans, and the Hebrew navy, based in Tyre and Sidon, remained a mighty force in the Mediterranean prior to the arrival of Alexander of Macedon. In *On History*, he characterized the Second Temple Period as the "Second Hebrew Empire," led by a high priest king,[218] indicating that at the early stages of his intellectual development he considered ancient Judaism capable of functioning as a territorial-political factor. The Hasmonean semi-independent kingdom, albeit forming through a religious war waged by Jews and making Judaism its official religion, was modeled after the Hellenic states, meaning that its cultural composition was syncretistic and religiously tolerant (and therefore despised by the Pharisees). This neo-Hellenic fiefdom reinforced local patriotism, which, though only a faint reminder of the Hebrew glory of old, was nonetheless animated enough to confront the Roman Empire.

The millennium starting with the Assyrian attack in 740 BCE and ending with the great anti-Roman rebellions in Judea in the first and second centuries CE is described by Horon as an extended twilight of the Hebrew national culture and outlook, "transitional stages and not an ending."[219] This period was characterized by national/denominational ambiguity, with elements of Hebrew nationalism and Jewish universalism both participating in its shaping, even if unequally: "For a long time, the vital forces of the [Hebrew] people resisted the verdict of mummificators [from the school of Ezra and Nehemia]."[220]

A subliminal memory of a sovereign national existence continued to manifest itself in various—though usually dim—ways throughout Jewish history: "[F]rom the days of Nehemias to the days of Bar Kochba and even much later," Horon states, "the history of Judaism is largely the history of the struggle between the new conception, the caste-conception, and the forces still faithful to the old ideal of Hebrew nationhood. The terrible wars with the Romans were not only wars against a foreign oppressor, but civil wars between the Hebrew and the Jewish brand of the same people."[221] As late as the seventh century, Hebrew Galilee had struggled against Byzantium until the Arab incursion put an end to the cultural dominance of the Hebrew language in the region. Some of the Hebrews' national characteristics, like commercial skills, a sense of universal mission, and complexes, either of inferiority or superiority, were carried over by the Jews into the Diaspora. Consciousness of a Hebrew national belonging was demonstrated by both Apostle Paul and Josephus Flavius.[222]

Yet ultimately Horon regards the rise of Judaism as a tangible symbol and the most potent expression of the Hebrews' historical catastrophe: "Judaism . . . is contemporary with the decline of the Hebrews, their last struggles and their destruction . . . [It] is the expression as well as the consequence of this destruction." This means that, historiosophically, "the Jewish centuries play the part of a Middle Age between a great past and a future, which, we hope, will not be unworthy of our beginnings."[223] Emphasizing his dual contention that the Hebrews are not the same as Jews and that the preservation of Hebrew heritage under a Jewish cover, however imperfect, enabled the Hebrews' national renaissance, he writes: "[N]ot all the descendants of the ancient Hebrews entered the Jewish caste; likewise, not all the Jews descend from the Hebrews. But it must be stressed that Judaism . . . played a major part in the beginnings of the modern Hebrew revival by transmitting these ancient national traditions to the new Hebrews of the 20th century."[224]

Conceived this way, Judaism's dialectical role in Hebrew national history is *both* a repudiation *and* a continuation of the Canaanite legacy: "[Judaism] is not a continuation of the ancient Hebrew culture but its negation; . . . Judaism . . . emerged from the Hebrew prophecy, but eventually turned hostile to the Land of the Hebrews and its heritage,"[225] nonetheless, "Judaism, to the extent that it preserved and transmitted the knowledge of the [Hebrew] language . . . made a cardinal contribution to the Hebrew national revival."[226] Horon's analogy for the relation between Hebrew heritage and Judaism is that of the Roman Empire in relation to the Byzantine Empire, respectively.[227] Accordingly, Judaism, after being "purged" of monotheistic additions, can assist in reclaiming the Hebrew pre-Judaic foundational myth.

While Judaism was gaining ground in the Hebrew east, Carthage carried on the torch of Hebrew nationalism in the west.[228] Carthage's downfall in the Third Punic War coincided with the emergence of the Hasmonean kingdom, which defied the Seleucids and checked the growing might of Rome. Cultural influence followed political power, inducing masses all over the Mediterranean to accept the Hasmoneans' supreme god YHWH and its Jewish cult. From Libya to Rome, numerous Canaanite and autochthonous communities converted to Judaism; many by will and some by force. This way, the Canaanite Hebrew Diaspora was soon replaced by a Jewish Diaspora, which merged with newly converted locals, few of whom spoke Hebrew. This is the true explanation for the astonishingly rapid and wide dissemination of originally xenophobic Judaism: its proselytes were drawn to a *victorious* religion, whose social base was the Canaanite colonists of the Mediterranean, and not the supposedly vanquished exiles from Judea after the crushing of the anti-Roman rebellions. Most important, Horon dates the increase in the Mediterranean Jewish population *before* the alleged dispersal in the wake of the disasters of 70 and 135 CE. He argues that Jewish historiography, which pinned the blame for the exile on the Romans, originated in the Pharisees' hostility to any form of Hebrew statehood that did not conform to their version of YHWH cult. The narrative that makes the Jewish exile a result of a military defeat is a fable, and quite a tendentious one: "[This view], rooted in historical ignorance, is in reality drawn from a malevolent fabrication of the fathers of the Church, who were keen to prove that this is how god punished the Jews for the crucifixion of Christ."[229]

As mentioned above, Horon asserts that the sociocultural dialectics of national versus denominational persisted into the first centuries of the Common Era. He points out that Pharisee Rabbinic Judaism did not prevail at once after the demise of the Bar Kochba state in 135 CE; moreover, a current that Horon calls "militant Judaism," although suppressed in rabbinic literature, survived at least until the eighth century CE. It is to its influence that some of the best-known cases of mass conversion to Judaism must be attributed, from the Ḥimyarite kingdom in modern-day Yemen and the Berbers in North Africa, to the Khazars in the Volga basin.[230] This tendency was nonetheless not potent enough to reverse the tide of history, when congregations overtake *ummas* as its chief protagonists. Such a state of affairs, Horon indicates, can be diagnosed by a nationally minded historian only as "nonhistory." "Inasmuch as we are or try to be Hebrews," he concludes, "Judaism is the very symbol of our defeat and the very shape of our exile."[231]

The above allows us to infer that Horon's—and, by extension, "Canaanite"—historical thinking distinguishes two ontological conditions relative to history: being "subject" versus being "object." The former implies an active role in history and the capability of influencing or even shaping it by collective or individual agency. The latter means the opposite: being inactive and influenced by, rather than influencing the, flow of historical time; as Anwar Abdel-Malek puts it, it means being "passive, non-participating . . . above all, non-active, non-autonomous, non-sovereign with regard to itself."[232] Horon's reasoning is obviously insubordinate to the Zionist philosophy of history.

A chain of correlating elements in his historiographical narrative that fits each of the two historical conditions outlined above—subjectivity-Hebrews-"golden age" versus objectivity-Jews-"Middle Ages"—shows that Horon gradually since the 1940s came to conceptualize being Jewish as being *inherently* bereft of historical agency and sovereign will. The discussion in chapter 4 will demonstrate that the drive to regain historical agency for the Jews (making them "subjects" rather than "objects" of history) was Zionism's chief imperative; its supposed failure was, in turn, the Young Hebrews' source of motivation.

The Hebrew "Middle Ages" begin when national outlook is finally overtaken by communal outlook and Jews no longer care about shaping their own history in a sovereign way. Hence, what is the "golden age" for Christianity and "prehistory" for Islam is for the Hebrews the beginning of "a *long* night between a day and another one"[233]: it is the nature of the outlook, and not stages of material development, that defines the essence of the macrohistorical phase. The "postnational" period into which the Land of Kedem lapsed with the emergence of Judaism nearly two millennia ago is dismissed by Horon as

> not an active history but passive deeds . . .[234]; this is no longer a national history—neither of a consolidated *umma* in its ancient shape nor of a territorial-political *leom* in its modern form. Throughout [this] long period . . . the forefront of history was occupied by religions, communities, and clans, various houses of duchy and royalty, and not by structures that can be described as "national" [*leumiim*]. In this medieval world the Land of Kedem . . . mutated from a homeland of a particular *umma* into a holy land.[235]

Chapter 3

From Denomination to Nation

Adya Horon's Politics

The Jews in Horon's Perspective

It should come as no surprise that, for the most part, Horon's periodization of the Hebrew commemorative narrative excludes the Jews from the Hebrew "golden age," though a connection between the two is acknowledged. The relative paucity of references to Jewish post-Hebrew history in Horon's writings was undoubtedly dictated by Horon's understanding of his mission as being principally that of a *Hebrew* national historian; moreover, he arrived at it quite early in his career, as the following passage from *On History* testifies:

> If it were written on the cover, or at least humbly stated in the foreword to, say, Renan's study: *The History of the Semitic Element in Israel*; or in Dubnov's later volumes: *The History of Anti-Semitism and the Jews' Legal Status Throughout the World Today*—I would not protest. I would not trouble myself with reading either. But since is it stated plain and simple: *The History of the Jewish People, The History of Israel,* etc.—I am left with no choice but to "demand my money back" with indignation from the book-vendor.[1]

Horon's aversion to a deterritorialized (thus, nonnational) Jewish history means that his scant references to Jews are limited to two issues, one historical, the other sociopolitical: tracing their ethnic origins and analyzing their contemporary social status. In both cases, the outcomes of Horon's inquiry sharply contradict the Jewish-Zionist historiographical paradigm, which identifies most Jews as the descendants of the ancient Israelites exiled from the Land of Israel after the defeats of the anti-Roman rebellions in 70 and 135 CE.

Horon's version of the emergence of Judaism and the Jewish Diaspora, investigated in the previous chapter, highlights the multi-ethnic and cosmopolitan nature of both the Mosaic religion and of its community of followers. Nonetheless, his understanding that a cultural and linguistic continuity between Hebrews and Jews exists makes Judaism a historically legitimate, albeit transitory, stage between the "golden age" of the past and its reclamation in the future: "To me, the *bulk* of the Jews were included in [Hebrew history], by their obvious past; and Judaism was but one of the historical manifestations of Hebrew life, with a beginning and perhaps an end: a phenomenon of 'Middle Ages,' yet still an inseparable part of the total flow of events and developments; certainly not something ANTI-Hebrew, or out of the Hebrew horizons altogether."[2]

This continuity is certainly not a biological one. In the late 1930s, Horon wrote that the only thing keeping Jews together—with neither common language nor territory to share—is the fact that they were the historical successors of the Hebrews.[3] At the same time (also, and particularly, later) Horon pointed to the diverse origins of major Jewish communities. For instance, "In the veins of the North-Western African Jewry . . . as well as in the veins of the Sephardic Jewry there undoubtedly flows more Carthaginian that Jewish blood, strictly speaking."[4] Hence, the western Canaanites of Carthage (mixed with the autochthonous Libyans/Berbers) are the progenitors of North African Jewry, while the Carthaginians who settled in the Iberian Peninsula become in Horon's account the forefathers of Sephardic Jewry. Other significant Jewish societies emerged in the centuries after the Hebrews' demise as an *umma* as a result of "militant"—that is, proselytizing—Judaism: the "Yemenites" hail from the Judaized Ḥimyarites; the emergence of Ashkenazi Jews (Horon's own community) is explained in accordance with the theory of East European Jewry's descent from the Turkic Khazars, as supposedly demonstrated by their complexion and temper; Ethiopian Jewry also originated from indigenous converts.[5] The Jews' natural habitat is therefore the deterritorialized Diaspora, and if Jews do attempt to transition toward a Hebrew national existence and "normalization," this would perforce mean an abandonment of their Jewish character.[6]

A modernist nationalist who treats the nation as an "imagined community"—that is, a real one regardless of the historical credibility of its ideologues' claims to authenticity—might argue that a rejection of the racial-biological concept of origins does not automatically nullify a group's claim to nationhood. According to such viewpoint, the Jews might still constitute a nation despite not being a true *ethnie*. Horon, who, as explained above, adheres not to the modernist but the territorialist model of the nation, refuses to acknowledge them as such. The Jews, he claims, are above all not a nation because they don't possess a defined territory to identify with and therefore lack a national outlook. Instead, Jews comprise a faith-community coalesced by a spiritual culture and heritage (that includes a distorted memory of the Hebrew age), which functions in a rigid system of codified principles, leaving the question of identity outside the individual's choice.

Echoing Max Weber's insights on the Jews as pariahs,[7] Horon classifies such a community as a "caste" or *millet*. The latter is an Ottoman loanword designating "a body or quasireligious, quasiracial class, to which a man belongs by the virtue of his birth and which he can abandon only with great difficulty."[8] *Millets*, or confessions/denominations, "may stand anywhere between the ethnic group, the tribe, the clan, and what we call churches in the Western world. But mostly they act and feel like castes—with loyalty bestowed upon an ideal, ritual way of life and upon such men and women as follow it from birth. Territorial bonds, political affiliation, and formal citizenship play a secondary role."[9] A caste, like a nation, might possess a common culture, language, and aspirations, but would lack the key national criterion of a common territory. Castes quickly degenerate into racism (since "origins" mean the world to them); into atrophy of the political sense; into a lack of patriotism; and into social impermeability, conservatism, religiosity, ritualism, and a tendency toward particular economic roles and specializations.[10] All these traits apply perfectly to Diaspora Jewry.

The *millet* system, Horon continues, was introduced by the Ottoman Empire to manage its numerous ethnoreligious communities by allowing them autonomy in matters of faith and communal life in exchange for political submissiveness: a model directly borrowed from the Persian Empire.[11] One of the Ottoman *millets* was, of course, the Jews; and despite the vast differences between the Ottoman Empire and the European West, Horon does not believe that the western Jews' situation differed (at least until modernity) in any substantial way from that of their eastern "brethren": "A typical instance of caste within the Western world is of course Jewry; is or *was*, until quite recently. For in spite of the impassioned biases of both Anti-Semitism and Zionism, Jewry never was a physical 'race,' nor a nation, but quite definitively a caste: something more than a mere church; a religion which controlled the entire life of its members, irrespective of their country of residence, their language, political affiliation, etc."[12]

Horon's definition of the caste/*millet* is deterministic: one cannot alter it from within, and it will stubborntly resist any long-term transformations. The italicized *was* in the above citation does not imply Horon's tacit acceptance of the Zionist maxim that the Jews transformed themselves by their own efforts from a caste into a nation, but it points to an entirely different historical trajectory. Jewish existence outside of history as objects, Horon wrote in 1939, was feasible in premodern (that is, prenational) Europe, when Jews were both economically useful and served as a reminder of the "truthfulness" of Christianity. Yet Protestant reaction against the papacy and the parallel emergence of new non-Jewish economic middle classes destabilized the economic and spiritual basis of Jewish existence. Jews started to migrate en mass to Eastern Europe, where nationalism was not yet known and the social "state of matter" of caste could therefore endure. By the eighteenth century, Judaism experienced its own crypto-pagan Hassidic "Reformation" against the most inhumane and ossified forms of caste existence.[13] This paralleled two other developments: the arrival of the national idea and industrial revolution in Eastern Europe, and the loss by a significant number of Jews of their traditional religious faith. With Ashkenazi Jews experiencing an exponential population growth thanks to modernization coupled with the loss of their traditional place in the economic structure and of their spiritual nourishment, the Jewish traditional way of life was fundamentally shattered. The caste became an anomaly in a modern world of nations, and hence, argues Horon in a manner similar to Jabotinsky's justification of the "anti-Semitism of things,"[14] Jew hatred is a normal reaction to the abnormality of a caste that had lost its raison d'être but is yet to find a new one.

Resistance to anti-Semitism is futile, Horon seems to suggest on the eve of the Holocaust: the only thing remaining to do is to await the inescapable Deluge while building an Arc. There are, in fact, three competing "projects" for the Arc: assimilation, meaning the adoption of the majority's national outlook (branded by Horon a "collective suicide"); social revolution, which in the Jewish case would serve as a sublimation of messianism; and Zionism. The latter is unsatisfactory given the huge opposition it encounters both among traditional and assimilated Jews. In Palestine, Zionism is coerced by Britain into surrender, while the Hebrew revival in Canaan takes place under Zionist banners but to an entirely different effect. It is therefore useless to attempt to persuade the world that something Jewish is happening in Palestine, while something Hebrew is finally occuring in Canaan, concludes Horon in his review of the "catastrophic" situation of the late 1930s.[15] Traditional Judaism must therefore succumb to the onslaught of modernity: it will crumble, but it will not abandon its nature. In this respect, Horon is actually not very far from the reasoning of Baruch Kurzweil.

If Jews do not constitute a nation, Zionism obviously does not qualify as a national movement. We saw in the previous chapter that Horon attributes the Jewish historiographical paradigm of dispersal following the destruction of the Second Temple by the Romans to a "malevolent fabrication" by the patriarchs of Christianity. This "anti-Semitic fable" was internalized by the Jewish Diaspora, which based its spiritual tradition on decrying the Galut and yearning for a messianic restoration in a rebuilt Jerusalem.[16] This tradition was transferred into the Zionist philosophy of history, which substituted the divine agent of redemption with a human-secular one, leaving the other essential elements intact, above all that the Jews are a single nation suffering in an exile that is temporary by nature. This lack of a proper conception of history, one that would not be enslaved to prenational paradigms of a Diaspora denomination, meant that "for half a century," Horon said in 1945, "Zionist thought feeds on the Jewish conception of our past, and is therefore trying to do something self-contradictory . . . to build a territorial nation and a state on the philosophy of a church."[17] In order to placate its numerous Jewish opponents of various persuasions, Zionism diluted whatever national character it had by internalising the principles of every possible human ideology from Marxism to religion.[18] Wielding this argument of organic continuity between traditional Judaism and Zionism, and the resultant intellectual and political dead-end, Horon mounts a radical attack on Zionism, with the intention of undermining its intellectual foundations and, in consequence, its politics.

While the charge that Zionism mirrored anti-Semitism was not peculiar to Horon, many opponents of Zionism singled it out for adopting the racial principles of the "new" nineteenth-century anti-Semitism that accompanied the growth of nationalism in Europe.[19]

Horon looks deeper by claiming that it is actually the "old" religious, and specifically Christian, anti-Semitism that Zionism incorporated into its worldview and commemorative narrative. Zionism becomes in Horon's analysis not so much a *reaction* to the anti-Semitic racism of modernity (though he does not deny it altogether) but an *extension* of a premodern anti-Semitic theology, whose Christian sources, in turn, reach back to the first monotheistic universal faith, Judaism. The implication is that the Jews, being a *millet*/caste, were incapable of adequately utilizing the nationalist grid of concepts; they were thus deterministically left to toy with an outdated confessional worldview, trying to adapt it to a sociopolitical reality that was changing beyond recognition. Zionism, Horon concludes, is just another stage in the historical decay of Judaism in the twentieth century; it is a "last attempt of Judaism to outlast itself, to gain a new lease on life."[20] Its midway position between Judaism's "racial or religious superstitions" and the palpable facts of the Hebrew rebirth has very quickly become unworkable,[21] and, having started as a rebellion against traditional Judaism, it ended up creating in 1948 a "pilgrim state."[22]

Horon draws a number of parallels between Judaism and Zionism in order to deprecate both. So much as Judaism was foreign to the Land of Kedem, Zionism is an "international Jewish agency" whose central aim is to solve a vague "Jewish problem" that afflicts the Jewish masses "around the Carpathians, between the Danube and the Dnieper."[23] Since a "Jewish problem" is global in scope, Zionism's simultaneous contention that the Jews constitute a single nation whose sovereign identity is expressed by Israeli statehood is self-contradictory, and the whole idea is mocked by Horon as "a dream of tradition dreamt up by the Jewish Diaspora."[24] Horon accuses the Zionists of functioning as outside agents who import values and problems that are alien to the Land: "Among the many foreign influences which play a part in the Levantine imbroglio . . . we must mention Zionism . . . from a geographical standpoint . . . Zionism is indeed an outside factor."[25] Zionism's utilisation of the name "Palestine" is yet another evidence of foreignness since the toponym is derived from a non-Semitic people coming from beyond the sea, and therefore represents an extrinsic, non-Hebrew, point of view.[26] Zionism's downfall is presaged: "Zionism, as it [is], must fail. Not just that it *may* fail, —but that it *must*. At least from the only point of view I [am] interested in, from the point of view of the *Hebrew* national revival."[27]

The renewed Jewish emigration to Palestine/Israel offers another case of continuity between Jewish history and Zionism. Horon regards *'aliya* a reenactment of the "Return to Zion" during the age of Cyrus—the same migration that had originally brought the confessional outlook to the Land of Kedem and turned Canaan into a "holy land." Just as in the sixth century BCE, the allegiance, material resources, and spiritual values of nineteenth- and twentieth-century Jewish immigrants lay outside the Land: Persia was replaced by the European and American Jewish Diaspora, while the role of Cyrus's court was taken over by the British Empire.[28] The latter exploited Zionism to pursue its own geopolitical interests in the eastern Mediterranean, which were ultimately incompatible with Zionist objectives. An unequal relationship with London meant that Zionist-British covenant was a gamble that backfired: referring to the 1917 Balfour declaration, Horon states that it was delivered to a "people not yet resurrected, but already betrayed"[29] and describes it as an imperialist self-serving tool rather than a true help to the Yishuv.[30] British perfidy is also visible in the alleged gerrymandering of the electoral districts of Jerusalem—a city with a 20 percent Muslim population and a two-thirds Hebrew majority, according to Horon—in order to artificially create an Arab-dominated municipality.[31] In collusion with France, the British played Zionism and Pan-Arabism against each other, delimiting the constituent states of the Land of Kedem in a way that entrenched the two movements' dependency upon their imperial overlords.[32]

Scrutinizing Zionism from the standpoint of its own principles, Horon concludes that it was, all in all, a miserable failure. Acknowledging that the movement had a role in shaping the Hebrew-speaking Yishuv ("for better or worse") and in fostering Jewish immigration to the "Land of Israel," he observes that Jews en masse rejected the Zionist appeal. Since the "Jewish problem" was at base a sociocultural question (finding a place where the Jewish community could thrive), it could be resolved by exchanging one universal outlook for another: either by migration to America or conversion to Soviet-style communism. Those who chose neither were in due course decimated by the Holocaust, so Zionism lost the bulk of its potential addressees.

As for the remainder, Horon calculates that only 10 percent of Diaspora Jewry eventually ended up in Palestine/Israel, the overwhelming majority being Sephardi Jews. Many of them, he remarks, were not driven by the pull motive of Zionist idealism, but by various religious or economic push factors. In that sense, Palestine/Israel did not differ from any other migration-absorbing country.[33]

Hebrew nation formation in the Land of Kedem therefore took place in defiance of Zionism's stated goals, yet those Jews who did come to the Land, whether due to Zionism or not, became a central element of this sociocultural process. Expressing his frustration with the doctrinarism of Yonatan Ratosh, who insisted on excluding Jews from Hebrew nation formation, and taking the chance that modern Jews would retransform themselves back to Hebrews for very real,[34] Horon wrote about the need for a large-scale immigration to Israel that would draw upon the Jewish Diaspora in the main—also in order to secure strict delimitation between Jews remaining abroad and Hebrews in the Land of Kedem: "If there is not a very substantial liquidation of the Jewish Diaspora, we will never cease to be 'crucified' on the horns of the dilemma: 'World Jewry' versus 'Hebrew Nationhood'; on the other hand, we need at least several millions of additional immigrants to achieve a sufficient demographic basis for the Hebrew Renaissance . . . This does not exclude non-Jewish immigrant; on the contrary."[35]

This is Horon's deterministic thinking: the geophysical environment will perforce prevail over ideological-cultural residues that are incompatible with it, regardless of their own potency. An ages-old regularity was repeated: once Jewish migrants had established themselves in the Land of Israel, environmental determinism acted to consolidate them into a different national community. The society shaped in Canaan since the late nineteenth century (primarily, though not exclusively, of Jewish extraction[36]) developed over time a sentiment of nativeness. A fresh national outlook deriving from Hebrew antiquity enabled the transformation of a Hebrew-speaking society into a modern *leom*. It thus could not but be inherently distinct from the nonnational Jewish *millet*, despite the genetic ties between the two. This is how Horon sums up the disposition of the newly formed nation:

> As to the renaissance of the Hebrew nation, which is emerging in front of our eyes in its country, still half-consciously . . . [it] matures by striking new roots in that same ancient land. What is buried in this land fertilizes also life above; and since the deeper layer is Hebrew-Canaanite, the new Hebrew nation tends to grow in the Canaanite direction, whether the powers that be wish it or not; . . . when growing, [the Hebrew nation] begins developing self-consciousness, in a natural way, that is, at least subconsciously, defying the education it receives (or refuses to receive) at school.[37]

To this Zionism remained blind: "The Hebrew movement," Horon claims, "by its very nature denies the possibility of a *Jewish* nationalism or a *Jewish* nation"[38] since "the organs of Zionism do not express and cannot express the Hebrew national movement."[39] Ergo, the Hebrew foundational myth, if it is to serve an evolving nation, must necessarily revert to the Hebrew "golden age," reducing the two thousand years of Jewish history of dispersal into a "Middle Ages" intermezzo.

When Horon was involved with the Hebrew Committee of National Liberation during the 1940s, he explicitly subscribed to its idea of the Hebrew nation as comprising *both* the Hebrews in Palestine *and* stateless Jewish refugees from the Holocaust in Europe.[40] In 1945, he assessed the numerical potential of the Hebrew nation at 3–4 million people, 25 percent of whom were already in the Levant.[41] This corresponded with the statement made by the head of the committee, Hillel Kook, that "the Zionist formulae of a 'Jewish people' may rightly or wrongly be interpreted as applying to about twelve or fourteen million people," while the true number of Hebrews to be repatriated from Europe was around 2.5 million.[42] This starkly contradicted the vision of exclusively non-Jewish Hebrew nationhood promulgated by the "Canaanites," and Ratosh condemned the Hebrew Committee extremely harshly for such a "compromise."[43] Later on, as Horon grew closer to Ratosh's approach, he came to treat the Hebrew Committee's attitude as a tactical concession.[44]

Horon dates the emergence of modern Hebrew national consciousness to the First World War, when the Yishuv made first organized attempts to win independence by force, citing the pro-British NILI spy network in Ottoman Palestine and the Hebrew Battalions within the British army in the Middle East. Horon invariably associates any expression of Hebrew national sentiment in the first half of the twentieth century (which he contrasts to "Jewish-style" lobbying by official Zionist leadership that resulted in the Balfour declaration)[45] with the ideological and political legacy of Jabotinsky. However, he adds, only in 1939 did Hebrew nationalism find expression in a concrete political platform, which implies the founding of La Renaissance Hébraïque in Paris and the Committee for the Consolidation of the Hebrew Youth in Tel Aviv.[46]

Horon takes a measure of care before announcing the existence of a nation totally independent of its Jewish lineage. Writing shortly after the establishment of Israel, he cautiously states that "it would be an error to assume that the Jews, or specifically the *Israelis*, are already a nation, or even a unified group . . . [The Sabras <native Israelis>] . . . are visibly the basis and ferment of an emerging Hebrew nationhood, but they still have to assimilate a discordant majority of foreign Jews and native non-Jews."[47] Nonetheless, Horon is optimistic: "Nobody with first-hand knowledge may honestly deny that many Israelis are lukewarm Zionists or no Zionists at all."[48] Privately, he believed (or took the effort of conveying the impression of believing) that by the late 1950s the Young Hebrews will have become the intellectual and perhaps also the political leaders of Israel.[49] On Israel's ninth independence day, Horon was already persuaded that "almost all of [the Jews in the Levant] have become ISRAELIS."[50] Having moved to Israel in 1959, Horon's writings in the 1960s and 1970s betray his belief that by this time the Hebrew Israelis have entirely detached themselves from their Jewish past to form a fully fledged nation:

> This nation possesses an established character, its own identity, albeit informally: it is Hebrew linguistically, territorially and existentially. The rising Sabra generation regards itself as Hebrew in a self-evident way, without any special education. Whoever is not a Jew—a Druze, for instance—can feel himself a Hebrew here and be an equal citizen of Israel; without converting to Judaism, obviously, and without declaring allegiance to a fictional "Jewish state" . . . As a national reality, our Israel is not a *Judenstaat* . . . On the contrary, the state is Hebrew de-facto; that is, by the nature of things, based on a territorial-linguistic reality, without any particular consideration of one's racial origins or religious awareness.[51]

Elsewhere, Horon formulates this even more succinctly: "The Canaanite language is coming back to life in the State of Israel";[52] therefore "it is easier for us to understand a Phoenician inscription than parts of the Book of Samuel, because the language we speak is more like Phoenician than the Judean dialect."[53]

By the late 1960s, Horon had calculated that the Sabras constituted almost half of Israel's population (including Palestinians in the territories captured in 1967),[54] capable of assimilating both Arabs and Jews from abroad, not unlike the way ancient Hebrews assimilated North African and Mesopotamian invaders and migrants. However, the Sabras' numerical predominance in Israel is not translated into sociocultural hegemony; in effect, the Israeli Zionist sociocultural system wages a *Kulturkampf* against the Hebrews, eliciting their all-too-natural enmity.[55]

This friction in outlook and disposition between Israelis and their authorities perpetuates a constant tension within the state. Horon goes as far as to suggest that in 1948 the Hebrews swapped the British occupation for the Zionist one, since Zionism, which promoted a Jewish historical vision and politics, did not *lead* the Hebrews toward independence (as distinct from *participated in* the independence struggle). Unlike the British, though, the Zionists laid a specific claim upon the hearts and minds of Hebrew Israelis, resulting in what Horon describes as an uneasy ambivalence of accommodation and rejection, whereby the "Zionist regime . . . is dangerously balanced on the edge of a sharp inner contradiction."[56]

Israel's precarious condition is exemplified by the very name picked for the state in 1948. The name "'Israel,'" Horon writes, "resurrected from Biblical antiquity—seems to strike a compromise between Zionists who conceived of a racially or religiously *Jewish* structure, and such home-grown patriots who fought for a modern, national *Hebrew* commonwealth, without racial and religious limitation."[57] This vagueness stems from the multitude of meanings packed into the denominator "Israel": Does it refer to "tribes migrating to Mesopotamia, hailing from Libya and Egypt or native to Canaan? Or the kingdom of Saul and David, the house of Omri, and the house of Jehu? Or perhaps it indicates 'Knesset Iśrael,' [that is,] a figure of speech . . . which denotes all Jewish congregations wherever they are?"[58] Horon's argumentation is an attack on Jewish-Zionist axiological geography: whereas the name "the Land of Kedem" possessed a "positive" degree of ambiguity, allowing it to express the Hebrew national outlook in its vast entirety, the name "Israel" is presented as an example of a "negative" ambiguity since it symbolizes the Zionist establishment's attempt to escape the tackling of the chief existential questions facing the state and its society.

When Israel was only a few years into its existence, Horon interpreted the above ambiguity as reflecting its situation as "an incipient nation [that] still lack[ed] definition, in practice as well as in theory, as to its ties with international Jewry, with the non-Jewish sections of its own population, and with the broader territory to which it belongs."[59] Yet the more Horon became confident of the disparity between the

Jews and the Hebrew Israelis, this situation came to symbolize for him Israel's, so to speak, "schizophrenic" condition, in both its domestic and foreign policy. Israel's "schizophrenia" is summarized in the following way: "The growing, modern society of Hebrew-speakers in Israel cannot become an integrated, leading national group in a progressive Levant, while remaining at the same time the spearhead of international Zionism, whose proclaimed aims are more or less racialist and more or less theocratic."[60] The core problem of Israel's politics is that the state *denies its own raison d'être,* which Horon recognizes as "becoming a framework for a nation forming in its own land" rather than serving as a "museum of Jewish antiquity" or "a 'ghetto' for an obsolete Zionism."[61]

Even Israel's independence war of 1948 was, to a large extent, a war not *for*, but *against*, Hebrew self-determination. The war, Horon points out, resulted from a prolonged process of territorial partitions that the Land of Kedem was subjected to under Anglo-French imperial tutelage and that contravened both the Land's geophysics and the Hebrews' national outlook. Horon names as the starting point for this process the Sykes-Picot Agreement of 1916 that detached Jordan's "Northern Bank"[62] from its two remaining banks, followed by the creation in 1923 of the Kingdom of Transjordan on the Eastern Bank. Next, in 1937, the Peel Commission laid out its proposal for dividing the Western Bank, recycled in the 1947 UN partition plan for Palestine. The Zionist leadership used the 1948 war to suppress and coopt the fury of the Hebrew youth against this breaking up of their homeland, which had been on the rise since the 1930s.[63]

As a result, the Zionists managed to establish in Israel a regime derided by Horon as "a racist narrow-minded Jewish theocracy"[64] or a "kingdom of fanatical rabbis,"[65] which inherited the Ottoman *millet* system. Describing his impressions of the Israeli social structure formed during his first stay there, Horon saw "a magnificent marriage of 'managerial socialism' with a High Middle Ages theocracy."[66] Under this "divide and rule" neo*millet* system Israel's citizenry is atomized into racialized or religious subgroups and subsectors vying with each other for access to limited material resources in a "socio-feudal" system of allocation, sustained by foreign donations. The society comprises the privileged connected institutionally with the MAPAI regime; the nouveaux riches; "flowers grown in concentration camps," who ended up in Israel for lack of better choice; and native Hebrew Israelis, who are completely excluded from their country's affairs.[67]

In the late 1960s, Horon charted a "pyramid of Israeli community-classes," at the top of which he placed the Zionist establishment, of mostly Ashkenazi origin. Immediately below, he located the mass of Ashkenazi Jews; next came the Sephardic and Oriental Jews, and then, in descending order, the "loyal" non-Jewish citizens ("the Druze, the Bedouin tribes, etc."), the various Christian and Muslim denominations, and finally the "non-citizen inhabitants of Jerusalem" and "subjects and refugees beyond the 'Green Line.' "[68] In that context, Horon expressed a certain sympathy for the struggle of the Mizrahi "Black Panthers" movement against the ethnosocial discrimination by the ruling Ashkenazi classes, since those were led mainly by francophone North African Jews—heirs of Hebrew Carthaginians, in Horon's eyes. He went as far as suggesting that the poverty enclaves of Mizrahi Jews were "ghettoes" that ought to be dismantled and their inhabitants incorporated into Israeli society in the same way as the Gaza refugees should be absorbed into Hebrew Israel.[69]

Its parliamentary system notwithstanding, Israel is essentially an undemocratic state, due to the selective conscription duty it implements, the lack of separation between religion and state (the latter utilizing its own legal instruments to enforce the former), and its refusal to introduce unitary secular education, perpetuating instead the division of Israeli society into castes and sects. Since Zionism never attempted "to develop a new science of Hebrew history, and to discover the true proportions of our destiny,"[70] it is unsurprising that the Israeli education, by excluding from its curriculum the geomorphological and human history of the land (with its significant non-Jewish chapters) in favor of a cosmopolitan and exterritorial "Jewish consciousness,"[71] works against the formation of a unified nation and contradicts the values and worldview of Israeli youth and schoolchildren. Until the Israeli schooling system is appropriately "de-Judaized" (by the introduction into the curriculum, inter alia, of topics unrelated to Jewish history, such as accounts of the Crusades by both Christian and Muslim authors), it is better, Horon suggests, to limit it to the provision of professional qualifications.[72]

Horon also asserts that Israeli policy on citizenship and immigration stands in stark contrast both to liberal democratic values and to the self-preservation imperative of a national state. Its most blatant manifestation is the "Ingathering of the Exiles" principle, which favors Jews of deprived socioeconomic background over "productive" non-Jews. Since non-Jews are by rule unwelcome in Israel, Horon observes that those who manage to make their way into it are forced either to undergo a humiliating process of conversion to Orthodox Judaism or to fabricate a Jewish ancestry.[73] His indignation at this state of things was so profound that he openly accused the Israeli ruling establishment of acting according to Nazi-like logic (which is not very surprising given that he traces Zionism's intellectual origins to an anti-Semitic myth): "In the state of Israel there develops a class of people, who might be defined as 'Marranos' or 'grandchildren of a non-Aryan grandmother,' in a manner reversing the medieval Spanish laws or the Nazi Nuremberg laws."[74] In private, Horon's denunciation of Israeli citizenship and nationality regime was even fiercer. This is how he referred to the Law of Return in a letter from May 1966:

> On principle, this is racist or theocratic law, without precedent in modern history apart from the Nazi Nuremberg laws. It accords citizenship to anyone born to a Jewish mother . . . and gives the status of tolerable citizens of a second degree, liable to expulsion, to all natives based on the "race" or "religion" of their father—in case their mother is not considered a full Jew (the Nazis traced the race to grandparents, we to the mother, that's the only difference) . . . This Law of Return is, in addition, non-implementable and was never implemented. That is, it was implemented in a "selective" way, by encouraging some to come and excluding others, according to their service to the "cause," which is simply the judeo-theocratic and pseudo-socialist establishment which in fact governs us . . . I therefore support the abrogation of this immoral, racist, arbitrary and non-implementable Law, which is in fact a hindrance in our opinion to immigration, not to speak of assimilation of the entire population into a single nation made up of equal citizens.[75]

In view of this judgment, it is not at all surprising that Horon opted not to accept Israeli citizenship under the Law of Return in 1959, but to undergo a naturalization process completed in 1964.

Whilst taking part in a debate at the Club for Hebrew Thought in 1966, Horon drew another parallel between Israel and Nazi Germany. Asserting that Israel's Arab citizens were in a position comparable to that of German Jews in the early days of Nazism, he suggested that this was due to the deeply ingrained Jewish mentality with its theologically ordained racism: "A good Jew and a good Zionist regards any non-Jew in Israel as a potential enemy. It took us eighteen years to achieve what took Germany just a few years with respect to detaching a part of the population from identification with the nation."[76] Thus, any "Arab problem" within Israel is of Israel's own making, as long as the state refuses to define the body politic territorially. Developing such parallels further, Horon compared Israel to the medieval Crusader Kingdom,[77] as the head of the Club, Aharon Amir, had done several years earlier,[78] and warned against Israel turning into a state resembling apartheid South Africa, in which Israeli Jews were the Afrikaners. Such a state, Horon cautioned, whose policies generate negative net migration (he was speaking at the peak of the mid-1960s economic crisis) and whose society lacks a positive sense of identification with it, will need to subsist on military power, making its inevitable collapse a question of time.[79]

The same structural weakness, Horon asserts, permeates Israel's foreign relations and, in consequence, undermines its geopolitical status and strength. An analogy is implicitly created between Israel "from within" and Israel "from without": whereas "from within" Israel pretends to be a "Jewish state" while not being such de facto, "from without" Israel is strategically the strongest state in the Land of Kedem, yet unable to make appropriate use of its superiority due to its clientelist dependence upon foreign powers—by which Horon means worldwide Zionism and the United States. Both are naturally uninterested in Israel breaking free from their patronage, but so is the Israeli regime, which is organically tied to the clientelist pattern of social relations that suited the Jewish Diaspora but became anomalous in a modern polity. As long as Israel consents to be a "Holy Land" for the American Jewish Diaspora, Horon warns that it will never achieve fiscal independence, and, by obvious extention, cultural and political sovereignty, whose best safeguard would be knowledge-based economic policy rather than economics reliant on heavy industry or agriculture.[80] Horon sardonically describes this state of affairs as "a ghetto wielding decisive military power over significant parts of two continents"[81] and accuses Israel of "micromania." Israel's heads of state and the military, afflicted with "Jewish mentality," treat war achievements as merely a bargaining chip for "leaving Israel alone" instead of using them to reshape the entire Land of Kedem—a strategic imperative for Israel and a liberating perspective for all its inhabitants.[82]

For Horon, Israel's position as an "armed ghetto" imbued with existential fears and unwilling to take up the initiative offered by its geophysical and geopolitical advantages is a deadly dangerous aberration, particularly after the 1967 war, when Israel held back from annexing the captured territories and granting their inhabitants full citizenship. Instead, he laments, it introduced a dual administration: by extending its military occupation over close to a million persons living beyond the "Green Line" while keeping its parliamentary regime within the confines of pre-1967 Israel, it entrenched the neo*millet* system[83] and obstructed the "natural" course of history, which replaces premodern *millets* with modern nations.

Nonetheless, Horon adds, Israel's regional isolation, although a manifestation of Jewish xenophobia, has ironically contributed to its geopolitical empowerment. Cut off from the Land of Kedem's hinterland, Israel directed by default its strategic efforts westwards, turning into a prominent Mediterranean naval force.[84] Furthermore, "prompted by enemies and *alleged* friends,"[85] it invested heavily in knowledge-based industry (not only military), propelling itself to the status of a leading economic power in the region. Thus, Horon could write back in 1952, "The Israelis are today the most compact and the strongest single element in the entire Levant, from almost any standpoint, and not alone from the standpoint of military superiority."[86] This way, Canaan (Israel + Lebanon) followed the logic embedded in its history from antiquity and became the most populous and culturally and economically advanced district of the Land of Kedem[87]—a bridgehead for a larger Hebrew liberal-democratic polity, once Israel finally overcomes its mental inferiority vis-à-vis the Jews, the superpowers, and the Arabs.

The Arabs in Horon's Perspective

It is telling that Horon opens his discussion of the "Arab question" with a survey of the Arabs' ancient history, just as he had approached the "Jewish question." Yet, having critically reviewed Arab historiography, Horon does not construct a positive alternative for it. This is reasonable: as a Hebrew national historian, it is not his task to provide the Arabs with a new commemorative narrative once he had, to his understanding, demolished the existing one. He merely remarks that an Arab national entity and identity might, and perhaps should, emerge in the Arabian Peninsula (and, as we shall quickly see, nowhere else);[88] he thus leaves the task of writing a genuinely Arab national history to his putative Arab counterpart. Other methodological similarities in the way Horon treats Jewish and Arab history will become apparent in the following discussion.

Historical and philological analysis is once again mobilized to undo what Horon perceives as the false mythology at the cornerstone of most modern Arab politics. His starting piece of evidence for the lack of contemporary Arab nationalism's grounding in provable historical realities is the etymology of the word "Arab." This, he explains, is a *hapax legomenon* in the Arabic language, its root (*'rb*) used for no other meanings and being actually a loanword from Hebrew that stands as a synonym for "Bedouin," that is, "man of the steppe." The loan is proved by Horon by pointing out that the Hebrew root for the words "steppe" and "Arab" (*'rv*) also covers meanings like "evening" and "west" (see chapter 2), while the Arab counterparts of the last two words are derived from an entirely different root, *ghrb*.[89]

Likewise, the Arabs' mythical ancestors Ismā'īl (the Hebrew Ishmael) and Qaḥṭān have evidently Hebrew names that originated outside the Arabian Peninsula and remain meaningless in Arabic. Horon notes that Qaḥṭān hails from "an older Hebrew patriarch," while the geographical etymology of Ishmael and his legendary mother, Hagar, points to North Africa. This makes him kin to some of the Hebrews' totemic ancestors, in particular Shimon, whose name is derived from the same root as Ishmael, *shm'*. The root literally means "hearing" but is used to indicate "one who hears [that is, commands] a language."[90] Ishmael's original domain, as detailed in the Bible, is Ḥaṿila in the Sahara Desert, and his physical description—half man, half wild ass—is explained by Horon as symbolizing the economic realities in the northern part of the African continent in the fourth to third millennia BCE. It is there that the wild ass was first domesticated and subsequently used as a transport animal, carrying precious goods from the Sahara to Egypt and thence to the westernmost environs of the Land of Kedem. The transport leaders, Horon adds, often donned animal masks (supposedly to enhance the goods' smooth transfer by keeping the animals calm), which in time acquired sacral-totemic meaning, with the ornamental and cultic motif of part man, part animal quickly spreading to early Pharaonic Egypt.

As to Hagar, Horon states that its root is also a Semito-Hamitic one, appearing in two versions, *hgr* and *hṿr*, both indicating "pregnancy," "parenthood," and other notions from the same semantic field. The legendary figure of Hagar, he suggests, probably originated in the matriarchal Libyan tribe of Hawwara (corrupted sometimes to Haggara), which bequeathed a trace of its existence to the Hoggar/Ahaggar mountain range in modern-day Algeria. The Hawwara's totem was a snake, which Horon identifies as evidence of an ethnocultural connection with the Levitic mythical sphere, where the figures of Ishmael and Levi's brother Shimon also belonged.[91]

Horon lets his reader infer that the Hagar and Ishmael myth arose in a similar way to other North African Hebrew myths that later merged into the Canaanite Abrahamic mythology, except that the former came to occupy a prominent place in Arab mytho-history. He argues that this was quite a late development since nomadic Bedouin Arabs cannot be identified as a separate group before the early first millennium BCE, while the Ishmael myth is certainly much older. Moreover, in ancient Arabic literature, the "sons of Ismāʻīl" denoted those migrating toward Arabia from the northwest (that is, from the Land of Kedem), and not an autochthonous peninsular element. The reason for the myth's prominence, Horon concludes, was probably Prophet Muhammad's legendary descent from the Ishmaelites.[92] He adds that the name of Muhammad's hometown of Mecca supposedly came from non-Arabic, southern Semitic sources,[93] thus suggesting a close intellectual link between Islamic and Arabic mytho-history, which is crucial to his attack on the political tenets of allegedly secular Pan-Arabism.

The Prophet's activity is classified by Horon as another case of "militant Judaism." At the outset of Muhammad's preaching, Jews were culturally and politically prominent in the Arabian Peninsula, particularly along its southern and northern rims (Kingdom of Ḥimyar and Canaan respectively), and therefore Muhammad imitated initially some Jewish traditions, such as praying toward Jerusalem.[94] The first Muslim community is labeled by Horon a "crypto-Judaic sect": "[P]rimitive Islam can be defined as an exiguous form of Judaism grafted onto local pagan traditions and placed within easier reach of the Bedouin mentality."[95] It is only when the Jews of Yathrib (now known as Medina) refused to accept Muhammad as their spiritual teacher that the latter broke away from Judaism, going on to found an authentically Arab creed, which inherited the Judaic theocratic conceptions of Ezra and Nehemia but cleared them of ethnic xenophobia.[96]

When speaking of "Arabic Islam" Horon does not suggest a new theological quality (save, perhaps, for the composition of the Qur'ān in Medina *after* Muhammad's death,[97] whose very name is inspired by the Hebrew name for the Old Testament, Miḳra[98]), but merely that the new religion was preached mainly to Bedouins, making the Arabian Peninsula its stronghold. Purely Arabic Islam, however, did not last long: the political and military vacuum resulting from the protracted Persian-Byzantine wars in the Land of Kedem provided an opportunity for Muhammad's successors to turn what started as Bedouin booty forays into permanent control. Horon notes at the same time that when faced with a more formidable enemy outside the Land of Kedem, like the Berber Jews, the Arabs' military advances slowed down considerably. North Africa was, in effect, never completely Islamized, leaving room for the potential development of Berber national identity.[99] He ridicules the historians "infatuated by the Arab mirage" who saw in the Arab "miraculous" military successes a reenactment of the conquest of Canaan by the sons of Israel.[100]

Horon observes that the transfer of the Muslim caliphate's capital outside Arabia, first to Damascus under the Umayyad dynasty (an Arabo-Syro-Greek kingdom, in his description), and then to Baghdad (a Persian toponym), symbolized the renewal of the old Persian Empire in an Islamic shape and the complete loss by early Islam of its Bedouin-Arab character. By that time the Arabs were already being overwhelmed, both numerically and culturally, by converts to Islam who used their new religion to establish their primacy in the Muslim world: "Islam, far from signifying the Arabization of Africa and the Orient, was . . . the means by which the Africans and Orientals *got rid* of the Arabs; the . . . neophytes . . . created international Islam and thereby defeated Arabism."[101] On a similar note, Horon states that the Islamic invasion of southwest Europe by recently Islamized Berbers actually signified the return to the Iberian Peninsula of the Hamito-Semitic element that had been all but extinguished after Hannibal's downfall.[102]

The Arabian Peninsula declined as a result into provincial insignificance, roamed by anarchic, superficially Muslim Bedouins and controlled only very loosely by the caliphs. The Muslim Empire became a huge and precarious patchwork of multiethnic, multilinguistic and multicultural denominations, often prone to ferocious internecine fighting, and perfected the *millet* system. This societal structure is likened by Horon to Latin Christendom—a typically medieval system of semiautonomous communities and tribes, united only by faith (quite incompletely so, bearing in mind the various heterodox sects of Islam and the extant non-Muslim denominations) and the literary Arabic sacral tongue. This is a demonstrably nonnational premodern reality in which the primary allegiance is given to one's own ethnoreligious group rather than to an abstract political structure like the state.[103]

The Arabs' minority status in present-day Muslim societies—not exceeding 15 percent, according to Horon—allows him to draw a distinction between Arabic speakers and Arabs proper, or true Arabs. He conceives of the former as the autochthonous inhabitants of the Muslim-conquered lands, who converted to Islam and adopted the Arabic language, thus "receiv[ing] Arabism as a bacterial infection" (*sic*!).[104] It was they who contributed most to the splendor of classical Arabic culture, while retaining a vivid memory of their non-Arabic and non-Islamic pedigree. True Arabs, as Horon defines them, are the original inhabitants of the Arabian Peninsula,[105] the desert-roaming Bedouins and their progeny. True Arabs persist in a premodern tribal framework and have no understanding or interest in modern nationalism, let alone an Arab one (they are also quite indifferent to faith, Horon remarks, but anyway constitute a mere 1 percent of all Muslims worldwide).[106]

Horon's determinist methodology is displayed with full force in the above argumentation, not only in its environmental aspect (one cannot be a true Arab outside Arabia), but also in its sociocultural aspect (true Arabs by the very nature of their Bedouin way of life are incapable of supratribal solidarity). Notably, such classification of true Arabs owes a lot to the Arabic sociophilological tradition, which celebrated the Bedouin way of life as "purely Arab" and whose primary exponent was the great Islamic medieval scholar Ibn Haldoun,[107] whom Horon readily cites.[108] As it also informed French colonial policy in the Middle East and North Africa, it is hardly surprising to identify an intellectual affinity between a Francophile like Horon and French perceptions of the "Arab world."

The Arabs' factual history and contemporary sociocultural reality as presented by Horon stand in stark contradiction to their image in Arab nationalist ideology. This ideology exploits two myths of origin that Horon seeks to undermine. One is the concept of the Arabian Peninsula as the Semites' ethnocultural cradle, derived, as observed above, from Ibn Haldoun and propagated by Ernest Renan. This essentialist concept ascribes to "Semites" inherent linguistic, physical, or racial traits and portrays the Arab Bedouins as the "unspoilt" perennial brothers of the modern-day inhabitants of the Middle East, including the Jews. The other, arising logically from the first, is that the Arabic language is the oldest of Semitic languages, from which all others have in due course developed. Both ideas are utterly baseless, Horon argues, and their presence in otherwise serious scholarship skews contemporary Semitic studies toward such misconceptions as that the "Semites" were a separate race originating among the camel-riding Bedouins, who spoke an isolated language.

We saw above that Horon dated the emergence of the Arab Bedouin culture to the early first millennium BCE, when Hebrew culture was in its prime; hence the latter could not take its origins from the Bedouins. As for the theory of the Semitic languages' origin in Arabia, he flatly rejects it as defying all linguistic and archaeological evidence. Horon claims that these languages and their speakers' cultures actually developed to the northwest of Arabia, that is, in the Hebrew-Mediterranean cultural sphere and under strong African influence. Arabic, he states, *was* of course indigenous to the Arabian Peninsula, emerging only upon the arrival of Hebrew-Semitic speakers. Yet this merely proves its peripheral status in the Semito-Hamitic world, both in terms of territory and time, and its preservation of archaic features points to its remoteness from linguistic developments taking place in the Semitic heartland. Nonetheless, he laments, the theory became popular thanks to its attractiveness as a romantic-orientalist myth and its political usefulness for Arab nationalism.[109]

Horon identifies the causes of this ominous popularity in the primacy of the philological paradigm in nineteenth-century European—especially German—ethnography, which mechanically transferred its principle of "one language per one *ethnos*" onto what it termed the "Arab World" (a misnomer from the very start, since most of the "Arab countries" are located outside Arabia proper), in blatant disregard of its variegated cultural and linguistic make-up. The very idea that ethnic belonging can be reduced to linguistic identification is denounced by Horon as racist and anti-Semitic. Literary Arabic language, he asserts, fulfils a role not unlike that of Latin in medieval Europe, a sacral nonspoken language (Horon emphatically insists that the nineteenth-century Arabic literary renaissance, the Nahḍa, had no national undertones or effects). Accordingly, he says, the only real "Arab unity" possible is indeed a linguistic one, which by his definition is innately nonnational: otherwise, the "Arabs" exhibit no cohesive properties whatsoever.[110] "The theory is false," he ends with a warning, "and its proper place is in the annals of European Romanticism from the previous century, and not in contemporary informed criticism. It would have made no sense to argue against it, had it not been meanwhile transformed into a political propaganda-tool."[111]

The political ideology that wields this tool is none other than Pan-Arabism, whose very name suggests a wide scope of linguistic and geographic references. Horon traces Pan-Arabism's origins to a sinister alliance struck between European imperial interests in the Middle East and local petty careerists who were looking for a new anchor after the collapse of the Ottoman Empire with its cozy *millet* system. Most of the local early adherents of Pan-Arabism were not of true Arab stock, and many were non-Muslims[112] who sought a cohesive framework in a vision of an Arabic cultural-political unity that would bypass religious limitations. The "Arab myth" became in due course the Middle Eastern counterpart of the "Aryan myth." The expansionist desires harbored by Pan-Arabists, Horon warns, are equally perilous for Middle Eastern non-Arab nations and communities as the Nazi ideology was for Europe.[113]

Those who did the most to foment the reductionist image of the Middle East as a uniform Arabo-Islamic space in order to dominate the Middle East were the British. The origins of the British method are traced by Horon to India, where, he says, they first learned to manipulate Muslim needs and wishes against the non-Muslim majority by mobilizing or bribing local Muslim agents. The British later applied this method in the Levant, having intervened in its affairs in the early twentieth century to keep French and Zionist advances at bay and to secure a strategic superiority in the Suez Canal neighborhood. For this end, Horon writes, London did not hesitate to introduce into the Land of Kedem a concept foreign to its inhabitants' medieval-like system of ideas and values—that of an Arab world unified by language and religion. By disregarding local cultural and ethnolinguistic, as well as geophysical and strategic realities, and cynically playing their local proxies against each other,

> the English fostered since 1915 the crude legend of Lawrence's Arabia, of a "Revolt in the Desert" which never took place. What actually happened was that England found stooges among an obscure Arab Sunnite dynasty from Mecca, the Hashemites, whom she imposed or tried to impose as kings and princes upon alien lands: Upon a heterogenous [*sic*] Iraq . . . created so as to ensure British control over the Kirkuk-Persian Gulf oilfields; Upon Syria

> also, a scheme foiled by the French when they expelled Lawrence's protégé, the Hashemite prince Faysal; Upon Transjordan, the larger part of Palestine, which was torn away from it . . . in order to check the growth of Zionist colonization, although Zionism provided the sole legal and moral basis for the entire British Palestinian Mandate. When the senior Hashemite, the "king" of Hejaz, proved too fickle, he was chased away by another royal puppet of England . . . Ibn-Saud, the Bedouin leader of the puritanical Wahabite [*sic*] sect . . . During and after World War II, Churchill conceded his Saudi fief . . . to Roosevelt; while [Anthony] Eden became the main architect of an Arab League.[114]

The result was a "weird cocktail of eastern and western imperialism, oil interests, ignorant Muslim lords and vane Islamic princes and tyrants, inciting together a mob of dubious 'Arabs,' "[115] but enjoying no authentic mass constituency. In present times, Horon continues, the British way of managing the Middle East was inherited by the political classes of the United States, in particular the State Department, whose officials are pushing toward an alliance with a fictional uniform Arab cultural and political power to the exclusion of Israel. Other members of the pro-Arabist lobby in America are the Arab foreign students funded by their governments and the American oil corporations working in the Middle East. Paradoxically, all serve purposes consonant with the geopolitical objectives of the Soviet Union, for whom Pan-Arabist activists serve as useful pawns to remove western regional influence. On that level, Pan-Arabism is indeed "similar to other contemporary teachings, such as racialism and communism . . . a pseudo-scientific myth and a tool of political deception."[116]

Horon contrasts Anglo-American imperialism in the Middle East and North Africa with French-style imperialism, thereby offering a glimpse into some definitive features of his thinking. His condemnation of the former is ferocious. Not only does it carry the blame for making Pan-Arabism an active political factor, which entered the void left by the discredited *Mare Nostrum* ideology of Italian fascism,[117] resulting in the British ceding control of the movement to local political adventurers such as Gamal 'Abd an-Nasir.[118] It is also guilty of keeping territories under British control backward, poor, and undeveloped. Horon asserts that between 1919 and 1945, British-ruled Levant lost between 8 and

10 million lives, which in relative numbers means that British atrocities were as heinous as those of the Nazis and the Soviets.[119] Palestine is the only prospering British colony thanks to the Hebrews, who had to labor under the double yoke of British imperialism and its Zionist proxies. "Today," Horon wrote in 1945, "Zionism is a vassal of London, a client of a certain Jewish-American bourgeoisie, and represents neither the immigrant (. . .) nor the Hebrew colonist."[120] Either way, Horon concludes that foreign intervention yielded a Middle East sliced up into ramshackle statelets. These were deliberately delimitated so as to remain unstable and dependent upon extraregional powers, whether France and Britain formerly or the USSR and USA presently, and thus elicited no authentic local patriotism.[121]

Against British imperialism, with its guiding principle of "unite [the Arabs] and rule [the Middle East],"[122] the French imperialists' policy of "divide and rule" is afforded much greater leniency on Horon's part. France based its colonial rule on the exploitation of local ethnocultural diversities, which supposedly made it more sensitive to the actual make-up of the Land of Kedem. Horon notes with alarm at the same time the influence of the "pro-Arab" (hence, pro-British) school in French politics, at whose feet he lays the blame for the antagonization of the Berbers and the consequent "loss" of North Africa to Pan-Arabism. French colonial rule was characterized, according to Horon, by economic and social progress unmatched in any other part of the Middle East under foreign rule, save Palestine. Urbanization (began by the Carthaginians), population growth, and the discovery and development of oil and other natural resources made the relinquishment of North Africa, especially Algeria, a tragic blunder, which resulted in the growing dependency of the West on what Horon somewhat scornfully terms "Arab oil," with gloomy political consequences.[123]

A topic quite central to Horon's discourse (at least before 1962) is his strong support for the French in the Algerian War of 1954–1962, including an early warning that de Gaulle, whom Horon had hated with a passion since World War II, might bring about France's withdrawal from Algeria. His support for the ultimately losing side was based not only on the strategic calculations alluded to briefly above; in the public talks he gave in Israel during the early 1960s Horon argued repeatedly that Israel (the modern incarnation of Hebrew power in the eastern Mediterranean) and Algeria (its counterpart in the western Mediterranean since Carthage) shared common historical, social, and therefore political, features and objectives. Both were immigration countries forging local territorial national identity out of heterogeneous ethnic components. Horon stated that the European colonists, the pieds noirs—who were not exclusively French but also Corsican, Alsatian, Italian, Spanish, and Jewish (as well as Berbers, Qabilians, and even assimilated Arabs)—were Algeria's Sabras "firmly rooted in their new homelands."[124] They were no less indigenous than the Arabic-speakers, whose presence in the Algerian littoral was anyway very negligible. Thus, Israel's and French Algeria's common purpose was to curtail Pan-Arabism's advance in the eastern and western Mediterranean respectively. In case of victory, Horon concluded, a Hebrew Israel would guarantee France's continued presence in North Africa as a block to British Arabist designs.

Horon refers to the FLN rebellion as "a foreign invasion by Pan-Arabist imperialism" and also points out—correctly—that more Muslim Algerians fought on the side of France than of the FLN: "The Muslim revolt in Algeria is also an inter-Muslim civil war." The FLN's Pan-Arabist dream (as Horon sees it) of unifying North Africa is therefore doomed to fail due to the ethnic diversity of the area and its non-Arab character; in fact, the only agent capable of bringing this unity about is none other than the French.[125] Horon interprets Soviet support for the FLN in the same vein: cynical political calculation in view of the USSR's oppression of its own Muslim population, whose real objective is to take over as patrons of Pan-Arabism from the British and steer it toward Soviet imperialist interests.[126]

This particular standpoint, I believe, throws an especially revealing light on Horon's general position with regard to national liberation. It would appear that he did not perceive national sovereignty as an absolute value. National independence was dear to him and the Young Hebrews only insofar as it was attained on the basis of principles they regarded as progressive, such as secularism and liberalism. With those values ascribed to the French, who were facing a Pan-Arabist and Islamic-influenced mutiny, it was obvious that Horon would embrace the former's cause. He clearly preferred an "enlightened" colonialism to a potentially illiberal independence, and indeed claimed that not all foreign intervention against Pan-Arabism must necessarily be denounced as "colonialist."[127]

So, Horon maintains, Pan-Arabism, conceived by European intelligentsia and British colonial designs, is enmeshed in a web of internal contradictions, which he undertakes to disentangle. Its greatest weakness, he argues, is its inherent foreignness to the area it pretends to unite and represent: the vague concept of an "Arab world" raises linguistic identification above the geographical and therefore expresses no territorial national outlook.[128] This identification is based on literary Arabic ("a half-dead language, renewed recently for educational, administrative, and journalistic purposes"[129]), suppressing local indigenous and Arabic-derived vernaculars, which are for the most part mutually unintelligible and thus obstruct the imagined Arab linguistic kinship. Horon insists furthermore that the areas where various versions of Arabic predominate are in reality much thinner than they are held to be in Western and Israeli popular consciousness, comprising in fact less than half of the whole "Arab world." He even produces a map of the spread of the Arabic language, juxtaposing it to the geographical span of other languages and dialects spoken in the "Arab world."[130] Asserting that the only language that has entirely vanished from the Middle East is Assyro-Babylonian,[131] Horon implies that other non-Arab languages continue to exist either latently or in full force, and, in appropriate circumstances, might become national tongues again.

Another principal weakness of Pan-Arabism is its supposedly organic link to Islam, a religion that most of Pan-Arabism's alleged adherents profess and that supplies it with a historiographical base and most of its sociopolitical terminology (in one place Horon actually accuses Pan-Arabism of serving as a "front" for a makeshift Pan-Islamic caliphate).[132] Western Orientalism, which rarely considered Islam outside the Arabic framework, is complicit in disseminating the view that the Arab and Muslim civilizations are overlapping.[133] However, as Horon's argument goes, a social organization based on Islam (or any monotheistic religion, for that matter) is inimical to modern national society by organizing a strict hierarchical and discriminatory order of premodern communities, where people lead an involuntary way of life, women are not considered fully human, and homosexuality proliferates (*sic*!).[134] Furthermore, given that the core of Pan-Arabism's foundational myth is the multiethnic age of classical Islam, Pan-Arabism's historiographical foundation naturally fails to provide a suitable "golden age" for an authentic national idea. Exposing yet another Pan-Arabist paradox, Horon writes that the Bedouins' supposed indifference to nationalism and their damaging impact on the economy makes them agents of dubious value at best, which leaves Pan-Arabism with no choice but to rely on the meagre Arabophone Sunni and Christian urban intelligentsia as its actual backbone.

Moreover, the true number of nationally inclined Arabs is much lower than is presented in Pan-Arabist propaganda. Refuting what he calls "the 100-million myth" (referring to the supposed Arab population of the Middle East mentioned by Pan-Arabism's supporters), Horon sets out to uncover the inaccuracies and deliberate exaggerations that purportedly abound in censuses all over the Arab world. He asserts that Arab population numbers are wildly inflated and are often contradictory and not based on any real estimates, and he proposes an alternative "Arab statistics," whereby the "true" number of Arabic speakers does not exceed 55 million. These millions, Horon claims, are interspersed among a great diversity of non-Arabs disinclined toward Pan-Arab nationalism or lost altogether in the immensity of the scarcely populated deserts.[135] Horon discloses that his calculations are based on reports by "serious and trustworthy travellers," including at least one by the radical Revisionist Wolfgang von Weisl, "which the author . . . has had the opportunity to consult since 1934."[136]

Horon concludes his statistical review by stating that the image of a tiny Israel facing a hostile Arab "ocean" is wholly fictitious, given the abundance of different ethnocultural groups in the "Arab world" who pose a direct challenge to Pan-Arabism's unitary vision by subverting the idea of a common Arab heritage. Their ethnolinguistic diversity, Horon claims, is being deliberately obfuscated for ideological reasons, both by Pan-Arabism and by Zionism. The "Arab world" is actually divided into at least four distinct geopolitical zones consisting of the Maghreb, the Nile basin, the Land of Kedem, and the Arabian Peninsula, each of which is torn between several rival foci of power. The main (and contending) foci of Pan-Arabism in the Land of Kedem are Damascus, Baghdad, Amman, and Beirut, all of which Horon describes as extremely precarious due to the large numbers of non-Sunnis under their control. The Arab League is therefore hardly anything more than a propaganda body, as it neither represents a tangible political reality, nor does it advance any meaningful political programme. Pan-Arabism failed to win a wide indigenous support base, Horon points out, since there exist no authentic national constituencies in the wider "Arab world" and in the Land of Kedem, save for the incipient Hebrew identity in Israel and perhaps in Lebanon, both of which are located outside Pan-Arabism's sphere of direct influence.[137]

Although Horon's treatment of Arabs is tainted with determinism and even essentialism, reflecting his standpoint on "objectivity" versus "subjectivity" in history (he depicts the Arabs as mostly passive recipients of colonialist conspiracies), it is nevertheless remarkable. We should keep in mind that Horon struggled to expose Pan-Arabism as void of positive content at the peak of its successes, during the 1950s and the 1960s. Given its post-1967 decline, one cannot but appreciate in retrospect Horon's far-sightedness—which does not necessarily mean subscribing to his particular mode of argumentation against Pan-Arabism.

What then are the true aims of Pan-Arabism, this "nationalism *sans* nation,"[138] which is "short on history but large over space"?[139] Upholding the homogeneous ideal of a unitary "Arab world" imported from European Orientalism indicates a desire to suppress all other aspirations and ideologies that might undermine the fantasy of Pan-Arab singularity. Pan-Arabism is an imperialism *directed internally*, the objective of which is to impose a single social, political, and cultural platform from the Maghreb to Iraq. Horon's natural conclusion is that Pan-Arabism is the "Arab" peoples' greatest adversary because it strives not only to forge a political framework repellent to them but also to force upon them an apparently nonexistent identity, thereby stifling any potential territorial-linguistic ethnic identification based on a defined geophysical space and an autochthonous vernacular. By attempting to crossbreed religious and linguistic affiliations, Pan-Arabism becomes a barrier to the emergence of a liberal-territorial nationalism in the Middle East and promotes what Horon sees as backward, oppressive, and overreaching sociocultural organization. Hence, he argues, the popularity of communism in the region as an expression of the desire to escape the Arab-Muslim oppression.[140]

In Horon's eyes, of all the states of the Land of Kedem, Israel and Lebanon are the most advanced culturally and economically, at least since the Mandates. Constituting an alternative model of social and national organization to Pan-Arabism, however faulty, they break up the "Arab world" in two. They are the least of all "Arab," keeping their Arab Sunni population (by force, in post-1967 Israel) remote from Pan-Arabist influences, and since Hebrews and Lebanese have mutually more in common than each of them has with Muslims, they possess the best chances of developing into *staatsnation*. For this reason, Pan-Arabist regimes will never accede to the existence of a non-Arab polity in Pan-Arabism's supposed zone of domination. Any attempt to come to reason with it amounts at best to naïveté, since the most a Pan-Arabist regime might propose is for Israel to become an ethnoreligious autonomy under its auspices, "a Lebanon for the Jews."[141]

Horon concludes that geography's deterministic logic, which makes Canaan the pivot of the Land of Kedem, means that the decisive battle between Pan-Arabism and its opponents tending to territorial nationalism must take place there. Such a battle will determine more than the political course the Land should take; it will decide whether it will survive as a separate geopolitical unit or be swallowed up by the "Arab world."[142] The same logic also enforces the persistence since antiquity of stable geopolitical tendencies. Horon depicts the twentieth-century strategic and military conflict between Israel and Egypt as a continuation by 'Abd an-Nasir of Pharaonic, Ptolemaic, Fatimid and Muhammad Ali's attempts to control Canaan from the Nilotic capitals. Likewise, the Israeli-Iraqi 1967 air battles are conceptualized as a modern-day expression of the geopolitical rivalry between Western and Eastern Riverlands.[143]

It is worth reemphasizing Horon's insistence on the existence of a latent alliance between the "two equally pernicious fictions—Zionism and Pan-Arabism,"[144] so much so that in a letter to Eri Jabotinsky, he wrote only half-jokingly that he considered Israel an undeclared member of the Arab League.[145] Both subscribe to the image of a small and detached Israel within a hostile (and entirely homogeneous) "sea" of Arabs; both originate outside the Land of Kedem, serving as foreign pressure agents; both rely on a nonnational foundational myth; finally, both subvert emergent national outlooks, obstructing Hebrew renaissance.[146]

Given that the systematic differentiation between Arabs "proper" and "improper" is a central tenet of Horon's political thinking, the place he accords "untrue" Arabs in his picture of the sociocultural make-up of the Middle East and his geopolitical programme for the region needs to be examined in some detail. Sedentary Sunni Arabic-speakers apart, Horon presents all other denominations and communities of the Eastern Mediterranean as either potential or actual opponents of Pan-Arabism. For the sake of his argument, he quite indiscriminately lumps together almost all Middle Eastern minorities (some of them constituting majorities or pluralities in their respective areas[147]), regardless of religious, ethnic, or social background and affiliation. Such a common denominator is both deterministic and negative: what brings all these groups together in Horon's eyes is their non-Sunni identity, which presumably entails an inclination to resist Pan-Arabism.

This inclination is assumed to feed upon the non-Sunnis' memory of their pre-Islamic origins, although Horon admits that there exists no precise correlation between adherence to non-Sunni belief and an anti-Arabist standpoint (and vice versa). For instance, as mentioned above, the Sunni Bedouins, though being accorded the role of the "authentic folk" organically tied to their land in the Pan-Arabist worldview, emerge in Horon's analysis as hostile, or at least useless, to Pan-Arabism, due to their reputed lack of attachment to modern nationalism. The hard core of adherents of Pan-Arabism remains the thin layer of urban intelligentsia, which constitutes a mixture of various ethnic elements, both indigenous and migratory, that switched to Arabic after the arrival of Islam. A case in point is "the Muslim bourgeoisie of Fez [that] is made in large part of Judeo-Berber converts to Islam and Moors chased out of Spain."[148] Hence, even by Horon's method, authentic Arab descent combined with a profession of Sunni Islam would not automatically correspond to an allegiance to Pan-Arabism, although such correspondence is crucial to the Pan-Arabist ideological structure and, in a reverse manner, to Horon's own politics.

Accordingly, many prominent Pan-Arabists belong to the huge demographic category that Horon names "the Arabianate" (*'arbaim* in Hebrew, singular *'arbai*).[149] This word is a neologism, coined probably by Yonatan Ratosh, who used it liberally in his own political writings. As the linguist Michal Ephratt (Ratosh's sister-in-law) explains, the Hebrew affix "i" was introduced by Ratosh to denote "pseudo."[150] *'Arbai* would thus indicate "pseudo-Arab,"[151] that is, one upon whom identification with the broadly conceived Arab identity had been forced at some point generations ago. The descendants of the first "Arabianate" in time came to form huge ethnic groups, Arabic by tongue but not by origin.

Reviewing the area to which Pan-Arabism lays claim from the Maghreb to Iraq, Horon lists and enumerates both the "Arabianate" and the non-Arabic-speaking communities and minorities opposed to Arab nationalism either outwardly or latently. In North Africa, these are chiefly the Berbers who, though professing Islam, are of indigenous stock and, historically, are related to the Canaanites of Carthage. The area is additionally inhabited by Semito-Hamitic local African peoples. In western Asia, the most prominent ethnic minority is the Kurds, who are heterogeneous both by religion and language: among the Kurds there are Sunnis, Shiites, and Yazidis, as well as Kurdish-, Arabic-, and Persian speakers. Horon is clearly supportive of Kurdish national aspirations, though he mentions that Kurdish nationalists probably exaggerate their nation's spread both statistically and geographically. Other significant ethnic minorities he cites are the Christian Armenians and the Muslim Circassians.

In Egypt, the most prominent minority are the Christian Copts, to whom Horon devotes a separate review of a history of the Copts by his American acquaintance Edward Wakin (himself a Christian from Lebanon).[152] In it he observes that the Copts are Egypt's most ancient and original inhabitants, who, historically and culturally, are related to the Hebrew Canaanites. They are also the country's eponyms[153] and ancestors of its Muslim majority, which more willingly subscribes to Egyptian territorial nationalism than to a Pan-Arabist slogan. "Napoleon, who had an eye for detail," Horon writes elsewhere, "and rarely erred in his political judgement, did not see any Arabs when he uncovered the heritage of the Pharaohs and established the new Egypt"[154] since "Egyptians speaking their own dialect of Arabic are no more Arabs than English-speaking Irishmen are Englishmen."[155] Horon, as other Young Hebrews, speaks warmly of the "Pharaonic" Egyptian nationalism promulgated since the 1920s, especially by the Copt Salāma Mūsa. He sees in it a potential ally for Hebrew nationalism and wishes the Copts perseverance in withstanding the "Pan-Arabist assault" led by Egypt's president, Gamal 'Abd an-Nasir (above all an enemy of his own people), even if their variation of monophysite Christianity tends to remain aloof from mundane matters. He suggests they politicize their refusal to become "Arabs," to bring about an Egyptian version of the Kemalist revolution in Turkey and tear Egypt away from the sphere of Pan-Arabism.[156]

Of particular importance are the various Christian churches and denominations in Western Asia and the Land of Kedem, most significant of whom are the Maronites dominating in Lebanon. The strong connection between Lebanese Christians and the French is cited by Horon as evidence of the Maronites' progressive role in the Land of Kedem. He expresses his admiration for the pro-Western nationalistic factors in Lebanon, referring to the founder of the Phalange party, Pierre Gemayel, as "one of the greatest men of his country"[157] who would lead it out of the Arab League, and suggesting that the Phalange's ideology is quite compatible with that of the Young Hebrews.[158] He also recalls an event from the closing stages of the 1948 Israeli independence war, when the IDF invaded Lebanon. Some Maronite notables are said to have used the occasion to voice their hope that Israel would annex the Shiite-dominated environs of Tyre in the south of the country. Israel refrained from doing so, which Horon condemns as betrayal of potential allies.[159]

Horon does not omit lesser churches like the Melkites, the Assyrians, the Jacobites, or the Protestant and the Orthodox—though he remarks of the former that it is regionally significant only inasmuch as its adherents communicated British influence, while the latter colluded with the Pan-Arabists.

The Christian communities are followed by the Druze and the Shiites—the latter comprising the majority of Iraq's population and also highly influential in Lebanon—and other heterodox communities like the Syrian Nusayris (otherwise Alawites). Horon emphasizes these communities' pre-Arab origins, which indicate a Hebrew lineage: Phoenician for the Maronites, Ishmaelite for the Druze, and Canaanite for the Nusayris. This fact, he believes, can and *should* catalyze a political action against Pan-Arabism, and he berates western Christianology for neglecting the Oriental churches, who were left to their own devices when facing a Muslim-Arabist onslaught.[160]

Whether Horon was aware of the methodological flaws of his indiscriminate classification of all non-Arabs and non-Sunnis as actual or potential enemies of Pan-Arabism remains an open question. Yet, being ideologically bent on contrasting the Arabs as a "faux-nation" to the Middle Eastern minorities as potential nations, he went as far as to argue that some of the Arabianate communities, such as the Maronites, the Copts, and the Shiites, though currently functioning as castes and religious sects, in fact possess numerous ethnic or even national attributes.[161] During the Islamic reign, he wrote, many communities that wished to preserve their identity and traditions, or simply to escape the inherent instability of war-torn Islamdom, fled to remote and isolated areas where they went into forced or voluntary seclusion. As a result, these minorities developed a strong attachment to their territories, whether ancestral or new, and thus began developing a national outlook. The Maronites' attachment to Mount Lebanon or the Copts' identification with the Nile Valley, Horon hopes, could become the spiritual source of their modern national identity.[162]

It is Horon's contention that the joined forces of Canaan—Lebanon, Israel, and any other adjacent minority willing to take part—will fulfill its "manifest destiny" in the Land of Kedem by launching a liberation war against all imported and hostile ideologies and agencies. Despite Canaan's limited space ("6 or 7 per cent of the immense area of the five states" [comprising the Land of Kedem][163]), this is the most advanced part of the Land in cultural, economic, technical, and strategic terms; it is also the most densely populated (8 million in Horon's day, half of the entire sedentary population of the Land of Kedem by his calculations). No less important, with Arabic-speaking

Sunnis constituting no more than a third of its entire population (and a quarter of them are "neutralized," as Horon puts it,[164] from active participation in Pan-Arabist politics by being under Israeli rule after 1967), it is the least "Arabianate" of the Land's regions. The remaining two-thirds are split into numerous minorities, grouped in several foci of latent or active resistance to Pan-Arabism: Israel, Lebanon, the Nusayri Syrian littoral, and the Druze-dominated mountains in southwest Syria. Since these areas produce "practically all fighting men of value . . . Kurds, Circassians, Druses [*sic*]; Alawites, Maronites, Assyrians; and last but not least—the Israelis,"[165] the Pan-Arab rulers of the remaining parts of the Land of Kedem will not be able to repel their advance when the day comes.[166]

One of the arguably most intriguing, albeit sporadic, elements of Horon's discussion of the difference between Arab and Arabianate identity is what might be termed "the Palestinian issue." In Horon's lifetime, regional-territorial Arab nationalism was yet to rise to prominence, hence the question of Palestine as a matter separate from Pan-Arab politics did not receive due attention in the Israeli mainstream sociopolitical discourse. We have seen how much space Horon devoted in his writings to Pan-Arab nationalism, placing under its banner even such a clearly Arab territorial-nationalist program as the FLN's demand for an independent Algeria. He simply did not live to see Arab territorial nationalisms, including the Palestinian one, reaching their full force in the post-Nasir age. Therefore, in order to gain insight into the ways Horon tackled the Palestinian issue we must painstakingly collect his passing references to it, dispersed throughout his writings.

The Young Hebrews had debated the Palestinian issue as early as the 1940s in a way that radically deviated from the Zionist consensus, which, broadly speaking, regarded Palestinian collective aspirations (whether acknowledging them as a nation or not) as entirely incompatible with the goals of the Jewish national movement. Horon's Israel-based "Canaanite" colleagues approached the Palestinian question rather instrumentally, above all as a means to attack the Zionist regime in Israel. Yet by doing so, they managed to undermine some of Israel's most revered truths with respect to the course of the 1948 war and the emergence of the Palestinian refugee problem. They had devoted growing attention to it since the mid-1960s, when the PLO started to emerge as a serious factor in Middle Eastern politics.[167] Horon's references to the Palestinians, even before his final move to Israel in 1959, did not diverge significantly from the other Young

Hebrews' statements on the topic and were similarly iconoclastic with respect to the Zionist consensus.

Since Horon classifies the Arabic-speaking residents of the Land of Kedem as largely Arabianate, the Palestinians constitute no exception. In Horon's historiography, the Palestinians are simply the descendants of those indigenous Hebrews who converted initially to Judaism, then to Christianity, and finally to Islam, and he mentions their alleged Hebrew origins at least twice.[168] His overall picture of the modern Palestinian ethnogenesis is dialectic since he takes into account the immigration into Canaan of Arabic speakers from neighboring countries, attracted by Canaan's speedy economic development in the age of the Hebrew revival.[169] Hence, the Palestinians, as all other peoples and communities in the Land of Kedem, are of mixed stock, both indigenous Hebrew and foreign. The political implication of this argument is that Palestinians lack an inherent positive identity and are certainly no more "native" than the Hebrews descended from Jewish migrants. Being "pseudo-Arabs" of Hebrew origin, the only national identity they can plausibly adopt, Horon hints (and other Young Hebrews state openly), is the Hebrew identity. It is therefore the Hebrews' task to attract the Palestinians to the Hebrew sociocultural sphere, so they are able to find their historically legitimate identity instead of the one that was allegedly foisted on them. This is why Horon writes with such satisfaction about what he interprets as a gradual coming-together between Israelis and Palestinians after 1967, on both sides of the "Green Line."[170] He is aware at the same time that Israel's undemocratic character would repel any serious attempt by Palestinians to assimilate, confessing shortly before his death his fear that "we face all the dangers of the Franco-Algerian non-integration, but since we have no de Gaulle [who would withdraw from the West Bank] . . . I am optimistic."[171]

Horon also addressed the Palestinian refugee problem, aiming to disassemble its destructive potential directed at Israel. Unlike many Israelis, he did not deny that mass population removal took place in 1948, writing in 1952 that "the Israeli method . . . sometimes amounted to expulsion."[172] All the same, he asserted that the numbers of Palestinian refugees were severely inflated, in line with his unmasking of "sham" Arab statistics,[173] and occasionally cast doubt upon the political and moral validity of this designation by putting the word "refugees" into inverted commas.[174] Israel's 1948 wartime and postwar policy, which strove to dispose of as many Arabic speakers as possible, was vociferously denounced by the Israel-based Young Hebrews, who regarded it as a manifestation of the xenophobic Jewish Diaspora mentality and the Jews' inability to create a genuine national state founded on ethnic pluralism.[175] In parallel, they interpreted the politicization of the Palestinian refugee problem, post-1948, as a Pan-Arabist stratagem to bring Israel down and suggested to diffuse it along with the Zionist neo*millet* system by incorporating and assimilating the Palestinians into Israel.[176] If such policy were implemented, the Young Hebrews claimed, the process already taking place naturally beyond the "Green Line" would merely be institutionalized, throwing the door open onto a much broader restructuring of the entire Land of Kedem.

The Path to "Kedem Union"

Having analyzed Horon's picture of the past and the conclusions arising from it that pertain politically to the present, we can now direct our attention to Horon's program for the future, whose underlying motive is the transformation of the "Land of Kedem" from a *geohistorical* to an active *geopolitical* notion. In the early 1950s, when he had only started to approach the topic, Horon had more of a poetic vision than a detailed plan of action in mind:

> The alternative should be described as the Hebrew or Semitic renaissance of the Levant, that is the rebirth of Hebrewland, of the Levant and Euphrates country. Any of these expressions will do, *provided they are taken geographically and historically, not in any racial or sectarian sense.* This renaissance is no mere dream—it is starting already, from the shores of the Mediterranean Sea, in ancient Canaan or Phoenicia, in present-day Israel and Lebanon. The extraordinary comeback of little Israel, the stubborn resistance of little Lebanon to Arab leveling, make sense only if they are the conclusion as well as the beginning of *something bigger than they themselves.* Their success shows once more that the roots of reality, in this ruined country, go deeper than the Islamic layer, deeper even than Christendom and Judaism, to the rock-bottom of the Hebrew, the Phoenician, the Semitic—the ever-classical Orient. And both *history and geography make it quite certain* that the new growth from the

> old roots shall spread to all the area of the Levant, up to and beyond the Euphrates.[177]

Though depicted in broad strokes, this passage contains most of the ideological principles of the Hebrew national revolution in the Land of Kedem, to the development of which Horon devoted the remaining two decades of his life. In a talk given that same year to the Asia Institute, he had already moved from vision to proposal:

> The requirements for a positive, constructive solution of the interlocked problems of Near East and North Africa . . . are as follows:
>
> 1. Genuine, objective information about, and understanding of the area . . . ;
> 2. Recognition of the basic fact that there are no Arab nations outside Arabia, and that nationhood in general is just starting on its modern road in this area;
> 3. The encouragement of such trends as lead toward national solidarity and organization within territorial (geographical-historical) frameworks . . . ;
> 4. Open and genuine separation of Church and State, and a common resistance of all men of good will to the encroachments of theocracy, of any and every theocracy;
> 5. Continued help by all free people from overseas . . . ;
> 6. First and foremost: without waiting for external help, the peoples directly concerned should work together, according to principles of self-help and mutual help, so as to resist the threat of Pan-Arabism, and the even greater threat . . . which must follow in its wake.[178]

Taken together, these as well as other fragments help us to extricate the values that underscore Horon's understanding of the Land's envisioned transformation:

- The national liberation of the Land of Kedem must be based on a territorial conceptualization of the nations' right to self-determination. "Any political solution," he writes, "must take into account the territorial strongholds already in the possession of major communities, as well as their historical rights to certain homelands."[179]

- Such conceptualization can be formulated only when based on a "correct" historiographical image, which explains the ages-long connection between nations and their lands; the deeper the Hebrew past is studied, the stronger a national outlook will be enhanced in the present, becoming a driving force for political and strategic initiative. The national-historical heritage, once uncovered and adequately internalized, "is destined to cause a revolution in our views of the Land's past and its place in world culture, a revolution of which we have meanwhile witnessed only the early buds."[180]

- Pursuing national liberation in the Land of Kedem means striving to achieve a harmonious unity between the Land's geographical reality, its political reality, and its peoples' mental horizons; Country, State, and National Identity must, roughly, become one. Geohistory possesses its own inescapable logic, by which nations with a developed "national outlook" must abide in order to persist as nations. "The national principle of the unity of the homeland rests upon two mutually-reinforcing pillars: the common sense inscribed onto any map and the historical right." This is due to the existence of "a historical-geographic logic enforcing itself upon the entire people (*'am*), [and] a natural imperative of geophysics."[181] In the case of the Land of Kedem, this dictates a renewed "conquest of Canaan" by the modern Hebrews.

- With national outlook reestablished throughout the Land of Kedem, any external antinational ideologies and agencies, such as Zionism and Pan-Arabism, or foreign imperialist pressure factors like the USA and the USSR, will be driven away; local societies and governments will no longer serve as their pawns or proxies.

- The borders cutting through the Land of Kedem, charted by European imperialist forces and maintained by their

Cold War heirs and local subcontractors, disregard historical, cultural, linguistic, and geographical realities; they therefore *must* be violated if the Land of Kedem is to shake off its colonial legacy. "All the Land's borders—external or internal—originate mostly in recent times, whether as ostensible 'ceasefire' lines or as a result of foreign intrigues . . . [S]uch borders are endowed with no sanctity."[182]

- This geopolitical dynamic must start with Canaan so that Canaan's cultural, strategic, and economic primacy becomes also political, allowing it to fulfill its liberating potential for the Land of Kedem.[183]
- The bottom line is that "a significant part of our population will remain non-Jewish."[184]

Particularly noteworthy in this context is Horon's contempt for Israeli statehood and its limitations, in contrast to certain Zionist (and post-Zionist) views of the Jewish state as a "goal attained." Israel's boundaries, in his perspective, constitute a colonial legacy that is inimical to a genuine national existence and suppresses the Hebrew national outlook. Keen to bring this point home, Horon came quite close to the rhetoric of *lebensraum* when explaining that Israel's "artificial" pre-1967 borders are unsustainable in physical terms: "The partition boundaries closing upon our land . . . do not contain enough soil and water to sustain a people [*'am*] standing on its feet."[185]

With the Hebrew liberation designed to unfold throughout the entire Land of Kedem, Horon insisted that Israel in its given borders should not elicit any authentic patriotism since "we do not want people to be faithful to their Jordanian, or Syrian, or even Lebanese passports, *and most of us refuse to take very seriously even the Israeli state as a final expression of our nationhood*."[186] A Jewish "ghetto state" lacks any chance of survival;[187] it is therefore legitimate only insofar as it constitutes "a transitional stage in a nation formation process."[188] That this will one day be achieved remained beyond all doubt for Horon, who, apart from relying on the logic of geography, was a believer in a Nietzschean historical "element" encased in the common vital will of the Nation:

> There exists a collective WILL TO POWER AND SELF-FULFILMENT which, however you look at it, you must

> call HEBREW (it is not Jewish, nor is it simply Israeli). This collective will, rather mysterious in its origins, ill-determined as to its present shape, incoherent as to its precise aspirations, exists nevertheless and has carried "little Israel," even before its creation, against the more obvious "currents of historical determinism," making it one of the POWERS of the world, even and especially in the military field. Against all odds—I believe in this WILL, and I am not an isolated eccentric.[189]

For Israel to become the bridgehead of the Hebrew liberation war, a profound internal transformation is imperative beforehand to fix Israel's shortcomings as a self-defined "Jewish state." Horon outlines in several places some of the components of this envisaged metamorphosis: the deconstruction of the socio-sectarian "ghettos" for non-Ashkenazi Jews (which effectively entails the abandonment of Ben-Gurion's population disbursement policy);[190] the introduction of a new educational system that would affirm liberal-secular values instead of Jewish-Zionist self-seclusionary indoctrination, instill an admiration for the Hebrew national past, and promote an attachment to the Land of Kedem's vast territories beyond Israel's existing boundaries;[191] "a separation of religion and state, an equality of duties and rights irrespective of faith and communal belonging, a unitary secular school, a common draft;"[192] last, about which Horon is somewhat less straightforward, the annexation of all territories beyond the "Green Line" occupied in 1967 and the indiscriminate granting of Israeli citizenship to their inhabitants, one of the aims being the solution of the refugee problem.

This "separation between Israel and Judaism"[193] and Israel's subsequent de-Zionization ought to become the first stage in a centrifugal dynamic that would engulf the entire Land of Kedem. Its geopolitical realignment must start with the adjustment of Israeli borders to the geophysical conditions in its immediate vicinity. This would mean capturing the three banks of the Jordan in the north and east and reaching Israel's southern natural limits along the Suez Canal by appropriating the Sinai Peninsula.[194] The latter would curb Arabist Egypt's eastward expansionist ambitions and facilitate its turn toward a "Pharaonite" African identity and raison d'état.[195] A regime change in Egypt and the states comprising the Land of Kedem from Pan-Arabist to liberal-territorial would allow Israel to forge a web of regional strategic alliances to roll the liberation march forward. This is how Horon envisioned this march before 1967:

> First and foremost, we must aim to move the Lebanese state and the Druze Mountain from the hostile camp to our own—not by *annexation* by Israel but by *incorporation* within Israel. There is no other way to solve the Jordan water issue and to secure our entry, *when the day comes*, to Transjordan as well. This operation is not merely military—since . . . this is a much more complex strategic question: ideational, political, economic. *We should not refrain from applying force*, since our potential allies are currently captured by the enemy. To enable them to negotiate with us we must release them, we must break the existing borders, and this cannot be done without warfare. *Yet military victory is but a means*; and as such it will do no good unless we use other means as well . . . For we speak here of winning allies and not of just expanding Israeli territory; of liberating non-Arab peoples [*'ammim*], victims to Pan-Arabism, and *not of expelling further refugees*; of renewing the independence of the Druze Mountain . . . or of redeeming the independence of Maronite Lebanon, and not of "Judaizing" them in a Jewish state—for they will never "Judaize," nor do we harbor such intent. *The aim is to gain partners, not slaves* . . . We must prepare for the day when we will move to the headwaters of the Jordan, to Lebanon, and the Druze Mountain, as liberators and not as conquerors.[196]

Horon did not hesitate to describe his plan as "aggression" (*toḳpanut*),[197] though the precise meaning of the term and the implications of its usage remain somewhat vague in his public pronouncements. Horon certainly did not dream of an Israeli conquest of the Land of Kedem informed by Israel's 1948 strategy (hence the reference to "further refugees" above) and made clear more than once that he envisaged a multifaceted operation, both military and nonmilitary, perhaps foreshadowing what in the early twenty-first century became known as "hybrid warfare." The liberation of the Land of Kedem would involve political and ideological agitation for a Hebrew national-liberal vision (both within and without Israel), cultural and economic pressure, diplomatic maneuvering, and finally, armed intervention. In letters written to members of the Kedem Club, Horon professed his conviction that a "warlike situation" was to be an indispensable and constant component of Israel's regional policy and, in fact, of its entire existence as a state and society. "The trouble with Israel is not that it is too aggressive, but not aggressive enough," he wrote. "Of course, aggressiveness alone will solve nothing; but conversely, nothing will be solved without aggressiveness . . . You cannot change the nature of any country by mere propaganda . . . ; it takes also sheer force . . . Our problem is not how to avoid war, but how to win it." Consequently, he suggested that "wisdom would be to build our entire program on the assumption that the warlike situation is basic to our entire future for at least the present generation."[198]

In 1965, that is, two years before the June 1967 war, Horon had, to some degree, foreseen a war resulting from the Zionist–Pan-Arabist deadlock and hoped that its outbreak would amend not only the "errors" of 1948, but also of the 1956 Sinai campaign, which the Young Hebrews saw as a "missed opportunity."[199] In other words, if the 1948 war is regarded by the Jews as their independence war, the upcoming war must be the war for Hebrew independence. And this would mean a war not *against* the "Arabianate" but *with* them and on *their behalf*. Whatever the weight of the military action and its nature, it was depicted by Horon as a common task for all enemies of Pan-Arabism, and not as a Zionist military raid whose aim would be to reestablish the status quo ante. "Who amongst us steps forward without withdrawing immediately?" Horon queries Zionist Israel's supposedly short-sighted military doctrine.[200]

Shortly after the 1967 war, Horon wrote, somewhat hopefully, that "any probable frontier change would tend to further enlarge [Israel]"[201] and used the opportunity to produce a more detailed provisional outline of the Hebrew revolutionary liberation. He proposed a three-stage process, starting with "Greater Israel" within its "security borders," as the 1967 ceasefire lines came to be known. Israel must achieve truly "secure borders" by obtaining territorial and strategic control over four focal points: the "Litani border" (southern Lebanon, the same area that Israel supposedly failed to annex in 1948–1949), the "Horan border" (the Druze Mountain in southwest Syria), the eastern bank of the Jordan (obliterating in effect the Hashemite "British protectorate in disguise"[202]), and the Suez Canal.[203] The next stages are described as follows:

> Due to the military and political circumstances it seems that we shall witness an incorporation-becoming-annexation throughout all of Israel's "security borders," with their

> population included . . . A second natural stage might manifest itself as a Canaan Union—composed of Greater Israel, Maronite Lebanon, the Druze Mountain, with the participation of any local factor interested in peace and prosperity. The Canaan Union, which will draw in the best progressive forces of the Land of Kedem, must be expected to attract the rest of its suppressed inhabitants from within and without, encouraging them to establish together the Kedem Union all over the Land.[204]

The dynamic would therefore lead from Greater Israel through the Canaan Union to the Kedem Union, which will "facilitate the liberation, the development, and the progress also in neighboring African and Asiatic countries."[205] In this connection, Horon reminds his readers that he was one of the first Hebrew political thinkers to call for the enhancement of contacts between the Hebrews and "non-Arab" (Sub-Saharan) Africa, even before the establishment of Israel,[206] and on one occasion suggests the forming of a North–South geopolitical axis, composed of Cyprus, Lebanon, Israel, and Ethiopia (to check Egyptian southward expansionism).[207]

The Kedem Union would disengage from the Cold War, thereby radically tipping the global strategic balance between East and West. Horon is equally hostile to both blocs, regarding the Soviet Union quite insightfully as above all a Russian national state and the United States as heir to British colonialism, and therefore an undeclared ally of Pan-Arabism (and not an ally of Israel, as Israeli common perception has it).[208] A "Hebrew foreign policy," he suggests, would challenge the paradigm prevalent in the Middle East that in order to survive, one must be aligned with one of the superpowers; in the early 1950s Horon already saw the future Hebrew national power as a dominant "third power" among the superpowers in tandem with France. Such development, he believed, would stem the drift of postcolonial states and movements, led by Pan-Arabism, toward Soviet tutelage. The USSR, Horon argued in 1958, is able to make advances on the world stage despite its technological inferiority compared to the West due to a profound sense of moral power, justice, and mass-mobilizing idea, while the West persists in a defensive posture behind a mental "Maginot Line." A similar feeling of moral superiority, if adopted by the Hebrews, will be able to propel a de-Zionised Israel within the Kedem Union onto a leading global position. A deep revision of received principles and notions of international relations, state ideologies, and historical conceptions would ensue, averting a nuclear catastrophe leading to a postatomic "decline of the West" prophesized by Spengler.[209]

One might wonder how much the Kedem Union would have resembled the ancient Hebrew statehood as reconstructed by Horon. While Horon did not dwell much on the exact shape and make-up of the Kedem Union, he was doubtlessly inspired by the ancient system of Hebrew regional alliances, which held a whole civilization together without impinging upon local tribal and princely powers. "We are the re-builders of David's Empire," he reminded Eri Jabotinsky and Shmuel Rosoff in 1956,[210] and in his last days, he professed, "I believe more and more that the stars are favorable to a Hebrew empire."[211]

With a measure of safety, it can be stated that he envisioned a modern liberal-democratic republic, stating at least twice that it was supposed to be a federation.[212] We can surmise that this federation would have been structured as a rather loose polity of voluntary members sharing the vision of the classical Hebrew period as their golden age but enjoying wide autonomy. Indeed, Eri Jabotinsky, in his blueprint for the future political structure of the Levant prepared for the Kedem Club, stated that due to "the ancient character and deep tradition of the peoples involved," the autonomy enjoyed by member states of the Hebrew federation would be wider than that of the US states.[213] Moreover, such federation, the Club assured, would not be a Hebrew replica of the Arab League but a qualitatively different organism in which "the exaggerated importance of state-boundaries would . . . disappear gradually."[214]

Interestingly, Horon did not insist on Hebrew being the exclusive language of the federated Kedem Union, but he predicted a fusion of all local languages, Hebrew, Arabic, and English.[215] Ultimately, the most important matter for him was that the Hebrew national outlook would once again be free and sovereign in the Hebrew homeland, and not the technical particularities of the Land's future structure.

Chapter 4

The Hebrew Foundational Myth in a Comparative Perspective

"Canaanism" Contrasted to Zionism

The preceding chapters analytically dissected the positions taken by Adya Horon regarding the historical, historiographical, and political aspects of what he saw as the emergence of a modern territorial Hebrew nation and its foundational myth. They traced the link between his conception of what *was*, what *is*, and what *ought to be* in the Land of Kedem and examined to what degree his vision of the past dictated his future program on the one hand and how his concept of a new geopolitical settlement in the Middle East assimilated his historiographical observations on the other. That being done, it can be established definitively that Horon was above all a nationalist public intellectual. His output fully meets the definition of a national commemorative narrative that provides not only a comprehensive alternative to both the Zionist and the Arabist national narratives of the past, but also a dissenting vision for the future. Ultimately, Adya Horon attempted to shape a community of memory that would transgress the confines set by the mutually hostile but typologically similar Zionist and Pan-Arabist commemorative narratives.

This observation will be the guiding principle of the present chapter, which offers a detailed comparative analysis of "Canaanism" and the other political-national ideologies present in the Middle East in the twentieth century with which "Canaanism" engaged in debate and polemics: Zionism (both Labor and Revisionist), post-Zionism, and territorial nationalisms in select Arabophone countries. I believe that equitable juxtaposition of "Canaanism" and Zionism opens new epistemological perspectives: though disparate in resources and public impact, they are classified here as belonging, each on its own terms, to the same sociocultural phenomenon of nationalisms in competition.

In asserting this, I conclude that the Hebrew national ideology was, at its core, independent of Zionism, both intellectually and politically. Any analysis of the Young Hebrews that, by neglecting Horon's input to the ideological edifice, reduces them to a bizarre offshoot of Zionism that developed its inherent assumptions to their logical extreme, as proposed by Yaacov Catz[1] or more recently Yaacov Yadgar,[2] or to a pathological deformation of Haskalah tropes, as suggested by Baruch Kurzweil, let alone to an artistic coterie that toyed with geopolitical fantasies, must therefore be seen as founded on deficient empirical evidence. The following analysis wishes to demonstrate that despite the numerous and at times decisive overlaps between "Canaanism" and Zionism—especially in its Revisionist form—the former cannot be regarded as ancillary to the latter. This is because not only were the historiographical cores of these ideologies incompatible, but so were such basic notions as what makes *a* nation, and what the human and the geographical ranges are that are covered by the ideologies in question. In other words: what is *the* nation, and where precisely does its country lie?

These divergences hold the key to understanding where "Canaanism" parted ways with Zionism. The former's vision of the past, as formulated by Horon, was more inclusive than the latter's: by extending its commemorative narrative to the whole Land of Kedem, it integrated non-Jews on an equal footing with Jews—as long as both accepted "Hebrew" as the defining code of their national existence. Zionism, contrariwise, positioned its master commemorative narrative within an ethnoreligious frame of reference, which is inegalitarian by definition. Essentially, then, the intellectual and political rivalry between "Canaanism" and Zionism was a manifestation of the clash between a modernist and a primordialist vision for the nation, respectively, for its delimitation, and for the moral and practical contents of its political sovereignty. The "Canaanites" were among the first to realize, shortly before the establishment of Israel, and following them Hillel Kook and the Hebrew Committee of National Liberation, that clinging to an illiberal discursive framework of ethnonationalism determined by premodern criteria of ethnoreligious identity, whether Jewish or

Muslim, would lead to the creation of a tribalist "ghetto state" that would stifle any secular and nondenominational voices.

The introduction discussed how nations can become "zones of conflict" (in John Hutchinson's phrase)[3] over the commemorative narratives elaborated by intellectuals to guide the shaping of their nations' identity.[4] It also pointed to a visible parallel between the status of the dominant narratives and their authors on the one hand, and the status of the sidelined narratives and their authors on the other. It was argued that the intellectuals whose national vision wins popular support, and therefore becomes channeled through mass national politics and media (often losing a lot of its original shape and intentions in the process) often accrue enough social and moral capital to become the nation's elite. Inversely, those intellectuals who formulate alternative national visions but fail to move beyond a small circle of followers become a counterelite, with a huge gap obtaining between their usually meagre social capital within society at large and their moral capital within their tightly-knit communities of devotees.[5]

It is this study's contention that the disagreement between Zionist historians and Adya Horon over the meaning and usefulness of ancient Hebrew history to Israeli nation formation exemplifies this phenomenon. While most of the events constituting ancient Hebrew history were common to Zionism and "Canaanism," in each case, they were proposed to be remembered differently, by applying different techniques for remembering and forgetting—and then by translating them into dissimilar political conclusions about the present and the future. Prasenjit Duara observes that, depending on the social, cultural, and political setting in which the national idea is taking root, certain elements of the past floating in the nation's cognitive space are favored over others during the formulation of national historiographies. The differences between national pasts correspond to the choices made regarding these elements of memory: societies and nations, both among themselves and within themselves, differ by their methods of selection and arrangement of their history's building blocks and the "architecture" of their commemorative narratives.[6] In Duara's perspective, Horon on the one hand and Zionist intellectuals on the other hardened *differently* the mental borders around various elements of national history: what Horon left "soft" and thereby excised from the main stream of the Hebrew national narrative was "hardened" by the Zionists, and vice versa. The use of the past by the "Canaanites," concludes James Diamond, was "different in content but no different in function from that of Zionism."[7]

Horon's life circumstances narrated in chapter 1 make it clear that despite the moral capital he enjoyed as a key figure within the Young Hebrews (especially in his later years), the Hebrew Committee of National Liberation, the Levant Club, and La Renaissance Hébraïque, his social capital remained rather low. His struggle to maintain a decent material existence (in which he was in any case more successful than Yonatan Ratosh, who spent his life in relative poverty) emerges as highly informative when compared to the social comfort enjoyed by two prominent intellectuals of mainstream Zionism, Ben-Zion Dinur and Yehezkel Kaufmann, both of whom have greatly contributed to the shaping of a Jewish-Zionist national community of memory.

Dinur, besides being a prolific historical writer, served during the early 1950s as the Israeli minister of education and chairman of the Israeli Holocaust memorial museum Yad Ṿashem, and thus he played a key role in instilling the Holocaust as a central symbol of Israeli identity.[8] Kaufmann, a professor of biblical studies at the Hebrew University, authored the *History of the Israelite Faith*,[9] for which he received the Israel Prize in 1958. The core argument of this multivolume magnum opus was that the ancient Israelites developed their monotheistic Jehowist faith much earlier than mainstream (Protestant-inspired) biblical criticism acknowledges, and claimed that the absence of mythological-pagan elements characterized the Israelites from the earliest stages of their development as a nation. That is, their unique deity did not represent any natural "primordial realm," which in paganism was usually embodied by various "naturalistic" gods of the skies, seas, earth, otherworld, and so on, but was single, omnipresent, and omnipotent. In effect, Kaufmann denied that any substantial cultural, ethnic, or religious bonds existed between the Israelites and the Canaanites.

While the aim of this study is not to evaluate critically Kaufmann's historiography, or to defend Horon's, for the purpose of the present discussion, some major drawbacks evident in Kaufmann's work cannot be ignored. Kaufmann premises his argument mainly on textual silence: he treats the apparent lack of biblical evidence for Israelite pagan mythology as positive proof of the nonmythical character of early Judaism. Moreover, Kaufmann appears to accept the historical accuracy of most of the biblical narrative.[10] In the introduction to his work, Kaufmann proclaims his disagreement with standard biblical criticism, stating that his object is the formulation of a new scholarly paradigm whereby "Israelite religion was an original creation of the people of Israel. It was absolutely different from anything the pagan world ever knew; its monotheistic world view had no antecedents in paganism," and that therefore biblical criticism's "basic postulate—that the priestly stratum of the Torah was composed in the Babylonian exile, and that the literature of the Torah was still being written and revised in and after the Exile—is untenable."[11] As Gabriel Piterberg reminds us, Kaufmann's approach was by and large rejected by the scholarly community, which judged his methodology to be out of date.[12] Therefore, in this discussion, Kaufmann's output is treated not as a dispassionate examination of ancient history, but as a polemical statement in the service of a contemporary ideology, much like Horon's writings. And although Horon never states so openly, the thrust of his argument in *Ḳedem Ṿa'erev* is directed beyond all doubt against the premises and theses of Kaufmann's *History of the Israelite Faith.*[13]

Kaufmann's image of a faith interlocking with, and defining a, national identity that highlights the Jews' perennial uniqueness and separateness from their sociocultural environment throughout the ages, bespeaks of his distrust in myth as a vital culture-forging element. He seems to treat mythology as a primitive vestige doomed to die out once a more "progressive" (by implication, universalist-monotheistic) worldview spreads among the faithful. Kaufmann thus adopts an essentialist position that pagan-territorial religion is by definition more "backward" than universal-cosmopolitan faith, a Hegelian idea directly attacked by Horon.[14] In his critique of the Young Hebrews, Baruch Kurzweil traced the "antimythical" standpoint shared by Kaufmann to the Dutch philosopher Johann Huizinga,[15] who contrasted the supposedly barbarian mythos (the irrational element) with the supposedly cultural logos (the rational element). On this basis Kurzweil concluded that the instrumentalization of the ancient Hebrew myth by the Young Hebrews' historiography was a symptom of cultural degradation:

> But when logic and logos—a religio-moral base—cease to determine men's views, they pin their hopes on myth . . . The "Young Hebrews" are not the first to put their faith in the renewal of myth. As a matter of fact, theirs is a belated discovery. For over a century, the world has been suffering from various returns to the mythical. Thus far, the flights to the realm of the mythical have brought

> mankind nothing but disaster. One may assume that the "Young Hebrews" have yet to learn this sad chapter of European thought. One quotation from Huyzinga [*sic*] will suffice: "The process of barbarization occurs when myth displaces logos in the life of an ancient culture." This playing with myth is unfailing evidence of confused thought. He who opposes Judaism in the name of modern progressive thought places himself in questionable position when he seeks to prove his sense for practical reality by argument borrowed from myth.[16]

This passage exemplifies a number of weaknesses in Kurzweil's (and, by extension, Kaufmann's) method, especially the implied belief that the Young Hebrews were potentially following the path of Nazism in their Nietzschean fascination with ancient mythology. The latter Kurzweil clearly considers in a limited manner, as a kind of literary sublimation of barbaric primordial instincts, which cannot in any way be compatible with reasonable thinking on history, let alone on politics. Such a position, however, was made outdated by developments in the late twentieth-century philosophy of history, which not only does not consider myth and historiography as antinomy, but actually tries to reconcile the two. For if the historian (or, for that matter, a national ideologue relying on history) has "to distill from . . . history its meaningful unity,"[17] then an essential characteristic of modern history writing is its reliance on mythical narrative forms. Myth is, as Anthony Cohen points out, "an expression of the way in which people cognitively map past, present and future"[18] and thus supplies the structure of historical thinking and a legitimizing device for political action. Another Cohen, Percy, writes that as a narrative of origins imbued with sacred quality, "myth" works to anchor the present in a series of significant past events and thus merges with "history."[19] This merger is enabled by accepting that both myth and history deal with aesthetic and literary questions attendant upon the weaving of a story, which, in order to present itself as logically coherent, must allow for creative treatment of the historical source material.[20] At the same time, as noted by Uriel Abulof, myths "offer insight into the dynamics of existential doubt,"[21] which political ideologies attempt to allay.

In contrast to Kaufmann, Horon represented a historiosophical standpoint most probably derived from (or at least influenced by) Friedrich Nietzsche's perception of myth and mythology as indispensable sources of positive vital collective energy. Therefore, the indirect dispute between Horon and Kaufmann can be regarded as yet another instance of a clash between the worldviews of Nietzsche and Huizinga—despite the latter's acceptation of national sentiment as deeply rooted in human nature.[22]

If, by advocating a form of scripturalism, Kaufmann had set out to reverse the influence of biblical criticism on modern Jewish identity, he had certainly not achieved his objective. The impact of critical Jewish studies, otherwise *Wissenschaft des Judenthums*, upon the (European, mainly) Jews' perception of their position in the modern world is undeniable, though its exact manner and extent are still subject to scholarly debate. "Time" and "place" in Jewish consciousness underwent an enormous shift toward secularization beginning with the eighteenth century.[23] The dissemination of Enlightenment values and critical scholarly approach to biblical heritage gradually gnawed away at the pious reverence many Jews held for their antiquity: in effect, the cyclical time-concept characteristic of sacral history, which Jews traditionally believed could only be broken eschatologically, was replaced by a linear one, where the past no longer constituted an ideal model for the future but every historical period was governed by its own intrinsic rules.[24] Jews became aware of history's forward movement and came to treat the "here and now" as worthy of remembrance and record, as well as liable to shaping by their own concerted efforts.[25] As explained by Nahum Glatzer, the "profanization" of the Jewish weltanschauung preconditioned the emergence of a secular history of Judaism:

> [T]he quest for a philosophy of Jewish history constituted a definite departure from the thinking of the past. The motifs of classical thought about the meaning of Israel—exile, suffering for the love of God, *galut* as punishment and purification, as a preparation for the world to come, messianic redemption—lost their relevance. The religious inquiry, an inquiry from within, was replaced by a historicism that attempted to view Jewish history from without. In order to retain the right to exist in the present, Judaism had to be explained in terms of world history.[26]

The principle underpinning Jewish nationalism in modern times was most efficiently summarized by David Biale: "[T]he task of Zionism was to 'return the Jews to history,' to turn them into active subjects rather than passive objects,"[27] and considered in greater detail by Alan Dowty: "Zionists sought to escape from the particularism of the Jewish past and to rejoin history by recasting Jewish life into new universal molds provided by modern ideology . . . They felt that 'the course of Jewish history must be reversed'; the significance of Zionism was nothing less than 'the re-entry of the Jewish people into the world political arena.' "[28]

The Jews' desire to enter secular history as active agents, and to exchange the "objective" stance toward history for a "subjective" one by assuming responsibility for their own fate, extended, as Nadia Abu el-Haj reminds us, not just to the current moment but to the historical past as well, in the form of a claim for a symbolic sovereignty over it.[29] Political Zionism, which struggled for (and ultimately won) Jewish political sovereignty, is therefore a variant of this overarching principle, whose multitudinous expressions did not always harmonize with the Zionist interpretation of Jewish history and national reawakening.[30] The task at hand was actually much greater: to alleviate the widespread Jewish sentiment of "exclusion from history," augmented—as Amos Funkenstein argues[31]—by a modernist historiographical paradigm that attributed agency only to actual wielders of material or political power. Yet, by accepting this paradigm, Jews, Azizza Khazzoom points out, "placed the legitimate judges of Jewish acceptability outside the Jewish world," trading home-grown values for an external promise of acceptance that was not universally honored.[32]

As with many other national "awakenings," the Jewish awakening of the eighteenth to twentieth centuries granted teleological value to Jewish mundane existence. The material world became the arena in which the liberation of the Jews was to be attained without (or not exclusively with) the Messiah's participation. Similarly, the material place, whether the Land of Israel or the Diaspora countries, which had previously lingered outside history in the mental image of Jewish existence, became an active element in the drive for national resurgence. The Jewish case was special in this regard since for the absolute majority of Jews the national "homeland" lay far away and for centuries was hardly anything more than a realm of theological fantasies;[33] accordingly, actual Jewish migration to the Land of Israel and its physical rediscovery and desacralization became central for secular Zionism. Zionist geography can thus be described as highly vitalistic: the new muscular Jew treading upon the Land was returning to Mother Nature (and to history) through physical effort.

Following the establishment of the State of Israel, the bond with the Land was facilitated further through public and state-sponsored means, such as hiking trips, the founding of agricultural settlements, and the extension of official patronage over archaeological research, making it a key element of Israeli "civil religion." "Not a strictly academic activity," as noted by Neil Asher Silberman, "but rather a tangible means of communication between the people and the land."[34] Baruch Kimmerling notes that the elements of Jewish tradition that became central in Zionism through their role as symbolic connectors to the Land (such as the Hanukkah and the 15th of Shvaṭ festivals, or the Masada myth, whose transformation into intensive cultural symbols in Zionism is explored by Yael Zerubavel[35]), were marginal in the Diaspora tradition.[36] Zerubavel complements Kimmerling's analysis by observing that before becoming a dominant paradigm in the Yishuv and then in Israel, Zionist innovatively secular historiography was initially a *subversive* "countermemory" to the traditional Diaspora theocentric historiography.[37]

One of the key tools employed in formulating the new Zionist geography and facilitating the Jews' reentry into secular-material history was the biblical text. No longer a repository of transcendental truths, it became a secular "textbook" for the history and geography of the Land of Israel. With the "profane" Bible becoming one of the central symbols of the Zionist revolution, its cult encompassed the Yishuv,[38] bypassing the Diaspora religious tradition, whose main cultural document was the Talmudic legal code, and putting forward a claim of continuity with the Land's national-territorial history.[39] Yaacov Shavit maps this process in the following way: "[F]or secular nationalists, the Bible was not important as the repository of a theological claim to Palestine; the Bible's value consisted in the objective historical account of the Jews' title to the land, borne out by archaeological evidence. Given the historical, nontheological use to which the Bible was put, it was part and parcel of Jewish modernity and thus stood in the foundation of secular Israeli society, exerting a romantic and conservative influence simultaneously."[40]

A national movement like many others, Zionism was trapped in the paradox of attempting to recreate a "golden age" while simultaneously crafting a wholly new forward-looking sociocultural structure. The Jews' past in the Land of Israel was an obvious inspiration;[41] at the same time, the state the Zionist movement aspired to create was meant, at least on the rhetorical level, to be morally "ideal," its structure and civil religion drawing from both the ethos of the biblical prophets and the values of the Enlightenment. In the words of David Ben-Gurion, uttered two years after the formation of the state,

> The existence of the Jewish people is characterized by a unique ideational dimension . . . The Jewish people is distinguished by its historic messianic conception: it . . . lives in excited anticipation of a future golden age of universal peace and the rule of justice on earth . . . There is no contradiction between national independence and a universal vision, between national uniqueness and universal attributes. The creation of the state is the beginning of national redemption; it also signals the onset of universal redemption.[42]

As several scholars have noted,[43] and as Ben-Gurion himself alluded to in the above words, the nationalist commonplace dialectic of past versus future was accompanied, in the case of Zionism, by a particular versus universal dialectic. As explained by Allon Gal: "Another basic characteristic of Zionism's ethno-symbolism is its strong bent towards moral and social renewal. Typically, the nationalist renaissance was conceived also in ethical-universalistic terms. Significantly, the same historical memories and myths that nurtured the nationalist urge . . . also served to nourish the moral quest."[44]

Eric Cohen observes that since the tension between the universal and the particular in nationalism "reflects a conflict between two basic principles in the idea of statehood: the liberal idea of the state as a political formation based on the voluntary consensus of its citizens and the nationalist idea of the state as the political expression of a primordial group," it is not unique to Israel. However, in the Israeli case, it became more salient, since it "reflect[ed] . . . a dilemma inherent in Jewish religious ethics."[45] The quest for the "perfect" (Jewish) society and polity highlights Zionism's teleological character, which incorporated much of traditional Jewish messianism. In Ben-Gurion's language, Jewish political sovereignty was akin to "national redemption." This secular messianism replaces the *agent* of redemption (the Zionist pioneer substitutes the Messiah of the House of David) but keeps the *historical-teleological movement* essentially unchanged.

However, by co-opting Jewish messianism, Zionism became trapped in an internal contradiction. Whereas in traditional Jewish historiography the final redemption was *integral* to its concept of historical time, the Zionist philosophy of history was, at least rhetorically, based on *rupture* with what had preceded Zionism. The Israeli historian Shmuel Almog described this contradiction quite poignantly as a foretold break with Jewish history that was historically determined therein:[46] that is, if Jewish history by its own internal logic is to reach its Hegelian Absolute in a national redemption that rebels against Jewish tradition, then the history's *telos* is its own violation!

This paradox originated, according to Almog, in the Zionist conceptualization of Jewish history as integral and continuous, and of the Jews as a nation united by its past.[47] Zionism wished simultaneously to release itself from the Jewish past (which it tended to describe in strongly derogatory terms, with both Shmuel Almog[48] and Yael Zerubavel[49] seeing it as a concession to anti-Semitism, and Aziza Khazzoom as an internalization of European colonialist-Orientalistic tropes directed at Pale of Settlement Jews[50]) and to maintain a measure of continuity with it, being aware that total rupture meant the annulment of Zionism's historical legitimation. Indeed, this "illusion that Zionism could escape the legacies—negative and positive—of the Jewish past, through an exercise of sheer ideological will" is categorized by Alan Dowty as no less than a "self-deception" and "conceit."[51] This, then, is the source of the question over which so many bright Jewish minds spent innumerable sleepless nights since the late nineteenth century: whether to consider Zionism a rebellion against the Jewish past or merely its transformation.[52]

Following Dowty and other scholars, I contend it is more helpful to understand Zionism as a *partial continuation* rather than a *complete break* with the Jewish history that preceded it. As summarized neatly by Baruch Kimmerling: "There is . . . no basis for the claim . . . that Zionism was in opposition to the Jewish religion. While Zionism was a revolt against specific institutional, political and social expressions of the Jewish religion . . . it included many components which were borrowed from the Jewish religion."[53] Alan Dowty makes a similar assertion that "the very legitimacy of the entire [Zionist] enterprise . . . rested, in the end, on Jewish history and religion,"[54] while Shmuel Almog, conscious of disagreements on the matter in the higher echelons of Zionism,[55] concludes that "between the two poles of continuity and rejection, Zionism established itself on a broad common base best described as dialectical continuity with the past."[56]

Yaacov Yadgar attributes the integration of elements of Jewish heritage into the Zionist ideology and the Israeli raison d'état to a biased reading of Jewish history by the founders of Zionism who, inspired by Enlightenment epistemology, separated between the spiritual and material aspects of Jewish tradition, in defiance of the lived experience of historical Jewry. Zionism was therefore left uninterested in providing a positive normative alternative to what it regarded as an outdated Jewish way of life, resorting in the end to an ethnoracial "objective" interpretation of the identity category of "Jew."[57] "The State of Israel," Yadgar says, "has never attempted to build an Israeli national identity that would be liberated, so to speak, from what the secular outlook itself understands as Jewish religion."[58] Last, Meron Benvenisti reflects gloomily that "the attempt to create a secular substitute for religious faith fashioned from materials drawn from the religious tradition could not possibly succeed in the long run."[59]

This understanding of Zionism's bondage to Judaism is shared (on Jewish religious grounds) by James Diamond, who found himself concurring with the "Canaanites" when writing that "Zionism in its classical manifestation *was* a substitute for Judaism. This is common wisdom among historians and everyone familiar with the modern Jewish experience. The power of Ratosh's thought is that it ceaselessly reminds us that Zionism, because it was at bottom something *ersatz*, rests on false premises. For you cannot found Jewish life and identity on a secular basis without taking leave of Judaism and transforming them into something brand new."[60]

With so many students of Zionism sharing this approach, we may speak of a scholarly consensus that vindicates at least this element of the "Canaanite" critique of Zionism.[61] The continuity between traditional Diaspora Judaism and its alleged opposite—Zionism—was manifested on several levels, including values, symbols, and practice. The sociologist Oz Almog identified and analyzed a number of key symbolic formulae that were carried over from Judaism to Zionism:[62] deliverance from enemies (Gentiles in traditional Judaism; Arabs in Zionism); the few against the many (the Diaspora versus the Gentile world; the Yishuv versus the Arab world); Isaac's binding (a myth of self-sacrifice for higher aims, whether religious or secular[63]); eschatological deliverance (the messianic element common to Judaism and Zionism); and the Land of Israel as inviolably belonging to Jews whether by divine decree or by their own determined decision. However, Almog, Zerubavel,[64] and Dowty[65] point out that in secular Zionism these cultural formulae were no longer embedded in a Jewish theological or philosophical interpretation, which relegated them to metahistory as the "essential truths" of Jewish existence. As James

Diamond put it, Zionism was willing "to play fast and loose with powerful religious ideas and symbols, and to appropriate them in a wholly secular context."[66] Thus, the *content and application* of these symbols radically changed in the transposition from Judaism to Zionism, yet their *essential mythic core* remained intact. On that, Zerubavel comments that "the Zionist collective memory did not invent new mythical structures. Rather, it promoted a closer association between existing Jewish myth plot structures and certain periods in Jewish history and reinterpreted their meaning";[67] for example, by refraining from introducing new festivals and holidays, instead assigning new meanings to existing ones, sometimes in a manner that contradicted their original sense.[68] Dowty is similarly unequivocal:

> They [the Zionists] did not reject the past outright, but combed it for what might be useful in building the future; "continuity was crucial: the Jewish society at which they aimed . . . had to contain within it the major elements of the Jewish heritage." The past was invoked and reinterpreted in order to restore Jewish dignity . . . ; precedents for "new" Zionist departures were sought in the historical sources . . . Holidays and national symbols were also inevitably drawn from the past, even if attempts were made to alter their content and significance.[69]

No less important is Almog's observation that pre-1948 Hebrew society in Palestine, whose chief sociological symbol was the Sabra, a native-born "new Jew,"[70] still remained organically tied to the Jewish system of norms and values. Almog diagnoses the Sabras' attitude to this system as "a complex and convoluted combination of rejection and acceptance,"[71] insisting that the "civil religion" established by Zionism possessed important structural and ideational similarities to the Diaspora communal-religious organization:

> In the end, as much as the Sabra tried to be a "new Jew" and distance himself from Jewish religion as his pioneer fathers commanded, this distance was only apparent. In fact, his entire being and essence spoke of Jewishness—the gatherings in youth group clubhouses, which were something like Hasidic yeshivot; the tribal solidarity and mutual responsibility; the sing-alongs and mandatory folk dancing;

> the Jewish myths that nourished his world; his aspiration to be learned in the pioneer doctrine; the sense of chosenness that filled him; and the tribal endogamy that separated him from the Arab *goy*—all these characterized the generation of the new Jews. *They were, as their name suggests, new but at base still Jews.*[72]

Almog designates the Sabras' antagonism toward their Jewish ancestors, which they conflated with the elder Zionist generation, a "conformist rebellion" that strives to strengthen the precarious values instilled by the forefathers rather than to reject them outright.[73] The Sabras' disdain was directed at the elders' pompous rhetoric (popularly lampooned as "Zionism within quotation marks") and not at the fundamentals of the ideology they espoused, in an oedipal mixture of an inferiority complex and a sense of superiority, the "founding fathers" being both greater "pioneers" and more "Jewish" than their "children." Yael Zerubavel concurs: "Zionism . . . sought to induce a 'fundamental' rather than a 'radical' transformation."[74]

With Zionist values, norms, and cultural codes established as maintaining closer linkage to Jewish heritage than Zionism was willing to admit, we can appreciate more clearly the difference between Jewish and Hebrew nationalism. Perhaps the latter's most striking characteristic is the absence of the basic legitimacy problem haunting the former—the lack of congruence between land, language, and nation, which, as indicated above, was resolved by the retention in Zionist ideology and discourse of traditional Jewish religious elements that emphasized ethnocultural continuity over territorial and linguistic discontinuity. Menachem Friedman explains: "[W]hile in every 'normal' national movement, the link between the territory and the nation is natural and is not cast in doubt, as far as the Zionist movement is concerned, the link between Palestine and the Jewish nation *is not based on living reality*; in other words, the residence of the Jewish nation in Palestine is not based on actual reality but on historical memories, links and sentiments. These memories and sentiments are an essential part of Jewish tradition."[75] "Canaanism," like Zionism, accepts the imperative of a break with Jewish history but does not regard this break as integral to the very logic of this history, as the Zionist philosophy of history needs to do in order to validate the Zionist political and state-building project in historically plausible terms.

I believe that the origin of this difference lies in the fact that the Jewish and Hebrew myths of origin belong to different categories of national foundational myths, whose typology was discussed in the introduction. Zionist historiography adopted from its Jewish predecessor the idea of the organic "eternal nation";[76] it thus mainly relied on what is variously termed a "genealogical myth of origin" (Anthony Smith), a "myth of biological descent" (John Coakley), or a "myth of continuity" (Steven Knapp). Whatever the designation, this myth in all its forms implies an unbroken temporal sequence between the Jewish golden age in antiquity and the renaissance in modernity.[77] As opposed to that, the insistence on the sociocultural discontinuity between the ancient Hebrews and the Jews on the one hand, and between the Jews and the modern Hebrew nation, on the other, is central to Horon's historiography. In Anthony Smith's terminology, the "Canaanite" foundational myth would therefore meet the definition of an ideological myth, one that is conscious of the lack of genetic bonds between national "forefathers" and "descendants" but instead "shift[s] the emphasis away from imputed blood ties to territorial association with a particular landscape and soil."[78] In Coakley's terms, Horon's historiography would make a national "myth of cultural affinity," while Knapp would define it as a "myth of analogy." Horon's apparatus of ideological legitimization, which fuses an image of a potent regional power with an image of a pristine pagan agrarianism,[79] thus offers a literally radical alternative to the Zionist one, different at its philosophical core as well as in its practical implications.

The opposing types of foundational myths adopted by Zionism and "Canaanism" point to another fundamental, though perhaps less clear-cut, difference between the two ideologies. It quite visibly emerges that they were at odds over the definition of national identity per se. Zionism rather paradoxically considered all those who professed the Jewish faith as belonging to the Jewish nation, portraying them at the same time as the factual descendants of those Jews who went into exile in the first centuries CE. Zionism thus subscribed to a rigid form of perennialism in its conceptualization of what constitutes a nation, adopting a "communalist" mode of thinking whereby a shared religious background implies "common social, political and economic interests."[80] Moreover, as observed by Shmuel Almog, if Zionism wished to offer a viable alternative to assimilation, it had no choice but to define Jewish nationhood in essentialist terms of a single-fate community shaped by primordial and eternal blood ties that would by law of nature defeat any attempt to acculturate in the surrounding society.[81] Contrariwise, the Young Hebrews, who adopted the "national outlook" approach, advocated a less teleological perception as to which group constituted a nation. They did not tie national identity ontologically to any particular historical epoch, whether modernity or antiquity, because, as explained in chapter 2, "national outlook" could develop at any time and in any place, given suitable geophysical and social conditions.

The dissimilar, though partly overlapping, notions of "national homeland" in Zionism and "Canaanism" are another instance of their fundamental difference. As opposed to "Canaanite" inclusivist desire to incorporate large populations and tracts of land without enforcing Jewish ethnocultural supremacy, Zionist expansionism was always checked by its unwillingness to include large non-Jewish populations within its sphere of control. Consequently, the Zionist outlook, which, as argued above, is informed by ethnoreligious criteria, is prone to exclusivism dictated by the type of the origin myth it had adopted.[82]

The practical effects of threading such path is revealed in an almost casual remark by Shmuel Almog: "the Zionists had always displayed a greater willingness to understand and even accept the mood of anti-liberal nationalism, while assuming a place for uniquely Jewish nationalism alongside it."[83] Yadgar likewise observes that "one can indeed expect other, 'less-liberal,' segments of Israeli society to be more clearly committed to what is, at base, an ethnonationalist or racial discriminatory scheme of application of civil, if not human, rights; in which case, it may be seen simply as an *Israeli manifestation of right-wing European nationalism*."[84]

The Young Hebrews' awareness of the "ideological" (in the meaning used by Anthony Smith) nature of their foundational myth, ever since the first article of *On History* celebrated the Mexicans' patently doctored adoption of the Aztec patrimony as their own national legacy, is succinctly formulated in Horon's summation of his own life work: "How do you abolish a false belief?—By another, *better myth*."[85] And elsewhere: "[I]n order to succeed, the Hebrew movement needs first and foremost the guiding spirit of a new 'myth'—based on the re-discovery of the Semitic Orient in its ancient glory." But "what if it fails?," Horon immediately asks. "Nothing can be expected in that case but a series of Zionist 'crusades' and 'Arab' counter-crusades, leaving the Levant in its present state of a desert."[86]

The adoption of an "ideological" foundational myth led "Canaanism" out of the nationalist paradox of the nation being simultaneously ever-ancient and ever-young. The very name of "Young Hebrews" reflected the cult of youth widespread in the Yishuv[87] and the primacy of the nationalist ideal future over the past, making them more future-oriented than the Zionists. Taken in this perspective, the discord between Zionism and "Canaanism" is typical of the dilemma faced by emergent nationalist movements in postcolonial states of migration: whether to bond the national myth of origin to the history of the settlers' mother country or to place it in the actual non-European historical-geographical setting.[88] Zionism remained ambivalent in this regard, attempting to strike a balance between an allegiance to the continuity of Jewish history of the Diaspora and the local setting of the biblical drama and expressing its attachment to the land by primordial kinship connections.[89] "Canaanism" chose to anchor its foundational myth exclusively in the "homeland," on which it relied more in symbolic than purely organic terms.

On this basis, what credit can we give to the Young Hebrews' contention that theirs was a more liberal and less self-contradictory ideology than Zionism? The social scientist Will Kymlicka's benchmarks for liberal nationalism, enumerated by Mazen Masri, include "having a more open definition of the national community that goes beyond race, ethnicity or religion; a thinner conception of nationality which allows individuals from different ethnocultural backgrounds to become full and equal members of the nation; recognition of national minorities in terms of public space, symbols and self-government; and the acceptance of the legitimacy of multinational states in which more than one nation can coexist."[90]

Kymlicka's criteria show that "Canaanism" only partially met the definition of a liberal nationalism. While its concept of national community certainly went "beyond race, ethnicity or religion" by advocating an egalitarian nation blind to "different ethnocultural backgrounds," it insisted on a uniformly Hebrew public sphere and, as we saw in the previous chapter, had especially low tolerance for Arab nationalist iterations. Since "Canaanite" inclusivism did not entail a recognition of the "Arabianate" communities' inherent right to pursue, develop, and express politically their own cultural, linguistic, and religious heritage, as this would have compromised the project of a secular Hebrew nationhood, the ideology's critics suggested that behind its liberal vocabulary actually lurked an aggressive Hebrew expansionism. Boas Evron, for instance, drew parallels between the "Canaanite" vision of a future Hebrew cultural-political space and the Germanization policies in the parts of Poland included in the Second Reich,[91] and Diamond dismissed the whole concept as "preposterous" in light of the projected resistance of "non-Jewish entities."[92]

The tension between the liberal and the "imperialist" motifs in "Canaanism" will be more exhaustively addressed in the conclusion; presently, however, it remains to be observed that in light of Kymlicka's criteria Zionism is notably less liberal than "Canaanism." It operates an ethnoreligious definition of the national community, which makes it next to impossible for "individuals from different ethnocultural backgrounds to become full and equal members of the [Jewish] nation" (except for a Halakhic conversion), and it actively represses Arab collective presense and expression in Israel's public and symbolic spheres.[93]

Common to the Young Hebrews and the Zionists was historical determinism, whereby macrohistorical developments were bound to "prove" each ideology's claim to truth. However, the direction this determinism took in each case was polarized: while Zionism interpreted the unavoidable outcome of Jewish history in optimistic terms of revival and regeneration, "Canaanism" pinned its trust on the inevitable substitution of a primordial ethnocommunity with a modern territorial nation. It prophesied the total decline of Jewry in its premodern shape, as Horon made clear in his January 1947 address to the Hebrew Committee of National Liberation: "We are now witnessing the last chapter in the history of Judaism: the more or less complete . . . assimilation of the Jews . . . as well as their physical extermination."[94] Despite Zionist optimism regarding the fate of the Jews, Zionism's key premise remained negative—I mean here the "rejection of the Diaspora" principle—while "Canaanism," which affirmed Hebrew nationhood, was ultimately premised on more positive foundations.[95]

With these insights in mind, we can now proceed to a more detailed comparison of Zionism and "Canaanism" as rival national ideologies. The Young Hebrews' inclusivity as opposed to Zionism's exclusivity is assessed most efficiently when we look into the respective delimitation of the nation adopted by these ideologies. The Hebrew-speaking Yishuv constitutes an overlapping element, being the stem of the prospective nation in both visions. However, in Zionism, the Yishuv was to maintain dialectical relations of rejection and interdependence, both politically and practically, with the Diaspora; thus, Zionism's call and field of activity were limited to world Jewry conceptualized ethnoreligiously. "Canaanism" on its part detached this connection in favor of a cultural-political alliance with the "Arabianate" Hebrews of the Land of Kedem, irrespective of their origins and creed. A formulaic expression of the above would look like this:

- Yishuv + Jewish Diaspora = Zionism;
- Yishuv + Land of Kedem inhabitants = "Canaanism."

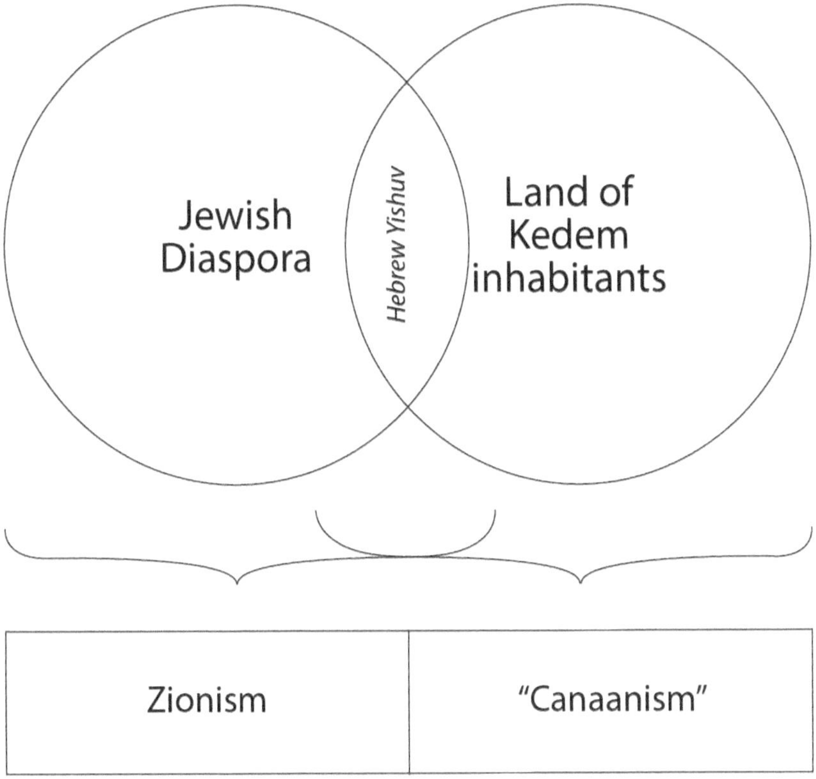

Figure 4.1: Nation delimitation in Zionism and "Canaanism." *Source*: Created by the author.

Such fundamental disagreement over the identification and the boundaries of the putative nation should lay to rest, I believe, any suggestion that "Canaanism" was, in the words of James Diamond, "the first critique that arose from *within* Zionism."[96] We may rather speak of certain discursive components or ideological images shared by both ideologies, or, to apply Gil Eyal's term, "liminal areas" where identities variously share and mix symbols, myths, temporal visions, social values, modes of behavior, language codes, and so on.[97]

An instance of a "liminal area" in the early twentieth century was a highly orientalistic strain of early Zionist theory and practice known as "romantic Zionism." This form of attraction toward the Arab Palestinian population by the Hebrew settlers is described by Oz Almog as disdain mixed with admiration for the Arab world and the "East" more generally, an admiration that, as Aziza Khazzoom reminds us, could only develop once European Jews settling in Palestine had a firm mental picture of themselves as part and parcel of the "Western" world and its culture.[98] This attitude imagined and pictured Palestinian Arabs as the "authentic" descendants of ancient Jews who had preserved their vitalistic attachment to their land throughout the ages "unsullied" by the Diaspora or modern civilization, and as such were worthy of emulation as the opposite of the stereotypical (anti-Semitic) image of the Diaspora Jew. At the same time, they were portrayed as hostile, backward, and in need of a "civilizing" hand by the supposedly more advanced Jews. The interaction between Zionist settlers and Palestinian Arabs was adapted by the Zionist national mythology into a "reconciliation" between the brothers torn apart by history, Isaac and Ishmael.[99]

However, this strain in Zionism died out as a consequence of the escalation of the Arab-Jewish conflict, with the Palestinians eventually recognized as a distinct community with competing claims.[100] "Canaanism," as demonstrated in chapter 3, managed to preserve the idea of a Hebrew-Palestinian kinship, premised on environmental determinism, whereby Palestinians were regarded as actual or potential Hebrews due to their shared geophysical space and not to any imputed genealogical closeness. "Romantic Zionism," contrariwise, developed its idea of a Jewish-Arab kinship on the racialist premises of a supposed common historical descent, which proved unsustainable in the face of the growing enmity between Jews and Palestinians.[101]

It has already been noted above that the findings of biblical criticism could only be incorporated into the Zionist worldview to a limited degree since the justification of Zionism's geopolitical program relied on the assumption of the historical veracity of at least part of the biblical narrative. Although Zionist discourse has thoroughly secularized the Bible, Zionism never subjected the Bible to such a devastating critique as Horon did.[102] The Zionist triad of "Golden Age"—"Middle Ages"—"Renaissance" reflected, by and large, the Jewish understanding of history. In Jewish and Zionist historiography the Golden Age ends only with the destruction of the Second Temple in the first century CE, while the appearance of Zionism in the late nineteenth century heralds the end of the "dark Middle Ages" of Exile.[103] In Horon's historiography, each of these elements is dated earlier than its Zionist equivalent: the Golden Age begins to fade when Judaism emerges in the Babylonian Exile in the mid-first millennium BCE, and the age of the Renaissance sets in when Hebrew ethnogenesis starts in the Land of Kedem in the mid-nineteenth century, several decades before Zionism. By shifting its periodization limits backwards, "Canaanite" historiography was able to put a claim for a greater authenticity and better grounding in the past than Zionism.

Finally, and ironically only at first sight, the Young Hebrews were in fact more friendly to Jewish tradition than Zionism due to their deterministic contention that premodern Jewry could meaningfully exist as a social and historical entity exclusively within a communal framework. This is appreciated by a number of observers, some reli-

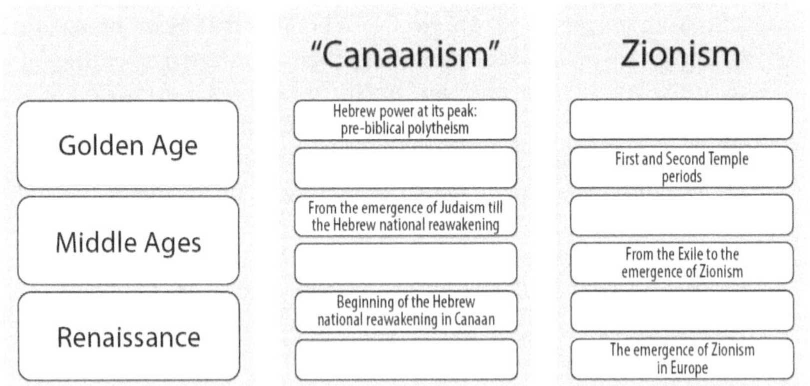

Figure 4.2: Comparative periodization in "Canaanism" and Zionism. *Source*: Created by the author.

giously devout, like James Diamond, who writes that "in its negation of Jewish *nationhood*, 'Canaanism' actually reaffirms Jewish *religion*,"[104] and some secular, like Boas Evron ("He who regards himself a national Hebrew or Israeli . . . is the only one who can treat Diaspora Jews as equals, whose existence possesses intrinsic value"[105]) or Asher Nehor ("The *Alef* people . . . come as far as . . . immortalizing the mysterious entity called 'world Jewry')."[106]

Zionism's attempt to transform Judaism into an ideology of secular redemption generated the anxiety of prominent religious and Zionist thinkers like Baruch Kurzweil, Martin Buber, Gershom Scholem, and Yeshayahu Leibowitz, each of whom, in his own way, accused secular Zionism of endeavoring to twist Judaism's shape by force.[107] Contrariwise, the Young Hebrews never declared an ontological war on "religion as the natural modality of the Jewish experience and the Diaspora as its historical locus,"[108] but only insofar as it was perceived to hinder the crystallization of the Hebrew national identity in Canaan. "Canaanite" theory accepted the possibility of a peaceful coexistence between religious and national identifications, if separation of religion and state were truly enforced in Israel. Ratosh made this point precisely, when in his rebuttal of Baruch Kurzweil he accused him of missing the fundamental fact of the formation of a Hebrew nation that required its own channels of expression and that "the Jewish question [was] a communal, international question . . . [and] dissimilar to questions of self-determination and questions of existence and the future of the Hebrew nation, which are local in nature." Moreover,

> [the Young Hebrews] do not . . . demand that Jews cease being Jews, or that they redefine their emotional attitude to Judaism. We do not care at all if Judaism persists for thousands of years, in any shape . . . or it perishes at some point. We do not inquire after solutions for problems of Jewry and Judaism . . . We do not fight Judaism for its own sake. We fight to prevent it from occupying a place to which is cannnot lay a rightful claim—in the country's politics and its civic legislation, in the sphere of civic values, so that it does not obstruct the free development of our secular culture.[109]

In focusing upon Zionism's manifestations of continuity with traditional Judaism and the Diaspora heritage, we must not overlook

Zionism's internal dialectics. While the Young Hebrews preferred to present themselves as hostile to both right- and left-wing Zionism,[110] they could not deny that their biographical and, to a significant extent, intellectual origins lay in the Revisionist camp founded and led by Zeev Jabotinsky from the mid-1920s. Closer examination of the ideological principles and methods of both "Canaanism" and Revisionism exposes a number of pronounced similarities related both to the intellectual content of the ideologies and to the social background of their adherents.

First, the "Canaanites" and the Revisionists shared a positive national approach by framing their struggle as a struggle *for* a certain aim, not only to *escape* some difficulty haunting the Diaspora. Second, while for socialist Zionism the polemical defense of the Jews' right to the Land of Israel was an imperative, often decorated with promises of prosperity for its Arab inhabitants, Jabotinsky rejected this as a preposterous weakness that exposed the moral doubt at the bottom of Zionism's raison d'être: "Only those with crippled spirits, with a diaspora psychosis," he claimed, "made these [questions about the right of the Jews to Palestine] into a 'problem' which must be investigated and proved."[111] In a similar vein, the Young Hebrews viewed Canaan within the Land of Kedem as the natural homeland of the Hebrew nation, whose right to it required no apology.

Other elements common to Jabotinsky's political thought and to "Canaanism" were a liberal approach to questions of societal and economic life, enhanced by a staunch secularism. The latter point, however, requires some clarification, since Jabotinsky's attitude to Judaism, as shown by Jan Zouplna,[112] evolved over time. Remaining steadfast in his rejection of the legalistic aspects of Halakhic tradition (the "outward" facet of Judaism; what Eri Jabotinsky, following Horon, called "an artificial wall of precepts and laws"[113]), in the 1930s Jabotinsky gradually embraced, albeit hesitantly, the "interior" aspect of Judaism. He understood the latter in a manner not dissimilar from Aḥad Ha'am's Hegelian approach to spiritual Jewish heritage as the inner essence of faith and tradition that had kept the Jews nationally distinct throughout the Exile and that was now passing on its torch to Zionism.[114] Now leading his own movement and looking to absorb into it the widest circles possible, even at the cost of watering down certain principles, Jabotinsky stood up to defend this standpoint at the New Zionist Organization foundation congress in 1935. As we saw in chapter 1, this aroused the ire of several secularist Revisionists,

Horon amongst them,[115] whose dogmatic attitude on this point, to use Gramscian language, was a corollary of his nonhegemonic position within the Revisionist movement. Jabotinsky the Zionist was ultimately unwilling to break with Judaism entirely, and, in consequence, his standpoint on political matters, such as Arab nationalism or the British policy in the Middle East, also diverged from the positions adopted by the Young Hebrews.

A form of environmental determinism was shared by Revisionism and "Canaanism." Jabotinsky might have borrowed from Herder the idea that a nation's geographical and historical conditions shape its "essence," which survives even when the nation abandons its original place of habitation.[116] In his writings from the first decade of the twentieth century, Jabotinsky attributed the preservation of Jewishness during the two millennia of Exile to a "genetic memory" that passed down the ages and defined what he termed the nation's racial [*sic*] uniqueness.[117] Dissenting radically from his mentor on that point, Horon rejected any notion of a genetic continuity or affinity among the Jews.

There were additional points of convergence between Revisionism and "Canaanism," mostly on matters related to history, as is evidenced by the enthusiastic reception of Horon's publications by some of Betar's leaders in the 1930s (see chapter 1). The Revisionists celebrated the ancient Hebrew statehood and its regional potency, whose source of power they had identified in the Hebrews' attachment to their land.[118] Thus, vitalism was more pronounced in Revisionism than in socialist Zionism.[119] The Revisionists also subscribed to the idea of the Hebrews' cultural affinity with the Mediterranean rather than with the Arab "Orient"; hence their theoretical and practical interest in Hebrew seafaring enabled the formation first of Rodêgal and then of the naval school at Civitavecchia.[120] Finally, the Revisionists accepted that Judaism's expansion over the Mediterranean in the first centuries CE resulted from active colonization and prozelytization rather than from dispersal.[121]

At bottom, however, Jabotinsky's over-all conception of Jewish history remained quite distant from Horon's historiography, a distance that the similarities listed above were insufficient to bridge. Jabotinsky's historical attitude, when not instrumental, was most faithfully expressed in his December 1938 letter, in which he beseeched Horon not to discount Jewish traditional interpretation of the Bible in favor of an innovative philological analysis and advised him "not to succumb to the urge to blemish Israel for the glory of the Hebrews or to blemish monotheism for the benefit of paganism."[122] Jabotinsky's novel *Samson*, which, as explained above, was a key source of inspiration for Horon in the 1930s, portrays the ancient Jews as pagans but newcomers distinct from the native Canaanites. At no stage could Jabotinsky's vision of the present and the future be described in any way as "Canaanite."

These observations on the ideational differences and similarities between "Canaanism" and Zionism can be matched by another one, concerning the social background of the adherents of both movements. Socialist Zionism chiefly represented the poverty-stricken shtetls of Eastern Europe and the underclass Jewish proletariat. Socialism was therefore the predominant worldview among the core of the "second *'aliya*" (1904–1914) pioneers who shared this background. They formed the backbone of the Zionist and Israeli elite up to the 1970s due to their dominance during the early twentieth-century Jewish settlement of Palestine.[123] Conversely, the Revisionists mobilized their human resources mainly from among well-to-do bourgeois assimilated Jewish families, whose liberal values placed them closer in outlook to the "first *'aliya*" (1882–1904) settlers. The "first *'aliya*'s agricultural colonies permitted private ownership and were maintained by hired (mainly Arab) labor.

The same social origins also characterized most of the Young Hebrews. In this context, it is possible to identify "Canaanism" as a locus for expressing the social values peculiar to their class, with an explicit secular, even anti-Jewish, bent. Revisionism meanwhile remained the ideological front for the assimilated Jewish bourgeoisie who were unwilling to relinquish their heritage entirely.

With this in mind, we are able to evaluate the Young Hebrews' positive references to the first *'aliya,* whose bourgeois values were suppressed almost to the point of oblivion by the radical-minded "second *'aliya*" founders of the Zionist "workers' society" that militated against Diaspora "shopkeeper mentality."[124] The Young Hebrews asserted that the Hebrew national identity started to develop during the first *'aliya* period, if not earlier, which made the second *'aliya* a "usurper" of sorts. Researchers agree that a native Hebrew culture had begun to take shape in Palestine by the opening years of the twentieth century, though they portray it in much more ambiguous colors than the Young Hebrews. A system of symbols and values new to Jewish culture undoubtedly formed during the nation formation processes that were taking place in Palestine in the late nineteenth century, such as the ethos of progress and renewal inspired by the ideal past.[125]

The Young Hebrews were then at least partially right in claiming that the first *'aliya* potentially led to the development of a new nation. However, what they did not consider was that the first *'aliya* imagined itself as *the* Jewish national culture and was far from repudiating the legacy of the Diaspora. The "liminal area" of late nineteenth-century Palestine fused native Hebrew elements with Arab indigenous cultural symbols, western concepts of progress and liberation, biblical romanticism, Turkish-Ottoman influences, and cultural elements imported from the first *'aliya* immigrants' native countries. This eclectic mix, Yafa Berelowitz observes, hindered to some extent the crystallization of a purely new Hebrew-Jewish identity.[126]

In brief, the first *'aliya* worked out several key elements that inspired the Young Hebrews, such as the desacralization of time and space, the drive to create a new culture and a new identity free from the "ailments" of the Diaspora, an ethos of nativeness and attachment to the place, the recovery of a foundational myth anchored in the local biblical past, and—to a measure—a liberal socioeconomic worldview. It was at the same time rather remote from the ideal picture the "Canaanites" drew of a non-Zionist and non-Jewish national renaissance-in-the-making frustrated by the Zionist "invasion."

"Canaanism" as a Precursor of Post-Zionism?

The centenary of the first *'aliya* in the early 1980s roughly coincided with the transfer of political hegemony in Israel from Zionist Labor to the Likud Party, which had grown out of the Revisionist movement. The beginning of the decline of Zionist Labor was arguably one of the signals forecasting the emergence of a post-Zionist school of thought in Israeli political and intellectual life, with a symbolic bridge linking late nineteenth-century first *'aliya*, mid-twentieth-century "Canaanism," and late twentieth-century post-Zionism. All three phenomena represented, each in its own way, a sceptical attitude to the socialist principles and slogans that lay at the core of second *'aliya* Labor Zionism. Numerous researchers have traced post-Zionism's pedigree to the Young Hebrews (though not necessarily to Horon's historiography); they did not, however, usually dwell on the exact nature of this connection.[127] The section that follows intends to fill this gap.

Chapter 1 devoted significant space to the exploration of Horon's role in bringing about the ideological rupture between Zionism and the Hebrew Committee of National Liberation. The committee was the first organization within the broad stream of Zionism to self-identify as "post-Zionist" in December 1947, when its leader Hillel Kook responded to the UN plan regarding the partition of Palestine on the pages of the *New York Herald Tribune*:

> What does a Jewish State mean? Will it be a kind of Jewish Vatican? Will the Jewish government represent the Jews of the world? Will all the Jews in the world eventually move to the Jewish State, or will they become part of a special international nation?
>
> Clearly, it should be understood, we of the Hebrew Liberation Movement oppose the concept of a "world Jewish nation," which strives, through the Jewish Agency, to place the label of "Jewish State" on the thirteen per cent of Palestine which has not been surrendered to the Arabs. In view of the fact that more than ten million Jews live outside of Palestine, and are not in D. P. camps or in danger, but enjoy full citizenship in many lands, the insistence upon a world Jewish Nation is bound to ensnare many good Americans, Frenchmen, Englishmen, etc., who are Jews, in a difficult and ugly situation. [. . .]
>
> [The Jewish Agency's] proposed ghetto-like "Jewish State" will only perpetuate the abnormality of the Jewish position.
>
> [. . .]
>
> It is our conviction that the decision of the United Nations offers a choice between a Jewish State as a unique entity, a religious-cultural-political center for World Jewry, or a Hebrew Republic of Palestine, as a normal and modern nation without any ties or ramifications among these citizens of other lands who are of Jewish faith.
>
> The crux of our program lies in a sharp separation between "The Jews," as a religion, and the Hebrews, as a nation. [. . .] We are neither anti nor non-Zionist. We are post-Zionist.[128]

This rupture persisted after the establishment of the state in the activity of the Committee's successors in Israeli public life: the

"Lamerḥav" faction within the Ḥerut party (1949–1950) and the Kedem Club in Haifa (mid-1950s). The platform adopted by Lamerḥav came very close in several respects to the Young Hebrews' ideology. It insisted that Israeli state apparatus must override the interests of global Zionist organizations in the state's internal affairs and that Israel must represent only its citizens regardless of ethnicity and not world Jewry at large. The faction's members, including Eri Jabotinsky and Hillel Kook, advocated the total separation of religion and state to be enshrined in a written constitution, attempted to fight off the monopolization of Israeli economy by the socialist-bureaucratic institutions of the "workers' society" and called for Israel's reorientation toward the Levant, where it was supposed to take on a leading geopolitical and cultural position as a viable alternative to Arab nationalism.[129]

The principles informing the activity of both Lamerḥav and the Kedem Club were laid out in detail by Eri Jabotinsky in an article he had published in a brochure put out by the Levant Club in the USA in 1952,[130] which, after Hillel Kook's "Post-Zionism" from December 1947, is probably the second utterance of the term "post-Zionism" in print, this time in connection with the establishment of Israel and the attendant conclusion of the historical mission of Zionism. Jabotinsky writes, "Today Zionism as such has ended by achieving fulfilment. We are now in what should be called the 'post-Zionist period' in Hebrew history,"[131] and he explains that this is so not only because Zionism can have no more claim to usefulness after achieving its declared objective, but also because the self-identification of the majority of Hebrew-speaking Israelis is hardly Jewish. The source of the crisis in Israeli public life, exacerbated by a lack of a constitution, is the refusal by the Zionist leadership to accept this state of things and to redirect Israel's raison d'état onto tracks commensurate with the vital interests of Israeli society as interpreted by Jabotinsky and his colleagues from the Kedem Club.

The outlook of the Kedem Club was formulated in the sharpest terms possible by its co-founder Shmuel Rosoff, in a letter written on a Kedem Club letterhead in November 1956 to Shmuel Merlin (a former member of the Hebrew Committee of National Liberation and its leader at some point, later a member of Lamerḥav), where he speaks of "the necessity to underline and proclaim the anti-Jewishness [*sic*!] of Israel." To Rosoff, who came from a family integrated into Russian culture (a classmate of Vladimir Nabokov in early twentieth-century St. Petersburg, he maintained a lifetime correspondence with him), "Jewishness" meant the whole gamut of anti-Semitic stereotypes that people like him struggled to release themselves from, a struggle that, in his opinion, stood the greatest chance of success in a de-Zionized Israel:

> Israel came into being as a Revolt against Jewishness—against Diaspora, against the Ghetto life, Ghetto-thinking, and the whole bundle of concepts which the Wandering Jew carries on his back [. . .] A vision of Israel as a liberal civilised nation freed of its Jewish complexes, freed of the isolationism of the Rabbinical "chosen Race" mentality—freed of its dependence on Diaspora and its shameful "Schnorr-industry"; Israel boldly and truly fulfilling an internal policy of civil equality and creating a type of an Israeli citizen inspired by ideals of Progress, Justice and Goodness [. . .] We are Israelis—not another Jewish community, not a Centre of World Jewry, not an East-End of the World! [. . .] It leaves the Diaspora-age behind and enters into a new age of Regional Renaissance.[132]

The need to distinguish between Jews and Israelis in legal and practical terms—not only in moral terms à la Rosoff—as a sine qua non for Israel's "normalization" and a safeguard for its sovereign existence was emphasized a number of times by Eri Jabotinsky. In a memorandum prepared for the Kedem Club, he argued: "Shaking off the unnatural bonds with the voluntary ghettoes inhabited today by the Jews of the free world is a simple security imperative: today the world regards us as just another Jewish community, and the world knows perfectly well what is habitually done with Jewish communities."[133] In the same document Jabotinsky formulated at length his thoughts on this differentiation, which offer a glimpse on how he understood the issue of the delimitation of Israeli and Jewish identities and the ways they work against each other as long as civic and religious identities remain conflated:

> A. An Israeli is any person who due to certain circumstances is a citizen of Israel. This is exclusively a formality and has no bearing on this person's opinions, feelings or origin.
>
> B. A Jew is any person throughout the world that belongs in one way or another to the Jewish religion and Judaism without any bearing on this person's patriotic sentiments.

C. A Zionist once meant a person who wished to abandon Diaspora life in order to come to this country and live like a Hebrew. It was a Hebrew-in-the-making. Today the adjective has lost its precision and is applied to a foreign (non-Israeli) Jew who is positively disposed toward Israel without any intention of joining it. (*I believe that today, after the Zionist period has come to an end by accomplishing its objective, we must not employ the hollow word Zionist*).

D. A Hebrew is a person that sees himself part of the renewed nation. His being Hebrew is dictated exclusively by his internal feeling. This is not similar to his being a Jew: most of the Jews, even in the free world, do not tie their own fate or the fate of their children to our fate and have no plans to do so in the future. This is not similar to his being an Israeli, since there are many Israelis who do not regard themselves as part of the sovereign Hebrew nation (and this includes both Jewish and non-Jewish elements—especially among the orthodox and the communists) [. . .] Clear things must be said to the Jews of the world: we the Hebrews are interested in immigrants. We are interested above all in a Jewish *'aliya* and therefore the gates of our country stand open to you, on the condition that you become Hebrews by disconnecting yourselves from the countries to which you now belong. With Jews who refuse to do so we shall continue to maintain good relations subject to our interests but maintaining awareness that those are foreigners.[134]

None of the above, however, will be achieved "as long as our leaders see themselves as emissaries and agents of world Jewry" content with establishing a "truncated Jewish State on the small beachhead around Tel Aviv," in Eri Jabotinsky's contemptuous words.[135]

This passage is very useful in contemplating the distance Eri Jabotinsky came to obtain from his father: Jabotinsky the elder, an ethnonationalist at the bottom of his soul, once declared that "[w]e [the Zionists] were never guilty of confusing concepts . . . in arguing that nationalism is by any means related to citizenship."[136] Jewish political-territorial affiliation in the Diaspora by Zeev Jabotinsky's understanding was not to imply a national identification, which was to remain separate and ideally crystalized in Zionism. His son, however, in differentiating between Israelis and Hebrews, wished to acknowledge the continued existence of a Jewish communal identity in Israel, which was to neither overlap with the state nor to dictate its legislation or moral content. His starting point was that being a Jew did not in and of itself imply belonging to a nation, quite the opposite from his father's intent.

Ever since Hillel Kook declared in December 1947 that "the Hebrew Liberation Movement oppose[s] the concept of a 'world Jewish nation' " and that "the crux of our program lies in a sharp separation between 'The Jews,' as a religion, and the Hebrews, as a nation,"[137] the Young Hebrews and the post-Zionists shared an operational assumption regarding the nonnational character of Diaspora Jewry, which was framed exclusively as an ethnoreligious community. This alone suffices to diagnose the 1940s–1950s post-Zionism as *anti*-Zionist since the dispute between it and Zionism (of all persuasions) revolved around basics rather than secondary principles or practical policy. A concomitant—and this time unstated—deterministic assumption shared by the Young Hebrews and the post-Zionists was that whatever Zionism managed to achieve in terms of the formation of the nucleus of a Hebrew nation in Palestine was in spite of itself. Zionism thus functioned within a framework of historical laws and circumstances greater than itself, and it is for this reason that Eri Jabotinsky believed to be within his rights to assert that "the term Hebrew used by us is but a new and more definite name for an old concept." This concept he attributed to both his father and to Theodor Herzl, writing that what they had meant by "Jews" was now more effectively encapsulated by "Hebrews."[138]

Yet here also emerge the cracks between the "Canaanites" and the post-Zionists. Whereas the latter openly acknowledged the positive historical role of Zionism (Hillel Kook wrote in December 1947: "We recognize the great merits of that movement in the past—in a free Palestine monuments and highways will be named in its honor") and considered it a legitimate stage in history that had made itself obsolete by victory in 1947–1948 (Kook again: "the Zionist program is today archaic"),[139] the former—or, at least, the circle around Yonatan Ratosh—judged Zionism to be inherently nonnational, an illegitimate usurper of the Hebrew national revival and certainly not an assisting factor in the formation of the Hebrew nation or the establishment of Israel. Horon, as we saw in chapter 3, fluctuated between these two positions: in the 1960s he condemned Zionism for functioning as a worldwide charity preoccupied with seeking a solution to a humanitarian Jewish problem (echoing Israel Scheib-Eldad's denunciation of Zionism on similar grounds in the 1940s[140]), yet at the same period he made the point at least twice that the pre-1948 period was the "Zionist epoch," which by implication meant that the post-1948 stage was "post-Zionist,"[141] thus granting Zionism historical legitimacy. Like Eri Jabotinsky but unlike Ratosh, Horon was willing to accept a widespread Jewish immigration to Israel, though after 1948 he did not defend this standpoint by portraying Jews as the descendants of the ancient Hebrews, as did Jabotinsky and Hillel Kook, and as Horon himself did in the 1930s.[142] Although one of the articles in Eri Jabotinsky's "Jews and Hebrews" was a direct retelling of Horon's historical findings as supposedly the legitimizing apparatus for the Hebrew Committee's repudiation of Zionism, this seems to be more an expression of Jabotinsky's personal sympathies than a principled statement.

The tactical alliance between the post-Zionists and the Young Hebrews, if there ever was one apart from personal contacts, rested more on a shared program concerning the future of Israel than on a common vision of the past or a common geographical outlook.[143] This lack of full acceptation by the post-Zionists of "Canaanite" historiography and geopolitics led in time to further divergences in political outlook: later in their lives, Kook and Merlin strongly advocated the establishment of a Palestinian state on both banks of the Jordan in a federation with pre-1967 Israel as an indispensable condition for the normalization of Israel's national existence and the peaceful conclusion of the Israeli-Arab conflict.[144] In effect, as observed by Uri Ram, post-Zionism succumbed to Zionism's inherent need of historical myth making grounded in the Jewish legacy,[145] and by the early 1960s vanished from the Israeli public stage. It was reborn in a very different shape only in the 1990s, a development that will be examined below.

All in all, the 1940s–1950s post-Zionism was undoubtedly an example of the "latent" existence of "Canaanism" in Israeli public life, as suggested by James Diamond.[146] It is noteworthy, then, that a different instance of latent "Canaanism" was displayed by none other than Israel's first prime minister, David Ben-Gurion. His fascination with the First Temple age, mentioned earlier, did not escape the attention of some Israeli intellectuals, who accused Ben-Gurion of being a "Canaanite."[147] This was not the only aspect of his activity that challenged Zionist ideological assumptions or foci of power.

During the early 1950s Ben-Gurion heralded the idea of "étatism" (*mamlakhtiyut*), which promoted the superiority of Israel over the Diaspora as a substitute for a "worn" Zionism and as a new focus of societal allegiance, in which a centralized bureaucratic mechanism takes over the nation-building tasks performed in the prestate phase by voluntary, informal, and occasionally clandestine bodies. In 1953 he even announced his resignation from World Zionist Organization.[148]

Although he was clearly aware that the new Israeli society, whose members did not necessarily subscribe to the ideology professed by the second *'aliya* veterans, required a different "civil religion," Ben-Gurion stopped short of declaring Zionism entirely obsolete. Anita Shapira attributes this to his inconsistent politics,[149] but I believe there were profounder reasons for this. As argued by Eric Cohen, the "étatist" idea proved to be an insufficient alternative to Zionism by failing to fulfill the role of the "melting pot" for Israel's highly heterogeneous society, since it canceled out the Zionist image of the past in favor of a future-oriented model of identity without proposing any alternative historiography.[150] As a result, Ben-Gurion had no choice but to revert to Zionism as the state ideology.

Over the next decades, Zionism underwent what Cohen calls "routinization," and by the late 1980s, he claims, it had naturally run its course. Therefore, a new "post-Zionist" age was inescapably looming.[151] Other researchers have mapped a more turbulent process for the renewed emergence and dissemination of the post-Zionist standpoint as the 1990s approached. Baruch Kimmerling attributed it to the growing pluralization of Israeli society that accompanied the decline of the Labor hegemony.[152] Alain Dieckhoff pointed to the geopolitical shocks experienced by Israel in the 1960s and 1970s in the wake of the occupation of the Palestinian territories in 1967.[153] Assaf Likhovski indicated the paradigm shift that Israeli academia underwent as state archives were declassified in the late 1980s and a new and less ideologically committed generation of researchers educated abroad came of (intellectual and professional) age.[154] Abu el-Haj interprets post-Zionism as a tool in the struggle led by the Israeli secular classes against the ascendancy of the orthodox and the national-religious camps in Israeli political and social life.[155] Finally, Daniel Gutwein emphasizes the Israeli middle classes' aspiration to dismantle the socialist-collectivist structure designed by the Labor Zionists in order to advance a neoliberal economic ideology and policy answering their material needs.[156]

Although drawing on a rather unidimentional class analysis, Gutwein's argument is especially valuable in our context, since it demarcates two kinds of contemporary post-Zionism, the "leftist" and the "rightist." Both, Gutwein asserts, serve the aim of "neutralizing the electoral advantage and the political power accumulated by the 'others,' and transferring the control of key state systems to the market and the professional institutions"[157] by "fighting the Zionist ethos, whose collectivist foundation legitimized top-down design of economy, society and culture."[158] He claims that "leftist" and "rightist" post-Zionisms are the convergence of two extremes:

> Right and left post-Zionism, each in its own way, struggle against the radical-collectivist ethos of Zionism . . . Right and left post-Zionism are inspired by opposing intellectual traditions and define themselves by means of rival ideologies; at the same time . . . they are potential political partners . . . Both make use of the category of "the Jew" in order to dismantle Israeli collective identity as defined by "the Zionist." The left sees the dissolution of Zionist collectivism as the first step in transforming Israel from an "ethno-democracy" . . . into a multicultural, universalist democracy; whereas the right uses "the Jew" to replace Zionism with an alternative "more Jewish" collective identity. Both ideologies employ arguments from the arsenal of the politics of identity to undermine the hegemony of Labor Zionism . . . Both view the collectivism that characterizes Zionism as a source of oppression and prefer free-market capitalism to the regulating force of the state.[159]

Gutwein closes his analysis by suggesting that modern-day post-Zionism is *not* a subversive ideology, but serves the up-and-coming classes and their dominant agenda, which, at least in socio-economic terms, he identifies as right wing.[160] Eran Kaplan's observation that the post-Zionists "are the cultural and intellectual heirs of Jabotinsky's Revisionist vision, which sought to free the Zionist movement from the perceived tyranny of the Laborites" is, for all intents and purposes, a statement to the same effect.[161]

A question now in order is the nature and the extent of the differences between the post-Zionism that accompanied the emergence of Israel and the post-Zionism that burst onto the public stage in the fifth decade of the state's existence. Very few writers drew any connections between the two, at best treating the former as a historical incident that had left meager traces in Israeli public life and collective consciousness. In general terms, the difference between the two generations of post-Zionism can be condensed to the observation that while the 1940s and 1950s post-Zionism largely sprang from the internal logic of Zionism, considering it a historically *justified,* and now *completed,* historical stage, the 1990s post-Zionism was the product of a dialectic cross-fertilizing of intrinsic developments and extrinsic impacts. Apart from questioning Zionist political principles, it made itself heard in numerous spheres: it is a critical academic approach, particularly in Israeli historiography, sociology, and archaeology (the latter casting doubt upon the veracity of the biblical story used as the Zionist commemorative narrative and on the Zionist interpretation of newer Jewish history);[162] it is a self-declared literary-cultural revolution whose aim is to release Hebrew letters and arts from Zionism's ideological shackles;[163] it might also be interpreted as a state of mind widespread in a society aspiring for a new "civil religion" once Zionism had ceased to fulfil the task.[164] Last, the dissemination of deconstructivist and postmodernist methods in the humanities finds reflection in the rejection by Israeli post-Zionist academic circles of the "oppressive" narrative of Zionism in favor of a more pluralistic approach to the Israeli past and present, and to identity issues.

Asima Ghazi-Bouillon and Laurence Silberstein maintain that the adoption of postmodernist and deconstructivist approaches is what makes a "genuine" post-Zionist scholarship,[165] yet this argument seems to overlook the complexity of the 1990s post-Zionism and its extra-academic sources and effects. Silberstein himself pays great attention to the pre-1990s "positivist" critics of Zionism, among whom he marks out the ex-"Canaanite" Boas Evron,[166] thus indicating his awareness of the "Canaanite" lineage of post-Zionism. Elsewhere he states plainly: "If Canaanism can be said to represent an early effort to construct a post-Zionist ideology for the generation of the 1940s and 1950s, Boas Evron . . . offers a lucid formulation of a post-Zionist ideology for the generation of the 1980s and 1990s."[167]

Evron's writings resonate with the Young Hebrews' critique of Zionism (despite all his disagreements with "Canaanism"), thus, one can indeed regard them as an intellectual bridge between the two generations of post-Zionism, given that Evron was personally involved in both. His standpoint is "post-Canaanite" inasmuch as it rejects some of this ideology's blatantly nationalistic and expansionist elements but retains its liberal components.[168] Joseph Gorny remarks that "post-Canaanite" liberals like Evron have abandoned the Young Hebrews' historical-territorial myth and acknowledged the bond between Israeli/Hebrew and Jewish history (in particular, he argues that Evron's contention that East European Jewry developed a national character of its own is inspired by Bundism[169]). Back in 1984, Evron stated that he regarded himself as a "post-Zionist" (using the Hebrew form *betar-tsiyoni*, which was later marginalized by the presently used *posṭ-tsiyoni*), meaning one who "desir[es] a state indifferent to its citizens' religious and national affiliations, which has no binding institutional links to the Jewish Diaspora, all of whose citizens are legally equal in theory and practice—and that does not regard itself as a body loyal to a certain ideology or mission, but its only obligations are toward its citizens."[170] Into this camp he corrals, postmortem, Yonatan Ratosh.

Boas Evron is additionally significant in the present context on account of his magnum opus, *National Reckoning*.[171] A public intellectual more than a professional academic, Evron undertook in this large volume to deconstruct the Zionist historical master narrative and to denounce the policies practised by Israel, proposing instead a picture of Hebrew and Jewish history that would facilitate the construction of a liberal and secular Israel and establish peaceful relations with the Palestinians and the Arab world. His objective is therefore similar to that of Horon (who is not listed among his sources), given the shared assumption that an adequate understanding of history is a prerequisite for adequate politics built on a liberal-national ethos. Yet he also dissents from Horon by his fierce denunciation of the Israeli right wing (especially in its religious shape) and his acceptance of the legitimacy of Arab and Palestinian nationalism. Although Evron was too young to have played any part in the activities of the Hebrew Committee of National Liberation (and during the 1950s initiated, with Uri Avnery, the "Semitic Action," which looked favorably upon Arab anticolonial nationalism),[172] his views closely reflect those of Hillel Kook in his later years. To the best of my knowledge, Evron's is the only book written before the series of titles by Shlomo Sand[173] (who admits to being inspired by Evron) that had the aim of supplying second-generation post-Zionists with a historical master narrative that would have the potential to furnish solutions to the acute questions of Israeli identity.

It would seem that the sharpest difference between the two generations of post-Zionism is that while the first generation kept largely within the nationalist framework of thinking, developing an Israeli and regional raison d'état and geopolitical vision in the name of Hebrew national liberation, second-generation post-Zionism is—except for the association led by Ratosh's youngest brother Uzzi Ornan, "I am an Israeli"[174]—either indifferent to nationalism or actively hostile to it. Nonetheless, one finds among the utterances of first-generation post-Zionists (who, it should be restated, emerged from right-wing Zionism) prescient warnings about the prospects for Palestine if a "Jewish" state was to form there. For example, in January 1948, an anonymous writer in the Hebrew Committee's journal *The Answer* discussed the self-contradictory nature of the Zionist planning:

> The Zionist spokesmen have tied themselves into knots trying to define a "Jewish State." But however they twisted and turned and evade[d] it, it still boils down to something very suspiciously like a theocratic state. And so they switched. What they wanted they said was a "democratic Jewish State." Which is like saying that they want a white blackbird. Because if it is white, it isn't a blackbird, and if it is a blackbird, then it can't be white. Either it is a "Jewish State" in which case the citizens of the state are Jews, and non-Jews are something else but not first-class citizens. Or else it is a democratic state and it doesn't matter whether its citizens are Jews or non-Jews. And if it is a democratic state and all citizens enjoy full equality under the law regardless of whether they are Jews or not, what on earth makes it Jewish?[175]

Moreover, some of the practical solutions proposed by first-generation post-Zionists to the gravest political questions posited by Israel's formation anticipated to some extent similar proposals raised by the second generation during the 1990s. In his 1956 letter to Shmuel Merlin, Shmuel Rosoff described the then relatively fresh issue of Palestinian refugees as "*our* [Israel's] problem" that "stands in our way as a great obstacle to any further progress."[176] To Horon's dissatisfaction, who warned from the United States that such moves played into the hands of anti-Israeli circles in the West, the Kedem Club prioritized the solution of the refugee problem in its "Tentative Formulation for a Program of Action" and suggested that the Palestinian refugees be resettled in Jordan, which it considered inseparable from historical Palestine. Were the Hashemite British pawns to be overthrown, Jordan could subsequently choose either to federate with Israel ("thus returning to the Palestine Refugees a stake in the whole of Palestine," the option the club clearly preferred) or remain independent. Refugees who declined such resettlement would be fully compensated.[177]

Eri Jabotinsky actively engaged in support of the Maronite deportees from Bir'am, evicted from their village in northern Israel by the Israeli army in December 1948 on the excuse of security and with a promise to return within a few weeks—a promise broken by all Israeli governments without exception.[178] He authored memoranda advocating their cause[179] and spoke on their behalf from the Knesset tribune, thereby making the issue of Bir'am (and another Christian village in the north, Iqrit[180])—into which he also drew Uri Avnery[181]—one of the first instances of practical cooperation between first-generation post-Zionists (who considered it a threshold condition for the formation of an Israeli-Lebanese anti-Arabist alliance) and radical anti-Zionist left-wingers (for whom this issue was inseparable from the broader question of the Palestinian Right of Return). This tallied with Jabotinsky's general inclination to include Arabic speakers in the body politic of Israel as an inseparable part of its society rather than a recognized national minority,[182] an inclination informed by his strong belief in the voluntary character of all nations (which shows, inter alia, that he did not accept Horon's method of environmental determinism). In the words of his memorandum to the Kedem Club, "This definition [of a national identity] is not outstandingly innovative: it is based on the principle of a person's right to define himself. This principle means that if you wish to know which nation one belongs to, go and ask him: if he says he's a Frenchman, you ought to believe him, since the right to determine this is exclusively his own."[183]

The Israeli public discourse is occasionally enlivened by journalistic quips that had Zeev Jabotinsky lived longer, he would today, on account of his secular liberalism and opposition, at least at a certain stage, to the removal of Arabs from Palestine,[184] be classified as a leftist and meted out the according treatment by public opinion.[185] In view of what has been established above—that post-Zionism straddles the line between "Canaanism" and Jabotinskian political philosophy—it is worthwhile, in concluding this section, to look deeper into certain central components of the latter and see how they manifest themselves in the post-Zionism of both generations.

Three strands of Jabotinskian thinking, to which we may apply the designations of positivism, legalism, and monism, become particularly pronounced upon examination. In brief, positivism meant conceptualizing Zionism as a struggle for Jewish revival without producing tortured ideological justifications for the Jews' right to Palestine, which was deemed beyond question; legalism meant opting for a legally binding acquisition of the entire Land of Israel for the Jewish people (including the possibility of tactically abandoning outposts and territories if clinging to them would interfere with this aim) against Labor Zionism's preferred policy of slow accumulation of faits accomplis; monism was formulated by Jabotinsky to mean that the Zionist struggle could not tolerate any ideological ambiguity, such as Labor's socialist inclinations, demanding instead that all efforts be concentrated on the attainment of a Jewish majority in Palestine under British imperial protection, to be followed by sovereignty.[186] After this objective was won, Jabotinsky continued, only then would there be room to work out the ideal social order for the Jewish state. Unsurprisingly, Jabotinsky's preferences tended toward a democratic-liberal one, though he did not rule out socialism outright.[187]

Viewed from this perspective, first-generation post-Zionism is simply the monism principle put into practice. Those among Jabotinsky's disciples who remained faithful to the liberal component of his legacy viewed the establishment of Israel as the end of the monist era and concluded that a democratic-liberal polity must come into being. While Zeev Jabotinsky did not directly claim that the establishment of a Jewish state *must* entail the end of Zionism, his son actually subscribed to this very notion. Together with his colleagues from the Hebrew Committee, Lamerḥav, and the Kedem Club, whose views on Jewish nationalism were significantly transformed under Horon's influence and by their American experience, he argued for a state that would not discriminate in favor of Jews. By advocating a policy of color-blind immigration matching the state's needs and the readmission of Palestinian refugees, he was ready to see Israel's Jewish "element" diluted. Second-generation post-Zionists similarly reiterate the call for the termination of Zionism once its goals had been achieved, though they, understandably enough, avoid invoking Jabotinsky.

Jabotinsky's legalistic outlook as the second element that underpins post-Zionism is expressed in the post-Zionist call (in both generations) for the adoption by Israel of international legal norms that would rid Israeli society of the instrumentalist approach to rule of law guided by tactical or ideological considerations, which Ehud Sprinzak termed "illegalism."[188] Consequently, if some territories are held in contravention of these norms, they should be abandoned. In contemporary Israel, second-generation post-Zionism sees such withdrawal as enabling the continued existence of the state, whereas those parts of the right that still deem themselves "Jabotinskian" interpret this step as a necessary price to pay for an international legal recognition of Israel's grip over other territories that are more important ideologically or strategically. Both are nevertheless ready to make major territorial concessions since, as explained by Baruch Kimmerling, "one assumes that the students of the school of Jabotinsky, who did not see settlement as the practical expression of Zionism, found it far less difficult to take such a step [of evacuating Jewish settlements] . . . than did the members of the Labor parties."[189] Kimmerling explains further that "this was consistent with the original ideology of Revisionist (and Political) Zionism, which downplayed the role of settlements per se . . . and emphasized more general political processes, which were seen as more crucial in determining the fate of the Jewish nation."[190]

The third Jabotinskian element, positivism, reverberates in Boas Evron's statement, uttered back in 1970, that "our existence . . . is justified because we exist."[191] These words echo Jabotinsky's reference, cited earlier, to the "crippled spirits" that make the Jews' unalienable right to the Land of Israel a matter of "investigation." The standpoint that upholds a liberal vision of an Israeli nationhood free of ideological "excuses" implies that Israel would not require any raison d'être beside the mere fact of its existence as the national state of the Israelis. Such a view has yet to be adopted by Israel's authorities, who as recently as 2013 in a response to a lawsuit brought by Uzzi Ornan to recognize the existence of the Israeli nation argued that "the identification of a national community does not depend on individuals' subjective determination" (*sic*!).[192]

"Canaanism" in a Regional Perspective

One of the criticisms directed at Baruch Kurzweil's analysis of the Young Hebrews was its narrow Judeo-centric focus that reduced the movement to an anomaly within Jewish intellectual history. Critics pointed out that Kurzweil took no notice of other nationalist-territorial ideologies analogous to "Canaanism" that competed with Pan-Arabism for the loyalty of the inhabitants of the Middle East.[193] Yaacov Shavit probably had this critique in mind when he included in his study a chapter on the Egyptian, Turkish, Syrian, and Lebanese varieties of territorial nationalism,[194] observing that "Canaanism" was "a Palestinian Jewish variation" thereof.[195]

Of the plethora of territorial nationalisms in the Arabic-speaking Middle East,[196] three ideologies in particular stand out as comparable to Hebrew territorial nationalism, due to matching principles and geopolitical outlooks. These are the "Phoenicianist" ideology in modern-day Lebanon, which imagines the Lebanese nation as non-Arab by origin and culture, and locates its golden age in the Phoenician period;[197] the Egyptian "Pharaonic" ideology, which by questioning the weight of Arabic and Islamic components in Egyptian identity seeks to ground it in Egypt's pre-Islamic past, whose most potent symbol is the kingdom of the Pharaohs;[198] finally, the "Pan-Syrian" ideology advocated by the Syrian Social National Party (Parti Populaire Syrien) established and led by Anṭūn Sa'āda, which is actually more "regional" than strictly statist-territorial.[199]

A central, albeit not exclusive, part in the formulation and dissemination of these ideologies was performed by members of ethnoreligious minorities in these countries, chiefly Christians of various denominations: Salāma Mūsa in Egypt; Anṭūn Sa'āda in Syria; Charles Corm, Charles Malik, Michel Chiha, and Sa'īd 'Aql in Lebanon. As demonstrated above, Horon considered the movements inspired by these ideologies a form of resistance by the "Arabianate" descendants of indigenous Hebrews to Pan-Arabist encroachment and oppression. Personal parallels can be drawn between the leaders of the Young Hebrews in Israel and their counterparts among the Arabic-speaking Middle Eastern territorialists. Thus, Horon's opposite numbers are arguably Salāma Mūsa in Egypt and Anṭūn Sa'āda in Syria, who both attempted to anchor their political ideology in a historical commemorative narrative meant to lend it credibility as historically "unavoidable" and more faithful to historical truth than the "fraudulent" historiography of Pan-Arabism. Yonatan Ratosh's counterparts would then be the Lebanese poets Sa'īd 'Aql and Charles Corm, who expressed their yearnings for a Christian-Lebanese national renaissance in lyrical language: French in Corm's case, and literary Arabic or colloquial Lebanese in the case of 'Aql.

All these movements shared central characteristics derived from their common intellectual origins and historical trajectory, first of which would be their nearly coterminous emergence in the first half of the twentieth century. This period was characterized by the arousal of popular interest in the Middle East's pre-Islamic past, prompted by groundbreaking archaeological discoveries like the finding of Tutankhamun's tomb in Egypt in 1922 or the unearthing of the Ugarit texts in Syria in 1929 (whose function as the impulse for Horon to start rethinking Hebrew ancient history was discussed in chapter 1).[200] These discoveries made local golden ages accessible to counterbalance the Pan-Arabist outlook, which legitimized the idea of an Arab national unity by relying above all on linguistic criteria. Middle Eastern territorial nationalists, much like the "Canaanites," were compelled therefore to sideline the suprastatist language-based conception of nationality, in some cases going as far as to advocate the adoption of the local colloquial as the language of the national culture. Some, like Salāma Mūsa in Egypt and Sa'īd 'Aql in Lebanon, even propagated the replacement of Arabic script with a Latin-based alphabet that was ostensibly more suited to local phonetics (an idea entertained by the Young Hebrews and Zionist Revisionists as well with regards to Hebrew). Promoters of Middle Eastern territorial nationalisms frequently resorted to forms of environmental determinism, which saw national identity as a fusion of attachment to the native soil with local language and culture. The "Pharaonic" nationalists regarded the Nile valley as the cradle of Egyptian identity, while the "Phoenicianists" made the Lebanon mountain range their primary symbol. Last, as observed by Yaacov Shavit, most of these movements exhibited a dialectical tension between liberal impulses and inspiration by the French pre-Second World War radical right.[201]

The Pan-Syrian nationalist Anṭūn Sa'āda's arguments mirrored most closely the ones promulgated by Horon and his fellow "Canaanites." First, Sa'āda's map of "Greater Syria" matched almost exactly Horon's map of the Land of Kedem;[202] only the ethnonyms derived from this political geography diverged, with Horon's "Hebrews" becoming in Sa'āda's parlance "Syrians." Second, above any other territorial nationalism in the Arabic-speaking Middle East, Sa'āda's ideology was strictly secular and inclusivist, disregarding any confessional differences between the inhabitants of "Greater Syria" and inviting them all to partake in his political project.[203] Finally, like Horon, Sa'āda interpreted Pan-Arab nationalism as a front for Islamic expansionism. Thus, in three major areas, "Canaanism" and "Pan-Syrianism" overlapped: in environmental determinism, in territorial outlook, and in geopolitical regional analysis.

"Canaanism" and "Phoenicianism," too, shared a political lexicon, with terms and notions used by the one side reflected in corresponding terms employed by the other. The ancient Hebrews were paralleled by the ancient Phoenicians; modern Hebrews were paralleled by modern Lebanese or Maronites (a suggestion implicit in certain forms of "Phoenicianism" was that a "genuine" Lebanese was a Maronite, or at least a Christian); Canaan was paralleled by Lebanon; finally, the demonic role of Zionism in "Canaanism" was mirrored, starting from the 1920s, in "Phoenicianist" nationalism by Pan-Arabism. Some "Phoenicianist" thinkers adopted an environmentally deterministic perspective on nation formation.[204] Also noteworthy is the fact that the Lebanese public intellectuals and writers who spearheaded "Phoenicianism" were usually well-to-do urban dwellers who espoused a national-liberal outlook in the socioeconomic sphere befitting their class interests.[205]

These significant areas of convergence cannot, however, obfuscate the deep disparities that remained between the Young Hebrews' ideology and those of its counterparts all around. Actually, sometimes what seemed a point of agreement turned out to be a bone of contention: to take just one example, both Horon and Sa'āda believed that the Umayyad caliphate was more Syrian than Arabo-Islamic.[206] However, for Sa'āda, the Umayyad period (661–749 CE), when Damascus was the caliphate's capital, was Greater Syria's historical golden age, whereas Horon, as demonstrated in previous chapters, regarded the Islamic age as history's nonnational age par excellence. Another example is the affinity with French culture and nation-building methods shared by "Canaanites" and "Phoenicianists." Yet, whereas the former remained opposed to European colonialism in the Levant (though less so in North Africa), some circles among the latter were explicit in their support for a continued French presence in the Eastern Mediterranean.[207] The "Phoenicianists'" attachment to French culture and language, which for some of them (mainly those based in Beirout) was the main medium of literary and political expression to the exclusion of Arabic, cast doubt upon their claim to Lebanese "indigeneity" and detached them from the majority of the Lebanese Arabophone public, including Christians. Modern Hebrew was for Horon and the "Canaanites" a symbol of the Hebrew nation's national and cultural rejuvenation; literary Arabic, conversely, contained for the "Phoenicianists" a potent irredendist threat, while the Lebanese colloquial never underwent such language corpus-planning and status-planning processes as did Hebrew to be considered fit for a unique language of a territorial-national renaissance. Hebrew tongue had no rivals for its role as the medium of Hebrew national resurgence in the "Canaanite" outlook; "Phoenicianism" treated language with greater suspicion, with the Beirout Lebanese nationalist intellectuals, such as Corm, opting for French and the mountain-based "Phoenicianists," like 'Aql, electing to express themselves in literary Arabic or colloquial Lebanese.

Differences between "Canaanism" and "Phoenicianism" also arose due to the latter's more prominent status in Lebanese public life. "Phoenicianist" ideology was consequently more complex and intricate than the more dogmatic "Canaanism" in Israel, with pronounced variances concerning the envisaged future of Lebanon between the Francophone Beiroutis and the Arabophone mountaineers, not least concerning Lebanon's relationship with Zionism and Israel.[208] Some Muslim Lebanese intellectuals were also involved in the propagation of "Phoenicianism," having adopted Ernest Renan's thesis that the entire population of the Levant migrated from the Arabian Peninsula, which effectively "arabized" the ancient Phoenicians.[209] "Phoenicianism" was also increasingly out of touch with the majority of Lebanese Christians, who prioritized good relations with the Muslims and the Druze to cordial relations with Israel as a condition of Lebanon's continued existence. Cultural outlooks diverged between the "Phoenicianists" and the "Canaanites," the former's Christianity making the ancient Phoenicians' paganism a rather unsuitable material for a national myth of origins. Thus, the poet and businessman Charles Corm insisted that Baal worship—for him, the ancient Phoenicians' "national" cult—was actually an early form of monotheism,[210] while Horon regarded Hebrew paganism as the source of a national vital energy that in modern times justified a secularist outlook and social order.

Lebanese "Phoenician" nationalism compared to Hebrew nationalism possessed a very strong religious component, its "inclusivism" by and large not extending beyond Lebanon's various Christian denominations. During the 1950s and 1960s the Young Hebrews in Israel and Horon in the United States were ready to overlook this quite major point for strategic reasons. Indeed, the paeans to Lebanese religious particularism appended to Ratosh's *1967—Uma Hal'a?*, let alone the explicitly Islamophobic statements (on Christian grounds) by the "Friends of Lebanon" from New Mexico reproduced in the memoranda and newspapers of the Levant Club, make for quite an odd reading compared to the Young Hebrews' aggressively secularist platform. Horon, who among the Young Hebrews was most actively involved in creating what he called "some kind of Lebanese anti-Arab and pro-Israeli trend among the Amero-Lebanese,"[211] was best aware of these specifics. This is why he grasped the counterproductivity of approaching the still very much sectarian Maronites, who often borrowed the jargon of American religious right, with ideas directly inspired by French secularism, and was willing to compromise on otherwise fundamental matters, such as separation of religion and state. As we saw in chapter 1, he chided both the Young Hebrews and the Kedem Club for their unwillingness to tone down their demands on these subjects.

Although Horon commented that the ideology of Pierre Gemayel's Katā'ib seemed to him perfectly compatible with that of the Young Hebrews,[212] he also admitted on a number of occasions that Lebanese nationalism, oblivious to the subtleties of identity dilemmas in the Yishuv and Israel, was more "Zionist" than "Canaanite."[213] For example, it appreciated no meaningful distinction between Hebrew, Jew, and Israeli—a difference to which Eri Jabotinsky devoted quite a long disquisition cited above. Furthermore, the writings of leading Maronite nationalists show that their enthusiasm for Zionism and Israel was not at all that unequivocal. Many of them supported a form of alliance between the two states, either explicit or clandestine,[214] harboring reservations all the same about Israel's policy and its geopolitical orientation. In 1955, the Lebanese intellectual Charles Malik wrote that if Israel wanted to move from functioning in wartime conditions to a regional peaceful coexistence, it needed to reform profoundly its own raison d'état.[215] Malik, Michel Chiha, Philip Hitti and Sa'īd 'Aql deplored the establishment of Israel as a Western-colonialist entity within the Middle East that threatened Lebanon's existence, although 'Aql switched to a pro-Israeli position during the Lebanese civil war in the 1970s.[216] In addition, the "Phoenicianists" limited their geopolitical outlook to Lebanon alone and seldom considered "Greater Syria" or "Levant" a geohistorical unit to identify with. Anṭūn Sa'āda, who did just so, accordingly branded "Phoenician" nationalism sectarian and isolationist.[217] Hence, Yaacov Shavit concludes that whereas the "Phoenicianists" were the Young Hebrews' potential allies, the Pan-Syrianists could not but become their sworn enemies.[218] Indeed, the Young Hebrews' very few references to Pan-Syrianism are universally hostile: Horon mentions in passing "the Greater Syria dream,"[219] which he ascribes to Syrian Christians, while Ratosh makes it plain that Anṭūn Sa'āda led "an Arabianate fascistic unity party."[220]

These differences cannot be explained merely by political disagreements. A more profound divergence, based on historiographical outlook, existed between the Young Hebrews and their "Arabianate" counterparts. All of them, in one way or another, used environmental determinism to formulate their visions of history and politics. However, none of the states surrounding Israel was coping with mass immigration on the scale of Israel, which as a result faced the problem of a glaring discontinuity between the golden age and the present, and the ensuing problem of a feeble state legitimacy. The Arab states' population was imagined to have survived on its native land throughout the centuries, with unbroken roots reaching back to history's obscurest moments; therefore, the foundational myth used by the Arabic-speaking counterparts of "Canaanism" was a genealogical myth of continuity and not an ideological myth of discontinuity. This, in consequence, located such ideology as Lebanese "Phoenicianism" or Egyptian "Pharaonism" intellectually closer to Zionism and may explain why no cooperative links between the Young Hebrews and the "Arabianate" territorial nationalists in the Land of Kedem were established in any meaningful form or to any long-lasting impact. Neither was such cooperation facilitated by Horon's insistence that "[t]here are no Phoenicians—only seagoing Hebrews: there is no Phoenician language, it is just good plain Hebrew."[221] While "Phoenicianists" did acknowledge the affinity between the language of the Phoenicians and ancient Hebrews, which for some of them justified collaboration with the Zionist movement, it is difficult to imagine any of them accepting Horon's disqualification of the ethnic denominator "Phoenicians" as foreign (Greek) and agreeing to call their presumed historical ancestors "Hebrews" instead.

Conclusion

What Counts as a Failure?

In the foregoing discussion of Adya Horon's historiography and its meaning in the context of mid-twentieth-century politics of Israel and the Middle East, I have argued that the "Canaanite" insistence on grounding local political identities in a territorial framework constituted a liberal alternative to Zionism's politicization of ethnoreligious communal identification. It now remains to examine why the Young Hebrews were ultimately pushed to the margins of Israeli sociocultural life and Horon's interpretation of the Hebrew past was never accorded the scholarly standing he believed to be its due.

Some of the authors cited in this book have attempted to explain the Young Hebrews' demise both as an organized movement and as an intellectual option in the Israeli "marketplace of ideas" between the 1950s and the 1970s. Yaacov Shavit considers the "Canaanite" "escape from Judaism" a failed radical nativist reaction to the blurring of the classical Zionist dichotomy of Jew/Hebrew that took place after 1948.[1] This position was thoroughly and convincingly refuted by Boas Evron, who demonstrated that "Canaanism" actually peaked *before* 1948.[2] James Diamond arrives at a more nuanced explanation for the Young Hebrews' failure, yet one that betrays his incomplete awareness of the role of Horon's historiography in the ideology's structure, coupled with his tacit belief in the plausibility of the Zionist commemorative narrative:

> Ultimately ["Canaanism"] represented a metamorphosis of Jewish identity into something that *had no defined historical precedent* or definable content. In other words, when

> "Canaanism" sought to act on the secular impulses that were so clearly manifested in early Zionism and to actualize them by severing the tie to the Jewish past, *it had no available model or context upon which to predicate the new secular self-understanding it asked of its adherents. The appeal to a prebiblical "Hebrew" past was more a fillip than a plausible option* . . . Secularism as the upshot of modernity and the Emancipation could be appropriated by Jews as individuals but there was as yet no way for Jews to do this meaningfully as a collective entity *without some recourse to the Jewish past and the Jewish religion*, as the Zionist experience shows. "Canaanism" held out a transformation into an unknown world *with no real past to structure its vision*.[3]

Earlier in his book, however, Diamond attempted to balance the social function of "Canaanite" and Zionist historiographies, asserting that the latter was more compelling to the Israeli Jewish public due to it ultimately hinging on Jewish tradition, not because of its scholarly "truthfulness":

> [I]t is not that "Canaanism" rests on a historiography that is debatable or even spurious; it is that this historiography has not been socially validated and accepted as normative by a body politic . . . *[I]t may not be any more or less debatable than the reconstruction of Jewish history that Zionism offers.* But it has been around for less time and . . . it is much less compatible with the theistic norms of Jewish religion than is Zionist historiography.[4]

Diamond does not stop at his otherwise entirely correct assertion that "Canaanism" was above all a modern nationalism—by excluding Horon's vision of the Hebrew golden age from his analysis of the movement, he makes it a nationalism of the present and denies it the historical depth it so clearly possessed. As a result, both Diamond and Shavit remain within the boundaries of Baruch Kurzweil's paradigm that reduced each and every form of inside intellectual protest against the Jewish spiritual legacy to the self-destructive "antivocational" tendency of the secularized and modernized Jewish culture. By reading "Canaanism" as a derivative of Zionism, they find themselves confining the phenomenon represented by the Young Hebrews within the philosophical and temporal limits of Jewish identity and history. Such methodology not only collides head on with the Young Hebrews' own stated principles, leading Shavit and Diamond to take up the morally indefensible position of "knowing better" than the objects of their analysis who they "really" were; it also leaves them with no choice but to take sides—even if implicitly—in the dispute between Zionism and "Canaanism."

This book refuses to take for granted the teleological perspective of either ideology. Multiple nations face more than one choice in their path to self-definition; eventually one prevails and the others survive, if at all, only as reminders of the victorious vision's potential vulnerability. I see no compelling reason to regard the conflict between Zionism and "Canaanism" as anything else but a case of this model, in which the former managed to win a mass following, both in the Diaspora and within the Yishuv, while the latter did not. James Diamond rightly points out that the causes of this outcome combined internal weaknesses with unfavorable external circumstances, advising that "[w]e need to locate the sources for 'Canaanism's' failure to challenge Zionism and develop into a serious alternative to it both in the 'Canaanite' ideology and in the historical and social realities of the society to which it was addressed."[5]

Before discussing those causes, I wish to restate that I regard as fundamentally correct the basic "Canaanite" contention that a new Hebrew national identity evolved in Mandatory Palestine in the first part of the twentieth century.[6] However, what the Young Hebrews apparently failed to grasp was that the mere existence of a Hebrew national identity did not by itself validate the "Canaanite" version of Hebrew nationalism or its historical commemorative narrative, leading to a natural detachment from the Jewish background. Some Palestinian native-born Hebrew-speakers, such as Boas Evron, were ready to go that far, seeing in "Canaanism" a long-sought answer for a semiconscious intellectual hunger that would give intellectual shape to the Hebrews' intuitive feeling of disengagement from the Jewish Diaspora heritage.[7] However, "[r]ootednedss in the land and in the language is itself no guarantee that a cultural revolution will transpire":[8] even before 1948 the overwhelming majority of Hebrew youth, to whom the "Canaanite" appeal was addressed, did not find the Young Hebrews' ideology either intellectually eye-catching or practically useful in helping to dispose of the British Mandate. "Canaanite" understanding of Hebrew nationhood diverged significantly from

Hebrew youth's self-perception, which remained in manifold ways tied to Jewish identity, history, and legacy, as traced in chapter 4 by Oz Almog in his analysis of the "New Jew's" sociocultural characteristics. These characteristics the "Canaanites" based in Israel could only frame in an "either-or" binary relation with the putative characteristics of Hebrew nationhood,[9] despite Horon's insistence in his letters from the United States that Jewish history remains an inseparate part of the Hebrews' background.

The title of an article published by 'Amos Ḳenan in 1949—"Hebrews and not Sabras"[10]—captured this incongruity between young Hebrews and the "Young Hebrews." In it Ḳenan accused the first generation born to Jewish immigrants to Palestine of being spellbound by the Diaspora value-world of Zionism and suggested that the resultant crisis-consciousness among the Sabras could only be overcome by adopting the broad territorialist Hebrew outlook, which will finalize the transition from a hybrid Sabra identity to a full Hebrew native identity. Ḳenan thus revealed that the "Canaanites" had some sense of their appeal being directed at a basically nonexistent target audience of anti-Zionist Hebrew-speaking youngsters whose identity was shaped exclusively by the landscape and language of Canaan.

In fact, the Hebrew identity, inasmuch as it had developed, was significantly less self-confident and at the same time much more "Jewish" than the Young Hebrews were willing to admit. Several decades later, Ḳenan recanted his arguments, admitting that he had come to realize the incompatibility of the values of the "1948 generation" with the values propagated by the Young Hebrews, which seemed simplistically rigid against the complex interplay of Jewish and non-Jewish elements of Israeli identity.[11] Other members of Ḳenan's generation viewed things similarly; for example, the Israeli sociologist Dan Horowitz confessed:

> I remained indifferent to Canaanism's nativist motif that disregarded our being children of immigrants . . . We did not require the Canaanite ideology . . . since the Zionist ideology—in its version that was palatable to us—regarded Hebraism [*sic*] as the realization of Jewish auto-emancipation and the expression of its transition from a dispersed community to a nation. This way we could share the Hebrew experience and the Erets-Israeli sentiment . . . without implying any denial of the Yishuv's bond to the Diaspora.[12]

The writer Hanoch Bartov, who, though born in Mandatory Palestine, hailed from an observant family, denounced the "ideal Sabra" image as a "narcissist mythology," stating that in his eyes the real "story . . . [was not of] the imagined Sabra Hebrew which is dissimilar to the Jew, but the true one—the story of new immigrants, their children, and their children's children."[13] Bartov did not make it clear though whether the sociocultural construct he criticized had *never* existed (meaning that the "ideal Sabra" image was completely false in his eyes) or whether it *did* exist, but did not encompass all native-born Hebrew-speakers like himself (meaning that the image was only partially adequate).[14] What is certain is that the awareness of being Jewish was central to Bartov's experience as a Hebrew-speaking native of Palestine.

The generation of Ḳenan, Horowitz, and Bartov was dubbed the "1948 generation," to emphasize the formative role the war for Israel's independence played in shaping their collective identity. Many of them perceived the war as a critical breaking point, following which the native Hebrew national ethos, such as had developed by this time, went into swift and sharp decline, with the denominator "Hebrew" becoming complementary for "Jew" rather than a rhetorical or moral opposite.[15] The deaths of approximately six thousand Israeli fighters in the war left the generation demographically decimated. Referring to the damage done to the Hebrew feeling of national selfhood by such a proportionally high number of casualties, 'Amos Ḳenan described it somewhat insensitively as the Israeli equivalent of the Holocaust.[16] Another prominent member of the 1948 generation, Uri Avnery, stated bluntly that native Hebrew culture was "murdered" that year.[17]

The Holocaust and its aftermath were also important factors in suppressing Hebrew national identity.[18] Hanoch Bartov vividly described his experiences as a Jewish Brigade soldier in postwar Europe, when he came to realize the dimensions of the catastrophe,[19] stressing at least twice that this realization caused him "to tear away from my heart any remaining Canaanite strings, such as had existed within me."[20] Viewing the emotions described by Bartov from a somewhat different angle, Avnery, who as a Jewish child in Weimar Germany witnessed the rise of Nazism, branded it quite derisively a "Jewish reaction" thriving on "bad conscience" awoken by the destruction of the Diaspora so reviled heretofore in mainstream Zionist discourse.[21] The fact that this reversal of attitude toward the Diaspora hit the "Canaanites" hardest shows that Hebrew youth remained insensitive to the delicate nuances separating the Zionist "negation of the Diaspora," which was in principle hostile to Jewish nonsovereign existence abroad, from the "Canaanite" rejection of Diaspora influences *within* Hebrew society, while remaining declaratively indifferent to the Diaspora itself.

Interestingly, the Young Hebrews and their associates were quite slow to recognize the ominous implications of the Holocaust becoming one of the key symbols of the emerging Israeli nationhood[22] for their ideology. As it was taking place, Yonatan Ratosh explicitly denied any connection between the Holocaust and the formation of the "Canaanite" movement: "The Committee for the Consolidation of the Hebrew Youth does not address you since so-and-so Jews were exterminated in such-and-such Diaspora, and the Yishuv's relative weight has increased by such-and-such degrees in the arithmetic of the Jewish global dispersal."[23] Ten years later, Eri Jabotinsky was also unable to apprise the increasingly dominant weight of Holocaust memory in Israeli nation building, with the scandal over reparations from West Germany raging around: "The *only* point concerning the Jewish past which *may* still arouse some Israelis to passion is Germany. But then it is with many a problem of *personal vengeance*."[24] At later stages, when the Holocaust had made itself evident in Israeli public life, the Young Hebrews loudly protested against the instrumentalization of this "manufactured trauma" in entrenching the siege mentality of Israeli society by emphasizing, among other things, that the Nazi atrocities were not limited to Jews. For this they incurred the wrath of a society accustomed to an ethnoparticularistic view of the Holocaust.[25]

The next crucial factor in the stifling of Hebrew national identity was the massive immigration to Israel between 1948 and 1952 of approximately 700,000 Jews, which relegated native Hebrews to the position of a small and mostly powerless minority. Various statistics concerning the growth of the Yishuv up to 1948 unequivocally prove native Hebrews' numerical insignificance, a situation that 1948 and its aftermath only aggravated. Ron Kuzar writes that back in 1918 the Jewish population of Palestine numbered 85,000, among them 30,000 native Hebrew-speakers;[26] thirty years later, according to Yaacov Shavit, the figures had risen to 716,000 and 253,000 respectively.[27] Bartov cites calculations by the historian Emmanuel Sivan that demonstrate that in 1948 less than 40 percent of the male adult population of the Yishuv was native-born;[28] the sociologist Oz Almog puts their numbers at a mere 20,000.[29] The calculations of a contemporary observer show that by late 1951 Israel's population had already numbered 1,400,000

Jewish people, of whom only 340,000 were native-born, and of the latter only 100,000 were adult.[30]

These statistics, however inconsistent, tend to agree on two counts: that, as observed by Oz Almog (and cited in the previous chapter), the native Hebrews' symbolic power far exceeded their numerical strength; and that, despite their cultural predominance in certain spheres of the prestate Yishuv, after 1948 they were too few and weak to resist the suppression of their national identity by the Zionist leadership (and probably reluctant to do so altogether). Uri Avnery grudgingly admitted his generation's defeat in words attesting to bitter nostalgia, uttered on the eve of the fortieth anniversary of Israel's establishment:

> A new culture emerged in the country since 1948, no longer "Hebrew" but "Israeli" . . . It absorbed some of the traits of the preceding "Hebrew" culture, emptying them of their true content and turning them into caricatures . . . A new chapter began approximately forty years ago. It must be approved of, as any living, emerging, and evolving culture deserves of approval. Yet it must be understood that this is not a continuation of what was beforehand.[31]

This admission by Avnery concedes that an Israeli culture shaped by national sovereignty is dissimilar from both traditional Jewish culture and the Hebrew national culture formed in the pre-1948 stage of nonsovereignty.[32] "Israeli culture," writes Diamond, "developed in ways quite different from what Ratosh [or] Kurzweil . . . expected . . . A transformation of consciousness did occur in Israel, but not the one Ratosh sought."[33] The establishment of Israeli statehood accelerated the processes of ethnogenesis, which, while subsuming Hebrew nationalism, created a wholly new national identity—yet linked in myriad ways to its past legacy—that contained both secularism and religious sentiment in a tense balance. Gideon Katz explains that

> . . . Hebrew culture—the culture that took shape during the period of the pre-state Yishuv—was not able to create a consistent religious tradition, nor was it able to acquire the authority necessary to replace religious tradition. These problems were not resolved within the framework of Israeli culture, that is, within the culture that developed after the

> founding of the state. Indeed, new and difficult problems then arose. Israeli culture is comprised of segmented subcultures that together do not compose a whole, unified cultural matrix.[34]

If this matrix was to persist, a recourse to a premodern religious communitarian legacy was in a way prefigured in the Zionist project with its concessions to traditionalism. The path paved by the Young Hebrews led in an opposite direction by delineating the most radical proposal for a reformulation of social relations between modern state and society on the one hand and premodern legacy on the other (which, in the Israeli case, was particularly diverse). Such a proposal at its core demanded that Jews cease being Jews (or limit their understanding and experience of Jewishness only to religious or folkloristic aspects), which was not in any form palatable either to the absolute majority of pre-1948 Hebrews or post-1948 Israelis. The actual dynamic was the reverse: the Israeli nation's collective values, symbols, experiences, and historical consciousness are in a state of a perpetual drift away from the elements that constituted Hebrew national identity, shifting from a focus on "Israel" as a modern and rational political structure with known borders to a focus on the "Land of Israel" as an ethnoreligious mythical and inherently vague symbol.

The social scientist Baruch Kimmerling dates the beginning of the growth in tribal-like ethnocentricity in Israeli society to the first decade of the state's existence. The 1967 war and the subsequent takeover by the descendants of the Revisionist movement of state power in 1977[35] only speeded up a "continuous Israeli shift toward a less tolerant and more nationalistic interpretation of Zionist ideology."[36] Polls conducted in the 1960s and 1970s, coinciding with the curbing of the Young Hebrews' organized activity, confirmed that by this time their ideal of a secular-territorial nation functioning in an inclusive democratic system detached from primordial criteria of identity had become irrelevant to the overwhelming majority of Israelis, most of whom chose to identify as "Jews."[37] "In answer to the question—'Are we in Israel an inseparable part of the Jewish people throughout the world or do we belong to a separate people formed here—Israelis?'—96 per cent of the religious, 87 per cent of the traditional, and 76 per cent of the nonreligious in [a] 1974 study identified with 'the Jewish people' throughout the world."[38] Another mid-1970s' poll showed that support for "Canaanite"-style secularism in Israel oscillated around 5 percent,[39] a situation that even the most outspoken post-Zionists were unable to reverse.

Summarizing this state of affairs James Diamond points out that "an Israeli nativism has certainly developed since 1948, but it is a nativism in which the Jewish component has persisted with increasing strength,"[40] and therefore "an elite, if it is truly to function as such, cannot be in opposition to the norms and values of the society of which it is a part. Because the 'Canaanites' were by their own definition anti-Zionist, they were in effect cut off from their society, unattached to its basic assumptions and so devoid of cultural influence."[41] Consequently, the Young Hebrews' principled position precluded them from being anything other than a counterelite, whose importance, as Diamond acknowledges, lies not in their numerical strength or political agency, but in the "intensity and consistency" of the questions raised and issues tackled.[42] Thanks to that, the debate over the "Canaanite" challenge never disappeared from Israeli public discourse, even if Horon himself vanished from popular memory.

The divergent development trajectories of Israeli society and the "Canaanite" ideology show that the post-1948 facts on the ground defeated Horon's idealist environmental determinism. The Young Hebrews, who refused to abandon their assumption that artificially created colonial boundaries could not compete with the allegedly fixed laws of political geography embodied in the geophysical unity of the Land of Kedem, were uniquely slow to realize that the Israeli nation, though forming in, and identifying with, the "circumscribed" borders of the "Zionist statelet," nevertheless developed an authentic national outlook and identity (Uzzi Ornan accepted this as late as the 1990s, by which time he gave up on the "Canaanite" historical vision).[43]

Moreover, when put into a comparative perspective, the Young Hebrews' belief in the artificiality, and therefore the untenability, of the Land of Kedem's post–World War I internal borders as sources of national identification appears to rest on flimsy foundations. Several political scientists and scholars of nationalism have demonstrated that the geographical delimitations made by colonial powers in actual fact not infrequently correlated to preexisting divisions within the colonized societies.[44] This ensured the postcolonial survival of these borders, notwithstanding their supposed artificiality and external imposure, and their transformation into foci of national sentiment and allegiance. Therefore, Israeli national identity, as well as other state-formed identities in the Land of Kedem, are distinct and authentic, despite the internal tensions that threaten from time to time to rip them apart, as demonstrated by the Lebanese (1958, 1975–1990) and Syrian (1976–1982, 2011–) civil wars. The Young Hebrews, transfixed on Pan-Jewish or Pan-Muslim "macro"-identities, missed the fact that "micro"-identities, even if colonial in origin, can be equally vigorous.

Throughout their writings, the Young Hebrews, and Horon above all, displayed discomfort with the persistence of postcolonial identities and geopolitical structures in the Land of Kedem and the larger Middle East that appeared to defy environmental determinism. From a postcolonial perspective, their ideology can be seen as a discursive attempt to chart a path out of the vexing paradox of Israel's colonial origins and postcolonial contemporaneity. The role and meaning of imperial and colonial experience in modern Jewish history have been scruitinized in recent years by critical historians and social scientists, with many interpreting Israel's settler-colonial character as a fundamental structural feature of the society and the state.[45] Others emphasize the differences between "typical" settler colonialism and Israel's unique features, such as serving as a haven for a persecuted minority with no allegiance to any overseas imperial power, or the Yishuv's sustained attempt to reach economic autarchy that ruled out exploitation of "native" labor.[46] Others yet examine how colonialism, anticolonialsm and postcolonialism interact in the ongoing process of Israel's state and nation building.[47] Regardless of specific opinions on Israel, this scholarship highlights that Jews' entry into modernity, however defined, took place not so much in the context of West European state-nationalism as in the imperial (within Central and Eastern Europe) and colonial (in North Africa and the Middle East) contexts,[48] meaning that "beginning in the nineteenth century and continuing well into the twentieth, the empire became a privileged site for working out the meaning and the contours of Jewish political identities,"[49] including the Zionist one. Adopting the praxis and discourse of settler colonialism—a colonialism that aspires not to exploit the "natives" but to eliminate and supplant them either physically or politically[50]—led to the development within Israeli society of what David Ohana calls "the Crusader anxiety," the fear that Israeli nation building amounts to a modern repetition of the medieval Crusader state building in the Levant.[51] The Sabra consciousness of committing a violent conquest of a land in which they are not genuine natives is what, according to 'Amos Ḳenan's article cited above, differentiates them from the "true" Hebrew natives and is the source of their spiritual crisis.[52]

In that sense, Zionism as seen by the Young Hebrews is indeed a settler-colonial movement with no chances of long-term success. Hence, the discursive differentiation they made between Sabra identity and Hebrew identity was at bottom a matter of life and death for the latter. The Young Hebrews' national foundational myth therefore functioned on account of its radical difference to the Jewish-Zionist one as an instrument of what Lorenzo Veracini calls "self-indigenizing," a perpetual process of developing a native identity: "Being the subject of indigenising processes is not the same as being indigenous, and one type of being rules the other out; this is why settlers can never become 'natives.' The question then is how to be efficient self-indigenisers. The fundamental, that is, the foundational stories must change: a degree of indigeneity, even if not unqualified indigeneity, can be acquired."[53] The unstated realization that the farthest the Hebrew nation can achieve on its self-indigenizing path is to become "creole" rather than as native as the Arab Palestinians is the source of the Young Hebrews' intense interest in cases of "successful" settler colonialism, such as the North American one,[54] and Horon's close attention and sympathy to the pieds noirs in French North Africa.

The parallels between the pieds noirs and Israeli Jews have, unsurprisingly, attracted the interest of scholars of settler colonialism. Joshua Cole mapped the common to the triangular relationship between native Algerians, pieds noirs and metropolitan France, and to the uneasy balance between their counterparts in the Eastern Mediterranean: Palestinians, Jewish settlers, and the British, respectively.[55] Such comparative perspective is valid as long as the Yishuv is conceptualized as exclusively Jewish and Zionist. However, in light of the "Canaanite" emphasis on the Hebrews' nativeness to the Land of Kedem that goes hand in hand with an entrenched hostility to both Zionism and British colonialism, I believe that a more informative comparison would be to the Afrikaners of South Africa and their position vis-à-vis the British on the one hand and the native Africans on the other. A detailed investigation into the sources and transmutations of Afrikaner nationalism is beyond the scope of this book; what is significant at present is that both its similarities and the dissimilarities to "Canaanite" Hebrew nationalism are quite striking.

Afrikaners, as much as the pieds noirs and the Hebrews (in the "Canaanite" perspective), developed their own national identity over a couple of centuries, starting from the Dutch and Huguenot merchants who began settling in the Cape Colony in the late seventeenth century.

The Afrikaners' feeling of being native to South Africa was rooted in an attachment to the land and in their creole language (Afrikaans), whose role in the consolidation of Afrikaner ethnonational identity was not unlike the Hebrew language's role in the formation of the Yishuv as a separate ethnocultural body. In the nineteenth and early twentieth centuries, Afrikaner identity was further consolidated by the protracted conflict with the British colonizing power, whose highlights were the Great Trek to South African hinterland that started in 1838 and the two Anglo-Boer wars, as well as the economic deprivation in the wake of those wars that created a large impoverished class of mostly Afrikaans-speaking Whites. Symbolically significant is also the fact that Afrikaner "moment of redemption" came, like Israel's, in 1948, when the National Party rose to power and within a few years converted the British Dominion of South Africa into a republic and instituted Apartheid.

Thus far, however, the similarities go. The institutionalization of Apartheid brought to the fore the racist side of Afrikaner nationalism. Seeking not integration but separation under White patronage from the Blacks and Asians, Afrikaner nationalism used racial rather than territorial or environmental determinism to codify skin color hierarchies (whereas the Young Hebrews argued that Arabs' "inferiority" was cultural and political, never genetic). The numerical ratio of Afrikaners, British and non-White nations in South Africa also meant that, unlike initial Zionist settler colonialism seeking the elimination of the natives, White colonization of South Africa represented exploitation colonialism that sought to police the presence of the indigenous people while exploiting their labor instead of removing them.[56] Thus, the mass presence of a Black majority in a White minority-run political structure generated a demographic angst among the Afrikaners, who justified both Apartheid and economic exploitation of the Blacks as necessary bulwarks against being overwhelmed by statistics. They also developed a self-justifying "Zionist" myth as pioneers in an empty land that only subsequently attracted Black migration.[57]

Another striking difference between Afrikaner and Hebrew nationalism was the former's strongly religious character, based on a fundamentalist interpretation of Calvinism, which portrayed the Afrikaners as "God's chosen people, destined to bring civilisation and Christianity to the southern tip of Africa."[58] And while religion nourished Afrikaners' sense of historical mission and common historical origins, they had no local equivalent of the Hebrew ancient history to develop a master commemorative narrative legitimizing their forward-looking political and cultural vision.[59] In a sense, Afrikaner nationalists had no "Horon" of their own (although, arguably, they had a "Ratosh").

If the Afrikaners had developed any form of an "anti-colonial" sentiment, it was akin to nineteenth century creole nationalism in America, which overthrew European overseas control in order to pursue exploitation colonialism without sending the profits to the mother country.[60] Afrikaner anticolonialism, directed against the British Empire, was most strongly expressed in semimilitarized radical organizations that in the 1940s not only started to threaten the Afrikaner establishment ascending to power but also served as a conduit into South Africa for Nazi ideas.[61] A Hebrew-Palestinian parallel to this phenomenon would be the LEHI underground: a radical anti-British organization, which at an early stage of its activity made two failed attempts to reach understanding with Nazi Germany, was perceived as a menace by the Yishuv's leadership, and of all clandestine organizations in the Yishuv was under the strongest influence of "Canaanism."

A central feature of Horon's methodology, in both its historiographical and geopolitical aspects, and at the same time its largest weakness, is his reliance on deterministic analytical mechanisms. This tends to spill over into all-out essentialism, such as his insistence that modern nations and primordial denominations or ethnocommunities are, by their very nature, mutually exclusive.[62] Craig Calhoun defines essentialism as "a reduction of the diversity in a population to some single criterion held to constitute its defining 'essence' and most crucial character . . . often coupled with the claim that the 'essence' is unavoidable or given by nature."[63] Anwar Abdel-Malek understands essentialism as an analytical attitude whereby "an essence should exist . . . which constitutes the inalienable and common basis of all things considered; this essence is both 'historical,' since it goes back to the dawn of history, and fundamentally a-historical, since it transfixes the being . . . within its inalienable and non-evolutive specificity."[64]

In true positivist fashion, Horon arms himself with what he identifies as the stable rules of historical and social development, which loom large over his otherwise thoughtful and complex exploration of ancient Hebrew history. His trust in the joint influence of space and time on sociocultural *longue durée* processes renders his writings highly teleological, if not outright "religious,"[65] which leads him to downplay or ignore facts that seem to contradict his macrohistorical vision. Such an approach certainly did a disservice to the Young Hebrews' political vigor: having persuaded themselves that history was deterministically on their side, in a sense they fell into a political complacency, relying on history's "stable laws" to "do the job" in their stead. A political movement that implicitly claims its prognoses will be realized anyway, no matter what obstinate reality says, cannot be overly attractive to activists.

Moreover, the Young Hebrews tend to persist in a kind of cognitive dissonance: for although Horon admits that a "false myth" should be replaced by a "better myth" (worked out by himself), this does not lead him to question the factual veracity of the historical elements he uses to construct his Hebrew national counterhistoriography. He maintains that it is enough to apply "logical" argumentation grounded in "unbiased" facts of history in order to deconstruct "false" identities (such as the "Arabianate") and to release their carriers from the inhibitions imposed by "regressive" primordial social categories, such as the ethnocommunity or the *millet*. This trust in the power of rationality as an instrument of national liberation is all the more striking given that, on the face of it, Hebrew nationalism is by itself no more "rational" than its Zionist and Pan-Arabist rivals.

Horon's approach exemplifies what the introduction referred to as "category error," that is, the application of one's own categories of analysis to a reality that might resist them as irrelevant or misplaced. As explained by Laurence Silberstein, category error means placing "the practices [of the phenomena analyzed] in the wrong category or discursive framework," mistakenly assuming that "they share the same interpretive premises as their . . . critics."[66] We can only surmise that when decyphering the Ugarit texts under Virolleaud in the early 1930s, Horon was so struck by his discovery of an ancient Hebrew civilization that he became convinced that once historical reality (and the political conclusions arising from it) are thoroughly explained to the Jews and Arabs of the Land of Kedem, they will cast aside the "backward" system of sociocultural relations in which they linger and replace it with a more "advanced" structure grounded in "objective" historical truth. He did not sway from this conviction, rather unwilling to recognize the possibility that the past that was of direct relevance to him as an ideologue of the Hebrew national revival might appear shadowy or wholly unappealing to those inhabitants of the Land of Kedem who identified with a different national vision, however "false."[67] In the one instance he did seem to apprehend this particular weakness, he actually suggested to take up violent and potentially destructive measures, such as "immigration, re-education, expulsion, massacre, re-settlement, or whatever other combination of means," to beat down Pan-Arabism.[68]

This unusual candor compels us to look deeper into the nature of the liberalism the Young Hebrews claimed to profess. The urge to put to practice progressive social principles within the framework of a nation-state established by settler colonial migrants from Europe means that "liberalism" in Israel is inherently circumscribed by its historical circumstances and political context. Crucially, in the history of the Zionist movement, the only consistently liberal platform was the one developed by the Revisionist movement, which the "Canaanites" carried over to Hebrew nationalism. The late nineteenth-century European liberalism that Jabotinsky tried to infuse the Jewish national movement with took shape on the uniquely modern crossroads of post-1789 sensitivity to individual and civil rights in Europe with "scientifically" rigid racial and class hierarchies dictating the practice and ideology of colonialism in Africa and Asia by the same European powers that at home ostensibly took the lessons of the French Revolution to heart.[69] The modernity conundrum of liberal rights with strings attached by the republican ideal was solved through a claim made by imperialist powers, including France in North Africa and Great Britain in India and the Eastern Mediterranean, that they ruled over the "natives" in the name of secular and rational values of technical and moral progress and development. Such self-imbibed sense of "historical responsibility" toward societies occupying "lower levels" of sociocultural development (measured by supposedly objective and rational benchmarks of empirical science) ended in justifying each and every act of colonial coercion, violence, and atrocity. Imperialism outside Europe and national statehood within Europe were the two polygons in which European modernity tested its own principles of enlightenment,[70] leading often, in the words of Yaacov Yadgar, to "pervasive xenophobia and continuous bloodshed [due to] conflation of territory, sovereignty, and identity."[71]

The limits of liberal tolerance toward premodern corporate identities undermining the republican body politic were defined as early as in 1789 by the Revolutionary aristocrat Stanislas de Clermont-Tonnerre, who advocated to the French National Assembly "accord[ing] everything to Jews as individuals" but "refus[ing] everything to the Jews as a nation." He cautioned that French Jews "should not be allowed to form in the state either a political body or an order. They must be citizens individually . . . If they do not want to be citizens, they should say so, and then, *we should banish them*."[72] "Fraught with contradictions since its emergence in eighteenth-century Europe," writes Shira Robinson,

> liberal thought has always been predicated on exclusions of gender, religion, race, and class in the name of public order, while the idealistic pursuit of the "common good" has served regularly to justify coercion against individuals or groups who do not fit this definition. The point is not simply that liberal ideas have produced a wide range of political forms, but that their very oscillation between freedom and compulsion, universalism and particularism, has helped to fuel Western imperial conquests in Asia, Africa, and the Pacific, where the same tensions have infused the techniques and rationalizations of rule.[73]

Liberal-colonial sentiments of benevolence toward the Arab natives were not foreign to Zionist political mythology and discourse, with their insistence on the blessings of European technological modernity that Jewish settlers were bringing to Palestine, alongside feelings of contempt and superiority.[74] A liberal sensitivity also manifested itself in the Zionist objective of attaining a Jewish numerical majority in Palestine prior to determining the country's poltical structure, although, when in the 1930s the attainment of this goal appeared beyond immediate reach and Nazi persecution became a pressing factor, some Zionist officials advocated a Jewish minority dictatorship.[75] Claiming to act as the political representation of the entire Jewish nation, the Zionist movement was able to uphold at least on the discursive level its democratic credentials as a speaker for the majority of Palestine's either actual or prospective inhabitants. The same maneuver was performed by the Hebrew Committee of National Liberation, which argued that Hebrews in Palestine and Hebrews in exile, taken together, are able to put forward a democratically valid claim for the entirety of Palestine.[76]

Unlike the Zionists, the Hebrew Committee was ready to accept Arab Palestinians as members of the Hebrew democratic body politic and equal participants in Hebrew sovereignty. Neither they, however, nor the Young Hebrews were ready to tolerate any Palestinian corporate identity that would express Arab national aspirations within the Hebrew political structure and space. Horon's plan for a federal Kedem Union approved of cultural pluralism to accommodate "Arabianate" ethnoreligious communities, yet the vision was overall unwelcoming to deterritorialized Muslim and Arab identities. Those were pictured according to the liberal-colonial worldview as underdeveloped and requiring a Hebrew benign hand to acquire the social and cultural traits permitting the full enjoyment of liberal democracy.

A final observation would be that "Canaanism" can be considered a failure only when judged by its own stated program. However, its indirect influence on Israeli sociocultural thought and politics is evident even today in certain spheres (this is what Diamond's "latent Canaanism" suggests). First among them is post-Zionism, whose connections to "Canaanism" and to Horon in particular were explored in the preceding chapter and elsewhere.[77] Eri Jabotinsky's intellectual and personal indebtedness to Horon stands out in this connection, but the list of Horon's other "influencees," nearer and farther, is impressive by any standard. These include not only Yonatan Ratosh, Aharon Amir, Esra Sohar, and Hillel Kook, four individuals in whose dealings Horon was deeply involved personally, but also names that come to mind less immediately, such as Abraham Stern; Boris Souvarine; Yirmiyahu Halpern; Jacques Soustelle; Israel's senior naval officers who studied in Civitavecchia; members of La Renaissance Hébraïque, Hebrew Committee of National Liberation and Levant Club; a number of Ḥerut politicians interested in Horon's advocacy of the pied noir cause (like Knesset member Avraham Drori,)[78] and other adversaries of Pan-Arabism from Morocco to Lebanon, who took the impulses provided by Horon beyond the borders of Israel and disseminated them in their own circles. Horon usually did not bother himself with claiming credit, professing in one of his letters his persuasion that Hebrew nationalism will in the end win hearts by slow and steady work: "We [need to] have the patience to wait until somebody else picks up some of our ideas (because our ideas are unavoidable . . .); this . . . was my own experience all my life, from Bergson to Begin."[79] When asked by his daughter why he so greatly admired Napoleon despite his ultimate personal and political defeats, Horon reportedly replied that the measure of a man was the breadth of his vision, and not the practical failure.[80] *Toutes proportions gardées*, I believe the same applies to Horon himself.

Perhaps a few words are in order here about the life-long relationship between Horon and Ratosh. Its occasionally tumultuous nature is evidenced by both eyewitnesses and correspondence between the two (see chapter 1), revolving mainly around the role each of them played in shaping "Canaanism" and the differences among them in the interpretation of ancient Hebrew history sustaining "Canaanite" politics. Yehoshu'a Porat's biography of Ratosh tends to play down Horon's influence by limiting it to clarifying and sharpening notions and ideas preexisting with Ratosh,[81] although Ratosh himself famously described his meeting with Horon as a "liberating shock,"[82] albeit only after Horon's death. Ratosh's achievements as poet and intellectual aside, it is quite obvious that his historical thinking was in many ways more simplistic than Horon's. The latter, for instance, would hardly have condoned the sweeping assertion made by Ratosh that *any* utterance in the Bible contradicting the monotheistic spirit of Judaism *must* be treated as an authentic residue of pre-Judaic Hebrew paganism and therefore trustworthy and genuine evidence of a bygone age.[83]

This could have easily soured Horon's contacts with the other Young Hebrews, such as Aharon Amir, who continued to consider Horon a Diaspora Francophile Jewish intellectual. Horon's different biographical background and role within "Canaanism" (a latecomer to Israel rather than a native Hebrew, a professional historian rather than writer or artist), as well as his uneasy character meant that he could find precious little common language with the other Young Hebrews. At the end of the day, Horon remained an external observer of Israeli society, whose accelarated desecularization and re-Judaization since 1967[84] was undoubtfully a cause of anxiety for him in his final years, an anxiety moderated only by his deterministic faith that laws of historical development will see Hebrew national idea triumphing.

All this said, the foregoing observations are by no means intended to justify a reverse historical determinism: namely, that the present dominance of Zionism (and, for a certain period contemporaneous with Horon's lifetime, of Pan-Arabism) suggests that the factual historical dynamic proves the inherent "correctness" of Jewish nationalism. To accept this would be tantamount to supplying Zionist ideological framework with a retroactive justification that echoes its teleological character. The fact that for the present time Zionism prevailed, and "Canaanism" did not, does not in itself "acquit" the former or "condemn" the latter in the eyes of history.

I believe, moreover, that the vulnerability of Zionism is implied in its currently confident position in the public life of Israel. In the first two decades of the twenty-first century, the illiberal processes that Baruch Kimmerling cautioned against in the mid-1980s[85]—perhaps unaware that he was repeating the Young Hebrews' grim predictions from the early 1950s—have drastically sped up. Uri Ram, who identifies ideologically with second-generation post-Zionism, anxiously observes that Jewish-Israeli national identity, constituted on the grounds of politicized religious sentiment, is increasingly being privileged in the public and statutory spheres over democratic principles.[86] Yaacov Yadgar's leading argument is that the ongoing politicization of Jewish identity, as practiced in the State of Israel, cannot be but inherently illiberal due to its ethnonationalist character, which distills this identity from a mixture of religious and biological criteria.[87] And indeed, since 2001 the Likud governments (whose abandonment of the liberal aspects of Jabotinsky's legacy in favor of Judeo-centric ethnoreligious chauvinism is meticulously traced by Colin Shindler[88]) have enacted a string of legislative proposals with the purpose of elevating the Jewish ethnonational character of Israel over its rump civic-liberal features and of cementing the Jewish collective dominance over the political system and resource allocation. As a result "the emphasis on Israel's Jewish identity is so great so as to sideline the state's commitment to democratic principles."[89] All this is accompanied, in Shindler's words, by "a dilution of intellectual thought on the right . . . coloured by a crude populism."[90]

The ongoing Israeli-Palestinian conflict, especially after the collapse of the Oslo process in 2000 ended promises of liberalization in the spheres of politics and societal values, provides a contextual explanation for this. But beyond that, this tendency, which enjoys broad legitimacy among Jewish Israelis, exposes a suppressed feeling of insecurity over the existence of the state. Such existential insecurity may point to the faltering of Israel's settler-colonial project, whose most blatant features have been transferred since 1967 beyond the Green Line,[91] and which expresses itself in the repeated demand made by the Israeli political class for an affirmation of Israel's "right to exist as a Jewish state" externally and internally.[92] Internally, Israeli Jews' "demographic angst" bespeaks in Yaacov Yadgar's eyes a lack of any substantial positive content to secular Jewish nationalism apart from maintaining a numerical Jewish majority defined in "objective," "biological" rather than in moral-spiritual terms.[93] With the deepening of Israel's existential crisis, a new positive content or inspiration for a uniquely Israeli nationhood may one day be rediscovered in the writings of Adya Horon and Yonatan Ratosh.

Appendix A[1]

The Hebrew Movement—An Outline

By Horon

. . . , the Mediterranean, January 1947

Written by special commission of the Hebrew Committe [*sic*] of National Liberation, Paris-Washington, the then political representative abroad of the National Military Organization ("Irgun"), by A. Horon ('Adyah Ḥoron).

Historical Introduction: The Ancient Hebrews

In ancient times the Hebrews had their own territory, their frontiers, their place under the sun. This Hebrew territory was called most often "The Country" (ha-Aretz, in Hebrew), also "The Hebrew Land" or "Heber" (Ever, in modern Hebrew), or "The Land of the River" (Ever ha-Nahar, in Hebrew)—a land stretching from Egypt to beyond the Euphrates River.

The western part of this country, along the Mediterranean, well-watered and thickly-populated, was by far the most important part of the Hebrew land. The overall name of this Mediterranean region is Canaan, in Hebrew, or Phoenicia, as the Greeks later called it. Canaan, or Phoenicia, therefore, is almost synonymous with "The Hebrew Land" and designates the essential western half of it.

Canaan, the Hebrew land, comprised not only the territory of the Kingdom of Israel, but also the territories of all the other Hebrew or Canaanite kingdoms, such as Edom, Juda, Moab, Tyre, Hamat, etc.

The Hebrews, including the Canaanites, had a common civilization and a common language: "the tongue of Canaan," as the Bible puts it, or Hebrew. Canaanite, Phoenician and Hebrew are equivalent terms designating a single language.

For several thousand years the Hebrews were a powerful people, including not only the clans and tribes of the League of Israel but also many other clans and tribes, city-states and kingdoms, such as the sea-going Phoenicians, the glorious Tyrians who were the founders of the overseas empire of Carthage.

When their day was done, after long and bloody wars, the Hebrews lost their sovereignty and the very soil of their homeland.

******

I.

Past and Present Facts

1. Who Are the Jews?

The Jews are a relatively late phenomenon, and their very name appears late in Hebrew history. They are the followers of Judaism, members of the Jewish church-community; they were recruited not only from the ranks of the former tribe of Juda, but also among the various Hebrew groups and non-Hebrew peoples in and around the Mediterranean basin.

Judaism, which was formed only on the eve of the Christian era, never coincided with a territory and never sought to be a nation. In contrast with Hebrewism (the Hebrews and their land), Judaism is a church and a religion, and Jewry is not a nationality nor a territorial and political entity. Jewry, in scientific terms, is a *caste*: a caste of religious rather than "racial" origin.

Not all the descendants of the ancient Hebrews entered the Jewish caste; likewise, not all the Jews descend from the Hebrews. But it must be stressed that Judaism has taken over and preserved most of the surviving Hebrew traditions and played a major part in the beginnings of the modern Hebrew revival by transmitting these ancient national traditions to the new Hebrews of the 20th century.

In the Middle Ages, Judaism discharged a peculiar economic function throughout the Mediterranean area, and, although persecuted by Christendom and Islam, was tolerated by the feudal world which derived more profits than disadvantages from its existence.

In modern times, the Jewish caste declined while sovereign territorial nations were growing. During the 19th and 20th centuries, it broke up and actually ceased to exist as a distinct social body. We are now witnessing the last chapter in the history of Judaism: the more or less complete, more or less final assimilation of the Jews, in one part of the world, as well as their physical extermination under the pretext of "racialism," in another part of the world.

2. *What Is Jewry Today?*

Today, Jewry is in the process of complete disintegration. Between one quarter and one third of the Jews in the world have been annihilated; the remainder are either being absorbed and assimilated by foreign nations or pushed farther down the road to physical and spiritual destitution, outlawry and ultimate destruction. On the other hand, a parallel process of reconstruction is gaining momentum every year: the vanguard of the Hebrew rebirth in Canaan is consolidating itself and becoming the spearhead of a new nation: the Hebrew nation, already deeply rooted in its own soil.

What, therefore, are Jewry and Judaism today? It is a fact that most Jews do not really practice Judaism, as a religion, any longer—in spite of which they are still encompassed by the "Jewish question."

If Judaism is taken to mean world Jewry, then it is only an empty word, for there exist no real bonds between the Jews of the world, no geographic bond, no common language, no common ideal leading to a common goal. They have not even a common understanding of their plight and of the broad interests they might share. The anti-Semitic persecutions constitute neither a positive definition nor an effective bond.

The Jewish communities and groups in the various continents have needs and aspirations which are far apart, and their attitude toward the Hebrew rebirth differs widely from group to group, from country to country. While most European Jews, for instance, aspire to be repatriated and to become Hebrews, most American Jews, despite the great interest they show in the Hebrew movement and the help they give it, do not in actual fact join its ranks and do not intend to join, at least for the time being.

To sum up: Judaism today is nothing but a religion observed by a minority of Jews. Jewry, as such—that is, as the sum total of the Jews in the world—has become merely an abstract notion.

3. *What Are the New Hebrews?*

The modern lack of understanding, the ignorance of true facts relating to Hebrew history and present-day Jewry, and the current use of distorted, improper terms and concepts are symbolical of the utter confusion which prevails in the minds of Jews and non-Jews alike all over the world. This confusion is one of the main obstacles to a constructive solution both to the "Jewish question" and to a problem still greater, the Hebrew rebirth in the frame of a Near East renaissance.

It is therefore essential to define in the clearest way what are the new Hebrews and who are the people claiming membership in the rising Hebrew nation.

"The Hebrews" comprise today:

a. The Hebrew settlers already rooted in the Hebrew land, forming there the nucleus of a reviving nation,

b. Those who want to join the Hebrew nation through an act of free choice and will,

c. Those who are in need of a Hebrew republic, and who must join the Hebrew nation as their only means of physical and spiritual salvation. This category includes mainly the hundreds of thousands, indeed the millions of oppressed or uprooted Jews and so-called "Non-Aryans," for whom there is no more room in the world outside the Hebrew nation—since nationhood is the law of the modern world. For every man and woman in this category the liberation of the Hebrew land and the creation of a Hebrew Republic is a question of life and death.

The difference between the three categories, however, is purely academic. Whether forced by circumstance or impelled by conviction, or simply because they are Hebrews by birth, the Hebrews share a common interest which makes them a tangible national body.

This community of interest is the achievement of the territorial possession of their country and its political liberation. This interest, shared by all the Hebrews, is at the same time the necessary condition of their national and individual survival.

4. The "Jewish Question" and the Near East

A. The Jewish Minorities

Whether they practice the Jewish religion or not, the Hebrews have hardly any positive interest in common with the "Jews"—that is, with those who consider themselves Jewish merely in the so-called "racial" or the denominational sense. In other words, the Hebrews have little in common with the Americans, the Englishmen and others of Jewish *origin* or *religion*, insofar as these latter desire to remain and succeed in remaining what they are today: members of other nations, foreign to the Hebrew nation.

Between the Jews and Hebrews as defined above, there is no strong bond of common interests. Yet there would be no necessity of conflict, if the two terms were as clearly separated as are the realities which they define. In that case, there might even be a common meeting ground: the Jews cannot dwell in peace where they are unless the Hebrews in exile leave and go to their country on the eastern shores of the Mediterranean; and the revival of the Hebrews cannot come about unless they relinquish their present status as Jews and renounce the claim to a double nationality.

B. The Failure of Zionism

The failure of Zionism, so obvious today, is due to the constant confusion of the two terms and of the two conceptions—Hebrew and Jew. This movement allows its members to be, at one and the same time, both English and Hebrew—which is nonsense. Dr. Weizmann, as the leader of the Zionist movement and a subject of His Britannic Majesty, has been the living symbol of this confusion and of the resulting impotence.

The time has come to put an end to a situation which permits every foreigner of Jewish descent or religion to speak in the name of the Hebrews. No other nation would permit anything of this kind. No American would permit a German to pose as a spokesman of the Americans under the pretect [*sic*] that both their countries are mostly protestant and include individuals of the same "race."

The Hebrew movement, which comprises all persons who are Hebrews or intend to become Hebrews, but who are not necessarily all of Jewish origin or religion, is the only legitimate expression of the rising Hebrew nation. It should be able to speak in its own name, through its own spokesmen who claim no allegiance to any foreign power.

C. The "Arab League" Fiction

Zionism, which was founded on the false assumption that Jewry is a national entity, has become an unworkable compromise between the superstitions of a "racial" or religious Judaism and the realities of the Hebrew rebirth in the Hebrew land. Zionism, however, is not the only misconception which stands in the way of the Hebrew renaissance and prevents a positive solution of the Near Eastern problem.

Pan-Arabism, and its political exponent, the so-called Arab League, has even less right to existence than Zionism. Pan-Arabism is based on the recent and erroneous assumption that all or most peoples speaking dialects derived from Arabic form a single homogeneous Arab nation or group of nations. In actual fact, the Arab League expresses mainly the selfish interests of an exceedingly small minority of feudal landlords and petty tyrants in the pay of British imperialism. Some of them are mere quislings, and some, inspired by Islamic superstitions, dream of restoring a fanatical and anachronistic Islam. In any case, few of these men are of Arab origin, none of them care for a genuine emancipation of the Arabic-speaking peoples, and all of them live as parasites by exploiting the ignorant Moslem masses, which they purport to represent, masses which have never had a chance to express their own wishes or to promote their own interests.

D. Enslavement of the Near East

Not only the Hebrew land, but the whole Near Eastern area of which it is a part, is directly or indirectly dominated by British colonialism, occupied by British forces, enslaved by British quislings and misled by British puppets. These puppets, these quislings are recruited from the Jewish Agency or the Arab League and represent nothing but two equally pernicious fictions—Zionism and Pan-Arabism.

In the present set-up, the masses of people directly and vitally interested in a positive solution of the Near Eastern problem are the only ones who are never consulted or considered. These masses comprise, on the one hand, the Hebrews of all categories, and on the other, the various local Near Eastern communities, Moslem, Christian, Jewish and other. There is every reason to believe that the Hebrews will find ways to work in accord with these communities to the common benefit of the Near East, of which the Hebrews are an essential part—provided that the relations between the Hebrews and their Near East neighbors are based on the complete and genuine independence of the Near Eastern countries and on their progressive development.

II.

The Fight for Freedom and Rebirth

1. The Hebrew Resistance

For many years now, the more active elements in the Hebrew land and in the Hebrew movement have realized that neither Britain, as a mandatory power, nor a Zionism protected by the British, should be trusted with ensuring even the most elementary conditions necessary for the Hebrew rebirth, or with seeking a constructive solution to both the Jewish question and the Near Eastern problem.

During and after the war the British dropped their last pretenses [*sic*] of being honest trustees for Hebrew interests and for the interests of other peoples native to the colonial or semi-colonial Near East. On the one hand, they have tried to enslave, and have succeeded in enslaving, through the agency of a small minority of quislings and political parisites [*sic*], the popular masses of the countries now grouped in the so-called Arab League. On the other hand, they have fought by the most inhuman means the Hebrew repatriation from Europe, and have thereby caused, in complicity with the Nazis, the wholesale slaughter of at least two thirds of European Jewry—millions of innocent men, women and children—who relied on the false promises of their alleged "friends" and "allies" of the Western world.

During the war, the Hebrew armed forces, underground, semi-legal, or officially recognized, —numbering many tens of thousands of fighters and grouping in their ranks most of the able-bodied Hebrew men in Canaan—accepted a truce with the British tyrants in order to fight the most dangerous common enemy, Nazi Germany. The Hebrew armed forces played a major part (proportionately a much greater part than the English soldiers) in repelling Rommel, in spearheading the Free French re-conquest of Syria and Lebanon, and in smashing the Nazi-organized rebellion in Iraq. This fight carried Hebrew units all the way from the Levant to Libya and Greece, to Tunisia and Italy, and even to the Rhine. The reward of the Hebrews has been the slaughter of their relatives in Europe, the herding of the survivors into concentration camps even after the end of the war, and more than that, political treachery in the Hebrew land.

While endeavoring to stamp out Hebrew repatriation efforts, the British are trying—although without success—to crush Hebrew resistance and to instigate attacks on the Hebrew population by Moslem mercenaries, most of whom are in no sense Arabs, even though Britain parades them as such. Above all, Britain tries, by partitioning an already partitioned Palestine, by manouvering [*sic*] the puppets of the Arab League, into positions of control and by appeasing a defeatist Zionism with promises of a tiny Jewish Ghetto, to ensure once and for all British imperial domination in the Near East, at the cost of the vital interests and of the very lives of all Near Eastern peoples, including the Hebrews.

*2. The Irgun and the Hagana**

Contrary to British propaganda and the allegations of some frightened Zionists, there are no "terrorists" in Palestine. There is no "minority of extremists" trying to impose its will on a dissenting population. Events have proved that a great majority of the local population, whatever their origin and religion, are in sympathy with the fighters for Hebrew liberation and back them either actively or passively, despite the tremendous pressure exerted by British military terror, by British intrigue, by the unceasing attempts of Britain to "divide and rule"—and also despite the subservience of many elements in the British-sponsored Jewish Agency and in the British-owned Arab Higher Committee of Palestine.

If civil war has not broken out between the various sections of the population and between the two main groups of Hebrew armed forces, the Irgun and the Hagana, it is only because the great majority of fighting men in the Hebrew land do not want to fight each other.

---

*"Irgun Tsvai Leu'mi" in English means "National Military Organization." "Hagana" means "Defense."

They are willing, rather, to fight shoulder to shoulder to throw out the common British enemy.

There are only two differences between the less numerous and more active Irgun and the larger Hagana, whose units are being kept in reserve:

a. The Irgun is organized for attack on the aggressor, whereas the Hagana, grouping a good half of the able-bodied Hebrew population, is mainly an organization for self-defense.

b. The higher-ranking officers of the Hagana are controlled by the Jewish Agency, whereas the independent Irgun recognizes as its political representatives the independent Hebrew Committee of National Liberation.

3. The Hebrew Committee of National Liberation

The Committee was constituted in Washington in 1944 in order to give some kind of expression to the Hebrew national movement and to prepare the ground for a political leadership in the fight for freedom and rebirth.

The Hebrews have as yet no recognized status. Before the creation of the Committee, many millions of men, cut off from other human communities by the bestiality of their enemies, the treachery of their "protectors" and the desertion of their "friends," had no one to represent them, to voice their needs, to formulate their claims, to guide their efforts toward liberation. They had nothing that could confer a meaning on their immense sacrifice and suffering, a meaning that only a *flag* can give.

For, all the slogans of the United Nations, unfortunately, did not apply and do not yet apply to the Hebrews. They are among the national groups which the Big Three ignore. The Big Three ignore their distress and even pretend to ignore their very existence.

From whom comes the mandate to the members of the Hebrew Committee of National Liberation? First of all, from themselves. The Hebrew Committee members declare that they belong to no nation but the Hebrew nation now being reborn. The first right of every man is to represent *himself*.

Furthermore, there exist today in the Hebrew land and abroad, millions of people whose only hope of physical and spiritual salvation is the establishment of a Hebrew nation and Republic, of which they would become part. Those are Hebrews in the making. Foreign oppression has closed their channels of self-expression. They can only be represented by those among them who dare raise their voice, unfurl their flag, and fight.

It must be stressed again that the Hebrews in Canaan are subject to the most brutal foreign occupation, and that the organs of Zionism do not express and cannot express the Hebrew national movement. The Jewish Agency leaders, in particular, cannot be considered other than as puppets, forced to take their orders from the mandatory power, whether they like it or not.

III.

Toward Hebrew Independence

1. Program of the Hebrew Movement

The Hebrew movement, of which both the Irgun and the Hebrew Committee are only expressions, has an immediate aim which can be summed up in one sentence:

> THE LIBERATION OF THE HEBREW NATIONAL TERRITORY OF ALL FOREIGN OCCUPATION AND THE SPEEDY REPATRIATION OF THE LARGE NUMBERS OF JEWS AND SO-CALLED "NON-ARYANS" WHO WANT TO BECOME HEBREWS AND THUS TO ESCAPE THE PHYSICAL AND SPIRITUAL DESTRUCTION WHICH THREATENS THEM IN THE NEAREST FUTURE.

The Hebrew nation cannot be reconstituted under the "protection" of foreign bayonets. Likewise, the solution of the internal problems of the Hebrew land and state concerns only the two elements which are directly involved:

a. The natives and residents of this land, whatever their "race" or religion.

b. The persons to be repatriated, and other immigrants.

One thing is clear: the Hebrew movement strives neither for a "Jewish Palestine" nor for a "Moslem Palestine." It strives to build *one* nation, *to create one single Republic*—the Hebrew Republic. This Republic will accept all those individuals who want to be part of it, and will grant a status of complete civil equality to every group, religious or other, that would prefer to retain its moral, social, cultural autonomy.

2. The Hebrew Republic and Its Territory

The Hebrew movement does not recognize the past partitions of the Hebrew country, that is, of the country on both sides of the Jordan, and will never accept the present situation, illegally enforced by a treacherous "mandatory power" which divides the land into Trans-Jordan and Palestine west of the Jordan. The Hebrew country on both sides of the Jordan corresponds to the minimum territorial program of the Hebrew national movement, for the following chief reasons:

a. The harnessing of the Republic, without which this Republic will never be economically viable and politically independent.
b. Nothing less than this territory is required to provide for:
    1. the solution of the "Jewish question" by means of Hebrew repatriation, and
    2. the welfare of the present water-resources of the Jordan river-basin is a vital prerequisite for a normal development of the Hebrew and future inhabitants of the land, without resorting to the preposterous scheme which plans evictions and *forced* transfers of population.
c. This minimum territory, corresponding very roughly to what is today called Palestine and Trans-Jordan, is already the result of a partition operated upon the territorial body of the historic Hebrew land, ancient Canaan. In fact, the minimum territory of the Hebrew Republic represents only the southern half of ancient Canaan.

The Hebrew movement is therefore committed to fight not only any further partition of Palestine, in whatever shape and under whatever pretenses [*sic*], but also to fight the continuation, as well as the formal or *de facto* recognition of Trans-Jordan's status as a separate political body, either under British mandate or as a fictitiously "independent" state. The Hebrew movement will fight to the bitter end, against whatever array of foes, for the integrity of this minimum territory, without which the Hebrew Republic will remain but an empty dream.

3. The Need for a Provisional Hebrew Government

The Draft Constitution of the Hebrew Republic can be prepared only by a completely independent Provisional Hebrew Government, and converted into a final Constitution only by the free approval of the people of the land, including both the people already settled there and those to be immediately repatriated—no discrimination being made on grounds of "racial" origin or religious denomination, and no qualifications required except loyalty to the Hebrew Republic and a minimum amount of cultural and political education.

Obviously, the Provisional Hebrew Government must and will represent a combination much broader than the Hebrew Committee and the Irgun of today. The Provisional Government must comprise spokesmen of all the Hebrews in the country and abroad, resident on the land or wishing to be repatriated. These spokesmen can and should belong not only to the Jewish denomination, but also to other religious communities—Christian, Moslem, etc. All members of this Government will work on a footing of complete equality for the liberation of the common fatherland and the revival of its glorious civilization. Together, they will lay down the foundation of a common Hebrew Republic.

The British, their quislings and their puppets are trying hard to stamp out by a propaganda of lies as well as by sheer violence the rising tide of the Hebrew movement, and to strike deadly blows at the well-organized and seasoned fighting forces of the Hebrews. Events are developing fast, Zionism is falling apart, and the way may soon be clear for the creation of the Provisional Government.

This Government answers an urgent need. It should not be a mere "government in exile." It should be a Government of all the forces striving for the rehabilitation of one of the oldest countries and cultures in the world, of one of the greatest nations in [history]: Canaan and the Hebrews. It will be, in part, an Underground Government, fighting side by side with the men which it must lead to victory; and, only in part, a Government in Exile, negotiating abroad with friendly powers and organizing the migration of the Hebrews back to the homeland—an armed migration if need be.

Appendix B[1]

Adolphe Gourevitch
Associate Professor,
The Asia Institute, New York

Community Center
270 W. 89th St.,
New York, N.Y.
November 23, 1952

Pan-Arabism

The claims of Pan-Arabism rest on the following assumptions: the unproven statement that there exists a solidly "Arab" world, stretching from the Atlantic to at least the borders of Persia; the argument that this area is Arab because its people are allegedly Arabic-speaking; or, which is a quite different argument, because they are overwhelmingly Moslem. And thus, playing on both these unrelated assumptions, Pan-Arabism tends to fade into Pan-Islam—swallowing up half of Africa, all the Middle East, much of Central Asia, Pakistan, Indonesia and what not.

The picture is vague—may be purposely so. There is great danger in this vagueness, which allows public opinion to play with fire, instead of learning the true facts.

One should remark that this vague picture of an "Arab World" is of quite recent origin. Until the 19th century, people were conscious of the presence and importance of the Moors in the West, in what was known as Barbary—and of Turks, Levantines, Egyptians and Arabs in the East, in the Ottoman Empire. Even in Arabi[c] usage itself, and in Arabic literature until recently, the word "Arab" was reserved for such tribes and individuals who were, or claimed to be, of Arabian origin. But these true Arabs (chiefly nomadic Bedouins) were, outside Arabia proper, only a small minority of limited importance.

Pan-Arabism was first born in some of the romantic notions of 19th century Europe. Oddly enough, the great French scholar and writer Ernest Renan (who started the game of putting the Biblical Hebrews in Bedouin garb) played father to Pan-Arabism: oddly enough, i.e., considering present-day relations between France and the Arab League.

But the real promoters, the political promoters of Pan-Arabism were the English in the 20th century. Suffice to mention the Oxford school and the Colonia[l] Office, Lawrence of Arabia, the Hashemite kingdoms sponsored by London, the Saudi kingdom sponsored by the English administration of India (and now taken over by some American oil interests), and last but not least, the Arab League itself, initiated by none other than Mr. Eden.

Thus Arab "nationalism," of which we hear so much, is a misnomer. It did *not* originate in any national movement of Arabia, of Arabia proper, or of people who are, or think of themselves sincerely as Arabs, as *ONE ARAB NATION*. If we want to understand the true meaning of Pan-Arabism and of its political exponent, the Arab League, we have to realize first of all the basic facts of a vast geographic area, the very vastness and diversity of which precludes any such facile description as that of an "Arab World."

Let's call it instead, tentatively, the world of *NEAR EAST AND NORTH AFRICA*.

This immense area forms a natural and geopolitical unit, comprising all the southern half of the Mediterranean sphere and stretching from the Atlantic to the mountains of Asia proper, that is to Armenia and Western Iran. Southward, this area stretches across the Sahara toward what is known as Black Africa, as far as the Upper Nile and Ethiopia. Thus defined, the area is twice larger than Europe, and almost as large as North America. Its strategic importance is crucial: it lies in the center of the continents and the major seas of the Old World.

On the whole, the Near East and North Africa are underpopulated—60–65 millions conservatively, of whom the majority live along the Nile and its tributaries, or in the coastlands of North-West Africa, or in the narrow stretch of the Levant coast, including chiefly Israel and Lebanon. In these lands along the Mediterranea[n] however, the density of population is fairly high—especially so in Egypt.

All in all, the regional contrasts are very conspicuous. To feel these contrasts, it is enough to enumerate the four chief regions into which the area may be subdivided:

1. North Africa to the west of Egypt;
2. The Nile basin, including Egypt, the Anglo-Egyptian Sudan, Ethiopia;
3. The Arabian Peninsula—practically a desert, but a desert that contains both the symbols of original Islam and the oil wells of ARAMCO;
4. The Levant—with the foreland of Israel and Lebanon and the hinterland of Syria, Jordan and Iraq.

The history of the area, and of all its regions, may be described as one of past greatness, of utter decay in recent centuries, and—in some few parts—of present-day attempts at revival.

Past Greatness: Proceeding from east to west, it is enough to mention the names of Babylon and Assyria, thus evoking the ancient civilization of the Mesopotamian Semites; the name of Canaan, the biblical and classic civilization of the Hebrews or Phoenicians (these two terms cover in fact a single reality, a single society and language); the name of Pharaonic, pyramid-building Egypt; and, in most of North Africa, the names of the Libyans and Moors, the oldest indigenous white men of Africa, who are none else but the Berbers of today.

The Arabs came in much later, especially in the early Middle Ages, and after the first spread of Islam lost most of their historic importance. The medieval greatness of Oriental Islam was due chiefly to Syrians, Egyptians, Persians and Tur[ks,] not all of them Moslem, and mostly not Arabic-speaking. As to the grandeur of Moorish civilization, to which Europe owes so much, its centers were in North Afric[a] and in Spain; its builders in all fields of endeavor were chiefly Berbers, often Jews, almost never Arabs.

The recent phase of decadence—which, however, has lasted for several centuries—can be summarized as the decay of the Ottoman Empire, the enfeeblement of civilization, the disappearance of national conscience, the dying out of man himself, the *progress of the desert*.

Finally, if we may speak with some hope of a modern revival, it is so far only in a few lands closest to the Mediterranean, such as French North Africa, Israel an[d] Lebanon. It should be noticed that both the tremendous increase in population in these countries (as well as in Egypt) since the 19th century, and the first foundations of modern civilization there were brought about not by any Arab revival—but to the contrary, by the cooperation of non-Arab peoples, the peoples of northern Africa and Israel and Lebanon, with settlers who came from overseas to develop their new homelands.

Thus, it is hardly fair, and highly misleading, to dismiss the French venture in North Africa as sheer colonialism, or imperialism.

One should even say that the chief imperialistic threat to the peoples dwelling south and south-east of the Mediterranean comes precisely from the Arab League, from its shallow and aggressive Pan-Arabism. In fact, it is aggression wanting to impose the will of one section, the Arabs or self-proclaimed Arabs, upon the rest of the people. Furthermore, it is a doubly dangerous aggression because of the very shallowness of Pan-Arabism, which cannot solve any problem in this area of the world, and therefore threatens to throw it open to Communism—for Communism thrives only and solely on unsolved problems.

As to the question of *language*, on which Pan-Arab claims are so largely based, one should stress the following three facts:

1. Since the beginnings of history, peoples of the area of the Near East and North Africa have been speaking languages which are mostly akin—forming what is known to scholars as the *HAMITO-SEMITIC* family of languages. This family, to the south of the Mediterranean, has played a part not unlike that of the Indo-European to the north of it. Now Arabic is one of the latest among Hamito-Semitic languages and cannot validly represent them all.

2. Even today, such languages as Berber in the West, Hebrew, the Kushitic and Semitic languages of Sudan and Ethiopia in the East, together with non-Hamito-Semitic tongues such as Kurdish, claim nearly half the population in the area. In fact, outside Arabia proper, not a single one of the main regions may be described as solidly Arabic-speaking.

3. Furthermore, here as elsewhere, language and political allegiance are unrelated. For instance, the Arabic-speaking Lebanese are most emphatically a non-Arab people, and often proclaim it quite vocally.

Thus, there is no good proof of the existence of any Arab nation or nations outside the Arabian Peninsula.

One may even have the gravest doubts about the existence today of *any* nation properly speaking, in any modern or western sense of the word, within the entire area. Even the more advanced, or more compact peoples such as the Berbers in the West, the Egyptians on the Nile, the Abyssinians in Ethiopia, the Israelis and Lebanese in the Levant, carry with them, maybe, the wish, the hope, the will of becoming nations, but still—they are just at the beginning of the modern road to nationhood.

Indeed, most of the area is still living within the framework of tribal loyalties and religious castes. Theocracy is rampant in most of the states of the Arab League—and in some others. There is not only the reactionary, medieval, selfish theocracy of *SUNNITE* (that is Orthodox) *ISLAM*, but also, in Israel, the narrow-minded, racialist Judaic theocracy of some of our Jewish fanatics. Not only is the area suffering from the mutual distrust of Christians, Moslems and Jews, but it is torn by the endless and hopeless strife of sects and communities within each of the major religions—Sunnites against the dissenting Shiites, liberal and orthodox Jews, and the many denominations of Christians. Within such a framework, Pan-Arabism is particularly harmful, because it really represents a conspiracy of the most backward and unscrupulous elements of Sunnite theocracy.

Let's analyze more precisely this *THREAT OF THE ARAB LEAGUE*:

It works against the interests—material and spiritual, individual and national—of the people themselves. There is no hope of progress, enlightenment[,] freedom, prosperity, either for the elite or for the masses, either for the majorit[y] races or the minorities in each country—within the frame of Pan-Arabism. Thus, Pan-Arabism prevents the national growth and ultimate independence of any and all the countries of the Near East and North Africa.

The threat, today, is quite direct and open, in such cases as Israel, Lebanon and Morocco.

But this same threat exists—indirect, subtle and nonetheless dangerous—in other cases, because it prevents the creation of the very conditions required to ensure the freedom and independence of modern nations, and thus helps foreign influence, foreign interests, foreign overlordship to endure and entrench themselves. The examples of Jordan, Iraq and many others are eloquent enough.

Finally—by keeping the peoples backward, ignorant, underfed, divided by sectional hatreds and bloodshed, Pan-Arabism unavoidably paves the way for the great common enemy of mankind: *COMMUNIST TYRANNY*. One need not belabor this point. The irresponsible blackmail which consists in threatening, or directly [?] hinting, about comin[g] to terms with Communism is heard often enough from the lips of Pan-Arab and Pan-Islamic spokesmen, and of some of their Western supporters.

*

What are the *REQUIREMENTS FOR A POSITIVE, CONSTRUCTIVE SOLUTION* of the interlocked problems of Near East and North Africa—a solution which Pan-Arabism does not offer? They are as follows:

1. Genuine, objective information about, and understanding of the area, instead of the prevailing biases and misinformation;
2. Recognition of the basic fact that there are no Arab nations outside Arabia, and that nationhood in general is just starting on its modern road in this area;
3. The encouragement of such trends as lead toward national solidarity and organization within *TERRITORIAL* (geographical-historical) frameworks, within *COUNTRIES*—rather than according to racial and denominational prejudices, within caste and church tyrannies;
4. Open and genuine separation of Church and State, and a common resistance of all men of good will to the encroachments of theocracy, of any and every theocracy;
5. Continued help by all free people from overseas—a help that should not be disrupted by uncritical outcries against alleged "colonialism"; for each case should be studied on its own merits, not as an illustration of extraneous, ideologica[l] biases;
6. First and foremost: without waiting for external help, the peoples directly concerned should work together,

according to principles of self-help and mutual help, so as to resist the threat of Pan-Arabism, and the even greater threat of Communism which must follow in its wake.

[. . .]

Appendix C[1]

Letter from Adya Horon to Eri Jabotinsky and Shmuel Rosoff (excerpts)

New York, February 10. 1956
Messrs. E. Jabotinsky & S. Rosoff
HAIFA
Dear friends Eri and Mulia:

[. . .]

If you stand for freedom of conscience, then it must also include the freedom of the other man's conscience. I definitely dislike your "liberalism" (I was always a rabid "reactionary") yet I have to tolerate it, because I want to cooperate with you on a level of decency. [. . .] There are people who have all kinds of sentiments; "liberalism" is not the only possible attitude. If your "separation of church and state" includes, for instance, enforced atheism, then count me out.

(d) This, finally, brings us to the *Statement of the Kedem Club*. [. . .] I gave certain specific advice, not only in my name, but more important—in the name of the leadership of the Levant Club here; and we also made very outspoken reservations on certain vital points. Nothing of this seems to have influenced you in any way, and we even failed to get any clear acknowledgment from you about the question marks which we had raised. Nevertheless, as you well know, we did everything on our part to support your efforts and give them publicity whenever you gave us any occasion to do so. We at once utilized that opening chapter in your first "green" (mimeographed) statement—the only one which lent itself to publication here—and had it published with favorable comments in the Lebanese Gazette. When you asked us to make a propaganda-drive at the Technion Middle East Conference in New York, last November, we did so, though it was n o t easy, and stressed very much the existence of Club Kedem in Haifa [. . .]

Now we have before our eyes your final printed statement, which differs in several important ways from your original declaration [. . .]. Far from amending the original definitions in a sense more acceptable to our common action, it goes further away from both our original premises and our subsequent remarks, doubts or warnings.

I'll try to be more specific, on some very striking points:

—"Kedem" is now not a "Hebrew" liberal, but an "Israeli" liberal club. We already objected to the adjective "liberal"—which is not an [*sic*] Hebrew word anyhow, and which in French, English and American has quite different, in part opposite connotations. In America it is often used as a disguise of more or less extreme leftism. In English it may imply certain particular views on economics. At best, especially in French, it implies a certain general softness in character, a yearning for the Nineteenth century, which is rather confusing in an association that comes out obviously for some bold and "fighting" ideas. Maybe you have in mind "liberalism" as applied to the religious and racial issues only—but this is far from clear.

What is even worse: the change from "Hebrew" to "Israeli." Especially in the context of the word "Kedem." "Kedem" denotes a historico-geographical area—the Levant—while "Israel" is taken as a concrete State, with definite boundaries and a passport. The two simply do not go together. With the word "Hebrew," the term "Kedem" made sense: at least in Israel, and among many of our Lebanese friends abroad, and all those who are in any way aware of the various uses to which "the Hebrews" as a concept was put by individual writers as myself, Shelaḥ, etc [*sic*], or by organizations such as the Hebrew Committee, the Alef group, or even in the usage of the Hebrew language itself—this Ever or "Hebrewland" is more or less co-extensive with our Levant, it represents a historical claim of leadership for the future, a certain historical doctrine of the past, etc. [. . .] Everybody could understand, or be made to understand, that Club Kedem is to some extent in line with a very comprehensive and if you want "liberal-minded" interpretation of the phenomenon: "Hebrew national renaissance," of which Israel is but a first concrete manifestation, a bridgehead (in spite of the narrower, or even contradictory, Zionist-Jewish restrictions) and to which we would like to add, first of all, the Christian, Maronite-led elements among the Lebanese, also the Druzes, and ultimately some other "minorities"—until we could expand in the shape of a federation of the Levant, based mainly on the concrete fact of the existence of two non-Moslem, non-Arab states, Israel and Lebanon. Etc. etc.

Now all of this has become quite hazy, the word "Hebrew" has disappeared from your title, and I really don't know what you are talking about.

[. . .] Even as it stands now, your statement, except for the jarring paragraph still concerned with Pan-Arabism, puts you in the eyes of a casual reader in the camp of our worse [*sic*] enemies rather than in that of our allies. If you cannot see that, if you continue to have any illusions about the nature, for instance, of the Am. Council for Judaism, [. . .] then it would be better to devote your attention to other things than practical politics. But I cannot credit you with so much naiveté. I imagined that you simply yielded to pressure [. . .]. And this is wrong. We must be flexible, even tolerant—yes; but there is a minimum, a hard core of principles on which we cannot yield.

—By a queer contradiction, while yielding on the most fundamental point in phraseology ("Hebrews"), you remain unbending on some other issues which are highly controversial, or irrelevant, and in any case irking to many of those people who are actually prepared to work with us, or are indeed working with us, in the first, vital phase of our "foreign affairs" relationships.

I allude to the separation of "Church" and "State" issue, and on the issue of "Two Passports." As to the first one, I need not tell you—as I have already done so time and again—that I wholeheartedly agree with you on the matter IN ITSELF: indeed, I was among the very first men, perhaps actually the first one, to raise publicly the warning that Jewish religion and Hebrew nationhood should n o t be treated as a single, indivisible phenomenon; this is not exactly the same as "separating church and state," but admittedly it comes very close to it. But this is neither here nor there. Since the beginning of our talks about creating a "club" in Israel, I stressed the obvious fact that we needed several different associations: one to accomodate [*sic*] the "liberals" who fought against Judaic theocracy, another to enhance a "Lebanese-Phoenician" sentiment among Maronites ("Cedar of Lebanon" club, was one suggestion), etc [*sic*]—and still another one (KEDEM) to group and coordinate all such men and activities who agreed on the broad Levant issue based on Israeli-Lebanese cooperation, whatever the differences of such men on other topics, e.g., the "religious" topic. I pointed out that it would be impossible to reconcile an appeal to Maronite particularism today (which is still very much enmeshed in the church-peculiarities of the Maronites' Aramaic Catholicism) and a vigorous stand on behalf of French-type secularism . . . You would not listen, not even reply, and the matter is still sticking out of your pamphlet with utter irrelevance.

As to the "passport" issue: I personally did not object to it, maybe it has a paedagogic [*sic*] value, though it is rather absurd to be so rabidly "passport"-minded in an association whose main point is the non-recognition of existing passports as far as they are tokens of the sacrosanct character of states whose validity we do not recognize: we do not want people to be faithful to their Jordanian, or Syrian, or even Lebanese passports, and most of us refuse to take very seriously even the Israeli state as a final expression of our nationhood . . . It is chiefly the American passport which is a nuisance (and a convenience) for some of us. Let's say so. I gladly admit that while I am a holder of an American passport you may exclude me from the honor of joining your "Israeli" club (here you are logical: a "Hebrew" club would hardly have to exclude anybody on the strength of a mere passport, for there is no Hebrew state or super-state as yet: it has the advantages and disadvantages of being an aim, not an accomplished fact). But the way in which you overstress the point, on the same level as your other declarations of principle, makes the entire thing quite petty and ridiculous in a KEDEM (super-state Levant) context. You are pushing yourselves into the position of a "side-show" [. . .]. Let me try and explain the matter again:

I am simply appalled at the recurrent trend, among those who are my witting and unwitting "pupils" in the doctrine of a Hebrew (as distinct of [*sic*] a self-contradictory "Jewish") nationalism: I mean, their trend to *narrow down*, more and more, an originally *expansive* idea. Please re-read my articles in *Shem 1939* [. . .]; or my lecture on "*Hebrews and Jews*" in 1945, before members of the incipient Hebrew Committee of National Liberation and Amer. League for a Free Pal [. . .]. Or indeed any other text of mine [. . .]. I always conceived of the Hebrew phenomenon as of something very broad—in its historical past, in its geographic location, in its present potentialities, in its future destiny. To me, the bulk of the Jews were included in it, by their obvious past; and Judaism was but one of the historical manifestations of Hebrew life, with a beginning and perhaps an end: a phenomenon of "Middle Ages," yet still an inseparable part of the total flow of events and developments; certainly not something ANTI-Hebrew, or out of the Hebrew horizons altogether. But in addition to Jews, I always claimed other potential or actual groups amenable to this common definition: the "Phoenicians" in the past, today the Aramaic-nurtured

Maronites, are typical examples; and I had nothing against the idea of "assimilating" by and by still other groups, even "Arab" groups, into our "imperialistic" conception of Hebrewism. Logically, it had to represent THE ALTERNATIVE to Pan-Arabism; especially in all the Levant, but more generally, at least as one of the important factors, within the Mediterranean area.

The "Hebrew Committee" (so named under the pressure of Eri, and with the sympathy of Merlin rather than of Peter Bergson) restricted the definition of "Hebrews" (for obvious tactical reasons) to the Jews residing in Palestine and the inmates of European concentration camps.

Then came the ALEF group of Shelaḥ. I have the greatest respect for Shelaḥ as a writer and a thinker, I consider him highly original and valuable, I have learned much from him. Yet of course he is basically my "pupil." With him, "the Hebrews" became an "ANTI-Jewish" concept—which was paedagogically [*sic*] useful for a while, but dialectically absurd. People came to understand the ALEF attitude as a denial of plain facts, which actually it tended to become . . . A narrowly 19-th century French conception of purely territorial nationhood (which Shelaḥ had learned in Paris, and partly from me—though I use it *cum grano salis*, and he doesn't) led to the Aharon Amir type of exaggeration: (Hannibal *not* part of the Hebrew stream, because it is out of "our" territory, as if people were merely plants, and had no feet to travel with . . .) with a consequent fight against Jewish immigration as such (utterly absurd, in practice and theory).

And now you come, with echoes from the last-phase Alef and the "League against religious Coercion" [*sic*], and narrow down Hebrewism to the holding of a SINGLE passport by Israeli residents (so that an Arab with a Mappai scrap of paper may be a member of your club, but I cannot—which I do not resent, of course, if it can do you any good). The logic of your evolution has finally forced you to renounce . . . even the name "Hebrew."

Very well, then. What next?

—Next, logically enough, comes the statement, prominently displayed, about your concern as to the fate of the Arab refugees. You did not consult us on the matter. In the broad world, the stressing of this issue will be interpreted as a not-so-tacit alliance with the pro-Arab thesis. Nobody will understand that you mean to solve the refugee problem within the framework of an anti-Arab, "greater Hebrew" federation of the Levant, and the expansion of Israel's own borders. Or do you mean so?

How did it come about? [. . .]

I think the answer lies in the following three deficiencies: —lack of patience with the theoretical elaboration of our movement, as to principles, strategy and tactics; —too great impatience as to immediate practical achievements (the fright of becoming a "side-show"); —and more than anything else, lack of the essential prerequisite, which is an *act of faith,* not an exercise in merely political logics. But these are things which I would like to point out again, more explicitly, within a more systematic context toward the end of this long letter.

However it may be, we here cannot make any profitable use of your first, and so far unique, publication: the Statement of the Kedem Club. Your intentions would be entirely misunderstood by any and every audience abroad—except perhaps by our mortal foes, who would read into the Kedem Club program another "anti-Zionist" (i.e., anti-Israel) declaration, and nothing else. The situation is the more annoying inasmuch as you deemed it advisable to designate us, the Levant Club, as your correspondents in the USA—at a moment when your own stated program has become to a large extent quite incompatible with our own line of conduct. As your and our organizations are not simply commercial publishing shops, the word "correspondent" implies of course a basic identity of views, which does not at all appear from the existing publications; these show rather that there is n o identity of views.

Would it not have been better to approach the problem gradually, to publish a few occasional papers, and let the issue simmer down, —instead of issuing, after one year's effort, a statement of principles with which we are now quite stuck??

If you still consider it as possible to publish papers less at variance with our original idea, and with the tactical situation in the U.S.A., we could certainly help you distribute it [*sic*] here. I'll give you one instance: due to our work at the American Technion Society, we have the permission, and have been given the facilities, to distribute materials in all the nearly 70 local chapters of this important organization in the U.S.A. What a natural thing it would have been to distribute in such a way the literature of a Kedem Club of Haifa, some whose leaders are actually members of the Haifa Technion?

[. . .]

(III) *Current activities.* Before asking you a similar question about what you do or intend to do in Israel, I must give you a clearer idea about our situation and outlook here.

a) What I am doing, with the help of a very few active friends and the occasional backing of a somewhat larger number of sympathizers, amounts to the following:

—We wanted first of all to build up a strictly limited but steadily-flowing activity, such as to create the fact of some kind of Lebanese anti-Arab and pro-Israeli trend among the Amero-Lebanese, and some kind of cooperation between—let us say, pro-Israeli American Jews and pro-Lebanese American Christians. In this limited task we have succeeded, but at a price of constant, exacting effort. [. . .] We know now that an entire Maronite community of 15,000 members can stand, like and espouse a fighting program, and consider this practically anonymous A. H. as "an obvious old Maronite of the Phoenician brand." [. . .] Also, we have gotten some of our message across the seas—to Paris, Lebanon and Israel.

In Paris, "Est et Ouest" (the fortnightly review of the Association d'Etudes Politiques et Economiques Internationales, whereof B. Souvarine is one of the leading spirits) is now devoting a column in each issue to our affairs [. . .];

We have private reactions from Lebanon, showing that some of our stuff gets through; from time to time we are being violently attacked in the pro-Arab press, which is not a bad sign.

In Israel [. . .] *Herut* has given us some journalistic support. Lately, we felt there was a slackening—maybe because there were delays in the sending of our materials from here. This is bad: it seems that we are almost the only source and the only "prodder." [. . .]

Yet we are nearing here a certain *point of saturation*. What we are doing is really *smuggled* through: there is no understanding and no diplomatic tact anywhere among the "Jewish" and "Zionist" leadership, and we do not expect it to develop at any time in the future; nor is the Lebanese leadership in America more intelligent. We had not only successes, we had also failures. Even so, what we have achieved is definitely more than zero:

We have a non-negligible network of publications:

As-Sabah weekly, all Arabic		c. 2000 circulation;
Leb. Gazette, increasingly Engl.		c. 2000—& growing fast;
Middle East Press Review, monthly		c. 8000—id.
Levant Memoranda	id.	c. 3000—(which is close to our maximum needs at present)

Excepting the purely local audiences, which may still grow indefinitely, we service well over 10,000 readers (excluding duplications) of only the relatively "high-level" type (Congressmen, Newscommentators [*sic*], leaders of communities, etc [*sic*]) and we receive almost daily requests.

[. . .]

[W]e got a few orders from other than "rightist" sources: e.g., the University, the Ministry of Religious Affairs, etc. We are sending now the stuff also to the Keneset [*sic*]—which did n o t react.

Does our work serve any purpose? In moments of fatigue, we tend to doubt it. But, reasonably speaking, this is not so: we *have* made a point; we cannot create events, and the current may be strongly against us; but we attract the attention of those concerned to such facts as do exist. For instance, our network has contributed to the Lebano-American outcry against the Syro-Lebanese alliance, and the latter has certainly contributed to stop this alliance. Even your official circles are not entirely irresponsive (though I doubt their intelligence and sincerity); for instance, we got requests for additional copies of our material about the Lebano-American reaction to the Syro-Lebanese pact project. [. . .]

All this is something, but it is very little.

It cannot grow, unless we find new ways and means.

And we shall not find them in the Zionist-Israeli officialdom, alas.

[. . .]

I also hold that the time is approaching when we shall have no choice but to revert to certain pre-1948 methods. And I am having certain talks with representatives of the qualified right-wing authorities.

[. . .] In the early thirties I was already considered as a crank ("side-show"). Yet I am very patient, and between 1938 and 1948 I saw full justification for all I was preaching and doing. Do you suppose that conditions are basically different today? I don't think so.

[. . .]

(IV) *What next*? There is much truth and wisdom in Mulia's "pessimistic" letter. Actually, we a r e a side-show, never were anything else, and cannot become anything else, except if:

a) we get financial means, sufficient for:

—travel, and therefore personal meeting, e.g., in Paris;

—feeding at least part of our activities from our own, rather than from "smuggled" sources;

b) we have the patience to wait until somebody else picks up some of our ideas (because our ideas are unavoidable, even and especially if "everything goes to hell," as it well seems to go); this is an experience which Eri's father had time and again, in his lifetime and more so—posthumously; also (not that I dare make any comparisons) it was my own experience all my life, from Bergson to Begin for instance (even now there are around Begin a number of such who are willing to "pick up"); so that I am less concerned than Mulia with the side-show position because I am used to it.

The question, for us, (for you as well as for me, and quite independently of whether we march together, or work independently, with or without quarrels) is really a different one:

WHAT DO WE WANT? As the saying goes, one cannot have the pie and eat it. And this is precisely, in short, my reproach to your Kedem Statement and to what seems to be your entire way of acting.

—Do you want to be in the middle of a street show? Then join Begin; (if he will let you)—for Ben-Gurion will certainly n o t let you.

—Or join me, in the hope that ultimately the "pre-1948" methods will result in some noise in the middle of various streets (I cannot guarantee that I shall have anything to do with it, except the literary or conversely—the confidential provocation; but you may chose [*sic*] the middle of the street if you so want;

[. . .]

BUT PERHAPS you are not really interested in all that, but only in ultimate results. This, in 1956, requires a crusading spirit and an almost boundless readiness of self-sacrifice [. . .]. If so, you will not ask questions about "side-" or "main shows," but set an ultimate goal clearly before your eyes, and, after analyzing the situation, define the principles and seek the ways and means for its attainment. An attainment which may require many years. In fact, generations. And bring you glory, or oblivion, or nothing at all but worries and daily doubts. I don't care. My mind was made up on these questions several d e c a d e s ago. I am a side show, but still going on. [. . .]

(V) *PRINCIPLES.* [. . .]

AIM: HEBREW RENAISSANCE. *Territorial shape of it*: from the existing beachhead of Israel, with the additional flanking bastion of the Maronite Mountain—to a controlling position in the Mediterranean Levant—later on, to the Euphrates—finally, to what Shelaḥ calls Erets ha-Perat, meaning Ever, in Hebrew. Perhaps ultimately with some additional frills in the broad world around the Mediterranean. *Human shape of it*: most of the Jews must become Hebrews; as long as most of the Jews remain what and where they are, Israel will be their "Holy Center" [. . .] Most of the population on this territory must become Hebrew also—by immigration, re-education, expulsion, massacre, re-settlement, or whatever other combination of means. "Most" need not mean 51 per cent at the beginning—it may be 30 per cent, but factually predominant—until the final result is acquired, in whatever number of generations. This is the way. Raq kakh. *Spiritual shape of it*: we cannot dictate it in advance as to details. Obviously "Judaism" has been only the "mummy" of our past and a "preserver" for our future. Yet a man is blind in spirit if he does not see that our way is, in the last resort, a profoundly mystical one. "Atta beḥartanu"? Yes, Amen. If you deny this, you deny everything. You are on your way to create a Hebrew dialectical variant of the future Arab World. You become a mere slave to "reasonable statistics" and other instruments of modern deception. IT IS BECAUSE OF THAT, precisely, that we cannot agree with the sham-Messianism of our current Zionists, and with the petty racialism of our Jews. Ours is r e a l l y a mission, which has worked political miracles, and will change the face of o u r world, and even turn all kind of humans into members of the new Hebrew nation.

STRATEGY: While the AIM is an ACT of FAITH, and cannot depend on the transient outlook of 1956, our strategy must be guided by ACTS OF REASON, and therefore based on a reasonable, cool, objective analysis of ways and means:

WE NEED A DOCTRINE, which is not something you can improvise in a few months, and which needs the give-and-take of discussion, trial and error: it will not jump out, fully armed, from the brain of a Jupiter. But here are the guiding lines:

DOCTRINE of the past (re-creation of a Hebrew conception of history, and therefore of the entire world of the Hebrews) in order to sustain the ACT of FAITH; OUR NEW BIBLE, completing the old one;

—*of the present*: especially, correct analysis of our territory and our area—which will show, of course, the necessity of starting from Lebanon and Israel, and of helping the French to cling to Algeria; and of *bodily* defeating "the Arabs" and driving them to a position of helplessness all around the Central Sea (a big program: nothing less will do)

—*of the future*: something *instead* of Marx, instead of Jefferson, instead of the preaching of rabbis and modern medicine-men. And this will certainly not be a democratic doctrine of "pursuit of happiness," but an aristocratic one of "fulfilment."

TACTICS: One principle is enough at this moment: —WE MUST START TO SPREAD OUR CREDO on the EDUCATIONAL LEVEL. We cannot yet implement it OPENLY in politics. The time is NOT YET. We must act, perforce, as "side-shows," or as "educators," or both. For how long? Who knows?

That's all today. Shalom.

A. G.

Appendix D[1]

Letter from Adya Horon to Eri Jabotinsky and Shmuel Rosoff (excerpts)

New York, April 3, 1956
Messrs E. Jabotinsky & S. Rosoff
HAIFA
Dear friends Eri and Mulia:

The reasons why I am so late in replying to the various letters which I received separately from each of you are, in the main, the following: a) On the whole, I did not feel you have answered my long message of February 10, and I hoped for complementary information; b) Some of the points answered seem to raise only new questions; c) Points concerning the future of Club Kedem and its proclaimed ideology seem to deepen, rather than to narrow, the gulf which already existed between us; d) Eri and Mulia do not seem to agree on some vital points, though I am not sure that I quite understand the reasons and scope of the divergence; e) I felt really discouraged: my long message has not brought clarity in our relationship, or rather—while renewing the personal contact—has only stressed the differences in political thinking, if any; f) Last but not least, my health has been so poor, lately, that I just managed to fulfil my current duties, and had to postpone any lengthy correspondence.

In addition to shorter, personal letters, I would like today, again, to try my hand at a lengthy message, directed at both of you (as I still cannot see clearly where you disagree, and as each of you seems aware of the letters written to me by the other). This letter should also contain that criticism, about the new project of a "Manifesto," which Mulia asked me to voice as soon as possible.

[. . .]

I will try, first of all, to answer the main points in your letters in their approximate chronological order. Then I will criticize the draft Manifesto. Then outline my own views. And finally try and submit a concrete program of action, taking into account our aim & position. Thus, my program for today is the following: (I) Answers to specific points; (II) Criticism of the Draft Memorandum; (III) My own views; (IV) Proposal of action. (The latter, open to *your* criticism).

*

(I) Answers to specific points in your letters.

[. . .]

I can't follow you in your analysis of the tensions around Israel. That your G<overnmen>t has been piling up "suicidal" mistakes seems quite certain. But even if its policy would have been wise, the result would not have differed much. The growth of Pan-Arabism cannot be stopped by wisdom alone; it cannot be stopped without continued military action (by Israel and by France, I don't see today any other candidates); the trouble with Israel is *not* that it is too aggressive, but not aggressive enough; of course, aggressiveness *alone* will solve nothing; but conversely, nothing will be solved without aggressiveness. I see a lot of constructive criticism in what Herut is saying, but I am afraid that your criticism leaves out the decisive factor: military action.

[. . .]

In fact, it seems to me that the *warlike* situation, which has been with us all the time, is nothing new, and that there is no means, and no need, of changing it. Wisdom would be to build our entire program on the assumption that the warlike situation is basic to our entire future for at least the present generation. Otherwise we are building on smoke, like Brith-Shalom for instance.

In this respect Israel is in a position very similar to that of a very large section of the world.

[. . .]

Eri writes: "On the matter of the name of the Club, I am more of your way of thinking than of Rosoff's; I want to use the word Hebrew. About 'Liberal' I have no feelings. Here it means simply anti-theocratic. . . . I consented to leave out 'Hebrew' under pressure [. . .]" My criticism was (not only in my long letter of February 10, but throughout our correspondence for a year or so) precisely that you could not reconcile, within a *single* Club of such type, so many problems of terminology and indoctrination. "Hebrew Israeli Liberal Kedem Club" was looking in too many directions at once. What I advised was the following: "Kedem Club" is self-sufficient as a determination—if the central aim, at this stage and for this particular audience, is to further the idea of certain regional interests (in the region of Kedem, i.e., the Levant) which certain ethnic groups have in common, in the face of the Pan-Arab offensive. A "Club" being something else than a party or a tightly-knit organization, should not undertake more than it can perform. As to the "Liberal" angle (whatever it means) it should be pursued in some other framework, because not everybody who likes the Kedem idea will like the Liberal trend. Similarly, the "Hebrew" indoctrination cannot be pursued very far in a "Levant" or a "Kedem" club, nor in any "club" as such. Hebrew indoctrination would rather be a matter of publications, on the one hand, and of more or less "fanatical" trends or groups, such as the Alef group in the past, or what is perhaps wrongly known as the "Canaanite" trend. Whether, ultimately, such indoctrination would lead to the rise of a party or parties, or influence the thinking of existing parties, is still another question.

Of course your local Maronites know next to nothing about the Hebrew ideology. This is a fact. We have no quarrel about it. But *if* "one of the purposes of Kedem is this indoctrination," then we find ourselves again in a vicious circle.

[. . .]

The "Arab refugees" problem. Nobody can overlook or minimize it. That's not the question. Noise is being made all over the world about it, against Israel; a simple mention of the problem in a Statement of Principles is either too much, or not enough. It is a question of proportions and of elaboration, I can't see how you can treat it separately from the entire issue of our aims. We must have solutions for the refugee problem in the framework of a different Levant and a greater Israel; in the present frame of reference there is no solution, as you well know—only a systematic use of the refugees against Israel. Contacts with refugees? On what basis? How do you visualize that? What can "we" (Kedem, Levant Club, etc?—or the Israeli Government, which is something very different) offer them in the present situation? Isn't it too late, or too early, to seek contacts with them? Maybe you have local information which I lack. On the whole, I don't think we can separate this issue from our entire problem. To say this is not to minimize the issue, on the contrary.

[. . .]

I am quite aware of the facts you quote: the pressure of Pan-Arab propaganda, (which is very well perceptible not only in the Middle East, but throughout the world, quite especially in the USA), the great difficulties in speaking with "Arabs" in terms of a Hebrew terminology (this applies also to Jews, by the way), the lack of confidence in our real intentions, etc, etc.

But that is not the point. Before determining the tactics (and phraseology) to be followed in each particular case (in each stage, in front of each particular audience, in each particular geographic location etc) we should clearly determine OUR AIMS, and our STRATEGY. For whom? For ourselves. FIRST OF ALL FOR OURSELVES. You apparently think it useless, or worse ("Navigating in the right direction . . . but forgetting the petty obstacles"; or restricting oneself to the "select few"). But I am quite sure that this is THE FIRST PREREQUISITE of ANY fruitful action. I felt this way a year ago, and even years ago. BUT I AM EVEN MORE CERTAIN OF IT NOW, because the last year, and the current correspondence, have proved beyond doubt that Mulia, Eri and Adyah are UNABLE so far to agree among themselves on a sufficiently clear and elaborated ideology as to aims and strategy (to say nothing of tactics . . .) So how can you hope to agree with the "masses," either "Arab" or "Jewish"?

Anything worthwhile, in the field of political action, must be matured AT FIRST among the "select few," then only applied to the "man in the street." Any other procedure is irresponsible amateurishness or empty demagoguery. The French, or the Russian Revolution (not that I admire either of them) were not engineered in a few years; they matured after a century (the Enlightenment, or the evolution from Marx to Lenin) of dreams and research, by "select few." You are impatient? Me too. Something can and should be done at once, even now. Agreed. But the point is precisely: what should be done IN RELATION TO THE AIMS, not what we could do for the pleasure of doing something.

In reading and re-reading your letter and your draft-memorandum, I become more convinced that y o u are the dreamer, and I the realist. For indeed:

—We are at war; but you close your eyes to it; you try to find such words as would not imply a "Jewish ruse" to "divide and rule," whereas everybody, at present, especially "Arabs," will interpret any words whatsoever spoken by us, as a "Jewish ruse." They may be wrong in the adjective "Jewish," as far as our subjective intentions are concerned—but whoever we are, we must indeed "try to divide" them in order to survive (to say nothing of our "rule"). However, neutral, liberal, progressive and unoffensive, your phraseology will not attract people who are afraid of you, or hate you, or think that your enemies are stronger than you.

I understand very well that you cannot start speaking, with even those few non-Jews who are potentially sympathetic, on the basis of a Hebrew ideology which is not understood even by Jews, except a handful of them. But we may start with such words as Levant, Kedem, etc., on condition that the orientation is clear from the beginning: it is anti-Pan-Arab; it considers the Arabs as intruders in the Levant rather than its "natural rulers," etc. We can *seek* for allies only among those who are threatened by Pan-Arabism. Which, today, rules out probably *most* of those men who do consider themselves Arabs. We may try to talk some of them (Christians, Shiite minorities such as the Druses and Alawites, etc) out of "being Arab," but this can be done only inasmuch and insofar as we challenge openly (by words *and* military deeds) the rule of Arabism in the Levant. This is elementary. You cannot change the nature of any country by mere propaganda, be it even so wise and appeasing; it takes *also* sheer force. Everybody understands that a war is going on in the Levant; the question is only—what is the meaning of this war? Between whom is it waged? What are the war aims? Or if you wish—the "peace aims." (Which makes no difference in current "democratic" terminology, where almost every word is meant to be a lie).

I don't see where the *war* comes in in your picture.

[. . .]

(II) The new Rosoff-Polkes (?) draft of a Kedem Memorandum.

It is with a heavy heart that I do my friendly duty and give my opinion, as requested. I can't understand why you still need this opinion after having developed a phraseology which, as you must be aware, goes from bad to worse from *my* point of view.

1. The "Land of Ur"? I can take it only as a joke, and a bad joke at that. "Hebrew" was too obscure, or too Jewish, or too traditional, and anyhow unsuitable, or what not; you had, instead, the noncommittal Levant, or Kedem; or, in a pinch, Uriel's "Erets ha-Perat" . . . But no, somebody pops up and proposes the Land of Ur.

Who ever heard about such a land? Archeologists [*sic*], on the one hand, and readers of the Bible on the other. In archeology [*sic*], Ur is a Sumerian city, quite excentrically [*sic*] located from our point of view, and quite dead from any point of view . . . Not even Semitic in the broadest sense . . . And in the Bible it is mentioned ONLY ONCE, as the native town (not land)* of Abraham, in just ONE form of his legend . . . UR-KASDIM?

A good name for some new Masonic Lodge of Chaldean Astrologers (not that I mind). Have you all had a sunstroke?

I assume that the hidden hint of Mr. Polkes (with whom I do not wish to polemize) was to Our Father Abraham, the symbol of the allegedly common Semitic Judeo-Arab, or Judeo-Islamo-Christian origins.

Delicately implied, of course, not brutally stated in so many words. Brith-Shalom, or Ihud, on the largest scale, with pseudo-mystic overtones. A good start for Liberals.

By the way, the Nile Delta and the Persian Gulf are not South and North, but West and East of each other. And the Fertile Crescent is an invention of Prof. Breasted, of Chicago University, NOT "known since olden days." Whether it be or not "the cradle of European civilization" is a debatable question, and an irrelevant one.

2. This paragraph is much too vague. Either you attack Pan-Arabism or you don't. The British-founded Arab League is no longer the sole, or the main agent of Pan-Arabism. What about Egypt's Pan-Arabism, which is disrupting the Arab League? What about the Baghdad Pact, which in a sense revives a Moslem-Ottoman-British imperialism? Who are the bad foreign wolves? The USA? The USSR? Or both? And what about France? And can we today divorce this problem from the broader issues of Afro-Asian Pan-Islamism, Egyptian megalomania, the so-called East and West rift, etc[.] At the present stage, I cannot conceive of any short, slogan-like answers. I think we should concentrate on a single "wolf": Pan-Arabism, and define why it is the main menace to the area.

3. Why are the Arabs the first-mentioned people in the Land of Ur? Is Arabia also included in this mysterious Land of Ur? Whether its present inhabitants can develop this land (why like California??

*"ארץ מולדתו" is certainly a gloss by some late redactor, who had no exact notion about "אור-כשדים."

I doubt whether everybody will appreciate this particular symbol of Paradise) is highly questionable, among other things—because of conditions described in No. 2 above. And do we want it to be developed only, or chiefly by its inhabitants? What about immigrants? How was California developed? By the local Indians?

4. Israel's future tied up with the Land of Ur, as developed by its present inhabitants? or [*sic*] by these, plus a lot of immigrants? Is Israel's future tied with the OPENING UP of the area, or is Israel to be integrated with the Arabic-speaking California of the future? *Dvie bolshiye raznitsy* [two huge differences], as they say in Odessa.

The kind invitation to the "nationally minded Jews in the Diaspora" is self-contradictory in many ways: "nationally Jewish," or "Urish," or what? (For, of course, you do not dare saying: nationally Hebrew). Right now, otherwise it will be too late? Or can they come, say, in the next generation? What is the deadline? Isn't it a Zionist statement? Even for Zionists, it will seem obscure: too little, or too much. And why should they come? To cease being "wandering Jews" in America or in Morocco (not the same situation, *at present*)? To become Judeo-Arabs instead of Judeo-Americans? Will Israel be a clearly defined political body distinct from World Jewry? Actually, it is already distinct. Too much, for some; too little, for others. You cannot get rid of so many problems in so few ambiguous words . . .

5. Speaking of the L and of Ur, there is no reason to single out Israel alone for "liberalization." Everything is relative. Within the area concerned, Israel is about the most "liberal" land today, with perhaps the exception of Lebanon. If I were an Israeli (which I am only potentially, as I lack your precious passport) I would resent this paragraph as discriminatory. Israel is too Jewish? Fine. And what about Syria and Iraq, are they not slightly theocratic, in the Moslem sense, which is rather worse than the Jewish? You should ask for all these reforms in all the "States of Ur," or in none.

6. Very incongruous to see, after No. 5, this No. 6 with its moral-religious preachings. I am not necessarily proud that this area gave birth to Judaism and Christendom; but if I were proud of it, I would not see in this fact any guarantee for Goddess Progress; Judaism believed in the Messiah, not in Progress; Christendom in the Christ; both believed in Original Sin (righty so, in my opinion). As to the third member of the trinity—Mohammedanism—why do you include it here? It was n o t born in the "Land of Ur" (unless you include Arabia in it); it conquered this land by violence and plunder, and still

continue [*sic*] plundering it out. Your kind advances to prospective Moslem audiences are somehow irreconcilable with your hymn to individual freedom, tolerance, etc.

Your concluding paragraph is the most contradictory of all. If your call will not be heard across the borders of Israel, why bother about it?

(III) My Own Views

[. . .]

FIRST VIEW: a year of discussion proves we still do not know what Club Kedem is. The first (green) draft of a Kedem pamphlet was in my opinion far better than any of its proposed "improvements."

I propose to drop for the time being any attempt at issuing a Manifesto, and start trying to create a Publication. AFTER we have created such a forum and compared the various papers which will appear in it, we may revert to the drafting of a Manifesto.

"Kedem Club" would be enough for me; I do not insist on "Hebrew" at this stage; I have no right to veto the adjective "Israeli"; it is not worthwhile to change stationery only because of the addition "liberal." But no lands of UR, please, otherwise I am out, definitely and finally.

SECOND VIEW: you should stop considering me as a theorist or a dreamer, and yourselves as practical men. I don't see where you have achieved m o r e in practice than I have. If you feel the need to consult me, it must mean that my "theories" are of some practical help.

THIRD VIEW: we must try and agree among ourselves, first of all. In words that are clear and unambiguous to ourselves. Then, and only then, shall we be able to find the proper phraseology to convey our message to the various audiences. So let us start thinking aloud, for the benefit of the "select few"—Eri, Mulia, myself, and perhaps a handful of other "initiates."

I REFER YOU BACK TO Chapter (V) in my Febr. 10 letter, "PRINCIPLES."

For me, it would be pointless to continue this correspondence if you do not agree with me, in substance, with the paragraph entitled "AIM." Please re-read it. You did not react to it. Permit me to stress here some particularly relevant points:

HEBREW RENAISSANCE: that's how we call it among ourselves, and that's how we hope it shall be called ultimately. You may explain it, when needed, as "Progress of the Levant," "Brotherly federation of the Fertile Crescent," or what not (though it will not seem at all a progress from the point of view of Arabism, and is not compatible with Moslem Brotherhood). On the other hand, you may also explain it, when needed, as the true fulfilment of Zionism, of the Messianic hopes, or anything of this kind. But this changes nothing in the aim as defined.

Territorially you cannot jump from Israel to the Fertile Crescent without transition. The progression is mapped out. We cannot but rely on the existing pathos of "Erets Yisrael âl shte gedot ha-Yarden," enlarged by the neighborhood of the Druze and Maronite bastions—Then only comes the notion of Canaan—the maritime or Mediterranean Levant—and Ever in its most limited sense, the "Greater Syria" of the Arabs. All the Fertile Crescent (Ever âl shte gedot ha-Perat) is only the final aim.—This progression is not arbitrary, it is implied in our history, geography and geo-politics. Many of your present difficulties (and those of Alef) come from this lack of transitions. We are already within reach of a factual preponderance in "Canaan"; Maronites and Druzes are much more concrete neighbors and potential allies than—say, the Kurds. I speak of course of the Maronites as a Lebanese element, not of the handful of forgotten friends in Bir'am.—From the *human* viewpoint: it is preposterous to renounce the idea of a more or less massive immigration from abroad, for many years, decades, and perhaps generations to come. On the one hand, if there is not a very substantial liquidation of the Jewish Diaspora, we will never cease to be "crucified" on the horns of the dilemma: "World Jewry" versus "Hebrew Nationhood"; on the other hand, we need at least several millions of additional immigrants to achieve a sufficient demographic basis for the Hebrew Renaissance (I do not claim that a "mathematical" majority is essential). This does not exclude non-Jewish immigrant; on the contrary; (Italians, some day? Re-immigration of the Lebanese Christians? etc). And all this ties us necessarily with overseas problems. I cannot stress too much that the tendency to "regional autarcy [*sic*]," so conspicuous in Alef's writings and in your own Kedem pronouncements, is a dangerous *delusion* as far as the present and near future are concerned. In this connexion: I ABSOLUTELY REFUSE TO UNDERSTAND WHY A JEW (OR NON*JEW) FROM ACROSS THE SEAS IS NECESSARILY A "STRANGER" WHILE ANY KIND OF ARAB FROM ACROSS THE DESERT IS EO IPSO AN INDIGENOUS, RIGHTFUL INHABITANT. Also, why the imperialism of the Zionists, the French, or even the British, is necessarily less justifiable than that of the Egyptians, who are interfering no less glaringly in "our" area.

OUR INDEPENDENCE, as a region, our NATIONAL and FEDERAL AUTARCY, is an AIM, it is not an existing condition. We have to fight for it as conquerors, colonizers, or what have you, against other conquerors and colonizers.—This is the truth, and to hide it would profit only the Pan-Arab thesis.

BY THE WAY, we can exploit whatever local patriotism does exist in the area by stressing that the only important element interested in shaping ultimately this area as an INDEPENDENT federation are we ourselves; Pan-Arabism is n o t an alternative, its capital will be in Cairo, or in Mecca, or in Moscow—not in Haifa, Beirut or Damascus.

BUT PERHAPS THE MOST IMPORTANT THING IS THE FOLLOWING: none of this can be achieved without warfare. Without a more or less permanent warlike situation interrupted from time to time by "rounds" or "thrusts." These things are not done otherwise. Our problem is not how to avoid war, but how to win it. If you don't agree with me (and with the great majority of our youth, I believe), then I will call you dreamers and go my own way.

I am not talking of things which are so remote, so distant in the future . . . A "second round" may come this year, or next year, or in a few years. We must of course assume that we shall win it in the military sense. (You know as well as I do that should we be beaten, there will be no further problems to discuss). And it very important to prepare for the "post-war" policy after the "second round," so that the suicidal errors of the present regime are avoided, and a better basis created for a "third round," etc.

In these conditions, it would make sense to discuss the Maronite problem, the question of refugees, of what we may offer to allies, neighbors, vassals, and beaten enemies . . . Otherwise, we have nothing to offer, and nobody to talk to.

The "pacifistic" strain in your papers is either a tribute to current political hypocrisy (then it is superfluous), or it is a "ruse" which may deceive only yourselves.

Generally speaking, we live in a world where politics must appeal to the worst part in man's nature (fear, greed, vanity, self-love) as much as to its best parts (idealism, love of fellow men, creative imagination); we live indeed in such a world since many thousand years already.

It may be expedient to talk in the language of progress, democracy, etc. But not among ourselves. We are after something very specific (a *mission*—yes, call me a fanatic, even a religious fanatic), we are the re-builders of David's Empire; we are not builders of Utopias or reformers of Human Nature. Whatever good we shall bring to men will be only incidental. This is why, incidentally, I am quite sure that we shall bring more good than the professional pacifists, reformists and social utopists, from Jesus to Trotzky.

[. . .]

Let's put it otherwise. Words are so ambiguous, especially in our times. I will try to clarify my philosophy as to "aims" and as to the general style of the action needed to reach the aims, by examining the concept of "integration" (between Israel and the Levant, or Fertile Crescent, or Middle East, or whatever it be).

A lot of people and groups, inside and outside Israel, speak about "integration." You do, very prominently. Alef did. Ihud does. Mr. Allen, of the U.S. State Department, does. I do. But the notion is ambiguous.

The ambiguity exists in each of the terms which make up the proposition: "Israel to be integrated with the area." The "area" is still indeterminate, "Israel" still dynamic, the "integration" itself may mean next to anything. Is the area something which *we* shall determine, or something given by others, and in which we shall be swallowed up? Is it our immediate neighborhood of the Mediterranean Levant, or the broader geo-political entity of the Levant and Euphrates? [. . .] Or perhaps the "Middle East" of current international phraseology—really an Afro-Asian "PANISLAMIA"—Or, on the contrary, a classical Mediterranean world, of which we would be the easternmost representatives, and in which France, Italy, Greece, North Africa would play a prominent part? Mr. Allen wants us to integrate with an American-controlled Moslem "Middle East," some of our Leftists dream of integration in a Communist-controlled Panislamia. There are Jews, and Israelis, who would accept the fantasy of a Judeo-Arab Golden Age (like the one which never existed in the Middle Ages) wherein we would be a kind of Junior Partner of Panarabism. Maybe there are a few Arabs (today less than ever) who would accept Israel as a half-Jewish vassal—like Lebanon (a half-Christian vassal of the Arabs).

I think we want exactly the opposite. We want to *integrate* our area, not to be integrated in some variant of a more or less Moslem area. We want to be the determining factor, not the determined result; the subject of history, not its object. Our attitude is aggressive, imperialistic, colonialist, aristocratic, etc. etc.—all adjectives which are not popular, though the things which they describe have never been more active than today.

I know that "WE" does not mean "the Jews"; not even "the Israelis." But this is not important. There exists a collective WILL TO POWER AND SELF-FULFILMENT which, however you look at it, you must call HEBREW (it is not Jewish, nor is it simply Israeli). This collective will, rather mysterious in its origins, ill-determined as to its present shape, incoherent as to its precise aspirations, exists nevertheless and has carried "little Israel," even before its creation, against the more obvious "currents of historical determinism," making it one of the POWERS of the world, even and especially in the military field. Against all odds—I believe in this WILL, and I am not an isolated eccentric. In religious terms, you may call it, like the Crusaders of 800 years ago, a divine will ("Dieu le veult," the war cry of the Crusaders). One must be blind not to see these things, which have helped us so far to overcome absolutely overwhelming odds in the purely material, statistical numerical field.

I don't believe in the might of numbers. And you don't. Otherwise you would not be living in Haifa, and there would be no Haifa.

We are in the position of the mythical David before Goliath. The question is h o w to bring the giant down, not whether giants can be brought down. Only big monsters can be humbled, and they are always humbled by little heroes. I do not feel pessimistic, in this present world-wide zoological garden of groggy dinosaurs, provided that we ourselves have the courage, and especially the p a t i e n c e, of playing our little heroic parts. The only danger which might threaten us would be to lose confidence, or interest, in this greatest of all shows, wherein we are called to participate in our appointed, if still obscure, places.

I don't know whether I have succeeded to convey to you something of my deeper convictions; whether they sound intelligible to you, or whether they must remain a personal idiosyncrasy.

**

****

After these views about "Aims," I must develop some points concerning the *STRATEGY* (I am still using the somewhat arbitrary classification of Ch. V, "Principles," in my *Febr. 10* letter, to which I refer you again).

I will have to skip, today, the "Doctrine of the past," and that of "the Future." I realize that I shall have to make a very great effort, in the coming months and years, to bring forth my expected contribution in the field of history. Circumstances, the pressure of events, the untold difficulties of the task itself, have prevented me from publishing more than a few fragments of what I have collected, matured and even written down over the years. I feel deeply guilty for achieving so little—guilty before myself as well as before all those *few* people who expected more. But this is something which I myself will have to make good. As to the doctrine of the Future, which seems to interest Mulia quite particularly, here I have much less to say "in public." It is perhaps an even more difficult field than "the Past."

A field which we should start tackle as soon as possible is that of our doctrine concerning the *PRESENT*.

First of all, we much achieve a clear analysis of the present situation. Many of the tacit or explicit assumptions not only of "Zionism," but of "Israeli policy," or even of the "Alef-Kedem" tradition, are simply outdated. I am speaking here of the assumptions concerning the world around Israel, not the trends within Israel.

Israel, more than ever, is thrust in the very middle of world affairs. Not only is it unrealistic to shut oneself up in the provincial dialogue of "Zion" versus "Jewish Diaspora," but it is not even sufficient to replace it by the "Alef" dilemma of Hebrew nationhood versus Pan-Arabism within a closed arena such as the Levant.

The fate of Israel shall be determined—or Israel shall determine her own fate (there is an abysmal difference between the two phrases)—in relation to forces and to areas which criss-cross each other, and which are in certain respects much broader, in others—narrower, than those which have been usually considered hitherto.

I cannot deal with all these questions here, they will require a more lengthy analysis. Let me only formulate a few thoughts, slogan-like:

- Pan-Arabism has politically "come of age." It is no longer merely a "tool" of British imperialism. It is on the rampage, very much on its own. It is bursting out of the British framework of the Arab League (it may disrupt this framework entirely), and the main center of the commotion seems now in Cairo. The rabidly Moslem (not nationalist . . .) character of this Pan-Arabism is also becoming more apparent, contrary to some of its phraseology.
- The decaying "Quatrième République" of France, despite all blunders and surrenders, has been involved willy-nilly

in a "warm" war with Pan-Arabism, because of the objective inability of France to surrender Algeria. There are many signs that the French may become, from potential allies, actual allies of Israel.

- A Mediterranean policy has therefore become of vital importance for us. It remains to be really formulated, and advocated.
- For the first time, the Soviets seem to make an effort in order to subvert (China-like, mutatis mutandis) the Middle East and Africa. Their success would mean such an overwhelming catastrophe for the entire West that even the idiots in London are beginning to be frightened by the perspective.
- American policy continues to be one of utter stupidity (from the American point of view) combined with petty private interests (Oil, etc)—but there is a growing opposition to it, not only because of the "Jewish vote" (though you should not underestimate Jewish opinion here). Because of the peculiar structure of the USA, there is a limit to what the State Department can do. Whereas there is no limit to what the Kremlin does. Therefore, while Washington acts as our enemy, Moscow remains nevertheless a more dangerous enemy. We cannot yield to any pressure from our "leftists": reliance on the USSR would be even more suicidal than on the USA. We should rely on neither.
- The technology of total war has become so frightening and unpredictable, that it has frightened the BIG TWO into . . . relative military stalemate, or even impotence, contrary to appearances.
- In a certain sense, Egypt and Israel are now among the Big Military powers, because they can fight, to a certain extent, without scaring the wits off each other.
- This entire situation has great drawbacks, of course, but also great opportunities. We seem more isolated than ever. But given the right maneuvering [*sic*] and the proper aggressiveness, we are less isolated than we ever

were; because there is a certain West, a certain Europe, a definite Algeria, etc. etc., which may ultimately help us fight and beat Pan-Arabism militarily, as a question of vital self-interest.

- None of the potentialities will become actual merely by themselves. This is why analysis and political enlightenment are still useful, even at this late stage. In Israel, in France, in the USA, etc. Otherwise, if we merely drift, then we must rely chiefly on the probable blunders and bragadaccio [*sic*] . . . of the Moslems, who have so largely contributed to beat themselves in 1948.

I would like to add a few words about the inner political situation in Israel: from my readings of the Israeli press (I follow it rather closely) I have gained the impression that Herut is n o t s o f a r from adopting, at least verbally and superficially, a "foreign policy" line which comes close to the above considerations. Perhaps it is due to the Jabotinskian mental heritage, which is certainly a better method of thinking than that derived from Marx cum Ahad ha-Am. Perhaps some slight touches are also due to our own preachings over the years.

WHY don't you consider some contact with Herut? Is it a question of unpleasant personalities, or do you hope to find any other channel of fruitful opposition in the near future?

I am convinced of the congenital incapacity of Mappay (whether Ben-Gurion or Sharrett) to develop the really aggressive policy which is required. And Ahdut ha-Avodah will n e v e r outgrow its marxist [*sic*] superstitions. So you simply c a n n o t discount Herut. And why should you?

By the way, the more I live, the more I feel among "the children of Zeev Jabotinsky," no matter what. That Eri is his son is not a sufficient reason to renounce his tradition.

(IV) My Proposal of Action, right now, will be very brief:

a. Keep the Kedem Club alive, but only as a center of debate, not as a "political party," for it will not succeed in this; it will not succeed even in drafting a Manifesto . . .

b. Start PUBLICATIONS. A good QUARTERLY, for instance, or even non-periodical pamphlets. As a "PUBLISHER," you may submit to the public a lot of controversial, or even contradictory, ideas, and thus use to good effect whatever ideas, materials, proposals you have developed. [. . .]

c. I must "keep on ice" any other proposals I might have. For you never did react to my various hints as to the possibility of initiating some kind of new "movement" of a Mediterranean nature (based on connexions between Israelis, French and Lebanese). I keep some contacts with all these elements, and there are signs of interest also among at least two "Moslem anti-Arab" personalities, one a Berber, the other a Kurdish leader. But I will not be able to exploit these opportunities unless there is some kind of organizational, ideological and financial basis for it. I am past hoping to gain anything by further "infiltration" of "official" or "semi-official" circles. Neither can I see that you will outgrow in the near future your present state of "crisis." I am sounding very cautiously the right-wing opposition. [. . .] Not that I have any illusions. But there are still a number of decent men in the right-wing leadership (not too influential, perhaps, when all is said). Should I keep you posted on these things, or is it entirely beyond your sphere of interests? You never replied, except by complete silence.

. . .

I must of course elaborate on points (a) and (b) of this chapter IV.

a. Nothing is easier than let "Kedem Club" go to the dogs, through inner disagreements and sheer disgust. I PAT YOU ON THE BACK AND PAT MYSELF ON THE BACK in an effort to persuade ourselves that we should n o t let all this go to the dogs. You have created some kind of a framework, keep it functioning, this is a prerequisite for any further development. As you cannot agree among yourselves, and with us here, as to the precise formulation of our common aims,—drop the attempt at an official formulation for the time being, and start to educate your audience on the p r o b l e m, if not yet on its exact solutions.

b. For reasons which are not entirely dissimilar from your circumstances—the Levant Club has become, in the main, a center of publications. However modest, it is useful, as such, and would not be useful at all without publications. BUT OF COURSE, a center of publications in Haifa—a "KEDEM PRESS" beside the Kedem Club (just as there is a Levant Press beside the Levant Club here)—would be of much greater importance. It might provide the real answer to your problems at the present stage.

I can promise you my full cooperation, if you decide to start publishing: my cooperation as a contributor, an agent abroad, an "advertiser" of your publications, within and without the Levant Club. The Levant Club might perhaps help you in getting across an English, perhaps also a French version, of your message.

It would be idle to go into concrete suggestions, proposals and plans, as long as I don't know whether you will publish.

*

**

. . . And now, l'Envoi . . .

It is of course discouraging to end a letter on page 14, close-typed at that . . . Words, words, words, and perhaps no nearer to a real message.

Nothing can replace those talks "in Paris, or Haifa," which we should have had a year ago. It might be several years before I come to see you, and then, in all probability, I will settle down, or at least try to settle down. Haifa is my preferite [*sic*] choice.

I still expect additional answers from both of you, and still hope that our correspondence will not prove unfruitful.

Shalom
Yours
A. G.

Notes

Introduction

1. The role of intellectuals in formulating national ideologies is debated in a large body of literature. This chapter relies on the insights of Stefan Berger, "The Power of National Pasts: Writing National History in Nineteenth- and Twentieth-Century Europe," in Stefan Berger (ed.), *Writing the Nation: a Global Perspective* (Basingstoke: Palgrave Macmillan, 2007), 32–46; John Breuilly, "Nationalism and the Making of National Pasts," in Susana Carvalho and François Gemenne (eds.), *Nations and Their Histories: Constructions and Representations* (Basingstoke: Palgrave Macmillan, 2009), 7–28; Robert J. Brym, *Intellectuals and Politics* (London: George Allen & Unwin, 1980); John Burrow, *A History of Histories: Epics, Chronicles, Romances and Inquiries from Herodotus and Thucydides to the Twentieth Century* (London: Penguin Books, 2009), 453–57, 462–66; John Coakley, "Mobilizing the Past: Nationalist Images of History," *Nationalism and Ethnic Politics* 10 (4), 2004, 535–40; Margarita Díaz-Andreu, "Nationalism and Archaeology," *Nations and Nationalism* 7 (4), 2001, 430–36; Geoff Eley, "Nationalism and Social History," *Social History* 6 (1), 1981, 96–99; Miroslav Hroch, "From National Movement to the Fully-Formed Nation: The Nation-Building Process in Europe," *New Left Review* 198, 1993, 3–20; Michael Kennedy and Ronald Grigor Suny, "Introduction," in Ronald Grigor Suny and Michael D. Kennedy (eds.), *Intellectuals and the Articulation of the Nation* (Ann Arbor: University of Michigan Press, 1999), 2, 25–27; Michael Keren, *Ben-Gurion and the Intellectuals: Power, Knowledge, and Charisma* (DeKalb, Illinois: Northern Illinois University Press, 1983); Michael Keren, *The Pen and the Sword: Israeli Intellectuals and the Making of the Nation-State* (Boulder and London: Westview, 1989); George Konrád and Ivan Szelényi, *The Intellectuals on the Road to Class Power* (tr. Andrew Arato and Richard E. Allen) (Brighton: Harvester, 1979); Charles Kurzman and Lynn Owens, "The Sociology of Intellectuals," *Annual Review of Sociology* 28, 2002, 63–90; David M. Potter, *The South and the Sectional Conflict* (Baton Rouge: Louisiana State University Press, 1968), 34–59; Katherine Verdery, "Civil Society or Nation? 'Europe' in

the Symbolism of Romania's Postsocialist Politics," in Suny and Kennedy (eds.), *Intellectuals and the Articulation of the Nation*, 301–340; Yael Zerubavel, *Recovered Roots: Collective Memory and the Making of Israeli National Tradition* (Chicago and London: University of Chicago Press, 1995), 10–12.

2. For a still valuable (though presented from a Zionist vantage point) review of Zionism's relations with its ideological rivals, including "Canaanism," see Ḥaim Avni and Gide'on Shim'oni (eds.), *Hatsiyonut Umitnagdeha Ba'am Hayehudi* (Jerusalem: Hasifriya Hatsiyonit, 1990).

3. See Yaacov Yadgar, *Israel's Jewish Identity Crisis: State and Politics in the Middle East* (Cambridge: Cambridge University Press, 2020), who argues that the reason for the retention of Jewish primordial identity markers as the formal gateways to Israeli body politic is that Zionism was never able (or willing) to provide a satisfying and normatively complete answer to the question "Who is a Jew?" that would fully replace the traditional definition of Jewishness.

4. Uriel Abulof, *The Mortality and Morality of Nations: Jews, Afrikaners and French Canadians* (Princeton, NJ: Princeton University Press, 2015), 212.

5. Ehud Ben-'Ezer, *En Shaananim Betsion: Śiḥot 'Al Meḥir Hatsiyonut* (Tel Aviv: 'Am 'Oved, 1986), 246.

6. A detailed history of the Young Hebrews as a movement is provided in James S. Diamond, *Homeland or Holy Land? The "Canaanite" Critique of Israel* (Bloomington/Indianapolis: Indiana University Press, 1986), and Yehoshu'a Porat, *Shelaḥ Ve'eṭ Beyado: Sipur Ḥayav̱ Shel Uriel Shelaḥ (Yonatan Raṭosh)* (Tel Aviv: Maḥbarot Lesifrut, 1989).

7. The precarious position of Hebrew in the Yishuv is explored by Liora R. Halperin, *Babel in Zion: Jews, Nationalism, and Language Diversity in Palestine, 1920–1948* (New Haven: Yale University Press, 2015).

8. These are the criteria of national identity listed by Yonatan Ratosh in his "Epistle to the Hebrew Youth" (1943), the first "Canaanite" public document (Yonatan Raṭosh, *Reshit Hayamim: Petiḥot 'Ivriyot* [Tel Aviv: Hadar, 1982], 35).

9. See, for instance, Herman van der Wusten, "The Occurrence of Successful and Unsuccessful Nationalisms," in Ronald J. Johnston, David B. Knight and Eleonore Kofman (eds.), *Nationalism, Self-Determination and Political Geography* (London, New York, Sydney: Croom Helm, 1988), 193–94.

10. Zerubavel, *Recovered Roots*, 6–7.

11. Saul Dubow, "Afrikaner Nationalism, Apartheid and the Conceptualization of 'Race,'" *Journal of African History* 33, 1992, 225.

12. Ana María Alonso, "The Effects of Truth: Re-presentations of the Past and the Imagining of Community," *Journal of Historical Sociology* 1 (1), 1988, 41.

13. E.g., Alraïd, "Ob Istorii (Zhaloba Profana)," *Rassviet* 27 (6), 8.2.1931, 6; Zeev Ben-Shlomo, "Masa' Bemerḥav Hazmanim: Śiḥa 'Im Hahisṭorion 'Adya Ḥoron," *Ma'ariv*, 16.9.1949, 6; 'A. G. Ḥoron, *Ḳedem Va'erev: Kna'an—Toldot Erets Ha'ivrim* (Tel Aviv: Dvir, 2000), 345.

14. Ron Kuzar, *Hebrew and Zionism: A Discourse Analytic Cultural Study* (Berlin, New York: Mouton de Gruyter, 2001), 207.

15. Yehoshu'a Porat, "Kna'aniyut 'Ivrit Ukhna'aniyut 'Arvit," in Dani Ya'aḳobi (ed.), *Erets Aḥat Ushe 'Amim Ba* (Jerusalem: Magnes, 1999), 84–88.

16. Bo'az 'Evron, "Hama'aśe—Uvavuato Haaḳademit," *Yedi'ot Aḥaronot*, 2.3.1984, 20.

17. Yair Sheleg, "Hakna'ani Harishon," *Haarets* (Friday supplement), 28.4.2000, 49.

18. Ḥanan Eshel, "Hatagliyot Haarkheologiyot Umif'al Ḥayaỵ Shel 'A. G. Ḥoron," in Ḥoron, *Ḳedem Ṿa'erev*, 29–32.

19. Asher Kaufman, *Reviving Phoenicia: The Search for Identity in Lebanon* (London: Tauris, 2004), 11.

20. In this book's geohistorical context this issue was investigated by Gil Eyal, *The Disenchantment of the Orient: Expertise in Arab Affairs and the Israeli State* (Stanford: Stanford University Press, 2006), and Laurence J. Silberstein, *The Postzionism Debates: Knowledge and Power in Israeli Culture* (New York and London: Routledge, 1999).

21. See especially Reinhart Koselleck, *Futures Past: On the Semantics of Historical Time* (tr. Keith Tribe) (Cambridge and London: MIT Press, 1985), who speaks of a "positional commitment" that in modernity becomes a "presupposition of historical knowledge," and John H. Rowe, "The Renaissance Foundations of Anthropology," *American Anthropologist* 67, 1965, 1–20.

22. Walker Connor, "The Timelessness of Nations," *Nations and Nationalism* 10 (1–2), 2004, 45.

23. Kaori O'Connor, "Cuisine, Nationality and the Making of a National Meal: The English Breakfast," in Carvalho and Gemenne (eds.), *Nations and Their Histories*, 159 (emphasis added).

24. See John Breuilly, "The Sources of Nationalist Ideology," in John Hutchinson and Anthony D. Smith (eds.), *Nationalism* (Oxford: Oxford University Press, 1994), 104–8; Eyal Chowers, "Time in Zionism: The Life and Afterlife of a Temporal Revolution," *Political Theory* 26 (5), 1998, 661–62; Prasenjit Duara, *Rescuing History from the Nation: Questioning Narratives of Modern China* (Chicago and London: University of Chicago Press, 1995), 4, 17–20, 87; Carlton J. H. Hayes, "Contributions of Herder to the Doctrine of Nationalism," *The American Historical Review* 32 (4), 1927, 719–36; Georg W. F. Hegel, *The Philosophy of History* (New York: Dover, 1956), 1–110; Johann G. Herder, *Against Pure Reason: Writings on Religion, Language, and History* (tr., ed. and intr. Marcia Bunge) (Minneapolis: Fortress, 1993).

25. Kennedy and Suny, "Introduction," 2–3.

26. Coakley, "Mobilizing the Past," 546–47.

27. Mary Matossian, "Ideologies of Delayed Development," in Hutchinson and Smith (eds.), *Nationalism*, 221–23.

28. Coakley, "Mobilizing the Past," 546.

29. O'Connor, "Cuisine, Nationality and the Making of a National Meal," 159.

30. Anthony D. Smith, "Ethnic Myths and Ethnic Revivals," *European Journal of Sociology* 25 (2), 1984, 292–97; Anthony D. Smith, *Myths and Memories of the Nation* (Oxford and New York: Oxford University Press, 1999), 57–68, 264.

31. Steven Knapp, "Collective Memory and the Actual Past," *Representations* 26, 1989, 129.

32. Coakley, "Mobilizing the Past," 542–45.

33. Baruch Kurzweil, "Ha'ḥidush' Bemered Ha"ivrim-Haḥadishim,'" *Beṭerem*, 1.1.1948, 13–15.

34. Baruch Kurzweil, *Sifrutenu Heḥadasha—Hemshekh o Mahapekha?* (Tel Aviv: Schocken, 1965), 270–300. An abridged English version of his large essay exists as well (Baruch Kurzweil, "The New 'Canaanites' in Israel," *Judaism* 2 (1), 1953, 3–15), to which I will be referring further.

35. Kurzweil, "The New 'Canaanites,'" 11–12. For Kurzweil's thought in general, see Ben-'Ezer, *En Shaananim Betsion*, 209–22; Baruch Kurzweil, *Bamaavaḳ 'Al 'Erke Hayahadut* (Tel Aviv: Schocken, 1969); Kurzweil, *Sifrutenu Heḥadasha*; Dan Miron, "Modern Hebrew Literature: Zionist Perspectives and Israeli Realities," *Prooftexts* 4 (1), 1984, 60–62; Gabriel Piterberg, *The Returns of Zionism: Myths, Politics and Scholarship in Israel* (London and New York: Verso, 2008), 179–85. For the background of his interest in the Young Hebrews, see Ben-'Ezer, *En Shaananim Betsion*, 215; Dan Laor, *Hamaavaḳ 'Al Hazikaron: Masot 'Al Sifrut, Ḥevra Ṿetarbut* (Tel Aviv: 'Am 'Oved, 2009), 282–95; Porat, *Shelaḥ Ṿe'eṭ Beyado*, 267–69.

36. Kurzweil, "The New 'Canaanites,'" 8, 9.

37. Colin Shindler, *The Rise of the Israeli Right: From Odessa to Hebron* (New York: Cambridge University Press, 2015), 34.

38. Kurzweil, "The New 'Canaanites,'" 11.

39. Yadgar, *Israel's Jewish Identity Crisis*, 25 (repeated on 190).

40. For a stingy parody of the Zionist "Rejection of the Diaspora," see Haim Hazaz, "The Sermon," in Robert Alter (ed.), *Modern Hebrew Literature* (New York: Behrman House, 1975), 271–87. For a discussion of the Young Hebrews' enthusiastic reception of the story, published originally in 1942 (which suggests they missed its satirical edge), see Laor, *Hamaavaḳ 'Al Hazikaron*, 233–49.

41. Anthony P. Cohen, *The Symbolic Construction of Community* (London and New York: Routledge, 1993), 40, 73.

42. Aharon Amir, *Ṿaani Besheli: 'Iyunim Utguvot, 1944–1996* (Tel Aviv: Yaron Golan, 1997), 111.

43. For more exhaustive comments on Scholem's thought, see Daṿid Oḥana, *Lo Kna'anim, Lo Tsalbanim: Meḳorot Hamitologia Haiśreelit* (Jerusalem: Keter, 2008), 258–66; David Ohana, *The Origins of Israeli Mythology: Neither Canaanites nor Crusaders* (tr. David Maisel) (New York: Cambridge University Press, 2012), 90–95; Piterberg, *The Returns of Zionism*, 155–91.

44. Kurzweil, *Bamaavaḳ 'Al 'Erke Hayahadut*, 97–240; Oḥana, *Lo Kna'anim, Lo Tsalbanim*, 266–72.

45. Kurzweil in addition overlooked Scholem's vehement hostility to "Canaanism" (Ben-'Ezer, *En Shaananim Betsion*, 300–1, 310–13).

46. Ya'aḳov Shaviṭ, *Me'ivri 'Ad Kna'ani—Praḳim Betoldot Haideologia Ṿehauṭopia Shel "Hatḥiya Ha'ivrit": Mitsiyonut Radiḳalit Leanṭi-Tsiyonut* (Jerusalem: Domino, 1984); Yaacov Shavit, *The New Hebrew Nation: A Study in Israeli Heresy and Fantasy* (London: Frank Cass, 1987).

47. Shaviṭ, *Me'ivri 'Ad Kna'ani*, 15, 68; Shavit, *The New Hebrew Nation*, 78.

48. Shaviṭ, *Me'ivri 'Ad Kna'ani*, 13, 68–69, 112, 167, 169; Shavit, *The New Hebrew Nation*, 77, 160.

49. For a penetrating criticism of Shavit's study made by a former "Canaanite," see Bo'az 'Evron, "Hama'aśe—Uvavuato Haaḳademit."

50. Diamond, *Homeland or Holy Land?*, 5.

51. Diamond, *Homeland or Holy Land?*, ix–xi. See James S. Diamond, *Baruch Kurzweil and Modern Hebrew Literature* (Chico: Scholars, 1983).

52. Kurzweil, "The New 'Canaanites,'" 7.

53. Diamond, *Homeland or Holy Land?*, 5, 67, 165.

54. Diamond, *Homeland or Holy Land?*, 9–23.

55. Diamond, *Homeland or Holy Land?*, 50.

56. Diamond, *Homeland or Holy Land?*, 124.

57. To name just a few examples: Nurit Gerts and Raḥel Weisbrod (eds.), *Haḳvutsa Hakna'anit—Sifrut Ṿeideologia* (Tel Aviv: Open University, 1986); Laor, *Hamaavaḳ 'Al Hazikaron*, 259–81; Dan Laor (ed.), *Yonatan Raṭosh: Mivḥar Maamre Biḳoret 'Al Yetsirato* (Tel Aviv: 'Am 'Oved, 1983); Yehuda Libes, "Mitos Tiḳun Haelohut: Ḳabalat Hazohar Ṿeshirat Raṭosh," *Alpaim* 7, 1993, 8–26; Ḥaim Pesaḥ, "'Ezra Pound, Yonatan Raṭosh Ṿehashira Ṿehaideologia Hakna'anit," *Moznaim* 24 (3–4), February–March 1982; Elliott Rabin, "'Hebrew' Culture: The Shared Foundations of Ratosh's Ideology and Poetry," *Modern Judaism* 19 (2), 1999, 119–32; Ziṿa Shamir, *Lehatḥil Mealef: Shirat Raṭosh, Meḳoriyuta Umeḳoroteha* (Tel Aviv: Haḳibbuts Hameuḥad, 1993); Ya'aḳov Shaviṭ, "Hayaḥasim Ben Idea Lepoetiḳa Beshirato Shel Yonatan Raṭosh," *Hasifrut* 17, 1974, 66–91; Judd L. Teller, "Modern Hebrew Literature of Israel," *Middle East Journal* 7 (2), 1953, 182–95.

58. Sh. Shifra, "Shira Keḥubba" (an interview with Yonatan Ratosh), *Davar*, 27.8.1971. Ratosh asserted the same in a letter to Horon from 1967 (Yonatan Raṭosh, *Mikhtavim [1937–1980]* [Tel Aviv: Hadar, 1986], 301).

59. Kurzweil, "The New 'Canaanites,'" 12.

60. For instances of framing "Canaanism" as a Jewish phenomenon, see Avni and Shim'oni (eds.), *Hatsiyonut Umitnagdeha Ba'am Hayehudi*, 327–50; Katell Berthelot, Joseph E. David and Marc Hirshman (eds.), *The Gift of the Land and the Fate of the Canaanites in Jewish Thought* (Oxford: Oxford University Press, 2014), 7.

61. For an example of such attitude see Gide'on Shim'oni, "Haleumiyut Hayehudit Kileumiyut Etnit," in Yehuda Reinharz, Yossef Shalmon and Gide'on

Shim'oni (eds.), *Leumiyut Ṿepolitiḳa Yehudit: Perspeḳṭivot Ḥadashot* (Jerusalem: Zalman Shazar Center, 1997), 81–92; Gideon Shimoni, *The Zionist Ideology* (Hanover and London: Brandeis University Press, 1995), 3–51.

Chapter 1

1. Jabotinsky Institute Archive (hereinafter JIA), File 11/18/4a, record dated 13.7.1963 (in French with occasional English phrases). Jabotinsky incorporated most of the data from this record into the chapter on Horon in his father's biography ('Eri Jabotinsky, *Avi, Zeev Jabotinsky*, [Jerusalem, Haifa, Tel Aviv: Steimatzky, 1980], 127–38). Aharon Amir partly relied on the record for his own biographical essay on Horon (Aharon Amir, "Petaḥ Davar: Ḥoron Beerets Ha'ivrim," in Ḥoron, *Ḳedem Ṿa'erev*, 17–27).

2. Yohanan Petrovsky-Shtern, *The Golden Age Shtetl: A New History of Jewish Life in East Europe* (Princeton and Oxford: Princeton University Press, 2014).

3. Benjamin Nathans, *Beyond the Pale: The Jewish Encounter with Late Imperial Russia* (Berkeley, Los Angeles, London: University of California Press, 2002).

4. Petrovsky-Shtern, *The Golden Age Shtetl*, 21. Nathans cautions not to conflate Jewish Russification with assimilation, given that most Russian-speaking secular Jews did not convert to Christianity, and that thanks to their traditional background in Jewish learning, they were by far more literate and therefore more culturally adept than their Russian neighbors. They thus quickly found themselves under the double fire of anti-Semitism on the one hand and suspicion of "apostasy" by *shtetl* Jews on the other (Nathans, *Beyond the Pale*, 112, 377).

5. Nathans, *Beyond the Pale*, 59; Petrovsky-Shtern, *The Golden Age Shtetl*, 345.

6. In the words of Horon's wife, Ada Gour, to Yehoshu'a Porat (Porat, *Shelaḥ Ṿe'eṭ Beyado*, 121): "You are lucky to be born in this country [the Land of Israel], this saved you from this revolting phenomenon" (Yiddish-speaking traditional Jews). A similar view is expressed by the author of Horon's obituary: "[H]e certainly had nothing in him of the Jewish town, for the simple reason that he was a man of culture [*sic*!]" (Sh. Yoḥana, "'Adya Zikhrono Livrakha," Yonatan Ratosh Archive, Genazim Institute, file 719/k-351).

7. Horon record (JIA/11/18/4a); Amir, "Petaḥ Davar," 19; email message from Margalit Shinar, 8.11.2009.

8. Horon's letter to Eri Jabotinsky, 18.7.1955 (JIA/4/4-4a).

9. Hillel Kook Archive (hereinafter HKA), file 31.

10. To mention just four pre-eminent Jewish men of letters among the "White" emigration: Mark Aldanov (né Landau, 1886–1957), Don-Aminado (né

Aminadav Shpoliansky, 1888–1957), Sasha Chornyi (né Glickberg, 1880–1932), and David Knut (1900–1955). The latter was vocal in his support for Zionism and took particular interest in its Jabotinskian brand. For a discussion of the Jewish involvement with the anti-Bolshevik "Whites," see Taro Tsurumi, "Jewish Liberal, Russian Conservative: Daniel Pasmanik between Zionism and the Anti-Bolshevik White Movement," *Jewish Social Studies: History, Culture, Society* 21 (1), 2015, 151–80.

11. For an analysis of *Samson*, see Eran Kaplan, *The Jewish Radical Right: Revisionist Zionism and its Ideological Legacy* (Madison: University of Wisconsin Press, 2005), 144–46. A similar perception of the relations between official Revisionism and its radical wing was developed independently by Ratosh, who ultimately became convinced that the latter was complicit alongside mainstream Zionism in the prolongation of the British Mandate (Diamond, *Homeland or Holy Land?*, 30–33).

12. I am grateful to Horon's daughter Margalit Shinar for sharing with me a detailed description of the event in an email message from 8.11.2009. See also Amir, "Petaḥ Davar," 20.

13. Email from Margalit Shinar, 8.11.2009, 16.11.2009.

14. For a critical review of Ben-Yehuda's life and place in Israeli collective memory, see Kuzar, *Hebrew and Zionism*, 41–120.

15. Cited in Kuzar, *Hebrew and Zionism*, 62.

16. The manual by Meyer Lambert was "undoubtedly the worst Hebrew grammar book ever published," Horon comments in his record.

17. Jabotinsky, *Avi, Zeev Jabotinsky*, 79. Aharon Amir's personal impression of Horon was that while he was "brilliant, brimming, talkative, true intellectual," he was also a pure theoretician who would prefer the publication of an ancient Hebrew poetry to any specific political action (Aharon Amir's diary, 25.9.1949, Genazim Institute, file 31296-k; I am indebted to Dr Shai Feraro for bringing this source to my attention).

18. A. Horon, "Hebrews and Jews: A Lecture Delivered in April 1945, New York, to the Leadership and Secretariat of the Hebrew Committee of National Liberation and the American League for Free Palestine," 15 (HKA/36).

19. Eri Jabotinsky remarks that before coming to Betar, Horon had an episode in the socialist Hashomer Hatsa'ir (Jabotinsky, *Avi, Zeev Jabotinsky*, 140), which is not corroborated in Horon's account.

20. Souvarine authored the earliest biography of Stalin to be published in the West, in 1935. Souvarine's papers are divided between the Houghton Library in Harvard University and the library of the Graduate Institute in Geneva. His biography (Jean-Louis Panné, *Boris Souvarine: le premier désenchanté du communisme* [Paris: Robert Laffont, 1993]) is focused almost exclusively on his relations with the communist movement.

21. Horon record (JIA/11/18/4a); Jabotinsky, *Avi, Zeev Jabotinsky*, 78; *Le Cran* 2, January 1931, 6 (handwritten notes on the margins of an article by

Mirkine); "L'Histoire du Betar en France," *Revue de la France Libre*, February 1951; obituary in *Hamashķif*, 23.1.1945, 4; Yirmiyahu Halpern, "Hamefaķed Victor Mirkine," *Hamashķif*, 8.3.1945, 3; Jean-François Muracciole, *Les Français Libres, l'Autre Résistance* (Paris: Tallandier, 2013). Details on Mirkine's military career can be found on https://www.ordredelaliberation.fr/fr/les-compagnons/669/victor-mirkin.

22. On Arber's activity in Betar, see Shindler, *The Rise of the Israeli Right*, 86–87.

23. Horon record (JIA/11/18/4a); interview with E. Jabotinsky, 1968 (HKA/35); Jabotinsky, *Avi, Zeev Jabotinsky*, 78.

24. On the self-defense school and its clash with the Tel Ḥai Fund, see Horon record (JIA/11/18/4a); JIA/32/2/21-l; JIA/33/2/21-l.

25. Porat, *Shelaḥ Ve'eṭ Beyado*, 31–32.

26. Amir, "Petaḥ Davar," 23; Porat, *Shelaḥ Ve'eṭ Beyado*, 31. Amir hints that in 1948 Abravaya served as an agent of the Israeli intelligence.

27. See a letter by Horon to Eri Jabotinsky, 14.6.1937 (JIA/16/14/4-a); Porat, *Shelaḥ Ve'eṭ Beyado*, 135.

28. Zeev Jabotinsky, "Civitaveccia," *Hayarden*, 10.12.1935, 2.

29. Horon record (JIA/11/18/4a); *Le Cran* 2, January 1931; Horon Archive (containing drafts of charts, maps and statistical calculations in Horon's handwriting); Yirmiyahu Halpern, "Tsir Rodêgal—Mikhtav Miparis," *Ha'am*, 7.6.1931. Halpern, who was strongly impressed by Horon's historiography in what concerns Hebrew naval achievements in antiquity, incorporated it in his book on the history of Hebrew seafaring (Yirmiyahu Halpern, *Teḥiyat Hayamaut Ha'ivrit* [Tel Aviv: Hadar, 1961]). Halpern's book, a fascinating mélange of historiography, anecdotes, personal reminiscences, and party propaganda, is an extremely valuable, though highly partisan, source on the beginnings of seafaring in the Hebrew Yishuv; on Halpern himself, see Jabotinsky, *Avi, Zeev Jabotinsky*, 113–16.

30. Undated lettercard from Horon to E. Jabotinsky (JIA/4/4-4a).

31. Undated letter from Horon to E. Jabotinsky (JIA/4/4-4a).

32. See text in JIA/4/4-4a, on a Rodêgal letterhead, dated to 25.8.1931. The text is in Hebrew, but in Latin letters, a point of importance to which I will return later.

33. "Le cran" is a naval technical term, but also means "courage" in French. The third issue is twice as short as the preceding two, which points to the dwindling funds of Rodêgal.

34. The issues of *Le Cran* in Horon's archive bear handwritten annotations that allow identification of Horon's contributions to the journal.

35. See announcements in *Le Cran* and *Rassviet* (27 [3], 18.1.1931, 12: Rodêgal ball on 31.1.1931; and 27 [13], 29.3.1931, 10: a lecture by Horon titled "War, Peace and Zionism," on 5.4.1931).

36. There was another Rodêgal group established in Latvia in 1933, but it had nothing in common with Horon's organization, and the similarity of names was probably coincidental (Halpern, *Teḥiyat Hayamaut Ha'ivrit*, 222).

37. Horon record (JIA/11/18/4a); Amir, "Petaḥ Davar," 22–23; Ch. Ben-Yerucham, *Sepher Bethar—Ḳorot Umḳorot*, vol. 1 (Jerusalem, Tel Aviv: Publishing Committee of Sepher Bethar, 1969), 308–9, 362; Halpern, *Teḥiyat Hayamaut Ha'ivrit*, 63; Jabotinsky, *Avi, Zeev Jabotinsky*, 128, 130–31, 152–56; 'Eri Jabotinsky, "Or Hayareaḥ Goneṭ Hirhurim," *Ḥerut*, 21.8.1949, 2; Orna Miller, "'Habaṭalion Heḥatukh' Ṿehanṭiyot Ha'kna'aniyot' BaETZEL Uvitnu'at Haḥerut—Me'haṿa'ad Ha'ivri' 'Ad 'Lamerḥav': Opozitsiya Lehanhagat HaETZEL Ṿe'Ḥerut,'" *'Iyunim Bitḳumat Iśrael* 14, 2004, 164; Porat, *Shelaḥ Ṿe'eṭ Beyado*, 126–27.

38. "Gedor" was Horon's neologism for "order," but it did not survive into modern Hebrew, which uses the word "misdar."

39. Horon record (JIA/11/18/4a); Jabotinsky, *Avi, Zeev Jabotinsky*, 13.

40. On the Betar naval school in Civitavecchia, see Ben-Yerucham, *Sepher Bethar*, vol. 1, 361–62; Ch. Ben-Yerucham, *Sepher Bethar—Ḳorot Umḳorot*, vol. 2 (1) (Jerusalem, Tel Aviv: Publishing Committee of Sepher Bethar, 1973), 169–72; Ch. Ben-Yerucham, *Sepher Bethar—Ḳorot Umḳorot*, vol. 2 (2) (Jerusalem, Tel Aviv: Publishing Committee of Sepher Bethar, 1975), 421–27, 553–56, 680–88, 778–81, 885–86; Halpern, *Teḥiyat Hayamaut Ha'ivrit*, 104–221; Kaplan, *The Jewish Radical Right*, 155–58; Porat, *Shelaḥ Ṿe'eṭ Beyado*, 127. That Betar managed to open a naval school in Mussolini's Italy is indicative of the attitude of Jabotinsky's movement to Italian fascism before it shifted to anti-Semitism in 1938 (one of whose casualties was the school itself). This topic has been extensively debated elsewhere (e.g., Daniel Kupfert Heller, *Jabotinsky's Children: Polish Jews and the Rise of Right-Wing Zionism* [Princeton: Princeton University Press, 2017], 6–12, 68–103; Kaplan, *The Jewish Radical Right*, 138–40, 149–58; Vincenzo Pinto, "Between *Imago* and *Res*: The Revisionist-Zionist Movement's Relationship with Fascist Italy, 1922–1938," *Israel Affairs* 10 (3), 2004, 90–109; Shindler, *The Rise of the Israeli Right*, 104–9; Dan Tamir, *Hebrew Fascism in Palestine, 1922–1942* [Basingstoke: Palgrave Macmillan, 2018]), and there is no need to dwell on it here.

41. On *On History*, see also Porat, *Shelaḥ Ṿe'eṭ Beyado*, 124–25; Yaacov Shavit, "Hebrews and Phoenicians: An Ancient Historical Image and its Usage," *Studies in Zionism* 5 (2), 1984, 164–67; Shaviṭ, *Me'ivri 'Ad Kna'ani*, 74–81; Shavit, *The New Hebrew Nation*, 80–85.

42. Alraïd, "Les Hébreux et Canaan," *Cahiers du Betar* 8, 1932, 2–4; Alraïd, "Esquisses d'Histoire Hébraïque," *Cahiers du Betar* 1, 10.2.1934, 4–10.

43. Porat, *Shelaḥ Ṿe'eṭ Beyado*, 127.

44. Protocol of the first Betar world congress, Danzig, 12.4.1931–16.4.1931 (JIA/1/29/2b).

45. JIA/1474: letter to seaman Grigory Wishniac, 21.2.1932; JIA/2958: letter to Aharon Zvi Propes, 27.11.1935; JIA/7128: letter to Eri Jabotinsky, 22.11.1935.

46. Letter from Ada Steinberg to Eri Jabotinsky, 5.6.1935 (JIA/4/4-4a). Ada Steinberg's mother was Zeev Jabotinsky's sister-in-law by second marriage (Jabotinsky, *Avi, Zeev Jabotinsky*, 138; Porat, *Shelaḥ Ṿe'eṭ Beyado*, 121).

47. Jabotinsky, *Avi, Zeev Jabotinsky*, 127.

48. Jabotinsky, *Avi, Zeev Jabotinsky*, 137.

49. Both were initially published in Yiddish, then republished in Hebrew (a peculiar step by Jabotinsky, given his well-known dislike of the "jargon," which probably points to a feeling of urgency to reach as broadest an audience as possible): Zeev Jabotinsky, "Mitologie fun Knaan," *Der Morgn Zhurnal*, 19.7.1931, 5; Zeev Jabotinsky, "Hamitologia Shel Kna'an," *Bamaḥane*, 21.8.1931, 2; Zeev Jabotinsky, "Israel un Carthage," *Haynt*, 22.1.1932, 5–6; Zeev Jabotinsky, "Iśrael Ṿeḳartago," *Ḥazit Ha'am*, 5.2.1932, 1.

50. Jabotinsky, *Avi, Zeev Jabotinsky*, 133.

51. Jabotinsky, *Avi, Zeev Jabotinsky*, 127, 137–38.

52. Jabotinsky's biographer Shmuel Katz cites Horon's words that "had Jabotinsky lived in ancient Rome he would have been declared a god" (Shmuel Katz, *Lone Wolf: A Biography of Vladimir (Zeev) Jabotinsky*, vol. II [New York: Barricade Books, 1996], 1316). Katz also quotes Horon's testimony on how Jabotinsky wrote the Betar anthem, one of whose rhymes was contributed by Horon (Adolph [*sic*] Gourevitch, "Jabotinsky and the Hebrew Language," in Joseph B. Schechtman, *Rebel and Statesman: The Vladimir Jabotinsky Story—The Last Years* [New York: Thomas Yoseloff, 1961], 594–95; 'A. G. Ḥoron, "Jabotinsky Ṿehaśafa Ha'ivrit," in Joseph B. Shechtman, *Zeev Jabotinsky: Parshat Ḥayaṿ; Sefer Shlishi: 1935–1940* [Tel Aviv: Ḳarni, 1959], 354–55; Shmuel Kats, *Jabo: Biografiia Shel Zeev Jabotinsky*, vol. 2 [Tel Aviv: Dvir, 1993], 863–64; Katz, *Lone Wolf*, 1331–32; Dan Miron, "Trumato Shel Zeev Jabotinsky Lashira Ha'ivrit Hamodernit," in Avi Bareli and Pinḥas Ginossar [eds.], *Ish Basa'ar: Masot Umeḥḳarim 'Al Zeev Jabotinsky* [Śde Boḳer: Ben-Gurion University, 2004], 246).

53. The other two were the Holocaust and the "Algerian treason" (by which Horon means de Gaulle's withdrawal from Algeria in 1962; this is a very significant aspect of Horon's mature politics that will be explored later in this book).

54. Letter by Zeev Jabotinsky to Eri Jabotinsky, 14.9.1935 (JIA/7121). For broader discussion of Jabotinsky's attitude to religion, see Jabotinsky, *Avi, Zeev Jabotinsky*, 95–106; Jan Zouplna, "The Evolution of a Concept: The Relationship between State and Religion in the Thought of Vladimir Jabotinsky, 1919–1940," *Journal of Modern Jewish Studies* 4 (1), 2005, 13–31.

55. Yosef Heller, *LEḤI: Ideologia Ṿepoliṭiḳa, 1940–1949* (Jerusalem: Keter, 1989), 236, n. 170.

56. Yavneh became the site of a religious academy in the aftermath of the Jewish anti-Roman Great Rebellion in 65–73 CE, while Samaria was the capital of the biblical Kingdom of Israel. The two are used respectively as prototypes of a deterritorialized and depoliticized Judaism ("a symbol of excessive spirituality and national defeatism" [Shmuel Almog, *Zionism and History: The Rise of a New Jewish Consciousness* (New York and Jerusalem: St. Martin's and Magnes, 1987), 124]), and a territorial sovereign national existence.

57. Amir, "Petaḥ Davar," 23–24; Ben-Yerucham, *Sepher Bethar*, vol. 2 (2), 513–18 (notably, this is the only place in this Betar chronicle that Horon is described as the ideologue of "Canaanism"); M. Benediktov, "Kongress Novoy Sionistskoy Organizatzii," *Rassviet*, n.d. (HKA/32); Halpern, *Teḥiyat Hayamaut Ha'ivrit*, 213; Horon record (JIA/11/18/4a); Jabotinsky, *Avi, Zeev Jabotinsky*, 131–32; Katz, *Jabo*, 942–43; Asher Nehor, "'Umma 'Ivrit'—Mahi?," *Ḥerut*, 19.8.1949, 5; Porat, *Shelaḥ Ṿe'eṭ Beyado*, 128–31; Shavit, *The New Hebrew Nation*, 29; Schechtman, *Rebel and Statesman*, 287; Shechtman, *Zeev Jabotinsky*, 28.

58. Jabotinsky, *Avi, Zeev Jabotinsky*, 133.

59. See, for example, letters by Jabotinsky, 8.2.1936 (JIA/3013) and 23.12.1938. For the original text of the latter in Russian, see JIA/3896. Jabotinsky, *Avi, Zeev Jabotinsky*, 134–35, contains a Hebrew translation. Horon replied to this letter on January 9, 1939 (he mentions this in his record), but I was unable to locate it in the archives.

60. For a fuller discussion of this topic see Roman Vater, "Hebrew as a Political Instrument: Language-Planning by the 'Canaanites,'" *Journal of Semitic Studies* 62 (2), 2017, 485–511.

61. Jabotinsky, *Avi, Zeev Jabotinsky*, 133.

62. E. Jabotinsky lists some of the Fund's achievements: funding the naval school in Civitavecchia, funding of the construction of the first glider in Palestine, funding the erection of the Revisionist Party headquarters in Tel Aviv, etc. (Jabotinsky, *Avi, Zeev Jabotinsky*, 132–33). Horon asserts in his record that it was he who designed the symbol of the Tel Ḥai Fund, some of whose elements were preserved in the symbol of the National Sick Fund in Israel.

63. Ben-Yerucham, *Sepher Bethar*, vol. 1, 45, 159, 359; Ben-Yerucham, *Sepher Bethar*, vol. 2 (1), 148; Ben-Yerucham, *Sepher Bethar*, vol. 2 (2), 556–58, 688–89, 886–88; Gourevitch, "Jabotinsky and the Hebrew Language," 582; Ḥoron, "Jabotinsky Ṿehaśafa Ha'ivrit," 332; Horon's letter to E. Jabotinsky, 14.6.1937 (JIA/16/14/4a); Horon record (JIA/11/18/4a); 'Eri Jabotinsky, "Or Hayareaḥ Goneṭ Hirhurim," *Ḥerut*, 19.8.1949, 5; Jabotinsky, *Avi, Zeev Jabotinsky*, 130–33, 152–53; Porat, *Shelaḥ Ṿe'eṭ Beyado*, 128, 132–33.

64. Jabotinsky, *Avi, Zeev Jabotinsky*, 132.

65. Horon, "Hebrews and Jews" (HKA/36).

66. Oḥana, *Lo Kna'anim, Lo Tsalbanim*; Ohana, *The Origins of Israeli Mythology*.

67. For a useful summary of these elements, see Shaviṭ, *Me'ivri 'Ad Kna'ani*, 74–89.

68. Amir, "Petaḥ Davar," 20; Adolphe G. Horon, "Canaan and the Aegean Sea: Greco-Phoenician Origins Reviewed," *Diogenes* 58, 1967, 40; 'A. G. Ḥoron, "Kna'an Ṿeyaṿan Bitḳufat Habronza," in Yonatan Raṭosh (ed.), *Minitsaḥon Lemapolet: Measef* Alef (Tel Aviv: Hadar, 1976), 212; Porat, *Shelaḥ Ṿe'eṭ Beyado*, 121, 132; Shavit, *The New Hebrew Nation*, 26; email from Margalit Shinar, 8.11.2009; letters from Ada Gour to E. Jabotinsky, 20.11.1935,

15.6.1937, letters from Horon to E. Jabotinsky, 20.5.1936, 22.9.1936, 14.6.1937, letter from E. Jabotinsky to Horon, 22.6.1937 (JIA/4/4-4a); Asia Institute booklet (JIA/16/14/4a). Ada Gourevitch was at the same time studying for a degree in physiology at the Sorbonne (undated letter from Ada Gour to E. Jabotinsky (JIA/4/4-4a)).

69. Roundtable in *Hakarat He'avar Betoda'at He'amim Uvtoda'at 'Am Iśrael: Ḳovets Hartsaot Shehushme'u Bakenes Hashlosha-'aśar Le'iyun Behistoria (Ḥanuka 5728)* (Jerusalem: The Historical Society of Israel, 1969), 141–42. For the meaning of the Ugarit discovery for contemporary Middle Eastern nationalist ideologies, see Miller, " 'Habaṭalion Heḥatukh,' " 165; Porat, *Shelaḥ Ṿe'eṭ Beyado,* 121–23, 139–42; Shaviṭ, *Me'ivri 'Ad Kna'ani,* 46–47, 87–89, 232–33; Shavit, *The New Hebrew Nation,* 85–86, 92–95.

70. See Binyamin Eliav, *Zikhronot Min Hayamin* (Tel Aviv: 'Am 'Oved, 1990). His daughters, Ya'el Loṭan (1935–2009) and Miri Eliav-Feldon, are both prominently associated with the Israeli radical Left.

71. Porat, *Shelaḥ Ṿe'eṭ Beyado,* 157; Shaviṭ, *Me'ivri 'Ad Kna'ani,* 83.

72. Ben-Yerucham, *Sepher Bethar,* vol. 2 (1), 152; Porat, *Shelaḥ Ṿe'eṭ Beyado,* 128; Shavit, "Hebrews and Phoenicians," 171; Shaviṭ, *Me'ivri 'Ad Kna'ani,* 55.

73. See Horon's letter to E. Jabotinsky, 14.6.1937 (JIA/16/14/4a).

74. Horon record (JIA/11/18/4a); E. Jabotinsky interview (HKA/35); Jabotinsky, *Avi, Zeev Jabotinsky,* 142–43.

75. For a detailed discussion of the circumstances that brought Ratosh to Paris, see Porat, *Shelaḥ Ṿe'eṭ Beyado,* 80–120, 135–49.

76. Yonatan Raṭosh, "Shira Ṿeideologia (b): Kakh Hayiti Le'kna'ani,' " *Yedi'ot Aḥaronot,* 20.2.1981, 23. See also Raṭosh, *Reshit Hayamim,* 12–15; Roman Vater, "Down with Britain, Away with Zionism: The 'Canaanites' and 'Lohamey Herut Israel' between Two Adversaries," *Melilah* 10, 2013, 29–35.

77. Jabotinsky, *Avi, Zeev Jabotinsky,* 79.

78. Jabotinsky, *Avi, Zeev Jabotinsky,* 130.

79. Jabotinsky, *Avi, Zeev Jabotinsky,* 130.

80. Porat, *Shelaḥ Ṿe'eṭ Beyado,* 74–75, 81, 89–91, 111, 136–42.

81. Jabotinsky, *Avi, Zeev Jabotinsky,* 130; Porat, *Shelaḥ Ṿe'eṭ Beyado,* 74–75, 89–91, 133, 150; Raṭosh, *Mikhtavim,* 303–4, 306; email from Margalit Shinar, 11.11.2009. More information on the intellectual bond between Horon and Ratosh can be found in Amir, "Petaḥ Davar," 26–27; Diamond, *Homeland or Holy Land?,* 34, 37–38; Porat, *Shelaḥ Ṿe'eṭ Beyado,* 142–43, 153–56, 390–91; Raṭosh, *Mikhtavim,* 23, 28; Raṭosh, *Reshit Hayamim,* 8, 12–15, 29–31; Shaviṭ, *Me'ivri 'Ad Kna'ani,* 63–66; Shavit, *The New Hebrew Nation,* 43–46.

82. Porat, *Shelaḥ Ṿe'eṭ Beyado,* 205–6.

83. For an analysis of the 1940 split, see Heller, *LEḤI*. Uri Avnery poignantly describes the shock and the disarray caused by Stern's split in the ranks of the ETZEL, with the Second World War in the background (Uri Avnery, *Opṭimi* I [Tel Aviv: Yedi'ot Aḥaronot, 2014], 109–15).

84. Porat, *Shelaḥ Ṿe'eṭ Beyado,* 219. On the connection between Ratosh and Stern, see Heller, *LEḤI,* 194–95, 512; Zeev Ivianski, *LEḤI—'Iśvat Rishona:*

'Iyunim Benaftule Teḳufa Ṿaderekh (Tel Aviv: Yair, 2003), 520–77 (a very elaborate discussion of the connection between "Canaanism" and LEHI, but written with a polemical objective from the standpoint of standard Zionism); Porat, *Shelaḥ Ṿe'eṭ Beyado*, 204–23; Raṭosh, *Mikhtavim*, 51–72; Raṭosh, *Reshit Hayamim*, 22–28. This boasting of Ratosh (who lived until 1981) concerning his influence on Stern (who died at the hands of the British police in 1942) made 'Amos Ḳenan, an intellectual and writer who was affiliated with the "Canaanites" in the late 1940s, remark with irritation in 1977 that he disliked "living people wielding influence over dead people" (interview with 'Amos Ḳenan, *Proza*, August–September 1977, 4).

85. Porat, *Shelaḥ Ṿe'eṭ Beyado*, 209.

86. It is traced quite efficiently by Heller, *LEḤI*.

87. Jabotinsky, *Avi, Zeev Jabotinsky*, 130.

88. See announcement in *Le Judaïsme Sephardi*, 66, December 1938, 148.

89. See previous endnote (Ratosh is identified as "M[onsieur] U[riel] Halpérine").

90. Porat, *Shelaḥ Ṿe'eṭ Beyado*, 133.

91. As recently as June 1937, in his letter to E. Jabotinsky, Horon proposed to accept the partition of Palestine as delineated by the Peel Commission and to manipulate it according to the needs of Zionism.

92. Porat (*Shelaḥ Ṿe'eṭ Beyado*, 150) identifies Belial correctly as G. Blumberg, whereas Tamir (*Hebrew Fascism in Palestine*, 197) misattributes this pseudonym to Horon. My thanks go to Christine Blumberg and Henriette Asséo for confirming the pseudonyms.

93. Email from Margalit Shinar, 7.11.2009.

94. For a discussion of the Egyptian/Canaanite deity Hor/Horus/Horon and its derivatives, see W. F. Albright, "The Canaanite God Ḥaurôn (Ḥôrôn)," *The American Journal of Semitic Languages and Literatures* 53 (1), 1936, 1–12; W. F. Albright, "The Egypto-Canaanite Deity Haurôn," *Bulletin of the American Schools of Oriental Research* 84, 1941, 7–12; Guy and Noga Darshan, *Hamitologiya Hakna'anit* (Tel Aviv: Mapa, 2009), 149–50; John Gray, "The Canaanite God Horon," *Journal of Near Eastern Studies* 8 (1), 1949, 27–34; 'A. G. Ḥoron, "Haḳedem Ha'ivri," in Raṭosh (ed.), *Minitsaḥon Lemapolet*, 227; 'A. G. Ḥoron, "Hakoptim—'Hamitsrim Haamitiim,'" *Ḳeshet* 6 (4), 1964, 180; Ḥoron, *Ḳedem Ṿa'erev*, 167–68, 172, 175, 298.

95. Margalit Shinar (email, 7.11.2009) attests that since the late 1920s, her father was being teasingly called "l'autre Adolphe," which only increased his dislike of his own given name.

96. Cited by Diamond, *Homeland or Holy Land?*, 36. Also A. Gour, "Hébreux et Juifs" (1939?; the National Library of Israel, file S39 B426), 31.

97. In a letter of May 1936 to E. Jabotinsky, Horon expressed a strong indignation with the *havlaga* (JIA/4/4–4a).

98. Porat, *Shelaḥ Ṿe'eṭ Beyado*, 151–53.

99. G. Belial, "Peuple Sans Terre, Terre Sans Peuple" (Central Zionist Archives, file A549/19–54).

100. This point betrays a clear influence by Yonatan Ratosh, who in the wake of the Peel Commission report in summer 1937 (that is, before he became a "Canaanite") published for the first time in the Revisionist press an open call for the disposal of the British Mandate and the establishment of an independent state by the Yishuv (See "'Einenu Neśuot El Hashilṭon," in Raṭosh, *Reshit Hayamim*, 42–59). Jabotinsky's rejection of this project pushed Ratosh away from Revisionism and toward the ideas propagated by Horon.

101. Avnery, *Opṭimi* I, 156.

102. Josef Ostermann, "Ben 'Ivriyut Leyahadut," *Haḥevra* 2 (19–20), October 1941, 300–1; Josef Ostermann, "Hamitos Shel Bene 'Ever," *Haḥevra* 2 (21–22), November 1941, 319–20; Josef Ostermann, "Apologia," *Haḥevra* 2 (23–24), December 1941, 325–26, 336; Ariel Avnery, "'Shem' Soter Ṿeḳore," *Haḥevra* 2 (27–28), March 1942, 363–64 (this issue contains another article signed by Josef Ostermann). See also "Ariel" [Avnery], "Isṭraṭegia Shel Ta'amula 'Ivrit," *Haḥevra* 6 (78), September 1946, 97–98. It is noteworthy that the first of these articles was accompanied by an editorial note promising an article that would refute *Shem*'s historical vision so enthusiastically endorsed by Avnery.

103. On *Shem*'s influence on Avnery, see Diamond, *Homeland or Holy Land?*, 43; Nitsa Er'el, *'Bli Mora Bli Maśo Panim': Uri Avnery Ṿe'Ha'olam Haze'* (Jerusalem: Magnes, 2006), 26–28; Porat, *Shelaḥ Ṿe'eṭ Beyado*, 182. On Avnery's politics and its convoluted relation to "Canaanism," see Uri Avnery, *Milḥemet Hayom Hashvi'i* (Tel Aviv: Daf Ḥadash, 1969), 145–80; Uri Avnery, "Haemet 'Al Hakna'anim," *Proza* 17–18, 1977, 26–27; Avnery, *Opṭimi* I, 152–81; Diamond, *Homeland or Holy Land?*, 93–95, 150–51, 161; Er'el, *'Bli Mora Bli Maśo Panim,'* 13–36; Oḥana, *Lo Kna'anim, Lo Tsalbanim*, 123–24; Porat, *Shelaḥ Ṿe'eṭ Beyado*, 182–84, 307–10; Shaviṭ, *Me'ivri 'Ad Kna'ani*, 145–54; Shavit, *The New Hebrew Nation*, 135–46, 148–53; also email from Margalit Shinar, 11.11.2009.

104. Dan Tamir, "Some Thoughts about Hebrew Fascism in Inter-War Palestine," *Zeitschrift für Religions- und Geistesgeschichte* 63 (4), 2011, 376. The brochure was brought to him by Ratosh upon his return from Paris (Ivianski, *LEḤI*, 537).

105. *Haḥevra* 3 (37–38), February 1943, 466 contains an announcement of Wańkowicz's forthcoming lecture in Tel Aviv on the "Birth of Zionism."

106. There are indeed records of meetings between Stern and high-ranking Polish civil and military officials in Palestine (Heller, *LEḤI*, 269, n. 257). Some aspects of these contacts are examined by Dominika Cholewinska-Vater, "Contested Loyalties in War: Polish-Jewish Relations within the Anders Army" (PhD dissertation, University of Manchester, 2019) and David Engel, "The Frustrated Alliance: The Revisionist Movement and the Polish Government-in-exile, 1939–1945," *Studies in Zionism* 7 (1), 1986, 11–36.

107. Shaviṭ, *Me'ivri 'Ad Kna'ani*, 90–91; Shavit, *The New Hebrew Nation*, 27, 46–47.

108. Porat, *Shelaḥ Ṿe'eṭ Beyado*, 134–35, 153.

109. *Hakarat He'avar*, 143.

110. Avnery, *Opṭimi* I, 158.

111. Eliav, *Zikhronot Min Hayamin*, 138.

112. Porat, *Shelaḥ Ṿe'eṭ Beyado*, 134. Similar suggestions were made by Avraham Stern early in the war (Heller, *LEḤI*, 514).

113. Porat, *Shelaḥ Ṿe'eṭ Beyado*, 153.

114. For a thorough discussion of the social and political atmosphere in 1930s France, see Michael R. Marrus and Robert O. Paxton, *Vichy France and the Jews* (Stanford: Stanford University Press, 1995), 34–71.

115. "Documents sur le National-Socialisme," présentés par Brice Parain & George Blumberg, *La Nouvelle Revue Française*, 1.8.1933, 234–62. I am grateful to Christine Blumberg and Henriette Asséo for drawing my attention to this source.

116. Sheleg, "Hakna'ani Harishon."

117. Alice Sen, "Slida 'Amuḳa," letter to *Haarets* Friday supplement, 12.5.2000, 4.

118. Horon record (JIA/11/18/4a); Jabotinsky, *Avi, Zeev Jabotinsky*, 135; Porat, *Shelaḥ Ṿe'eṭ Beyado*, 156; Sen, "Slida 'Amuḳa"; email from Margalit Shinar, 8.11.2009. On the Emergency Rescue Committee, see Andy Marino, *A Quiet American: The Secret War of Varian Fry* (New York: St. Martin's, 1999). On wartime Jewish emigration from France to the USA, see Marrus and Paxton, *Vichy France and the Jews*, 114, 161–64.

119. His wife Marcelle Cazés, son Jean-Pierre Jossua, and father-in-law managed to escape from France to Argentina via Portugal in 1942, while Leon Jossua willingly stayed behind to continue in the Resistance. After the war, Jean-Pierre Jossua converted to Catholicism, took orders, and became a renowned Dominican theologian and writer. He briefly recalls La Renaissance Hébraïque and Horon in his unpublished "En causant avec Edward Kaplan" (a professor emeritus of philosophy in Brandeis University, specializing in interfaith dialogue). Thanks are due again to Christine Blumberg and Henriette Asséo.

120. This is the explanation given by Edmond Asséo in his unpublished memoirs, as communicated to me by Christine Blumberg and Henriette Asséo. Yehoshu'a Porat, *Shelaḥ Ṿe'eṭ Beyado*, 157, explains the change as a measure to elude any association with Maurras, who now became one of Pétain's strongest advocates.

121. And not in 1949, as claimed by Porat, *Shelaḥ Ṿe'eṭ Beyado*, 264, who relied on a faulty recollection by Ada Gour.

122. D. Gil'adi, "'Masada' Asher Bemaḥane Compiègne," *Ma'ariv*, 17.5.1963, 6.

123. Yosef Ariel, "Mistorin Ushmo 'Masada,'" *Ma'ariv*, 28.5.1963, 20.

124. Yad Ṿashem, file M/25. Further information regarding La Renaissance Hébraïque and *Shem* is in Amir, "Petaḥ Davar," 25–26; Jabotinsky, *Avi, Zeev Jabotinsky*, 133, 135–36; Porat, *Shelaḥ Ṿe'eṭ Beyado*, 132–33, 149–53; "L'aventure de SHEM" (unpublished text by Christine Blumberg and Henriette

Asséo; an abridged version is in Henriette Asséo, Annie Bellaïche-Cohen, Muriel Flicoteaux, Corry Guttstadt, Xavier Rothea, Sabi Soulam, Alain De Toledo (eds.), *Mémorial des Judéo-Espagnols Déportés de France* [Paris: Éditeur Muestros Dezaparesidos, 2019, 325–27]); personal information provided by Christine Blumberg and Henriette Asséo.

125. Porat, *Shelaḥ Ve'eṭ Beyado*, 421, no. 90.

126. Both Marrus and Paxton, *Vichy France and the Jews*, 310–15, Samuel Moyn, *A Holocaust Controversy: The Treblinka Affair in Postwar France* (Hanover and London: Brandeis University Press, 2005), 13–19, and Adam Rayski, *The Choice of the Jews Under Vichy: Between Submission and Resistance* (tr. Will Sayers) (Notre Dame: University of Notre Dame Press, 2005), 211–17, devote some attention to "Massada," but make no mention of *Shem* or of both movements' interest in Hebrew history. Rayski and Moyn discuss in some detail Kadmi-Cohen's entanglement with the Vichy authorities, with Moyn wondering about the extent this might have influenced the future life choices of Kadmi-Cohen's son, Jean-François Steiner, author of the scandalous *Treblinka: The Revolt of an Extermination Camp* (Paris: Fayard, 1966) and husband of the granddaughter of the Wehrmacht field marshal Walther von Brauchitsch.

127. Anon., "Livres Recemment Parus," *Le Cran*, no. 2, January 1931, 23.

128. Jabotinsky, *Avi, Zeev Jabotinsky*, 135; Porat, *Shelaḥ Ve'eṭ Beyado*, 156; Sen, "Slida 'Amuḳa"; email from Margalit Shinar, 8.11.2009. Schechtman's biography of Jabotinsky erroneously relates that Horon accompanied Zeev Jabotinsky in his final days in America (Shechtman, *Zeev Jabotinsky*, 168). This is plainly impossible, since Horon's daughter Alice was born in Nice on August 13, 1940, exactly a week after Jabotinsky's death in New York (letter from Horon to Eri Jabotinsky, 20.8.1940 [JIA/4/4-4a]).

129. Horon record (JIA/11/18/4a); email from Margalit Shinar, 8.11.2009.

130. According to his obituary notice, published in *Ma'ariv*, 24.9.1972, Horon headed the Russian and French translation service.

131. Ben-Shlomo, "Masa' Bemerḥav Hazmanim"; 'A. G. Ḥoron, *Erets-Haḳedem: Madrikh Hisṭori Umdini Lamizraḥ Haḳarov* (Tel Aviv: Ḥermon, 1970), back cover; Jabotinsky, "Or Hayareaḥ Goneṭ Hirhurim," 19.8.1949; Panné, *Boris Souvarine*, 296; email from Margalit Shinar, 8.11.2009; letter from E. Jabotinsky, 22.1.1944 (JIA/11/18/4a).

132. On that matter see Kaufman, *Reviving Phoenicia*, 78.

133. Yad Vashem, file M25/10.

134. The main scholarly works dealing with the "Bergson group" and the traces it left in Israeli politics are Eran Kaplan, "A Rebel with a Cause: Hillel Kook, Begin and Jabotinsky's Ideological Legacy," *Israel Studies* 10 (3), 2005, 87–103; Rebecca Kook, "Hillel Kook: Revisionism and Rescue," in Mark LeVine and Gershon Shafir (eds.), *Struggle and Survival in Palestine/Israel* (Berkeley, Los Angeles, London: University of California Press, 2012), 157–69; Rafael Medoff, *Militant Zionism in America: The Rise and Impact of the Jabotinsky Movement in the United States, 1926–1948* (Tuscaloosa and London: University

of Alabama Press, 2002); Rafael Medoff and David Wyman, *A Race against Death: Peter Bergson, America, and the Holocaust* (New York: New, 2002); Miller, "'Habaṭalion Heḥatukh'"; Sarah E. Peck, "The Campaign for an American Response to the Nazi Holocaust," *Journal of Contemporary History* 15 (2), 1980, 367–400; Monty Noam Penkower, "In Dramatic Dissent: The Bergson Boys," *American Jewish History*, 1.3.1981, 281–309; Monty Noam Penkower, "Vladimir (Ze'ev) Jabotinsky, Hillel Kook-Peter Bergson and the Campaign for a Jewish Army," *Modern Judaism* 31 (3), 2011, 1–43; Louis Rapaport, *Shake Heaven and Earth: Peter Bergson and the Struggle to Save the Jews of Europe* (Jerusalem: Gefen, 1999); Arye Bruce Saposnik, "Advertisement or Achievement? American Jewry and the Campaign for a Jewish Army, 1939–1944: A Reassessment," *Journal of Israeli History* 17 (2), 1996, 193–220; Avi Shilon, "Milḥemet Sheshet Hayamim Ṿehit'orerut Hara'ayon Hakna'ani," *'Iyunim Bitḳumat Iśrael* 11, 2017, 102–29; Judith Tydor Baumel, *The "Bergson Boys" and the Origins of Contemporary Zionist Militancy* (Syracuse: Syracuse University Press, 2005); Judith Tydor Baumel, "The IZL Delegation in the USA 1939–1948: Anatomy of an Ethnic Interest/Protest Group," *Jewish History* 9 (1), 1995, 79–89; Roman Vater, "Pathways of Early Post-Zionism," in Frank Jacob and Sebastian Kunze (eds.), *Jewish Radicalisms: Historical Perspectives on a Phenomenon of Global Modernity* (Berlin/Boston: de Gruyter Oldenbourg, 2020), 23–74; David S. Wyman, "The Bergson Group, America, and the Holocaust: a Previously Unpublished Interview with Hillel Kook," *American Jewish History* 89 (1), 2001, 3–34. Original materials produced by the "Bergson group," which make it possible to trace its eight-year-long activity (1940–1948) as well as its ideological metamorphoses, are located in the Hillel Kook Archive in Śde Boḳer. It is notable that the Hebrew Committee's main channel to the Hebrew Yishuv in real time was through the periodical *Haḥevra* (particularly in the years 1944–1947), in which just a few years previously Uri Avnery had published his enthusiastic review of *Shem*. The Hebrew Committee is mentioned also in Halpern, *Teḥiyat Hayamaut Ha'ivrit*, 276; Jabotinsky, *Avi, Zeev Jabotinsky*, 136, 157–63; Natan Yalin-Mor, *Loḥame Ḥerut Iśrael: Anashim, Re'ayonot, 'Alilot* (Jerusalem: Shiḳmona, 1974), 249–50, 382.

135. Shechtman, *Zeev Jabotinsky*, 270, reports a clandestine meeting between Horon and Begin that took place in January 1947, following which, according to Eri Jabotinsky, Begin came to see "a deep moral truth" in the Horon-Kook distinction between "Hebrews" and "Jews" (Eri Jabotinsky, "Jews and Hebrews" [JIA/3/13/410]), which influenced ETZEL's subsequent political rhetoric. This shift, however, was apparently not for the long haul: in Israel's history Begin is remembered as one of its most "Jewish" politicians, to whom the right of the Jews to the Land of Israel was grounded in the Bible's factual veracity (Shindler, *The Rise of the Israeli Right*, 6, 269).

136. "A Nation Is a Sovereign Will, Letter by A. G. Horon," *The Answer* 2 (8–9), 29.8.1944 (HKA/41).

137. For instance, "Declaration of Principles of the Hebrew National Movement," 10.4.1944 (JIA/3/52p); "Hebrews and Jews: A Lecture Delivered

in April 1945, New York, to the Leadership and Secretariat of the Hebrew Committee of National Liberation and the American League for Free Palestine" (JIA/4/52p; HKA/36); "The Hebrew Movement—An Outline," January 1947 (JIA/2/52p; HKA/36).

138. HKA/1.

139. Horon, "Hebrews and Jews" (HKA/36; emphasis added).

140. JIA/3/13/410.

141. Cited in Shavit, *The New Hebrew Nation*, 70.

142. Horon, "The Hebrew Movement" (JIA/2/52p; HKA/36).

143. Horon, "The Hebrew Movement" (JIA/2/52p; HKA/36).

144. Raṭosh, *Reshit Hayamim*, 170–71. A Hebrew-language ideological manifesto of the Hebrew Committee, which illustrates the differences between its platform and "Canaanism," is found in Shaviṭ, *Me'ivri 'Ad Kna'ani*, 191–201. LEHI also denounced Kook for his willingness to forego a mass Jewish immigration, for his pretence to construct a focus of Hebrew power outside Palestine, and for his pro-American (i.e., proimperialist) leanings (Heller, *LEḤI*, 212, 554, no. 71; Ivianski, *LEḤI*, 554).

145. HKA/30.

146. HKA/25; HKA/50; JIA/7/1/4ḥ.

147. An exhaustive exploration of all these questions and other related issues is provided in my "Pathways of Early Post-Zionism."

148. Email from Margalit Shinar, 8.11.2009.

149. Jabotinsky, *Avi, Zeev Jabotinsky*, 79. A similar assessment is given by Uri Avnery, *Opṭimi* I, 157. For a contemporary's observation of the ideological differences between Horon and Kook (as well as other "Canaanite"-inclined groups), see Iśrael Segal, "'Ivrim' Ỵ'ihudim': Giglulaỵ Shel Re'ayon," *Haḥevra* 7 (82), March 1947, 186–88.

150. Letter from Horon to E. Jabotinsky, 16.3.1953 (JIA/4/4-4a).

151. HKA/48; HKA/49.

152. Jabotinsky, *Avi, Zeev Jabotinsky*, 136.

153. Untitled document, Ratosh Archive, file 719/k-359 (with the following hand-written annotation: "Written in Paris, early summer 1948—for, and by request of, the Irgun (through their Plenipotentiary to France, and the European Inspector of the Commander-in-chief, Beigin)").

154. Letter from Ada Gour to E. Jabotinsky, 20.11.1948; letters from Horon to E. Jabotinsky, 29.3.1949, 8.4.1949, 11.4.1949 (JIA/4/4-4a); Aharon Amir's diary, 25.9.1949 (Genazim Institute, 31296-k).

155. Horon's source was the 1949 Johannesburg edition of *Taryag Millim*, which used the Latin alphabet for a more efficient inculcation of Hebrew among adult learners. For the 1950 edition, Horon produced two appendices in which he commented on some outdated features of Jabotinsky's Hebrew based on his observations of the language spoken in Israel and also introduced a few "Canaanite" glosses (Vladimir Jabotinsky, *Taryag Millim* [Jerusalem: Eri

Jabotinsky, 1950]; Gourevitch, "Jabotinsky and the Hebrew Language," 584, 599; Ḥoron, "Jabotinsky Ṿehaśafa Ha'ivrit," 362).

156. See 'A. G. Ḥ., "Afriḳa: Prehisṭoria," "Ameriḳa: Prehisṭoria," "Asia: Prehisṭoria," "Iberia: Prehisṭoria," "Iberim," "Iṭalia: Prehisṭoria," "Eropa: Prehisṭoria," in *Encyclopaedia Hebraica* (vols. 2–5) (Jerusalem, Tel Aviv: Haḥevra Lehotsaat Entsiḳlopediot, 1950–1953).

157. Letter by Horon to the editorial board of *Alef*, 22.12.1950 (Ratosh Archive, file 719/690).

158. Porat, *Shelaḥ Ṿe'eṭ Beyado*, 262–63; letter from E. Jabotinsky to S. Halperin, 28.11.1949; letter from Horon to E. Jabotinsky, 17.1.1953 (JIA/4/4-4a).

159. Email from Margalit Shinar, 8.11.2009.

160. A document preserved in Horon's archive (file "Canaan—fundamental principles") refers to "Horon's house, 50 yards from the Jordanian border, TALPIOT, facing Mount Nebo."

161. Letter from Horon, October 1950 (JIA/4/4-4a).

162. Letter from E. Jabotinsky to Horon, 6.11.1950 (JIA/4/4-4a).

163. Letter from Horon to the editorial board of *Alef*, 22.12.1950 (Ratosh Archive, 719/690); letter by Horon to Aharon Amir, 22.9.1951 (correspondence between Adya Horon and Aharon Amir, in private possession, courtesy of Kedem Auction House and Dr Shai Feraro).

164. Letter from Horon to E. Jabotinsky, 15.10.1955, also letter from Horon to E. Jabotinsky, 19.7.1955 (JIA/4/4-4a).

165. Letters from Horon to E. Jabotinsky, 4.11.1952, 6.11.1952 (JIA/4/4-4a).

166. Email from Margalit Shinar, 8.11.2009.

167. On the Asia Institute see http://www.iranicaonline.org/articles/asia-institute-the-1.

168. For materials related to Horon's involvement in the Asia Institute and the ensuing scandal, see Horon Archive, Asia Institute files, and JIA16/14/4a.

169. Aharon Amir's diary, 1.4.1951, 9.5.1951, 16.9.1952 (Genazim Institute, 31296-k); letter from Yair Evron to Horon, 17.1.1951, letter from Horon to Aharon Amir, 19.2.1951 (Aharon Amir's correspondence, in private possession, courtesy of Kedem Auction House and Dr Shai Feraro); Porat, *Shelaḥ Ṿe'eṭ Beyado*, 249–50, 263–66. See also *Alef*, May 1951, September 1952, December 1952.

170. Letters from Horon to E. Jabotinsky and other Israeli addressees, 21.12.1951, 16.3.1953, 2.5.1955 (JIA/4/4-4a). Their contact was re-established only in the late 1960s (letter by S. Rin to Horon, 23.6.1967; Ratosh Archive, file 719/626).

171. Svi Rin, "The Narrative Literature in the Bible" (postgraduate seminar essay, University of Kentucky, 1955; Svi Rin Archive, Genazim Institute, file 395/k-11).

172. Letter from Horon to E. Jabotinsky, 26.1.1955 (JIA/4/4-4a).

173. Correspondence between Horon and the Young Hebrews, 1950–1952 (Aharon Amir's correspondence, in private possession, courtesy of Kedem

Auction House and Dr Shai Feraro; Ratosh Archive, files 719/210, 719/398, 719/401, 719/690, 719/722); letters from Horon to E. Jabotinsky, 6.11.1952, 17.1.1953, 20.12.1954, 4.2.1955, 2.5.1955 (JIA/4/4-4a); letter from Horon to E. Jabotinsky and S. Rosoff, 10.2.1956 (HKA/32); Horon Archive, file "Canaan—fundamental principles."

174. Aharon Amir's diary, 25.9.1949 (Genazim Institute, 31296-k).

175. See chapter 3 for further discussion.

176. For Kedem Club materials, see JIA/1/12/4a and JIA/3/12/4a; HKA/32; Israel State Archives, file GL-17109/33 (I thank Dr Shai Feraro for sharing the latter source with me). For an analysis of the club's activity in the context of the 1950s post-Zionism consult my "Pathways of Early Post-Zionism," esp. 50–60.

177. This topic (and the "Canaanite" input into it) is expanded upon in chapter 4.

178. Asher Kaufman (*Reviving Phoenicia*, 131) mentions the Paris-based Lebanese expatriate organization Nova Phoenicia and its journal *La Revue du Liban et de l'Orient Méditerranéen*. I found no evidence of any contacts between them and Horon, but it is plausible to assume that Horon was at least aware of their existence.

179. Letter from Horon to E. Jabotinsky, 26.1.1955 (JIA/4/4-4a). The names are noted down for posterity: Louis Anter, Fouad Farris, Chekri Kanaan, Lee Kanaan, Peter Mundaleck (all American Lebanese Christians), Mordecai Ben-Emek (otherwise Morton Dolinsky from Betar, who was observant), M. Z. Frank (affiliated with MAPAI), Adolphe Gourevitch (Horon, an anti-Zionist "Canaanite"), Murray K. Josephson and Herbert A. Kampf (member of the Zionist Organization of America).

180. This is made abundantly clear in articles penned by two ideologues of Maronite "Phoenician" nationalism, reproduced in a Hebrew translation in an appendix to Yonatan Raṭosh, *1967—Uma Hal'a?* (Tel Aviv: Ḥermon, 1967) (Elias Rabbabi, "Al Tiṭ'u Bazehut," 89–91; Albert Ghosn, "Hamaronim—'Am Halevanon," 92–103), as well as by the statements of a New Mexico–based organization called "Friends of Lebanon," whose declared purpose was "perpetuating the State of Lebanon as a Christian nation" (see *Memorandum no. 3* of the Levant Club, June 1955; Israel State Archives, file GL-17109/33).

181. Copies of these newspapers were preserved in Horon's archive but were disposed of at a certain point, due to their "obsolescence" and "irrelevance," as explained to me by Margalit Shinar. The Israel State Archives, file GL-17109/33, contain one bilingual issue of *The Lebanese Gazette—Leesan Al-Adl* (September 2, 1955), but Horon's contribution there is in English (A. H., "The Phoenician Column").

182. A. Gourevitch, "Arabia's Mythical Millions" (1955 typescript, JIA/8/52p); Adolphe Gourevitch, "Pan-Arabism," *Land Reborn* (a publication of the American Christian Palestine Committee) 4 (3), May–June 1953,

5 (JIA/16/14/4a); A. G. Horon, "Is there an 'Arab Civilization'? Islam and Arabism," *Commentary*, November 1958, 411–19.

183. Book prospectus in Horon Archive, Asia Institute files; letter from Horon to E. Jabotinsky, 12.2.1953 (JIA/4/4-4a). Horon suggested that Jabotinsky, who opened his own publishing house to put out the collected writings of his father (as supposedly no state-sanctioned publisher would do so at the time), would produce its Hebrew version.

184. Letter from Roland Laudenbach to A. Gourevitch, 22.11.1955; letter from Horon to E. Jabotinsky, 2.5.1955 (JIA/4/4-4a).

185. For instance, A. G. Horon, "Le Mythe Panarabe dans le Vide Oriental et Africain," *Est & Ouest*, 1-15.7.1957, 3–6; A. G. Horon, "L'URSS 'Amie' de l'Islam," *Est & Ouest*, 1-15.1.1958, 1–3; A. G. Horon, "Le Panarabisme," *Le Contrat Social* 1 (3), July 1957, 149–56; A. G. Horon, "La Grande Illusion," *Le Contrat Social* 2 (2), March 1958, 63–68; A. G. Horon, "Les Arabes depuis l'Islam," *Le Contrat Social* 2 (3), May 1958, 135–42; A. G. Horon, "Après Juin," *Le Contrat Social* 11 (6), November–December 1967, 367–72. The remainder of Horon's contributions was book reviews, and some of these reviews and articles Horon published simultaneously in English and Hebrew as well. See correspondence between Horon and Souvarine on that matter (and others) in Boris Souvarine's papers, Houghton Library, Harvard University, bMs Fr 375 (509).

186. Israel State Archives, file GL-17109/33.

187. For this biography (both its English and Hebrew versions) Horon supplied information about Jabotinsky's linguistic and literary activities, translated some of his poetry from Russian and Italian (Joseph B. Schechtman, *Rebel and Statesman: The Vladimir Jabotinsky Story—The Early Years* [New York: Thomas Yoseloff, 1956], 7–8; Schechtman, *The Vladimir Jabotinsky Story—The Last Years*, 536–545; Shechtman, *Zeev Jabotinsky*, 320), and contributed a whole chapter on Jabotinsky as a man of letters. Perhaps not incidentally since choosing this particular topic for Horon to tackle helped obscure his political disagreements with Jabotinsky.

188. Horon later made an apparently fruitless attempt to become a freelance writer for *Ḥerut* (correspondence with *Ḥerut* editor Aizik Remba, 1957–1958, JIA/25/4-141).

189. Memorandum of discussion with Col. Katriel S., 15.12.1954 (JIA/16/14/4a).

190. Apart from the publications of the Levant Club (*Behind the Arab Curtain* and the *Levant Memoranda*), most of the information concerning the club comes from correspondence between Horon and Eri Jabotinsky (JIA/4/4-4a; HKA/32).

191. For a contextual discussion of the Lebanese-Israeli contacts in the 1940s through the 1950s, see Laurie Zittrain Eisenberg, "From Benign to Malign: Israeli-Lebanese Relations, 1948–1978," in Clive Jones and Sergio

Catignani (eds.), *Israel and Hizbollah: An Asymmetric Conflict in Historical and Comparative Perspective* (London and New York: Routledge, 2010), 10–18; Laurie Eisenberg, "History Revisited or Revamped? The Maronite Factor in Israel's 1982 Invasion of Lebanon," *Israel Affairs* 15 (4), 2009, 373–81; Benny Morris, "Israel and the Lebanese Phalange: The Birth of a Relationship, 1948–1951," *Studies in Zionism* 5 (1), 1984, 125–44; Benny Morris, *Righteous Victims: A History of the Zionist-Arab Conflict, 1881–2001* (New York: Vintage, 2001), 494–98; Eyal Zisser, "The Maronites, Lebanon and the State of Israel: Early Contacts," *Middle Eastern Studies* 31 (4), 1995, 889–918.

192. See letters from Horon to E. Jabotinsky, 20.12.1954, 2.5.1955, 10.2.1956, 3.4.1956 (JIA/4/4-4a; HKA/32).

193. An interview with Temsamani (conducted by the Levant Club's "special correspondent"—Horon, in all probability) is reproduced in *Memorandum no. 8* of the Levant Club, October 1955 (Jabotinsky Institute Archive, file 31/18/4a). Horon himself referred to the Istiqlal as representation of the Arab minority in Morocco against the Berber (supposedly pro-French) majority (A. G., "Pan-Arab Propaganda," *Memorandum no. 4* of the Levant Club, June 1955; Israel State Archives, file GL-17109/33).

194. Letters from Horon to E. Jabotinsky, 6.11.1952, 12.12.1954, 9.9.1955 (JIA/4/4-4a).

195. Email from Margalit Shinar, 15.11.2009. Souvarine's help is mentioned by Horon in his record to Eri Jabotinsky.

196. Memorandum of discussion with Col. Katriel S., 15.12.1954 (JIA/16/14/4a).

197. Letter from Horon to E. Jabotinsky, 13.2.1955 (JJIA/4/4-4a).

198. Letter from Horon to A. Guillaume, 24.9.1953 (Horon Archive, Asia Institute files).

199. Letter from Horon to E. Jabotinsky, 26.1.1955 (JIA/4/4-4a).

200. Avnery, *Opṭimi* I, 180, 535–36. Avnery, who at that time was strongly advocating Algerian independence (while most of Israel's political elite sided with the French), calls Soustelle a "fascist."

201. Letter from Horon to A. Remba, 29.5.1957 (JIA/25/4-14l); Porat, *Shelaḥ Ve'eṭ Beyado*, 264. See also correspondence between Horon and the French consulate in New York (Horon Archive, Asia Institute files).

202. Letter from Horon to E. Jabotinsky, 19.11.1958 (JIA/4/4-4a).

203. His wife and daughters had moved there a few months earlier. Postcard from Ada Gour to E. Jabotinsky, 12.10.1958; letter from Horon to E. Jabotinsky, 19.11.1958 (JIA/4/4-4a); email from Margalit Shinar, 15.11.2009.

204. Letter from Horon to E. Jabotinsky, 2.5.1955 (JIA/4/4-4a).

205. Email from Margalit Shinar, 9.11.2009. Horon mentions his fruitless contacts with Zeev Ya'vets from Tel Aviv University in a letter to E. Jabotinsky of 11.12.1964 (JIA/4/4-4a).

206. Email from Margalit Shinar, 8.11.2009.

207. Letter from E. Jabotinsky to Justice Jacob Ziegelman, 3.1.1969 (JIA/11/184a).

208. Evgenii Belyaev, *Arabs, Islam and the Arab Caliphate in the Early Middle Ages* (tr. Adolphe Gourevitch) (Jerusalem: Israel Universities Press, 1969). Horon explained his motives for translating the book in a short article written for Boris Souvarine (A. G. Horon, "Un Arabisant Soviétique," *Le Contrat Social* 12 (1), January–March 1968, 77–79). Belyaev's book, according to Horon, was outstanding in comparison to the usual output of Soviet academe, given that Belyaev's insights on the origins of Islam were not too remote from his own (though it is possible that Horon crafted upon him his own ideas, as his "translator's notes" scattered throughout the book suggest).

209. Anwar G. Chejne, "*Arabs, Islam and the Caliphate in the Early Middle Ages* by E. A. Belyaev; Adolphe Gourevitch," *Journal of the American Oriental Society* 92 (1), 1972, 112–13; G. E. von Grunebaum, "*Arabs, Islam and the Arab Caliphate in the Early Middle Ages* by E. A. Belyaev," *Speculum* 45 (3), 1970, 453–55; Ira M. Lapidus, "*Arabs, Islam and the Arab Caliphate in the Early Middle Ages* by E. A. Belyaev; A. Gourevitch," *International Journal of Middle Eastern Studies* 2 (1), 1971, 86–87; Wilferd Madelung, "*Arabs, Islam and the Arab Caliphate in the Early Middle Ages* by E. A. Belyaev; Adolphe Gourevitch," *Journal of Near Eastern Studies* 31 (2), 1972, 128–29; Ehud Ya'ari, "Muḥammad Be'enaim Marksisṭiyot," *Davar*, 7.7.1970, 7.

210. Ḥoron, *Erets-Haḳedem*, 165; emails from Margalit Shinar, 8.11.2009, 9.11.2009, 15.11.2009.

211. Itsḥaḳ Oren and Michael Zand (eds.), *Kratkaia Evreiskaia Entsiklopediia* (Jerusalem: Keter, 1976–2005).

212. Materials related to these talks (posters, announcements, outlines, questions from the audience, etc.) are preserved in Horon's archive.

213. Reference to a Jewish "glorified ghetto" as an antithesis to a Hebrew nation-state is made by Yonatan Ratosh as well (Raṭosh, *Reshit Hayamim*, 170).

214. Reproduced by kind permission of Margalit Shinar.

215. Yigal Bin-Nun archive.

216. See materials pertaining to the planning and the preparation of the series and the book in Ratosh Archive, files 719/k-351, 719/k-353, 719/k-361, 719/k-365; letter from Horon to B. Souvarine, 5.1.1967 (Boris Souvarine Papers, Houghton Library, Harvard University, bMs Fr 375 (509)).

217. These reservations (some of them going back to the 1930s) Ratosh laid out in a broad letter he sent to Horon in January 1967 (Raṭosh, *Mikhtavim*, 300–9). Ratosh expressed his criticism of the club also in a couple of letters to Horon from 1965 through 1966 (Ratosh Archive, files 719/400, 719/402).

218. Porat, *Shelaḥ Ṿe'eṭ Beyado*, 333–38; Sheleg, "Hakna'ani Harishon."

219. Diamond, *Homeland or Holy Land?*, 95–96, points out that it was rather the secular, not the religious, members of the Greater Israel Movement who torpedoed the cooperation with Amir's Action Staff (the religious, like

Amir, saw in secular-socialist Zionism an adversary). Eri Jabotinsky also participated in the Greater Israel Movement, by his own admission, out of strategic considerations: as a committed secularist and post-Zionist, he could hardly have any common goal with national-religious rabbis.

220. Email from Margalit Shinar, 11.11.2009; also Porat, *Shelaḥ Ṿe'eṭ Beyado*, 338–40.

221. Sh. Yoḥana, "'Adya Zikhrono Livrakha," Ratosh Archive, file 719/k-351.

222. S. Rin's letter to Horon, 23.6.1967 (Ratosh Archive, file 719/626).

223. Raṭosh, *1967—Uma Hal'a?*.

224. Horon's hand-written comments to Ratosh's booklet, dated to 15.7.1967, are preserved in Ratosh Archive, file 719/k-356. See also Horon's French-language review of Ratosh's booklet (Horon, "Après Juin").

225. The typescripts of the talks carry numerous hand-written amendments by Ratosh that are incorporated into later versions (Ratosh Archive, files 719/k-351, 719/k-360).

226. Emails from Margalit Shinar, 9.11.2009, 11.11.2009; also Porat, *Shelaḥ Ṿe'eṭ Beyado*, 343–48, 364, 368.

227. Materials related to "Bene Kna'an" are located both in Horon's archive (file "Canaan—fundamental principles") and in Ratosh's archive in the Genazim Institute (file 719/142). The "Nimrodites" included Horon's daughter Margalit Gour, her future husband, 'Ami Śenir (born Schechter, later changed to Shinar), Yigal Bin-Nun, Ratosh's son Śaharon Shelaḥ, and Sami Gohar. The Nimrod Archive forms part of Horon's estate. On "Nimrod," see Oḥana, *Lo Kna'anim, Lo Tsalbanim*, 143–46. On *Erets-Haḳedem*, see letter from Margalit Gour to Yigal Bin-Nun, 25.11.69 (Yigal Bin-Nun archive); Moshe Giora, "Hateza Hakna'anit—Bemisparim Uv'uvdot," in Raṭosh (ed.), *Minitsaḥon Lemapolet*, 285–87; Baruch Nadel, "'Mea Milion Ha'aravim'—Lo Mea Milion Ṿelo 'Aravim," *Yedi'ot Aḥaronot*, 8.7.1970, 17; ad in *Haarets*, 7.5.1970. Selected pages from *Erets-Haḳedem* were reproduced in *Alef* and "Nimrod" publications, also after Horon's death.

228. Letter from Horon to B. Souvarine, 16.5.1971, Boris Souvarine Papers, bMs Fr 375 (509).

229. Letters from E. Jabotinsky to Horon, January–March 1969 (JIA/11/184a).

230. Letter from Horon to E. Jabotinsky, 31.3.1969 (Horon Archive, file "Canaan—fundamental principles").

231. Porat, *Shelaḥ Ṿe'eṭ Beyado*, 264, 345.

232. Letter from Horon to E. Jabotinsky, 11.12.1964 (JIA/4/4-4a).

233. Email from Margalit Shinar, 6.3.2017.

234. This fact prompts another question, that of the legal status of Horon's family during their stay in Israel in 1949 and 1950. They obviously could not be Israelis in the legal sense since until 1952, when the Israeli nationality law was promulgated, "the legal status of Israeli citizenship [. . .]

did not exist" (Lauren Banko, *The Invention of Palestinian Citizenship, 1918–1947* [Edinburgh: Edinburgh University Press], 2016, 210; see also Shira Robinson, *Citizen Strangers: Palestinians and the Birth of Israel's Liberal Settler State* [Stanford: Stanford University Press, 2013], 68–112; Louis A. Warsoff, "Citizenship in the State of Israel—A Comment," *New York University Law Review* 33, 1958, 857; and Ori Yehudai, *Leaving Zion: Jewish Emigration from Palestine and Israel after World War II* [Cambridge: Cambridge University Press, 2020], 72–73). Mazen Masri writes that in lieu of a formally encoded nationality, Israeli residency as defined in the Law and Administration Ordinance of 1948 functioned as a surrogate citizenship prior to 1952, though Israeli residents were still technically stateless (Mazen Masri, *The Dynamics of Exclusionary Constitutionalism: Israel as a Jewish and Democratic State* [Oxford: Hart, 2017], 83–85).

235. Raṭosh (ed.), *Minitsaḥon Lemapolet*, 3, 345–46.

236. Letter from Ada Gour to Boris Souvarine, 1.10.1972, Boris Souvarine Papers, bMs Fr 375 (509).

237. Sh. Yoḥana, "'Adya Zikhrono Livrakha," Ratosh Archive, file 719/k-351.

238. Rebecca Kook (ed.), *Hillel Kook / Shmuel Merlin: Hitkatvut, 1965–1986* (Haifa: University of Haifa Press, 2022), 236.

239. "'A. Gourevitch-Ḥoron—Limnuḥot," *Ma'ariv*, 22.9.1972, 5. The note refers to Horon as to "one of the important theoreticians of the national movement," though without specifying *which* national movement it was.

240. Sh. Yoḥana, "'Adya Zikhrono Livrakha," Ratosh Archive, file 719/k-351.

241. Letters from Ada Gour to Boris Souvarine, 24.9.1973, 18.8.1976, Boris Souvarine Papers, bMs Fr 375 (509).

Chapter 2

1. Alraïd, "Ob Istorii (Zhaloba Profana)," 6.

2. Examples: Adolphe Gourevitch, "The Semitic Levant: Present Conditions," *The Levant: Behind the Arab Curtain* (New York: Levant, 1952), 12, 13; 'A. G. Ḥoron, "Iśrael Ṿehamitos Ha'aravi," *Haumma* 8, 1964, 502.

3. Porat, *Shelaḥ Ṿe'eṭ Beyado*, 134. It must be noted that both Porat (*Shelaḥ Ṿe'eṭ Beyado*, 418) and Shavit (*Me'ivri 'Ad Kna'ani*, 9) relied on a translation of *On History* and did not consult the Russian original.

4. Alraïd, "Ob Istorii (Zhaloba Profana)," 6.

5. Alraïd, "Ob Istorii: Ob'yedinitel'noe Dvizheniie XIV–XII Vekov," *Rassviet* 27 (16), 19.4.1931, 6 (emphasis added).

6. Horon, "Le Monde des Hébreux" (JIA/5/52p).

7. The following studies were particularly helpful: Benedict Anderson, *Imagined Communities: Reflections on the Origin and Spread of Nationalism* (rev. ed.) (London, New York: Verso, 1991); Craig Calhoun, *Nationalism* (Buckingham:

Open University Press, 1997); Walker Connor, *Ethnonationalism: The Quest for Understanding* (Princeton: Princeton University Press, 1994); Eric Hobsbawm and Terence Ranger (eds.), *The Invention of Tradition* (Cambridge: Cambridge University Press, 1983); Azar Gat, *Nations: The Long History and Deep Roots of Political Ethnicity and Nationalism* (Cambridge: Cambridge University Press, 2013); Hutchinson and Smith (eds.), *Nationalism*; Alexander J. Motyl, *Revolutions, Nations, Empires: Conceptual Limits and Theoretical Possibilities* (New York: Columbia University Press, 1999); Smith, *Myths and Memories of the Nation*; Yasir Suleiman, *The Arabic Language and National Identity: A Study in Ideology* (Washington: Georgetown University Press, 2003); Suny and Kennedy (eds.), *Intellectuals and the Articulation of the Nation*; Geneviève Zubrzycki, "The Classical Opposition between Civic and Ethnic Models of Nationhood: Ideology, Empirical Reality and Social Scientific Analysis," *Polish Sociological Review* 3, 2002, 275–95.

8. Suleiman, *The Arabic Language*, 4–9, 20–27.

9. Smith, *Myths and Memories of the Nation*, 13.

10. Smith, *Myths and Memories of the Nation*, 230–31.

11. Calhoun, *Nationalism*, 99. For a more thorough discussion of these two approaches, see Daniele Conversi, "Mapping the Field: Theories of Nationalism and the Ethnosymbolic Approach," in Athena S. Leoussi and Steven Grosby (eds.), *Nationalism and Ethnosymbolism: History, Culture and Ethnicity in the Formation of Nations* (Edinburgh: Edinburgh University Press, 2007), 15–30; Zubrzycki, "The Classical Opposition."

12. Hobsbawm and Ranger (eds.), *The Invention of Tradition*.

13. Gat, *Nations*.

14. Gat, *Nations*, 263, offers the quite illuminating observation that nations that are ostensibly purely "political" or "civic" are actually driven by strong ethnic tensions and allegiances. He writes, "Hardly any nation exists based solely or even mainly on political allegiance to state and constitution" (213).

15. Suleiman, *The Arabic Language*, 7. See also Hroch, "From National Movement to the Fully-Formed Nation," 4; Ronald G. Suny and Michael D. Kennedy, "Toward a Theory of National Intellectual Practice," in Suny and Kennedy (eds.), *Intellectuals and the Articulation of the Nation*, 383–384.

16. Horon, "Le Monde des Hébreux" (JIA/5/52p).

17. Wilhelm Gesenius, *A Hebrew and English Lexicon of the Old Testament* (tr. Edward Robinson) (Oxford: Clarendon, 1906), 766, notes the similarity of roots but does not identify "paternal uncle" as the etymological source of "people" (*'am*).

18. Horon, "Le Monde des Hébreux" (JIA/5/52p).

19. Ludwig Koehler and Walter Baumgartner, *The Hebrew and Aramaic Lexicon of the Old Testament* (Leiden: Brill, 1994), 62 concur.

20. Ḥoron, *Ḳedem Ṿa'erev*, 145, 152; 'A. G. Ḥoron, "'Olam Behashḳafa 'Ivrit. Bene 'Ever: Motsa Miben 'Ame Haadama, Ṿehitnaḥalut Bikhna'an,"

Ḳeshet 9 (1), 1966, 133, 140. Horon's *leom* therefore evokes Smith's *ethnie*, since both are based on imaginary kinship ties.

21. Ḥoron, *Ḳedem Ṿa'erev*, 106–8, 145, 152, 155; Ḥoron, " 'Olam Behashḳafa 'Ivrit. Bene 'Ever," 140, 143; 'A. G. Ḥoron, " 'Olam Behashḳafa 'Ivrit. Reshit Yeme Ḳedem: Ben Yam Ṿenahar," *Ḳeshet* 8 (3), 1966, 124–25.

22. 'A. G. Ḥoron, " 'Olam Behashḳafa 'Ivrit. Maamar Rishon: Dvar Petiḥa," *Ḳeshet* 8 (1), 1965, 103; Ḥoron, *Ḳedem Ṿa'erev*, 46.

23. For more on this linguistic distinction in Russian, see Gat, *Nations*, 359–60 (footnote).

24. In spite of that, the Hebrew translation of one of the *On History* articles, appended to Shavit's book, makes use of the term *leom* and its derivatives (Shaviṭ, *Me'ivri 'Ad Kna'ani*, 172).

25. See, for instance, Ḥoron, *Ḳedem Ṿa'erev*, 46, 47; Ḥoron, " 'Olam Behashḳafa 'Ivrit. Maamar Rishon," 102, 103; Gourevitch, "The Semitic Levant," 14–15; 'A. G. Ḥoron, "Shlemut Hamoledet Ṿekhibush Hashalom," *Ḳeshet* 7 (4), 1965, 156–57.

26. "Testimony," by 'A. G. Ḥoron, regarding the term "Hebrew Nation" (Ratosh Archive, file 719/k–352). A somewhat similar document prepared probably by Horon or Aharon Amir is located in Boris Souvarine's archive ("Note sur 'la definition legale du "juif" par l'Etat d'Israel,' " Boris Souvarine Papers, bMS Fr 375 (1826)).

27. Ḥoron, *Ḳedem Ṿa'erev*, 48; Ḥoron, " 'Olam Behashḳafa 'Ivrit. Maamar Rishon," 104; his reference is to Poland.

28. Alraïd, "Yevrei i Khanaan: Istoricheskiie Ocherki," *Rassviet* 27 (51), 20.12.1931, 6. Compare Anthony Smith, *Myths and Memories of the Nation*, 108: "Clearly, ancient Israel in the later Second Temple Era was well on the way to becoming a nation . . . [However], it is easy [in this context] to fall into the trap of a retrospective nationalism."

29. Ḥoron, *Ḳedem Ṿa'erev*, 47–48; Ḥoron, " 'Olam Behashḳafa 'Ivrit. Maamar Rishon," 104.

30. Horon, "Le Monde des Hébreux" (JIA/5/52p).

31. Ḥoron, *Ḳedem Ṿa'erev*, 33.

32. Ḥoron, " 'Olam Behashḳafa 'Ivrit. Bene 'Ever," 140.

33. Gourevitch, "The Semitic Levant," 15.

34. Ḥoron, *Ḳedem Ṿa'erev*, 47; Ḥoron, " 'Olam Behashḳafa 'Ivrit. Maamar Rishon," 103.

35. Suleiman, *The Arabic Language*, 166.

36. 'A. G. Ḥoron, "Toledot Haarets Hi Hahisṭoria Haleumit," *Alef*, November 1971, 3. Horon's two examples are France and Italy, both of which are populated by nations with very tenuous genetic connections to their ancient inhabitants.

37. Ḥoron, *Ḳedem Ṿa'erev*, 47, 57; Ḥoron, " 'Olam Behashḳafa 'Ivrit. Maamar Rishon," 103, 115. Also Gourevitch, "The Semitic Levant," 15.

38. Ḥoron, *Ḳedem Ṿa'erev,* 70.

39. Ḥoron, *Erets-Haḳedem,* 68. It is notable that in the *On History* series, which lacked the theoretical basis of environmental determinism, Horon made a number of references to "white peoples" (for instance, Alraïd, "Yevrei i Rim: Istoricheskie Ocherki," *Rassviet* 28 (4), 24.1.1932, 5). Even his later writing was not fully clear of racial thinking, as his passing reference to the Indo-Europeans' craniological legacy in the Western Mediterranean demonstrates (Ḥoron, *Ḳedem Ṿa'erev,* 314).

40. "Testimony," by 'A. G. Ḥoron (Ratosh Archive, 719/k-352), also Ḥoron, "Toledot Haarets."

41. Anderson, *Imagined Communities;* Suleiman, *The Arabic Language.*

42. Ḥoron, "Iśrael Ṿehamitos Ha'aravi," 512.

43. Gourevitch, "The Semitic Levant," 14–15; Ḥoron, *Ḳedem Ṿa'erev,* 49–51, 118–23; Ḥoron, " 'Olam Behashḳafa 'Ivrit. Maamar Rishon," 106–8; 'A. G. Ḥoron, " 'Olam Behashḳafa 'Ivrit. Mishpaḥat Ḥam Ṿeshem: Leshonotehen Ṿiḥasehen," *Ḳeshet* 8 (4), 1966, 160–66.

44. Ḥoron, *Ḳedem Ṿa'erev,* 48; Ḥoron, " 'Olam Behashḳafa 'Ivrit. Maamar Rishon," 105.

45. Horon, "Hebrews and Jews" (HKA/36), 11.

46. An alternative term was "natural outlook" (*hashḳafa ṭiv'it*), which Horon used on occasion in the early 1960s ("Club 59" lectures, Horon Archive). The implicit analogy between nationalism and natural disposition is telling.

47. Ḥoron, *Ḳedem Ṿa'erev,* 47; Ḥoron, " 'Olam Behashḳafa 'Ivrit. Maamar Rishon," 103, 104.

48. Ḥoron, *Ḳedem Ṿa'erev,* 34; Ḥoron, " 'Olam Behashḳafa 'Ivrit. Maamar Rishon," 97 (emphasis added).

49. Ḥoron, *Ḳedem Ṿa'erev,* 36.

50. Ḥoron, *Ḳedem Ṿa'erev,* 33–34; Horon, "Le Monde des Hébreux" (JIA/5/52p); Ḥoron, " 'Olam Behashḳafa 'Ivrit. Maamar Rishon," 96–97.

51. Hence Tyre's title among the Hebrews, "Heart of the Seas," and Jerusalem's "Support of the Pole" (Horon, "Le Monde des Hébreux" [JIA/5/52p]).

52. Horon, "Le Monde des Hébreux" (JIA/5/52p).

53. Ḥoron, *Ḳedem Ṿa'erev,* 228, 291, 294; Horon's letter to Pierre and Nathalie Delougaz, 8.9.1944 (Boris Souvarine Papers, bMS Fr 375 (2011)); compare Gesenius, *A Hebrew and English Lexicon,* 412.

54. Horon's letter to Pierre and Nathalie Delougaz, Boris Souvarine Papers, bMS Fr 375 (2011).

55. "Śiḥa 'Al Toledot Haarets," 30.10.1971, typescript (Ratosh Archive, file 719/k-190).

56. Ḥoron, *Ḳedem Ṿa'erev,* 38–39.

57. 'A. G. Ḥoron, "Erets Haḳedem Uvene Shem: Hatfisa Hageografit Shel Ha'ivrim Haḳadmonim," *Alef,* January 1972, 3; Ḥoron, *Ḳedem Ṿa'erev,* 35–36, 148–56; Ḥoron, " 'Olam Behashḳafa 'Ivrit. Bene 'Ever," 137–44. Neither Gesenius,

A Hebrew and English Lexicon, 9–10, 526–27, nor Koehler and Baumgartner, *The Hebrew and Aramaic Lexicon*, 14–16, support such far-reaching interpretation.

58. See also Gesenius, *A Hebrew and English Lexicon*, 326; Koehler and Baumgartner, *The Hebrew and Aramaic Lexicon*, 325.

59. Horon, "Hebrews and Jews" (HKA/36), 12–13; see also Gour, "Hébreux et Juifs," 4–6; Horon, "Le Monde des Hébreux" (JIA/5/52p). Compare Koehler and Baumgartner, *The Hebrew and Aramaic Lexicon*, 1548–51.

60. The Indo-Iranian counterpart to "Sons of Shem" is "Arians," which similarly denotes "well-bred aristocrats" (Horon, "Le Monde des Hébreux" [JIA/5/52p]).

61. Horon, "Le Monde des Hébreux" (JIA/5/52p).

62. Gourevitch, "The Semitic Levant," 12; Ḥoron, *Ḳedem Ṿa'erev*, 39–42; Horon, "Le Monde des Hébreux" (JIA/5/52p).

63. *Tsvat Rishona*, 75 (Yigal Bin-Nun Archive).

64. Alraïd, "Yevrei i Rim," 5.

65. Ḥoron, "Toledot Haarets."

66. Horon, "Hebrews and Jews" (HKA/36), 4–5.

67. Ḥoron, *Ḳedem Ṿa'erev*, 60; Ḥoron, " 'Olam Behashḳafa 'Ivrit. Maamar Rishon," 118–19.

68. Horon, "Hebrews and Jews" (HKA/36), 5.

69. Alraïd, "Ob Istorii (Zhaloba Profana)," 7.

70. Alraïd, "Ob Istorii (Zhaloba Profana)," 7.

71. Horon, "Hebrews and Jews" (HKA/36), 4.

72. Horon, "Le Monde des Hébreux" (JIA/5/52p).

73. Horon, "Hebrews and Jews" (HKA/36), 8.

74. If such connections are acknowledged at all, Horon remarks, they are concentrated on the Hebrews' contacts with Europe in the Western Mediterranean, side-lining the no less significant contacts with Africa, whose role in ancient global history was tremendous and whose inhabitants were not regarded by ancient history writers as inferior.

75. Horon, "Hebrews and Jews" (HKA/36), 4–5, 8–9; Ḥoron, *Ḳedem Ṿa'erev*, 42–46, 135–37; Horon, "Le Monde des Hébreux" (JIA/5/52p); Ḥoron, " 'Olam Behashḳafa 'Ivrit. Maamar Rishon," 98–102; Ḥoron, " 'Olam Behashḳafa 'Ivrit. Mishpaḥat Ḥam Ṿeshem," 178–80.

76. Horon, "Hebrews and Jews" (HKA/36), 4–5; Ḥoron, *Ḳedem Ṿa'erev*, 141–42; Horon, "Le Monde des Hébreux" (JIA/5/52p); Ḥoron, " 'Olam Behashḳafa 'Ivrit. Bene 'Ever," 129–30.

77. Hayden V. White, *Metahistory: The Historical Imagination in Nineteenth-Century Europe* (Baltimore: Johns Hopkins University Press, 1973), 15–16, 163–90.

78. Oḥana, *Lo Kna'anim, Lo Tsalbanim*, 46–47.

79. Kaplan, *The Jewish Radical Right*, 35–37. For Spengler's impact on extremist Revisionists in Palestine in the 1930s, see Peter Bergamin, *The Making of the Israeli Far-Right: Abba Ahimeir and Zionist Ideology* (London: Tauris, 2020).

80. Perhaps a less discernible inspiration for Horon might be the nineteenth-century British thinker Lord Acton, who emphasized the fundamental tie between ancient nationhood and paganism (Nissim Rejwan, *Israel in Search of Identity: Reading the Formative Years* [Gainesville: University Press of Florida, 1999], 22).

81. Hayes, "Contributions of Herder," 722–27, 733.

82. Ḥoron, *Ḳedem Ṿa'erev*, 120–21; Ḥoron, "'Olam Behashḳafa 'Ivrit. Mishpaḥat Ḥam Ṿeshem," 162.

83. Alraïd, "Ob Istorii (Zhaloba Profana)," 7; Adolphe Gourevitch, "Pan-Arabism," talk given in New York, 23.11.1952 (Horon Archive, Asia Institute files; see also Appendix B).

84. Compare Belial, "Peuple Sans Terre."

85. 'A. G. Ḥoron, "Erets Haḳedem," in Raṭosh (ed.), *Minitsaḥon Lemapolet*, 40.

86. A. Red-Or, "Haḳdama," in Ḥoron, *Erets-Haḳedem*, V.

87. Horon, "Canaan and the Aegean Sea," 59; Ḥoron, *Ḳedem Ṿa'erev*, 36, 39, 62; 'A. G. Ḥoron, "'Olam Behashḳafa 'Ivrit. Hadvarim Haṭromiim: Toledot Adam Beezor Hayam Hatikhon," *Ḳeshet*, 8 (2), 1966, 113. See also Gesenius, *A Hebrew and English Lexicon*, 869–70.

88. Gourevitch, "The Semitic Levant," 11. One can observe a seeming inconsistency in Horon's reasoning here since he rejects the designation "Orient" ("East"), while one of the meanings of Ḳedem is exactly the same. Apparently Horon rejected the former as implying "east to Europe" and thus being based on an extrinsic vantage point, while the latter meant "east of the Mediterranean," preserving the intrinsic point of view.

89. Letter from Horon to Aharon Amir, 22.9.1951 (Aharon Amir's correspondence, in private possession, courtesy of Kedem Auction House and Dr Shai Feraro).

90. Gourevitch, "The Semitic Levant," 10.

91. Gourevitch, "The Semitic Levant," 10, 12; also Ḥoron, *Erets-Haḳedem*, 56.

92. 'A. G. Ḥoron, "Beriat Artsenu Lefi Mimtsae Hageologia," *Alef*, January 1972, 3; Ḥoron, "Haḳedem Ha'ivri," 215–16.

93. Ḥoron, *Ḳedem Ṿa'erev*, 61; Ḥoron, "'Olam Behashḳafa 'Ivrit. Hadvarim Haṭromiim," 113.

94. Ḥoron, *Ḳedem Ṿa'erev*, 48–49; Ḥoron, "'Olam Behashḳafa 'Ivrit. Maamar Rishon," 105 (emphasis added).

95. Ḥoron, *Ḳedem Ṿa'erev*, 49; Ḥoron, "'Olam Behashḳafa 'Ivrit. Maamar Rishon," 105 (emphases added). See also Gourevitch, "The Semitic Levant," 10; Ḥoron, *Erets-Haḳedem*, 54, 104; Horon, "Hebrews and Jews" (HKA/36), 16; Horon, "Le Monde des Hébreux" (JIA/5/52p); A. G. Horon, "The Pan-Arab Myth in the Mideastern Vacuum," Levant Club, *Memorandum no. 17–18*, 1957, 3. Elsewhere Horon (*Erets-Haḳedem*, 122) annexes Cyprus to the Land

of Kedem, apparently the first Mediterranean island to be colonized by the Hebrews during the second millennium BCE (Horon, "Le Monde des Hébreux" [JIA/5/52p]).

96. Ḥoron, *Ḳedem Ṿa'erev*, 63–65; Ḥoron, "'Olam Behashḳafa 'Ivrit. Hadvarim Haṭromiim," 114. For the Land of Kedem's natural structure in greater detail, see Ḥoron, *Erets-Haḳedem*, 54–65; Ḥoron, *Ḳedem Ṿa'erev*, 61–67, 76; Ḥoron, "'Olam Behashḳafa 'Ivrit. Hadvarim Haṭromiim," 113–16, 123.

97. Ḥoron, "'Olam Behashḳafa 'Ivrit. Maamar Rishon," 108. See also Ḥoron, *Ḳedem Ṿa'erev*, 51, 65–66, 90, 106, 112; Ḥoron, "'Olam Behashḳafa 'Ivrit. Hadvarim Haṭromiim," 115, 116, 132; Ḥoron, "'Olam Behashḳafa 'Ivrit. Reshit Yeme Ḳedem," 124, 128.

98. Ḥoron, *Ḳedem Ṿa'erev*, 93, 114; Ḥoron, "'Olam Behashḳafa 'Ivrit. Hadvarim Haṭromiim," 134; Ḥoron, "'Olam Behashḳafa 'Ivrit. Reshit Yeme Ḳedem," 130; Horon, "Le Monde des Hébreux" (JIA/5/52p).

99. Ḥoron, *Erets-Haḳedem*, 54, 106–7.

100. Hence, the Sinai Peninsula, though part of the Land of Kedem, does not belong to Canaan.

101. Ḥoron, *Ḳedem Ṿa'erev*, 39.

102. Horon, "The Hebrew Movement—An Outline" (JIA/2/52p; HKA/36, 4). The editors of Horon's posthumous publication also stressed Canaan's centrality within the Land of Kedem by subtitling *Ḳedem Ṿa'erev* "a history of Canaan and the Land of the Hebrews." However, Canaan's regional predominance is questioned in more recent scholarship (see Anson F. Rainey, "Who Is a Canaanite? A Review of the Textual Evidence," *Bulletin of the American Schools of Oriental Research* 304, 1996, 11).

103. Ḥoron, "Erets Haḳedem," 40; Ḥoron, *Erets-Haḳedem*, 100–1, 140; Ḥoron, "Haḳedem Ha'ivri," 216; Ḥoron, *Ḳedem Ṿa'erev*, 37, 39, 159–60; Ḥoron, "'Olam Behashḳafa 'Ivrit. Bene 'Ever," 146.

104. Ḥoron, *Ḳedem Ṿa'erev*, 158. Compare Gesenius, *A Hebrew and English Lexicon*, 716–20, who disagrees.

105. Gourevitch, "The Semitic Levant," 12; Ḥoron, *Erets-Haḳedem*, 56–60; Ḥoron, "Haḳedem Ha'ivri," 217; Ḥoron, *Ḳedem Ṿa'erev*, 157–59; Horon, "Le Monde des Hébreux" (JIA/5/52p); Ḥoron, "'Olam Behashḳafa 'Ivrit. Bene 'Ever," 145. Horon rejects the identification of the Hebrews as hailing from the Akkadian Khabiru since this would be incompatible with the Hebrews' indigenousness to the Land of Kedem (Ḥoron, *Ḳedem Ṿa'erev*, 159; Ḥoron, "'Olam Behashḳafa 'Ivrit. Bene 'Ever," 145–46), although in *On History* he supported this etymology (Alraïd, "Ob Istorii: Istoki Yevreiskago Plemeni [1]," *Rassviet* 27 [7], 15.2.1931, 4).

106. Ḥoron, *Ḳedem Ṿa'erev*, 140–41; Ḥoron, "'Olam Behashḳafa 'Ivrit. Bene 'Ever," 128–30. See the next section for a more exhaustive discussion of Horon's approach to the Bible's "usefulness" as a historical source.

107. Ḥoron, *Ḳedem Ṿa'erev*, 147; Ḥoron, " 'Olam Behashḳafa 'Ivrit. Bene 'Ever," 135 (emphasis added).

108. 'A. G. Ḥ., "Asia: Prehisṭoria," 922–23; Ḥoron, *Ḳedem Ṿa'erev*, 50–53, 67–104, 122–29, 138; Horon, "Le Monde des Hébreux" (JIA/5/52p); Ḥoron, " 'Olam Behashḳafa 'Ivrit. Hadvarim Haṭromiim," 116–35; Ḥoron, " 'Olam Behashḳafa 'Ivrit. Maamar Rishon," 107–10; Ḥoron, " 'Olam Behashḳafa 'Ivrit. Mishpaḥat Ḥam Ṿeshem," 166–71, 182; Ḥoron, " 'Olam Behashḳafa 'Ivrit. Reshit Yeme Ḳedem," 114–23; 'A. G. Ḥoron, draft for a talk for Club for Hebrew Guidance, 27.11.1971 (Ratosh Archive, file 719/k-351).

109. Ḥoron, *Ḳedem Ṿa'erev*, 94; Ḥoron, " 'Olam Behashḳafa 'Ivrit. Hadvarim Haṭromiim," 135.

110. Ḥoron, *Ḳedem Ṿa'erev*, 34, 43, 345; Ḥoron, "Kna'an Ṿeyaṿan Bitḳufat Habronza," 211; Ḥoron, " 'Olam Behashḳafa 'Ivrit. Maamar Rishon," 97, 98.

111. Alraïd, "Ob Istorii: Istoki Yevreiskago Plemeni (4)," *Rassviet* 27 (11), 15.3.1931, 4–6.

112. Horon writes that the Jews had dreamed "for forty centuries" of Palestine as their homeland (Alraïd, "Ob Istorii: Ob'yedinitel'noe Dvizheniie," 6; Alraïd, "Yevrei i Khanaan," 8). In the mid-1940s Horon wrote: "We are the successors, and even, *to a certain degree*, the descendants, of the Phoenicians" (Horon, "Hebrews and Jews" [HKA/36], 18; emphasis added). Contrast this to his later statement that the ancient Hebrews were "our [modern Hebrews'] national, albeit not racial, forefathers" (Ḥoron, "Haḳedem Ha'ivri," 258).

113. Alraïd, "Ob Istorii: Ob'yedinitel'noe Dvizheniie," 6, speaks of "Palestine and neighboring countries," and refers to Mesopotamia as a foreign land (Alraïd, "Ob Istorii: Istoki Yevreiskago Plemeni [1]," 4).

114. Alraïd, "Ob Istorii: Istoki Yevreiskago Plemeni (3)"; *Rassviet* 27 (9), 1.3.1931, 5.

115. Alraïd, "Ob Istorii: Istoki Yevreiskago Plemeni (1)," 4.

116. Alraïd, "Yevrei i Rim," 5.

117. Alraïd, "Yevrei i Rim," 5, 7.

118. Alraïd, "Yevreiskaiia Imperiia Tri Tysiachi Let Nazad (Istoricheskiie Ocherki)," *Rassviet* 28 (1), 3.1.1932, 4.

119. Alraïd, "Les Hébreux et Canaan," 2–4.

120. Alraïd, "Esquisses d'histoire hébraïque," 4–10.

121. The Russian word *iudei* (which is etymologically derived from the Hebrew word for "Jew," *yehudi*) means one who observes the Mosaic faith, while the word *yevrei* (etymologically derived from the Hebrew word for "Hebrew," *'ivri*) designates both a member of the Jewish nation and an adherent of the Jewish religion. The meanings thus overlap rather than diverge, so an attempt to juxtapose *iudei* to *yevrei* would be senseless linguistically and logically. Many years later, in 1969, Horon burst out in frustration from a meeting with newly arrived immigrants from the Soviet Union in Israel, exclaiming "[T]hey don't understand a thing!" (personal communication by

Dr Yigal Bin-Nun, July 2014). Apparently, his attempt to explain the difference between "Hebrews" and "Jews" in Russian ran up against a wall.

122. Yet it was entirely missing from *On History*.

123. S. G., "Méditerranée," *Le Cran* 2, January 1931, 1–4.

124. Ḥoron, "Haḳedem Ha'ivri," 239–40; 'A. G. Ḥoron, "Śiḥot 'Al Ḳadmoniyut Haarets: Nisayon Leshiḥzur 'Yetsiat Mitsraim' Ṿe'khibush Kna'an,' Bamitologia Uvamtsiut," *Ḳeshet* 16 (3), 1974, 132.

125. Horon, "Hebrews and Jews" (HKA/36), 12.

126. Ḥoron, "Haḳedem Ha'ivri," 239–40; Ḥoron, "Śiḥot 'Al Ḳadmoniyut Haarets," 132.

127. Horon, "Canaan and the Aegean Sea," 39.

128. Horon, "Hebrews and Jews" (HKA/36), 11.

129. Horon, "Le Monde des Hébreux" (JIA/5/52p). For other declarations to a similar intent, see Ḥoron, "Haḳedem Ha'ivri," 234; Ḥoron, *Ḳedem Ṿa'erev*, 53–54, 146, 303; Ḥoron, "'Olam Behashḳafa 'Ivrit. Bene 'Ever," 135; Ḥoron, "'Olam Behashḳafa 'Ivrit. Maamar Rishon," 111; Ḥoron, "Śiḥot 'Al Ḳadmoniyut Haarets," 123.

130. Horon, "Le Monde des Hébreux" (JIA/5/52p).

131. Ḥoron, *Ḳedem Ṿa'erev*, 247, 253. See also Ḥoron, "Haḳedem Ha'ivri," 225; Ḥoron, *Ḳedem Ṿa'erev*, 217, 224, 322.

132. Krinka Vidaković Petrov, "Memory and Oral Tradition," in Thomas Butler (ed.), *Memory: History, Culture and the Mind* (Oxford, New York: Basil Blackwell, 1989), 77–96.

133. Donald R. Kelley, "Ideas of Periodization in the West," in Q. Edward Wang and Franz L. Fillafer (eds.), *The Many Faces of Clio: Cross-Cultural Approaches to Historiography, Essays in Honor of Georg G. Iggers* (New York, Oxford: Berghahn Books, 2007), 17–27.

134. Ḥoron, *Ḳedem Ṿa'erev*, 129, 297; Ḥoron, "'Olam Behashḳafa 'Ivrit. Mishpaḥat Ḥam Ṿeshem," 170; Ḥoron, "Śiḥot 'Al Ḳadmoniyut Haarets," 124.

135. Horon, "The Hebrew Movement—An Outline" (JIA/2/52p; HKA/36), 4.

136. Ḥoron, *Ḳedem Ṿa'erev*, 127–28; Horon, "Le Monde des Hébreux" (JIA/5/52p); Ḥoron, "'Olam Behashḳafa 'Ivrit. Mishpaḥat Ḥam Ṿeshem," 169–70; A. H., "The Phoenician Column," *The Lebanese Gazette—Leesan Al-Adl* 41 (3), 2.9.1955, 1–2 (Israel State Archives, file GL-17109/33).

137. Ḥoron, *Ḳedem Ṿa'erev*, 140, 158; Ḥoron, "'Olam Behashḳafa 'Ivrit. Bene 'Ever," 128. See also Alraïd, "Ob Istorii: Istoki Yevreiskago Plemeni (2)," *Rassviet* 27 (8), 22.2.1931, 9; Alraïd, "Ob Istorii: Istoki Yevreiskago Plemeni (3)"; Alraïd, "Ob Istorii: Istoki Yevreiskago Plemeni (4)," 6; Ḥoron, "Haḳedem Ha'ivri," 239; Ḥoron, *Ḳedem Ṿa'erev*, 136, 156–58, 296–302; Ḥoron, "'Olam Behashḳafa 'Ivrit. Mishpaḥat Ḥam Ṿeshem," 180; Ḥoron, "Śiḥot 'Al Ḳadmoniyut Haarets," 132. The sweeping identification of Hebrews and Canaanites is disputed by other scholars (Rainey, "Who Is a Canaanite?," 5–6, 9, 10).

138. Alraïd, "Ob Istorii: Istoki Yevreiskago Plemeni (1)," 4; Alraïd, "Ob Istorii: Istoki Yevreiskago Plemeni (4)."

139. Horon, "Hebrews and Jews" (HKA/36), 20; see also Horon, "Le Monde des Hébreux" (JIA/5/52p).

140. 'A. G. Ḥ., "Afriḳa: Prehisṭoria," 339–40; 'A. G. Ḥ., "Asia: Prehisṭoria," 924; Alraïd, "Ob Istorii: Istoki Yevreiskago Plemeni (3)," 5; Ḥoron, "Haḳedem Ha'ivri," 225–26; Ḥoron, *Ḳedem Ṿa'erev*, 179–80, 246–56, 264, 280, 300; Horon, "Le Monde des Hébreux" (JIA/5/52p); Ḥoron, "Śiḥot 'Al Ḳadmoniyut Haarets," 116, 122.

141. Ḥoron, *Ḳedem Ṿa'erev*, 182–206.

142. Ḥoron, *Ḳedem Ṿa'erev*, 222.

143. Ḥoron, *Ḳedem Ṿa'erev*, 224.

144. Ḥoron, *Ḳedem Ṿa'erev*, 186.

145. Ḥoron, *Ḳedem Ṿa'erev*, 222. Gesenius, *A Hebrew and English Lexicon*, 212, 397, does not support this particular contention. For other examples of wordplays symbolizing geo-cosmic elements that were assimilated into the ancient Hebrews' beliefs, see Steven Grosby, "The Successor Territory," in Leoussi and Grosby (eds.), *Nationalism and Ethnosymbolism*, 108–9.

146. Horon, "Canaan and the Aegean Sea," 45; Ḥoron, *Ḳedem Ṿa'erev*, 186, 190, 223, 249, 293–95.

147. Ḥoron, *Ḳedem Ṿa'erev*, 77, 151, 198–200; Horon, "Le Monde des Hébreux" (JIA/5/52p); Ḥoron, "'Olam Behashḳafa 'Ivrit. Bene 'Ever," 139; Ḥoron, "'Olam Behashḳafa 'Ivrit. Hadvarim Haṭromiim," 124–25; Ḥoron, "'Olam Behashḳafa 'Ivrit. Reshit Yeme Ḳedem," 134.

148. Reflections of these stories can be identified as well in the ancient literature of the Greeks and the Berbers (Horon, "Le Monde des Hébreux" [JIA/5/52p]).

149. Peter Burke, "History as Social Memory," in Thomas Butler (ed.), *Memory: History, Culture and the Mind*, 104.

150. Ḥoron, *Ḳedem Ṿa'erev*, 203–4.

151. Ḥoron, *Ḳedem Ṿa'erev*, 160–81, 207–13, 275–79; Ḥoron, "'Olam Behashḳafa 'Ivrit. Reshit Yeme Ḳedem," 133–38; Ḥoron, "Śiḥot 'Al Ḳadmoniyut Haarets," 116, 123–27.

152. Babylon's most enduring legacy is the mystery play involving the deities Istar and Marduk, whose latest incarnation is the Jewish Purim carnival with its heroes "Esther" and "Mordechai" (Horon, "Le Monde des Hébreux" [JIA/5/52p]).

153. Ḥoron, "Haḳedem Ha'ivri," 234–38; Ḥoron, *Ḳedem Ṿa'erev*, 173–75, 273, 277–83; Ḥoron, "Śiḥot 'Al Ḳadmoniyut Haarets," 127–29; also Gat, *Nations*, 53.

154. Alraïd, "Ob Istorii: Istoki Yevreiskago Plemeni (2)," 8–9; Ḥoron, "Haḳedem Ha'ivri," 237–38; Ḥoron, *Ḳedem Ṿa'erev*, 277–78, 280–83; Ḥoron, "Śiḥot 'Al Ḳadmoniyut Haarets," 129–31.

155. Alraïd, "Ob Istorii: Istoki Yevreiskago Plemeni (3)," 5.

156. 'A. G. Ḥ., "Eropa: Prehisṭoria," 141–42; 'A. G. Ḥ., "Iberim," 608, 615–16; Ḥoron, "Haḳedem Ha'ivri," 234–37; Ḥoron, *Ḳedem Ṿa'erev*, 143–62, 267–75, 283–302; Ḥoron, "'Olam Behashḳafa 'Ivrit. Bene 'Ever," 131–47; Ḥoron, "Śiḥot 'Al Ḳadmoniyut Haarets," 127–29.

157. This view is shared by the biblical scholar Umberto Cassuto (Moshe Daṿid Ḳassuṭo, *Haela 'Anat: Shire 'Alila Kna'aniim Mitḳufat Heavot* [Jerusalem: Bialik Institute, 1958], 20), a rabbi and certainly not a "Young Hebrew."

158. Ḥoron, "Haḳedem Ha'ivri," 237; Ḥoron, "Śiḥot 'Al Ḳadmoniyut Haarets," 130; Jabotinsky, *Taryag Millim*, 109.

159. This etymology is supported by the existence of a wave-shaped Egyptian hieroglyph, which supposedly stood for "the land of the Hebrews" (see illustration in Ḥoron, *Ḳedem Ṿa'erev*, 213).

160. Alraïd, "Ob Istorii: Ob'yedinitel'noe Dvizheniie," 7 (here Horon suggests that the Hyksos invaded Canaan from the north and were subsequently accompanied by the Hebrews into Egypt); Alraïd, "Ob Istorii (Prodolzheniie)," *Rassviet* 27 (18), 3.5.1931, 7; Ḥoron, "Haḳedem Ha'ivri," 238–39; Ḥoron, *Ḳedem Ṿa'erev*, 158, 255–56, 274, 309–10, 317–18; Ḥoron, "Śiḥot 'Al Ḳadmoniyut Haarets," 131.

161. Gour, "Hébreux et Juifs," 6.

162. Horon, "Hebrews and Jews" (HKA/36), 17.

163. Jabotinsky, *Taryag Millim*, 109. A brief historical overview of the Phoenicians is provided by Kaufman, *Reviving Phoenicia*, 3.

164. Horon, "Canaan and the Aegean Sea," 60–61; Ḥoron, *Ḳedem Ṿa'erev*, 312.

165. Horon, "Le Monde des Hébreux" (JIA/5/52p).

166. In a private letter dated May 13, 1966, Horon extensively dwells on the various forms of the word "bull" in both Semitic and non-Semitic languages, pointing to their common origins (Horon Archive).

167. Horon, "Le Monde des Hébreux" (JIA/5/52p).

168. Supported by Gesenius, *A Hebrew and English Lexicon*, 402.

169. This is challenged by Rainey, "Who Is a Canaanite?," 11.

170. Compare Gesenius, *A Hebrew and English Lexicon*, 504–5.

171. 'A. G. Ḥ., "Iṭalia: Prehisṭoria," 731; Alraïd, "Finikiitzy: Istoricheskiie Ocherki," *Rassviet* 27 (52), 27.12.1931, 6–8; Horon, "Canaan and the Aegean Sea"; Ḥoron, "Haḳedem Ha'ivri," 239; Ḥoron, *Ḳedem Ṿa'erev*, 185, 302–12; Ḥoron, "Kna'an Ṿeyaṿan Bitḳufat Habronza"; Ḥoron, "Śiḥot 'Al Ḳadmoniyut Haarets," 131–32. This is precisely the thesis of Michael Astour's famous (and controversial) *Hellenosemitica* (Michael C. Astour, *Hellenosemitica* [Leiden: Brill, 1965]). Astour was Horon's classmate in Paris in the 1930s and mentions him favorably in a letter to Boris Souvarine from September 26, 1965 (Boris Souvarine Papers, bMS Fr 375 [45]). Horon cites both Astour and his doctoral advisor Cyrus H. Gordon (an equally controversial figure) in his discussion

of the Greek-Canaanite connection. Asher Kaufman (*Reviving Phoenicia*, 4, 144, 212–13) traces the thesis to early-twentieth-century researches of Victor Bérard, one of Horon's teachers.

172. Horon, "Canaan and the Aegean Sea," 59.

173. Ḥoron, "Kna'an Ṿeyaṿan Bitḳufat Habronza," 214.

174. In a sense, this is a reversal of etymological fortunes: the very name of the European continent is derived from an extrinsic (to Europe) Hebrew Semitic source.

175. 'A. G. Ḥ., "Iberim," 607–10 (additional etymologies are on 610–12); Ḥoron, "Haḳedem Ha'ivri," 244, 245; Ḥoron, *Ḳedem Ṿa'erev*, 152, 200, 311, 326, 382; Jabotinsky, *Taryag Millim*, 109.

176. Ḥoron, *Ḳedem Ṿa'erev*, 317.

177. Horon, "Le Monde des Hébreux" (JIA/5/52p).

178. Alraïd, "Yevrei i Khanaan," 6. Despite the importance of this theme for Horon's historiography, its later espousal (Ḥoron, "Haḳedem Ha'ivri," 240–60; Ḥoron, *Ḳedem Ṿa'erev*, 313–45) is noticeably shorter than the preceding chapters, devoted to the processes that led to Hebrew nation formation, since Horon had not had the time to develop it fully before passing away.

179. Horon, "Le Monde des Hébreux" (JIA/5/52p).

180. Horon, "Hebrews and Jews" (HKA/36), 17; also Gour, "Hébreux et Juifs," 7.

181. Accordingly, the dispute between the YHWH prophet Elijah and the Baal priests (1 Kings 18) is "a sorcerers' quarrel" (Ḥoron, "Haḳedem Ha'ivri," 247; Ḥoron, *Ḳedem Ṿa'erev*, 329). Further evidence for the pagan nature of the YHWH cult was his designation as "Adonay," a name whose grammatical plural form betrays a polytheistic source, and whose meaning ("Lord") was a synonym for *Ba'al* (local lord god of a particular territory). YHWH thus was simply a Baal of the Israelites (Horon, "Le Monde des Hébreux" [JIA/5/52p]).

182. Horon Archive, file "Canaan—fundamental principles."

183. Alraïd, "Ob Istorii: Istoki Yevreiskago Plemeni (2)," 9; Alraïd, "Ob Istorii: Istoki Yevreiskago Plemeni (4)," 4–5; Ḥoron, "Haḳedem Ha'ivri," 247; Ḥoron, *Ḳedem Ṿa'erev*, 195, 220, 267, 319–20, 328–29.

184. Alraïd, "Ob Istorii: Ob'yedinitel'noe Dvizheniie," 7.

185. Ḥoron, *Ḳedem Ṿa'erev*, 325. Gesenius, *A Hebrew and English Lexicon*, 187, traces the name to the ancient Israelite sun god Dodo, of whom Horon makes no mention at all.

186. Alraïd, "Yevreiskaiia Imperiia Tri Tysiachi Let Nazad"; Gour, "Hébreux et Juifs," 7–9; Ḥoron, "Haḳedem Ha'ivri," 240–45; Ḥoron, *Ḳedem Ṿa'erev*, 221, 313–27, 364.

187. Gour, "Hébreux et Juifs," 9; Horon, "Le Monde des Hébreux" (JIA/5/52p).

188. Alraïd, "Yevreiskaiia Imperiia Tri Tysiachi Let Nazad," 4.

189. The biblical scholar Norman Gottwald argues somewhat similarly that YHWH cult began as an egalitarian protest movement against the Canaanite hierarchy (Knapp, "Collective Memory and the Actual Past," 126–27).

190. ʻA. G. Ḥ., "Afriḳa: Prehisṭoria," 346; ʻA. G. Ḥ., "Iberia: Prehisṭoria," 606; ʻA. G. Ḥ., "Iberim," 611–13; Alraïd, "Finikiitzy"; Alraïd, "Ierusalim i Karfagen: Istoricheskiie Ocherki," *Rassviet* 28 (3), 17.1.1932, 11; Alraïd, "Yevrei i Khanaan"; Alraïd, "Yevreiskaiia Imperiia Tri Tysiachi Let Nazad"; Alraïd, "Yevreistvo Nakanune Stolknoveniia s Rimom: Istoricheskie Ocherki," *Rassviet* 28 (7), 14.2.1932, 10–11; Gour, "Hébreux et Juifs," 10; Ḥoron, "Haḳedem Haʻivri," 245–48; Horon, "Hebrews and Jews" (HKA/36), 20; Ḥoron, *Ḳedem Ṿaʻerev*, 327–32; Horon, "Le Monde des Hébreux" (JIA/5/52p); Horon's lecture at the Fisher Club, Raʻanana, 22.3.1960 (Horon Archive). For a summary of the recent historiography of Hebrew antiquity, including the debates over the extent and contents of its "national" character, consult Gat, *Nations*, 89–93.

191. *Tsvat Rishona*, 39 (emphasis added).

192. Letter from Horon to E. Jabotinsky and S. Rosoff, 10.2.1956 (HKA/32). See also "Club 59" lectures, Horon Archive.

193. Aharon Amir's diary, 25.9.1949 (Genazim Institute, 31296-k).

194. This can be gauged by comparing the extent of the relevant materials in *Minitsaḥon Lemapolet* and in *Ḳedem Ṿaʻerev*.

195. Horon, "Le Monde des Hébreux" (JIA/5/52p).

196. And not a whale, the present Hebrew meaning of the word *leṿiatan*. To the same totem Horon ascribes the legendary figure of Lot, Abraham's brother, as a personification of *Shalyaṭ*, an Ugaritic synonym of *Leviathan* (Ḥoron, *Ḳedem Ṿaʻerev*, 200). Compare Gesenius, *A Hebrew and English Lexicon*, 532.

197. Ḥoron, "Haḳedem Ha ʻivri," 231–34; Ḥoron, *Ḳedem Ṿaʻerev*, 241–46; Ḥoron, "ʻOlam Behashḳafa ʻIvrit. Bene ʻEver," 147–52; Ḥoron, "Śiḥot ʻAl Ḳadmoniyut Haarets," 120–21. This meaning is also preserved in the name of the Litani River in Lebanon (Ḥoron, *Ḳedem Ṿaʻerev*, 244–45).

198. Ḥoron, "Haḳedem Haʻivri," 232; Ḥoron, "Śiḥot ʻAl Ḳadmoniyut Haarets," 121. Another North African water-born (though not Levitic) legendary forefather is Joseph, whose name, Horon argues, is meaningless in Hebrew, but its original form (*ṿ-a-sif*) denotes in Libyan/Berber "of the river" (Ḥoron, *Ḳedem Ṿaʻerev*, 179–80, 363; Ḥoron, "ʻOlam Behashḳafa ʻIvrit. Bene ʻEver," 151). Gesenius, *A Hebrew and English Lexicon*, 415, sticks to the Hebrew interpretation of the name as theophoric (*Joseph* being a shortened form of *Jehoseph*). Ḥoron, *Ḳedem Ṿaʻerev*, 363, dismisses this interpretation as "wordplay."

199. This means that the root *mṿsh* is in the Hebrew Canaanite language synonymous with the root *ʻrv*, and the root *ḥṿl* is similar to *ḳdm*. Clans, deities, and legendary figures whose names are derived from these two roots (Moses being only one) appear throughout the Bible and extrabiblical literature as well (Horon, "Canaan and the Aegean Sea," 58; Ḥoron, "Haḳedem Haʻivri," 231; Ḥoron, *Ḳedem Ṿaʻerev*, 186–87, 190; Ḥoron, "ʻOlam Behashḳafa ʻIvrit. Bene ʻEver," 148; Ḥoron, "Śiḥot ʻAl Ḳadmoniyut Haarets," 120).

200. Ḥoron, "Haḳedem Haʻivri," 233–34; Ḥoron, *Ḳedem Ṿaʻerev*, 108, 232, 257, 261; Ḥoron, "ʻOlam Behashḳafa ʻIvrit. Reshit Yeme Ḳedem," 125; Ḥoron, "Śiḥot ʻAl Ḳadmoniyut Haarets," 122. Koehler and Baumgartner, *The Hebrew and Aramaic Lexicon*, 80, connect the etymology of Ephraim to "pasture land."

201. Ḥoron, *Ḳedem Ṿa'erev*, 265–67. Studies published after Horon's death confirmed that the figure of Joshua was most probably a concoction from the seventh century BCE, whose purpose was to lend historical credibility to King Josiah's religious reforms (Piterberg, *The Returns of Zionism*, 267–73).

202. Another African tradition imported by "sons of Ephraim" was circumcision.

203. Alraïd, "Ob Istorii: Istoki Yevreiskago Plemeni (3)," 5; Gour, "Hébreux et Juifs," 11; Ḥoron, "Haḳedem Ha'ivri," 230–34; Ḥoron, *Ḳedem Ṿa'erev*, 185–87, 203, 241–67; Ḥoron, "'Olam Behashḳafa 'Ivrit. Bene 'Ever," 147–52; Ḥoron, "Śiḥot 'Al Ḳadmoniyut Haarets," 119–23.

204. Horon, "Hebrews and Jews" (HKA/36), 21.

205. Horon, "Hebrews and Jews" (HKA/36), 21–22.

206. Ḥoron, *Erets-Haḳedem*, 82.

207. Ḥoron, "Haḳedem Ha'ivri," 249; Ḥoron, *Ḳedem Ṿa'erev*, 333.

208. Ḥoron, "Haḳedem Ha'ivri," 248; Ḥoron, *Ḳedem Ṿa'erev*, 332.

209. Horon, "Hebrews and Jews" (HKA/36), 24.

210. Interestingly, the idea that Ezra was the true author of the biblical canon, which Horon borrowed from biblical criticism, is found also in medieval Muslim apology and polemics (Jonathan Marc Gribetz, *Defining Neighbors: Religion, Race, and the Early Zionist-Arab Encounter* [Princeton: Princeton University Press, 2014], 78–79).

211. Ḥoron, *Ḳedem Ṿa'erev*, 195. Horon also took pains to undermine the Jewish biblical chronology by pointing to the Bible's inconsistency not only with the extra-biblical historical material, but to contradictions within the Jewish version of the Bible as well (Ḥoron, "Haḳedem Ha'ivri," 218–25; Ḥoron, *Ḳedem Ṿa'erev*, 142, 253–56).

212. Ḥoron, *Ḳedem Ṿa'erev*, 248.

213. Burke, "History as Social Memory," 103.

214. Alraïd, "Yevreistvo Nakanune Stolknoveniia s Rimom"; Gour, "Hébreux et Juifs," 11–14; Ḥoron, "Haḳedem Ha'ivri," 218–20, 223, 233, 248–51; Horon, "Hebrews and Jews" (HKA/36), 24; Ḥoron, *Ḳedem Ṿa'erev*, 146–47, 217–24, 247–48, 252–56, 332–34, 364, 366; 'A. G. Ḥoron, "Mitologia Umetsiut: 'Al 'Yetsiat Mitsraim' Ṿe'khibush Kna'an,'" *Alef*, May 1972, 4–5; Ḥoron, "'Olam Behashḳafa 'Ivrit. Bene 'Ever," 135; Ḥoron, "Śiḥot 'Al Ḳadmoniyut Haarets," 122.

215. Horon, "Hebrews and Jews" (HKA/36), 23.

216. Ḥoron, *Ḳedem Ṿa'erev*, 247.

217. Alraïd, "Yevrei i Rim: Istoricheskie Ocherki," 6–7.

218. Alraïd, "Ierusalim i Karfagen," 11.

219. Ḥoron, *Ḳedem Ṿa'erev*, 339.

220. Gour, "Hébreux et Juifs," 12–13.

221. Horon, "Hebrews and Jews" (HKA/36), 24. See also Alraïd, "Ierusalim i Karfagen"; Ḥoron, "Haḳedem Ha'ivri," 251–54; Ḥoron, *Ḳedem Ṿa'erev*, 54–55, 334–41; Horon, "Le Monde des Hébreux" (JIA/5/52p); Ḥoron, "'Olam Behashḳafa 'Ivrit. Maamar Rishon," 112–13.

222. Horon, "Le Monde des Hébreux" (JIA/5/52p).

223. Horon, "Hebrews and Jews" (HKA/36), 7–8.

224. Horon, "The Hebrew Movement—An Outline," JIA/2/52p; HKA/36, 5. Also Horon, "Hebrews and Jews" (HKA/36), 25; Ḥoron, *Ḳedem Ṿa'erev*, 249. Shavit's claim that "Canaanism" manifests "no evidence anywhere of willingness to recognize the fact that only the Jews of all the nations of the Ancient Near East throughout history carried the Hebrew heritage within the general Jewish heritage" (Shavit, *The New Hebrew Nation*, 120) must therefore be recognised as unfounded.

225. Ḥoron, "Haḳedem Ha'ivri," 250; Ḥoron, *Ḳedem Ṿa'erev*, 334.

226. Ḥoron, *Ḳedem Ṿa'erev*, 50, 249; Ḥoron, "'Olam Behashḳafa 'Ivrit. Maamar Rishon," 107.

227. Horon, "Le Monde des Hébreux" (JIA/5/52p).

228. Horon does not specify whether Carthage possessed a "national outlook" of its own, shaped by the North African littoral, but merely asserts that "inasmuch as a Hebrew history persists, it is concentrated mainly in the Canaanite overseas, from Tyre and Sidon to Carthage" (Ḥoron, *Ḳedem Ṿa'erev*, 335). He does however contrast the frailty of the Persian Empire, which could not oppose Alexander of Macedon, to the vibrancy of Carthage, which bore Hannibal, whom Horon regards as the greatest Hebrew warrior of antiquity ('A. G. Ḥ., "Iberim," 613; Alraïd, "Ierusalim i Karfagen," 12; Ḥoron, *Ḳedem Ṿa'erev*, 55, 334–38; Ḥoron, "'Olam Behashḳafa 'Ivrit. Maamar Rishon," 112). Speaking shortly after the North African campaign in the Second World War, Horon owned that "I feel that when Hebrew-speaking soldiers appeared in the field, in Libya and Tunisia and Italy, —the spirit of Hannibal must have recognized them as his own" (Horon, "Hebrews and Jews" [HKA/36], 20).

229. Ḥoron, "Haḳedem Ha'ivri," 257; Ḥoron, *Ḳedem Ṿa'erev*, 344. See also Alraïd, "Ierusalim i Karfagen," 12; Ḥoron, "Haḳedem Ha'ivri," 252, 255–57; Ḥoron, *Ḳedem Ṿa'erev*, 338–45. Ironically, some elements of Christian mythology (such as the doctrine of transubstantiation) are, in Horon's opinion, derived from ancient Canaanite legends (lecture to Tel Aviv University students, May 1966, Horon Archive).

230. Ḥoron, "'Olam Behashḳafa 'Ivrit. Maamar Rishon," 114–15; Ḥoron, *Ḳedem Ṿa'erev*, 56–57.

231. Horon, "Hebrews and Jews" (HKA/36), 7.

232. Cited in Edward Said, *Orientalism* (New York: Vintage, 1994), 97.

233. Horon, "Hebrews and Jews" (HKA/36), 8.

234. Ḥoron, *Ḳedem Ṿa'erev*, 56; Ḥoron, "'Olam Behashḳafa 'Ivrit. Maamar Rishon," 114.

235. Ḥoron, "Haḳedem Ha'ivri," 257–58; Ḥoron, *Ḳedem Ṿa'erev*, 345.

Chapter 3

1. Alraïd, "Ob Istorii (Zhaloba Profana)," 7.

2. Letter from Horon to E. Jabotinsky and S. Rosoff, 10.2.1956 (HKA/32); the final sentence is clearly a denunciation of Yonatan Ratosh's position.

3. Gour, "Hébreux et Juifs," 3, 9.

4. Alraïd, "Ierusalim i Karfagen," 12.

5. 'A. G. Ḥ., "Iberim," 613–14; A. Gourevitch, "Le Panarabisme" (JIA/6/52p), 14, 71, 77; Horon, "Les Arabes depuis l'Islam," 135, no. 2; Ḥoron, *Ḳedem Va'erev*, 57; Ḥoron, "'Olam Behashḳafa 'Ivrit. Maamar Rishon," 115.

6. Gour, "Hébreux et Juifs," 3–4.

7. Piterberg, *The Returns of Zionism*, 19–20.

8. Ḥoron, *Erets-Haḳedem*, 88.

9. Gourevitch, "The Semitic Levant," 16.

10. Gour, "Hébreux et Juifs," 15–16; Horon, "Le Monde des Hébreux" (JIA/5/52p).

11. Jonathan Gribetz defines the *millet* system functionally as "an arrangement [by which] the Ottoman government related to its various minority populations via their religious leadership" (Gribetz, *Defining Neighbors*, 19).

12. Gourevitch, "The Semitic Levant," 16.

13. In his letter to Horon from January 1967 Ratosh berates him for interpreting Hassidism in the late 1930s as an early sign of Hebrew national revival (Raṭosh, *Mikhtavim*, 305).

14. This part of Horon's analysis is subheaded "The Jewish Catastrophe; The Truth of Anti-Semitism" (Gour, "Hébreux et Juifs," 26). The anti-Semitism of Hitler, Horon writes in 1939 (!), is an exaggerated and modernized form of the sense of disaster that had accompanied Judaism since its crystalization as caste, being only a novel paroxysm of a perennial catastrophe.

15. Gour, "Hébreux et Juifs," 17–31.

16. Reformed Judaism deviated in the nineteenth century from this tradition, which Horon considered the only authentically Jewish one, and therefore held Reformed Judaism in contempt (email from Margalit Shinar, 6.12.2009).

17. Horon, "Hebrews and Jews" (HKA/36), 14.

18. Gour, "Hébreux et Juifs," 25–26.

19. Bo'az 'Evron, *Haḥeshbon Haleumi* (Tel Aviv: Dvir, 1988), 16–17, 93–98, 156–86; Boas Evron, *Jewish State or Israeli Nation?* (Bloomington and Indianapolis: Indiana University Press, 1995), 4–5, 41–44, 68–86; Piterberg, *The Returns of Zionism*, 30–36; Adam Shatz (ed.), *Prophets Outcast: A Century of Dissident Jewish Writing about Zionism and Israel* (New York: Nation Books, 2004), 108–17.

20. Horon, "Hebrews and Jews" (HKA/36), 14.

21. Gourevitch, "Le Panarabisme" (JIA/6/52p), 119; Horon, "The Hebrew Movement—An Outline" (JIA/2/52p; HKA/36), 8.

22. Horon Archive, file "Canaan—fundamental principles." Compare Diamond's observation of the "Canaanite" mind-set: "To the extent that Zionism represented and promoted this rejection of the Jewish past . . . to that extent was it on the right track. When, however, it made its peace with the

past . . . Zionism compromised and thus betrayed its revolutionary nature" (Diamond, *Homeland or Holy Land?*, 49). Consequently, the "Canaanites" are "suggesting that *in principle* Zionism and Judaism should really have nothing to do with each other" (Diamond, *Homeland or Holy Land?*, 120). For a summary of the "Canaanite" position against Zionism consult Diamond, *Homeland or Holy Land?*, 55–56, 62, 72–73.

23. Ḥoron, *Erets-Haḳedem*, 136; Ḥoron, *Ḳedem Ṿa'erev*, 59; Ḥoron, " 'Olam Behashḳafa 'Ivrit. Maamar Rishon," 117.

24. Ḥoron, "Shlemut Hamoledet," 155.

25. Gourevitch, "The Semitic Levant," 26.

26. Gour, "Hébreux et Juifs," 7; Horon, "Le Monde des Hébreux" (JIA/5/52p).

27. Horon, "Hebrews and Jews" (HKA/36), 15.

28. Horon even acidly referred to sixth-century BCE "Return to Zion" as to a "Babylonian-Persian Zionism" (Ḥoron, *Ḳedem Ṿa'erev*, 54; Ḥoron, " 'Olam Behashḳafa 'Ivrit. Maamar Rishon," 112; see also Alraïd, "Ierusalim i Karfagen," 12). However, he also likened the Cyrus Charter permitting exiled Hebrews to return to Jerusalem in the sixth century BCE to the Balfour declaration of 1917 (Alraïd, "Yevreistvo Nakanune Stolknoveniia s Rimom," 10) without intending this in a derogatory way.

29. Ḥoron, "Iśrael Ṿehamitos Ha'aravi," 508.

30. Ḥoron, *Ḳedem Ṿa'erev*, 59; Ḥoron, " 'Olam Behashḳafa 'Ivrit. Maamar Rishon," 117.

31. Gourevitch, "Le Panarabisme" (JIA/6/52p), 87.

32. Gourevitch, "The Semitic Levant," 26; Ḥoron, *Erets-Haḳedem*, 92, 96; Ḥoron, "Iśrael Ṿehamitos Ha'aravi," 508.

33. Gourevitch, "The Semitic Levant," 26; Ḥoron, *Erets-Haḳedem*, 136–37; Ḥoron, *Ḳedem Ṿa'erev*, 59; Ḥoron, " 'Olam Behashḳafa 'Ivrit. Maamar Rishon," 117; Ḥoron, "Shlemut Hamoledet," 155.

34. Horon, "Le Monde des Hébreux" (JIA/5/52p).

35. Letter from Horon to E. Jabotinsky and S. Rosoff, 3.4.1956 (JIA/4/4-4a); see also Gourevitch, "Le Panarabisme" (JIA/6/52p), 131.

36. Gourevitch, "Le Panarabisme" (JIA/6/52p), 115.

37. Ḥoron, "Haḳedem Ha'ivri," 259; Ḥoron, *Ḳedem Ṿa'erev*, 33; Ḥoron, " 'Olam Behashḳafa 'Ivrit. Maamar Rishon," 96.

38. Horon, "Hebrews and Jews" (HKA/36), 3.

39. Horon, "The Hebrew Movement—An Outline" (JIA/2/52p; HKA/36), 11.

40. Horon, "The Hebrew Movement—An Outline" (JIA/2/52p; HKA/36), 6.

41. Gourevitch, "Le Panarabisme" (JIA/6/52p), 121.

42. HKA/19.

43. Raṭosh, *Reshit Hayamim*, 171.

44. Letter from Horon to E. Jabotinsky and S. Rosoff, 10.2.1956 (HKA/32).

45. In this, Horon deviated somewhat from the Young Hebrews' historiography, which perceived the "first *'aliya*" (1882—1904) as the "true parent" of the Hebrew nation, by predating the Zionist-inspired "second *'aliya*" (1904–1914). Horon did, however, pay homage to a "first *'aliya*" contemporary, Palestine-born Avshalom Feinberg, who agitated for a joint Hebrew-Druze anti-Ottoman insurrection as early as the 1900s, in defiance of "objective [disadvantageous] conditions" and therefore mindful of history's "deepest" truths ('Adya Gur, "She'at Kosher—Lemi?," in Raṭosh [ed.], *Minitsaḥon Lemapolet*, 294–96).

46. Gourevitch, "Le Panarabisme" (JIA/6/52p), 123.

47. Gourevitch, "The Semitic Levant," 22. He reiterated this standpoint a year later ('A. Ḥoron, "Haimperializm Ha'arbai," *Alef*, 18, 1953, 5).

48. Gourevitch, "The Semitic Levant," 26.

49. Aharon Amir's diary, 25.9.1949 (Genazim Institute, 31296-k).

50. Horon, "The Pan-Arab Myth." Note the transition in Horon's usage of the term "Israelis" from a civic-political to a national signifier.

51. Ḥoron, "Shlemut Hamoledet," 156. See also 'Adya Gur, "Hem Niḳlaṭim Maher," in Raṭosh (ed.), *Minitsaḥon Lemapolet*, 323; Ḥoron, "Haḳedem Ha'ivri," 259.

52. Ḥoron, *Erets-Haḳedem*, 70.

53. *Tsvat Rishona*, 39.

54. Ḥoron, *Erets-Haḳedem*, 138–39. Back in 1952, Horon estimated that the Sabras were "not much more than one third of all the people in the state" (Gourevitch, "The Semitic Levant," 22).

55. Gourevitch, "The Semitic Levant," 26.

56. Gourevitch, "The Semitic Levant," 26.

57. Gourevitch, "The Semitic Levant," 26. See also Ḥoron, "Haḳedem Ha'ivri," 259; Ḥoron, *Ḳedem Ṿa'erev*, 59–60; Ḥoron, "'Olam Behashḳafa 'Ivrit. Maamar Rishon," 118.

58. Ḥoron, "Haḳedem Ha'ivri," 259.

59. Gourevitch, "The Semitic Levant," 16; see also Eri Jabotinsky, "Israel and Zionism: Why Israel Has no Constitution," *The Levant: Behind the Arab Curtain* (New York: Levant, 1952), 43–50, for a more detailed argumentation in this direction.

60. Gourevitch, "The Semitic Levant," 26–27.

61. Ḥoron, "Shlemut Hamoledet," 156.

62. For Horon's concept of Jordan's "three banks," see the previous chapter.

63. Ḥoron, *Erets-Haḳedem*, 100–3; Ḥoron, "Iśrael Ṿehamitos Ha'aravi," 517.

64. Ḥoron, "Haimperializm Ha'arbai," 5.

65. Horon's letter to B. Souvarine, 5.1.1967, Boris Souvarine Papers, bMs Fr 375 (509).

66. Letter from Horon, October 1950 (JIA/4/4-4a).

67. 'Adya Gur, "Pizur Hageṭṭaot," in Raṭosh (ed.), *Minitsaḥon Lemapolet*, 190–91; Letter from Horon, October 1950 (JIA/4/4-4a).

68. Horon's statistical estimate is 2,800,000 Israeli citizens, 100,000 noncitizen inhabitants of Israel (meaning primarily those living in annexed East Jerusalem), and almost a million of noncitizens beyond the "Green Line" (Ḥoron, *Erets-Haḳedem*, 134–35).

69. Gur, "Pizur Hageṭṭaot"; letter from Horon to B. Souvarine, 16.5.1971, Boris Souvarine Papers, bMs Fr 375 (509).

70. Horon, "Hebrews and Jews" (HKA/36), 14.

71. A reference to the introduction of the "Jewish consciousness" classes in Israeli schools in 1957, which the Young Hebrews unanimously condemned (Diamond, *Homeland or Holy Land?*, 83–84; see also Keren, *The Pen and the Sword*, 48, who comments that it is "[n]o wonder the Jewish-Israeli consciousness program soon took a religious turn" since the only specifically defined values in the program were the religious ones).

72. Ḥoron, "Beriat Artsenu Lefi Mimtsae Hageologia"; Ḥoron, "Toledot Haarets Hi Hahisṭoria Haleumit"; *Tsvat Rishona*, 38–41, 49.

73. 'Adya Gur, "28 Elef 'Anusim' Biśrael," in Raṭosh (ed.), *Minitsaḥon Lemapolet*, 120–21. In one of his letters, Horon suggested that Jewish immigration from the USSR, which intensified in the early 1970s, might assist in dismantling the Israeli "socio-feudal" order (letter from Horon to B. Souvarine, 16.5.1971, Boris Souvarine Papers, bMs Fr 375 [509]).

74. Gur, "28 Elef 'Anusim.'"

75. Typescript of a letter to David Bensoussan, 9.5.1966, Horon Archive (my translation from French).

76. *Tsvat Rishona*, 65–67.

77. *Tsvat Rishona*, 87–88.

78. Yehoshu'a Benṭov [Aharon Amir], "Mamlekhet Iśrael Hatsalbanit?," in Gerts and Weisbrod (eds.), *Haḳvutsa Hakna'anit*, 25–28. For the full weight of the "Crusader" charge against Israel consult Oḥana, *Lo Kna'anim, Lo Tsalbanim*, 291–348; Ohana, *The Origins of Israeli Mythology*, 131–81.

79. *Tsvat Rishona*, 65–67. In a private letter, Horon observed that "the desire of our princes (who are mostly Polish or otherwise Carpathian) is to establish here a South Africa supported by profitable pilgrimage" buttressed by "racial-theocratic theories" (letter from Horon to B. Souvarine, 16.5.1971, Boris Souvarine Papers, bMs Fr 375 [509]).

80. *Tsvat Rishona*, 87–88.

81. 'Adya Gur, "Ma'amad Shel Ma'atsama Ṿetakhsise Geṭṭo Bematsor," in Raṭosh (ed.), *Minitsaḥon Lemapolet*, 153–54.

82. Gur, "Ma'amad Shel Ma'atsama"; Ḥoron, "Iśrael Ṿehamitos Ha'aravi," 517.

83. Ḥoron, *Erets-Haḳedem*, 132.

84. Ḥoron, "Iśrael Ṿehamitos Ha'aravi," 501. The "marine" motif, so central to Horon's historiography, emerges here in a contemporary context.

85. Ḥoron, *Erets-Haḳedem*, 146 (emphasis added). The "alleged friends" probably refers to the United States and France.

86. Gourevitch, "The Semitic Levant," 22.

87. Ḥoron, *Erets-Haḳedem,* 140.

88. Ḥoron, "Iśrael Ṿehamitos Ha'aravi," 518; Ḥoron, "Shlemut Hamoledet," 157.

89. Ḥoron, *Ḳedem Ṿa'erev,* 226; see also Gesenius, *A Hebrew and English Lexicon,* 787–88.

90. See also Gesenius, *A Hebrew and English Lexicon,* 1035; Koehler and Baumgartner, *The Hebrew and Aramaic Lexicon,* 1576–77.

91. Belyaev, *Arabs, Islam and the Arab Caliphate,* 60, translator's footnote; Ḥoron, "Haḳedem Ha'ivri," 227–30; Ḥoron, *Ḳedem Ṿa'erev,* 228–41; Ḥoron, "Śiḥot 'Al Ḳadmoniyut Haarets," 117–19.

92. Ḥoron, *Ḳedem Ṿa'erev,* 226–28.

93. Belyaev, *Arabs, Islam and the Arab Caliphate,* 87, translator's footnote.

94. By asserting this, Horon ignores that the first Muslim direction of prayer (*qibla*) was the Meccan holy site of Ka'ba, which subsequently changed to Jerusalem and then reverted back ("qibla," *Encyclopaedia of Islam,* 2nd ed.), as well as the Ka'ba's pre-Islamic pagan significance.

95. Horon, "Is There an 'Arab Civilization'?," 412.

96. Gourevitch, "Le Panarabisme" (JIA/6/52p), 13–15; Horon, "Is There an 'Arab Civilization'?," 411–12; Ḥoron, "Iśrael Ṿehamitos Ha'aravi," 502–3; Ḥoron, *Ḳedem Ṿa'erev,* 57; Horon, "Les Arabes depuis l'Islam," 136; Ḥoron, "'Olam Behashḳafa 'Ivrit. Maamar Rishon," 115; Horon Archive, file "Canaan—fundamental principles."

97. Horon, "Is There an 'Arab Civilization'?," 418; Horon, "Les Arabes depuis l'Islam," 141. This, of course, parallels Horon's observation that the Bible in its current form, or major parts of it, was composed after the Hebrew nation's decay into Jewish denomination.

98. Gourevitch, "Le Panarabisme" (JIA/6/52p), 35.

99. Horon's lecture at the Fisher Club, Ra'anana, 22.3.1960 (Horon Archive).

100. Alraïd, "Yevrei i Khanaan," 8. This is one of only two references to the "Arab question" in *On History,* which lends credibility to Yonatan Ratosh's assertion that it was he who introduced Horon to this issue in the late 1930s (see chapter 1).

101. Horon, "Is There an 'Arab Civilization'?," 416 (emphasis added); Horon, "Les Arabes depuis l'Islam," 137; also Gourevitch, "Le Panarabisme" (JIA/6/52p), 21, 26.

102. 'A. G. Ḥ., "Iberim," 613.

103. Gourevitch, "Le Panarabisme" (JIA/6/52p), 12, 19, 32; Ḥoron, *Erets-Haḳedem,* 12, 16, 24–30, 88–89; Horon, "Is There an 'Arab Civilization'?," 412–18; Ḥoron, "Iśrael Ṿehamitos Ha'aravi," 503–6; Horon, "Les Arabes depuis l'Islam," 137–41; Ḥoron, *Ḳedem Ṿa'erev,* 57–58; Ḥoron, "'Olam Behashḳafa 'Ivrit. Maamar Rishon," 115–16.

104. Horon, "Les Arabes depuis l'Islam," 137.

105. Or, to be more exact, its central part, the Roman Arabia Deserta, which strongly differed ethnically, culturally, and economically from Arabia

Felix on the shores of the Red Sea and the Indian Ocean. Languages spoken in Southern Arabia, both ancient and modern, were hardly Arab, Horon claims, but a mixture of Semitic tongues with East African ones (Horon, "Le Monde des Hébreux" [JIA/5/52p]).

106. Gourevitch, "The Semitic Levant," 14, 17; Ḥoron, *Erets-Haḳedem*, 14, 22, 26, 42; Ḥoron, "Haimperializm Ha'arbai," 4; Horon, "Is There an 'Arab Civilization'?," 411, 418–19; Ḥoron, "Iśrael Ṿehamitos Ha'aravi," 506; Horon, "The Pan-Arab Myth in the Mideastern Vacuum," 4.

107. Ibn Khaldûn. *The Muqaddima: An Introduction to History* (tr. Franz Rosenthal, ed. and abr. N. J. Dawood) (Princeton: Princeton University Press, 1989), 91–122.

108. Horon, "Is There an 'Arab Civilization'?," 417.

109. In this capacity, the theory was promulgated by some Arab intellectuals like the Lebanese thinker Edmond Rabbath (Birgit Schaebler, "Writing the Nation in the Arabic-Speaking World, Nationally and Transnationally," in Berger [ed.], *Writing the Nation*, 184–85). For Rabbath's thought in detail, see Kaufman, *Reviving Phoenicia*, 205–9.

110. Adiag, "Comment s'est formée la mythologie arabe," *La Riposte*, 5.2.1948, 4, 6; Alraïd, "Ob Istorii: Istoki Yevreiskago Plemeni (1)," 5; Gour, "Hébreux et Juifs," 4–5; Gourevitch, "Le Panarabisme" (JIA/6/52p), 102–3, 109; Gourevitch, "The Semitic Levant," 13; Ḥoron, *Erets-Haḳedem*, 16, 34–35, 44, 70; Ḥoron, "Haimperializm Ha'arbai," 4; Horon, "Is There an 'Arab Civilization'?," 418; Ḥoron, "Iśrael Ṿehamitos Ha'aravi," 505–6; Ḥoron, *Ḳedem Ṿa'erev*, 129, 135–37, 227, 367–68; Horon, "Le Monde des Hébreux" (JIA/5/52p); Ḥoron, "'Olam Behashḳafa 'Ivrit. Mishpaḥat Ḥam Ṿeshem," 171, 178–80; *Tsvat Rishona*, 75–76.

111. Ḥoron, *Ḳedem Ṿa'erev*, 136; Ḥoron, "'Olam Behashḳafa 'Ivrit. Mishpaḥat Ḥam Ṿeshem," 179.

112. Horon attributes the *dhimmis'* (non-Muslims') Pan-Arabist zeal to their old desire to assimilate with the Muslim majority, comparing it to the Jewish assimilation drive in Europe and America, triggered by what he believed was a Jewish "inferiority complex" (Ḥoron, "Iśrael Ṿehamitos Ha'aravi," 508).

113. Adiag, "Le Panarabisme—une fiction au service de l'impérialisme britannique dans le Moyen Orient," *La Riposte*, 22.10.1947, 4–5.

114. Horon, "The Pan-Arab Myth in the Mideastern Vacuum," 6; for similar argumentation, see also Adiag, "Londres veut faire de la Méditerranée un lac anglais," *La Riposte*, 22.1.1948, 5; Gourevitch, "Le Panarabisme" (JIA/6/52p), 1, 13, 47–48, 118; Gourevitch, "Pan-Arabism"; 'A. Ḥoron, "MiNapoleon 'Ad Lawrence," *Alef*, May 1951, 11.

115. Ḥoron, "Iśrael Ṿehamitos Ha'aravi," 518

116. A. G., "Pan-Arab Propaganda," Levant Club, *Memorandum no. 4*, June 1955; M. Z. Frank, "The State Department and Israel," *Jewish Spectator*, February 1955, reproduced in the Levant Club, *Memorandum no. 2*, April 1955; see also the unsigned commentary in the same Memorandum (Israel State Archives, file GL-17109/33).

117. Gourevitch, "Le Panarabisme" (JIA/6/52p), 12.

118. Letter from Horon to E. Jabotinsky and S. Rosoff, 3.4.1956 (JIA/4/4-4a).

119. Adiag, "Le Panarabisme est un facteur de stagnation économique et de réaction sociale," *La Riposte*, 3.12.1947, 4–5; Adiag, "Pétroles du Proche-Orient," *La Riposte*, 2.1.1948, 8; Gourevitch, "Le Panarabisme" (JIA/6/52p), 57–60, 132.

120. Gourevitch, "Le Panarabisme" (JIA/6/52p), 122.

121. Gourevitch, "The Semitic Levant," 24–26; Ḥoron, *Erets-Haḳedem*, 30–33, 46–47, 92–99; Ḥoron, "Haimperializm Ha'arbai," 4; Ḥoron, "Iśrael Ṿehamitos Ha'aravi," 507–9; Ḥoron, *Ḳedem Ṿa'erev*, 60; Ḥoron, "'Olam Behashḳafa 'Ivrit. Maamar Rishon," 118; Horon, "The Pan-Arab Myth in the Mideastern Vacuum."

122. Gourevitch, "Le Panarabisme" (JIA/6/52p), 129.

123. Adiag, "Le Panarabisme est un facteur de stagnation économique"; Gourevitch, "Le Panarabisme" (JIA/6/52p), 57–60; Ḥoron, *Erets-Haḳedem*, 92–94; Horon, "The Pan-Arab Myth in the Mideastern Vacuum," 4; Horon's lecture at the Fisher Club, Ra'anana, 22.3.1960 (Horon Archive, and other drafts for talks on similar topics in his archive). For a profounder discussion of the differences between the British and the French colonialist attitudes, see Kaufman, *Reviving Phoenicia*, 13–15; Avi Shlaim, *Lion of Jordan: The Life of King Hussein in War and Peace* (London: Allen Lane, 2007), 1–37.

124. Levant Club, *Memorandum no. 2*, April 1955 (Israel State Archives, file GL-17109/33). In claiming so, Horon glosses over the blatant anti-Semitism widespread among the pieds noirs, many of whom celebrated the revocation by Vichy government in 1940 of the Crémieux Decree that in 1870 granted French citizenship to Algerian Jews (Marrus and Paxton, *Vichy France and the Jews*, 191–97; see also Sophie Roberts, *Citizenship and Antisemitism in French Colonial Algeria, 1870–1962* [Cambridge: Cambridge University Press, 2017]).

125. Adiag, "Vers un nouvel empire britannique en Méditerranée oriental," *La Riposte*, 9.1.1948, 4–5; Gourevitch, "Le Panarabisme" (JIA/6/52p), 70–71, 156; Horon, "The Pan-Arab Myth," 2; Letter from Horon to E. Jabotinsky and S. Rosoff, 3.4.1956 (JIA/4/4-4a); relevant unclassified materials in Horon's archive. In March 1960, Horon made the following prognosis, which can now be regarded only as inadvertent premonition: "In Algeria [the Jews] are full French citizens . . . and if Algeria remains French it is not to be expected that their prominent position in the life of the country, and of entire France, will change for the worse" (Horon's lecture at the Fisher Club, Ra'anana, 22.3.1960 [Horon Archive]).

126. Horon, "L'URSS 'amie' de l'Islam."

127. Gourevitch, "Le Panarabisme" (JIA/6/52p).

128. Adiag, "Le 'Monde Arabe' est une fiction," *La Riposte*, 29.1.1948, 2, 8. For more on language politics in Pan-Arab nationalism and its internal tensions, see Suleiman, *The Arabic Language*.

129. Ḥoron, *Erets-Haḳedem*, 16.

130. Ḥoron, *Erets-Haḳedem*, 16–21.

131. Gourevitch, "Le Panarabisme" (JIA/6/52p), 72.

132. Gourevitch, "The Semitic Levant," 25; Horon, "For a new American Policy South and East of the Mediterranean," 1951–52 (Horon Archive); Ḥoron, "Haimperializm Ha'arbai," 4; Ḥoron, "Hakoptim—'Hamitsrim Haamitiim,'" 182; Ḥoron, "Iśrael Ṿehamitos Ha'aravi," 510.

133. Horon, "Le Monde des Hébreux" (JIA/5/52p).

134. Ḥoron, *Erets-Haḳedem*, 90; Horon, "For a New American Policy" (Horon Archive). For a criticism of the determinist view of the supposed incompatibility between Islam and modern ethnic or national identity, see Haim Gerber, "The Muslim *Umma* and the Formation of Middle Eastern Nationalisms," in Leoussi and Grosby (eds.), *Nationalism and Ethnosymbolism*, 209–20.

135. The most detailed alternative "Arab" statistics from the mid-1940s are found in Gourevitch, "Le Panarabisme" (JIA/6/52p), 158–215. An updated calculation from 1955 is provided by Horon in Gourevitch, "Arabia's Mythical Millions" (JIA/8/52p). Other statistics of the population dynamics in the Levant and Mediterranean basin are from 1952 (Gourevitch, "The Semitic Levant," 29–30) and 1970 (Ḥoron, *Erets-Haḳedem*, 10). Unsurprisingly, Horon's touchstone is French statistical estimates from North Africa, which show a significantly reduced population density as opposed to comparable areas in (English-controlled) Middle East.

136. Gourevitch, "Le Panarabisme" (JIA/6/52p), 173. For von Weisl, see Dan Tamir, "'Dictate More, for We Should Obey Your Orders!' Cult of the Leader in Inter-War Hebrew Fascism," *Politics, Religion and Ideology* 14 (4), 2013, 449–67. For von Weisl's very questionable competence in all matters Arab, see a sarcastic observation by Hillel Cohen, *1929: Year Zero of the Arab-Israeli Conflict* (Waltham: Brandeis University Press, 2015), 101.

137. Gourevitch, "Le Panarabisme" (JIA/6/52p), 59, 140; Gourevitch, "The Semitic Levant," 9–10, 14, 16–17, 24–26; 'A. G. Ḥoron, "Bene Britenu Haṭiv'iim," *Alef*, June 1967, 2; Ḥoron, *Erets-Haḳedem*, 4–49, 124; Ḥoron, "Haimperializm Ha'arbai," 5; Ḥoron, "Iśrael Ṿehamitos Ha'aravi," 509–17; Ḥoron, *Ḳedem Ṿa'erev*, 227; Ḥoron, "Shlemut Hamoledet," 154–55; Horon, "The Pan-Arab Myth."

138. Ḥoron, *Erets-Haḳedem*, 48.

139. Ḥoron, "Iśrael Ṿehamitos Ha'aravi," 502.

140. Ḥoron, *Erets-Haḳedem*, 48; Horon, "For a New American Policy" (Horon Archive); Ḥoron, "Haimperializm Ha'arbai"; Horon, "The Pan-Arab Myth," 2.

141. Adiag, "Réalités du Proche-Orient: Le Liban," *La Riposte*, 14.3.1949, 8; Gourevitch, "Le Panarabisme" (JIA/6/52p), 90–94; Ḥoron, "Iśrael Ṿehamitos Ha'aravi," 501; Ḥoron, "Shlemut Hamoledet," 154. The Young Hebrews' severe dislike of Israel's peace camp, with its conciliatory attitudes toward variations of Arab nationalism, must be understood within this context.

142. Ḥoron, *Erets-Haḳedem*, 42; Ḥoron, "Haimperializm Ha'arbai," 5; Horon, "The Pan-Arab Myth," 5.

143. Ḥoron, *Erets-Haḳedem*, 50, 64–65.

144. Horon, "The Hebrew Movement—An Outline" (JIA/2/52p; HKA/36), 8.

145. Letter from Horon to E. Jabotinsky, 2.5.1955 (JIA/4/4-4a).

146. Ḥoron, *Erets-Haḳedem*, 124; Ḥoron, "Shlemut Hamoledet," 156.

147. Ḥoron, "Iśrael Vehamitos Ha'aravi," 516. For example, in the mid-1950s, the Levant Club assessed the number of Christians of all denominations in the Levant at 12 million (Levant Club, *Memorandum no. 2*, April 1955; Israel State Archives, file GL-17109/33).

148. Gourevitch, "Le Panarabisme" (JIA/6/52p), 70.

149. I am grateful to Dr Johannes Becke for suggesting this translation.

150. Michal Ephratt, "Iconicity, Ratosh's Lexical Innovations, and Beyond," *Semiotica* 157 (1/4), 2005, 91–92.

151. Horon, *Erets-Haḳedem*, 4, interprets the word *'arbai* as "Arab-like," "quasi-Arab," or "self-titled Arab."

152. Ḥoron, "Hakoptim—'Hamitsrim Haamitiim.'"

153. Horon ("Hakoptim—'Hamitsrim Haamitiim'") explains that the ethnonym *Copt* evolved from *Aegyptos*, which is a Greek form of the ancient Egyptian name *Hi-Kw-Ptḥ*, "Castle of the bull-god Ptah," the earliest name of Egypt's original capital, Memphis.

154. Ḥoron, "MiNapoleon 'Ad Lawrence," 11.

155. Horon, "Le Monde des Hébreux" (JIA/5/52p).

156. Gourevitch, "Le Panarabisme" (JIA/6/52p), 75; Ḥoron, *Erets-Haḳedem*, 36; Ḥoron, "Hakoptim—'Hamitsrim Haamitiim,'" 179–80. In a brief note written just a few months before the Free Officers' coup in Egypt and preserved in Horon's archive ("Egypt Today in the Opinion of Some Cultured Egyptians," 28.11.1951), Horon reported (based on personal conversations with Egyptian middle-class intellectuals) of a deep dissatisfaction with the Egyptian corrupt and inefficient ruling classes responsible for the 1948 blunder in Palestine in the name of an Arabist ideology that jeopardizes Egypt's uniqueness.

157. Ḥoron, "Shlemut Hamoledet," 160.

158. Letter from Horon to Y. Ratosh and other Young Hebrews, 19.4.1951 (Ratosh Archive, file 719/721); letter from Horon to E. Jabotinsky, 2.5.1955 (JIA/4/4-4a).

159. Ḥoron, *Erets-Haḳedem*, 130.

160. Gourevitch, "The Semitic Levant," 13–14, 18–20; Ḥoron, *Erets-Haḳedem*, 12–21, 36, 90, 108–31, 140–41; Ḥoron, "Haḳedem Ha'ivri," 255, 258–59; Ḥoron, "Hakoptim—'Hamitsrim Haamitiim,'" 179, 181–83; Ḥoron, "Iśrael Vehamitos Ha'aravi," 501; Ḥoron, *Ḳedem Va'erev*, 261, 342; Horon, "Le Monde des Hébreux" (JIA/5/52p); Ḥoron, "Shlemut Hamoledet," 158–60; Horon, "The Pan-Arab Myth."

161. Ḥoron, *Erets-Haḳedem*, 122; Ḥoron, "Shlemut Hamoledet," 158, 159.

162. Horon, "Is There an 'Arab Civilization?,'" 417–18. See also Ghosn, "Hamaronim—'Am Halevanon," who argues that the Maronites are a separate nation of non-Arab but Canaanite-Phoenician origin.

163. Gourevitch, "The Semitic Levant," 22.

164. Ḥoron, *Erets-Haḳedem*, 114.

165. Gourevitch, "The Semitic Levant," 24.

166. Gourevitch, "The Semitic Levant," 22–24; Ḥoron, *Erets-Haḳedem*, 108–15, 124, 140–41.

167. Roman Vater, "Beyond Bi-Nationalism? The Young Hebrews versus the 'Palestinian Issue,'" *Journal of Political Ideologies* 21 (1), 2016, 45–60.

168. Ḥoron, *Erets-Haḳedem*, 138; Ḥoron, "Haḳedem Ha'ivri," 259.

169. Gourevitch, "Le Panarabisme" (JIA/6/52p), 201–2015; Ḥoron, *Erets-Haḳedem*, 136. This position would have echoed the Israeli right-wing thesis that those who call themselves Palestinians (or Palestinian refugees) are in fact newcomers had it not been for the Young Hebrews' contention that the Hebrew revival took place outside Zionism.

170. Gur, "Hem Niḳlaṭim Maher"; 'Adya Gur, "Ḥufsha Beramallah," in Raṭosh (ed.), *Minitsaḥon Lemapolet*, 321–22.

171. Letter from Horon to B. Souvarine, 16.5.1971, Boris Souvarine Papers, bMs Fr 375 (509).

172. Gourevitch, "The Semitic Levant," 26; see also Ḥoron, "Shlemut Hamoledet," 160.

173. Ḥoron, "Iśrael Ṿehamitos Ha'aravi," 515.

174. Ḥoron, *Erets-Haḳedem*, 124, 128.

175. Benṭov, "Mamlekhet Iśrael Hatsalbanit?," 26; Yehoshu'a Benṭov, "Mesheḳ Shel 'Ayara," in Gerts and Weisbrod (eds.), *Haḳvutsa Hakna'anit*, 34; Raṭosh, *Reshit Hayamim*, 92, 95.

176. Moṭi Avi-Yair, "Ḳeliṭat Toshve 'Aza," in Raṭosh (ed.), *Minitsaḥon Lemapolet*, 98–99; Amnon Kats, "Me'aravim—Le'ivrim," in Raṭosh (ed.), *Minitsaḥon Lemapolet*, 83–89; Kuzar, *Hebrew and Zionism*, 227–28; Raṭosh, *1967—Uma Hal'a?*, 36, 43–44, 62–68, 74–75, 115–16. Horon's standpoint on the matter is expressed in Gur, "Pizur Hageṭṭaot," 191; letter from Horon to E. Jabotinsky and S. Rosoff, 3.4.1956 (JIA/4/4-4a).

177. Gourevitch, "The Semitic Levant," 28 (emphases added).

178. Adolphe Gourevitch, "Pan-Arabism" (talk at the Asia Institute, 23.11.1952 [Horon Archive, Asia Institute files]; reprinted in Hebrew with some variations in Ḥoron, "Haimperializm Ha'arbai," 5).

179. Horon, "The Pan-Arab Myth," 4.

180. Ḥoron, *Ḳedem Ṿa'erev*, 345.

181. Ḥoron, "Shlemut Hamoledet," 153.

182. Ḥoron, *Erets-Haḳedem*, 104; see also Ḥoron, *Erets-Haḳedem*, 54; Ḥoron, "Jabotinsky Ṿehaśafa Ha'ivrit," 339; Ḥoron, "Shlemut Hamoledet," 157.

183. Gourevitch, "The Semitic Levant," 24.

184. Gur, "Hem Niḳlaṭim Maher," 323.

185. Ḥoron, "Shlemut Hamoledet," 153.

186. Letter from Horon to E. Jabotinsky and S. Rosoff, 10.2.1956 (HKA/32; emphasis added); see also Ḥoron, "Shlemut Hamoledet," 157.

187. Gur, "Ma'amad Shel Ma'atsama," 154.

188. Ḥoron, *Ḳedem Ṿa'erev*, 59; Ḥoron, "'Olam Behashḳafa 'Ivrit. Maamar Rishon," 118; see also Gourevitch, "Arabia's Mythical Millions" (JIA/8/52p), 7; Gourevitch, "The Semitic Levant," 28; Ḥoron, "Shlemut Hamoledet," 156.

189. Letter from Horon to E. Jabotinsky and S. Rosoff, 3.4.1956 (JIA/4/4-4a).

190. Gur, "Pizur Hageṭṭaot," 191.

191. Ḥoron, "Shlemut Hamoledet," 161.

192. Ḥoron, *Erets-Haḳedem*, 150.

193. Horon Archive, file "Canaan—fundamental principles."

194. Ḥoron, *Erets-Haḳedem*, 52, 142; Ḥoron, "Shlemut Hamoledet," 153; Horon Archive, file "Canaan—fundamental principles."

195. 'Adya Gur, "'Teḳufat Hahamtana'—1972," in Raṭosh (ed.), *Minitsaḥon Lemapolet*, 166.

196. Ḥoron, "Shlemut Hamoledet," 160–61 (emphases added). See also Ḥoron, "Iśrael Ṿehamitos Ha'aravi," 518, where he cites as his finite ideal Jabotinsky's famous lines from his poem "The East Bank of the Jordan": "There he'll be saturated with abundance and happiness the son of Arabia, the son of Nazareth and my son" (citation from Arye Naor, "The Leader as a Poet: The Political and Ideological Poetry of Ze'ev Jabotinsky," *Israel Affairs* 20 (2), 2014, 177). Compare also the charter of "Club 59" from December 1959 (chapter 1).

197. Ḥoron, "Shlemut Hamoledet," 154.

198. Letter from Horon to E. Jabotinsky and S. Rosoff, 3.4.1956 (JIA/4/4-4a).

199. Ḥoron, "Shlemut Hamoledet."

200. Ḥoron, "Shlemut Hamoledet," 154, 157–58; see also Ḥoron, "Iśrael Ṿehamitos Ha'aravi," 518.

201. Ḥoron, *Erets-Haḳedem*, 132.

202. Gourevitch, "The Semitic Levant," 23.

203. Ḥoron, *Erets-Haḳedem*, 148–49.

204. Ḥoron, *Erets-Haḳedem*, 150. Very interesting is Horon's disclaimer that this prognosis is only approximate, based on opinions expressed by politicians (such as the Israeli-Christian member of the Knesset Rustam Bastūni, who partook in Aharon Amir's Club for Hebrew Thought, or the Syrian activist 'Abd al-Qādir), scientists (the "Canaanite" physicist Amnon Kats and the linguist Uzzi Ornan) and men of letters, like Ratosh, "whose words took the shape of a poetic vision years before the [1967] war" (Ḥoron, *Erets-Haḳedem*, 163).

205. Ḥoron, *Erets-Haḳedem*, 152.

206. Ḥoron, "Iśrael Ṿehamitos Ha'aravi," 519.

207. Levant Club, *Memorandum no. 2*, April 1955 (Israel State Archives, file GL-17109/33); notes for a talk to a Betar training camp in France in August 1963 (Horon Archive).

208. The theme of USA's detrimental influence upon Israeli geopolitics was developed later by Horon's disciple and friend Esra Sohar, *A Concubine in the Middle East: American-Israeli Relations* (tr. Laurence Weinbaum) (Jerusalem: Gefen, 1999).

209. Gur, "Teḳufat Hahamtana"; Horon, "For a new American Policy" (Horon Archive); Horon, "La Grande Illusion," 63–68; Ḥoron, "Shlemut Hamoledet," 161–63; Horon, "The Pan-Arab Myth," 7–8; letter from Horon to Y. Ratosh and other Young Hebrews, 26.12.1950 (Ratosh Archive, file 719/720); letter from Horon to E. Jabotinsky and S. Rosoff, 3.4.1956 (JIA/4/4-4a).

210. Letter from Horon to E. Jabotinsky and S. Rosoff, 3.4.1956 (JIA/4/4-4a).

211. Letter from Horon to B. Souvarine, 16.5.1971, Boris Souvarine Papers, bMs Fr 375 (509).

212. Letter from Horon to E. Jabotinsky and S. Rosoff, 10.2.1956 (HKA/32); letter from Horon to E. Jabotinsky and S. Rosoff, 3.4.1956 (JIA/4/4-4a).

213. Eri Jabotinsky, "Tentative Formulation for a Program of Action," Haifa, November 19, 1956 (HKA/32).

214. *The Lebanese Gazette—Leesan Al-Adl*, 8.7.1955 (Israel State Archives, file GL-17109/33).

215. *Tsvat Rishona*, 18.

Chapter 4

1. See Ivianski, *LEḤI*, 790, no. 1.

2. Yadgar, *Israel's Jewish Identity Crisis*, 162–64. This is not to say that "Canaanism" did not pick up themes that Zionism was reluctant to develop; I argue instead that it is wrong to view the Young Hebrews *only* in this perspective.

3. John Hutchinson, *Nations as Zones of Conflict* (London: Sage, 2005).

4. Clashes over what makes a nation are by no means unique to Israel or the Middle East. See Breuilly, "Nationalism and the Making of National Pasts," 17–19; Cohen, *The Symbolic Construction of Community*, 115–18; Duara, *Rescuing History from the Nation*, 10–16, 66; Smith, *Myths and Memories of the Nation*, 71, 86–87, 263. For an example of rival national visions for the same nation in the Ukrainian context, consider John-Paul Himka, "The Construction of Nationality in Galician Rus': Icarian Flights in Almost all Directions," in Suny and Kennedy (eds.), *Intellectuals and the Articulation of the Nation*, 109–64; for a similar phenomenon in the French context, see Michael Dietler, "'Our Ancestors the Gauls': Archaeology, Ethnic Nationalism, and the Manipulation of Celtic Identity in Modern Europe," *American Anthropologist* 96 (3), 1994, 584–605.

5. For a three-phased framework of the development of a national ideology from initial elaboration by a tiny core of historically minded intellectuals to a mass movement, see Hroch, "From National Movement to the Fully-Formed Nation," 6–10, and also Eley, "Nationalism and Social History," 100–3.

6. Duara, *Rescuing History from the Nation.*

7. Diamond, *Homeland or Holy Land?*, 69.

8. On Dinur's career, see Piterberg, *The Returns of Zionism*, 131–33, 140–45; Uri Ram, *Israeli Nationalism: Social Conflicts and the Politics of Knowledge* (London and New York: Routledge, 2011), 10–12, 15–24.

9. Yehezkel Kaufmann, *The Religion of Israel from Its Beginnings to the Babylonian Exile* (tr. and abr. Moshe Greenberg) (London: George Allen & Unwin, 1961).

10. For Kaufmann's version of the emergence of Judaism and the Israelite nation, generally in accordance with the biblical story, see Kaufmann, *The Religion of Israel*, 212–42. Ben-Zion Dinur was much more sceptical regarding the historical reliability of the Bible (Ben-Zion Dinur, "Hakarat He'avar Betoda'at Ha'am Uv'ayot Haḥeḳer Ba," in *Hakarat He'avar*, 12–19). In his historiographic credo (see Dinur, "Hakarat He'avar," 9–24), Dinur insisted on scholarly meticulousness in research while being aware that any history was written from a contemporary standpoint and therefore ought to be a pedagogical tool in nation building. Yitzhak Conforti, "Zionist Awareness of the Jewish Past: Inventing Tradition or Renewing the Ethnic Past?," *Studies in Ethnicity and Nationalism* 12 (1), 2012, 167, identifies such views with the "East European" historiographic school, which used the history of postimperial nations for mass nation-building projects in Europe after 1918.

11. Kaufmann, *The Religion of Israel*, 1–3.

12. Piterberg, *The Returns of Zionism*, 103–5, 278–79.

13. This, however, was noticed by both the author of the foreword to *Ḳedem Ṿa'erev* (Eshel, "Hatagliyot Haarkheologiyot Umif'al Ḥayaṿ Shel 'A. G. Ḥoron," 32) and David Ohana (Oḥana, *Lo Kna'anim, Lo Tsalbanim*, 107–8).

14. For a criticism of Kaufmann's historiography from a post-"Canaanite" perspective, see 'Evron, *Haḥeshbon Haleumi*, 115–27.

15. Kurzweil, *Sifrutenu Heḥadasha*, 284.

16. Kurzweil, "The New 'Canaanites,'" 9.

17. Koselleck, *Futures Past*, 214.

18. Cohen, *The Symbolic Construction of Community*, 99.

19. Percy S. Cohen, "Theories of Myth," *Man* (new series) 4 (3), 1969, 337–53.

20. This position was most comprehensively developed by Hayden White in his now-classical *Metahistory* (White, *Metahistory*) and revisited in his newest *The Practical Past* (Hayden White, *The Practical Past* [Evanston: Northwestern University Press, 2014]). See also Rebecca Collins, "Concealing the Poverty of Traditional Historiography: Myth as Mystification in Historical

Discourse," *Rethinking History: The Journal of Theory and Practice* 7 (3), 2003, 341–65; Claude Lévi-Strauss, *The Savage Mind* (London: Weidenfeld and Nicolson, 1966), 256–58; Mario J. Valdés, *A Ricoeur Reader: Reflection and Imagination* (Hemel Hempstead: Harvester Wheatsheaf, 1991), 105–6, 116.

21. Abulof, *The Mortality and Morality of Nations*, 186.

22. Gat, *Nations*, 215–16.

23. Chowers, "Time in Zionism."

24. For an exhaustive discussion of the shifts in the concept of historical time under the impact of modernity, see Koselleck, *Futures Past*.

25. See Iśrael Barṭal, " 'Al Harishoniyut: Zman Umaḳom Ba'aliya Harishona," in Yafa Berelowitz and Yosef Lang (eds.), *Leśoḥeaḥ Tarbut 'Im Ha'aliya Harishona: 'Iyun Ben Teḳufot* (Tel Aviv: Haḳibbuts Hameuḥad, 2010), 15–24, and, for a critical interpretation of this shift, Amos Funkenstein, "Collective Memory and Historical Consciousness," *History and Memory* 1 (1), 1989, 11–21. For a contemporary's evidence, see Zacharias Frankel, "Mada' Hayahadut—Ṭivo Ṿetafḳido," in Paul R. Mendes-Flohr (ed.), *Ḥokhmat Iśrael: Hebeṭim Hisṭoriim Ṿefilosofiim* (Jerusalem: The Historical Society of Israel, 1979), 113–14.

26. Nahum N. Glatzer, "The Beginnings of Modern Jewish Studies," in Alexander Altmann (ed.), *Studies in Nineteenth-Century Jewish Intellectual History* (Cambridge: Harvard University Press, 1964), 44.

27. David Biale, *Power and Powerlessness in Jewish History* (New York: Schocken Books, 1987), 137.

28. Alan Dowty, "Zionism's Greatest Conceit," *Israel Studies* 3 (1), 1998, 6.

29. Nadia Abu el-Haj, *Facts on the Ground: Archaeological Practice and Territorial Self-Fashioning in Israeli Society* (Chicago and London: University of Chicago Press, 2001), 257–58.

30. For scholarly opinions supporting such interpretation of the meaning of Zionism, see Glatzer, "The Beginnings of Modern Jewish Studies," 33–36; Kaplan, *The Jewish Radical Right*, 139; Zerubavel, *Recovered Roots*, 14. For a problematization of the tenets of the "return to history" idea in Zionism consult Piterberg, *The Returns of Zionism*, 245–49; Amnon Raz-Krakotzkin, "Exile, History, and the Nationalization of Jewish Memory: Some Reflections on the Zionist Notion of History and Return," *Journal of Levantine Studies* 3 (2), 2013, 37–70.

31. Funkenstein, "Collective Memory," 17.

32. Aziza Khazzoom, "The Great Chain of Orientalism: Jewish Identity, Stigma Management, and Ethnic Exclusion in Israel," *American Sociological Review* 68 (4), August 2003, 492.

33. For an overview of Jewish attitudes to the Land of Israel from antiquity to the present see Lawrence A. Hoffman (ed.), *The Land of Israel: Jewish Perspectives* (Notre Dame: University of Notre Dame Press, 1986); Avraham Ya'ari, *Mas'ot Erets Iśrael* (Tel Aviv: Modan, 1996).

34. Neil Asher Silberman, *Between Past and Present: Archaeology, Ideology, and Nationalism in the Modern Middle East* (New York: Henry Holt, 1989), 125.

On Zionist territorial vitalism, see Oz Almog, *The Sabra: The Creation of the New Jew* (tr. Haim Watzman) (Berkeley, Los Angeles, London: University of California Press, 2000), 138–39; Allon Gal, "Historical Ethno-Symbols in the Emergence of the State of Israel," in Leoussi and Grosby (eds.), *Nationalism and Ethnosymbolism*, 223; Eran Kaplan, "Decadent Pioneers: Land, Space and Gender in Zionist Revisionist Thought," *Journal of Israeli History* 20 (1), 2001, 1–3; Baruch Kimmerling, *Zionism and Territory: The Socio-Territorial Dimensions of Zionist Politics* (Berkeley: Institute of International Studies, University of California, 1983), 13–14, 201–5; Zerubavel, *Recovered Roots*, 15, 28–29. On the role of nationalist archaeology in Israel, see Abu el-Haj, *Facts on the Ground*; Amos Elon, "Politics and Archaeology," in Neil Asher Silberman and David B. Small (eds.), *The Archaeology of Israel: Constructing the Past, Interpreting the Present* (Sheffield: Sheffield Academic, 1997), 34–47; Michael Feige and Tsvi Shiloni (eds.), *Ḳardom Laḥpor Bo: Arkheologia Uleumiyut Beerets Iśrael* (Jerusalem: Ben-Gurion Research Institute, 2008); Yaacov Shavit, "Archaeology, Political Culture, and Culture in Israel," in Silberman and Small (eds.), *The Archaeology of Israel*, 48–61; Silberman, *Between Past and Present*.

35. Zerubavel, *Recovered Roots*.

36. Kimmerling, *Zionism and Territory*, 206.

37. Zerubavel, *Recovered Roots*, 14–15.

38. One of its chief "priests" was David Ben-Gurion (Anita Shapira, "Ben-Gurion and the Bible: The Forging of an Historical Narrative?," *Middle Eastern Studies* 33 (4), 1997, 645–74).

39. Almog, *The Sabra*, 160–61; Conforti, "Zionist Awareness of the Jewish Past," 163–65; Piterberg, *The Returns of Zionism*, 273–82; Ram, *Israeli Nationalism*, 21–22; Shapira, "Ben-Gurion and the Bible," 646–47; Anita Shapira, "The Bible and Israeli Identity," *AJS Review* 28 (1), 2004, 11–42; Shavit, "Archaeology, Political Culture, and Culture in Israel," 53–55. The role of the Bible as a cultural resource for nationalist ideologies is reviewed by David Aberbach, "Nationalism and the Hebrew Bible," *Nations and Nationalism* 11 (2), 2005, 223–42, and Kalman Neuman, "Political Hebraism and the Early Modern 'Respublica Hebraeorum': On Defining the Field," *Hebraic Political Studies* 1 (1), 2005, 57–70.

40. Shavit, "Archaeology, Political Culture, and Culture in Israel," 55–56.

41. This pertains more to the Second Temple and the Hasmonean period than to the First Temple era (Almog, *Zionism and History*, 17; Gal, "Historical Ethno-Symbols," 223, 225; Shapira, "The Bible and Israeli Identity," 11–15; Zerubavel, *Recovered Roots*, 23). In this respect, Ben-Gurion dissented from the Zionist intellectual mainstream by focusing his attention after 1948 on the First Temple period (Shapira, "Ben-Gurion and the Bible," 658–59).

42. Shapira, "Ben-Gurion and the Bible," 654, see also Oḥana, *Lo Kna'anim, Lo Tsalbanim*, 180.

43. Almog, *The Sabra*, 73–74; Eric Cohen, "Israel as a Post-Zionist Society," *Israel Affairs* 1 (3), 1995, 204; Gal, "Historical Ethno-Symbols," 227; Allon Gal, "National Restoration and Moral Renewal: The Dialectics of the Past in

the Emergence of Modern Israel," in Carvalho and Gemenne (eds.), *Nations and their Histories*, 172–88.

44. Gal, "Historical Ethno-Symbols," 227.

45. Cohen, "Israel as a Post-Zionist Society," 204.

46. Almog, *Zionism and History*, 23–83, 236.

47. See also Ram, *Israeli Nationalism*, 7, 9–10; Raz-Krakotzkin, "Exile, History, and the Nationalization of Jewish Memory," 44. Piterberg, *The Returns of Zionism*, 155–91, identified Gerschom Scholem as the intellectual father of the idea of a temporal rupture as its own *telos* (see introduction).

48. Almog, *Zionism and History*, 38.

49. Zerubavel, *Recovered Roots*, 14, 19.

50. Khazzoom, "The Great Chain of Orientalism," 492–93.

51. Dowty, "Zionism's Greatest Conceit," 1.

52. Almog, *Zionism and History*, 308–9; Ben-'Ezer, *En Shaananim Betsion*, 287–317; Diamond, *Homeland or Holy Land?*, 9–23; David Vital, "Zionism as Revolution? Zionism as Rebellion?," *Modern Judaism* 18, 1998, 205–15; Yadgar, *Israel's Jewish Identity Crisis*, 16.

53. Kimmerling, *Zionism and Territory*, 204. For a detailed description of components taken over from Judaism by Zionism, see Baruch Kimmerling, *The Invention and Decline of Israeliness: State, Society, and the Military* (Berkeley, Los Angeles, London: University of California Press, 2005), 191. For an analysis of the tension between Zionist theory and praxis in this regard, see Kimmerling, *The Invention and Decline of Israeliness*, 173–207.

54. Dowty, "Zionism's Greatest Conceit," 7.

55. Almog, *Zionism and History*, 95.

56. Almog, *Zionism and History*, 309.

57. Yadgar, *Israel's Jewish Identity Crisis* (esp. 27, 41, 75). Yadgar implies that the only viable way out of the philosophical and moral dead end that secular Zionism has brought itself into is the adoption of a non-Jewish definition of Israeli nationhood, that is, ascending the "Canaanite" path. This however has slim chances of realization given the Jewish Israeli public's opposition to such option (see conclusion for further discussion).

58. Yadgar, *Israel's Jewish Identity Crisis*, 27.

59. Meron Benvenisti, *Sacred Landscape: The Buried History of the Holy Land Since 1948* (tr. Maxine Kaufman-Lacusta) (Berkeley, Los Angeles, London: University of California Press, 2000, 250.

60. Diamond, *Homeland or Holy Land?*, 73.

61. Apart from the authors cited above, see also Conforti, "Zionist Awareness of the Jewish Past"; Gal, "Historical Ethno-Symbols"; Raz-Krakotzkin, "Exile, History, and the Nationalization of Jewish Memory," 48–54 (notably, Raz-Krakotzkin argues that the Zionist philosophy of history internalized to a large extent Protestant historiographical thought, as does Yadgar, though the two disagree on the effects of the adoption of Protestant epistemology on Jewish nationalist thinking); Zerubavel, *Recovered Roots*, 21–22, 217, 218.

62. Almog, *The Sabra*, 35–45.

63. For a harsh critique by Yeshayahu Leibowitz of the "secularization" of the myth of Isaac's binding from an orthodox religious position, see Ben-'Ezer, *En Shaananim Betsion*, 135.

64. Zerubavel, *Recovered Roots*, 16–33.

65. Dowty, "Zionism's Greatest Conceit," 7.

66. Diamond, *Homeland or Holy Land?*, 5.

67. Zerubavel, *Recovered Roots*, 217.

68. Zerubavel, *Recovered Roots*, 218. An example of a purely novel Zionist festival was Adar 11, the anniversary of the 1920 Tel-Ḥai incident, but it remained relatively marginal in the calendar of the Yishuv and the State of Israel (Zerubavel, *Recovered Roots*, 39–47, 84–95, 147–77).

69. Dowty, "Zionism's Greatest Conceit," 7.

70. Almog, *The Sabra*, 2, 3, 5–13, qualifies that the Sabras, being quite insignificant statistically (about 20,000 out of 650,000 in 1948), were not a "generation" in the biological sense, but a symbolic-cultural type formed by a particular socialization context, whose cultural significance greatly exceeded its numerical strength.

71. Almog, *The Sabra*, 35.

72. Almog, *The Sabra*, 265 (emphasis added). See furthermore: Almog, *The Sabra*, 18–22, 226–27; Yafa Berelowitz, "Hamoshava Ha'ivrit: Reshita Shel Tarbut Erets Iśreelit," in Berelowitz and Lang (eds.), *Leśoḥeaḥ Tarbut 'Im Ha'aliya Harishona*, 70–109; Itamar Even-Zohar, "Hatsmiḥa Ṿehahitgabshut Shel Tarbut 'Ivrit Meḳomit Ṿilidit Beerets Iśrael, 1882–1948," *Ḳatedra*, 16, 1980, 165–89; Arieh B. Saposnik, *Becoming Hebrew: The Creation of a Jewish National Culture in Ottoman Palestine* (Oxford: Oxford University Press, 2008); Zerubavel, *Recovered Roots*, 27–28. A member of the Sabra generation, the writer Hanoch Bartov tellingly titled his autobiographical essay: "A Hebrew person was expected, yet there grew a Jew" (Ḥanokh Barṭov, *Ligdol Ṿelikhtov Beerets Iśrael*, Or Yehuda: Zmora-Bitan, 2007, 132–42).

73. Almog, *The Sabra*, 149–52, 260.

74. Zerubavel, *Recovered Roots*, 27.

75. Cited by Kimmerling, *Zionism and Territory*, 205 (emphasis added). The same argument is made by Michael Keren, *The Pen and the Sword*, 18–19.

76. Almog, *Zionism and History*, 17–18.

77. For a brief discussion of the debates within Zionism on how the connection between past and present be conceptualized and implemented, see Almog, *Zionism and History*, 306.

78. Smith, "Ethnic Myths and Ethnic Revivals," 295.

79. For an investigation of these two images, consult Matossian, "Ideologies of Delayed Development." Matossian's analysis, which pertains to third-world postcolonial nationalism, implies these images' incompatibility. Horon, who integrates the two, nonetheless seems to share her understanding, when in his account of the downfall of the Hebrew power he tacitly accuses the

disaffected masses, who under the Prophets' guidance transformed YHWH's worship from a cult of the royal house to a protest symbol, of "lagging" behind Canaan's geopolitical ascendancy.

80. Radhika Seshan, "Writing the Nation in India: Communalism and Historiography," in Berger (ed.), *Writing the Nation*, 155.

81. Almog, *Zionism and History*, 41.

82. Anthony Smith, "Ethnic Myths and Ethnic Revivals," 296–97, accordingly observes that an inclusive approach is more characteristic of nationalist visions based on myths of ideological renewal rather than of those based on conservative genealogical myths.

83. Almog, *Zionism and History*, 215. When analysing early Zionism's objective of "the conquest of [Jewish Diaspora] communities," Almog highlights the Zionist leadership's disdain toward the principles and values of democracy developed from a minority position within worldwide Jewry in the early twentieth century. Another case in point is the Zionists' firm opposition to any kind of representative democratic structures for Palestine as long as the Arabs constituted a numerical majority in the country (Abulof, *The Mortality and Morality of Nations*, 192; Nimrod Lin, "'Al Ma Anaḥnu Medabrim Kesheanu Medabrim 'Al Medina? Maḥshavat Hamdina Hatsiyonit Biteḳufat Hamandaṭ Habriṭi," *Iśrael* 27–28, 2021, 187–212). Heller, *Jabotinsky's Children*, 8, 57, suggests an illuminating explanation as to why some Jews (and therefore also some Zionists) preferred in certain instances authoritarianism to democracy before the Second World War: they trusted that the former would keep anti-Semitism at bay, while the latter might set it on the rampage.

84. Yadgar, *Israel's Jewish Identity Crisis*, 64 (emphasis added). Elsewhere, Yadgar is explicit that the Zionist "objectivist" definition of Jewish identity is inspired by anti-Semitism (Yadgar, *Israel's Jewish Identity Crisis*, 10, 48).

85. Ḥoron, "Iśrael Ṿehamitos Ha'aravi," 518 (emphasis added).

86. Prospectus for "The Hebrew Land by the Euphrates" manuscript by Horon, preserved in his archive.

87. Almog, *The Sabra*, 80–82; Zerubavel, *Recovered Roots*, 27.

88. Stefan Berger, "Introduction: Towards a Global History of National Historiographies," in Berger (ed.), *Writing the Nation*, 5–6; Natividad Gutiérrez Chong, "Ethnic Origins and Indigenous People: An Approach from Latin America," in Leoussi and Grosby (eds.), *Nationalism and Ethnosymbolism*, 312–24. This claim is made here notwithstanding Zionism's uniqueness, as its "mother-country" was the entire Jewish Diaspora.

89. Kimmerling, *Zionism and Territory*, 214.

90. Masri, *The Dynamics of Exclusionary Constitutionalism*, 42.

91. 'Evron, *Haḥeshbon Haleumi*, 363–67; Evron, *Jewish State or Israeli Nation?*, 215–18. This, of course, is a wholly speculative comparison, since the Young Hebrews never came even close to any of the achievements of the German Empire in terms of expansion and dominance.

92. Diamond, *Homeland or Holy Land?*, 72.

93. Masri, *The Dynamics of Exclusionary Constitutionalism*; Shourideh C. Molavi, *Stateless Citizenship: The Palestinian-Arab Citizens of Israel* (Leiden, Boston: Brill, 2013); Robinson, *Citizen Strangers*; Yadgar, *Israel's Jewish Identity Crisis*.

94. Horon, "The Hebrew Movement—An Outline" (JIA/2/52p; HKA/36).

95. Vital, "Zionism as Revolution?," 207.

96. Diamond, *Homeland or Holy Land?*, 5.

97. Gil Eyal, *Hasarat Haḳesem Min Hamizraḥ: Toledot Hamizraḥanut Be'idan Hamizraḥiyut* (Jerusalem: Van Leer Institute, Haḳibbuts Hameuḥad, 2005), 13–21; Eyal, *The Disenchantment of the Orient*, 7–16.

98. Khazzoom, "The Great Chain of Orientalism," 495–96.

99. On "romantic Zionism," see Almog, *The Sabra*, 185–90; Berelowitz, "Hamoshava Ha'ivrit," 96–100; Hillel Cohen, "Masorot Muslemiyot Meshupatsot 'Al Shivat Iśrael Leartso Baśiaḥ Hatsiyoni-Meshiḥi," *Jama'a*, 10, 2003, 169–85; Eyal, *Hasarat Haḳesem Min Hamizraḥ*, 22–43; Eyal, *The Disenchantment of the Orient*, 33–61; Gribetz, *Defining Neighbors*, 123–26, 237; Oḥana, *Lo Kna'anim, Lo Tsalbanim*, 357–59; Ohana, *The Origins of Israeli Mythology*, 73–74, 182–84; Saposnik, *Becoming Hebrew*, 146–68, 181–82. The occasional treatment by the Zionist elites of Sephardic and Arabic-speaking Jews as possible "interlocutors" between the Occident and the Orient can be seen as a subtendency of "romantic Zionism" (Almog, *The Sabra*, 186; Berelowitz, "Hamoshava Ha'ivrit," 98–99; Saposnik, *Becoming Hebrew*, 169–73). Some Mizrahi Jewish intellectuals in Ottoman and Mandatory Palestine were indeed ready to take upon themselves the task of mediation, alarmed by the prospect of an intractable conflict developing at their doorstep due to Zionist colonization, all the while professing loyalty to the Jewish national movement (see Moshe Behar and Zvi Ben-Dor Benite (eds.), *Modern Middle Eastern Jewish Thought: Writings on Identity, Politics, and Culture* [Waltham: Brandeis University Press, 2013]; Abigail Jacobson and Moshe Naor, *Oriental Neighbors: Middle Eastern Jews and Arabs in Mandatory Palestine* [Waltham: Brandeis University Press, 2016]).

100. Notably, Revisionist Zionism preceded Labor Zionism in this regard (Kimmerling, *Zionism and Territory*, 185).

101. Klaus Hofmann, "Canaanism," *Middle Eastern Studies* 47 (2), 2011, 274. Interestingly, Palestinian nationalism has relatively recently produced its own version of a "Canaanite" ideology that depicts modern-day Palestinians as descendants of the ancient Canaanite peoples who dwelt in the Land before the Israelite invasion from Egypt, implied to be analogous to the Zionist migration (Shavit, *The New Hebrew Nation*, 101–3; Ifraḥ Zilberman, "Kna'aniyut Falesṭinit," in Ya'aḳobi (ed.), *Erets Aḥat Ushne 'Amim Ba*, 96–102). It is quite ironic that in order to demolish the Zionist claim to the Land, the Palestinians resorted to the Jewish-biblical narrative whereby the Exodus was a historical fact.

102. For an example of a Zionist historiographic argument against "Canaanite" historiography, see Av. N. Polaḳ, "Tefisat Hahisṭoria Ha'ivrit—Keytsad?," *Beṭerem*, January 1950, 35–40. Curiously, this is the same author

who wrote a book attempting to prove the Khazarian origins of Ashkenazi Jews (A. N. Polaḳ, *Kazariah: Toledot Mamlakha Yehudit Beeropa* [Tel Aviv: The Bialik Institute, 1951]). See also Shavit, *The New Hebrew Nation*, 183, no. 4.

103. Kaplan, "Decadent Pioneers," 3; Kaplan, *The Jewish Radical Right*, 114; Zerubavel, *Recovered Roots*, 16–33.

104. Diamond, *Homeland or Holy Land?*, 99. Also Diamond, *Homeland or Holy Land?*, 68, 73, 102.

105. Ben-'Ezer, *En Shaananim Betsion*, 171.

106. Nehor, "'Umma 'Ivrit'—Mahi?," 5.

107. Ben-'Ezer, *En Shaananim Betsion*, 56–61, 214–17; Kurzweil, *Bamaavaḳ 'Al 'Erke Hayahadut*, 166–83, 184–240; Kurzweil, *Sifrutenu Heḥadasha*, 190–224; Oḥana, *Lo Kna'anim, Lo Tsalbanim*, 181–88, 263–64, 272–89.

108. Diamond, *Homeland or Holy Land?*, 99.

109. Yonatan Ḳenan [Ratosh], "Izmel Yehudi Babe'aya Ha'ivrit," *Alef*, December 1952, 4–5. Horon was less generous in his treatment of Kurzweil, referring to him privately as a "zimniy durak" (Russian for "winter's fool," meaning a fool whose stupidity is not obvious to the naked eye) who writes in "yekkit," the supposedly pseudoscholarly jargon of German-speaking Jews (letter by Horon to E. Jabotinsky, 4.11.1952 [JIA/4/4-4a]). Other opponents of Kurzweil, not necessarily supportive of "Canaanism," likewise pointed out that his approach was reductionist or exaggerated the "threat" to Jewish culture (Laor, *Hamaavaḳ 'Al Hazikaron*, 282–95).

110. Aharon Amir, *Miṭ'ane Tsad: Leḳeṭ Maamarim, 1949–1989* (Tel Aviv: Yaron Golan, 1991), 136–38; Raṭosh (ed.), *Minitsaḥon Lemapolet*, 285–87.

111. Cited by Abulof, *The Mortality and Morality of Nations*, 139, and Kimmerling, *Zionism and Territory*, 189–90. For more on Jabotinsky's general stance on Zionism, see Vladimir Jabotinsky, *Izbrannoe* (Jerusalem: Biblioteka-Aliya, 1989), 200–229. With regards to the "Arab question," Jabotinsky never attempted to obfuscate his "realism" that the Arabs would never accede to a mass Jewish settlement of their own free will and therefore have to be coerced into its acceptation by an "Iron Wall" built jointly by Zionists and their colonial sponsors. See Jabotinsky's famous "The Iron Wall" and "On the Morality of the Iron Wall" (Jabotinsky, *Izbrannoe*, 230–43). For the implementation of the "Iron Wall" principle in Israeli policy toward the Arab states see Avi Shlaim, *The Iron Wall: Israel and the Arab World* (New York: Norton, 2000).

112. Zouplna, "The Evolution of a Concept."

113. Jabotinsky, "Jews and Hebrews" (JIA/3/13/410).

114. Shindler, *The Rise of the Israeli Right*, 37.

115. Zouplna, "The Evolution of a Concept," 23.

116. Hayes, "Contributions of Herder to the Doctrine of Nationalism," 722–26.

117. Refaela Bilski Ben-Ḥur, *Kol Yaḥid Hu Melekh: Hamaḥshava Haḥevratit Vehamdinit Shel Zeev Jabotinsky* (Tel Aviv: Dvir, 1988), 157–58, 163–66; see also Kaplan, *The Jewish Radical Right*, 48.

118. Kaplan, *The Jewish Radical Right*, 144; Shindler, *The Rise of the Israeli Right*, 38.

119. Kaplan, "Decadent Pioneers," 3–11; Kaplan, *The Jewish Radical Right*, 111–58.

120. Moshe Dotan, "Halashon Ha'ivrit Bemishnato Shel Zeev Jabotinsky," *Haumma*, 19 (3), 1981, 411–15; Kaplan, *The Jewish Radical Right*, 140–47.

121. Kaplan, *The Jewish Radical Right*, 143.

122. Jabotinsky, *Avi, Zeev Jabotinsky*, 134–35.

123. Dowty, "Zionism's Greatest Conceit," 9; Asima A. Ghazi-Bouillon, *Understanding the Middle East Peace Process: Israeli Academia and the Struggle for Identity* (London and New York: Routledge, 2009), 38–39; Kimmerling, *Zionism and Territory*, 18, 80–83.

124. Berelowitz, "Hamoshava Ha'ivrit," 105–9; Eliav, *Zikhronot Min Hayamin*, 57. Recent research indicates that Zionist-secular militancy characterized a very small but articulate minority of "second *'aliya*" immigrants, whose self-perception as groundbreaking pioneers came to dominate the historiography of early Zionism, obfuscating the broader commonalities between pre-1904 and post-1904 Jewish immigrants to Palestine (Gribetz, *Defining Neighbors*, 34).

125. Berelowitz, "Hamoshava Ha'ivrit," 70–94; Even-Zohar, "Hatsmiḥa Ṿehahitgabshut"; Saposnik, *Becoming Hebrew*.

126. Berelowitz, "Hamoshava Ha'ivrit," 95–96. Saposnik's *Becoming Hebrew* is a very detailed study of the germination of Hebrew culture during the late Ottoman period.

127. Diamond, *Homeland or Holy Land?*, 5, 95; Yosef Gorny, "Haliberalizm Habetar-Kna'ani—Gishot 'Akhshaṿiyot Bish'elat Hanormalizatsiya Shel Haḳiyum Haleumi Bimdinat-Iśrael," *Kiṿunim* (new edition) 1 (38), 1990, 45–57; Kaplan, "A Rebel with a Cause"; Miller, " 'Habaṭalion Heḥatukh' "; Oḥana, *Lo Kna'anim, Lo Tsalbanim*, 31–32, 239–41; Ohana, *The Origins of Israeli Mythology*, 21–23, 78; Ram, *Israeli Nationalism*, 112–13; Silberstein, *The Postzionism Debates*; Chaim I. Waxman, "Critical Sociology and the End of Ideology in Israel," *Israel Studies* 2 (1), 1997, 200.

128. Peter H. Bergson, "Post-Zionism" (HKA/30). For the full text of Kook's letter, see Vater, "Pathways of Early Post-Zionism," 26.

129. On the "Lamerḥav" faction in further detail see Miller, " 'Habaṭalion Heḥatukh,' " 168–84; Oḥana, *Lo Kna'anim, Lo Tsalbanim*, 239–40; Ohana, *The Origins of Israeli Mythology*, 76–77.

130. Jabotinsky, "Israel and Zionism."

131. Jabotinsky, "Israel and Zionism," 44.

132. Letter by S. Rosoff to S. Merlin, 18.11.1956 (HKA/32).

133. Memorandum by E. Jabotinsky for the Kedem Club, April 1954 (HKA/32).

134. Memorandum by E. Jabotinsky for the Kedem Club (HKA/32, emphasis added).

135. Jabotinsky, "Jews and Hebrews" (JIA/3/13/410); Memorandum by E. Jabotinsky for the Kedem Club (HKA/32).

136. Jabotinsky's speech to the 17th Zionist congress (1931), cited in Kaplan, *The Jewish Radical Right*, 48.

137. Peter H. Bergson, "Post-Zionism" (HKA/30).

138. Jabotinsky, "Jews and Hebrews" (JIA/3/13/410).

139. Peter H. Bergson, "Post-Zionism" (HKA/30).

140. See Iśrael Eldad, "Avne Yesod," in Avi Bareli and Pinḥas Ginossar (eds.), *Tsiyonut: Pulmus Ben Zmanenu—Gishot Meḥḳariyot Ṿeideologiyot* (Śde Boḳer: Ben-Gurion University, 1996), 453–465; Vater, "Down with Zionism."

141. Outline for a talk at a Betar camp in France in August 1963 (Horon Archive); Ḥoron, "Iśrael Ṿehamitos Ha'aravi," 501. In both cases, the receiving public were Revisionist Zionists, so Horon might have tactically moderated his language. This moderation was only partially effective: another article he had submitted to the Revisionist periodical *Haumma* was rejected and published instead in the "Canaanite" *Ḳeshet* (Ḥoron, "Shlemut Hamoledet," handwritten annotation on a print-out in JIA16/14/4a).

142. For a clarification on this point, consult Horon's letters in the appendices, Eri Jabotinsky's critical remarks on the Young Hebrews' ideology (Jabotinsky, "Israel and Zionism," 46–47; Porat, *Shelaḥ Ṿe'eṭ Beyado*, 264), and his memorandum for the Kedem Club that details his geopolitical plan for the Middle East after the defeat of Zionism and Pan-Arabism (HKA/32).

143. The idea of the Land of Kedem is absent from the writings of the Hebrew Committee, which concentrated on Palestine and Transjordan, yet recurs in the materials of the Kedem Club under the name "The Ever" or the "Federation of the Levant."

144. See an ad placed by Kook and Merlin in *Haarets* and other newspapers on April 18, 1975, and also Kaplan, "A Rebel with a Cause," 96–98, 102; Shilon, "Milḥemet Sheshet Hayamim," 104–5, 120–24, and my "Pathways of Early Post-Zionism" for a detailed exploration of the similarities and differences between "Canaanism" and post-Zionism.

145. Uri Ram, "Why Secularism Fails? Secular Nationalism and Religious Revivalism in Israel," *International Journal of Politics, Culture and Society* 21 (1/4), 2008, 57–73.

146. Diamond, *Homeland or Holy Land?*, 4, 6, 46, 77, 139.

147. Shapira, "The Bible and Israeli Identity," 31. We must place this invective hurled at Ben-Gurion by Hebrew University professors in the wider context of the tensions that persisted between the Israeli government and Jerusalem intellectuals in the 1950s and 1960s (Keren, *Ben-Gurion and the Intellectuals*; Oḥana, *Lo Kna'anim, Lo Tsalbanim*, 188–205).

148. Ben-'Ezer, *En Shaananim Betsion*, 64–82; Dowty, "Zionism's Greatest Conceit," 10–14; Yosef Gorny, "Hashniyut Beyaḥaso Shel Daṿid Ben-Gurion El Hatsiyonut," in Avni and Shim'oni (eds.), *Hatsiyonut Umitnagdeha Ba'am Hayehudi*, 437–45; Keren, *The Pen and the Sword*, 51; Shapira, "Ben-Gurion and

the Bible," 658–60, 667. Notably, the Young Hebrews commended Ben-Gurion for distancing himself from Zionism (Sh. Rotem [Moshe Giora Elimelekh], "Mashber Haknesiya Hatsiyonit," in Gerts and Weisbrod [eds.], *Haḳvutsa Hakna'anit*, 40–41).

149. Shapira, "Ben-Gurion and the Bible," 669.

150. Cohen, "Israel as a Post-Zionist Society," 206.

151. Cohen, "Israel as a Post-Zionist Society," 207–11.

152. Kimmerling, *The Invention and Decline of Israeliness.*

153. Alain Dieckhoff, *The Invention of a Nation: Zionist Thought and the Making of Modern Israel* (New York: Columbia University Press, 2003), 270–71.

154. Assaf Likhovski, "Post-post-Zionist Historiography," *Israel Studies* 15 (2), 2010, 4.

155. Abu el-Haj, *Facts on the Ground*, 272–76.

156. Daniel Gutwein, "Left and Right Post-Zionism and the Privatization of Israeli Collective Memory," in Anita Shapira and Derek J. Penslar (eds.), *Israeli Historical Revisionism: From Left to Right* (London and Portland: Frank Cass, 2003), 9–42; Daniel Guṭṿein, "Posṭ-Tsiyonut, Mahapekhat Hahafraṭa Ṿehaśmol Haḥevrati," in Ṭuvia Friling (ed.), *Teshuva Le'amit Posṭ-Tsiyoni* (Tel Aviv: Yedi'ot Aḥaronot, 2003), 243–73.

157. Guṭṿein, "Posṭ-Tsiyonut," 251.

158. Guṭṿein, "Posṭ-Tsiyonut," 262.

159. Gutwein, "Left and Right Post-Zionism," 34.

160. Gutwein, "Left and Right Post-Zionism," 35–38; Guṭṿein, "Posṭ-Tsiyonut," 249–50.

161. Kaplan, *The Jewish Radical Right*, 176. Kaplan's later study, *Beyond Post-Zionism* (Albany: State University of New York Press, 2015), abandons this line of examination that would trace the connections between historical rightist thought in Zionism and the modern post-Zionist challenge to it in favor of an aesthetic analysis of post-Zionism's cultural manifestations.

162. Interestingly, post-Zionist biblical archaeology with its insistence on the historical marginality of the kingdoms of David and Salomon sharply contradicts Horon's findings (Elon, "Politics and Archaeology," 38, 45; Shapira, "The Bible and Israeli Identity," 36–40; Neil A. Silberman, "Structuring the Past: Israelis, Palestinians, and the Symbolic Authority of Archaeological Monuments," in Silberman and Small (eds.), *The Archaeology of Israel*, 74–76).

163. Risa Domb, "Ideology, Identity and Language in Modern Hebrew Literature," *Israel Affairs* 7 (1), 2000, 71–86.

164. Dieckhoff, *The Invention of a Nation*, 273–81; Ohana, *The Origins of Israeli Mythology*, 21.

165. Ghazi-Bouillon, *Understanding the Middle East Peace Process*; Silberstein, *The Postzionism Debates*. Dieckhoff, *The Invention of a Nation*, 280, seems to share this viewpoint as well.

166. Silberstein, *The Postzionism Debates*, 69–84.

167. Laurence J. Silberstein, "*The New Hebrew Nation: A Study in Israeli Heresy and Fantasy* by Yaakov Shavit; *The Slopes of Lebanon* by Amos Oz; *Jewish Theocracy* by Gershon Weiler; *HaHeshbon HaLeumi* by Boas Evron," *International Journal of Middle Eastern Studies* 23 (4), 1991, 688.

168. Compare Evron's criticism of the Young Hebrews' ideology ('Evron, *Haḥeshbon Haleumi*, 351–73; Evron, *Jewish State or Israeli Nation?*, 205–22) with his criticism of the Zionist policy, ideology, and historiography ('Evron, *Haḥeshbon Haleumi*, 11–18, 93–86, 213–350, 408–25; Evron, *Jewish State or Israeli Nation?*, 41–67, 101–204, 242–54; Bo'az 'Evron, "Hatsiyonut—Mabaṭ Leaḥor," in Bareli and Ginossar (eds.), *Tsiyonut: Pulmus Ben Zmanenu*, 52–59).

169. Gorny, "Haliberalizm Habetar-Kna'ani," 47.

170. 'Evron, "Hama'aśe—Uvavuato Haaḳademit," 21.

171. 'Evron, *Haḥeshbon Haleumi*; English version: Evron, *Jewish State or Israeli Nation?*.

172. On "Semitic Action" and its brand of post-Zionism, see Uri Avnery, "Model Shel Iśrael Aḥeret—Arba'im Shana La'minshar Ha'ivri'," *Haarets*, 10.1.1997, D1 (and letters to the editor within the following fortnight); Avnery, *Opṭimi* I, 510–29.

173. Shlomo Sand, *The Invention of the Jewish People* (London: Verso, 2009); Shlomo Sand, *The Invention of the Land of Israel* (London: Verso, 2012). For a critical evaluation of Sand's oeuvre that examines its indebtedness to "Canaanite" historiography, see Derek Penslar, "Shlomo Sand's *The Invention of the Jewish People* and the End of the New History," *Israel Studies* 17 (2), 2012, 156–68.

174. The position of this association vis-à-vis "Canaanism" and second-generation post-Zionism is examined in my "Neither Canaanites nor Post-Zionists: Fighting for a Civic Israel," in Shai Feraro, Ofri Krischer (eds.), *New Studies on the Young Hebrews Movement* (Brill, forthcoming 2024).

175. HKA/25. In April 1945 Hillel Kook issued an open letter to Haim Weizman, president of the World Zionist Organization at the time, in which he debated in great detail the inconsequential nature of Zionism and the perils awaiting Palestine, Hebrews and Jews worldwide, if the Zionist program was to be implemented (for the text of the letter, see HKA/29, HKA/47).

176. Letter by S. Rosoff to S. Merlin, 18.11.1956 (HKA/32). Merlin, while a parliamentarian (!), advocated as early as in 1949 the return of the Palestinian refugees, whose numbers he wrongly estimated at three hundred thousand (Shmuel Merlin, "Towards Collapse or Prosperity; Problems of Israel's Economic Independence—Analysis and Outline of a Solution," 12.5.1949; HKA/8).

177. Jabotinsky, "Tentative Formulation for a Program of Action" (HKA/32); see also Kedem Club's statute from November 1956 (JIA/3/12/4a). This idea recently saw revival among certain circles of West Bank settler leadership, who declared their willingness to grant Israeli citizenship to Palestinians in case of annexation of the West Bank to Israel, though they

vehemently denied any associations with "Canaanism" (Ohana, *The Origins of Israeli Mythology*, 22–23).

178. Benvenisti, *Sacred Landscape*, 161–62, 325–26.

179. See memorandum by E. Jabotinsky in HKA/32.

180. A case of a third village that suffered a similar fate, Ghabassiyya, is less well-known, although its sheikh, Rabaḥ 'Awwaḍ, actively collaborated with the Zionists before 1948 (Hillel Cohen, *'Aravim Ṭovim—Hamodi'in Haiśreeli Ṿeha'aravim Biśrael: Sokhnim Umaf'ilim, MASHTAPIM Umordim, Maṭarot Ṿeshiṭot* ['Ivrit: Jerusalem, 2006], 45–47; Hillel Cohen, *Tsva Hatslalim—MASHTAPIM Falesṭinim Besherut Hatsiyonut, 1917–1948: Modi'in, Mediniyut, Hityashvut, Hitnaḳshuyot* [Ivrit: Jerusalem, 2004], 249–50, 257).

181. Avnery, *Opṭimi* I, 157.

182. Whereas his father favored a national-cultural autonomy for the Arab citizens of the future Jewish state (Bilski Ben-Ḥur, *Kol Yaḥid Hu Melekh*, 281–91, 329–32). For E. Jabotinsky's detailed standpoint on the issue (which paradoxically drew the condemnation of both Zionists and communists), see his speech in the Knesset on May 8, 1950, and the accompanying press reports on the ensuing scandal (JIA/5/13/410).

183. Memorandum by E. Jabotinsky (HKA/32).

184. Heller, *Jabotinsky's Children*, 251; Shindler, *The Rise of the Israeli Right*, 144.

185. See examples of evocation of Jabotinsky to support almost any cause in Israeli politics in the early twenty-first century in Heller, *Jabotinsky's Children*, 251.

186. It was against this order of priorities that Ratosh rebelled in his 1937 series of articles, "We Aspire to Power" (Raṭosh, *Reshit Hayamim*, 42–59), arguing that mathematical majority was not a precondition for sovereignty (but the Yishuv's technical and cultural superiority was) and that the British Mandate was a hostile foreign power and not protector. The issue of the Arab majority in Palestine was faced again by the Hebrew Committee of National Liberation, which "solved" it by counting among the Hebrews all Jewish refugees from Europe.

187. Eri Jabotinsky's sketch of his father's opinions on economics prepared for Hillel Kook in 1951 portrays him as a moderate social democrat (HKA/32). For the monism principle in detail, see Bilski Ben-Ḥur, *Kol Yaḥid Hu Melekh*, 227–334; Kaplan, *The Jewish Radical Right*, 31–50; Sasson Sofer, *Zionism and the Foundations of Israeli Diplomacy* (New York: Cambridge University Press, 1998), 211–13.

188. Ehud Sprinzak, *Ish Hayashar: I-Legalism Baḥevra Haiśreelit* (Tel Aviv: Sifriyat Po'alim, 1986).

189. Kimmerling, *Zionism and Territory*, 180.

190. Kimmerling, *Zionism and Territory*, 224; see also Abulof, *The Mortality and Morality of Nations*, 201–3; Kaplan, *The Jewish Radical Right*, 118; Shindler, *The Rise of the Israeli Right*, 353.

191. Ben-'Ezer, *En Shaananim Betsion*, 188.

192. Dalia Ḳarpel, "'Uzzi Ornan 'Adain Lo Ṿiter 'Al Ḥalom Haleom Haiśreeli," *Haarets*, 21.5.2015; Nili Osheroff, *Yotse Min Haklalim—'Uzzi Ornan: Sipur Ḥaim* (Jerusalem: Carmel, 2015), 137; Yadgar, *Israel's Jewish Identity Crisis*, 165. See also Vater, "Neither Canaanites nor Post-Zionists."

193. Michael Asaf, "Par'onim, Kna'anim A Ukhna'anim B," *Davar*, 3.10.1952; Laor, *Hamaavaḳ 'Al Hazikaron*, 293.

194. Shaviṭ, *Me'ivri 'Ad Kna'ani*, 46–53; Shavit, *The New Hebrew Nation*, 92–103.

195. Shavit, *The New Hebrew Nation*, 92.

196. See Amatzia Baram, "Territorial Nationalism in the Middle East," *Middle Eastern Studies* 26 (4), 1990, 425–48 for a useful overview.

197. Eliahu Elath, "'Phoenician Zionism' in Lebanon," *The Jerusalem Quarterly* 42, 1987, 40–49; Kais M. Firro, "Lebanese Nationalism versus Arabism: From Bulus Nujaym to Michel Chiha," *Middle Eastern Studies* 40 (5), 2004, 1–27; Albert Hourani, *Arabic Thought in the Liberal Age, 1798–1939* (Cambridge: Cambridge University Press, 2002), 285–91, 319–23; Kaufman, *Reviving Phoenicia*; Asher Kaufman, "'Tell Us Our History': Charles Corm, Mount Lebanon and Lebanese Nationalism," *Middle Eastern Studies* 40 (3), 2004, 1–28; Shavit, "Hebrews and Phoenicians," 163–64; Suleiman, *The Arabic Language*, 204–19.

198. Baram, "Territorial Nationalism," 429–33; Suleiman, *The Arabic Language*, 174–204.

199. Baram, "Territorial Nationalism," 433–39; Hourani, *Arabic Thought in the Liberal Age*, 317–19; Suleiman, *The Arabic Language*, 162–69.

200. Baram, "Territorial Nationalism," 429–30; Kaufman, "Tell Us Our History," 8; Miller, "'Habaṭalion Heḥatukh,'" 165–66; Shaviṭ, *Me'ivri 'Ad Kna'ani*, 47; Shavit, *The New Hebrew Nation*, 93–95.

201. Shaviṭ, *Me'ivri 'Ad Kna'ani*, 50; Shavit, *The New Hebrew Nation*, 93. Also Kaufman, "Tell Us Our History," 6.

202. Shaviṭ, *Me'ivri 'Ad Kna'ani*, 50; Shavit, *The New Hebrew Nation*, 97–98.

203. Suleiman, *The Arabic Language*, 165.

204. Kaufman, *Reviving Phoenicia*, 68.

205. Charles Corm, to give one example, was Lebanon's most successful car dealer.

206. Ḥoron, *Erets-Haḳedem*, 26; Hourani, *Arabic Thought in the Liberal Age*, 318.

207. Charles Corm specifically defined Lebanon's raison d'état as the perpetuation of its political dependency upon France to ward off Pan-Arabism and reportedly was "in panic" when the French mandate was terminated in 1943 (Kaufman, *Revivng Phoenicia*, 184, no. 7; Kaufman, "Tell Us Our History," 28).

208. Kaufman, *Reviving Phoenicia*, 158, 245.

209. Kaufman, *Reviving Phoenicia*, 3, 132, 195.

210. Kaufman, *Reviving Phoenicia*, 35, 146, 157; Kaufman, "Tell Us Our History," 11.

211. Letter by Horon to E. Jabotinsky and S. Rosoff, 10.2.1956 (HKA/32).

212. Letter by Horon to E. Jabotinsky, 2.5.1955 (JIA/4/4-4a).

213. Letters by Horon to E. Jabotinsky, 20.12.1954, 2.5.1955 (JIA/4/4-4a); letter by Horon to E. Jabotinsky and S. Rosoff, 3.4.1956 (JIA/4/4-4a).

214. During Israel's invasion of Lebanon in 1982 Aharon Amir initiated some common projects with intellectuals associated with the Katā'ib, but the Israeli government's disapproval eliminated further collaboration (Diamond, *Homeland or Holy Land?*, 96–97). For a detailed historical examination of the Maronites' (and other Lebanese Christians') cooperation with Zionism and Israel, consult Laurie Z. Eisenberg, *My Enemy's Enemy: Lebanon in the Early Zionist Imagination, 1900–1948* (Detroit: Wayne State University Press, 1994); Yusri Hazran, "A People That Shall Dwell Alone; Is That So? Israel and the Minorities Alliance," *Middle Eastern Studies* 56 (3), 2020, 396–411; Kristen E. Schulze, *Israel's Covert Diplomacy in Lebanon* (Basingstoke: Macmillan, 1998); Zisser, "The Maronites, Lebanon and the State of Israel."

215. Rejwan, *Israel in Search of Identity*, 98.

216. Kaufman, *Reviving Phoenicia*, 132, 167, 181.

217. Suleiman, *The Arabic Language*, 165. Interestingly, 'Aql began his public career in the 1930s as a Pan-Syrianist and follower of Sa'āda (Kaufman, *Reviving Phoenicia*, 172).

218. Shaviṭ, *Me'ivri 'Ad Kna'ani*, 51; Shavit, *The New Hebrew Nation*, 100.

219. Ḥoron, *Erets-Haḳedem*, 128.

220. Raṭosh, *Reshit Hayamim*, 93.

221. Horon, "Hebrews and Jews" (HKA/36), 17.

Conclusion

1. Shaviṭ, *Me'ivri 'Ad Kna'ani*, 158–71; Shavit, *The New Hebrew Nation*, 19–20, 64, 160–62.

2. 'Evron, "Hama'aśe—Uvavuato Haaḳademit."

3. Diamond, *Homeland or Holy Land?*, 118 (emphases added). Also Shavit, *The New Hebrew Nation*, 160.

4. Diamond, *Homeland or Holy Land?*, 71–72 (emphasis added).

5. Diamond, *Homeland or Holy Land?*, 76–77.

6. As does Diamond, *Homeland or Holy Land?*, 80, 110.

7. See Evron's confession to that effect, cited by Diamond, *Homeland or Holy Land?*, 80.

8. Diamond, *Homeland or Holy Land?*, 115.

9. Diamond, *Homeland or Holy Land?*, 86.

10. 'Amos Ḳenan, " 'Ivrim Ṿelo Tsabarim," in Gerts and Weisbrod (eds.), *Haḳvutsa Hakna'anit*, 42–43.

11. Interview with 'Amos Ḳenan, *Proza*, August–September 1977, 5–6. See also Diamond, *Homeland or Holy Land?*, 76, 104–5; Er'el, *'Bli Mora Bli Maśo Panim,'* 39–40; Oḥana, *Lo Kna'anim, Lo Tsalbanim*, 118–20.

12. Er'el, *'Bli Mora Bli Maśo Panim,'* 40.

13. Barṭov, *Ligdol Ṿelikhtov Beerets Iśrael,* 132, 157.

14. For other sociological portraits of the Sabra generation, see Almog, *The Sabra;* Er'el, *'Bli Mora Bli Maśo Panim,'* 38–39, 42–43; Avraham Shapira, "Spiritual Rootlessness and Circumscription to the 'Here and Now' in the *Sabra* World View," *Israel Affairs* 4 (3–4), 1998, 103–31; Bernard D. Weinryb, "The Lost Generation in Israel," *Middle East Journal* 7 (4), 1953, 415–29.

15. Shaviṭ, *Me'ivri 'Ad Kna'ani,* 162–63.

16. Interview with 'Amos Ḳenan, *Proza,* August–September 1977, 10; Er'el, *'Bli Mora Bli Maśo Panim,'* 53.

17. Uri Avnery, "Mot Nimrod," in 'Amos Ḳenan (ed.), *Omanut Hapisul Biśrael: Ḥipuś Hazehut* (Tefen: Open Museum, 1988), 29.

18. Diamond, *Homeland or Holy Land?,* 119.

19. Barṭov, *Ligdol Ṿelikhtov Beerets Iśrael,* 134–42, 150, 157.

20. Barṭov, *Ligdol Ṿelikhtov Beerets Iśrael,* 138, 140.

21. Avnery, "Mot Nimrod," 29.

22. On the role of the Holocaust in the formation of Israeli identity, see Idith Zertal, *Israel's Holocaust and the Politics of Nationhood* (Cambridge: Cambridge University Press, 2005).

23. Yonatan Raṭosh, "Ketav El Hano'ar Ha'ivri," in Raṭosh, *Reshit Hayamim,* 32 (written in 1943). Similar allegations were repeated by Ratosh a year later in "The Opening Discourse" (Raṭosh, *Reshit Hayamim,* 149–203). See also Diamond, *Homeland or Holy Land?,* 54–55; Shavit, *The New Hebrew Nation,* 62–63.

24. Jabotinsky, "Israel and Zionism," 46 (emphases added). This statement is especially striking given that Jabotinsky, a founding member of the ETZEL delegation to the USA (the "Bergson group" discussed in chapter 1), was one of the few people to grasp from the distance of America the extraordinary nature of the collective experience of the Holocaust in Jewish history as it was occurring. Apparently Jabotinsky somehow believed that this would not translate into an active component in the autonomous Israeli identity.

25. 'Uzzi Ornan, "Anaḥnu Kna'anim: Śiḥot 'Im Prof. 'Uzzi Ornan," *Svivot,* December 1994, 61–73; 'Uzzi Ornan, "Shoat Haḥinukh," *Svivot,* December 1994, 74–77; Porat, *Shelaḥ Ṿe'eṭ Beyado,* 302–307; Liat Steir-Livny and Ya'aḳov Shaviṭ, "Yonatan Raṭosh, 'Hakna'anim' Ṿeyaḥasam Lashoa, 1943–1953," in Dina Porat and Aviva Ḥalamish (eds.), *Shoa Mimerḥaḳ Tavo: Ishim Bayishuv Haerets-Iśreeli Ṿeyaḥasam Lanatsizm Ṿelashoa, 1933–1948* (Jerusalem: Yad Ben Tsvi, 2009), 85–99.

26. Kuzar, *Hebrew and Zionism,* 187. Both Gribetz, *Defining Neighbors,* 33, no. 71 and Morris, *Righteous Victims,* 698, no. 97 assert that the figure of eighty-five thousand is exaggerated.

27. Shaviṭ, *Me'ivri 'Ad Kna'ani,* 159.

28. Barṭov, *Ligdol Ṿelikhtov Beerets Iśrael,* 133–34. Mazen Masri (*The Dynamics of Exclusionary Constitutionalism,* 106) reaches a similar conclusion.

29. Almog, *The Sabra,* 5–13.

30. Weinryb, "The Lost Generation," 417. In a 1970 conversation with the Israeli poet Moshe Dor Ratosh admitted that while previously he had directed his appeal to about 15 percent of the Yishuv, the mass migration after 1948 reduced the native Hebrews' relative numbers to seven percent of the population (Moshe Dor, "Te'udat Hazehut Shel Yonatan Raṭosh," *Ma'ariv Yamim Ṿelelot*, 25.9.1970, 25).

31. Avnery, "Mot Nimrod," 30.

32. For the sake of the argument's brevity I shall presently overlook the role played in the making of Israeli national identity by non-Jewish Israelis.

33. Diamond, *Homeland or Holy Land?*, 114–15.

34. Gideon Katz, "The Israeli *Kulturkampf*," *Israel Affairs* 14 (2), 2008, 253.

35. Baruch Kimmerling, "Between the Primordial and the Civil Definitions of the Collective Identity: *Eretz Israel* or the State of Israel?," in Eric Cohen, Moshe Lissak, and Uri Almagor (eds.), *Comparative Social Dynamics: Essays in Honor of S. N. Eisenstadt* (Boulder and London: Westview, 1985), 262–83.

36. Yadgar, *Israel's Jewish Identity Crisis*, 6.

37. Kimmerling, "Between the Primordial and the Civil," 268–69. See also Abulof, *The Mortality and Morality of Nations*, 133–35.

38. Roselle Tekiner, "Race and the Issue of National Identity in Israel," *International Journal of Middle Eastern Studies* 23 (1), 1991, 44.

39. Charles Liebman and Eliezer Don-Yehiya, "What a Jewish State Means to Israeli Jews," in Sam Lehman-Wilzig and Bernard Susser (eds.), *Comparative Jewish Politics: Public Life in Israel and the Diaspora* (Ramat-Gan: Bar-Ilan University, 1981), 101–9.

40. Diamond, *Homeland or Holy Land?*, 84. Yadgar similarly observes that Jewish and Israeli identity for most (Jewish) Israelis became interchangeable, with the one implying the other and vice versa (Yadgar, *Israel's Jewish Identity Crisis*, 149).

41. Diamond, *Homeland or Holy Land?*, 114. The same perspective is shared by Nitsa Er'el, *'Bli Mora Bli Maśo Panim,'* 36, and Yaacov Shavit (Shaviṭ, *Me'ivri 'Ad Kna'ani*, 169; Shavit, *The New Hebrew Nation*, 160).

42. Diamond, *Homeland or Holy Land?*, 104.

43. See my "Neither Canaanites nor Post-Zionists."

44. Breuilly, "The Sources of Nationalist Ideology"; Benjamin Neuberger, "State and Nation in African Thought," in Hutchinson and Smith (eds.), *Nationalism*, 231–35; Crawford Young, "The Colonial Construction of African Nations," in Hutchinson and Smith (eds.), *Nationalism*, 225–31.

45. E. g., Yara Hawari, Sharri Plonski, and Elian Weizman, "Seeing Israel through Palestine: Knowledge Production as Anti-Colonial Praxis," *Settler Colonial Studies* 9 (1), 2019, 155–75; Yara Hawari, Sharri Plonski and Elian Weizman, "Settlers and Citizens: A Critical View of Israeli Society," *Settler Colonial Studies* 9 (1), 2019, 1–5; Omar Jabary Salamanca, Mezna Qato, Kareem Rabie, and Sobhi Samour, "Past Is Present: Settler Colonialism in Palestine," *Settler Colonial Studies* 2 (1), 2012, 1–8; Ethan B. Katz, Lisa Moses Leff, and

Maud S. Mandel, "Introduction: Engaging Colonial History and Jewish History," in Ethan B. Katz, Lisa Moses Leff, and Maud S. Mandel (eds.), *Colonialism and the Jews* (Bloomington and Indianapolis: Indiana University Press, 2017), 1–25; Masri, *The Dynamics of Exclusionary Constitutionalism*; Gabriel Piterberg, "The Zionist Settlement in Palestine as Settler Colonialism: The Formative Impact of the German Project in the Ostmark," *Orient: German Journal for Politics, Economics and Culture of the Middle East* 2, 2013, 24–29; Robinson, *Citizen Strangers*; Lorenzo Veracini, "What Can Settler Colonial Studies Offer to an Interpretation of the Conflict in Israel-Palestine?," *Settler Colonial Studies* 5 (3), 2015, 268–71.

46. Avi Bareli, "Forgetting Europe: Perspectives on the Debate about Zionism and Colonialism," in Shapira and Penslar (eds.), *Israeli Historical Revisionism*, 99–120; Moshe Lisak, "Sotsiologim 'Biḳortiim' Ṿesotsiologim 'Mimsadiim' Baḳehila Haaḳademit Haiśreelit: Maavaḳim Ideologiim O Śiaḥ Aḳademi 'Inyani?," in Bareli and Ginossar (eds.), *Tsiyonut: Pulmus Ben Zmanenu*, 60–98.

47. Derek J. Penslar, "Is Zionism a Colonial Movement?," in Katz, Leff, and Mandel (eds.), *Colonialism and the Jews*, 275–300; Derek J. Penslar, "What We Talk About When We Talk about Colonialism," in Katz, Leff, and Mandel (eds.), *Colonialism and the Jews*, 327–40; Derek J. Penslar, "Zionism, Colonialism and Postcolonialism," in Shapira and Penslar (eds.), *Israeli Historical Revisionism*, 84–98.

48. Katz, Leff, and Mandel, "Introduction," 2–5.

49. Katz, Leff, and Mandel, "Introduction," 16.

50. Muṣṭafa Kabha and Naḥum Ḳarlinski, "Mitaḥarut Ledu-Leumiyut: Hapardesanut Ha'aravit-Falesṭinit Ṿehayehudit-Tsionit Biteḳufat Hamandaṭ," *Iśrael*, 27–28, 2021, 141; Masri, *The Dynamics of Exclusionary Constitutionalism*, 15–20; Piterberg, "The Zionist Settlement in Palestine"; Elizabeth F. Thompson, "Moving Zionism to Asia: Texts and Tactics of Colonial Settlement, 1917–1921," in Katz, Leff, and Mandel (eds.), *Colonialism and the Jews*, 317–26.

51. Oḥana, *Lo Kna'anim, Lo Tsalbanim*, 291–348; Ohana, *The Origins of Israeli Mythology*, 131–81.

52. Ḳenan, "'Ivrim Ṿelo Tsabarim."

53. Veracini, "What Can Settler Colonial Studies Offer?," 270.

54. See *Ḳeshet*, 13 (4), 1971 (a special issue dedicated to the "American experience").

55. Joshua Cole, "Derek Penslar's 'Algebra of Modernity': How Should We Understand the Relation between Zionism and Colonialism?," in Katz, Leff, and Mandel (eds.), *Colonialism and the Jews*, 301–16.

56. Exploitation colonialism was typical to "first *'aliya*" agricultural settlements, which sought to integrate Arab Palestinian labor in their economic model. Settler colonialism was more pronounced in "second *'aliya*"'s economic segregation principles of "conquest of soil" and "conquest of labor" (Piterberg, "The Zionist Settlement in Palestine"). Derek Penslar argues that Israel's post–1967 control of the West Bank and the economic relations between

it and Israel per se represent a return to exploitation colonialism, as mass removal of Palestinians on the scale of 1948 was no longer possible (Penslar, "Is Zionism a Colonial Movement?").

57. Derek Jonathan Penslar, "What if a Christian State Had Been Established in Modern Palestine?," in Gavriel D. Rosenfeld (ed.), *What Ifs of Jewish History* (Cambridge: Cambridge University Press, 2017), 154–55. A comparable demographic fear of losing the Jewish majority to the Arabs developed among Jewish Israelis, to justify Israel's structural inequalities between Jews and Arabs (Yadgar, *Israel's Jewish Identity Crisis*).

58. Albert Grundlingh, "The Trajectory and Dynamics of Afrikaner Nationalism in the Twentieth Century: An Overview," in Lize van Robbroeck, Federico Freschi and Brenda Schmahmann (eds.), *Troubling Images: Visual Culture and the Politics of Afrikaner Nationalism* (Johannesburg: Wits University Press, 2020), 27.

59. For a discussion of Afrikaner nationalism, see Abulof, *The Mortality and Morality of Nations*, 227–300; Dubow, "Afrikaner Nationalism," 209–237; Hermann Giliomee, "Constructing Afrikaner Nationalism," *Journal of Asian and African Studies* 18 (1–2), 1983, 83–98; Grundlingh, "The Trajectory and Dynamics of Afrikaner Nationalism."

60. See Anderson, *Imagined Communities*, 47–65.

61. Grundlingh, "The Trajectory and Dynamics of Afrikaner Nationalism," 30–33. Grundlingh observes that Nazi "crude pseudo-scientific social Darwinism" could not make significant headways into the Afrikaner public sphere since Afrikaner nationalism was above all religious, and therefore the "affinity between Afrikaner nationalism and German national-socialism appeared to be mainly one of mutual ideological sympathy rather than any deep-seated structural similarity" (Grundlingh, "The Trajectory and Dynamics of Afrikaner Nationalism," 33).

62. This view is actually inconsistent with contemporary sociological knowledge. Clifford Geertz observed in 1963 that "primordial and civil sentiments are not ranged in direct and implicitly evolutionary opposition to one another" (cited in Kimmerling, "Between the Primordial and the Civil," 275).

63. Calhoun, *Nationalism*, 18.

64. Cited in Said, *Orientalism*, 97.

65. In a private letter from 1950, Horon expressed his confidence that when Hebrew nationalism reaches full bloom it will necessarily defeat the imperialist powers in the Middle East since unlike Zionism and Pan-Arabism, the Hebrew case is one of a genuine nationalism (letter from Horon to Y. Ratosh and the editorial board of *Alef*, 26.12.1950; Ratosh Archive, 719/720).

66. Silberstein, *The Postzionism Debates*, 177.

67. This particular weakness of the "Canaanite" ideology was eloquently dissected by Moshe Aṭṭer in his review of *Minitsaḥon Lemapolet* (Moshe Aṭṭer, "Ḥalomam Hamatoḳ Shel 'Hakna'anim,'" *Haarets* literary supplement, 12.11.1976).

68. See letter by Horon to E. Jabotinsky and S. Rosoff, 10.2.1956 (HKA/32), cited in Appendix C.

69. For the social significance of racial criteria as well as the persistence of religious criteria as salient identity markers in the Middle East in the late nineteenth century and early twentieth century, see Gribetz, *Defining Neighbors.*

70. Katz, Leff, and Mandel, "Introduction," 3–7.

71. Yadgar, *Israel's Jewish Identity Crisis,* 129.

72. Cited in Nathans, *Beyond the Pale,* 77 (emphasis added).

73. Robinson, *Citizen Strangers,* 6.

74. Abulof, *The Mortality and Morality of Nations,* 210; Morris, *Righteous Victims,* 42–45. As a matter of fact, Arab Palestinian peasants ridiculed "first *'aliya*" settlers' agricultural incompetence and their speakers utterly rejected the suggestion that Zionist settlement brought them any economic prosperity or cultural advancement (Rashid Khalidi, *Palestinian Identity: The Construction of Modern National Consciousness* [New York: Columbia University Press, 1997], 89–144; Morris, *Righteous Victims,* 45–66, 127).

75. Piterberg, *The Returns of Zionism,* 78. This was also Ratosh's proposition in his "We Aspire to Power" from 1937 (Ratosh, *Reshit Hayamim,* 42–59).

76. Similar claims to democratic representative rule were made by White settlers in Britain's African colonies with the explicit aim to exclude Blacks from governance (Dan Freeman-Maloy, "The International Politics of Settler Self-Governance: Reflections on Zionism and 'Dominion' Status within the British Empire," *Settler Colonial Studies* 8 [1], 2018, 89–90).

77. Vater, "Pathways of Early Post-Zionism."

78. Email from Margalit Shinar, 9.11.2009.

79. Letter from Horon to E. Jabotinsky and S. Rosoff, 10.2.1956 (HKA/32). In her email to me from 9 November 2009 Margalit Shinar mentioned her father's "strange lack of personal ambition—or the loss thereof pretty early in his life."

80. Email from Margalit Shinar, 8.11.2009.

81. Porat, *Shelaḥ Ve'eṭ Beyado,* 142–43, 153–56, 390–91.

82. Raṭosh, *Reshit Hayamim,* 12–15.

83. Yonatan Raṭosh, "Melekh Iśrael Harishon: Milḥemet Hashiḥrur Shel Shaul Ha'ivri," in Raṭosh, *Reshit Hayamim,* 115–17.

84. See Yoav Peled and Horit Herman Peled, *The Religionization of Israeli Society,* Abingdon: Routledge, 2019.

85. Kimmerling, "Between the Primordial and the Civil."

86. Ram, "Why Secularism Fails?."

87. Yadgar, *Israel's Jewish Identity Crisis.*

88. Shindler, *The Rise of the Israeli Right.*

89. Yadgar, *Israel's Jewish Identity Crisis,* 17. See also Molavi, *Stateless Citizenship,* 50–58, 71–75.

90. See Shindler, *The Rise of the Israeli Right,* 11–12, 360.

91. Piterberg, "The Zionist Settlement in Palestine," 26.

92. See Abulof, *The Mortality and Morality of Nations*, 211: "Even if the sense of belonging is emphasized, that very emphasis reveals a need for repeated confirmation."

93. Yadgar, *Israel's Jewish Identity Crisis*.

Appendix A

1. Source: JIA/2/52P (reproduced courtesy of Margalit Shinar and the Jabotinsky Institute in Israel).

Appendix B

1. Source: Adya Horon Archive, Asia Institute files (reproduced courtesy of Margalit Shinar).

Appendix C

1. Source: HKA/32 (reproduced courtesy of Margalit Shinar and the Ben-Gurion Research Institute for the Study of Israel and Zionism).

Appendix D

1. Source: JIA/4/4-4a (reproduced courtesy of Margalit Shinar and the Jabotinsky Institute in Israel).

Bibliography

Archives

Adya Horon Archive, Karme Yossef (in private possession)
Boris Souvarine Papers, Houghton Library, Harvard University
Central Zionist Archives, Jerusalem
Getzel Kressel Archive, Leopold Muller Memorial Library, Oxford
Hillel Kook Archive, Śde Boḳer
Jabotinsky Institute Archive, Tel Aviv
The National Library of Israel, Jerusalem
Yad Ṿashem Archives, Jerusalem
Yigal Bin-Nun Archive, Tel Aviv (in private possession)
Yonatan Ratosh Archive, Genazim Institute, Tel Aviv

Periodicals

Alef
The Answer
Haarets
Haḥevra
Hamashḳif
Ḳeshet
La Riposte
Le Cran
Le Judaïsme Sephardi
Ma'ariv
Proza
Rassviet
Yedi'ot Aḥaronot

Books, Articles, Speeches, Pamphlets, Notes, Memoranda, etc.

"'A. Gourevitch-Ḥoron—Limnuḥot." *Ma'ariv*, 22.9.1972, 5.
Aberbach, David. "Nationalism and the Hebrew Bible." *Nations and Nationalism* 11 (2), 2005, 223–242.
Abu el-Haj, Nadia. *Facts on the Ground: Archaeological Practice and Territorial Self-Fashioning in Israeli Society*. Chicago and London: University of Chicago Press, 2001.
Abulof, Uriel. *The Mortality and Morality of Nations: Jews, Afrikaners and French Canadians*. Princeton: Princeton University Press, 2015.
Adiag. "Comment s'est formée la mythologie arabe." *La Riposte*, 5.2.1948, 4, 6.
Adiag. "Le 'Monde Arabe' est une fiction." *La Riposte*, 29.1.1948, 2, 8.
Adiag. "Le Panarabisme est un facteur de stagnation économique et de réaction sociale." *La Riposte*, 3.12.1947, 4–5.
Adiag. "Le Panarabisme—une fiction au service de l'impérialisme britannique dans le Moyen Orient." *La Riposte*, 22.10.1947, 4–5.
Adiag. "Londres veut faire de la Méditerranée un lac anglaise." *La Riposte*, 22.1.1948, 5.
Adiag. "Pétroles du Proche-Orient." *La Riposte*, 2.1.1948, 8.
Adiag. "Réalités du Proche-Orient: Le Liban." *La Riposte*, 14.3.1949, 8.
Adiag. "Vers un nouvel empire britannique en Méditerranée oriental." *La Riposte*, 9.1.1948, 4–5.
A. H., "The Phoenician Column." *The Lebanese Gazette—Leesan Al-Adl* 41 (3), 2.9.1955, 1–2.
Albright, W. F. "The Canaanite God Ḥaurôn (Ḥôrôn)." *The American Journal of Semitic Languages and Literatures* 53 (1), 1936, 1–12.
Albright, W. F. "The Egypto-Canaanite Deity Haurôn." *Bulletin of the American Schools of Oriental Research* 84, 1941, 7–12.
Almog, Oz. *The Sabra: The Creation of the New Jew* (tr. Haim Watzman). Berkeley, Los Angeles, London: University of California Press, 2000.
Almog, Shmuel. *Zionism and History: The Rise of a New Jewish Consciousness*. New York and Jerusalem: St. Martin's and Magnes, 1987.
Alonso, Ana María. "The Effects of Truth: Re-presentations of the Past and the Imagining of Community." *Journal of Historical Sociology* 1 (1), 1988, 33–57.
Alraïd. "Esquisses d'Histoire Hébraïque." *Cahiers du Betar* 1, 10.2.1934, 4–10.
Alraïd. "Finikiitzy: Istoricheskiie Ocherki." *Rassviet* 27 (52), 27.12.1931, 6–8.
Alraïd. "Ierusalim i Karfagen: Istoricheskiie Ocherki." *Rassviet* 28 (3), 17.1.1932, 11–12.
Alraïd. "Les Hébreux et Canaan." *Cahiers du Betar* 8, 1932, 2–4.
Alraïd. "Ob Istorii: Istoki Yevreiskago Plemeni (1)." *Rassviet* 27 (7), 15.2.1931, 3–5.
Alraïd. "Ob Istorii: Istoki Yevreiskago Plemeni (2)." *Rassviet* 27 (8), 22.2.1931, 8–10.

Alraïd. "Ob Istorii: Istoki Yevreiskago Plemeni (3)." *Rassviet* 27 (9), 1.3.1931, 5–6.

Alraïd. "Ob Istorii: Istoki Yevreiskago Plemeni (4)." *Rassviet* 27 (11), 15.3.1931, 4–6.

Alraïd. "Ob Istorii: Ob'yedinitel'noe Dvizheniie XIV–XII Vekov." *Rassviet* 27 (16), 19.4.1931, 6–7.

Alraïd. "Ob Istorii (Prodolzheniie)." *Rassviet* 27 (18), 3.5.1931, 6–7.

Alraïd. "Ob Istorii (Zhaloba Profana)." *Rassviet* 27 (6), 8.2.1931, 6–8.

Alraïd. "Yevrei i Khanaan: Istoricheskiie Ocherki." *Rassviet* 27 (51), 20.12.1931, 6–8.

Alraïd. "Yevrei i Rim: Istoricheskie Ocherki." *Rassviet* 28 (4), 24.1.1932, 5–7.

Alraïd. "Yevreiskaiia Imperiia Tri Tysiachi Let Nazad (Istoricheskiie Ocherki)." *Rassviet* 28 (1), 3.1.1932, 4–5.

Alraïd. "Yevreistvo Nakanune Stolknoveniia s Rimom: Istoricheskie Ocherki." *Rassviet* 28 (7), 14.2.1932, 10–11.

Amir, Aharon. *Miṭ'ane Tsad: Leḳeṭ Maamarim, 1949–1989*. Tel Aviv: Yaron Golan, 1991.

Amir, Aharon. "Petaḥ Davar: Ḥoron Beerets Ha'ivrim." in 'A. G. Ḥoron, *Ḳedem Ṿa'erev: Kna'an—Toldot Erets Ha'ivrim*. Tel Aviv: Dvir, 2000, 17–27.

Amir, Aharon. *Ṿaani Besheli: 'Iyunim Utguvot, 1944–1996*. Tel Aviv: Yaron Golan, 1997.

Anderson, Benedict. *Imagined Communities: Reflections on the Origin and Spread of Nationalism* (rev. ed.). London—New York: Verso, 1991.

"Ariel" [Uri Avnery]. "Isṭraṭegia Shel Ta'amula 'Ivrit." *Haḥevra* 6 (78), September 1946, 97–98.

Ariel, Yosef. "Mistorin Ushmo 'Masada.'" *Ma'ariv*, 28.5.1963, 20.

Asaf, Michael. "Par'onim, Kna'anim A Ukhna'anim B." *Davar*, 3.10.1952, 2.

Asséo, Henriette, Annie Bellaïche-Cohen, Muriel Flicoteaux, Corry Guttstadt, Xavier Rothea, Sabi Soulam, Alain De Toledo (eds.), *Mémorial des Judéo-Espagnols Déportés de France*. Paris: Éditeur Muestros Dezaparesidos, 2019.

Astour, Michael C. *Hellenosemitica*. Leiden: Brill, 1965.

Aṭṭer, Moshe. "Ḥalomam Hamatoḳ Shel 'Hakna'anim.'" *Haarets* literary supplement, 12.11.1976.

Avi-Yair, Moṭi. "Ḳeliṭat Toshve 'Aza," in Yonatan Raṭosh (ed.). *Minitsaḥon Lemapolet: Measef* Alef, Tel Aviv: Hadar, 1976, 98–99.

Avnery, Ariel. "'Shem' Soter Ṿeḳore." *Haḥevra* 2 (27–28), March 1942, 363–364.

Avnery, Uri. "Haemet 'Al Hakna'anim." *Proza* 17–18, 1977, 26–27.

Avnery, Uri. *Milḥemet Hayom Hashvi'i*. Tel Aviv: Daf Ḥadash, 1969.

Avnery, Uri. "Model Shel Iśrael Aḥeret—Arba'im Shana La'minshar Ha'ivri.'" *Haarets*, 10.1.1997, D1.

Avnery, Uri. "Mot Nimrod," in 'Amos Ḳenan (ed.). *Omanut Hapisul Biśrael: Ḥipuś Hazehut*. Tefen: The Open Museum, 1988, 25–30.

Avnery, Uri. *Opṭimi* I. Tel Aviv: Yedi'ot Aḥaronot, 2014.

Avni, Ḥaim, and Gide'on Shim'oni (eds.). *Hatsiyonut Umitnagdeha Ba'am Hayehudi*. Jerusalem: Hasifriya Hatsiyonit, 1990.

Banko, Lauren. *The Invention of Palestinian Citizenship, 1918–1947*. Edinburgh: Edinburgh University Press, 2016.

Baram, Amatzia. "Territorial Nationalism in the Middle East." *Middle Eastern Studies* 26 (4), 1990, 425–448.

Bareli, Avi. "Forgetting Europe: Perspectives on the Debate About Zionism and Colonialism," in Anita Shapira and Derek J. Penslar (eds.), *Israeli Historical Revisionism: From Left to Right*. London, Portland: Frank Cass, 2003, 99–120.

Bareli, Avi, and Pinḥas Ginossar (eds.). *Tsiyonut: Pulmus Ben Zmanenu—Gishot Meḥḳariyot Veideologiyot*. Śde Boḳer: Ben-Gurion University, 1996.

Barṭal, Iśrael. "'Al Harishoniyut: Zman Umaḳom Ba'aliya Harishona," in Yafa Berelowitz and Yosef Lang (eds.), *Leśoḥeaḥ Tarbut 'Im Ha'aliya Harishona: 'Iyun Ben Teḳufot*. Tel Aviv: Haḳibbuts Hameuḥad, 2010, 15–24.

Barṭov, Ḥanokh. *Ligdol Velikhtov Beerets Iśrael*. Or Yehuda: Zmora-Bitan, 2007.

Behar, Moshe, and Zvi Ben-Dor Benite (eds.). *Modern Middle Eastern Jewish Thought: Writings on Identity, Politics, and Culture*. Waltham: Brandeis University Press, 2013.

Belial, G. [George Blumberg]. "Peuple Sans Terre, Terre Sans Peuple" (Central Zionist Archives, file A549/19–54).

Belyaev, Evgenii. *Arabs, Islam and the Arab Caliphate in the Early Middle Ages* (tr. Adolphe Gourevitch). Jerusalem: Israel Universities Press, 1969.

Ben-'Ezer. Ehud. *En Shaananim Betsion: Śiḥot 'Al Meḥir Hatsiyonut*. Tel Aviv: 'Am 'Oved, 1986.

Ben-Shlomo, Zeev. "Masa' Bemerḥav Hazmanim: Śiḥa 'Im Hahisṭorion 'Adya Ḥoron." *Ma'ariv*, 16.9.1949, 6.

Ben-Yerucham, Ch. [Ḥen-Melekh Mereḥavia]. *Sepher Bethar—Ḳorot Umḳorot*, vol. 1. Jerusalem—Tel Aviv: Publishing Committee of Sepher Bethar, 1969.

Ben-Yerucham, Ch. [Ḥen-Melekh Mereḥavia]. *Sepher Bethar—Ḳorot Umḳorot*, vol. 2 (1). Jerusalem—Tel Aviv: Publishing Committee of Sepher Bethar, 1973.

Ben-Yerucham, Ch. [Ḥen-Melekh Mereḥavia]. *Sepher Bethar—Ḳorot Umḳorot*, vol. 2 (2). Jerusalem—Tel Aviv: Publishing Committee of Sepher Bethar, 1975.

Benṭov, Yehoshu'a [Aharon Amir]. "Mamlekhet Iśrael Hatsalbanit?," in Nurit Gerts and Rachel Weisbrod (eds.), *Haḳvutsa Hakna'anit—Sifrut Veideologia*. Tel Aviv: Open University, 1986, 25–28.

Benṭov, Yehoshu'a [Aharon Amir]. "Mesheḳ Shel 'Ayara," in Nurit Gerts and Rachel Weisbrod (eds.), *Haḳvutsa Hakna'anit—Sifrut Veideologia*. Tel Aviv: Open University, 1986, 34–36.

Benvenisti, Meron. *Sacred Landscape: The Buried History of the Holy Land Since 1948* (tr. Maxine Kaufman-Lacusta). Berkeley, Los Angeles, London: University of California Press, 2000.

Berelowitz, Yafa. "Hamoshava Ha'ivrit: Reshita Shel Tarbut Erets Iśreelit," in Yafa Berelowitz and Yosef Lang (eds.), *Leśoḥeaḥ Tarbut 'Im Ha'aliya Harishona: 'Iyun Ben Teḳufot*. Tel Aviv: Haḳibbuts Hameuḥad, 2010, 70–109.

Berelowitz, Yafa, and Yosef Lang (eds.). *Leśoḥeaḥ Tarbut 'Im Ha'aliya Harishona: 'Iyun Ben Teḳufot*. Tel Aviv: Haḳibbuts Hameuḥad, 2010.

Bergamin, Peter. *The Making of the Israeli Far-Right: Abba Ahimeir and Zionist Ideology*. London: Tauris, 2020.

Berger, Stefan. "Introduction: Towards a Global History of National Historiographies," in Stefan Berger (ed.), *Writing the Nation: A Global Perspective*. Basingstoke, UK: Palgrave Macmillan, 2007, 1–29.

Berger, Stefan. "The Power of National Pasts: Writing National History in Nineteenth- and Twentieth-Century Europe," in Stefan Berger (ed.), *Writing the Nation: A Global Perspective*. Basingstoke: Palgrave Macmillan, 2007, 30–62.

Berger, Stefan (ed.). *Writing the Nation: A Global Perspective*. Basingstoke: Palgrave Macmillan, 2007.

Bergson, Peter H. [Hillel Kook]. "Post-Zionism" (HKA/30).

Berthelot, Katell, Joseph E. David, and Marc Hirshman (eds.). *The Gift of the Land and the Fate of the Canaanites in Jewish Thought*. Oxford: Oxford University Press, 2014.

Biale, David. *Power and Powerlessness in Jewish History*. New York: Schocken Books, 1987.

Bilski Ben-Ḥur, Refaela. *Kol Yaḥid Hu Melekh: Hamaḥshava Haḥevratit Ṿehamdinit Shel Zeev Jabotinsky*. Tel Aviv: Dvir, 1988.

Blumberg, Christine, and Henriette Asséo. "L'aventure de SHEM" (unpublished).

Breuilly, John. "Nationalism and the Making of National Pasts," in Susana Carvalho and François Gemenne (eds.), *Nations and Their Histories: Constructions and Representations*. Basingstoke: Palgrave Macmillan, 2009, 7–28.

Breuilly, John. "The Sources of Nationalist Ideology," in John Hutchinson and Anthony D. Smith (eds.), *Nationalism*. Oxford: Oxford University Press, 1994, 103–113.

Brym, Robert J. *Intellectuals and Politics*, London: George Allen and Unwin, 1980.

Burke, Peter. "History as Social Memory," in Thomas Butler (ed.), *Memory: History, Culture and the Mind*. Oxford, New York: Basil Blackwell, 1989, 97–113.

Butler, Thomas (ed.). *Memory: History, Culture and the Mind*. Oxford, New York: Basil Blackwell, 1989.

Burrow, John. *A History of Histories: Epics, Chronicles, Romances and Inquiries from Herodotus and Thucydides to the Twentieth Century*. London: Penguin Books, 2009.

Calhoun, Craig. *Nationalism*. Buckingham: Open University Press, 1997.

Carvalho, Susana and François Gemenne (eds.). *Nations and Their Histories: Constructions and Representations*. Basingstoke: Palgrave Macmillan, 2009.

Chejne, Anwar G. "*Arabs, Islam and the Caliphate in the Early Middle Ages* by E. A. Belyaev; Adolphe Gourevitch." *Journal of the American Oriental Society* 92 (1), 1972, 112–113.

Cholewinska-Vater, Dominika. "Contested Loyalties in War: Polish-Jewish Relations within the Anders Army" (PhD dissertation, University of Manchester, 2019).

Chowers, Eyal. "Time in Zionism: The Life and Afterlife of a Temporal Revolution." *Political Theory* 26 (5), 1998, 652–685.

Coakley, John. "Mobilizing the Past: Nationalist Images of History." *Nationalism and Ethnic Politics* 10 (4), 2004, 531–560.

Cohen, Anthony P. *The Symbolic Construction of Community*. London and New York: Routledge, 1993.

Cohen, Eric, "Israel as a Post-Zionist Society." *Israel Affairs* 1 (3), 1995, 203–214.

Cohen, Hillel. *'Aravim Ṭovim—Hamodi'in Haiśreeli Ṿeha'aravim Biśrael: Sokhnim Umaf'ilim, MASHTAPIM Umordim, Maṭarot Ṿeshiṭot*. 'Ivrit: Jerusalem, 2006.

Cohen, Hillel. "Masorot Muslemiyot Meshupatsot 'Al Shivat Iśrael Leartso Baśiaḥ Hatsiyoni-Meshiḥi" *Jama'a* 10, 2003, 169–185.

Cohen, Hillel. *1929: Year Zero of the Arab-Israeli Conflict*. Waltham: Brandeis University Press, 2015.

Cohen, Hillel. *Tsva Hatslalim—MASHTAPIM Falesṭinim Besherut Hatsiyonut, 1917–1948: Modi'in, Mediniyut, Hityashvut, Hitnaḳshuyot*. 'Ivrit: Jerusalem, 2004.

Cohen, Percy S. "Theories of Myth." *Man* (new series) 4 (3), 1969, 337–353.

Cole, Joshua. "Derek Penslar's 'Algebra of Modernity': How Should We Understand the Relation between Zionism and Colonialism?," in Ethan B. Katz, Lisa Moses Leff, and Maud S. Mandel (eds.), *Colonialism and the Jews*. Bloomington and Indianapolis: Indiana University Press, 2017, 301–316.

Collins, Rebecca. "Concealing the Poverty of Traditional Historiography: Myth as Mystification in Historical Discourse." *Rethinking History: The Journal of Theory and Practice* 7 (3), 2003, 341–365.

Conforti, Yitzhak. "Zionist Awareness of the Jewish Past: Inventing Tradition or Renewing the Ethnic Past?" *Studies in Ethnicity and Nationalism* 12 (1), 2012, 155–171.

Connor, Walker. *Ethnonationalism: The Quest for Understanding*. Princeton: Princeton University Press, 1994.

Connor, Walker. "The Timelessness of Nations." *Nations and Nationalism* 10 (1–2), 2004, 35–47.

Conversi, Daniele. "Mapping the Field: Theories of Nationalism and the Ethnosymbolic Approach," in Athena S. Leoussi and Steven Grosby (eds.), *Nationalism and Ethnosymbolism: History, Culture and Ethnicity in the Formation of Nations*. Edinburgh: Edinburgh University Press, 2007, 15–30.

Darshan, Guy and Noga. *Hamitologiya Hakna'anit*. Tel Aviv: Mapa, 2009.

Diamond, James S. *Baruch Kurzweil and Modern Hebrew Literature*. Chico: Scholars, 1983.

Diamond, James S. *Homeland or Holy Land? The "Canaanite" Critique of Israel*. Bloomington and Indianapolis: Indiana University Press, 1986.

Díaz-Andreu, Margarita. "Nationalism and Archaeology." *Nations and Nationalism* 7 (4), 2001, 429–440.

Dieckhoff, Alain. *The Invention of a Nation: Zionist Thought and the Making of Modern Israel*. New York: Columbia University Press, 2003.

Dietler, Michael. " 'Our Ancestors the Gauls': Archaeology, Ethnic Nationalism, and the Manipulation of Celtic Identity in Modern Europe." *American Anthropologist* 96 (3), 1994, 584–605.

Dinur, Ben-Zion. "Hakarat He'avar Betoda'at Ha'am Uv'ayot Haḥeḳer Ba," in *Hakarat He'avar Betoda'at He'amim Uvtoda'at 'Am Iśrael: Ḳovets Hartsaot Shehushme'u Bakenes Hashlosha-'aśar Le'iyun Behistoria (Ḥanuka 5728)*. Jerusalem: The Historical Society of Israel, 1969, 9–24.

"Documents sur le National-Socialisme," présentés par Brice Parain & George Blumberg. *La Nouvelle Revue Française*, 1.8.1933, 234–262.

Domb, Risa. "Ideology, Identity and Language in Modern Hebrew Literature." *Israel Affairs*, 7 (1), 2000, 71–86.

Dor, Moshe. "Te'udat Hazehut Shel Yonatan Raṭosh." *Ma'ariv Yamim Ṿelelot*, 25.9.1970, 25.

Dotan, Moshe. "Halashon Ha'ivrit Bemishnato Shel Zeev Jabotinsky." *Haumma* 19 (3), 1981, 409–417.

Dowty, Alan. "Zionism's Greatest Conceit." *Israel Studies* 3 (1), 1998, 1–23.

Duara, Prasenjit. *Rescuing History from the Nation: Questioning Narratives of Modern China*. Chicago and London: University of Chicago Press, 1995.

Dubow, Saul. "Afrikaner Nationalism, Apartheid and the Conceptualization of 'Race.'" *Journal of African History* 33, 1992, 209–237.

Eisenberg, Laurie. "History Revisited or Revamped? The Maronite Factor in Israel's 1982 Invasion of Lebanon." *Israel Affairs* 15 (4), 2009, 372–396.

Eisenberg, Laurie Z. *My Enemy's Enemy: Lebanon in the Early Zionist Imagination, 1900–1948*. Detroit: Wayne State University Press, 1994.

Eisenberg, Laurie Zittrain. "From Benign to Malign: Israeli-Lebanese Relations, 1948–1978," in Clive Jones and Sergio Catignani (eds.), *Israel and Hizbollah: An Asymmetric Conflict in Historical and Comparative Perspective*. London and New York: Routledge, 2010, 10–24.

Elath, Eliahu. " 'Phoenician Zionism' in Lebanon." *The Jerusalem Quarterly* 42, 1987, 38–56.

Eldad, Iśrael. "Avne Yesod," in Avi Bareli and Pinḥas Ginossar (eds.), *Tsiyonut: Pulmus Ben Zmanenu—Gishot Meḥḳariyot Ṿeideologiyot*. Śde Boḳer: Ben-Gurion University, 1996, 453–465.

Eley, Geoff. "Nationalism and Social History." *Social History* 6 (1), 1981, 83–107.

Eliav, Binyamin. *Zikhronot Min Hayamin*. Tel Aviv: 'Am 'Oved, 1990.

Elon, Amos. "Politics and Archaeology," in Neil Asher Silberman and David B. Small (eds.), *The Archaeology of Israel: Constructing the Past, Interpreting the Present*. Sheffield: Sheffield Academic, 1997, 34–47.

Engel, David. "The Frustrated Alliance: The Revisionist Movement and the Polish Government-in-exile, 1939–1945." *Studies in Zionism* 7 (1), 1986, 11–36.

Ephratt, Michal. "Iconicity, Ratosh's Lexical Innovations, and Beyond." *Semiotica* 157 (1/4), 2005, 83–104.

Er'el, Nitsa. *'Bli Mora Bli Maśo Panim': Uri Avnery Ṿe'Ha'olam Haze'*. Jerusalem: Magnes, 2006.

Eshel, Ḥanan. "Hatagliyot Haarkheologiyot Umif'al Ḥayaṿ Shel 'A. G. Ḥoron," in 'A. G. Ḥoron, *Ḳedem Ṿa'erev: Kna'an—Toldot Erets Ha'ivrim*. Tel Aviv: Dvir, 2000, 29–32.

Even-Zohar, Itamar. "Hatsmiḥa Ṿehahitgabshut Shel Tarbut 'Ivrit Meḳomit Ṿilidit Beerets Iśrael, 1882–1948." *Ḳatedra* 16, 1980, 165–189.

Evron, Boas. *Jewish State or Israeli Nation?*, Bloomington and Indianapolis: Indiana University Press, 1995.

'Evron, Bo'az. *Haḥeshbon Haleumi*. Tel Aviv: Dvir, 1988.

'Evron, Bo'az. "Hama'aśe—Uvavuato Haaḳademit." *Yedi'ot Aḥaronot*, 2.3.1984, 20–21.

'Evron, Bo'az. "Hatsiyonut—Mabaṭ Leaḥor," in Avi Bareli and Pinḥas Ginossar (eds.), *Tsiyonut: Pulmus Ben Zmanenu—Gishot Meḥḳariyot Ṿeideologiyot*. Śde Boḳer: Ben-Gurion University, 1996, 52–59.

Eyal, Gil. *The Disenchantment of the Orient: Expertise in Arab Affairs and the Israeli State*. Stanford: Stanford University Press, 2006.

Eyal, Gil. *Hasarat Haḳesem Min Hamizraḥ: Toledot Hamizraḥanut Be'idan Hamizraḥiyut*. Jerusalem: Van Leer Institute, Haḳibbuts Hameuḥad, 2005.

Feige, Michael, and Tsvi Shiloni (eds.). *Ḳardom Laḥpor Bo: Arkheologia Uleumiyut Beerets Iśrael*. Jerusalem: Ben-Gurion Research Institute, 2008.

Firro, Kais M. "Lebanese Nationalism versus Arabism: From Bulus Nujaym to Michel Chiha." *Middle Eastern Studies* 40 (5), 2004, 1–27.

Frankel, Zacharias. "Mada' Hayahadut—Ṭivo Ṿetafḳido," in Paul R. Mendes-Flohr (ed.), *Ḥokhmat Iśrael: Hebeṭim Hisṭoriim Ṿefilosofiim*. Jerusalem: The Historical Society of Israel, 1979, 112–114.

Freeman-Maloy, Dan. "The International Politics of Settler Self-Governance: Reflections on Zionism and 'Dominion' Status Within the British Empire." *Settler Colonial Studies* 8 (1), 2018, 80–95.

Funkenstein, Amos. "Collective Memory and Historical Consciousness." *History and Memory* 1 (1), 1989, 5–26.

Gal, Allon. "Historical Ethno-Symbols in the Emergence of the State of Israel," in Athena S. Leoussi and Steven Grosby (eds.), *Nationalism and Ethnosymbolism: History, Culture and Ethnicity in the Formation of Nations*. Edinburgh: Edinburgh University Press, 2007, 221–230.

Gal, Allon. "National Restoration and Moral Renewal: The Dialectics of the Past in the Emergence of Modern Israel," in Susana Carvalho and François Gemenne (eds.), *Nations and Their Histories: Constructions and Representations*. Basingstoke: Palgrave Macmillan, 2009, 172–188.

Gat, Azar. *Nations: The Long History and Deep Roots of Political Ethnicity and Nationalism*. Cambridge: Cambridge University Press, 2013.

Gerber, Haim. "The Muslim *Umma* and the Formation of Middle Eastern Nationalisms," in Athena S. Leoussi and Steven Grosby (eds.), *Nation-*

alism and Ethnosymbolism: History, Culture and Ethnicity in the Formation of Nations. Edinburgh: Edinburgh University Press, 2007, 209–220.

Gerts, Nurit, and Rachel Weisbrod (eds.). *Haḳvutsa Hakna'anit—Sifrut Ṿeideologia*. Tel Aviv: Open University, 1986.

Gesenius, Wilhelm. *A Hebrew and English Lexicon of the Old Testament* (tr. Edward Robinson). Oxford: Clarendon, 1906.

Ghazi-Bouillon, Asima A. *Understanding the Middle East Peace Process: Israeli Academia and the Struggle for Identity*. London and New York: Routledge, 2009.

Ghosn, Albert. "Hamaronim—'Am Halevanon," in Yonatan Raṭosh, *1967—Uma Hal'a?* Tel Aviv: Ḥermon, 1967, 92–103.

Gil'adi, D. "'Masada' Asher Bemaḥane Compiègne." *Ma'ariv*, 17.5.1963, 6.

Giliomee, Hermann. "Constructing Afrikaner Nationalism." *Journal of Asian and African Studies* 18 (1–2), 1983, 83–98.

Giora, Moshe. "Hateza Hakna'anit—Bemisparim Uv'uvdot," in Yonatan Raṭosh (ed.), *Minitsaḥon Lemapolet: Measef* Alef. Tel Aviv: Hadar, 1976, 285–287.

Glatzer, Nahum N. "The Beginnings of Modern Jewish Studies," in Alexander Altmann (ed.), *Studies in Nineteenth-Century Jewish Intellectual History*. Cambridge: Harvard University Press, 1964, 27–45.

Gorny, Yosef. "Haliberalizm Habetar-Kna'ani—Gishot 'Akhshaṿiyot Bish'elat Hanormalizatsiya Shel Haḳiyum Haleumi Bimdinat-Iśrael." *Kiṿunim* (new edition) 1 (38), 1990, 45–57.

Gorny, Yosef. "Hashniyut Beyaḥaso Shel Daṿid Ben-Gurion El Hatsiyonut," in Ḥaim Avni and Gide'on Shim'oni (eds.), *Hatsiyonut Umitnagdeha Ba'am Hayehudi*. Jerusalem: Hasifriya Hatsiyonit, 1990, 437–445.

Gour, A. "Hébreux et Juifs" (The National Library of Israel, file S39 B426).

Gourevitch, A. "Arabia's Mythical Millions" (JIA/8/52p).

Gourevitch, A. "Le Panarabisme" (JIA/6/52p).

Gourevitch, Adolph. "Jabotinsky and the Hebrew Language," in Joseph B. Schechtman, *Rebel and Statesman: The Vladimir Jabotinsky Story—The Last Years*. New York: Thomas Yoseloff, 1961, 577–599.

Gourevitch, Adolphe. "Pan-Arabism," talk given in New York, 23.11.1952 (Horon Archive, Asia Institute files).

Gourevitch, Adolphe. "Pan-Arabism." *Land Reborn* 4 (3), May–June 1953, 5.

Gourevitch, Adolphe. "The Semitic Levant: Present Conditions," in *The Levant: Behind the Arab Curtain*. New York: Levant, 1952, 9–30.

Gray, John. "The Canaanite God Horon." *Journal of Near Eastern Studies* 8 (1), 1949, 27–34.

Gribetz, Jonathan Marc. *Defining Neighbors: Religion, Race, and the Early Zionist-Arab Encounter*, Princeton: Princeton University Press, 2014.

Grosby, Steven. "The Successor Territory," in Athena S. Leoussi and Steven Grosby (eds.), *Nationalism and Ethnosymbolism: History, Culture and Ethnicity in the Formation of Nations*. Edinburgh: Edinburgh University Press, 2007, 99–112.

Grundlingh, Albert. "The Trajectory and Dynamics of Afrikaner Nationalism in the Twentieth Century: An Overview," in Lize van Robbroeck, Federico Freschi and Brenda Schmahmann (eds.), *Troubling Images: Visual Culture and the Politics of Afrikaner Nationalism*. Johannesburg: Wits University Press, 2020, 23–39.

von Grunebaum, G. E. "*Arabs, Islam and the Arab Caliphate in the Early Middle Ages* by E. A. Belyaev." *Speculum* 45 (3), 1970, 453–455.

Gur, 'Adya. "Hem Niḳlaṭim Maher," in Yonatan Raṭosh (ed.), *Minitsaḥon Lemapolet: Measef* Alef. Tel Aviv: Hadar, 1976, 323–324.

Gur, 'Adya. "Ḥufsha Beramallah," in Yonatan Raṭosh (ed.), *Minitsaḥon Lemapolet: Measef* Alef. Tel Aviv: Hadar, 1976, 321–322.

Gur, 'Adya. "Ma'amad Shel Ma'atsama Ṿetakhsise Geṭṭo Bematsor," in Yonatan Raṭosh (ed.), *Minitsaḥon Lemapolet: Measef* Alef. Tel Aviv: Hadar, 1976, 153–154.

Gur, 'Adya. "Pizur Hageṭṭaot," in Yonatan Raṭosh (ed.), *Minitsaḥon Lemapolet: Measef* Alef. Tel Aviv: Hadar, 1976, 190–191.

Gur, 'Adya. "She'at Kosher—Lemi?," in Yonatan Raṭosh (ed.), *Minitsaḥon Lemapolet: Measef* Alef. Tel Aviv: Hadar, 1976, 294–296.

Gur, 'Adya. " 'Teḳufat Hahamtana'—1972," in Yonatan Raṭosh (ed.), *Minitsaḥon Lemapolet: Measef* Alef. Tel Aviv: Hadar, 1976, 162–167.

Gur, 'Adya. "28 Elef 'Anusim' Biśrael," in Yonatan Raṭosh (ed.), *Minitsaḥon Lemapolet: Measef* Alef. Tel Aviv: Hadar, 1976, 120–121.

Gutiérrez Chong, Natividad. "Ethnic Origins and Indigenous People: An Approach from Latin America," in Athena S. Leoussi and Steven Grosby (eds.), *Nationalism and Ethnosymbolism: History, Culture and Ethnicity in the Formation of Nations*. Edinburgh: Edinburgh University Press, 2007, 312–324.

Guṭṿein, Daniel. "Posṭ-Tsiyonut, Mahapekhat Hahafraṭa Ṿehaśmol Haḥevrati," in Ṭuvia Friling (ed.), *Teshuva Le'amit Posṭ-Tsiyoni*. Tel Aviv: Yedi'ot Aḥaronot, 2003, 243–273.

Gutwein, Daniel. "Left and Right Post-Zionism and the Privatization of Israeli Collective Memory," in Anita Shapira and Derek J. Penslar (eds.), *Israeli Historical Revisionism: From Left to Right*. London and Portland: Frank Cass, 9–42.

Hakarat He'avar Betoda'at He'amim Uvtoda'at 'Am Iśrael: Ḳovets Hartsaot Shehushme'u Bakenes Hashlosha-'aśar Le'iyun Behistoria (Ḥanuka 5728). Jerusalem: Historical Society of Israel, 1969.

Halperin, Liora R. *Babel in Zion: Jews, Nationalism, and Language Diversity in Palestine, 1920–1948*. New Haven: Yale University Press, 2015.

Halpern, Yirmiyahu. "Hamefaḳed Victor Mirkine," *Hamashḳif*, 8.3.1945, 3.

Halpern, Yirmiyahu. *Teḥiyat Hayamaut Ha'ivrit*. Tel Aviv: Hadar, 1961.

Halpern, Yirmiyahu. "Tsir Rodêgal—Mikhtav Miparis." *Ha'am*, 7.6.1931.

Hawari, Yara, Sharri Plonski, and Elian Weizman. "Seeing Israel through Palestine: Knowledge Production as Anti-Colonial Praxis." *Settler Colonial Studies* 9 (1), 2019, 155–175.

Hawari, Yara, Sharri Plonski, and Elian Weizman. "Settlers and Citizens: A Critical View of Israeli Society." *Settler Colonial Studies* 9 (1), 2019, 1–5.
Hayes, Carlton J. H. "Contributions of Herder to the Doctrine of Nationalism." *The American Historical Review* 32 (4), 1927, 719–736.
Hazaz, Haim. "The Sermon," in Robert Alter (ed.), *Modern Hebrew Literature*. New York: Behrman House, 1975, 271–287.
Hazran, Yusri. "A People That Shall Dwell Alone; Is That So? Israel and the Minorities Alliance." *Middle Eastern Studies* 56 (3), 2020, 396–411.
Hegel, Georg W. F. *The Philosophy of History*. New York: Dover, 1956.
Heller, Yosef. *LEḤI: Ideologia Ṿepoliṭiḳa, 1940–1949*. Jerusalem: Keter, 1989.
Herder, Johann G. *Against Pure Reason: Writings on Religion, Language, and History* (tr., ed. and intr. Marcia Bunge). Minneapolis: Fortress, 1993.
Himka, John-Paul. "The Construction of Nationality in Galician Rus': Icarian Flights in Almost all Directions," in Ronald Grigor Suny and Michael D. Kennedy (eds.), *Intellectuals and the Articulation of the Nation*. Ann Arbor: University of Michigan Press, 1999, 109–164.
Hobsbawm, Eric, and Terence Ranger (eds.). *The Invention of Tradition*, Cambridge: Cambridge University Press, 1983.
Hofmann, Klaus. "Canaanism." *Middle Eastern Studies* 47 (2), 2011, 273–294.
Hoffman, Lawrence A. (ed). *The Land of Israel: Jewish Perspectives*. Notre Dame: University of Notre Dame Press, 1986.
Ḥ.[oron], 'A.[dya] G.[ur]. "Afriḳa: Prehisṭoria," *Encyclopaedia Hebraica*, vol. 5, 1953. Jerusalem, Tel Aviv: Haḥevra Lehotzaat Entsiḳlopediot, columns 329–347.
Ḥ.[oron], 'A.[dya] G.[ur]. "Ameriḳa: Prehisṭoria," *Encyclopaedia Hebraica*, vol. 4, 1952, Jerusalem, Tel Aviv: Haḥevra Lehotzaat Entsiḳlopediot, columns 167–175.
Ḥ.[oron], 'A.[dya] G.[ur]. "Asia: Prehisṭoria," *Encyclopaedia Hebraica*, vol. 4, 1952. Jerusalem, Tel Aviv: Haḥevra Lehotzaat Entsiḳlopediot, columns 915–931.
Ḥ.[oron], 'A.[dya] G.[ur]. "Eropa: Prehisṭoria," *Encyclopaedia Hebraica*, vol. 3, 1953. Jerusalem, Tel Aviv: Haḥevra Lehotzaat Entsiḳlopediot, columns 133–142.
Ḥ.[oron], 'A.[dya] G.[ur]. "Iberia: Prehisṭoria," *Encyclopaedia Hebraica*, vol. 2, 1950. Jerusalem, Tel Aviv: Haḥevra Lehotzaat Entsiḳlopediot, columns 599–606.
Ḥ.[oron], 'A.[dya] G.[ur]. "Iberim," *Encyclopaedia Hebraica*, vol. 2, 1950. Jerusalem, Tel Aviv: Haḥevra Lehotzaat Entsiḳlopediot, columns 607–616.
Ḥ.[oron], 'A.[dya] G.[ur]. "Iṭalia: Prehisṭoria," *Encyclopaedia Hebraica*, vol. 2, 1950. Jerusalem, Tel Aviv: Haḥevra Lehotzaat Entsiḳlopediot, columns 727–731.
Horon. "For a new American Policy South and East of the Mediterranean," 1951–1952 (Horon Archive).
Horon. "The Hebrew Movement—An Outline," January 1947 (JIA/2/52p; HKA/36).
Horon. "Le Monde des Hébreux" (JIA/5/52p).

Horon, A. "Hebrews and Jews: A Lecture Delivered in April 1945, New York, to the Leadership and Secretariat of the Hebrew Committee of National Liberation and the American League for Free Palestine" (HKA/36).

Ḥoron, 'A. "MiNapoleon 'Ad Lawrence." *Alef*, May 1951, 11, 15.

Horon, A. G. "Après Juin." *Le Contrat Social* 11 (6), November–December 1967, 367–372.

Ḥoron, 'A. G. "Bene Britenu Haṭiv'iim." *Alef*, June 1967, 2.

Ḥoron, 'A. G. "Beriat Artsenu Lefi Mimtsae Hageologia." *Alef*, January 1972, 3.

Ḥoron, 'A. G. "Erets Haḳedem," in Yonatan Raṭosh (ed.), *Minitsaḥon Lemapolet: Measef* Alef. Tel Aviv: Hadar, 1976, 40.

Ḥoron, 'A. G. *Erets-Haḳedem: Madrikh Hisṭori Umdini Lamizraḥ Haḳarov*. Tel Aviv: Ḥermon, 1970.

Ḥoron, 'A. G. "Erets Haḳedem Uvene Shem: Hatfisa Hageografit Shel Ha'ivrim Haḳadmonim." *Alef*, January 1972, 3.

Ḥoron, 'A. G. "Haimperializm Ha'arbai." *Alef*, 18, 1953, 4–5.

Ḥoron, 'A. G. "Haḳedem Ha'ivri," in Yonatan Raṭosh (ed.), *Minitsaḥon Lemapolet: Measef* Alef. Tel Aviv: Hadar, 1976, 215–260.

Ḥoron, 'A. G. "Hakoptim—'Hamitsrim Haamitiim.'" *Ḳeshet* 6 (4), 1964, 179–183.

Horon, A. G. "Is there an 'Arab Civilization'? Islam and Arabism." *Commentary*, November 1958, 411–419.

Ḥoron, 'A. G. "Iśrael Ṿehamitos Ha'aravi." *Haumma* 8, 1964, 501–519.

Ḥoron, 'A. G. "Jabotinsky Ṿehaśafa Ha'ivrit," in Joseph B. Shechtman, *Zeev Jabotinsky: Parshat Ḥayaṿ; Sefer Shlishi: 1935–1940*. Tel Aviv: Ḳarni, 1959, 328–362.

Ḥoron, 'A. G. *Ḳedem Ṿa'erev: Kna'an—Toldot Erets Ha'ivrim*. Tel Aviv: Dvir, 2000.

Ḥoron, 'A. G. "Kna'an Ṿeyaṿan Bitḳufat Habronza," in Yonatan Raṭosh (ed.), *Minitsaḥon Lemapolet: Measef* Alef. Tel Aviv: Hadar, 1976, 209–215.

Horon, A. G. "La Grande Illusion." *Le Contrat Social* 2 (2), March 1958, 63–68.

Horon, A. G. "Le Mythe Panarabe dans le Vide Oriental et Africain." *Est & Ouest*, 1–15.7.1957, 3–6.

Horon, A. G. "Le Panarabisme." *Le Contrat Social* 1 (3), July 1957, 149–156.

Horon, A. G. "Les Arabes depuis l'Islam." *Le Contrat Social* 2 (3), May 1958, 135–142.

Horon, A. G. "L'URSS 'Amie' de l'Islam." *Est & Ouest*, 1–15.1.1958, 1–3.

Ḥoron, 'A. G. "Mitologia Umetsiut: 'Al 'Yetsiat Mitsraim' Ṿe'khibush Kna'an.'" *Alef*, May 1972, 4–5.

Ḥoron, 'A. G. "'Olam Behashḳafa 'Ivrit. Bene 'Ever: Motsa Miben 'Ame Haadama, Ṿehitnaḥalut Bikhna'an." *Ḳeshet* 9 (1), 1966, 128–153.

Ḥoron, 'A. G. "'Olam Behashḳafa 'Ivrit. Hadvarim Haṭromiim: Toledot Adam Beezor Hayam Hatikhon." *Ḳeshet* 8 (2), 1966, 113–136.

Ḥoron, 'A. G. "'Olam Behashḳafa 'Ivrit. Maamar Rishon: Dvar Petiḥa." *Ḳeshet* 8 (1), 1965, 96–120.

Ḥoron, 'A. G. "'Olam Behashḳafa 'Ivrit. Mishpaḥat Ḥam Ṿeshem: Leshonotehen Ṿiḥasehen." *Ḳeshet* 8 (4), 1966, 160–184.

Ḥoron, ʻA. G. "ʻOlam Behashḳafa ʻIvrit. Reshit Yeme Ḳedem: Ben Yam Ṿenahar." *Ḳeshet* 8 (3), 1966, 114–139.
Horon, A. G. "The Pan-Arab Myth in the Mideastern Vacuum," Levant Club, *Memorandum no. 17–18*, 1957.
Ḥoron, ʻA. G. "Shlemut Hamoledet Ṿekhibush Hashalom." *Ḳeshet* 7 (4), 1965, 153–163.
Ḥoron, ʻA. G. "Śiḥot ʻAl Ḳadmoniyut Haarets: Nisayon Leshiḥzur ʻYetsiat Mitsraim' Ṿe'khibush Kna'an', Bamitologia Uvamtsiut." *Ḳeshet* 16 (3), 1974, 116–132.
Ḥoron, ʻA. G. "Toledot Haarets Hi Hahisṭoria Haleumit." *Alef*, November 1971, 3.
Horon, A. G. "Un Arabisant Soviétique." *Le Contrat Social* 12 (1), January–March 1968, 77–79.
Horon, Adolphe G. "Canaan and the Aegean Sea: Greco-Phoenician Origins Reviewed." *Diogenes* 58, 1967, 37–61.
Hourani, Albert. *Arabic Thought in the Liberal Age, 1798–1939*. Cambridge: Cambridge University Press, 2002.
Hroch, Miroslav. "From National Movement to the Fully-Formed Nation: The Nation-Building Process in Europe." *New Left Review* 198, 1993, 3–20.
Hutchinson, John. *Nations as Zones of Conflict*. London: Sage, 2005.
Hutchinson, John, and Anthony D. Smith (eds.). *Nationalism*. Oxford: Oxford University Press, 1994.
Ibn Khaldûn. *The Muqaddima: An Introduction to History* (tr. Franz Rosenthal, ed. and abr. N. J. Dawood). Princeton: Princeton University Press, 1989.
Ivianski, Zeev. *LEḤI—Tsvat Rishona: ʻIyunim Benaftule Teḳufa Ṿaderekh*. Tel Aviv: Yair, 2003.
Jabary Salamanca, Omar, Mezna Qato, Kareem Rabie, and Sobhi Samour. "Past Is Present: Settler Colonialism in Palestine." *Settler Colonial Studies* 2 (1), 2012, 1–8.
Jabotinsky, ʻEri. *Avi, Zeev Jabotinsky*. Jerusalem, Haifa, Tel Aviv: Steimatzky, 1980.
Jabotinsky, Eri. "Israel and Zionism: Why Israel Has no Constitution," in *The Levant: Behind the Arab Curtain*. New York: Levant, 1952, 43–50.
Jabotinsky, Eri. "Jews and Hebrews" (JIA/3/13/410).
Jabotinsky, ʻEri. "Or Hayareaḥ Goneṭ Hirhurim." *Ḥerut*, 19.8.1949, 5.
Jabotinsky, ʻEri. "Or Hayareaḥ Goneṭ Hirhurim." *Ḥerut*, 21.8.1949, 2.
Jabotinsky, Eri. "Tentative Formulation for a Program of Action," Haifa, November 19, 1956 (HKA/32).
Jabotinsky, Vladimir. *Izbrannoe*. Jerusalem: Biblioteka-Aliya, 1989.
Jabotinsky, Vladimir. *Taryag Millim*. Jerusalem: Eri Jabotinsky, 1950.
Jabotinsky, Zeev. "Civitaveccia." *Hayarden*, 10.12.1935, 2.
Jabotinsky, Zeev. "Hamitologia Shel Kna'an." *Bamaḥane*, 21.8.1931, 2.
Jabotinsky, Zeev. "Israel un Carthage." *Haynt*, 22.1.1932, 5–6.
Jabotinsky, Zeev. "Iśrael Ṿeḳartago." *Ḥazit Ha'am*, 5.2.1932, 1.

Jabotinsky, Zeev. "Mitologie fun Knaan." *Der Morgn Zhurnal*, 19.7.1931, 5.
Jacobson, Abigail, and Moshe Naor. *Oriental Neighbors: Middle Eastern Jews and Arabs in Mandatory Palestine*. Waltham: Brandeis University Press, 2016.
Jossua, Jean-Pierre. "En causant avec Edward Kaplan" (unpublished).
Kabha, Muṣṭafa and Naḥum Ḳarlinski. "Mitaḥarut Ledu-Leumiyut: Haparde-sanut Ha'aravit-Falesṭinit Vehayehudit-Tsionit Biteḳufat Hamandaṭ." *Iśrael* 27–28, 2021, 137–164.
Kaplan, Eran. *Beyond Post-Zionism*. Albany: State University of New York Press, 2015.
Kaplan, Eran. "Decadent Pioneers: Land, Space and Gender in Zionist Revisionist Thought." *Journal of Israeli History* 20 (1), 2001, 1–23.
Kaplan, Eran. *The Jewish Radical Right: Revisionist Zionism and its Ideological Legacy*. Madison: University of Wisconsin Press, 2005.
Kaplan, Eran. "A Rebel with a Cause: Hillel Kook, Begin and Jabotinsky's Ideological Legacy." *Israel Studies* 10 (3), 2005, 87–103.
Ḳarpel, Dalia. "'Uzzi Ornan 'Adain Lo Viter 'Al Ḥalom Haleom Haiśreeli." *Haarets*, 21.5.2015.
Ḳassuṭo, Moshe David. *Haela 'Anat: Shire 'Alila Kna'aniim Mitḳufat Heavot*. Jerusalem: Bialik Institute, 1958.
Kats, Amnon. "Me'aravim—Le'ivrim," in Yonatan Raṭosh (ed.), *Minitsaḥon Lemapolet: Measef* Alef. Tel Aviv: Hadar, 1976, 83–89.
Kats, Shmuel. *Jabo: Biografiia Shel Zeev Jabotinsky*, volume 2. Tel Aviv: Dvir, 1993.
Katz, Ethan B., Lisa Moses Leff, and Maud S. Mandel, "Introduction: Engaging Colonial History and Jewish History," in Ethan B. Katz, Lisa Moses Leff, and Maud S. Mandel (eds.), *Colonialism and the Jews*. Bloomington and Indianapolis: Indiana University Press, 2017, 1–25.
Katz, Ethan B., Lisa Moses Leff, and Maud S. Mandel (eds.). *Colonialism and the Jews*. Bloomington and Indianapolis: Indiana University Press, 2017.
Katz, Gideon. "The Israeli *Kulturkampf*." *Israel Affairs* 14 (2), 2008, 237–254.
Katz, Shmuel. *Lone Wolf: A Biography of Vladimir (Zeev) Jabotinsky*, vol. II. New York: Barricade Books, 1996.
Kaufman, Asher. *Reviving Phoenicia: The Search for Identity in Lebanon*. London: Tauris, 2004.
Kaufman, Asher. "'Tell Us Our History': Charles Corm, Mount Lebanon and Lebanese Nationalism." *Middle Eastern Studies* 40 (3), 2004, 1–28.
Kaufmann, Yehezkel. *The Religion of Israel from Its Beginnings to the Babylonian Exile* (tr. and abr. Moshe Greenberg). London: George Allen & Unwin, 1961.
Kelley, Donald R. "Ideas of Periodization in the West," in Q. Edward Wang and Franz L. Fillafer (eds.), *The Many Faces of Clio: Cross-Cultural approaches to Historiography, Essays in Honor of Georg G. Iggers*. New York, Oxford: Berghahn Books, 2007, 17–27.
Ḳenan, 'Amos. "'Ivrim Velo Tsabarim," in Nurit Gerts and Rachel Weisbrod (eds.), *Haḳvutsa Hakna'anit—Sifrut Veideologia*. Tel Aviv: Open University, 1986, 42–43.

Ḳenan, Yonatan [Ratosh]. "Izmel Yehudi Babe'aya Ha'ivrit." *Alef,* December 1952, 4–5.

Kennedy, Michael, and Ronald Grigor Suny. "Introduction," in Ronald Grigor Suny and Michael D. Kennedy (eds.), *Intellectuals and the Articulation of the Nation.* Ann Arbor: University of Michigan Press, 1999, 1–51.

Keren, Michael. *Ben-Gurion and the Intellectuals: Power, Knowledge, and Charisma.* DeKalb: Northern Illinois University Press, 1983.

Keren, Michael. *The Pen and the Sword: Israeli Intellectuals and the Making of the Nation-State.* Boulder and London: Westview, 1989.

Khalidi, Rashid. *Palestinian Identity: The Construction of Modern National Consciousness.* New York: Columbia University Press, 1997.

Khazzoom, Aziza. "The Great Chain of Orientalism: Jewish Identity, Stigma Management, and Ethnic Exclusion in Israel." *American Sociological Review* 68 (4), August 2003, 481–510.

Kimmerling, Baruch. "Between the Primordial and the Civil Definitions of the Collective Identity: *Eretz Israel* or the State of Israel?," in Eric Cohen, Moshe Lissak and Uri Almagor (eds.), *Comparative Social Dynamics: Essays in Honor of S. N. Eisenstadt.* Boulder and London: Westview, 1985, 262–283.

Kimmerling, Baruch. *The Invention and Decline of Israeliness: State, Society, and the Military,* Berkeley, Los Angeles, London: University of California Press, 2005.

Kimmerling, Baruch. *Zionism and Territory: The Socio-Territorial Dimensions of Zionist Politics.* Berkeley: Institute of International Studies, University of California, 1983.

Knapp, Steven. "Collective Memory and the Actual Past." *Representations* 26, 1989, 123–149.

Koehler, Ludwig, and Walter Baumgartner. *The Hebrew and Aramaic Lexicon of the Old Testament.* Leiden: Brill, 1994.

Konrád, George and Ivan Szelényi. *The Intellectuals on the Road to Class Power* (tr. Andrew Arato and Richard E. Allen). Brighton: Harvester, 1979.

Kook, Rebecca. "Hillel Kook: Revisionism and Rescue," in Mark LeVine and Gershon Shafir (eds.), *Struggle and Survival in Palestine/Israel.* Berkeley, Los Angeles, London: University of California Press, 2012, 157–169.

Kook, Rebecca (ed.). *Hillel Kook / Shmuel Merlin: Hitkatvut, 1965–1986.* Haifa: University of Haifa Press, 2022.

Koselleck, Reinhart. *Futures Past: On the Semantics of Historical Time* (tr. Keith Tribe). Cambridge and London: MIT Press, 1985.

Kupfert Heller, Daniel. *Jabotinsky's Children: Polish Jews and the Rise of Right-Wing Zionism.* Princeton: Princeton University Press, 2017.

Kurzman Charles, and Lynn Owens. "The Sociology of Intellectuals." *Annual Review of Sociology* 28, 2002, 63–90.

Kurzweil, Baruch. *Bamaavaḳ 'Al 'Erke Hayahadut.* Tel Aviv: Schocken, 1969.

Kurzweil, Baruch. "Ha'ḥidush' Bemered Ha''ivrim-Haḥadishim.'" *Beṭerem,* 1.1.1948, 13–15.

Kurzweil, Baruch. "The New 'Canaanites' in Israel." *Judaism* 2 (1), 1953, 3–15.

Kurzweil, Baruch. *Sifrutenu Heḥadasha—Hemshekh o Mahapekha?* Tel Aviv: Schocken, 1965.

Kuzar, Ron. *Hebrew and Zionism: A Discourse Analytic Cultural Study*. Berlin, New York: Mouton de Gruyter, 2001.

Laor, Dan. *Hamaavaḳ 'Al Hazikaron: Masot 'Al Sifrut, Ḥevra Ṿetarbut*. Tel Aviv: 'Am 'Oved, 2009.

Laor Dan (ed.). *Yonatan Raṭosh: Mivḥar Maamre Biḳoret 'Al Yetsirato*. Tel Aviv: 'Am 'Oved, 1983.

Lapidus, Ira M. "*Arabs, Islam and the Arab Caliphate in the Early Middle Ages* by E. A. Belyaev; A. Gourevitch." *International Journal of Middle Eastern Studies* 2 (1), 1971, 86–87.

Leoussi Athena S., and Steven Grosby (eds.). *Nationalism and Ethnosymbolism: History, Culture and Ethnicity in the Formation of Nations*. Edinburgh: Edinburgh University Press, 2007.

Lévi-Strauss, Claude. *The Savage Mind*. London: Weidenfeld and Nicolson, 1966.

"L'Histoire du Betar en France." *Revue de la France Libre*, February 1951.

Libes, Yehuda. "Mitos Tiḳun Haelohut: Ḳabalat Hazohar Ṿeshirat Raṭosh." *Alpaim* 7, 1993, 8–26.

Liebman Charles, and Eliezer Don-Yehiya. "What a Jewish State Means to Israeli Jews," in Sam Lehman-Wilzig and Bernard Susser (eds.), *Comparative Jewish Politics: Public Life in Israel and the Diaspora*. Ramat-Gan: Bar-Ilan University, 1981, 101–109.

Likhovski, Assaf. "Post-post-Zionist Historiography." *Israel Studies* 15 (2), 2010, 1–23.

Lin, Nimrod. "'Al Ma Anaḥnu Medabrim Kesheanu Medabrim 'Al Medina? Maḥshavat Hamdina Hatsiyonit Biteḳufat Hamandaṭ Habriṭi." *Iśrael* 27–28, 2021, 187–212.

Lisak, Moshe. "Sotsiologim 'Biḳortiim' Ṿesotsiologim 'Mimsadiim' Baḳehila Haaḳademit Haiśreelit: Maavaḳim Ideologiim O Śiaḥ Aḳademi 'Inyani?," in Avi Bareli and Pinḥas Ginossar (eds.), *Tsiyonut: Pulmus Ben Zmanenu—Gishot Meḥḳariyot Ṿeideologiyot*. Śde Boḳer: Ben-Gurion University, 1996, 60–98.

Madelung, Wilferd. "*Arabs, Islam and the Arab Caliphate in the Early Middle Ages* by E. A. Belyaev; Adolphe Gourevitch." *Journal of Near Eastern Studies* 31 (2), 1972, 128–129.

Marino, Andy. *A Quiet American: The Secret War of Varian Fry*. New York: St. Martin's, 1999.

Marrus Michael R., and Robert O. Paxton, *Vichy France and the Jews*. Stanford: Stanford University Press, 1995.

Masri, Mazen. *The Dynamics of Exclusionary Constitutionalism: Israel as a Jewish and Democratic State*. Oxford: Hart, 2017.

Matossian, Mary. "Ideologies of Delayed Development," in John Hutchinson and Anthony D. Smith (eds.), *Nationalism*. Oxford: Oxford University Press, 1994, 218–225.

Medoff, Rafael. *Militant Zionism in America: The Rise and Impact of the Jabotinsky Movement in the United States, 1926–1948*. Tuscaloosa and London: University of Alabama Press, 2002.

Medoff, Rafael, and David Wyman. *A Race against Death: Peter Bergson, America, and the Holocaust*. New York: New Press, 2002.

Merlin, Shmuel. "Towards Collapse or Prosperity; Problems of Israel's Economic Independence—Analysis and Outline of a Solution," 12.5.1949 (HKA/8).

Miller, Orna. "'Habaṭalion Heḥatukh' Vehanṭiyot Ha'kna'aniyot' BaETZEL Uvitnu'at Haḥerut—Me'hava'ad Ha'ivri' 'Ad 'Lamerḥav': Opozitsiya Lehanhagat HaETZEL Ve'Ḥerut.'" *'Iyunim Bitḳumat Iśrael* 14, 2004, 153–189.

Miron, Dan. "Modern Hebrew Literature: Zionist Perspectives and Israeli Realities." *Prooftexts* 4 (1), 1984, 49–69.

Miron, Dan. "Trumato Shel Zeev Jabotinsky Lashira Ha'ivrit Hamodernit," in Avi Bareli and Pinḥas Ginossar (eds.), *Ish Basa'ar: Masot Umeḥḳarim 'Al Zeev Jabotinsky*. Śde Boḳer: Ben-Gurion University, 2004, 187–251.

Molavi, Shourideh C. *Stateless Citizenship: The Palestinian-Arab Citizens of Israel*. Leiden—Boston: Brill, 2013.

Morris, Benny. "Israel and the Lebanese Phalange: The Birth of a Relationship, 1948–1951." *Studies in Zionism* 5 (1), 1984, 125–144.

Morris, Benny. *Righteous Victims: A History of the Zionist-Arab Conflict, 1881–2001*. New York: Vintage, 2001.

Motyl, Alexander J. *Revolutions, Nations, Empires: Conceptual Limits and Theoretical Possibilities*. New York: Columbia University Press, 1999.

Moyn, Samuel. *A Holocaust Controversy: The Treblinka Affair in Postwar France*. Hanover and London: Brandeis University Press, 2005.

Muracciole, Jean-François. *Les Français Libres, l'Autre Résistance*. Paris: Tallandier, 2013.

Nadel, Baruch. "'Mea Milion Ha'aravim'—Lo Mea Milion Velo 'Aravim." *Yedi'ot Aḥaronot*, 8.7.1970, 17.

Naor, Arye. "The Leader as a Poet: The Political and Ideological Poetry of Ze'ev Jabotinsky." *Israel Affairs* 20 (2), 2014, 161–181.

Nathans, Benjamin. *Beyond the Pale: The Jewish Encounter with Late Imperial Russia*. Berkeley, Los Angeles, London: University of California Press, 2002.

Nehor, Asher. "'Umma 'Ivrit'—Mahi?" *Ḥerut*, 19.8.1949, 5.

Neuberger, Benjamin. "State and Nation in African Thought," in John Hutchinson and Anthony D. Smith (eds.), *Nationalism*. Oxford: Oxford University Press, 1994, 231–235.

Neuman, Kalman. "Political Hebraism and the Early Modern 'Respublica Hebraeorum': On Defining the Field." *Hebraic Political Studies* 1 (1), 2005, 57–70.

O'Connor, Kaori. "Cuisine, Nationality and the Making of a National Meal: The English Breakfast," in Susana Carvalho and François Gemenne (eds.). *Nations and Their Histories: Constructions and Representations*. Basingstoke: Palgrave Macmillan, 2009, 157–171.

Oḥana, Daṿid. *Lo Kna'anim, Lo Tsalbanim: Meḳorot Hamitologia Haiśreelit.* Jerusalem: Keter, 2008.

Ohana, David. *The Origins of Israeli Mythology: Neither Canaanites nor Crusaders* (tr. David Maisel). New York: Cambridge University Press, 2012.

Oren, Itsḥaḳ, and Michael Zand (eds.). *Kratkaia Evreiskaia Entsiklopediia.* Jerusalem: Keter, 1976–2005.

Ornan, 'Uzzi. "Anaḥnu Kna'anim: Śiḥot 'Im Prof. 'Uzzi Ornan." *Svivot,* December 1994, 61–73.

Ornan, 'Uzzi. "Shoat Haḥinukh." *Svivot,* December 1994, 74–77.

Osheroff, Nili. *Yotse Min Haklalim—'Uzzi Ornan: Sipur Ḥaim.* Jerusalem: Carmel, 2015.

Ostermann, Josef. "Apologia." *Haḥevra* 2 (23–24), December 1941, 325–326, 336.

Ostermann, Josef. "Ben 'Ivriyut Leyahadut." *Haḥevra* 2 (19–20), October 1941, 300–301.

Ostermann, Josef. "Hamitos Shel Bene 'Ever." *Haḥevra* 2 (21–22), November 1941, 319–320.

Panné, Jean-Louis. *Boris Souvarine: le premier désenchanté du communisme.* Paris: Robert Laffont, 1993.

Peck, Sarah E. "The Campaign for an American Response to the Nazi Holocaust." *Journal of Contemporary History* 15 (2), 1980, 367–400.

Peled, Yoav, and Horit Herman Peled. *The Religionization of Israeli Society.* Abingdon: Routledge, 2019.

Penkower, Monty Noam. "In Dramatic Dissent: The Bergson Boys." *American Jewish History,* 1.3.1981, 281–309.

Penkower, Monty Noam. "Vladimir (Ze'ev) Jabotinsky, Hillel Kook-Peter Bergson and the Campaign for a Jewish Army." *Modern Judaism* 31 (3), 2011, 1–43.

Penslar, Derek. "Shlomo Sand's *The Invention of the Jewish People* and the End of the New History." *Israel Studies* 17 (2), 2012, 156–168.

Penslar, Derek J. "Is Zionism a Colonial Movement?," in Ethan B. Katz, Lisa Moses Leff, and Maud S. Mandel (eds.), *Colonialism and the Jews.* Bloomington and Indianapolis: Indiana University Press, 2017, 275–300.

Penslar, Derek J. "What We Talk About When We Talk about Colonialism," in Ethan B. Katz, Lisa Moses Leff, and Maud S. Mandel (eds.), *Colonialism and the Jews.* Bloomington and Indianapolis: Indiana University Press, 2017, 327–340.

Penslar, Derek J. "Zionism, Colonialism and Postcolonialism," in Anita Shapira and Derek J. Penslar (eds.), *Israeli Historical Revisionism: From Left to Right.* London and Portland: Frank Cass, 2003, 84–98.

Penslar, Derek Jonathan. "What if a Christian State Had Been Established in Modern Palestine?," in Gavriel D. Rosenfeld (ed.), *What Ifs of Jewish History.* Cambridge: Cambridge University Press, 2017, 142–164.

Pesaḥ, Ḥaim. "'Ezra Pound, Yonatan Raṭosh Ṿehashira Ṿehaideologia Hakna'anit." *Moznaim* 24 (3–4), February–March 1982.

Petrovsky-Shtern, Yohanan. *The Golden Age Shtetl: A New History of Jewish Life in East Europe*. Princeton and Oxford: Princeton University Press, 2014.

Pinto, Vincenzo. "Between *Imago* and *Res*: The Revisionist-Zionist Movement's Relationship with Fascist Italy, 1922–1938." *Israel Affairs* 10 (3), 2004, 90–109.

Piterberg, Gabriel. *The Returns of Zionism: Myths, Politics and Scholarship in Israel*. London and New York: Verso, 2008.

Piterberg, Gabriel. "The Zionist Settlement in Palestine as Settler Colonialism: The Formative Impact of the German Project in the Ostmark." *Orient: German Journal for Politics, Economics and Culture of the Middle East* 2, 2013, 24–29.

Polaḳ, A. N. *Kazariah: Toledot Mamlakha Yehudit Beeropa*. Tel Aviv: Bialik Institute, 1951.

Polaḳ, Av. N. "Tefisat Hahisṭoria Ha'ivrit—Keytsad?" *Beṭerem*, January 1950, 35–40.

Potter, David M. *The South and the Sectional Conflict*. Baton Rouge: Louisiana State University Press, 1968.

Porat, Yehoshu'a. "Kna'aniyut 'Ivrit Ukhna'aniyut 'Arvit," in Dani Ya'aḳobi (ed.), *Erets Aḥat Ushe 'Amim Ba*. Jerusalem: Magnes, 1999, 84–88.

Porat, Yehoshu'a. *Shelaḥ Ve'eṭ Beyado: Sipur Ḥayav Shel Uriel Shelaḥ (Yonatan Raṭosh)*. Tel Aviv: Maḥbarot Lesifrut, 1989.

"qibla," *Encyclopaedia of Islam*, 2nd ed.

Rabbabi, Elias. "Al Tiṭ'u Bazehut," in Yonatan Raṭosh, *1967—Uma Hal'a?* Tel Aviv: Ḥermon, 1967, 89–91.

Rabin, Elliott. "'Hebrew' Culture: The Shared Foundations of Ratosh's Ideology and Poetry." *Modern Judaism* 19 (2), 1999, 119–132.

Rainey, Anson F. "Who Is a Canaanite? A Review of the Textual Evidence." *Bulletin of the American Schools of Oriental Research* 304, 1996, 1–15.

Ram, Uri. *Israeli Nationalism: Social Conflicts and the Politics of Knowledge*. London and New York: Routledge, 2011.

Ram, Uri. "Why Secularism Fails? Secular Nationalism and Religious Revivalism in Israel." *International Journal of Politics, Culture and Society* 21 (1/4), 2008, 57–73.

Rapaport, Louis. *Shake Heaven and Earth: Peter Bergson and the Struggle to Save the Jews of Europe*. Jerusalem: Gefen, 1999.

Raṭosh, Yonatan. "Ketav El Hano'ar Ha'ivri," in Yonatan Raṭosh, *Reshit Hayamim: Petiḥot 'Ivriyot*. Tel Aviv: Hadar, 1982, 32–37.

Raṭosh, Yonatan. "Melekh Iśrael Harishon: Milḥemet Hashiḥrur Shel Shaul Ha'ivri," in Yonatan Raṭosh, *Reshit Hayamim: Petiḥot 'Ivriyot*. Tel Aviv: Hadar, 1982, 111–127.

Raṭosh, Yonatan. *Mikhtavim (1937–1980)*. Tel Aviv: Hadar, 1986.

Raṭosh, Yonatan. *1967—Uma Hal'a?*, Tel Aviv: Ḥermon, 1967.

Raṭosh, Yonatan. *Reshit Hayamim: Petiḥot 'Ivriyot*. Tel Aviv: Hadar, 1982.

Raṭosh, Yonatan. "Shira Ṿeideologia (b): Kakh Hayiti Le'kna'ani.'" *Yedi'ot Aḥaronot*, 20.2.1981, 23.

Rayski, Adam. *The Choice of the Jews Under Vichy: Between Submission and Resistance* (tr. Will Sayers), Notre Dame: University of Notre Dame Press, 2005.

Raz-Krakotzkin, Amnon. "Exile, History, and the Nationalization of Jewish Memory: Some Reflections on the Zionist Notion of History and Return," *Journal of Levantine Studies* 3 (2), 2013, 37–70.

Red-Or, A. "Haḳdama," in 'A. G. Ḥoron, *Erets-Haḳedem: Madrikh Hisṭori Umdini Lamizraḥ Haḳarov*. Tel Aviv: Ḥermon, 1970, III–VIII.

Rejwan, Nissim. *Israel in Search of Identity: Reading the Formative Years*. Gainesville: University Press of Florida, 1999.

Rin, Svi. "The Narrative Literature in the Bible" (Svi Rin Archive, Genazim Institute, file 395/k-11).

Roberts, Sophie. *Citizenship and Antisemitism in French Colonial Algeria, 1870–1962*. Cambridge: Cambridge University Press, 2017.

Robinson, Shira. *Citizen Strangers: Palestinians and the Birth of Israel's Liberal Settler State*. Stanford: Stanford University Press, 2013.

Rotem, Sh. [Moshe Giora Elimelekh]. "Mashber Haknesiya Hatsiyonit," in Nurit Gerts and Rachel Weisbrod (eds.), *Haḳvutsa Hakna'anit—Sifrut Ṿeideologia*. Tel Aviv: Open University, 1986, 40–41.

Rowe, John H. "The Renaissance Foundations of Anthropology." *American Anthropologist* 67, 1965, 1–20.

S. G. [Serge Halperin?]. "Méditerranée." *Le Cran* 2, January 1931, 1–4.

Said, Edward. *Orientalism*. New York: Vintage, 1994.

Sand, Shlomo. *The Invention of the Jewish People*. London: Verso, 2009.

Sand, Shlomo. *The Invention of the Land of Israel*. London: Verso, 2012.

Saposnik, Arieh B. *Becoming Hebrew: The Creation of a Jewish National Culture in Ottoman Palestine*. Oxford: Oxford University Press, 2008.

Saposnik, Arye Bruce. "Advertisement or Achievement? American Jewry and the Campaign for a Jewish Army, 1939–1944: A Reassessment." *Journal of Israeli History* 17 (2), 1996, 193–220.

Schaebler, Birgit. "Writing the Nation in the Arabic-Speaking World, Nationally and Transnationally," in Stefan Berger (ed.), *Writing the Nation: A Global Perspective*. Basingstoke: Palgrave Macmillan, 2007, 179–196.

Schechtman, Joseph B. *Rebel and Statesman: The Vladimir Jabotinsky Story—The Early Years*. New York: Thomas Yoseloff, 1956.

Schechtman, Joseph B. *Rebel and Statesman: The Vladimir Jabotinsky Story—The Last Years*. New York: Thomas Yoseloff, 1961.

Schulze, Kristen E. *Israel's Covert Diplomacy in Lebanon*. Basingstoke: Macmillan, 1998.

Segal, Iśrael. "'Ivrim' Ṿ'ihudim': Giglulaṿ Shel Re'ayon." *Haḥevra* 7 (82), March 1947, 186–188.

Sen, Alice. "Slida 'Amuḳa," letter to *Haarets* Friday supplement, 12.5.2000, 4.

Seshan, Radhika. "Writing the Nation in India: Communalism and Historiography," in Stefan Berger (ed.), *Writing the Nation: A Global Perspective*. Basingstoke: Palgrave Macmillan, 2007, 155–178.

Shamir, Ziva. *Lehatḥil Mealef: Shirat Raṭosh, Meḳoriyuta Umeḳoroteha*. Tel Aviv: Haḳibbuts Hameuḥad, 1993.

Shapira, Anita. "Ben-Gurion and the Bible: The Forging of an Historical Narrative?" *Middle Eastern Studies* 33 (4), 1997, 645–674.

Shapira, Anita. "The Bible and Israeli Identity." *AJS Review* 28 (1), 2004, 11–42.

Shapira, Avraham. "Spiritual Rootlessness and Circumscription to the 'Here and Now' in the *Sabra* World View." *Israel Affairs* 4 (3–4), 1998, 103–131.

Shatz, Adam (ed.). *Prophets Outcast: A Century of Dissident Jewish Writing about Zionism and Israel*. New York: Nation Books, 2004.

Shavit, Yaacov. "Archaeology, Political Culture, and Culture in Israel," in Neil Asher Silberman and David B. Small (eds.), *The Archaeology of Israel: Constructing the Past, Interpreting the Present*. Sheffield: Sheffield Academic, 1997, 48–61.

Shavit, Yaacov. "Hebrews and Phoenicians: An Ancient Historical Image and Its Usage." *Studies in Zionism* 5 (2), 1984, 157–180.

Shavit, Yaacov. *The New Hebrew Nation: A Study in Israeli Heresy and Fantasy*. London: Frank Cass, 1987.

Shaviṭ, Ya'aḳov. "Hayaḥasim Ben Idea Lepoetiḳa Beshirato Shel Yonatan Raṭosh." *Hasifrut* 17, 1974, 66–91.

Shaviṭ, Ya'aḳov. *Me'ivri 'Ad Kna'ani—Praḳim Betoldot Haideologia Ṿehauṭopia Shel "Hatḥiya Ha'ivrit": Mitsiyonut Radiḳalit Leanṭi-Tsiyonut*. Jerusalem: Domino, 1984.

Shechtman, Joseph B. *Zeev Jabotinsky: Parshat Ḥayaṿ; Sefer Shlishi: 1935–1940*. Tel Aviv: Ḳarni, 1959.

Sheleg, Yair. "Hakna'ani Harishon." *Haarets* (Friday supplement), 28.4.2000, 47–50.

Shifra, Sh. [Shifra Shmulevitch]. "Shira Keḥubba" (an interview with Yonatan Ratosh), *Davar*, 27.8.1971, 12, 14.

Shilon, Avi. "Milḥemet Sheshet Hayamim Ṿehit'orerut Hara'ayon Hakna'ani." *'Iyunim Bitḳumat Iśrael*, 11, 2017, 102–129.

Shim'oni, Gide'on. "Haleumiyut Hayehudit Kileumiyut Etnit," in Yehuda Reinharz, Yossef Shalmon and Gide'on Shim'oni (eds.), *Leumiyut Ṿepolitiḳa Yehudit: Perspeḳṭivot Ḥadashot*. Jerusalem: Zalman Shazar Center, 1997, 81–92.

Shimoni, Gideon. *The Zionist Ideology*. Hanover and London: Brandeis University Press, 1995.

Shindler, Colin. *The Rise of the Israeli Right: From Odessa to Hebron*. New York: Cambridge University Press, 2015.

Shlaim, Avi. *Lion of Jordan: The Life of King Hussein in War and Peace*. London: Allen Lane, 2007.

Shlaim, Avi. *The Iron Wall: Israel and the Arab World*. New York: Norton, 2000.

Silberman, Neil A. "Structuring the Past: Israelis, Palestinians, and the Symbolic Authority of Archaeological Monuments," in Neil Asher Silberman and David B. Small (eds.), *The Archaeology of Israel: Constructing the Past, Interpreting the Present*. Sheffield: Sheffield Academic, 1997, 62–81.

Silberman, Neil Asher. *Between Past and Present: Archaeology, Ideology, and Nationalism in the Modern Middle East*. New York: Henry Holt, 1989.

Silberman, Neil Asher, and David B. Small (eds.), *The Archaeology of Israel: Constructing the Past, Interpreting the Present*. Sheffield: Sheffield Academic, 1997.

Silberstein, Laurence J. "*The New Hebrew Nation: A Study in Israeli Heresy and Fantasy* by Yaakov Shavit; *The Slopes of Lebanon* by Amos Oz; *Jewish Theocracy* by Gershon Weiler; *HaHeshbon HaLeumi* by Boas Evron." *International Journal of Middle Eastern Studies* 23 (4), 1991, 686–693.

Silberstein, Laurence J. *The Postzionism Debates: Knowledge and Power in Israeli Culture*. New York and London: Routledge, 1999.

Smith, Anthony D. "Ethnic Myths and Ethnic Revivals." *European Journal of Sociology* 25 (2), 1984, 283–305.

Smith, Anthony D. *Myths and Memories of the Nation*. Oxford and New York: Oxford University Press, 1999.

Sohar, Esra. *A Concubine in the Middle East: American-Israeli Relations* (tr. Laurence Weinbaum). Jerusalem: Gefen, 1999.

Sofer, Sasson. *Zionism and the Foundations of Israeli Diplomacy*. New York: Cambridge University Press, 1998.

Sprinzak, Ehud. *Ish Hayashar: I-Legalism Baḥevra Haiśreelit*. Tel Aviv: Sifriyat Po'alim, 1986.

Steir-Livny, Liat, and Ya'aḳov Shaviṭ. "Yonatan Raṭosh, 'Hakna'anim' Ṿeyaḥasam Lashoa, 1943–1953," in Dina Porat and Aviva Ḥalamish (eds.), *Shoa Mimerḥaḳ Tavo: Ishim Bayishuv Haerets-Iśreeli Ṿeyaḥasam Lanatsizm Ṿelashoa, 1933–1948*. Jerusalem: Yad Ben Tsvi, 2009.

Suleiman, Yasir. *The Arabic Language and National Identity: A Study in Ideology*. Washington: Georgetown University Press, 2003.

Suny Ronald G., and Michael D. Kennedy. "Toward a Theory of National Intellectual Practice," in Ronald Grigor Suny and Michael D. Kennedy (eds.), *Intellectuals and the Articulation of the Nation*. Ann Arbor: University of Michigan Press, 1999, 383–417.

Suny, Ronald Grigor, and Michael D. Kennedy (eds.). *Intellectuals and the Articulation of the Nation*. Ann Arbor: University of Michigan Press, 1999.

Tamir, Dan. "'Dictate More, for We Should Obey Your Orders!' Cult of the Leader in Inter-War Hebrew Fascism." *Politics, Religion and Ideology* 14 (4), 2013, 449–467.

Tamir, Dan. *Hebrew Fascism in Palestine, 1922–1942*. Basingstoke: Palgrave Macmillan, 2018.

Tamir, Dan. "Some Thoughts about Hebrew Fascism in Inter-War Palestine." *Zeitschrift für Religions- und Geistesgeschichte* 63 (4), 2011, 364–381.

Tekiner, Roselle. "Race and the Issue of National Identity in Israel." *International Journal of Middle Eastern Studies* 23 (1), 1991, 39–55.

Teller, Judd L. "Modern Hebrew Literature of Israel." *Middle East Journal* 7 (2), 1953, 182–195.

Thompson, Elizabeth F. "Moving Zionism to Asia: Texts and Tactics of Colonial Settlement, 1917–1921," in Ethan B. Katz, Lisa Moses Leff, and Maud S. Mandel (eds.), *Colonialism and the Jews*. Bloomington and Indianapolis: Indiana University Press, 2017, 317–326.

Tsurumi, Taro. "Jewish Liberal, Russian Conservative: Daniel Pasmanik between Zionism and the Anti-Bolshevik White Movement." *Jewish Social Studies: History, Culture, Society* 21 (1), 2015, 151–80.

Tsvat Rishona: Hamo'adon Lemaḥshava 'Ivrit, Diyunim Ukhtavim, 1966 (n.d., n.p.).

Tydor Baumel, Judith. *The "Bergson Boys" and the Origins of Contemporary Zionist Militancy*. Syracuse: Syracuse University Press, 2005.

Tydor Baumel, Judith. "The IZL Delegation in the USA 1939–1948: Anatomy of an Ethnic Interest/Protest Group." *Jewish History* 9 (1), 1995, 79–89.

Valdés, Mario J. *A Ricoeur Reader: Reflection and Imagination*. Hemel Hempstead: Harvester Wheatsheaf, 1991.

Vater, Roman. "Beyond Bi-Nationalism? The Young Hebrews versus the 'Palestinian Issue.'" *Journal of Political Ideologies* 21 (1), 2016, 45–60.

Vater, Roman. "Down with Britain, Away with Zionism: The 'Canaanites' and 'Lohamey Herut Israel' between Two Adversaries." *Melilah* 10, 2013, 26–45.

Vater, Roman. "Hebrew as a Political Instrument: Language-Planning by the 'Canaanites.'" *Journal of Semitic Studies* 62 (2), 2017, 485–511.

Vater, Roman. "Neither Canaanites nor Post-Zionists: Fighting for a Civic Israel," in Shai Feraro, Ofri Krischer (eds.), *New Studies on the Young Hebrews Movement*. Brill, forthcoming 2024.

Vater, Roman. "Pathways of Early Post-Zionism," in Frank Jacob and Sebastian Kunze (eds.), *Jewish Radicalisms: Historical Perspectives on a Phenomenon of Global Modernity*, Berlin and Boston: de Gruyter Oldenbourg, 2020, 23–74.

Veracini, Lorenzo. "What Can Settler Colonial Studies Offer to an Interpretation of the Conflict in Israel-Palestine?" *Settler Colonial Studies* 5 (3), 2015, 268–271.

Verdery, Katherine. "Civil Society or Nation? 'Europe' in the Symbolism of Romania's Postsocialist Politics," in Ronald Grigor Suny and Michael D. Kennedy (eds.), *Intellectuals and the Articulation of the Nation*. Ann Arbor: University of Michigan Press, 1999, 301–340.

Vidaković Petrov, Krinka. "Memory and Oral Tradition," in Thomas Butler (ed.), *Memory: History, Culture and the Mind*. Oxford, New York: Basil Blackwell, 1989, 77–96.

Vital, David. "Zionism as Revolution? Zionism as Rebellion?" *Modern Judaism* 18, 1998, 205–215.

Warsoff, Louis A. "Citizenship in the State of Israel—A Comment." *New York University Law Review* 33, 1958, 857–861.

Waxman, Chaim I. "Critical Sociology and the End of Ideology in Israel." *Israel Studies* 2 (1), 1997, 194–210.

Weinryb, Bernard D. "The Lost Generation in Israel." *Middle East Journal* 7 (4), 1953, 415–429.

White, Hayden. *The Practical Past*. Evanston: Northwestern University Press, 2014.

White, Hayden V. *Metahistory: The Historical Imagination in Nineteenth-Century Europe*. Baltimore: Johns Hopkins University Press, 1973.

van der Wusten, Herman. "The Occurrence of Successful and Unsuccessful Nationalisms," in Ronald J. Johnston, David B. Knight and Eleonore Kofman (eds.), *Nationalism, Self-Determination and Political Geography*. London, New York, Sydney: Croom Helm, 1988, 189–202.

Wyman, David S. "The Bergson Group, America, and the Holocaust: A Previously Unpublished Interview with Hillel Kook." *American Jewish History* 89 (1), 2001, 3–34.

Ya'ari, Avraham. *Mas'ot Erets Iśrael*. Tel Aviv: Modan, 1996.

Ya'ari, Ehud. "Muḥammad Be'enaim Marksisṭiyot." *Davar*, 7.7.1970, 7.

Yadgar, Yaacov. *Israel's Jewish Identity Crisis: State and Politics in the Middle East*. Cambridge: Cambridge University Press, 2020.

Yalin-Mor, Natan. *Loḥame Ḥerut Iśrael: Anashim, Re'ayonot, 'Alilot*. Jerusalem: Shiḳmona, 1974.

Yehudai, Ori. *Leaving Zion: Jewish Emigration from Palestine and Israel after World War II*. Cambridge: Cambridge University Press, 2020.

Yoḥana, Sh. [Joanna Shelaḥ-Raṭosh]. "'Adya Zikhrono Livrakha" (Yonatan Ratosh Archive, Genazim Institute, file 719/k-351).

Young, Crawford. "The Colonial Construction of African Nations," in John Hutchinson and Anthony D. Smith (eds.), *Nationalism*. Oxford: Oxford University Press, 1994, 225–231.

Zertal, Idith. *Israel's Holocaust and the Politics of Nationhood*. Cambridge: Cambridge University Press, 2005.

Zerubavel, Yael. *Recovered Roots: Collective Memory and the Making of Israeli National Tradition*. Chicago and London: University of Chicago Press, 1995.

Zilberman, Ifraḥ. "Kna'aniyut Falesṭinit," in Dani Ya'aḳobi (ed.), *Erets Aḥat Ushe 'Amim Ba*. Jerusalem: Magnes, 1999, 96–102.

Zisser, Eyal. "The Maronites, Lebanon and the State of Israel: Early Contacts." *Middle Eastern Studies* 31 (4), 1995, 889–918.

Zouplna, Jan. "The Evolution of a Concept: The Relationship between State and Religion in the Thought of Vladimir Jabotinsky, 1919–1940." *Journal of Modern Jewish Studies* 4 (1), 2005, 13–31.

Zubrzycki, Geneviève. "The Classical Opposition between Civic and Ethnic Models of Nationhood: Ideology, Empirical Reality and Social Scientific Analysis." *Polish Sociological Review* 3, 2002, 275–295.

Index

1948 war, 4, 50–51, 128, 147, 149, 150, 156, 157, 211, 324n156, 346n56

Abraham (biblical figure), 72, 88, 91, 97, 110, 134, 313n196
Abravaya, Haim, 25, 27, 284n26
Acton, Lord, 306n80
"admiration toponyms," 79, 92
Africa, Northern, 55, 58, 72, 78, 83, 87, 89, 102, 104, 107, 114, 133–135, 136, 139–141, 146, 152, 158, 203, 217, 221, 313n198, 315n228, 323n135; Jews in, 60, 92, 118, 129, 135, 216; migrations from, 96, 97–98, 106–108, 126
Aḥad-Ha'am (Asher Hirsch Ginsberg), 16, 183; criticized by Baruch Kurzweil, 13
Aḥimeir, Aba, 38
Albright, William Foxwell, 44
Alef (journal), 4, 5, 54, 56, 65, 67, 182
Algeria, 41, 134, 141, 150, 217; independence war of, 56, 58–59, 60, 140–141, 149, 286n53, 298n200, 322n125. *See also* pieds noirs
'aliya, 122–123, 190; first, 185–186, 318n45, 345–346n56, 347n74; second, 185–186, 193, 336n124, 345–346n56
Amir, Aharon, 4, 15, 16, 25, 55, 61, 64–65, 106, 131, 223, 224, 282n1, 283n17, 299–300n219, 303n6, 342n214. *See also* Club for Hebrew Thought; *Ḳeshet*
Amorites, 98, 103
anti-Semitism, 21, 24, 39–40, 41, 50, 79, 100, 106, 120, 121–122, 130, 137, 171, 180, 188–189, 282n4, 285n40, 316n14, 322n124, 333n83, 333n84
anti-Zionism, 1, 3, 8, 9, 12, 13, 17, 40, 49, 61, 191–192, 198, 210, 215
antiquity, Hebrew, 2, 8, 9–10, 22–23, 28, 32–35, 37, 39–40, 51, 54, 59, 69, 72–115, 123, 124, 163–167, 169, 218–219, 224
'Aql, Sa'īd, 201–202, 204–205, 342n217. *See also* nationalism, Lebanese
Arab League, 56, 139, 143, 145, 147, 159. *See also* Pan-Arabism
Arabian Peninsula, 33, 79, 83, 133–137, 143, 204
"Arabianate" (Arabic-speaking non-Arabs), 145–150, 156–157, 177, 179, 201, 206, 220, 223
Arabs, history of, 132–137, 143–144; statistics of, 136, 142–143, 150, 323n135. *See also* identity, Arab
Arameans, 96

Asher (deity), 103, 110
Asia Institute, 53, 58, 152
Asséo, Edmond, 42–43, 291n120. *See also* "La Renaissance Hébraïque"; *Shem: Revue d'Action Hébraïque*
assimilation, Jewish, 19–21, 23, 39, 46, 49, 120–121, 175, 178, 185, 282n4, 321n112. *See also* Diaspora (Jewish); identity, Jewish
Assyria, 103–105, 108, 112
Astour, Michael, 311–312n171
Avnery, Uri, 59, 196, 198, 211, 213, 288n83, 298n200; attitude to "Canaanism," 40, 41, 290n102, 293n134

Baal (deity), 96–97, 107, 204, 312n181
Babylon, 78, 98, 105, 108–110, 165, 181, 310n152, 317n28
Bartov, Hanoch, 211, 212, 332n72. *See also* Sabras
Bedouins, 79, 83, 84, 129, 133–137; uselessness to Arab nationalism of, 136, 142, 146
Begin, Menachem, 41, 46, 51, 58, 61, 67, 223, 293n135. *See also* Ḥerut (party)
Ben-Eliezer, Arieh, 45
Ben-Gurion, David, 51, 55, 155, 170, 330n38; "Canaanite" tendencies of, 192–193, 330n41, 337n147, 338n148
Ben-Yehuda, Eliezer, 22
"Bene Kna'an" ("Sons of Canaan"), 66
Bérard, Victor, 33, 312n171
Berbers, 78, 102, 107, 114, 118, 135, 140, 141, 146, 298n193, 310n148. *See also* Africa, Northern; Algeria; Maghreb
Bergson, Peter. *See* Kook, Hillel
Betar, 21, 24, 25, 27, 28, 34, 56, 60, 184, 285n40, 296n179; Horon's role in, 23–25, 28, 31–32, 35, 91, 283n19, 286n52, 287n57. *See also* Jabotinsky, Zeev; Revisionism
Bible, 8, 20, 22, 32, 34, 44, 45, 72, 78, 82–84, 92–94, 96–100, 106, 107, 109–110, 127, 133, 167, 177, 181, 184, 186, 313n199, 314n210, 320n97; as historical source, 88, 91, 93–94, 99, 107, 110, 164–165, 169, 195, 224, 293n135, 314n211, 328n10, 338n162
Blumberg, George, 37–40, 42–43, 44, 52, 289n92, 291n121. *See also* "La Renaissance Hébraïque"; *Shem: Revue d'Action Hébraïque*

Canaan (land), 29, 38, 51, 74, 78, 82, 87–88, 91–93, 95–111, 121, 123, 124, 127, 132, 134, 135, 145, 148, 150, 151, 153–154, 182, 183, 203, 210, 307n100, 307n102, 311n160, 333n79; ties to ancient Greece, 100–102, 312n171; *see also* Kedem, Land of
Canaan Union, 158. *See also* Kedem Union
Canaanites (ancient), 28, 31, 33, 55, 72, 74, 94, 95–101, 107, 113–114, 118, 146–148, 164, 185, 325n162, 334n101, 309n137, 312n189; mythology of, 96–97, 99, 101, 103, 109, 134, 164, 289n94, 315n229. *See also* Hebrews (ancient)
Carmichael, Joel, 53
Carthage, 66, 92, 102, 104–106, 113, 118, 129, 140, 146, 315n228. *See also* Africa, Northern; Hannibal
"category error," 14–15, 220
"Center for the Hebrew Youth," 4, 54
Chiha, Michel, 201, 205. *See also* nationalism, Lebanese
Christianity, 58, 76, 82, 84, 91, 120, 121–122, 147, 150, 151, 204, 218,

282n4, 315n229; historiography, Christian, 81–82, 115
Civitavecchia, naval school in, 27–28, 184, 223, 285n40, 287n62. *See also* Betar; seafaring
Club 59, 61–64
Club for Hebrew Guidance, 5, 61, 65. *See also* Ratosh, Yonatan
Club for Hebrew Thought, 4, 61, 64–65, 130–131, 299n217, 326n204. *See also* Amir, Aharon
colonialism, British, 35, 39, 55, 123, 138–140, 158, 199, 217–218, 221, 347n76; French, 55, 123, 136, 139–140, 221
Committee for the Consolidation of the Hebrew Youth, 4, 125, 212. *See also* Ratosh, Yonatan
Copts, 147–148, 324n153. *See also* Egypt; nationalism, Egyptian
Corm, Charles, 201, 204, 341n205, 341n207. *See also* nationalism, Lebanese
criticism, biblical. See *Wissenschaft des Judenthums*
Cyrus (king of Persia), 108–109, 123, 317n28. *See also* Persian Empire, authority legitimacy in

David (king), 82, 91, 96, 103, 110, 127, 159, 170, 338n162
denominational outlook, 109, 114, 115, 122, 123
determinism, environmental, 75, 77, 84, 85, 102, 124, 132, 145, 153–154, 180, 184, 198, 202, 203, 206, 215, 216, 218, 304n39. *See also* identity, national
Diaspora (Jewish), 6, 13–14, 17, 26, 31, 32, 39–40, 46, 55, 82, 90, 92, 112, 118, 121–125, 131, 151, 168–169, 172, 173, 177, 179, 180, 182–186, 189–191, 193, 196, 209–212, 224, 333n83; as a *millet*, 119–120, 124; emergence of, 34, 82, 111, 113–114, 118. *See also* assimilation, Jewish; identity, Jewish
Dinur, Ben-Zion, 164, 328n10
Druze, 126, 129, 148–149, 156–158, 204, 318n45

Egypt, 18, 78, 86, 88, 89, 91, 92, 97–98, 100, 102, 103, 106, 108, 127, 133, 145, 147, 155, 158, 201–202, 324n153, 324n156, 334n101; center of Jewish preaching, 111; ruled by Hyksos, 99–100, 101, 102, 311n159, 311n60. *See also* Copts; nationalism, Egyptian
El (deity), 72, 103
Eliav, Binyamin, 33–34, 41, 288n70
Emergency Rescue Committee, 42
Encyclopaedia Hebraica, Horon's contribution to, 52
Enlightenment, 12, 13, 167, 170–172. *See also* Haskalah
essentialism, 83, 136, 143, 165, 175–176, 219–220. *See also* "category error"
ethnie, 70, 74, 119, 303n20. *See also* identity, national
ethnogenesis. *See* nation formation
ETZEL, 21, 34, 36, 38, 41, 45, 46, 51, 288n83, 293n135. *See also* Betar; Jabotinsky, Zeev; Revisionism
Euphrates, 69, 79, 87–88, 91, 95, 152; Land of, 86, 151. *See also* Kedem, Land of
Evron, Boas, 178, 182, 195–196, 200, 207, 209. *See also* post-Zionism
Exodus (legend), 88, 91, 97, 100, 106, 110, 334n101
Ezra (Scribe), 109, 111, 112, 134, 314n210. *See also* Judaism, emergence of

fascism, 15, 41–42, 81, 139, 206, 285n40

de Gaulle, Charles, 41–42, 44, 59, 65, 140, 150, 286n53
Ghedalia, Leon, 37, 43. *See also* "La Renaissance Hébraïque"; *Shem: Revue d'Action Hébraïque*
"golden age," 10–11, 80, 85, 94–95, 98, 102, 103, 115, 117, 118, 125, 142, 159, 169, 170, 175, 181, 201, 202, 203, 206, 208. *See also* myths, foundational
Gordon, Cyrus H., 311–312n171. *See also* Astour, Michael
Gour, Ada (née Steinberg), 24, 28, 51, 66, 67, 92, 282n6, 285n46, 288n68, 291n121, 298n203
Gourevitch, Arie Noah (Leon), 19–21, 22, 24, 27
Gourevitch, Rachel, 20, 22
Greater Israel Movement, 61, 65, 299–300n219

Hagar (biblical and koranic figure), 133–134
"Hagedor Ha'ivri" ("The Hebrew Order"), 27. *See also* "Rodêgal"
Haḥevra (journal), 40, 290n102, 290n105, 293n134
Halperin, Uriel. *See* Ratosh, Yonatan
Halperine, Serge, 24, 26, 92
Halpern, Yirmiyahu, 27, 45, 223, 284n29. *See also* Civitavecchia, naval school in; seafaring
Hannibal, 106, 135, 315n228. *See also* Carthage
Haskalah (Jewish Enlightenment), 12–15, 162
Hasmonean kingdom, 112, 113, 330n41
Hebrew Committee of National Liberation, 32, 45–53, 55, 61, 125, 162, 164, 178, 187–188, 192, 196, 197, 199, 222, 223, 293n134, 294n144, 337n143, 340n186; Horon's role in, 46–47, 125. *See also* Kook, Hillel; post-Zionism
Hebrews (ancient), 22–23, 28, 31, 32–33, 35, 37, 39, 40, 45, 49, 51, 70, 72–73, 77–115, 118, 126, 133, 137, 147, 150, 158, 184, 201, 203, 206, 220, 284n29, 305n74, 307n95, 307n105, 309n137, 310n145, 311n160, 317n28; decline of, 104–114, 118, 320n97, 332–333n79; emergence of, 69–70, 74, 83, 88–89, 92–93, 95, 99, 102–104; meaning of term, 88; relation to Jews, 81, 83–84, 90, 91, 96, 103, 112–113, 117–118, 175, 192, 308n112
Hebrews (modern), 3, 5, 6, 11, 14, 38, 40, 50, 62–63, 80, 123–128, 140, 144, 150, 153, 179, 180, 182, 183, 191, 203, 209–211, 212–214, 217, 222–224, 308n112, 315n228, 339n175; differentiation from Jews, 40, 46–48, 58, 65–66, 113, 124, 173–174, 175, 187, 188, 190–191, 205, 207, 209–211, 216–217, 293n135; emergence of, 5, 49, 82, 113, 123–126, 161, 181, 182, 185–186, 191, 318n45; statistics of, 125, 212–213, 340n186, 344n30
Hegel (Georg Wilhelm Friedrich), 10, 75, 165, 171, 183
Herder (Johann Gottfried von), 10, 84, 110, 184
Ḥerut (newspaper), 57, 297n188
Ḥerut (party), 46, 51, 57, 61, 188, 223. *See also* Begin, Menachem; ETZEL
Ḥimyar, 114, 118, 134
Hitti, Philip, 205. *See also* nationalism, Lebanese
Holocaust, 43, 44, 45, 49, 120, 123, 125, 164, 211–212, 286n53, 343n22, 343n24; "Canaanite" attitude to, 212
Huizinga, Johann, 165–167

identity, Afrikaner, 217–219, 346n61; Arab, 6, 17, 132–133, 136, 137,

144, 146, 149, 223, 320–321n105; Hebrew, 1, 5–7, 14, 17, 18, 38–40, 48, 65–66, 83, 102, 105, 123–128, 143, 150, 182, 185–186, 190–191, 209–214, 217; Israeli, 7, 17, 18, 125–129, 164, 172, 188–191, 193, 194, 196, 209–217, 225, 343n22, 343n24, 344n32, 344n40; Jewish, 3, 5–7, 14, 17, 21, 31, 38–40, 65–66, 119–125, 167, 172, 175–176, 189–191, 207–211, 216, 225, 278n3, 308–309n121, 321n112, 333n84, 344n40; national, 10, 11–12, 17, 29, 69, 70–77, 79, 84, 106, 119, 141, 152–153, 163, 165, 175–176, 198, 200, 202, 278n8, 302n14, 323n134, 328n5; postcolonial, 215–216

indigeneity, indigenization, 2, 95, 124, 203, 217, 307n105. *See also* identity, postcolonial; settler colonialism

Iran, 91, 102

Iraq, 138, 144, 145, 146, 148

Ishmael (biblical and koranic figure), 133–134, 180. *See also* Hagar

Islam, 55, 76, 83, 104, 115, 136, 138, 142, 146, 148, 150, 151, 201–203, 216, 223, 314n210, 320n94, 321n112, 323n134; emergence of, 134–136, 299n208

Israel (state of), 1–4, 6, 11, 14, 17, 18, 25, 37, 44, 50–66, 86, 88, 105, 123–128, 132, 139, 140–141, 143–145, 147–151, 154–158, 162–164, 169–172, 182, 185–201, 204–206, 207, 210–214, 216, 218, 221, 223–225, 293n135, 294n155, 298n200, 319n68, 327n208, 332n68, 345–346n56; as sectarian-denominational, 52, 56, 85, 122, 127–132, 150–151, 154–155, 172, 176, 178, 182, 194, 196, 200, 207, 212–215, 224–225, 278n3, 319n73, 319n79, 346n57; as settler-colonial, 2, 131, 216–218, 221, 225, 333n88, 345–346n56; citizenship in, 66–67, 126, 129–130, 155, 189, 300–301n234, 339–340n177; education in, 83, 124, 129, 155, 319n71; foreign relations of, 131–132; origins of name, 127; relations with Lebanon, 55–58, 147, 204–205, 342n214

Israel (kingdom), 104–105, 108, 286n56

Israel (tribal confederation), 84, 90, 95–97, 102–104, 107–108, 110, 118, 135, 159, 164–165

Israel Program for Scientific Translations, 60

Israelites. *See* Israel (kingdom; tribal confederation)

Jabotinsky, Eri, 19, 23, 24, 26–32, 34–39, 45, 47, 49, 50, 52–53, 55–58, 60, 66, 145, 159, 183, 188–192, 198, 199, 205, 212, 223, 282n1, 283n19, 297n183, 300n219, 340n182, 340n187, 343n24. *See also* Jabotinsky, Zeev; post-Zionism

Jabotinsky, Zeev (Vladimir), 21, 24–31, 34, 41, 47, 52, 57, 61, 92, 100, 120, 125, 183–185, 190–191, 194, 198–200, 221, 225, 285n46, 290n100, 326n196, 335n111, 340n182, 340n187; relationship with Horon, 19, 20, 24, 27–32, 286n49, 286n52, 292n128, 294n–295n155, 297n187. *See also* Betar; ETZEL; monism; Revisionism

Jacob (biblical figure), 72, 91, 95, 96, 103, 110

Jerusalem, 92, 104, 105, 109, 121, 123, 129, 134, 304n51, 317n28, 319n68, 320n94

Jordan (country), 49, 52, 86, 88, 128, 139, 154, 156, 157, 197–198, 295n160, 337n143
Jordan (river), 22, 49, 87–88, 128, 155–156, 157, 192
Joseph (biblical figure), 313n198
Jossua, Leon, 37, 42–44, 291n119. *See also* "La Renaissance Hébraïque"; *Shem: Revue d'Action Hébraïque*
Judaism, 3, 5, 16, 28, 30–32, 40, 72, 81–82, 84, 91, 93–96, 118, 120–122, 126, 130, 134, 150, 151, 155, 164, 166, 172, 175, 178, 182–184, 189, 207, 224, 286n56, 316n14, 316n16, 317n22; emergence of, 105, 106–115, 181, 184, 332–333n79; "militant," 82, 114, 118, 134; secularization of, 12–15, 167–173, 181. *See also* Diaspora (Jewish); identity, Jewish
Judea, 82, 97, 104, 105, 112, 114

Kadmi-Cohen, Yitzhak, 43–44, 292n126. *See also* "Massada" (group)
Katā'ib (Lebanese Phalange Party), 55, 57, 147, 205, 342n214. *See also* nationalism, Lebanese
Kaufmann, Yehezkel, 164–167
Kedem Club, 55, 57, 61, 156, 159, 188–189, 197–199, 205. *See also* Jabotinsky, Eri; post-Zionism; Rosoff, Shmuel
Kedem, Land of, 85–89, 91, 92, 94–99, 101–102, 104–107, 111–112, 115, 122–124, 127, 128, 131–135, 138, 140, 143–145, 147–156, 158–159, 161, 162, 179, 181, 183, 202, 206, 215–217, 220, 306–307n95, 307n100, 307n105, 337n143; formation of, 86; geography of, 86–88; meaning of name, 85–86, 306n88. *See also* Canaan (land)
Kedem Union, 67, 151, 158–159, 223, 326n204. *See also* Canaan Union
Ḳenan, 'Amos, 16, 210, 211, 216, 289n84
Ḳeshet (literary review), 4, 64, 80, 337n141. *See also* Amir, Aharon
Khazars, 82, 114, 118, 335n102
Kook, Hillel, 45–51, 66, 67, 125, 162, 187–188, 191–192, 196, 223, 294n144, 339n175, 340n187. *See also* Hebrew Committee of National Liberation; post-Zionism
Kurds, 102, 146, 149
Kurzweil, Baruch, 16, 81, 121, 182, 213, 280n35; interpreting "Canaanism," 12–16, 162, 165–166, 200, 208, 281n45, 335n109

"La Renaissance Hébraïque" (discussion club), 36–40, 41–45, 49, 125, 164, 223, 291n119. See also *Shem: Revue d'Action Hébraïque*
La Riposte (journal). See *The Answer* (journal)
"Lamerḥav," 188, 199. *See also* post-Zionism
languages, Semitic/Semito-Hamitic, 79, 89, 94–95, 133, 137, 311n166, 321n105
Law of Return, 66–67, 130. *See also* Israel (state of), citizenship in
Le Cran (journal), 26–28, 44, 92, 284n33, 284n34. *See also* "Rodêgal"
League against Religious Coercion, 4. *See also* Ornan, Uzzi
Lebanon, 18, 53, 55–58, 78, 86, 88, 99, 132, 143, 144, 147–149, 151, 156–158, 198, 201–205, 216, 223, 296n180, 313n197, 341n205, 341n207, 342n214. *See also* Levant Club; Maronites; nationalism, Lebanese

LEHI ("Fighters for the Freedom of Israel"), 4, 36, 67, 219, 288n83, 288–289n84, 294n144. *See also* Stern, Avraham
Levant, 7, 33, 62–64, 86, 101, 122, 125–126, 128, 132, 138–140, 151–152, 159, 176, 188, 203, 204, 205, 216, 323n135, 324n147
Levant Club, 55–58, 164, 188, 204, 223, 298n193, 324n147. *See also* nationalism, Lebanese
Levi (tribe), 106–110, 134, 313n198. *See also* Judaism, emergence of
Leviathan (legendary sea monster), 96, 106, 313n196
liberalism, 5–6, 21, 46, 59, 61, 81, 129, 141, 144, 155–156, 159, 170, 177–178, 183, 185–186, 189, 196, 198–200, 202, 203, 207, 225; limits of, 221–223
Libya, 91, 106, 108, 113, 127, 134, 315n228. *See also* Africa, Northern
"liminal areas," 180, 186
Lods, Adolphe, 33

Maghreb, 101, 104, 106, 108, 143, 144, 146, 298n193. *See also* Africa, Northern; Carthage
Malik, Charles, 201, 205. *See also* nationalism, Lebanese
Malinov, Zeev, 26–27. *See also* Civitavecchia, naval school in; "Rodêgal"; seafaring
Maronites, 55–58, 147–149, 156, 158, 198, 203, 205, 296n180, 325n162. *See also* nationalism, Lebanese
"Massada" (group), 43–44, 292n126. *See also* Kadmi-Cohen, Yitzhak
Mediterranean (region), 26, 33, 37, 55, 62, 64, 70, 77, 79, 82, 85–89, 91, 92, 97, 98, 100, 103–106, 108–109, 111–114, 123, 132, 137, 140–141, 145, 151, 184, 203, 217, 221, 304n39, 305n74, 306n88, 307n95
Merlin, Shmuel, 45, 188, 192, 197, 339n176. *See also* Hebrew Committee of National Liberation; Kook, Hillel; "Lamerḥav"; post-Zionism
Mesopotamia, 72, 78, 86, 88, 98, 126, 127, 308n113
millet (ethnoreligious caste), 119–120, 122, 124, 128, 132, 135, 138, 151, 220, 316n11. *See also* Diaspora (Jewish)
Mirkine, Victor, 24–26, 35. *See also* Betar; *Le Cran* (journal); "Rodêgal"
monism (Jabotinskian principle), 198–199. *See also* post-Zionism
monotheism, 82, 84, 91, 95, 99, 103, 106, 108–111, 113, 122, 142, 164–165, 184, 204, 224. *See also* Judaism, emergence of
Moses (biblical figure), 91, 97, 107–108, 110, 313n199
Muhammad (prophet of Islam), 134–135
Mūsa, Salāma, 147, 201–202. *See also* Copts; Egypt; nationalism, Egyptian
myths, foundational, 4, 8, 10–11, 22, 39, 70, 72, 75, 93, 110, 113, 125, 134, 136, 142, 145, 161, 165–166, 169, 173, 176–177, 186, 192, 196, 204, 217; typology of, 11, 175–176, 206, 333n82. *See also* "golden age"

narrative, commemorative, 8, 9, 10, 92, 106, 110, 117, 122, 132, 161–163, 195, 196, 201, 207, 209, 219
nation-building, 2, 3, 80, 103, 193, 203, 212, 216, 328n10. *See also* state-building

nation formation, 2, 6, 8, 11, 69–73, 75, 81, 84–85, 89, 123–124, 129, 150, 154, 163, 181, 182, 185, 191, 203, 213, 312n178
"national outlook," 62, 76–80, 83–87, 90, 92, 108–109, 112, 115, 119, 120, 124, 127–128, 142, 145, 148, 153–154, 159, 176, 210, 215, 304n46, 315n228; historiography based on, 79–81; historiography opposed to, 81–83. *See also* identity, national
nationalism, Arab. *See* Pan-Arabism
nationalism; Afrikaner, 217–219, 346n61; Egyptian, 18, 76, 147, 155, 201–202, 206, 324n156; Hebrew, 1, 2, 8, 12, 15, 17, 22, 23, 37, 38, 45, 46, 49, 84, 112, 113, 122, 125–127, 147, 156, 162, 174, 191, 201, 204, 209, 211, 213, 217, 218, 220, 221, 223, 224, 316n13, 346n65; Lebanese, 18, 55–58, 143, 147, 201–206, 296n178, 296n180; Palestinian, 2, 3, 48, 149–150, 180, 196, 222–223, 334n101
nationalism, Jewish. *See* Zionism
"New Jew," 2, 32, 173–174, 210. *See also* Sabras
"New Hebrew," 2, 113
New Zionist Organization, 30, 183. *See also* Jabotinsky, Zeev; Revisionism
Nietzsche, Friedrich, 13, 32, 40, 84, 154, 166–167
Nile, 69, 78, 86, 91, 143, 145, 148, 202. *See also* Egypt
"Nimrod" ("Canaanite"-influenced youth movement), 66, 300n227

On History (series of articles), 27–28, 34, 69, 73, 74, 80, 81, 90–91, 112, 117, 176, 301n3, 303n24, 304n39, 307n105, 309n122, 320n100. See also *Rassviet* (newspaper)
Ornan, Uzzi, 4, 197, 200, 215, 326n204

paganism, 29, 82, 84, 93–94, 100, 102, 105, 106, 110, 134, 164–165, 175, 184, 204, 224, 306n80, 312n181c, 320n94; geo-cosmical sources of, 96–97, 313n199; territorial nature of, 103, 108. *See also* polytheism
Pale of Settlement, 20, 171. *See also* Diaspora (Jewish)
Palestine, 1–5, 7, 21, 24, 26, 27, 29, 30, 33, 35, 38–43, 45, 48–50, 92, 121–123, 125, 139–140, 149, 169, 172, 174, 180, 183, 185–187, 191, 197–199, 201, 209–212, 219, 222, 287n62, 290n106, 294n144, 308n112, 308n113, 324n156, 333n83, 334n99, 336n124, 337n142, 339n175, 340n186; partition of, 50, 128, 140, 154, 187, 289n91
Palestinians, 2, 3, 38, 48, 50, 126, 130–131, 149–151, 180, 192, 193, 196, 217, 222, 225, 325n169, 334n101, 339n177, 345–346n56, 347n74; Hebrew origins of, 150, 180; refugees, 57, 149, 150–151, 155, 197–199, 325n169, 339n176, 340n180. *See also* nationalism, Palestinian
Pan-Arabism, 3–4, 6, 7–9, 17, 29, 36, 39, 40, 53, 55–56, 58–59, 61, 63, 123, 133, 138, 140–149, 151–153, 155–158, 184, 188, 196, 200–203, 220, 221, 223, 224, 321n112, 341n207, 346n65; as British instrument, 138–139, 141; as linguistic nationalism, 6, 76, 137, 142, 144, 202; founding myths of, 136–138, 142, 146; Islamic character of, 134, 142, 144, 202. *See also* Arabs, history of; statistics of; identity, Arab
Pan-Syrianism, 201–202, 205–206, 342n217. *See also* Sa'āda, Anṭūn
Persian Empire, 111, 123, 135, 315n228, 317n28; authority

legitimacy in, 108–111, 119. *See also* Cyrus (king of Persia)
Pharaonism. *See* nationalism, Egyptian
Phoenicianism. *See* nationalism, Lebanese
Phoenician (language), 95, 100, 105, 126, 151, 206
Phoenicians, 33, 34, 40, 45, 55, 100, 148, 201, 203–204, 206, 325n162
pieds noirs (French-speaking European settlers in Northern Africa), 59, 141, 217, 223, 322n124. *See also* Algeria, independence war of
polytheism, 93, 110, 312n181. *See also* paganism
post-Zionism, 18, 50, 55, 61, 154, 161, 186–200, 215, 223, 225, 300n219, 338n161, 338n162; Horon's role in formation of, 17, 47, 186–187, 199; Jabotinsky's impact on, 198–200. *See also* Club 59; Hebrew Committee of National Liberation; Kedem Club; Kook, Hillel; "Lamerḥav"

Rassviet (newspaper), 27, 29, 34, 90, 91. See also *On History*
Ratosh (Shelah), Joanna, 65, 67, 282n6
Ratosh, Yonatan, 1, 4–5, 7, 15–16, 36–37, 40, 42, 49, 51–52, 61, 64, 86, 124–125, 146, 164, 172, 182, 191–192, 196–197, 201, 204, 206, 212, 213, 219, 223, 225, 278n8, 283n11, 289n84, 290n100, 290n104, 299n213, 326n204, 340n186, 344n30, 347n75; relationship with Horon, 22, 25, 34–36, 54, 64–66, 106, 124–125, 223–224, 299n217, 300n225, 316n2, 316n13, 320n100
Renan, Ernest, 33, 83, 136, 204; impact on Horon, 84–85, 117
Revisionism (right-liberal stream within Zionism), 5, 8, 19, 21, 25–35, 37–40, 45, 47, 50, 51, 57, 143, 161–162, 186, 194, 200, 202, 214, 221, 283n10, 283n11, 285n40, 287n62, 290n100, 334n100, 337n141; similarities with "Canaanism," 183–185. *See also* Jabotinsky, Zeev; New Zionist Organization
Rin, Svi (Gamliel Heilperin), 54, 65
"Rodêgal" (youth movement for naval and aviation training), 25–28, 29, 38, 92, 184, 284n33, 284n36. See also *Le Cran* (journal); seafaring
Roman Empire, 90, 91, 104, 105, 111–113, 121, 286n52
Rosoff, Shmuel, 55, 159, 188–189, 197. *See also* Kedem Club

Sa'āda, Anṭūn, 201–203, 205–206, 342n217. *See also* Pan-Syrianism
Sabras (native Israelis), 126–127, 141, 173–174, 210–211, 216, 217, 318n54, 332n70, 332n72. *See also* identity, Hebrew; identity, Israeli; nationalism, Hebrew; "New Jew"
Scholem, Gerschom, 15, 182, 281n45, 331n47
seafaring, 26, 28, 89, 92, 100, 103, 105, 112, 132, 184, 284n29
Semites, 33, 34, 79, 82–83, 87, 93, 97–98, 136–137, 151, 176. *See also* languages, Semitic/Semito-Hamitic
Sephardic Jews, 92, 118, 123, 129, 334n99
settler colonialism, 2, 216–217, 218, 221–222, 225, 345n56. *See also* Israel (state of)
Shelah, Uriel. *See* Ratosh, Yonatan
Shem: Revue d'Action Hébraïque (journal), 38, 40, 41–43, 47, 49, 290n102, 291n120, 292n126,

Shem: Revue d'Action Hébraïque (journal) *(continued)* 293n134. *See also* "La Renaissance Hébraïque"
shtetl (East-European Jewish town), 19–20, 185, 282n4. *See also* Diaspora (Jewish)
Sohar, Esra, 64, 66, 85, 223, 327n207
Solomon (biblical figure), 82, 91, 93, 103–104
Souvarine, Boris, 24, 37, 42, 44, 57, 58, 223, 283n20, 298n195
Spengler, Oswald, 84, 159
state-building, 2, 3, 174
Stern, Avraham, 36, 40–41, 223, 288n83, 289n84, 290n104, 290n106, 291n112. *See also* LEHI
Syria, 33, 86, 88, 138, 149, 154, 157, 201–203, 205–206, 216
Syrian Social National Party, 201. *See also* Pan-Syrianism; Sa'āda, Anṭūn

Tammuz, Benyamin, 16
Tel Ḥai Fund, 25, 31, 287n62
Temsamani, Muhammad, 53, 58, 298n193. *See also* Maghreb
The Answer (journal), 47, 50, 197. *See also* Hebrew Committee of National Liberation
Tyre, 58, 100, 104, 105, 112, 147, 304n51, 315n228

Ugarit, 7, 33–34, 92, 94, 99, 107, 202, 220, 313n196. *See also* Virolleaud, Charles
Umayyads (dynasty), 135, 203

Virolleaud, Charles, 33, 44, 92, 220
von Weisl, Wolfgang, 40, 143, 323n136

"White" Russians, 21–22, 282–283n10. *See also* anti-Semitism
Wissenschaft des Judenthums, 8, 12, 32, 33, 81, 83–84, 164–165, 167, 180, 314n210

Yalin-Mor, Natan, 67. *See also* LEHI
Yemen, 78, 82, 114, 118
YHWH (deity), 102–106, 108–111, 113–114, 312n181, 312n189, 333n79. *See also* monotheism
Yishuv (Hebrew society in Palestine), 1, 2, 4, 5, 34, 35, 43, 46, 48, 52, 56, 90, 123, 125, 169, 172, 177, 178–179, 205, 209, 210, 212–213, 216–219, 284n29, 290n100, 293n134, 332n68, 340n186, 344n30. *See also* Hebrews (modern); identity, Hebrew

Zionism, 1–9, 11–18, 20–21, 23, 30–33, 35, 37, 38, 40, 45–47, 49–51, 55–58, 61, 90–92, 115, 120–125, 127–128, 131, 139–140, 143, 145, 149–150, 153, 161–162, 167–170, 183–188, 190–195, 197, 199–200, 203, 206–210, 213, 216, 217, 220–222, 224, 283n10, 283n11, 289n84, 289n91, 300n219, 317n28, 325n169, 331n57, 333n88, 334n100, 334n101, 338n148, 346n65; anti-democratic tendencies of, 333n83; anti-Diasporic, 9, 14, 84, 121–122, 178, 211–212, 280n40; as ethnoreligious/ethnonational, 6, 11–12, 17, 33, 46, 121–123, 125, 162, 175–180, 197, 207, 214–215, 224–225, 278n3, 331n57, 333n84; continuity with Judaism, 121, 171–174; fundamental differences from "Canaanism," 162–164, 174–182, 316–317n22, 327n2; historiography of, 16, 34, 45, 69, 90–96, 114, 118, 121, 127, 129–130, 161–175, 178, 180–181,

196, 207–208, 217, 316–317n22, 330n41, 331n61, 336n124; liberal aspects of, 221–222; perceived by Lebanese nationalists, 55–56, 58, 204–206; "romantic," 180, 334n99; teleology of, 6, 7, 17, 168, 170, 209, 224, 331n47. *See also* anti-Zionism; post-Zionism

www.ingramcontent.com/pod-product-compliance
Lightning Source LLC
Chambersburg PA
CBHW031702230426
43668CB00006B/84
9781438497655